The Official®

OLD BOOKS

❊

Marie Tedford
and
Pat Goudey

THIRD EDITION

House of Collectibles
The Ballantine Publishing Group   *New York*

To Marie's mother, and Pat's grandmother, Jenny, who could neither read nor write. She thought books were a frivolous pastime, but she would have thoroughly enjoyed the irony of this book.

Published by: House of Collectibles
201 East 50th Street
New York, NY 10022

Distributed by Ballantine Books, a division of Random House, Inc., New York, and simultaneously in Canada by Random House of Canada Limited, Toronto.

Grateful acknowledgment is made to Peter Fraser & Dunlop Group Ltd. for permission to reprint an excerpt from THE BAD CHILD'S BOOK OF BEASTS by Hilaire Belloc, first published by Gerald Duckworth & Co. Copyright © The Estate of Hilaire Belloc.

Manufactured in the United States of America

ISSN: 1073-8614

ISBN: 0-676-60157-X

Cover design by Kristine V. Mills-Noble
Cover photo © George Kerrigan

Third Edition: November 1999

10 9 8 7 6 5 4 3 2 1

CONTENTS

✳

Acknowledgments	iv
Introduction to the Third Edition	v
Market Review	3
A Closer Look at the Book Trade	6
Children's Books	14
The Internet	18
The Care and Repair of Old Books	21
How to Use This Book	29
Glossary	33
Abbreviations	60
Old Books Listing	63
Bibles Listing	381
Dealers	385
Recommended Periodicals and Research Resources	390

ACKNOWLEDGMENTS

✳

O ur thanks to the many booksellers who responded to our request for catalogues and to Swann Galleries, Pacific Book Auction Galleries, Donna Howard of The Eloquent Page bookshop in Vermont, and Lee and Grayce Nash of Authors of the West bookshop in Oregon, who provided information for the market review.

We thank the Vermont Antiquarian Booksellers who allowed us to use photographs from Pomfret Book Shows; and thanks to photographer Ilan Fisher of Sharon, Massachusetts, for the continuing use of his pictures.

Our gratitude also goes to Alan and Mary Culpin, booksellers from Austin, Texas, and Boulder, Colorado; Stephen Smith of Fair Haven, Vermont; Cattermole Books of Newberry, Ohio; Monroe Street Books of Middlebury, Vermont; Roger and Joan Bassett, Booksellers of Fullerton, Nebraska; and Barbara Harris Books of Guilford, New Hampshire. And once more, special thanks to Donna Howard at The Eloquent Page in St. Albans, Vermont, for information on Children's Books and for the new chapter on The Internet.

Thanks to Lief Laudamus of Leyden, Massachusetts, for his help with Bibles.

INTRODUCTION TO THE THIRD EDITION

✳

Interest in antiquarian books continues to grow. The market has always been brisk and steady, but it was a somewhat esoteric interest—well known to those who participated, all but invisible to those who didn't. Not so now, as we move into the twenty-first century.

Newcomers to the field have swelled the ranks of collectors and dealers alike, many of them entering the industry on the Internet. The general public, too, is more aware of rare and collectible books as valuable items for trade and investment. Perhaps more people can afford to buy collectible books, or perhaps the mania for collecting everything from advertising posters to Disneyana has spilled over into books.

Whatever the reason, heightened interest is propelling ever greater numbers of dealers and collectors into the field to search out those unique volumes to round out a collection, or to list on the Internet for sale.

This book is designed to help in that search. No one research volume can contain all the information an antiquarian book dealer or collector will need. The literature available and the new cyberspace websites include a considerable body of reference material for publication and price data. Cross-checking information on a book will help you ensure you've got the best price and accurate statistics. And searching multiple references can net you information on a book that's hard to find, but still a valuable item.

For this edition, we've combed our listings, updated prices, provided additional publication information, and added thousands of new volumes. We've also written a chapter on the Internet. We suggest you use the information we provide and consult many other sources. We've provided a list of resources at the back of the book, and we discuss websites in the Internet chapter.

We want this book to do more than tell you the going rate for a particular title. Books are much more than a commodity with a price tag. As always, our intention is to inform you, pique your interest, and even entertain you a bit, because we still think the best reason for developing an interest in books is for the sheer fun of it.

The Official® Price Guide to

OLD
BOOKS

❉

MARKET REVIEW

✳

A long with everything else, the world of commerce is rapidly evolving as individual countries combine their financial interests to create a global economy.

This new economy has weathered some serious stock market fluctuations over the past couple of years, including rapid rises and sudden downturns, or "corrections." Regions of the world are currently struggling to pull out of crippling economic depression, but the United States has so far been spared the worst of it.

Through it all, antiquarian bookselling remains a constant market. Sales typically fluctuate only slightly from year to year and decade to decade. Never a place to make a killing, the industry is a good solid endeavor that pays consistently when knowledgeably managed.

For the individual bookseller, the trick is to keep an eye on trends and be aware of genres that are rising and falling off. For the past few years, science fiction and related genres have gained strength. Children's series books are enjoying popularity now as well. Modern first editions are in a high-risk category that can achieve considerable short-term gains, but they carry the risk of sudden losses when popular authors fall from favor and prices for their books plummet.

In our chapter on the Internet, we discuss the effects of online buying in the book trade, particularly the drop-off in traffic at smaller bookshows. Many dealers have chosen to list their wares electronically and are doing well, but others prefer the hands-on approach and resist the pull toward computerized commerce.

Lee Nash of Dundee, Oregon, has been selling antiquarian books for 25 years. He and his wife, Grayce, own Authors of the West dealing in Western Americana, fiction, history, and travel. They also deal in Inkling books, featuring authors like C. S. Lewis and J. R. R. Tolkien. Nash, a retired academic, continues traveling to buy books for his shop, but he also uses the Internet. He planned to begin listing his stock online before the end of 1999.

Genres and authors that are strong in his region at the end of the decade include Willa Cather, John Steinbeck, and Wallace Stegner. Frank Waters has been gaining strength with books on New Mexico and Indian culture. Tony Hillerman's Navaho reservation mysteries are popular, as are books by A. B. Guthrie.

The Nash's have been selling C. S. Lewis and related authors for about five years and find that the market is growing. They feature American authors of similar religious and philosophical themes, including Madeleine L'Engle, author of *A Wrinkle in Time,* and New England novelist Frederick Buechner.

Marie's colleague Donna Howard deals extensively in doll books, finding the Internet an excellent marketing tool for these scarce collectibles. She lists reading copies in science fiction, mystery, horror, and romance, as well. Especially popular now are the Doll & Doll House books, Vermontiana, and reading copies of romance novels.

Pacific Book Auctions reported a record sale of a private collection of golf books in the summer of 1998. The collection of Joseph Murdoch—more than 1,200 books—brought excellent returns in the genre, with some books realizing prices in the $50-$500 range, but many reaching into four and five figures. A volume edited by Robert Clark, *Golf: A Royal and Ancient Game*, a presentation copy by Clark, realized $14,950 against an estimate of $5,000-$8,000. *Rules of the Thistle Club,* by James Cundell, one of only six such rule books printed before 1830, also brought $14,950 against an estimate of $10,000-$15,000.

The sale of several hundred books in the golf collection of John Downie in the fall of 1998 realized prices in the $50-$500 range, with many into four figures as well.

In other genres, Swann Galleries reported the sale of a first edition of Mary Shelley's *Frankenstein,* London, 1818, for $35,650 in April of 1997. An 1885 copy of *Huckleberry Finn,* tattered but signed by Twain, brought $21,850 in June of 1997.

Swann reports that art and architecture books are holding the public's attention and fetching strong prices, as are sports books. The gallery has instituted a special autumn sale in October, just before Halloween, featuring books on magic and related genres. With the success of the 1998 sale, the gallery plans to make it an annual event.

*Browsers among the stacks at the Vermont Antiquarian Booksellers'
Fair in Pomfret, Vermont. (Photo by Ilan Fisher)*

A CLOSER LOOK
AT THE BOOK TRADE

※

Thou art the book, the library
Where I look

—HENRY KING, BISHOP OF CHICHESTER

Whenever we mention that we're used and rare book dealers, we're met with a host of questions about books people have tucked away in an attic or closet. We suspect the world contains many would-be bookmen needing only a nudge to get them started. Below, we'll offer the nudge, try to dispel some of the mystery surrounding old books, and answer some questions we're often asked.

WHAT IS OLD IN OLD BOOKS?

This seems like a reasonable question, but instead of thinking in terms of "old," consider your books used, out of print, or rare. These descriptions apply to collectible books of all ages.

Rather than age, think about content: what is the book about and who wrote it? If you must choose between two books in good condition, one printed in London in 1632 by an obscure British poet no one has ever heard of, and the other a 19th-century tome on the American Indian published in New York, choose the one on the American Indian. There's a lively market for Native Americana and you'll likely find a customer for the book. The poetry is merely fun to have on the shelf because it's old. It isn't automatically a collector's item.

We don't think anybody knows what the cut-off date is for "antiquarian" books. Is it 19th century? Early 20th? Unless you are a rare book dealer focusing on the earliest printed material — incunabula or the first printed books in the new world — put actual age out of your mind and learn which books are sought by dealers and other collectors. You'll discover a busy trade in books from past centuries and books from last year — from the antiquarian to the modern first editions.

WHERE WILL I FIND GOOD BOOKS?

The first source that comes to mind is the antiquarian and collectible book dealer. For many genres, used-book stores will yield exactly what you're after, often at bargain prices. Throw in a little conversation with the bookseller, and you've found your book and learned something about your subject, too. Bought from a reputable dealer, the book has been pre-screened and you won't have to do further research to verify your find.

Booksellers consider other dealers a prime source of good stock. You can buy direct from dealers through bookstores, dealer catalogues, advertisements, industry periodicals, and at book fairs. As a beginner, attend the smaller regional fairs and shows that are popular all over the country. They're an education unto themselves.

Other excellent sources are flea markets, estate sales, auctions, the Salvation Army, antique stores, and garage sales. These are the places that professionals go to find books.

HOW GOOD ARE AUCTIONS FOR BUYING AND SELLING BOOKS?

Books at local auctions are plentiful and they're a fine source of collectibles, but you can't be sure of picking up a bargain any longer. In too many cases, except perhaps at exclusive rare book and collectible houses like Swann's, Christie's, and Sotheby's, the popularity of auctions has brought with it a kind of recreational bidder. In the heat of competition for an item, bidding may be driven much higher than a careful buyer would be willing to pay in a bookstore or in a private transaction.

Great books can still be had for excellent prices if buyers exercise caution, know how much they are willing to pay ahead of time, and sit on their hands when the bidding gets rowdy.

If you're selling books, auctions and dealers are on a par, each having their strong and weak points. On a particular day, if an auction attracts a spirited audience, you could do well. On an off day, you risk your books selling for less than you hoped. Selling through dealers requires more of your time and effort, but dealers have pipelines to collectors who may be looking for just the book you're selling.

In the final analysis, we can only tell you what is available. You must choose what's right for you.

WHAT BOOKS SHOULD I PICK UP?

There's no one answer to this question. Before you ask it, you have some decisions to make, and then the question will begin to answer itself. Are you buying books for investment or fun? Will you be a collector? Or a dealer? Will you specialize or be a generalist?

Carefully bought collectible books hold their value well and grow in value at a steady rate of up to 10% per year. They're a safe investment, but with rare exceptions, they're not speculative and most likely won't make you a killing.

As often as not, even those who collect as an investment wind up excited by the hunt and end up collecting for fun, too.

If you decide to specialize, whether bookseller or collector, learn all you can about your subject. Don't neglect allied subjects that broaden and flesh out your knowledge. Visit bookstores, talk to dealers, read dealer catalogues to see what's being offered and what someone else wants. Visit libraries.

Michael Ginsberg, a bookseller from Massachusetts and past president of the Antiquarian Booksellers Association of America (ABAA), recommends that you read the bibliographies of books related to your specialty; you'll discover other books to read and some you'll want to collect or stock in your store.

CATEGORIES, OR ANA

When you get more involved in books as a dealer or collector, you'll become familiar with references to the common genres and specialties, sometimes called "ana" (see Glossary). These will include topics from books on the settling of the Americas, native peoples, black studies, maritime trades, foreign countries, children's books, medicine, science, sporting books, zoology, anthropology, magic, antiques, the military, cooking, poetry, railroads, billiards, the radical labor movement, and on and on. Add to that limited editions, fine presses, fine bindings, illustrated books; the list doesn't end. And each genre has sub-genres, ad infinitum.

These categories help people to communicate. Dealers use them to describe their specialties and collectors use them to define their area of interest. But genres are not mutually exclusive — there's enormous overlapping — and they are just one tool for evaluating books.

AMERICANA VS. US-IANA

A very popular specialty is Americana, but what do bookmen mean by that term? Do they refer to books on the discovery, exploration, political, and cultural development of the United States? Or do they adopt the broader and truer meaning of the term and include all the Americas from Canada to Argentina?

In modern vernacular, the meaning of Americana has narrowed to refer to the United States and its territories though some dealers use it in the more inclusive form. To be technically correct when referring to the Unites States, the term US-iana was coined by bibliographer Wright Howes, author of *Howes USIANA* issued in 1954, but that term is less widely used.

WHAT ABOUT CONDITION?

This is probably the most important judgment you will make about a book you're buying or selling. Depending on its condition, a book can be a collector's item or just a nice book to read. We often see the same look of perplexity on the faces of people not in the trade when we reject the old book in their hand. "But it's old!"

No matter.

Unless the book is an Eliot Bible, or another great rarity, it must be in good condition — bindings attached, pages all there, illustrations accounted for, no underlining, no tears, and clean covers. If the book was issued with a dust jacket, the jacket must be present and in good condition, especially for modern first editions. The absence of the jacket radically reduces the value.

Sounds cranky, doesn't it? But we can't stress enough the importance of condition in collectible books. But don't throw away that intact book in less than good condition. Scholars, researchers, and recreational readers are another market for inexpensive reading copies.

HOW IMPORTANT ARE FIRST EDITIONS?

Rare book collectors want first editions because they reflect the first time these particular thoughts of an author appeared in print. They are percieved to be closest to the author's true intent. As further editions are issued, the supply of books is increased, thereby diminishing the value of succeeding editions. But relative scarcity of firsts remains constant.

As often as not, collectors don't read their first editions, but buy them to enjoy the possession of something rare and special, something others don't have. Scholars and readers will pay a price for later editions, but it will be a mere shadow of the price paid for a first edition.

Now, after having said that, let us confuse you further. Popular titles are often re-issued in limited editions. Printed on high quality papers, with fine bindings and slipcases, these commonly include illustrations by noted artists. Limited editions may command higher prices than first editions, since most are numbered and signed by the author, the artist, or both.

WHAT'S THE STORY ON MODERN FIRST EDITIONS?

If any area of book collecting is in danger of falling victim to fads, this is it. Modern first editions attest to the fact that a book can be published in the past year or two and already have a collectible price affixed, which nullifies the idea that age determines price.

Sue Grafton's crime novels have been popular with collectors of modern first editions over the past few years. Her first book, *"A" Is For Alibi*, published in 1982, has been offered at prices ranging from $150 to $1,000 depending on which catalogue you're looking at. But auctioneers and dealers report that Grafton's books, especially those further down the alphabet, haven't been leaving the bookshelves as quickly as they once did. Whether she and other currently popular writers like Tom Clancy, John Grisham, and Ann Tyler will have staying power in the collectible modern first edition category remains to be seen.

This is the way it is with modern first editions. Either the books become part of the popular culture — most notably through movies — or they are recognized as literature and are studied in the classroom, and their value remains high. Or they pass into oblivion and are relegated to the Penny Box.

A first edition of Raymond Chandler's 1939 mystery *The Big Sleep*, in a near perfect dust jacket, sold for $7,150 in 1992, more than twice what experts had estimated it would bring in. By 1996, experts were setting the price closer to $5,000. Even after all these years, the price fluctuated. Considered a classic in the genre for its era, *The Big Sleep* was also dramatized in a movie starring Humphrey Bogart. Was it exposure that brought the price up? What really sets the pace for what a book is worth? We suspect that whimsy has a lot to do with modern book trading.

Percy Muir had a wonderful discussion on the subject in his delightful publication *Book Collecting as a Hobby*. He says when a contemporary author is "hot" the demand for first editions will drive up the price. When the demand is satisfied, prices decline. If the author's work has lasting substance, collectors will rediscover him and prices will rise again.

Muir cautions, "Never, never collect an author when he is in the height of fashion." He advises anticipating who will be the next to rise, or waiting until authors have weathered the test of time.

The bottom line is, take care in buying and pricing. Watch trends, understand them, plan for them, but don't be swept up in them.

HOW DO I PRICE A BOOK?

The plain truth is, there is no right price for a used book. It's all subjective. The law of supply and demand is in play. During flush times, prices and sales soar, and in a lagging economy, they come back down. Market correction.

With a book in your hand, you'll do the research and then settle on a number. In the end, the value of a book is only what you or your customer is willing to pay. You will notice for some books we've listed that the price range is narrow. According to our sources, including dealers' pricing and auction records, folks agree on the current value of those books. For others, the range is hundreds or even thousands of dollars. These are actual prices people have asked for and paid. They reflect differing opinions from one dealer to another, or from one part of the country to another. Such disparities are common.

We've listed some titles more than once to show the difference in price between, for instance, trade and limited editions, the first edition and a later edition, a first edition with dust jacket and one without, or a signed copy and an unsigned one. We've assigned our prices assuming very good to fine condition, with the rare exception noted. Where you don't find the actual title you're after, but we list other titles by the same author, you've verified the author as collectible. You have more research to do, however, before you can price the book in your hand. Some authors have many titles to their credit, not all prized. The whole subject is fraught with cautions.

Talk to people in the business, consult price guides and dealer catalogues, visit antiquarian bookstores. Learn as much as you can and then learn some more.

Pricing stock for a shop begins when you buy the books. Will your initial investment be tied up for months or a year, or do you have a ready customer for the book? Do you have a shop with overhead costs or do you mail order?

As dealers, when we know exactly what book we're looking for, the quickest way to find it is through other professionals. That means we

A page with woodcut illustration from The History of Reynard the Fox, *printed in 1894 by David Nutt, London. It is included in Special Collections at the Bailey-Howe Library, University of Vermont.*

dealers often buy from each other and the price goes up as a book passes from hand to hand before it ever reaches the public. How many times can that happen? You must make these judgments based upon your growing knowledge of the business.

In the end, you're bound to make some mistakes. It's that kind of business.

CHILDREN'S BOOKS

✳

Child, do not throw this book,
Refrain from the unholy pleasure
Of cutting all the pictures out,
Regard it as your choicest treasure.

—HILAIRE BELLOC
A BAD CHILD'S BOOK OF BEASTS

In recent years, one category of old book collecting has attracted increasing interest from both the seasoned collector and the newcomer— children's books. Each year, prices rise but they don't put a damper on collectors' appetites for their coveted treasures. Perhaps nostalgia motivates this interest and a willingness to pay more, much as people's fondness for old toys is playing with those collectible prices. Or maybe mothers and grandmothers are looking for the books that delighted them as children to pass on to their own kids.

Whatever the motivation for collecting, the desirable classic authors—Carroll, Milne, Potter, Wiggin, Burgess and others too numerous to mention—take the lion's share of the market, but series books like the Hardy Boys and Nancy Drew are back in circulation and enjoying a renaissance.

Unlike collectors who covet the first edition, collectors of series books don't always consider it important, says Stephen Smith of Fair Haven, Vermont. And, besides, determining a first edition series book isn't so easy. The copyright page tells you little about which edition you're holding. In the series milieu, content is king because most collectors are baby boomers who read these books as children and want to read them again. To the hard-core collector, however, all the points are important; dust jacket, first edition, very good condition, rarity—and that applies to the series books as well.

"Without a doubt, Nancy Drew, the Hardy Boys and Tom Swift are the most popular and best known of the children's series," said Joan Bassett of Antiquarian and Collector Books in Fullerton, Nebraska. "Some of these series in dust jackets are extremely scarce and valued at hundreds of dollars. Often the last title in the series, with picture board covers, is the most valuable," she said, which sounds strange since we are conditioned to think in terms of *first editions*.

We consulted Donna Howard at The Eloquent Page in St. Albans, Vermont, and she tried to explain. First, children's series books can be known by their titles and by their place in the series, which is their number. "In the children's series, often, though not always, the last number or the last few numbers are considerably more expensive than earlier numbers," Donna said. For example, Cherry Ames books— the pictureboard book sells for $7.50, $12.50 or $15, she said. The last title of the series, *Ski Nurse, #27*, sells for $100-$150, if you can find it. This is because fewer books were published later in the series. As each new book in a series is produced, more copies of earlier titles are printed to meet a continued demand. The result, she says, is "the last numbers are usually printed once as the series goes out of print, therefore fewer copies are available to collectors and dealers." When publishers detect a slump in readership, too, they tend to publish smaller numbers of books or terminate publishing altogether. Donna commented, "You have the traditional mode of supply and demand working the marketplace."

The higher-number rule doesn't apply to all the series books, however. Those popular Hardy Boys and Nancy Drew books, most notably, have ongoing publication and follow the standard rule—the earlier the edition, the better.

Cattermole Books in Newberry, Ohio, doesn't deal in series books for children, but says the trade in classic children's books is great. Collectors are searching for illustrators whose drawings tickle their fancy or permit their imagination to re-create other worlds.

Valuable and collectible children's books are out there if you know what to look for, says Dick Chodkowski of Monroe Street Books in Middlebury, Vermont, and condition is most important. We know that children can read a book to death, but finding that well-loved book in very good condition is what renders it collectible. Dick cautions that some flaws are acceptable, such as cover wear or an owner's signature on a flyleaf— even a dust jacket can be missing— but a collector draws the line on books that are falling apart or have torn and scribbled pages.

Remember, too, the Middlebury bookseller advises, don't spurn a reprint, especially one in good condition. Unlike the modern first edition, juvenile reprints hold a higher percentage of their value, Dick says.

Clean, crisp books with clean dust jackets sell fast and best. And prices can be considerable. Beginners in the children's category are amazed how a dust jacket can add to the price of a book.

The mid 1930s through the 1950s were the true Golden Age of Children's books in America. There's also strong interest in the World-War air-combat series like Al Avery, R. Sidney Bowen, and Eustace Adams. Older series like Ruth Fielding and Rover Boys, Motor Cycle Boys, and Boy Scouts seem to be increasing in interest and value.

Bunny Brown, Bobbsey Twins, and Honey Bunch series are popular. Some of the less well-known series such as Six Little Bunkers and Curly Tops could be good items to pick up now, especially dust-jacketed copies.

Booksellers give the children's market an A+. Old favorite illustrators like Wyeth and Parrish still excite the buying public. In the series category Tom Swift is right up there. The time-honored Oz books are still commanding high figures.

Monroe Street Books offers these top post-1930s first edition titles:

1. *Little Black Sambo* by Helen Bannerman. This book   is becoming scarce.
2. *Eloise* by Kay Thompson, illustrated by Hillary Knight. The 1955 first edition in a dust jacket is valued over $100.
3. *Elves and Fairies* by Jane Werner, illustrated by Garth Williams. This golden book in nice condition can sell for $200.
4. *Cat in the Hat by Dr. Seuss.* A word of caution: his first editions can be difficult to identify.
5. *Little House on the Prairie* by Laura Ingalls Wilder. A winner with many children, and now with their parents and grandparents, who grew up on the books and reruns of the television series.
6. *Were the Wild Things Are/In the Night Kitchen* by Maurice Sendak. His early illustrated books are hard to identify in first editions, but he is worth every bit of trouble it takes to ferret him out.
7. *Madeline* by Ludwig Bemelmans. This delightful book and the other Madeline books can cost between $100-$200 in dust jackets.
8. Newberry Medal Titles. First editions of the books awarded this coveted title are always desirable.
9. Caldecott Medal Titles. Same as the Newberry titles. For further information, consult the *Horn Book Magazine.*
10. And no list would be complete without the charm and language of *Charlotte's Web* by E. B. White.

Among the ten most requested authors from the 1930s to the present are: Margaret Wise Brown, Lois Lenski, Roald Dahl, Eleanor Estes, Caroly Ryrie Brink, Jean DeBrunhoff, Marguerite De Angeli, Robert Lawson, William Steig, and Maud Hart Lovelace.

The most-wanted series books are: Nancy Drew, Hardy Boys, Tom Swift, Judy Bolton, Rick Brant, Ken Holt, Black Stallion Series, Thornton Burgess, Dr. Dolittle, Freddy the Pig, Landmark Books, and the Scribner's Illustrated Classics.

However, the Frank Baum Oz books, Uncle Wiggily, Mary Frances, Palmer Cox's Brownies, The Teenie Weenies, Joseph Altsheler's historical novels, Arthur Ransom, Rosemary Sutcliff, Volland Publishing and Leo Edwards' series still have special appeal for collectors and nostalgia buffs.

Now, if you are thinking into the future or you're making a list for your children to collect, keep these authors in mind: Brian Jacques, James Marshall, Gary Paulsen, Arthur Yorinks/Richard Egieski, Lisbeth Zwerger, Michael Hague, Susan Cooper, Ted Lewin and Jerry Pinkney, Daniel Pinkwater, Trina Schart Hyman, and the inimitable Chris Van Allsburg.

Alan Culpin at Abracadabra Booksearch International in Austin, Texas, says the children's book market there is doing very well. "It is one of the fastest growing sectors in the out-of-print book world, and shows no sign of declining," he says. The store lists some classic authors and illustrators who are still demanding attention: Rackham, Dulac, Nielsen, Parrish, Pogany, Tasha Tudor, as well as some new faces like Cicely Mary Barker, Margaret Tarrant, and E. H. Shepard.

"Fiction authors tend to be ephemeral, with names popping up only to disappear a year or so later," Alan said. Classic names from 1870 to the 1930s predominate, authors like Carroll, Milne, Potter, Barker, and others.

Oz-mania is still strong and the later but still fairly early Oz books are holding up in value, Alan says. New Oz collectors show up regularly. He says authors Margaret Sutton and Claire Bee are particularly strong.

The world of children's books is wide and varied and contains many subdivisions—picture books, series, chapter, pop-up, toy, fiction, non-fiction, illustrated, and more. One of the best ways to learn more is to read catalogues offered by dealers who specialize in them. We have space only to skim the surface of this delightful collecting category, so much more is out there. If your interest in collecting or selling leans toward the whimsical but you find yourself in a tangled forest with lurking goblins and roads to nowhere, just call on one of the booksellers who know all about goblins and magic forests and they will set you on the right road.

THE INTERNET

✳

Books are the legacies that a great genius leaves to mankind,
which are delivered down from generation to generation,
as presents to the posterity of those who are yet unborn.

—*THE SPECTATOR*, 1711

This volume will be on bookstore shelves "in the year 2000." To most of us, that phrase still sounds surreal. Over the years, talk of the year 2000 conjured up a world of robots and rocket ships, space stations and instant video communication with people on the other side of the planet. Wait a minute, that sounds like the world we live in. We've seen the future and it is now.

This technology leading us into the 21st century has changed the way we live and work. With the use of computers and the Internet, the whole landscape of business has shifted in the last decade and antiquarian and collectible books are no exception.

The Internet alone has had a greater effect on the book trade than any other factor in the latter half of this century. Instant access to markets the world over has changed the way many dealers buy and advertise their stock and the way collectors search for their treasures. Historically, dealers carried books catering to known buyers and to collectors interested in their own geographic region. Dealers set up informal networks among themselves to move regional books to areas where they would most likely find a waiting buyer.

With instant Internet access to buyers all over the world, dealers can now easily market regional books direct to the customer, rather than to a dealer in a distant locale.

Donna Howard of The Eloquent Page in St. Albans, Vermont, now lists her considerable stock of science fiction, fantasy, and horror—much of it in reading copies or paperbacks—on her Internet website. She attracts a clientele of collectors and readers alike and does a brisk business in these genres, even more so now that she's featured in cyberspace.

"We now get orders from people who never would have made it into the store," Donna said. "Orders from Malaysia, Indonesia, from Americans living abroad. They now have accessibility they never had before."

Catalogue advertising and dealer-to-dealer selling has changed with this new scenario, as has attendance at bookshows. Many dealers are less willing to spend the considerable time and resources to create and mail comprehensive print catalogues when so many serious collectors have access to the Internet. Book shows continue to draw dedicated bibliophiles, but casual buyers and investment-oriented collectors are attracted to the ease of cyber-commerce and attendance at some smaller regional shows has fallen off.

The pros and cons of the Internet for booksellers can be legitimately argued. One of the advantages of the net is the wealth of book titles available, titles heretofore completely unseen in some regions and so thought to be scarce. Prices can also be an eye-opener. Competition, keen among dealers, seems to be guiding prices now, bringing them into a more competitive range. The consumer profits from this adjustment.

Many dealers on the net offer more than just titles and prices. They provide extensive information not readily found in the past without time-consuming research. Both the collector and the dealer have much to gain surfing through these informational sites.

On the other hand, a new breed of buyer and seller has entered the market with the Internet. Many are people who have little expertise or interest in the books per se. With these newcomers, prices vary greatly as does their knowledge of the books they're trading in and the quality of their wares. Serious dealers and collectors should tread carefully when dealing with unknowns in cyberspace even though website host companies make every effort to monitor their sites. We have spoken to many customers who regularly use the internet to purchase books and their experiences have been mostly positive.

Several large websites have moved to the forefront of the industry, including Advanced Book Exchange at www.abebooks.com, Bibliofind at www.bibliofind.com, A Libris at alibris.com, Bookfinder at bookfinder.com, and ABAA Quick Finder at abaa-booknet.com. Barnes and Noble includes antiquarian titles among its offerings at www.barnesandnoble.com, as does the Internet bookselling giant Amazon.com.

Independent booksellers can subscribe to one of several group sites, set up a webpage and post books for sale, advertise wants and perform searches for clients, all for reasonable monthly fees usually based on the number of books posted or the amount of activity at the site. For newcomers to the Internet, technical support for managing the pages is readily available. Thousands of booksellers have availed themselves of these services or set up their own sites, including experienced dealers, long established auction houses, and brand new entrepreneurs.

Buyers can log onto these sites and search the dealer lists for specific books, or just browse among the many titles offered. As a buyer, know your books well and learn something about the dealer you're working with before committing your money to a sale. Check to see if the dealer has a return policy. For dealers, if you're new to the field, learn about the books, how to evaluate their rarity and condition, and how to properly describe them to a potential buyer before putting a price on them and posting them for sale to the world.

Marie's experience and that of her colleagues in Vermont and elsewhere has been that buying and selling on the Internet is a growing segment of their regular business, but some people are in the business for more than just a living. Traditional bibliophiles enjoy the hunt through the stacks, scouring the countryside for books long out of circulation, leafing through private collections to find the one or two treasures among them, holding history in their hands even if only for a moment. They enjoy the heft and feel of a book almost as much as the words and images on a page. These are among the esoteric pleasures of antiquarian bookselling and collecting that the Internet cannot replace.

Some dealers are resisting the "on line" mania, but the Internet has changed every facet of commerce on the planet and there's no turning back. How the world of antiquarian and collectible books will finally adapt to it remains to be seen.

THE CARE AND REPAIR
OF OLD BOOKS

❊

A few strong instincts, and a few plain rules.

—WILLIAM WORDSWORTH
ALAS! WHAT BOOTS THE LONG LABORIOUS QUEST?

AVOIDING DAMAGE

Though paper may be fragile, books are surprisingly durable if they are treated well. Proof of this is in the considerable number of incunabula that have survived from the Middle Ages in sturdy enough shape to delight collectors and continue serving as reference materials for serious scholars today.

Our own examination of a 300-year-old Eliot's *Natick Indian Bible* at the Boston Public Library revealed a book with pages solid enough to withstand the careful attentions of readers and researchers for many more years.

Even ignored and uncared for, an ancient tome left undisturbed and dry may survive without serious damage. A leather binding will certainly dry out and crack without proper dressing, but the pages of old books are stubbornly durable.

Unfortunately, newer books may not last so long. Modern paper manufacture produces a lot of paper fast, but the quality of the paper is inferior and it has a far shorter lifespan. The common product today has a high acid content that causes it to degrade, discolor, become brittle, and fall apart over a few decades. Pulp paper used in newspapers and cheap magazines shows this defect in the extreme, as newspapers yellow and become brittle after a mere few days. Unless the industry corrects this

21

problem, older books will be in better shape a hundred years from now than books printed last year.

Some chief enemies of books are:

FIRE. Fire has totally or partially destroyed many important libraries, often during war (for example, the burning of the Alexandrian Library by Caesar's troops, and the destruction of the Library of Congress in Washington by the British in the War of 1812), and sometimes by accident. The Jenkins Company of Austin, Texas, lost an extensive inventory to fire in December 1985. Fortunately some of the more valuable items—many acquired from other collection dispersal sales through the years—were stored in a large walk-in vault and survived the blaze.

Light or moderate fire damage to a book may be repaired. The binding can be replaced and page ends, if scorched, may be trimmed. If a badly scorched book is still worth the trouble, the leaves may be unbound and mounted by a professional bookbinder.

Some precautions can be taken to minimize the threat of fire damage to a collection. A book room should have fire retardant carpets; draperies and curtains should be kept at a minimum; upholstered and overstuffed furniture should be avoided. Glass enclosed bookshelves are safer than open shelves where fires are a risk. A fire extinguisher should be kept handy and the door kept shut when the room is not in use.

WATER. Books can be water damaged by floods, fire fighting efforts, plumbing problems, storms, or any occasion when water comes into contact with covers and leaves.

Whether or not a soaked book can be salvaged depends on the paper quality. Vellum can often take a soaking and be reconditioned. A good rag paper has the best chance, but the book must be dismantled and each leaf dried separately. Modern books on coated paper, such as art books, however, are a loss. The coating disintegrates and you're left with sticky goo and incomplete images on the pages.

Newspapers, too, cannot take moisture. They absorb water and return to the pulp they started from.

Properly drying out a book is a delicate process and should be done by a professional. Restoration is an expensive procedure, so a book should be evaluated carefully to determine whether it is worth the cost.

Some steps to take to guard against water damage include avoiding rooms with overhead water pipes for book rooms. (Be aware of kitchens and bathrooms on the floor above. Those pipes are not always visible, but they can still leak down onto your books if they burst.) Avoid basement rooms that may leak or be damp at best. Cover books carefully when transporting them.

EXCESSIVE HUMIDITY OR EXCESSIVE DRYNESS. Dry air damages leather bindings. Humid air breeds mold and mildew, curls paper, and loosens bindings. The ideal humidity for books is around 50%, give or take ten points. In a humid environment, without a dehumidifier, it's best to store books on open shelves rather than in glass cases where moisture can build up inside.

To help leather remain supple in all environments, but especially in dry air, treat regularly with a leather dressing. This will be taken up at greater length when we discuss leather care.

ROUGH HANDLING. Books that are improperly handled do not remain long in collectible condition. Be gentle when handling all books, not just those that appear fragile. Even a big, brawny folio can be easily damaged sometimes by the weight of its own pages pulling on the spine if it's not handled well.

Don't open any book too wide or press it flat on a table to copy from it, this cracks the hinges.

Older books with metal clasps require special handling. If the clasps are tight, don't tug at them to open them. Instead, gently squeeze the outer edges of the book until the clasps pop open easily. To close them, squeeze again and gently fit the clasps in place. If they won't close, don't force them. Over time these books, especially vellum, may have swelled and the clasps no longer fit. Leave them open or risk damaging the binding with too much squeezing.

IMPROPER STORAGE. A book can be damaged by improper shelving, though the harm is often done over time, almost imperceptibly, so you may not notice it's happening until it's too late. Common mistakes are wedging books too tightly on a shelf or letting books flop about on unfilled shelves, stacking books flat on their sides, one atop another, or shelving books on their fore-edge.

Most spine problems of folio books and larger are caused by shelving on the fore-edge, causing the books to develop loose sections or covers, bent edges and corners, and possibly damaged pages. While it's tempting to place a book that's too large for the shelf on its edge, you should resist the impulse. The weight of the pages will pull them away from the spine and you'll end up with a broken book.

If you can, stand large books on top of the bookcase supported by bookends. If you can't do this, place them flat on the bookshelf, but don't put other books on top of them.

LIGHT. Especially sunlight. Direct sunlight, the ultraviolet component, degrades many kinds of paper and fades the color—or "mellows" the bindings—of books that stand for long periods in the sun. Nothing is more discouraging than to see a table full of books at a flea market warping and wilting unprotected from a hot summer sun.

Bookcases shouldn't receive direct sunlight if it can be avoided, though indirect sunlight to brighten a room is okay. Interior lighting should be incandescent. Fluorescent light damages books.

INSECTS AND PESTS. A particularly nasty enemy of books is the bookworm. Not the bookish person devoted to reading, but insect larvae that feast on the binding and paste of books. Bugs, too, can wreak havoc on books. Some bugs, like silverfish, love a meal of sizing and starches used in the manufacture of paper. Some like the dyes and materials used in bindings like buckram.

The best recourse, if worms or insects are attacking your collection, is to call in a professional and have the entire house treated, but don't spray insecticide directly on your volumes. You may cause more damage than the bugs.

DISPLAYING YOUR BOOKS

BOOKSHELVES. You'd think it would be simple to figure out how to store and display your books. Put them on a bookshelf, of course. But, it's not so simple as it sounds. Many book enthusiasts think that old books belong in old bookcases and they will go out to an antique shop or an auction and buy the first old bookcase they see. Wrong.

It's important to look past the brass trimming and the darling, carved gargoyles to see how the bookcase is constructed. Are the shelves adjustable in height? Are they sagging, cracked, or splintered? Are all the shelf supports present? Are they sturdy enough to carry the weight of heavy books?

Whether or not your bookcase should have glass doors depends on several factors. Do you want the books handled? Are there children in the house too young to appreciate the delicacy of your treasures? Do you have pets who like to sit on top of a shelf of books? (Cats do.)

Glass doors are a great protection from dust and they cut down on the work you must do, as well as the wear and tear on your books, keeping the books clean. But they are bulky and stand between you and your collection in a way that open, inviting shelves don't.

BOOKENDS. Many bookends are collectible, from the Art Nouveau and the Arts and Crafts movements, stunning in brass, copper, and bronze. But do they do the job?

Bookends should keep your books from tumbling around and should support heavy volumes. If you find you're constantly repositioning and straightening or tightening them up, they aren't working and should be replaced. For the best service, and at a fraction of the cost of the fancy bookend, we recommend the metal L-shaped or T-shaped models in which the lower portion slides beneath the first several books. Be sure

The English were the masters at panel binding. It is very symmetrical and orderly. The material is black morocco, the tooling is in gold, and the spine has extra embellishing, c. 1690.

they're tall enough to support your books and that the edges are smooth and won't scuff the covers and pages.

BOOK REPAIR

We cannot emphasize too strongly leaving the repair of a rare book to a competent bookbinder. For those more common or moderately priced books, learning a few pointers on how to repair them yourself is worthwhile.

PROFESSIONAL BOOKBINDING. A good bookbinder is a valuable resource, and anyone interested in used and old books should know one. He's first-aid for books, rescuing broken and defective volumes from oblivion, making suggestions and offering alternatives you may not realize you had.

Do not order a complete new binding if the old, loose one is in fairly sound condition. A loose cover can be rehinged, and missing leather can be replaced. New bindings can be created in which usable portions of the old leather are inlaid into a leather of similar grain and color. The old spine—or what's left of it—can be reset into a new spine.

These procedures are expensive and probably not worth the cost unless your book has some special appeal or is particularly ancient or rare.

When pages or gatherings are loose, the book may need resewing. If the paper is too fragile to permit this, the book can be dismantled and the inner edges of the leaves can be attached to guards which are then sewn together. When guards are used, it is generally not possible to recase the volume—that is, return it to the original binding—because the page ends will protrude from the fore-edge. A new binding is necessary.

HOME REPAIR. You may try some home repair on mildly damaged books that are not so rare or expensive that a mistake would be a disaster. Some of the more common repairs are:

•*Loose Bindings.* Loose cloth bindings can usually be repaired by opening the book midway, laying it face downward, and brushing glue along the inner side of the spine. Do not use cement-type glues; polyvinyl acetate, such as Elmer's Glue-All, does the job best. Use it sparingly. When completed, place rubber bands around the book and allow it to dry for several hours.

•*Cracked Inner Hinges.* Inner hinges can be strengthened by folding a narrow strip of paper and pasting it along the hinge. The paper should be about as heavy as an index card for best results. Make sure it is neither too long nor too short.

•*Notations and Underlinings.* Markings done in pencil are easily—but gently!—erased. When the marks are in ink, nothing

Ever popular, The Complete Angler *(sometimes spelled* Compleat Angler), *by Isaac Walton (sometimes spelled Izaak Walton), in several incarnations, along with other books of the genre, are held in Special Collections at the University of Vermont's Bailey-Howe Library. Shown are (l. to r.) Izaak Walton and Charles Cotton,* The Complete Angler, *William Pickering, London, 1836; John Williamson,* The British Angler, *or a Pocket Companion for Gentlemen Fishers, 1740; Walton and Cotton,* The Complete Angler, *London, 1824; and Izaak Walton,* The Compleat Angler, *illustrated by E.J. Sullivan, J.M. Dent Co., London, 1896.*

removes them satisfactorily, and it is probably wise not to make the effort. The paper could be damaged by using strong cleansers or by scraping. At times, the notations might be of interest and could even provide evidence on the book's previous ownership (called provenance).

•*Torn Spines.* Spines are best treated by simply brushing a small quantity of glue on the torn sections, pressing them firmly into place, and allowing them to dry under the pressure of a rubber band.

•*Moisture.* Treat the book before the pages dry. Once stains are set by drying, they won't come out. Now the treatment we recommend may seem a little strange, but, if the book doesn't warrant professional attention, try this anyway.

First, mop any surface water by patting gently with soft paper towels. Place an oversized sheet of wax paper between all leaves that have gotten wet. In a wooden box about twice the size of the book, place an inch-thick layer of pipe tobacco and lay the book in it. Sprinkle a few more tobacco leaves over the book and seal the box tightly. Store the box in a dry place for several weeks. Some stains will probably remain, but they'll be less visible than if treatment had not been tried.

CARE OF LEATHER BOOKBINDINGS

Leather bindings, though more attractive than cloth, require more upkeep. Leather, an animal substance, has natural oils when new. As it grows old the oil dries out and the leather becomes brittle. Red dust on your bookshelves is a sure sign that your bindings are dry. At that point, emergency treatment is necessary. It won't cure damage that has already occurred but it will halt further deterioration.

Leather bindings must be dressed. This may not be the most pleasant chore, but it can be rewarding. Be sure to get a good leather care preparation, and use it intelligently. Too much will leave the binding sticky.

For best results, use a dressing made expressly for bindings such as the British Museum Leather Dressing. This old stand-by was once hard to get in America and collectors sent to London for it and paid the price. Today, it can generally be purchased in the states. Abide by the directions and don't be disappointed if the leather doesn't look polished. The aim in dressing leather is to give it a drink, not a shine.

Most old leathers will not polish and should not be expected to.

Give your leather-bound books a dressing about every six months. With regular care, any leather binding bought in good condition should remain so. But don't buy a shabby binding in the belief that it can be easily refurbished as this is impossible.

HOW TO USE THIS BOOK

�֍

Books are part of man's prerogative.

—SIR THOMAS OVERBURY

The books in this listing are arranged alphabetically by author's last name, or, if no author, by the title.

Categories of books such as Americana, Travel, Sporting, etc., have been dispensed with since most books can be assigned to more than one category. We believe our system is simpler and more "user friendly." We discuss genres and categories in the glossary, and again in our section on the book business. A careful reader will soon be able to determine the proper categories for whatever book is in question.

In most listings, the author's name is followed by the title, the place of publication and/or a date. Dates have been taken from the title page or the copyright page. In preferred bibliographic format, which we endorse and use in our own business, dates taken from the copyright page are in parentheses. We have endeavored to adhere to this style as closely as possible and, where the information was known, we have included parentheses for copyright page dates.

We have not limited ourselves to listing first editions, but we have identified first editions in the majority of cases. Where a question remains whether or not you have a first edition in hand, further research in reference bibliographies is called for. Several excellent research sources are listed at the back of this book.

In most cases, the number of pages in a volume is not given, but where we considered it helpful, or where identification of a work

Fine bindings on display at the Vermont Antiquarian Booksellers Fair in Pomfret, Vermont.

requires it, we have included page counts. Similarly, where illustrations include colored or engraved plates, we have included the number of plates in many cases, especially when identification of an important book is dependent on that information. (Note: When examining any volume, check the table of contents or list of illustrations against the plates present to be sure they are all accounted for, since some people remove plates from old books to frame and sell them separately.)

Readers will notice that many books listed are not first editions. Some titles are rare and valuable in whatever editions they appear. Later editions may contain signatures, provenance, or other attributes of note or may be illustrated by artists of great renown, making those editions more valuable than the first.

Unless otherwise stated, the prices given are for books in their original bindings except for those dating to the 17th century or earlier, in which case a good period binding is assumed.

Our prices reflect fair retail value based on a consensus of asking prices and realized prices of books on the open market over the past three years.

Dealers typically offer a 10–20% discount to other bookmen. A dealer may pay about 50% of retail for a book bought from a private individual if a customer is waiting in the wings for that book. For stock, a dealer will offer from 20% to 35% of a book's retail value.

If you should offer a dealer an extremely rare and sought-after book, the dealer may act as an agent to market the book and take only a commission on the sale. This happened to us recently when we discovered Professor Albert Einstein's signature on a dinner menu and program from a 1930s' TransAtlantic Ocean Liner. Prof. Einstein was on the program to entertain that evening playing his violin.We informed the owner, who was not aware of the signature, and with her permission sent the program to Swann Galleries in New York. We're not only thrilled to be the agents in this case, but discovering the signature was great fun.

Settling on prices for this guide, we used the tools available to us—auction records, dealer catalogues, conversations with booksellers, and 20 years experience in the trade—to give you the best estimates on the retail value of the books listed.

At times, the variation in our price listings reflects slight differences in the condition of books offered by different dealers. At times, it reflects the vicissitudes of the market, where a book may fetch a smart price in the mountains of New England and go far more cheaply in the deserts of Arizona. Or a dealer may offer a book at one price in his shop, while patrons of an auction house bought it at a far different price. We have not shied away from listing these broad ranges so the reader can see clearly the idiosyncrasies of the antiquarian book trade.

In all cases, books are assumed to be in at least very good condition, and where modern first editions are concerned, excellent condition. To realize their best price, modern firsts must have their dust jackets intact, but some listings clearly do not state dust jacket. These books have been

Children's books on display at the Vermont Antiquarian Booksellers' Fair in Pomfret, Vermont, in the booth of Roy and Jean Kulp of Hatfield, Pennsylvania. (Photo by Ilan Fisher)

offered or sold for a lower price than they would have fetched with the jacket. Still, many modern firsts, even without their jackets, are worth more than the $.50 charged at library sales, so we've included them here.

At all times, remember that this is a guide and not a guarantee of prices. The marketplace, forever in flux, determines the real value of used and old books.

We have endeavored to verify statistics for each listing, but no book of this type can guarantee freedom from error. The serious bibliophile will not depend on any one source, but will use multiple research tools to verify data on important books.

GLOSSARY

✳

A word fitly spoken is like apples of gold in pictures of silver.

—PROVERBS

ADDENDA (OR ADDENDUM). Supplemental material inserted at the end of a book.

ADVANCE COPY. Copies of a book issued ahead of schedule to gain final approval from the author or to send to reviewers before the edition is released. Sometimes the advance copies will be identical to the regular edition, but often they are not, at least to the extent that they are labeled advance copies. If the only difference is in style or color of binding, it may be difficult to determine later if the copies are an advance issue or simply a binding variant, which could be part of a normal trade run.

Collectors often value advance copies since they represent an early state of the text and, however rare the case, they may contain notations by the author.

ALL EDGES GILT. Indicates that all three edges of the leaves (top, bottom, and fore-edge) have been gilded. The term is abbreviated aeg or, if only the top edge is gilded, teg.

AMERICANA. In the strict sense, refers to material dealing with the American hemisphere. But today, the term more often refers narrowly and loosely to books, documents, pamphlets, and other printed material that shows why, how, when, and by whom the United States was developed.

ANA (OR IANA). Suffix denoting items related to a particular subject, be it a person, a time or place in history, or some such. For instance, Joyceiana is material relating in some way to James Joyce, even if the connection is remote. The heading covers such things as pamphlets, books, newspaper accounts, artifacts, and letters by, about, or to the subject.

Collecting ana (or iana) is widespread among those interested in a particular author or historical time or personality. Even those who have written only one book (or none) can be the subject of an extensive collection of written and artifact items. Institutions and libraries are notable collectors of ana.

ANTHOLOGY. A collection of short works, by one or more writers, in one book or set of volumes. Anthologies are most often collections of works that have appeared elsewhere.

ANTIQUARIAN BOOKSELLING. Sale of used, old, and rare books, printed fare, and related items; usually refers to trade in books out of print.

Until about the 12th century, most books were handcrafted in monasteries and churches and remained their property. Except to those who owned them and valued the information they contained, books had no intrinsic value unless they contained gold gilt or were inlaid with precious stones. Not until sometime around the 13th century, when craftspeople in the secular world began to make and sell books, adding topics like philosophy and literature, did books take on a broader commercial value.

Michael Olmert, author of the *Smithsonian Book of Books* (1992) remarks, "An intriguing question is when did books become valuable enough to steal?" Olmert says that thieves profited from stealing books once a commercial market for them was established. As proof that books were taking on value, he reports book owners of the 12th century began writing curses on their flyleaves to discourage theft, warning that whoever steals the books would be damned to hellfire.

Even as the first commercial markets were growing, bookmaking was done slowly by hand, comparatively few books were produced, and those that were were often custom made for specific buyers. Bookselling was primarily a second-hand business but was not yet antiquarian bookselling. Since bound books were still in their infancy, you wouldn't term their trade antiquarian.

By the 17th century, enough time had elapsed, printing had become mechanized, and enough books were in circulation for true antiquarian bookselling to arise in England, France, and elsewhere.

Few catalogues were issued at first. Most early shops gathered in clusters, such as those that sprang up in St. Paul's Churchyard, London. Most shopkeepers located in large cities, primarily in stalls with much of their material displayed on the sidewalk and very little within.

The PENNY BOXES that became such a favorite of the bargain hunters in later years were probably not present early on. Prints, engravings, maps, and such were sold by at least some dealers.

The emergence of the scholar-dealer—the collector at heart who studied his merchandise with interest—did not occur until the early part of the 19th century. By this time, bookselling was big business. The Bohn brothers of London are generally credited with giving birth to modern rare-book dealing. By 1900, at least a half dozen English dealers boasted inventories in excess of half-a-million volumes. Several German booksellers by this time had stocks even larger.

APPRAISAL. Estimation of the value of a book or a collection. An appraisal should be made by a qualified professional in the antiquarian book trade with the tools and the experience to do the job right. Some appraisers will offer an opinion based on a mere list and description of volumes, but that is not recommended. The value of a book depends on many factors, not the least of which is its condition. The best appraisals are done by experts who can hold the books in their hands and examine them in fine detail. This can't be done with a list.

AQUATINT. A method of etching that stresses soft tones and shades, resembling wash paintings. The French artist LePrince is generally credited with perfecting the process during the late 18th century. The technique became popular in Britain during the 18th and 19th centuries.

Sometimes aquatint printing was done in color and sometimes the coloring was added by hand later. When printing in colored aquatint, a separate plate for each color is necessary. A few famous artists such as Goya and Picasso experimented with the process.

ART PAPER. Shiny, coated stock on which most art books (or at least the illustrations) are printed. The paper ages badly and is easily damaged by moisture. Also, dirt stains cannot be removed without damaging the surface of the paper.

AS NEW. Showing no signs of wear; the book doesn't look used. Basically a British expression, Americans prefer MINT, which carries the same meaning.

ASSOCIATION COPY. A book that was part of the author's own library or was associated in one way or another with a famous person. It may be that the author inscribed the book to a friend, or the book may contain an inscription by another famous owner, perhaps a dedication or a presentation, or the book was merely included—without any inscriptions—in a famous person's library. But the point is, there must be proof that the book has been in the possession of someone famous.

The value of association copies to the collector derives from the book's connection to history, or in modern times, to people who are perceived as larger than life. If we were to learn that Abraham Lincoln had a favorite book of sonnets that he daily carried with him, we would love to have that book. It would be an association copy.

Association copies should be distinguished from signed copies, which proliferate these days with the popularity of book tours and autograph signings. And beware the forgeries! Experts in the trade can help you weed them out.

AUTHORIZED EDITION. Usually refers to biographies written with the approval or even help of the subject. The term is intended to draw attention and interest, but a drawback to authorized editions is the public perception that if the subject of a biography authorized the work, it wouldn't tell tales of the subject's secret life.

B.A.L. The *Bibliography of American Literature*, authored by Jacob Nathaniel Blanck and published in 1955 by the Yale University Press for the Bibliographical Society of America. Virginia Smyers and Michael Winship edited the work and later added a final volume. The seven-volume work is a detailed bibliography of important American literature through much of the 20th century and an indispensable research tool for the serious book person.

BASTARD TITLE. Another name for the **HALF-TITLE PAGE**, the leaf preceding the title page that carries the title in small print but no other information. Use of this page is a holdover from the incunabula days when the title page consisted of only this. It has no other real purpose and is retained in many volumes merely because old habits die hard. With a nod to decorum, many bibliographers referred to this as the "bas. title."

BAY PSALM BOOK. The first full-length American-printed book. Issued at Cambridge, Massachusetts, in 1640 by Stephen Daye, the name derives from the Massachusetts Bay Colony. Only 11 volumes are known to remain, all but one in public or institutional collections. The total number of copies printed isn't known, but is guessed to be from 100 to 300. Though the usual press run at the time was considerably more, experts theorize that Daye would not have had a large market for books printed locally and would have printed less than the usual number. The book was collected as a rarity as early as the mid 1700s. The actual title of Daye's volume is *The Whole Booke of Psalmes Faithfully Translated into English Metre*, but printers in Europe had produced works with similar titles, and therefore *Bay Psalm Book* more clearly distinguishes Daye's work from the others.

BEVELED EDGES. Angle-cut edges on wooden boards once used in bookbindings. They're of little consequence when judging the value of an antiquarian book.

Chapbooks were popular fare during the 19th century, often sold door-to-door by traveling salesmen commonly called chapmen. The collection pictured is included in Special Collections at the Bailey-Howe Library at the University of Vermont. Books pictured are (l. to r.): The Farm House, *Mahlon Day printer, early 1800s;* Cinderella, *J. B. Jansen, NY, 1830s;* The Red Squirrel, *A. Phelps, Greenfield, 1846;* Cinderella or The Glass Slipper, *H & E Phinney, Cooperstown, 1834;* Stories for Children About Whales, *Rufus Merrill, Concord, NH, 1843;* Cock Robin's Courtship and Marriage, *Sidney's Press, New Haven, 1824;* The Young Sailor, or The Sea Life of Tom Bowline, *Kiggins & Kellogg, NY, 1840s.*

BIBLIOGRAPHY. Commonly, a list of books organized by subject or author. For instance, libraries consider an author bibliography to be a list, as complete as possible, of all specimens of an author's work that have appeared in print.

The term has taken on an alternate meaning coming into its own now as the study of books themselves, including their origins, history, development, physical appearance, construction, and value.

BIBLIOMANIA. A preoccupation with books, a compulsion to be around them, learn about them, and own them. Booksellers and collectors are prone to this disease. The malady can be observed at library sales, auctions, and house sales.

BIBLIOPHILE. An ardent and avid book collector. One who loves books. A mild, benign form of bibliomania.

BIBLIOTHECA AMERICANA. A comprehensive directory of books on Americana, 29 volumes in all, dating from the coming of the Europeans to the 20th century. Begun by Joseph Sabin, who completed the first 13 volumes, the work was continued by Wilberforce Eames and completed by R. W. G. Vail.

BINDING COPY. A book in need of a new binding. A British term.

BINDINGS. The permanent cover of a book, not to be confused with a dust jacket. As soon as books were made of folded leaves instead of scrolls, they needed a proper covering. The earliest bindings were probably uncovered wooden boards with a hide spine—what we call today a **HALF-LEATHER** binding. This evolved into a full-leather binding. Early ornamentation on books consisted of painting and encrusting with jewels and bone carvings. In time, these gave way to **BLINDSTAMPING** and finally goldstamping.

Materials used over the centuries for binding books are numerous and even macabre. Most common were vellum, pigskin, calf, morocco, and various types of cloth or muslin. A practice arose during the Middle Ages of occasionally stripping the skin of slain enemy soldiers. One use of the leather made out of these skins: book bindings. (In some cathedrals in Europe one can still see doors covered in these human hides. Tour guides often hesitate to mention this fact.)

Collecting fine bindings is a major area of book collecting.

BLINDSTAMPING. Recessed or raised impressions on the bindings of books which are not inked or colored. Blindstamping did not originate with bookbinding but was long a popular means of hand-decorating leather. As a decoration for bindings, the process did not begin until the 12th century.

BOARDS. Uncovered hard cardboard, wooden boards, or boards covered with thin paper, linen, buckrum, etc., used as front and back covers in bindings. The term is a holdover from the early days of printing when books were bound with actual wooden boards held together by leather or buckram at the spine. In the bookselling trade today, "boards" refers to stiff bindings covered in paper instead of the more common cloth or even leather.

BOOK OF HOURS. Illuminated medieval prayer books. During the Middle Ages, wealthy patrons commissioned these stunning books for their personal use. They were prized for their calendars, which frequently featured pictures of month-by-month activities—planting in spring, harvesting in fall, etc.—providing historians with valuable insights into medieval society and habits. Small in size, handy to carry to church services, the books included psalms, litanies, and various offices of the church. The organization of these books was based on the church's prescribed daily schedule for devotions, hence the name *Book of Hours*.

BOOK OF KELLS. An Irish manuscript of Christian scripture from the 8th century. The opening page of each gospel is lavishly illustrated with brightly colored designs and images of saints and religious persons and events. Depictions of nature, such as animals, fish, and trees, abound throughout. The art of the monks and their use of color and whimsy shows the attainment of the Irish artists of the early Middle Ages. By the way figures are depicted in the hand illuminations, it is obvious artists of the day had not perfected the study of anatomy but that deficiency was made up for in their exquisite concepts of color and design. The folio manuscript is housed in the Library of Trinity College, Dublin, Ireland.

BOOKPLATES. A label identifying ownership usually pasted on the inside of a book cover. Older, intricately designed and executed bookplates are collectors' items in their own right. Some are delightful examples of art. Their use dates from the 15th century. If a modern bookplate is inserted by a person of no particular renown, the plate does not detract from the book; when properly applied, they do no harm, but they should not be affixed over existing plates or in such a way that they obscure important inscriptions or writings.

Plates of antiquity, either engraved by some famous craftsman or showing possession by some notable person, are highly sought after by collectors of bookplates but they really should not be removed from the books. Contrary to common belief, this practice damages the books and destroys evidence of a book's PROVENANCE, or history, an important phase of bibliography.

BOOK SCOUT. A person who beats the bushes looking for saleable books who then markets these finds to booksellers. Since a bookseller is often tied down with a shop, scheduling time for a buying trip can be a problem. Enter the bookscout. With no overhead and unfettered by the minutiae of a bookseller's store, scouts have time to ferret out books sitting on somebody's shelf in an attic or the eternal Friends of the Library book sale.

A bookseller might have several scouts scattered in different parts of the country haunting the flea markets, Salvation Army stores, and garage sales. But for the most part, scouts work independently, seeking out the bookseller with the strongest interest in their finds.

Often a person starting out as a scout develops into a fulltime bookseller. Scouts of the seedy, unsavory character described by John Dunning in his mystery novel, *Booked to Die* (1992), may exist somewhere, but our experience of scouts in New England (Marie started out as a scout 20 years ago) reveals a type of person who loves books to begin with and is delighted to chase them for booksellers.

TAMERLANE

AND

OTHER POEMS

BY A BOSTONIAN

Young heads are giddy and young hearts are warm
and make mistakes for manhood to reform.

Cowper

BOSTON:

CALVIN F. S. THOMAS . . PRINTER

1827

Facsimile title page

BOOK SIZES. Industry terms loosely inferring the size of volumes. The terms describe books according to their FORMAT (the way they are printed and bound) rather than actual measurements, giving the practiced professional only an indication of how big the books really are.

The common book size formats are folio, quarto, octavo, and duodecimo, indicating the manner in which the printer folds the paper sheets on which a book is printed to create leaves (pages). Regardless of the planned format, all sheets are fed through a press in full size and folded later into "quires." These are collected and bound together, the closed edges of the folded sheets are slit, and—presto—you have book.

If each printed sheet is folded once to create two leaves, the book becomes a folio, the largest format. If folded twice, we get four leaves, or a quarto, written "4to." Fold again and there are eight leaves, an octavo, or "8vo"; twelve leaves are duodecimo, "12mo." Keep going and you have progressively smaller sizes and larger numbers: 16mo, 24mo, 32mo, and 64mo. A 128mo format exists, but it's only seen in the very tiniest of miniature volumes.

You can't divine the actual measure of a book from the format, but is isn't a useless convention. What you can reliably ascertain from a statement of format is something about the shape of a volume. Octavos tend to be sleek, at least 1½ times tall as they are wide. Quartos tend to be squarish and dumpy. Folios are tall and well proportioned. The Gutenberg "Bible" is a folio. Most modern novels are 8vo's. Coffee-table art books are folios and large quartos.

BOOKWORMS. The larval stage of a beetle that likes to eat books, a pesty little worm that feeds upon the bindings and leaves. They've been preying on libraries since the very earliest times. These maggots were the scourge of monastic libraries in the Middle Ages. No area of Europe was free of the bookworm, and contrary to some beliefs, they did not seek out only filthy habitations but ate books in fine homes and libraries as well. Modern chemicals have virtually exterminated them.

BREAKER. Someone who takes books apart and then sells the parts separately, especially the illustrations. Breaking a book may bring a higher price for the parts than the book would fetch as a whole. When a book is so badly damaged that it cannot be repaired or recovered as a book, breaking is a way of preserving the plates and putting them into circulation.

Breaking books that are not otherwise damaged is looked down on by serious antiquarian booksellers and collectors as a horrendous practice.

BROADSIDE. A poster, announcement, or proclamation, usually printed on one side of a sheet and meant to be posted on a wall. Many a political statement was brought to the people's attention in this manner, even after the advent of newspapers. Old auction posters, especially horse auctions, might be adorned with an illustrated display of wares adding to the value and desirability of the artifact.

Broadsides are popular with collectors today.

BUCKRAM. A modern binding material very much like cloth but tougher and somewhat more attractive. Libraries most always have their books rebound in buckram. Inexpensive, buckram can be dyed all the colors of the rainbow, as well as goldstamped. The natural shade, which is rather like a cross between straw and wheat, is preferred by many.

Buckram bindings are often described in catalogues as cloth and vice-versa, a fact of life that collectors must endure.

CALF. Leather used for bookbindings.

CALLED FOR. Points mentioned in bibliographies that determine the edition of a book. For instance, if a handbook written by Smith says that a blank leaf follows the title in a certain edition of a certain book, then the blank leaf is "called for" for that edition and must be there for the book to be complete.

CAXTON, WILLIAM. The first English printer. Born at Kent, he started his business life as a mercer, or dealer in yarn goods, a trade he followed for most of his life, showing no particular mechanical skills or flair for literature. Around 1441, Caxton went to Burgundy. He spent most of his adult life on the continent. In 1471, he entered the service of the Duchess of Burgundy and, under her influence, he performed his first effort with books, translating the *Recuyell of the Historyes of Troye.*

On a visit to Cologne that year, he was apparently introduced to the art of printing, which he brought back to Bruges, setting about to give the city a printing press. Together with a Flemish calligrapher, Colard Mansion, Caxton issued the first English language book, the same *Recuyell.* After printing two more books with Mansion, Caxton returned alone to England and founded a printing office in the parish of Westminster.

Compared to the best French and Italian printing of the time, Caxton's books come off a sorry second. His fame has led many to assume that his talent as a craftsman and type designer must have been extraordinary, but this was not the case. He did, however, exert much influence upon his contemporaries and followers. He began with types modeled on German gothic and stuck with them to the end. This set the trend for English printers and it was not until a century after his death that the types were replaced by the more graceful Roman.

A craze for Caxtons among collectors began in the early part of the 19th century and has gathered steam ever since. The finest collections are at the British Museum and John Rylands Library. In the United States, the Morgan and Huntington libraries are notable for their Caxtons.

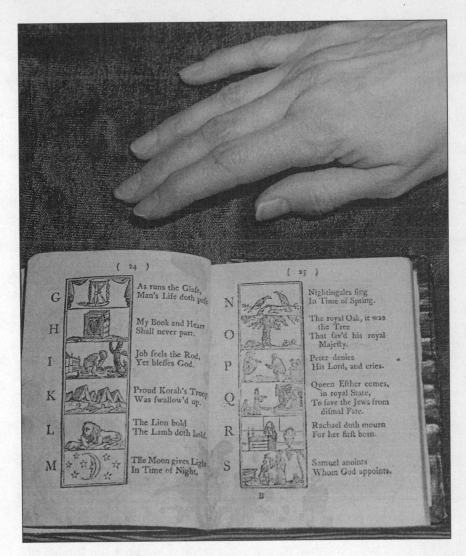

Two pages of The Boston Primer, *a popular chapbook, this one printed in 1811. Engravings illustrate the alphabet for young learners, and are a typical example of the style used on these popular little books. (Courtesy of the Trustees of the Boston Public Library. Photographed by Marilyn Green.)*

CHAPBOOK. A small pamphlet or booklet usually associated with children's stories or rhymes. Most are diminutive in size and illustrated with woodcuts. In the 18th century, itinerant peddlers, or "chapmen," hawked the booklets door to door. Because they were cheaply made, many of the books have not survived in very good condition, but those that have are highly prized and collectible.

CHEAP COPY. A defective copy which is being offered at a discount. The dealer wants the prospective buyer to be aware of the poor condition.

CLOTH BINDING. The ideal binding substance, cheap, durable, easy to apply, comes in a variety of colors. For modern books, cloth has replaced leather as the binding of choice. True, the disappearance of leather is lamentable, but the cost of leather binding would prohibit ownership of books to all but a limited class of collectors.

In the first years of cloth binding, publishers let their imaginations run wild. Every effort was made to ornament the bindings lavishly. The books were gilded and blindstamped using patterns copied from notable bindings of earlier ages. But unlike the books of old, gilding was done with large panel stamps impressed by machine rather than with tools worked by hand. The purpose was to make the public forget leather. It succeeded; out of sight, out of mind. In time, only connoisseurs who kept fine libraries retained any affection for leather. That is not to say, however, that we have become so undiscriminating that we cannot still appreciate a book bound in fine, soft leather.

CODEX. Applies to leaves bound in book form—this book you are holding, for example—as opposed to scrolls or tablets. The invention is generally credited to Roman legal clerics who grew weary of cumbersome scrolls and cut them down to convenient size. The practice made sense at a time when the whole process of managing information was time-consuming and laborious.

COLLATED. Inspected from cover to cover to be sure all pages, plates, maps, and the like are present, intact, and in their proper place. In the case of earlier books, a perfect copy—or comprehensive knowledge of one—is necessary to make a comparison when collating.

A good practice when purchasing a book is to check out the list of illustrations numbered in the contents and confirm that they are all there. If maps should be present, check them out. Nothing is more frustrating when you get home than to discover pages missing from a book you were all excited about purchasing.

And never, never send out a book to a dealer or customer before collating it. Selling a book with missing pages could be cause for manslaughter, or, more seriously, labeling yourself unprofessional.

COLOPHON. The "finishing touch." The tradition of medieval scribes when completing their manuscripts was to record, on the last page, their name and place of residence and, sometimes, the day on which the book was finished.

At times, the addition of a colophon was done out of vanity but, more often than not, such information was necessary. Without it, a printer or publisher could not identify an edition as his own, which might result in legal difficulties if the book were pirated or stolen by another printer.

The average colophon was a model of simplicity, one sentence or so, giving the essential facts. Colophons were replaced after the 16th century by information included on the title page. Still, some modern books, usually limited editions, still add a colophon, perhaps out of respect for tradition. You might find one that starts out: "This book was set on the monotype in Fournier. . . ."

CONDITION. The general state of a book. This singularly most important point cannot be overemphasized when considering whether to buy or sell a collectible book.

Like people, books are either in fine shape, very good shape, bad shape, or various states in between. As no hard and fast definitions exist, the terms used to designate a book's condition are subject to personal opinion. Having said that, we hasten to add that there is some agreement in the book trade as to what the terms mean.

•*Mint*. As new. Right off the press.

•*Fine*. Nearly new. Sometimes a dealer might overlap this with mint.

•*Very Good*. Definitely showing wear, but not damaged. Usually a clean, tight copy. Most collectible books fit this category.

•*Good*. Obviously read. Perhaps the cover shows moderate wear, a hinge is cracked in front or back, some minor spine fading might be present, the binding scuffed. Perhaps the book is even a little shaken, not quite as tight as it used to be. All in all, the condition shows the book has been around for a while and used. No really major defects.

•*Fair*. Worn and used. Cover soiled, scuffed, evidence of repairs, shaken, perhaps a page torn here or there. The book has definitely been around the barn.

•*Reading Copy*. About all it is good for. Or, it may interest collectors of modern first editions who keep their pristine copies on a shelf safe from prying hands but who may still want to read Hemingway or Faulkner. Reading copies come in handy for research.

Now when all is said and done, should a disheveled rare book come up at auction, you can bet your bottom dollar—and you might have to—that book will not lack for spirited bidding. So extenuating circumstances call for common sense. If a book is being purchased for investment, then by all means, abide by the most rigid rules of condition.

COPPER PLATE ENGRAVING. A process for producing prints and book illustrations. Plates were prepared by a battery-hammer method, then smoothed by rubbing with pumice and oilstone. Though costly and time-consuming, this method gave the best possible surface for engraving. The majority of English illustrated books of the 18th century used copper plates.

COPYRIGHT. The equivalent of a patent on a work of literature. A copyright prohibits anyone from reproducing the work, either in whole or in part, without consent of the copyright holder.

CURIOSA. In today's market, books that deal with off-beat subjects like a monograph on foot fetishes or the psychology of wearing hats. During the Victorian age, anything of a sexual nature was hidden under the heading of Curiosa. Today's bookseller has no problem with that subject and classifies erotic material where it belongs, under Erotica.

C.W.O. Cash with order. Most booksellers append this to their ads, safeguarding their interests, choosing not to send a book out to a customer before they have payment in hand. But through the years, we have never encountered a deadbeat customer or bookseller. We have sent out books before the check arrives, in particular, a $5,000 sporting book to a dealer with a fine reputation.

At times, we need to have a little faith in our fellow human beings. Of course, in this case, it was easy as we knew the man's character.

DAMP STAINS. Damage caused by excessive humidity, but not water as is sometimes thought. Books damaged by damp are ragged and musty rather than crisp.

Improper ventilation can cause as much damage as water. Humidity constantly above 70% can damage a book as it stands untouched in a bookcase. In a book with lovely plates, dampness can cause the pages to stick together. Pulling them apart damages the plates, thus greatly altering the value and esthetics of the book.

DAYE, STEPHEN. An important individual, the first man to print mechanically in America. Daye, a British locksmith, came to the Massachusetts Bay Colony in 1633. He and his son, Matthew, a printer's apprentice, set up a printing shop in Cambridge at Harvard College. The earliest surviving book of the Daye's press is commonly known as the *Bay Psalm Book,* after the colony where it was printed.

DELUXE EDITION. Meant to imply extraordinary production qualities; those books which, by superior design, type, paper, binding, or other factors, are set above the pale.

DISBOUND. Refers to a pamphlet or other brief work that once was part of a larger work and has been separated. Purists look down on this practice of removing the piece from the larger collection much as they look down on breaking a book.

DISCARD STAMP. A mark used by libraries when they are culling their collections to show the books have been released for sale or distribution. This is a matter of procedure to guard against theft and to show the book is legitimately no longer a part of the library collection. How nice when a librarian thinks like a book collector and carefully selects an unobtrusive place for the stamp.

DOG-EARED. Originally referred to the corners of pages that have become ragged or creased. Now, it applies to any pages that have the appearance of heavy use. One of the causes of dog-earing is the regrettable habit many readers have of turning down the corner of a page to mark their place. Thank goodness not all readers are guilty of this barbaric practice, choosing instead to use bookmarks.

DURER, ALBRECHT. A German artist, painter, and book illustrator at the turn of the 16th century, he was famous and in great demand for quality woodcuts used in book illustrations. Among his early works are the woodcuts for Sebastian Brant's famous *Ship of Fools*.

Most of Durer's fame came after 1500 when he was prolific in his output not only in book illustration but working in oils, watercolor, silverpoint, and other artistic media.

DUST JACKET (OR DUSTWRAPPER). The decorative paper cover that protects the binding from soil and wear. Jackets were sometimes used during the 19th century and if you found a volume with a jacket of such antiquity, hooray for you. Jackets for books dating back to the early part of the 20th century, too, are like icing on the cake. They're desirable, but hard to come by. For newer books, however—the MODERN FIRST EDITIONS—jackets are a must.

If a book such as William Faulkner's *Light in August* has no dust jacket, it can lose half or more of its value. Even reprints of Zane Grey or Edgar Rice Burroughs command higher prices when accompanied by dust jackets. A modern book with a jacket missing can be likened to an antique table without its legs.

EDGES. Refers to the three outer edges of the leaves. Style of edges is a very important part of a book's makeup, especially in fine or rare editions. New books are delivered to the binder in folded but uncut sheets, or gatherings, and the binder must separate the leaves by cutting the folds. The edges are usually trimmed to make them perfectly even. Books bound without trimming the edges, showing the original state of the paper with all its irregularities, are valued by some collectors. But then there is a collector for just about anything.

ELSE FINE. A term used after a recitation of a book's faults indicating that, otherwise, something is right with the book. The phrase "o/w very good," is more common.

ENGRAVING. Illustrations printed from a metal plate or wood block. Engravings on steel were developed in the 15th century, an improvement over wood that permitted more fine detail and delicate shading.

Collectors of engravings seek the early impressions in a print run, those among the first taken from a plate, as the fine lines of the engraved image sometimes wear down with repeated use.

EPHEMERA. Items that were meant to last a short time. Some booksellers abhor the myriad postcards, sheet music, and advertising paper that appear at book shows under this heading. But many of these items are extensions of book collecting that we accept as not only legitimate but desirable. Say you are putting together a collection of P. G. Wodehouse. Why would you reject the sheet music he wrote? Or the Christmas cards by Robert Frost to round out a collection of his books of poetry? Or the screen scripts written by now famous authors when they were down on their luck and needed to eat?

Ephemera is fun and exciting, and some very famous artists like Maxfield Parrish produced beautiful ads as well as book illustrations for some of the most sought-after children's books. Tucked into old volumes, many ephemera treasures have come to light. A stevensgraph or a hollow-cut silhouette, even a letter with historical information, are some of the bonuses possible when turning the pages of an old book.

A Burlington, Vermont, bookseller was a little chagrined when she learned she'd sold a book on Calvin Coolidge with a holograph letter tucked unnoticed among the leaves. The next day the customer returned and asked, did she have any more of those books with letters of the presidents inside?

ERASURES. Removal of underlining or notations with an eraser, discussed further under "Notations and Underlining" in the section on "Care and Repair of Old Books."

A bookseller may resort to erasing pencil or pen markings made by former owners of a book, generally by use of a wad of art gum or pencil eraser. Collectors have mixed feelings about notations and whether or not they should be removed. The value and rarity of a book will influence whether a book is rejected due to the presence of notations or purchased and lived with as is. For the bibliophile, a notation might suggest some continuity with the former owners and be cherished.

The erasures themselves should be clean and not leave unsightly blotches or destroy the print.

ERRATA. Mistakes in printing. The "errata leaf" is still used in cases where a blooper was spotted too late to correct the print run but early enough to bind a note into the book stating the error and correction. More frequently seen is the "errata slip," a small strip of paper containing the correction which may be pasted in the book, or laid-in loosely, after the book has been bound.

EX-LIBRARY (EX-LIB). Indicates the book belonged to a library or bears evidence of having been in a library collection, e.g., the library stamp, card pockets, or identifying marks on the spine. These books, unless they are exceedingly rare, are not often sought by collectors as they usually show considerable wear and damage due to use and library mutilation.

Ex-lib books are almost as difficult to sell as Book of the Month Club or Reader's Digest editions, although many catalogues feature ex-lib books.

FINE PRINTING. Any book in which the quality of type and layout are a main consideration. Books printed by individuals or presses which design their own type may rate as fine printing if the type is well designed. Such books do not necessarily have to be limited editions or kept from public sale. All the products of early typographers were sold on the general market, yet some represent excellent presswork. Had these men bought their types from foundries rather than having a hand in their design, their books might not be so respected.

FIRST EDITION. The first appearance of a book in print. Collectors refer to the first impression (print run) of the book as a true first edition. Identification of true first editions can be an art and even the most experienced booksellers and collectors run the risk of making an error.

The way printers specify the edition somewhere inside the book—or fail to give any indication at all of which edition it is—varies widely from printer to printer, era to era, and country to country. Best to go prepared with a pocket guide on the subject when browsing through bookstores, for you could not possibly keep in mind the vast number of codes that publishers have used or the legions of points that identify specific titles. Unfortunately, if a book does not readily admit in print to being a second or a third or a fifteen-thousandth edition, the uninformed public automatically assumes the book is a first. The collector or bookseller cannot afford this casual assumption as most collectors acquire first editions for many reasons, not least among them, investment.

FIRST IMPRESSION. The first time a set of plates has been used to print a book. Also called a **PRINTING.**

All impressions using the same set of plates constitute one edition, thus each edition can include more than one impression. Most sellers and collectors are speaking of the first impression of the first edition when discussing collectible **FIRST EDITONS.**

Miniature and micro books displayed by Isaiah Thomas Booksellers of Massachusetts at the Vermont Antiquarian Booksellers' Fair in Pomfret, Vermont. (Photo by Ilan Fisher)

FIRST THUS. Not the first edition, but you may see this used to describe an altered edition of an old book. Since the revised book is an edition unlike the original, perhaps issued by a different publishing house or illustrated by some other artist, the book can be presented as first thus. Like a distant cousin to the first edition.

FLYLEAF. Blank leaf after the front free endpaper, not always present. The term is often misapplied to the front endpaper.

FOLDING PLATES. Plates which fold out to a larger size than the book leaves. Volumes published by the Government Printing Office during the 19th century have many folding maps and color illustrations bound into the books. Guide books are designed with folding illustrations and maps, too. Through the years, unfortunately, folding plates begin to show wear and tear from handling.

FOLIO. A standard book size, measuring from about 12" tall on up. An atlas folio is 24", and an elephant folio is 20" or more. Audubon's *Birds of America* is a most valued natural history book measuring 37" tall.

FORE-EDGE. The outer edge of a book, opposite the spine.

FORE-EDGE PAINTING. Painting the edges of a book's leaves with a scene or other picture. The book must be held in a special press and while the leaves are slightly fanned out the artist paints or decorates the exposed fore-edges of the leaves. When the book is fully closed, the edge is gilded to conceal traces of the painting. But lightly fan out the edges, and the fore-edge painting can be a lovely surprise. Because the painting is hidden, a book with a fore-edge painting can go undetected, even by a knowledgeable bookseller, until the book is opened.

FORMAT. The size of a book determined by the specific number of times the original printed sheet of paper has been folded to form the leaves. For standard format sizes used in the booktrade, see **BOOK SIZE.**

FOXED. Discoloration with brown spots and blotches caused by microorganisms that find the paper in certain books appetizing. Dampness can encourage the problem. The spots are often dark and, when the foxing is heavy, can seriously detract from the value of an otherwise good book.

FRAKTUR. A German style of gothic or black-letter type. Fraktur was most prevalent at Augsburg and Nuremburg in the post-incunabula period when gothic had been almost totally dropped by French and Italian printers. Popular with the Pennsylvania Dutch, early birth certificates decorated and embellished with fraktur are becoming harder to find and more expensive to buy.

FRONTISPIECE. An illustration appearing opposite the title page. More often than not, the frontis (as abbreviated) is a portrait of the author, but in many books, the frontis is a lovely color plate or a steel engraving.

GILT EDGES. Gold applied to all three edges of a book's leaves. In book parlance, t.e.g. means top edge gilt, and a.e.g. means all edges gilt.

HALF-BOUND. A book with leather extending over the spine and about an inch or so along the front and back covers. The rest of the binding is either cloth or paper. If the spine is leather and the four corners of the book are covered in leather triangles, you have a book which is called three-quarter leather. Thought to be an English custom, the practice goes back to the 17th century, but did not become popular until the 18th century.

HALF-TITLE. Usually the first appearance of print in a volume, the title printed on an otherwise blank sheet before the title page. This is a holdover from the days of early printing when the title was the only information given on the title page.

The half-title is also known as **BASTARD TITLE.** Grant Uden in his book *Understanding Book Collecting*, puts this appellation down to the insensitivity of Americans who he says often adopt their own bibliographical terminology. But whosoever puts these terms together, all you have to remember is that the half-title is most often the first appearance of print in a volume.

In the past, when restoring a book, binders often discarded the half-title page. They may have considered it superfluous, and well it might be, unless you are a collector, and then that half-title page had better be there.

HEADBAND. A (usually) colorful band inside of the spine, sewn across the top of the leaves. In modern bindery, it has no function and is primarily decorative, if it is present at all. Headbands are more often seen in older books. The term is used to include the tailband (sewn across the bottom inside of the spine) as well.

HINGE. The ridge where the front or back cover meets the spine. When a book has a hinge crack, the cover is intact but loose. It definitely needs attention before worse can happen, which is separation of the covers from the book.

HOLOGRAPH. A document written wholly in the hand of the author. Although autograph collectors use the term more frequently, booksellers find it helpful to indicate more than mere inscription or presentation material on the flyleaf of a book; specifically, a laid-in letter or a MANUSCRIPT.

HORNBOOK. A sheet of paper, printed on one side with the alphabet or some other rudiments of school work, pasted onto a handled piece of wood then covered with transparent horn. In colonial America, these were a child's first school books. Used from the 16th to the 18th century, genuine hornbooks are rare, but imitation copies turn up now and then, no doubt prompted by the high price an original would command.

ILLUMINATED MANUSCRIPT. A work containing dazzling letters, initials, and sentence openings, hand decorated in bold colors and finished off with gold and silver. Spectacular and colorful, the art work did, in essence, brilliantly shed light upon the text. Manuscript illumination is known to have been practiced as early as the 5th century. Monks in the 7th and 8th centuries produced specimens of great artistry in Ireland, including the awe-inspiring *Book of Kells*.

Illuminating manuscripts remained the province of monastic scribes until the end of the 14th century when the commercial manuscript industry came into its own and the secular world took a serious interest in book ownership. Unfortunately, the invention of printing, which literally set the book business on its head, also contributed to the demise of the manuscript trade. By 1470, the German manuscript industry had virtually ceased to function; those of Italy and Spain gave way soon after. France was the last stronghold of illuminated manuscripts, turning out specimens of quality even after the age of INCUNABULA. But in the end, the writing was on the wall and manuscripts were only hand illuminated by special request.

IMPRESSION. In the strictest sense, a run of copies, large or small, ordered by a publisher from the printer at one time. After the first impression, other runs may be printed from the same setting of type, and are usually so noted. Collectors of first editions are actually looking for the first impression of the first edition of a volume, as all impressions taken from one setting of type constitute an edition.

In days past, when type was set in metal and was ungainly and difficult to store for long periods, a book that remained in demand after its first edition sold out was likely to need resetting before it could be reissued. Printings from the new set of type then constituted impressions of a second edition.

IMPRINT. The information at the foot of the title page that refers to the publisher or the place of publication. The book industry includes collectors who specialize in imprints. Those of the Revolutionary period and the Confederacy are especially prized.

INCUNABULA (INCUNABLE). Books printed on presses in the 15th century. The word is derived from the Latin root meaning "in the cradle," and indicates printing in its infancy. Incunabula is automatically valuable and collectible.

INDIAN BIBLE. The name commonly given to an edition of the Bible in a Native American language, an Algonquin dialect, translated and compiled by the Rev. John Eliot and published at Cambridge, Massachusetts, in 1663. The bible is also known as the Natick Bible and the Eliot Bible.

INSCRIBED COPY. A book carrying a signed inscription, usually saying something like "with regards to" or "for a special friend." Should the author of the inscription be famous, the book's value is enhanced. However, simply an inscription by the former owner, who may be a nice person, does not constitute an inscribed copy.

ISSUE. A term applied to a second printing (impression) of an edition that includes a change or correction—but not a complete resetting of type—made after the first impression is printed. Adding to the confusion are "states," or printings in which changes have been made during the print run. The terms are technical but important to the identification of older first editions. Many booksellers use "issue" and "state" interchangeably.

LAID IN. Refers to a piece of paper, such as a letter or a photo, placed in the book but not attached.

LEAF. A single sheet of paper, with a **RECTO** (front) page and a **VERSO** (back) page. Many people confuse pages and leaves. Pages are just one side of a leaf.

LIBRARY OF CONGRESS. America's largest library, located in Washington, D.C. Once founded as a working library for members of Congress, the library now holds not only government documents, but one of the largest collections of incunabula in the United States.

LIMITED EDITION. Special printing of a limited number of books. Printing and binding is often of a higher quality than the usual trade books or may be the product of a **PRIVATE PRESS.** The books are often numbered and signed by the author and illustrator, if there is one.

LIMP. Refers to bookbindings made of material that is not supported by boards. The cover is literally hanging limp. Limp vellum was first used as a trade binding for printed books almost since the beginning of typography and remained popular in Italian, Spanish, and Portuguese bindery during the 15th to 17th centuries. Limp bindings were often fitted with leather thong ties in place of clasps.

In the 19th century, limp leather was often used as a binding for bibles, giving way to imitation leather in later years.

LITHOGRAPHY. A principal method of printing developed in the 19th and 20th centuries, especially suited to reproducing drawings and illustrations. The process consists of printing from an impression drawn on smooth lithographic limestone using chemical inks. Many artists came to use the process to replace engraving, including the renowned Currier and Ives. Lithography is now a prominent art form.

LOOSE. A book that is in danger of separating from its binding. No longer held tight by the spine, the joints cannot support the weight of the book.

MANUSCRIPT. In the book world, refers to a handwritten document. Technically, a work written by hand, but in the modern world, a manuscript can be typewritten and still be considered a manuscript. The distinction is that it was not typeset or printed. If the writing is in the author's hand, it's termed a **HOLOGRAPH** manuscript. In the Middle Ages, monks copying sacred texts created **ILLUMINATED** (illustrated) manuscripts of great beauty, but with the invention and proliferation of mechanical printing, the practice died out.

MARBLED. A technique of decorating paper to create the effect of marble, mostly used for endpapers. Some examples have intriguing patterns that craftspeople today are duplicating to frame or to function as bookcovers.

MEZZOTINT. The process of engraving on copper plates.

MINIATURE. Actually not what you'd think, derived from "miniate" which means to paint with vermilion. The ancient artists who used this red paint were called miniators. Originally, miniatures referred to the colored drawings in early manuscripts.

MINT CONDITION. Like new. Right off the press.

MISPRINT. An error in printing, very important when identifying first editions. For instance, in the first American edition of Mark Twain's *Adventures of Huckleberry Finn* the word "saw" was printed incorrectly as "was" on line 23, page 57. Misprints are often among the important POINTS which must be present if a book is a true first edition.

MODERN FIRST EDITIONS. Includes books published since the turn of the 20th century. Here again in book parlance, phrases are evolving with time and most people use the term in reference to books from the 1920s on.

MOROCCO. Leather made from goatskin.

ND. No date of publication is given.

NP. No place of publication is given.

OCTAVO. The most common size/format of books. Usually seen expressed as "8vo," the most common octavos measure approximately 8" high.

OUT OF PRINT. No longer obtainable from the publisher.

PAMPHLET. A small work, issued unbound or in wraps, and usually sewn or stapled together.

PAPERBACK. Softcovered books, primarily books bound in heavy paper, published from the 1930s on. Today, early paperbacks are collectible and sought after, especially the Horror and Science Fiction genres.

The term is not to be confused with WRAPS, a thin paper cover.

PARTS. Books released in serial form or in installments. Many books started out this way and were only later published in book form. The works of Dickens followed this pattern—his *Dombey and Son* was printed in parts, 19 of the 20 parts in green pictorial wrappers, as were several of his other works. Amassing all the parts can be a daunting task since unprotected paper is fragile and many did not survive.

PENNY BOXES. Trays or boxes outside antiquarian bookshops where the bookseller puts cheap, miscellaneous stock to attract browsers.

PLATE. A full page devoted to an illustration, separate from the text pages of the book. The verso is blank.

POINTS. Characteristics which determine whether or not a book is a first edition. For instance, the first edition of a book may contain a specific spelling or other publishing mistake on a certain page that was corrected in later editions. The presence of the mistake is a point.

PRESENTATION COPY. Inscribed by the author as a gift. Not to be confused with a signature acquired by a total stranger who asked for the author's autograph in the book.

PRESS BOOK. A finely produced book, published by a private press, an individual, or established publisher for the sake of excellence in printing and binding and not necessarily for the book's literary value.

Prices run high on these specialties—from the outset, not just as collectibles—again for the high manufacturing standard, not because the book is wonderful literature, though it might be.

PRINT RUN. The number of volumes of a book run off the press at one time.

PRIVATELY PRINTED. Not produced by a publisher. The author pays for the publication out of his own pocket. Quite often the privately printed book was compiled for a select group of people, family or friends. Some very collectible books have been privately published, not the least of which was Edgar Allan Poe's *Tamerlane*, a copy of which recently sold at auction for a quarter of a million dollars.

PRIVATE PRESS. Publishers of limited editions or, simply, a single person producing (publishing) books.

PROVENANCE. The history of a book's ownership. Provenance may add to value if it shows prized associations. Many bibliophiles like information on the provenance of a book for its own sake. A love of old books and their history seem to go hand in hand.

QUARTER BOUND. Only the spine of a book is leather. The rest is boards or cloth.

QUOTES. The backbone of the bookseller's trade, a written description of a book with the asking price of the book stated. When quoting, use a 3" × 5" index card for each book quoted. Print the title, author, publisher, date, edition, number of pages, whether or not illustrations or maps are present, and the type of binding. Then carefully describe the condition. It is here a bookseller appreciates full disclosure of the defects. Even if you are as accurate as you know how to be, sometimes a dealer will envision something different and find the quote wanting. Include your name, address, and sale requirements and state whether the transaction is CWO (Cash With Order) or future billing.

READING COPY. A book that has seen better days, worn from use and in less than good condition. They're appreciated by scholars for research, but not by collectors unless the volume is exceedingly rare.

REBACKED. Fitted with a new spine and hinges. When considering such repairs, be prepared to pay well for a competent job. Unless you have a personal affinity for the book, before ordering any restoration by a professional book binder, have your volume appraised to see if it is worth the preservation cost.

REBOUND. Fitted with a new binding. Here again, as in the rebacked book, we are talking restoration and expensive repairs. Whenever this route is undertaken, opt for reattaching the original covers, if that is possible. Again, if you are selling the book, value should be there to justify the expense.

RECTO. In a book, the right-hand page, the front of the leaf.

REMAINDER. Selling book stock to a distributor at a considerable discount when the publisher believes the title has sold as many copies as it is likely to sell at full price in bookstores.

REPRINT. A reissue of a book previously published. A. L. Burt and Grosset & Dunlap reissued and made available many famous works to those who otherwise could not afford the first editions. In an elderly farm woman's house we visited in Vermont, the shelves in an upstairs bedroom were lined with books, reprints by Zane Grey, E. R. Burroughs, Dixon, Henty, Horatio Alger, and more. And proud she was that she had read them all.

REVIEW COPY. Complimentary copies of books sent to editors, journalists, and institutions, hoping for a review or at least a mention in their publications or programs.

RUBBED. Scratches or wear spots on leather bindings.

SABIN, JOSEPH. An English bookseller who emigrated to the United States and became one of the foremost authorities on Americana, setting about to publish a comprehensive bibliography of the genre. Unfortunately, Sabin lived to see only the first 13 volumes realized. Wilberforce Eames and R. W. G. Vail completed the monumental work, finishing with a total of 29 volumes.

SCUFFED. Worn, scratched, nicked.

SEARCH SERVICE. Precisely what the term implies, initiating a search for a title through dealership and trade channels. Lets say you want a particular book, and you cannot find it in a used bookstore. If you know the title and author, a bookseller will print an inquiry in the trade journals welcoming quotes from other dealers. Since these journals have wide exposure among booksellers, the likelihood of finding your book is strong.

Most booksellers now charge a basic fee for the service whether or not a book is found. Back in the good old days, Wright Howes noted in his Fall 1933 catalogue, "Out of print and scarce books sought for and reported free of charge." The times, they are a changing.

SPINE. The backstrip of a book.

STATE. Changes or corrections made during a print run. Sometimes used interchangeably with "issue," which indicates changes or corrections, but not a full resetting of the type, made between impressions.

SUNNED. Faded. The original color of the book loses brightness and freshness when exposed to direct bright light, especially sunlight.

THREE-QUARTER LEATHER. Leather on the spine and about an inch beyond, along with triangles of leather at the corners of the book. The rest of the binding could be cloth or boards.

TIPPED-IN. Glued in, as when illustrations are not bound into a book but glued in after binding. The technique is most often used to add glossy pictures or maps, with glue applied to the back of the illustration at the top only. Tipping-in was used to incorporate illustrations that would have been too expensive to print and bind into the book.

TISSUE GUARDS. Tissue paper bound into the book that protects the plates.

TITLE PAGES. The page at the front of each book which gives the title, author, publisher and, sometimes, the printing date. In most books, this information is on a recto page. Always consult the title page for pertinent information about a book; never depend upon what is printed on the spine or cover.

TOOLING. Impressing a design by hand in leather.

UNCUT. Untrimmed leaves. When sheets are printed, folded, and bound, the trimming process to open the leaves can miss some folds, leaving the pages uncut and unopened.

UNOPENED. Uncut leaves. Tearing can open them, but they remain uncut, though opened.

VELLUM. Calfskin binding. Also sometimes called parchment. Vellum and other leather bindings should be carefully cared for to keep them from drying and cracking (see "Care and Repair of Old Books").

VERSO. Left-hand page of a book, the back side of a leaf.

WANT LIST. A listing of books needed either to fill a dealer's bookshelves or to accommodate customers looking for particular works. Booksellers periodically send out want lists to other dealers. Often the bookseller will include a "permanent want list" in which case there is no cut-off date for acquiring those books, and duplicates may even be welcome.

WESTERN AMERICANA. The genre covering the settling of the American West and American western culture, including indigenous peoples. Everyone seems to want this category, and the prices are high for the really good stuff. The collector, of course, is looking for pioneer imprints, broadsides, handbills, documents, hand-written journey narratives, or ledgers. Books on Indians, explorations, outlaws, mining, and whatever else attested to the westward push are collectible.

WRAPPERS. Paper binding. This does not refer to modern paperbacks, which are bound in stiff paper with illustrations. The term refers to simple paper covering, sometimes plain paper serving also as a title page. Before modern bindings, books were often published with plain paper covers. Customers brought the works to their own binderies to have custom leather or cloth covers put on. Older pamphlets were often published with thin paper covers, or wrappers.

WRAPS. Same as wrappers.

THE

HOLIE BIBLE

FAITHFVLLY TRANS-
LATED INTO ENGLISH,
OVT OF THE AVTHENTICAL
LATIN.

Diligently conferred with the Hebrew, Greeke,
and other Editions in diuers languages.

With ARGVMENTS of the Bookes, and Chapters:
ANNOTATIONS. TABLES: and other helpes,
for better vnderstanding of the text: for discouerie of
CORRVPTIONS in some late tranflations: and
for clearing CONTROVERSIES in Religion.

BY THE ENGLISH COLLEGE OF DOWAY.

Haurietis aquas in gaudio de fontibus Saluatoris. Isaiæ. 12.
You shal draw waters in ioy out of the Sauiours fountaines.

Printed at Doway by LAVRENCE KELLAM,
at the signe of the holie Lambe.

M. DC. IX.

Title page of the first edition of the Roman Catholic Old Testament in English. It was printed in the city of Douai in France, spelled phonetically "Doway." It was considered unwise to attempt such a publication in England where Protestantism had been adopted as the state religion. The border is composed of a repetitive design common to printing of the era.

ABBREVIATIONS

�֎

Albany	Alb
All edges gilded	aeg
American Musuem of Natural History	AMNH
Association books	asso copy
Atlanta	Atl
Backed	bkd
Baltimore	Balt
Boards	bds
Boston	Bos
Black and white	b/w
British	Brit
Cambridge	Camb
Catalog	cat
Chicago	Chi
Cincinnati	Cinc
Cleveland	Cleve
Color, colored	clr
Copies	cc
Cover	cvr

Covered	cvred
Dust jacket/dust wrapper	dj
Edinburgh	Edin
Edition, edited	ed
Editor(s)	(ed)
English	Eng
Engravings	engr
Ex libris	ex lib
Facsimile	facs
First edition	1st ed
Folding	fldg
Frontispiece	frontis
Government Printing Office	GPO
Hard cover	hardcvr
Illustrated	illus
Impression	imp
Indianapolis	Ind
Inscribed	inscrb
Leather	lea
Limited edition	ltd
Lithographs	litho
London	Lon
Marbled	mar
Milwaukee	Milw
Minneapolis	Minn
Morocco	mor
Museum of Modern Art	MOMA
National Geographic Society	NGS
No date	nd
No place	np
Number	nbr
Oxford	Ox
Pages	pp
Philadelphia	Phila
Pittsburgh	Pitts

Photographs	photos
Printing	ptg
Providence	Prov
Rebacked	rbckd
Rebound	rbnd
Reprint	rprnt
Reproduction	repro
Revised	rev
Richmond	Rich
Sacramento	Sac
Salt Lake City	SLC
San Francisco	SF
Signed (by author)	sgn
Tipped-in	tip-in
Title has been abbreviated	. . .
Top edge gilded	teg
Toronto	Tor
United Kingdom	UK
University	Univ
Volumes	vols
Wrappers, soft covers	wrps

OLD BOOKS LISTING

*The University of these days
is a Collection of Books.*

—THOMAS CARLYLE

1875 Walter A. Wood's Harvesting Machines. Hoosick Falls, NY. wrps. fair circular, 6 chromo illus. .... *$85.00–$60.00*

A Scot (F. A. Bald). *Consistent Golf or How to Become a Champion.* Lon. Stockwell. 1st ed. illus. .... *$80.00–$120.00*

A'Beckett, Gilbert Abbott. *Comic History of England.* Lon. Bradbury, Agnew. (1964). illus. wood engraved plates, teg. .... *$35.00–$50.00*

Abbatt, William. *Battle of Pell's Point.* NY. 1901. illus. map ports. 500 cc. ....
.... *$50.00–$75.00*

Abbey, Edward. *Good News.* NY. Dutton. (1980). 1st ed. author's first novel, dj. ....
.... *$70.00–$100.00*

Abbot, Willis. *Soldiers of the Sea.* NY. 1918. illus. .... *$35.00–$75.00*

Abbot, Willis J. *Panama and the Canal.* NY. First Syndicate Pub. 1913. illus. photos, maps, red pictorial paste-down cvr. .... *$30.00–$50.00*

Abbott, Anthony. *The Shudders.* NY. Farrar & Rinehart. 1943. 1st ed. dj. ....
.... *$95.00–$125.00*

Abbott, Charles. *Primitive Industry: or Illustrations of the Handiwork . . .* Salem, MA. 1881. illus. .... *$75.00–$135.00*

Abbott, Charles D. *Howard Pyle: A Chronicle.* NY. Harper. 1925. 1st ed. illus. by Pyle.
.... *$70.00–$90.00*

Abbott, Wilbur. *Bibliography of Oliver Cromwell*. Harvard Pub Pr. 1929. illus. 2 portraits. .... *$50.00–$95.00*

Abe, Kobo. *Face of Another*. NY. Knopf. 1966. 1st ed. dj. .... *$20.00–$45.00*

Abe, Kobo. *Woman in the Dunes*. NY. Knopf. 1964. 1st Eng ed. dj. ..... *$55.00–$95.00*

Abel, Ernest L. *Scientific Study of Marihuana*. Chi. Nelson-Hall. 1976. 1st ed. dj. .... *$15.00–$25.00*

Abels, Jules. *Man On Fire* . . . NY. Macmillan. (1971). 1st ed. dj. .... *$20.00–$30.00*

Abercrombie, John. *Pathological & Practical Researches on Diseases of the Brain*. Phil. 1843. .... *$100.00–$200.00*

Aberle, David Friend. *Peyote Religion Among the Navaho*. Chi. Aldine. 1966. 1st ed. dj. .... *$65.00–$85.00*

Abernethy, John. *Surgical Works*. Lon. 1816. 2 vols. new ed. 1 plate, calf. .... *$100.00–$200.00*

Abrahams, Israel. *Book of Delight & Other Papers*. Phil. 1912. bds. ....*$15.00–$25.00*

Abrahams, Peter. *Wreath for Udomo*. NY. Knopf. 1956. 1st ed. dj. ..... *$35.00–$40.00*

Achatenere, Romulo. *Oh, mio Yemeya*. Cuba. Editorial Ed Arte. 1938. wrps. graphic by Hernadez Cardenas. .... *$75.00–$100.00*

Ackerman, Irving C. *Wire-haired Fox Terrier*. NY. 1928. illus. .... *$18.00–$30.00*

Acklen, J. T. *Tennessee Records*. Nashville. 1933. 1st ed. illus. .... *$40.00–$50.00*

Ackley, Edith. *Doll Shop of Your Own*. NY & Tor. Frederick A Stokes. (1941). 1st ed. dj sgn. .... *$25.00–$40.00*

Act for the Making of Bread. Lon. 1758. .... *$50.00–$75.00*

Activities of Ku Klux Klan Organizations in the United States.Wash. GPO. 1966. wrps. .... *$25.00–$35.00*

Acton, John. *An Essay on Shooting*. Lon. 1791. 2nd ed. gold tooled red lea. .... *$450.00–$550.00*

Adair, J. *Navajo & Pueblo Silversmiths*. Norman, OK. 1946. maps, charts, plates, dj. .. .. *$30.00–$40.00*

Adam, Franklin P. *Diary of Our Own Samuel Pepys*. NY. Simon & Schuster. 1935. 2 vols. 1st ed. .... *$50.00–$85.00*

Adamic, Louis. *Native Returns*. NY. Harper & Bros. 1934. 1st ed. .... *$25.00–$35.00*

Adams, A. L. *Field and Forest Rambles* . . . Lon. 1873. illus. .... *$75.00–$100.00*

Adams, Andy. *Log of a Cowboy*. Bos. 1903. 1st ed. illus. by E Boyd Smith, 2nd issue, maps, 6 plates. .... *$70.00–$85.00*

Adams, Andy. *Wells Brothers; The Young Cattle Kings*. NY. Grosset & Dunlap. 1911. illus. Boy Scout ed. .... *$15.00–$20.00*

Adams, Ansel. *An Autobiography*. Bos. 1985. wrps. dj. .... *$22.00–$85.00*

Adams, Ansel. *Born Free and Equal*. NY. US Camera. 1944. 1st ed. illus. scarce in dj. *$1,500.00–$1,800.00*

Adams, Ansel. *Camera and Lens Studio*. Morgan & Lester. 1948. 1st ed. dj. .... *$35.00–$48.00*

Adams, Ansel. *My Camera in the National Parks.* Yosemite National Park. Virginia Adams. 1950. illus. 97 pp, spiral-bound bds sgn. .... *$275.00–$450.00*

Adams, Ansel. *The Negative.* 1964. dj. .... *$20.00–$25.00*

Adams, Ansel. *Yosemite and the Range of Light.* Bos. 1979. illus. dj. . *$75.00–$125.00*

Adams, Ansel. *Yosemite Valley.* SF. 1959. 1st ed. pictorial wrappers. .. *$45.00–$100.00*

Adams, Ansel and Nancy Newhall. *Tetons & the Yellowstone.* Redwood City, CA. 1970. wrps. .... *$25.00–$95.00*

Adams, Ansel and Nancy Newhall. *Fiat Lux.* NY. McGraw-Hill. (1967). 1st ed. illus. sgn, dj. .... *$150.00–$250.00*

Adams, Ansel and Nancy Newhall. *Pageant of History in Northern California.* SF. American Trust Co. 1954. 1st ed. wrps. illus. spiral bound, sgn. .... *$100.00–$150.00*

Adams, Ansel and Nancy Newhall. *This Is the American Earth.* SF. Sierra Club. 1960. 1st ed. 89 pp, illus, dj. .... *$25.00–$75.00*

Adams, Austin. *Man John D. Spreckels.* San Diego. 1924. illus. .... *$15.00–$30.00*

Adams, Charles. *Lee At Appomattox and Other Papers.* Bos. Houghton Mifflin. 1902. 1st ed. .... *$35.00–$50.00*

Adams, Charles. *Origin & Development of the Pueblo Katsina Cult.* Tucson. Univ of Arizona Press. 1991. .... *$10.00–$20.00*

Adams, Charles Francis. *Confederacy and the Transvaal.* Bos. Houghton Mifflin. 1901. .... *$25.00–$50.00*

Adams, Charles Francis, Jr. *Notes on Railroad Accidents.* NY. 1879. cloth. .... *$50.00–$100.00*

Adams, D. *Hitchhiker's Guide to the Galaxy.* 1979. 1st ed. dj. .... *$12.00–$35.00*

Adams, Elizabeth Laura. *Dark Symphony.* NY. Sheed & Ward. 1942. 1st ed. dj. .... *$65.00–$100.00*

Adams, Emma H. *To & Fro, Up & Down in Southern California.* Cinc. 1888. 1st ed. 288 pp. .... *$25.00–$275.00*

Adams, Frank Davis. *Life and Times of Buckshot South.* NY. Dutton. 1959. 1st ed. dj. .... *$15.00–$35.00*

Adams, George. *Doctors in Blue.* NY. Schuman. (1952). 1st ed. .... *$50.00–$125.00*

Adams, George. *Treatise Describing the Construction, and Explaining the Use, of New Celestial and Terrestrial Globes.* Lon. pub by author. 1782. 5th ed. plates. .... *$300.00–$500.00*

Adams, Hannah. *An Abridgement of the History of New England . . .* Bos. Etheridge & Bliss. 1807. .... *$45.00–$60.00*

Adams, Henry. *Mont-Saint Michel and Chartes.* NY. Limited Editions Club. 1957. illus. with photos by Samuel Chamberlain, 72/1500 cc sgn. .... *$35.00–$50.00*

Adams, Herbert. *The Owl.* Lon. Harrap. (1937). 1st ed. .... *$60.00–$200.00*

Adams, John Couch. *Scientific Papers of.* Cambridge. University Press. 2 vols. 6 fldg charts. .... *$280.00–$500.00*

Adams, John D. *Arts-Crafts Lamps. How to Make Them.* Chi. 1911. illus. .... *$65.00–$85.00*

Adams, Joseph. *Salmon and Trout Angling*. NY. Dutton. 1923. 1st Amer ed. 288 pp. .. .. *$25.00–$65.00*

Adams, N. A. *Voyage Around the World*. Bos. Hoyt. (1871). illus. 3 plates cloth. .... *$35.00–$75.00*

Adams, Nehemiah. *South Side View of Slavery*. Bos. Marvin. 1854. .... *$30.00–$60.00*

Adams, Ramon F. *Come an' Get It*. OK. Univ of OK. 1st ed. dj. .... *$30.00–$45.00*

Adams, Ramon F. *Cowboy Lingo*. Bos. Houghton Mifflin. 1936. 1st ed. dj. .... *$75.00–$90.00*

Adams, Randolph. *Pilgrims, Indians & Patriots*. Bos. 1928. illus. .... *$30.00–$75.00*

Adams, Richard. *Tales From Watership Down*. Lon. (1996). 1st ed. dj. *$20.00–$35.00*

Adams, Richard. *Traveller*. NY. Knopf. 1988. 1st ed. dj. .... *$45.00–$80.00*

Adams, Richard C. *Delaware Indian Legend and the Story of Their Troubles*. Wash. private printing. 1899. 1st ed. illus. scarce. .... *$100.00–$125.00*

Adams, Samuel Hopkins. *Harvey Girls*. Cleve. World Pub. illus. Motion Picture ed. .. .. *$20.00–$30.00*

Adams, W. H. Davenport. *Famous Caves and Catacombs Described and Illustrated*. Lon. 1886. pictorial cloth. .... *$75.00–$100.00*

Adams, William Davenport. *Rambles in Book Land*. Lon. Elliot Stock. 1889. cloth. ... . *$25.00–$40.00*

Adams-Acton, Murray. *Domestic Architecture & Old Furniture*. Lon. nd. illus. .... *$120.00–$275.00*

Adanson, Michel. *Vogage to Senegal, the Isle of Goree, and the River Gambia*. Lon. Nourse & Johnston. 1759. 1st Eng ed. fldg map. .... *$300.00–$400.00*

Adcock, Thomas. *Sea of Green*. NY. Mysterious Press. 1989. 1st ed. dj.*$25.00–$45.00*

Addams, Jane. *Twenty Years at Hull House* . . . NY. Macmillan. 1911. 1st ed. illus. .... *$18.00–$25.00*

Addington, Sarah. *Boy Who Lived in Pudding Lane*. Bos. (1922). illus. *$30.00–$40.00*

Addison, Joseph. *Works of* . . . Lon. Cadell Y W Davis. 1811. 6 vols. .... *$375.00–$500.00*

Ade, George. *Artie*. Chi. 1896. 1st ed. .... *$35.00–$75.00*

Ade, George. *Fables in Slang*. Chi. 1900. sgn 1000 cc. .... *$65.00–$90.00*

Ade, George. *Forty Modern Fables*. NY. Russell. 1901. .... *$20.00–$30.00*

Adney, Edwin Tappan. *Klondike Stampede*. WA. 1968. illus. rprnt. ltd ed. .... *$50.00–$85.00*

Aesop's Fables. Lon. 1933. illus. by Arthur Rackham, new translation by Vernon Jones. .... *$75.00–$100.00*

Aesop's Fables for Children. Rand McNally & Co. (1919). 1st ed. illus. tall pictorial wrps. pictures by Milo Winter. .... *$20.00–$30.00*

Agassiz, L. *Geological Sketches*. Bos. Ticknor & Fields. 1866. .... *$45.00–$50.00*

Agassiz, L. *Lake Superior*. Bos. 1850. 15 plates, map. .... *$350.00–$525.00*

Agassiz, Louis. *Journal in Brazil*. Bos. Ticknor & Fields. 1868. .... *$50.00–$75.00*

Agassiz, Louis. *Structure of Animal Life: Six Lectures*. Scribner's, Armstrong. 1866. ...
.... *$50.00–$65.00*

Agatha, Sister M. *Texas Prose Writings*. Dallas. (1936). illus. frontis cloth scarce. ......
.... *$45.00–$100.00*

Agee, James. *Death in the Family*. Lon. Victor Gollancz. 1958. 1st ed. dj. ....
.... *$45.00–$125.00*

Agee, James. *Let Us Now Praise Famous Men*. Bos. Houghton Mifflin. 1960. illus. photos. .... *$20.00–$50.00*

Agricultural Implements and Machines. Bos. Ames Plow Co. 1901. illus. pictorial wrps. .... *$25.00–$30.00*

Aguilar, Grace. *Vale of Cedars and Other Tales*. Lon. 1902. illus. yellow cloth. ....
.... *$50.00–$100.00*

Aguilar, Grace. *Women of Israel*. NY. 1870. 2 vols. illus. 1st US ed. ....
.... *$100.00–$140.00*

Aickman, Robert. *Wine Dark Sea*. NY. Arbor House. (1988). 1st ed. dj. *$25.00–$35.00*

Aiken, Conrad. *Earth Triumphant*. NY. 1914. 1st ed. .... *$100.00–$150.00*

Aiken, Conrad. *Jig of Forslin*. Bos. 1916. 1st ed. .... *$75.00–$150.00*

Aiken, Conrad. *Senlin: A Biography*. Lon. Hogarth Press. 1925. 1st ed. *$75.00–$90.00*

Aiken, Conrad. *Short Stories*. NY. (1950). dj. .... *$25.00–$50.00*

Aiken, Joan. *Fit of Shivers*. Lon. Gollancz. 1990. 1st ed. dj. .... *$15.00–$30.00*

Aiken, Joan. *Skin Spinner's Poems*. NY. Viking. 1976. 1st ed. dj. .... *$15.00–$20.00*

Ainsworth, Ed. *Cowboy Art*. NY. World Publishing Co. (1968). 1st ed. illus. #222/1,000 cc, slipcase. .... *$180.00–$250.00*

Aircraft Yearbook for 1944. NY. Lanciar Publishers. (1944). annual ed. edited by Howard Mingos. photos, dj. .... *$45.00–$60.00*

Akers, Dwight. *Drivers Up*. NY. Putnam. 1938. 1st ed. .... *$20.00–$40.00*

Akers, Floyd. *Boy Fortune Hunters in Alaska*. Chi. Reilly & Britton. (1908). 1st ed. decal frontis. .... *$75.00–$150.00*

Akin, Otis F. *Reminiscences of the Klondike Rush of 1898*. 1st ed. wrps. ....
.... *$75.00–$100.00*

Akre, Nancy. *Miniatures*. Cooper-Hewitt Museum. (1983). 1st ed. illus. clr photos. .....
.... *$15.00–$20.00*

Albee, Edward. *Malcolm*. NY. 1966. 1st ed. dj sgn. .... *$85.00–$150.00*

Albee, Edward. *Who's Afraid of Virginia Woolf?* NY. 1962. 1st ed. dj. ....
.... *$120.00–$200.00*

Albert, Lillian. *Complete Button Book*. Doubleday. 1949. 1st ed. dj. .. *$65.00–$100.00*

Albion, Robert Greenhalgh. *Rise of New York Port*. NY. Scribner's. 1939. dj. ....
.... *$30.00–$40.00*

Albrecht, Arthur Amil. *International Seaman's Union of America* . . . GPO. 1923. wrps.
.... *$18.00–$25.00*

Alcoholics Anonymous. NY. Works. 1939. 1st ed. red cloth, dj. . *$2,000.00–$6,800.00*

Alcoholics Anonymous. 1948. 12th ptg. .... *$125.00–$150.00*

Alcoholics Anonymous. NY. Works. 1947. blue cloth, dj. .... *$325.00–$700.00*

Alcoholics Anonymous. 1st ed. 14th ptg, dj. .... *$350.00–$600.00*

Alcott, Louisa May. *An Old Fashioned Girl*. Bos. 1870. 1st ed. ads on copyright page, 2 plates. .... *$65.00–$150.00*

Alcott, Louisa May. *Aunt Jo's Scrap Bag*. Bos. Roberts. 1873. .... *$35.00–$45.00*

Alcott, Louisa May. *Little Men*. Bos. Roberts. 1871. 1st ed. 1st issue, green cloth. .... *$125.00–$150.00*

Alcott, Louise. *Jo's Boys*. Grosset & Dunlap. 1948. .... *$8.00–$14.00*

Alcott, Louise. *Little Men*. Grosset & Dunalp. 1973. .... *$10.00–$15.00*

Alcott, Louise. *Moods*. Bos. Loring. 1864. 1st ed. green cloth. .... *$75.00–$200.00*

Alcott, Louise May. *Under the Lilacs*. Goldsmith. dj. .... *$10.00–$20.00*

Alcott, William Tyler. *Book of the Stars for Young People*. NY. 1929. 5th ptg, plates, 411 pp. .... *$30.00–$45.00*

Aldis, Harry. *Printed Book*. Cambridge. University Press. 1941. 2nd ed dj. .... *$20.00–$35.00*

Aldrich, Herbert L. *Arctic Alaska and Siberia*. Chi/NY. Rand McNally. 1899. illus. photos, maps, blue cloth. .... *$145.00–$200.00*

Aldrich, Bess Streeter. *White Bird Flying*. NY. Appleton Century Crofts. 1931. 1st ed. dj. .... *$25.00–$40.00*

Aldridge, James. *Cairo Biography of a City*. Bos. Little Brown. 1969. 1st ed. illus. dj. .... *$15.00–$30.00*

Alekhine, Alexander. *My Best Games of Chess 1908–1923*. NY. Harcourt Brace. nd. .. .. *$15.00–$25.00*

Alexander, David. *Most Men Don't Kill*. NY. Random House. 1951. 1st ed. author's first novel, dj. .... *$35.00–$65.00*

Alexander, E. P. *Military Memoirs of a Confederate*. NY. 1907. 1st ed. illus. fldg map. .... *$100.00–$275.00*

Alexander, William. *History of Women*. Lon. Strahan and Cadell. 1779. 2 vols. 1st ed. scarce. .... *$400.00–$700.00*

Alexander, William. *History of Women*. Bristol. 1995. rprnt. .... *$125.00–$150.00*

Alexie, Sherman. *Lone Ranger and Tonto Fistfight in Heaven*. NY. Atlantic Monthly. 1993. wrps. advance proofs. .... *$35.00–$60.00*

Alexie, Sherman. *Lone Ranger and Tonto Fistfight in Heaven*. NY. Atlantic Monthly. 1993. wrps. 1st US ed. .... *$50.00–$75.00*

Alfred Stieglitz: Photographs & Writings. DC. National Gallery of Art. (1983). 1st ed. photo plates, folio, dj. .... *$60.00–$70.00*

Alger, Horatio. *Brave and Bold*. Cleve. World Pub. .... *$14.00–$16.00*

Alger, Horatio. *From Canal Bay to President*. NY. 1881. red-brown with lettering in gold. .... *$35.00–$75.00*

Alger, Horatio. *Silas Snobden's Office Boy*. Garden City. 1973. dj. ...... *$14.00–$25.00*

Alger, Horatio. *Strive and Succeed*. Bos. 1872. .... *$75.00–$95.00*

Alger, Horatio. *Young Miner*. SF. 1965. ltd 450 cc. .... *$45.00–$75.00*

Alger, William Rounseville. *Life of Edwin Forrest*. Phila. Lippincott. 1877. 2 vols. large 8vo, pictorial cloth, 864 pp, plates. .... *$85.00–$100.00*

Algren, Nelson. *Man with the Golden Arm*. NY. 1949. 1st ed. dj. .... *$30.00–$65.00*

Algren, Nelson. *Walk on the Wild Side*. Farrar, Straus & Cudahy. (1956). 1st ed. dj. .... *$35.00–$90.00*

Ali Baba and the Forty Thieves. Houghton Mifflin. 1950. 6 pop-ups. *$75.00–$125.00*

Alken, Henry. *Scraps From the Sketch Book*. Lon. 1823. illus. hand-clr plates, folio. ... . *$500.00–$650.00*

All About Hawaii, Standard Tourist Guide. Honolulu. 1928. 1st ed. wrps. illus. maps. .... *$60.00–$85.00*

Allan, William. *Army of Northern Virginia in 1862*. Bos/NY. 1892. 1st ed. maps. .... *$295.00–$300.00*

Allen, Charles Dexter. *American Book Plates*. NY. 1968. rprnt. .... *$20.00–$30.00*

Allen, Charles Dexter. *American Book-Plates*. NY. Macmillan. 1894. 1st ed. illus. .... *$85.00–$100.00*

Allen, Charles Dexter. *Classified List of Early American Bookplates*. NY. Grolier Club. 1894. wrps. illus. .... *$35.00–$45.00*

Allen, Harvey. *Israfel. The Life and Times of Edgar Allan Poe*. NY. Doran. 1926. 2 vols. scarce cloth. .... *$200.00–$250.00*

Allen, Henry. *Report of an Expedition to the Copper, Tanana and Koyukuk Rivers*. Wash. GPO. 1887. 5 large folding maps. .... *$75.00–$100.00*

Allen, Hervey. *Forest and the Fort*. NY. Farrar and Rinehart. 1943. 1st ed. dj. .... *$15.00–$25.00*

Allen, Hugh. *Story of the Airship*. Akron. 1942. illus. dj. .... *$35.00–$55.00*

Allen, John H. *Southwest*. Phil. Lippincott. dj. .... *$20.00–$30.00*

Allen, Lewis F. *American Herd Book*. Buffalo, NY. Jewett, Thomas & Co. 1846. 1st ed. frontis, plates. .... *$800.00–$1,000.00*

Allen, Miss A J. *Ten Years in Oregon*. Ithaca. 1848. 1st ed. 2nd issue. *$95.00–$300.00*

Allen, Ruth A. and Barton, Sam B. *Wage Earners Meet the Depression*. Austin. 1935. wrps. .... *$20.00–$35.00*

Allen, Steve. *Funny Men*. NY. Simon & Schuster. 1956. dj. .... *$15.00–$30.00*

Allen, Woody. *Side Effects*. Random House. 1980. 1st ed. dj. .... *$10.00–$24.00*

Allende, Isabel. *Of Love and Shadows*. NY. Knopf. 1987. 1st ed. dj. .... *$50.00–$75.00*

Allingham, Margery. *Gyrth Chalice Mystery*. Garden City. Doubleday Crime Club. 1931. 1st ed. dj. .... *$25.00–$45.00*

Allison, Willie (ed.). *First Golf Review*. Lon. Bonar. (1950). 1st ed. dj. *$40.00–$100.00*

Alliss, Percy. *Better Golf*. Lon. Black. 1926. 1st ed. illus. photos. .... *$70.00–$100.00*

Almack, Edward. *Bookplates*. Lon. Methuen & Co. 1904. illus. blue cloth. .... *$20.00–$40.00*

Almon W. Babbit, Delegate from Deseret. DC. 1850. .... *$65.00–$85.00*

Alther, Lisa. *Bedrock.* NY. Knopf. 1990. 1st ed. dj sgned. ....*20.00–$25.00*

Alther, Lisa. *Other Women.* NY. Knopf. 1984. 1st ed. dj. .... *$10.00–$20.00*

Altrocci, Julia. *Snow Covered Wagons.* NY. 1936. 1st ed. cloth. .... *$25.00–$35.00*

Alvarez, Julia. *How the Garcia Girls Lost Their Accents.* Algonquin. 1991. 1st ed. dj.
.... *$35.00–$88.00*

Alvarez, Julia. *In the Time of the Butterfly.* Chapel Hill. Algonquin Books. 1994. 1st ed. sgn, dj. .... *$35.00–$45.00*

Alvarez, Walter C. *Nervousness, Indigestion & Pain.* NY. 1943. 1st ed. bds. ....
.... *$25.00–$50.00*

Ambler, Charles Henry. *History of Transportation in the Ohio Valley.* CA. 1932. 1st ed. illus. .... *$125.00–$150.00*

Ambler, Eric. *Intercom Conspiracy.* NY. Atheneum. 1969. 1st ed. dj. .. *$20.00–$35.00*

Ambler, Eric. *Night-Comers.* Lon. Heinemann. 1956. 1st ed. dj. .... *$45.00–$60.00*

Ambler, Eric. *Passage of Arms.* NY. 1960. 1st US ed. dj. .... *$15.00–$20.00*

Ambler, Eric. *Story So Far: Memories and Other Fictions.* Lon. Weidenfeld & Nicolson. 1993. 1st ed. dj. .... *$15.00–$30.00*

Ambler, Louis. *Old Halls & Manor Houses of Yorkshire.* Lon. nd. illus. ....
.... *$100.00–$235.00*

American Bible Society. *Twelfth Annual Report of the* . . . NY. Fanshaw. 1928. wrps. .
.... *$15.00–$25.00*

American Boy's Book of Sports and Games . . . NY. (1864). illus. ... *$150.00–$350.00*

American Car and Foundry Company in Khaki; Its Production Achievements in the Great War. NY. 1919. 95 pp. .... *$50.00–$75.00*

American Jack Stock Stud Book. Nashville. American Breeders Association of Jacks and Jennets. 1891. Vol. III. .... *$100.00–$125.00*

American Jack Stock Stud Book. Nashville. American Breeders Association of Jacks and Jennets. 1891. Vol. I. .... *$100.00–$125.00*

American Line Type. Jersey City. American Type Founders. 1903. large 4to, 292 pp. ...
.... *$50.00–$75.00*

American Pioneer in Science, William James Beal. Amherst, MA. 1925. 1st ed. illus.
.... *$50.00–$75.00*

Ameringer, Oscar. *Yankee Primer.* Oklahoma City. American Guardian. 1933. 1st ed. wrps. 40 pp. .... *$25.00–$35.00*

Ames, Nathaniel. *An Astronomical Diary, of An Almanack* . . .*1760, 1761, 1762, 1763, 1764.* Bos. John Draper. (1759–1763). 5 almanacks bound together, cloth, lea label. .....
.... *$325.00–$385.00*

Amherst, Alicia. *History of Gardening in England.* Lon. 1896. illus. . *$90.00–$120.00*

Amis, Martin. *London Fields.* Tor. Lester & Orpen Denny. (1989). 1st Canadian ed, inscr, dj. .... *$75.00–$100.00*

Amory, Thomas C. *Life of Admiral Sir Isaac Coffin, Baronet* . . . Bos. 1886. 1st ed. illus.
.... *$25.00–$50.00*

Amsden, Charles Avery. *Navaho Weaving* . . . Glorietta, NM. 1974. illus. rprnt of 1934 ed. .... *$20.00–$30.00*

Amsden, Charles Avery. *Navaho Weaving, Its Technique and History.* Albuquerque. 1949. 2nd ed. clr repro laid in. .... *$70.00–$150.00*

Amsden, Charles Avery. *Prehistoric Southwesterners from Basketmaker to Pueblo.* LA. 1949. wrps. illus. .... *$30.00–$75.00*

Amundsen, Roald. *South Pole.* UK. 1996. illus. rprnt, dj. .... *$50.00–$75.00*

Amundsen, Roald. *South Pole.* NY. 1912. 2 vols. 1st ed. illus. maps. .... *$850.00–$2,000.00*

Andersen, Hans Christian. *Ice Maiden* . . . Lon. (1889). green cloth, gilt lettering, clr frontis. .... *$65.00–$100.00*

Andersen, Hans Christian. *Kate Greenaway's Original Drawings for The Snow Queen.* NY. Schocken Books. (1981). 1st ed. illus. gray cloth pictorial dj. .... *$15.00–$30.00*

Andersen, Hans Christian. *Nightingale and Other Stories.* NY/Lon. nd. 1st ed. illus by Edmund Dulac, tip-in clr plates. .... *$150.00–$200.00*

Andersen, Hans Christian. *Picture Book Without Pictures.* NY. 1848. 1st US ed. .... *$50.00–$60.00*

Andersen, Hans Christian. *Tumble Bug and Other Tales.* NY. Harcourt Brace. 1940. illus by Hertha List. red cloth over bds, dj. .... *$45.00–$100.00*

Anderson, C. W. *Blaze and the Gray Spotted Pony.* NY. Macmillan. 1968. 1st ed. scarce dj. .... *$30.00–$65.00*

Anderson, C. W. *Touch of Greatness.* NY. Macmillan. 1945. dj. .... *$20.00–$50.00*

Anderson, Charles C. *Fighting by Southern Federals.* NY. 1912. 1st ed. blue cloth .... *$85.00–$175.00*

Anderson, Christopher. *Annals of the English Bible.* NY. Carter. 1849. ncw cloth. .... *$50.00–$85.00*

Anderson, Eva Greenslit. *Chief Seattle.* Caldwell, IN. 1943. 1st ed. map. .... *$75.00–$115.00*

Anderson, Isabel. *Spell of Japan.* Bos. Page. 1916. illus. photos, folding map. .... *$20.00–$30.00*

Anderson, John. *American Theatre & Motion Picture in America.* NY. 1938. illus. .... *$30.00–$70.00*

Anderson, Kenneth. *Nine Man-eaters and One Rogue.* NY. Dutton. 1955. illus. b/w photos, dj. .... *$45.00–$65.00*

Anderson, Kent. *Sympathy for the Devil.* Garden City. Doubleday. 1987. 1st ed. author's first novel, sgn, dj. .... *$100.00–$200.00*

Anderson, Lawrence. *Art of the Silversmith in Mexico.* NY. 1975. 2 vols in one. rprnt. .... *$30.00–$45.00*

Anderson, Marian. *My Lord, What a Morning.* NY. 1956. 1st ed. dj. ... *$10.00–$20.00*

Anderson, Martha Jane. *Social Life and Vegetarianism.* Mt Lebanon. Chi: Guiding Star Printing House. 1893. 27 pp. .... *$50.00–$80.00*

Anderson, Mary. *Scenes in Hawaiian Islands & Calif.* Bos. 1865. illus. .... *$75.00–$100.00*

Anderson, Nels. *The Hobo* . . . Chi. Univ of Chi Press. 1923. 1st ed. illus. photos, cloth scarce. .... *$70.00–$85.00*

Anderson, Poul. *Flandry of Terra.* Phila. 1965. 1st ed. dj. .... *$25.00–$35.00*

Anderson, Poul. *Guardians of Time.* Lon. 1961. 1st ed. sgn. dj. .... *$120.00–$150.00*

Anderson, Poul. *Operation Chaos.* NY. 1971. 1st ed. dj. .... *$25.00–$35.00*

Anderson, Poul. *Perish the Sword.* NY. Macmillan. 1959. 1st ed. dj. .. *$50.00–$100.00*

Anderson, Poul. *Vault of the Ages.* Phil. (1952). 1st ed. author's first book. .... *$75.00–$125.00*

Anderson, R. C. *Rigging of the Ships in the Days of the Spritsail Topmast* . . . Salem. 1927. illus. plates, dj. .... *$65.00–$110.00*

Anderson, R. M. *Birds of Iowa.* Davenport. 1907. wrps. illus. .... *$20.00–$30.00*

Anderson, Romola. *Sailing Ship.* NY. 1926. illus. .... *$35.00–$50.00*

Anderson, Romola. *Sailing Ship.* NY. 1963. dj. .... *$15.00–$20.00*

Anderson, Rufus. *Hawaiian Islands.* Bos. Gould & Lincoln. 1864. 1st ed. illus. plates, maps. .... *$125.00–$375.00*

Anderson, Sherwood. *Many Marriages.* NY. 1923. 1st ed. dj. .... *$125.00–$185.00*

Anderson, Sherwood. *Poor White.* NY. Huebsch. 1920. 1st ed. dj. ... *$125.00–$300.00*

Anderson, Sherwood. *Puzzled America.* NY/Lon. Scribner's Sons. 1935. 1st ed. .... *$35.00–$55.00*

Anderson, Sherwood. *Tar.* NY. Boni & Liveright. 1926. 1st ed. 1/350 cc, sgn. .... *$100.00–$300.00*

Anderson, Sherwood. *Tar.* NY. 1926. 1st ed. dj. .... *$35.00–$50.00*

Anderson, William. *Japanese Wood Engravings.* Lon. Seely. 1895. 1st ed. illus. .... *$55.00–$70.00*

Andrade, E. N. *Structure of the Atom.* Lon. 1924. illus. 2nd ptg. .... *$15.00–$30.00*

Andrews, A. A. *Dirigible.* A L Burt. 1931. 1st ed. photoplay ed, no dj. *$15.00–$25.00*

Andrews, A. A. *Dirigible.* A L Burt. 1931. 1st ed. dj photoplay ed. .... *$85.00–$200.00*

Andrews, Allen. *Pig Plantagenet.* Viking. 1981. 1st ed. illus by Michael Forema, dj. ... . *$25.00–$35.00*

Andrews, Clarence L. *Story of Alaska.* Caxton, Caldwell. 1938. 1st ed. dj. .... *$25.00–$40.00*

Andrews, Eliza Frances. *War-Time Journal of a Georgia Girl 1864–1865.* NY. 1908. 1st ed. .... *$55.00–$85.00*

Andrews, Marietta M. *My Studio Window* . . . NY. Dutton. illus. .... *$25.00–$35.00*

Andrews, Roy Chapman. *On the Trail of Ancient Man* . . . NY. Putnam. 1926. illus. photos. 3rd ptg. .... *$35.00–$40.00*

Andrews, Roy Chapman. *Under a Lucky Star.* NY. Viking. 1943. 1st ed. .... *$15.00–$20.00*

Angelou, Maya. *And Still I Rise.* NY. 1978. 1st ed. dj. .... *$30.00–$40.00*

Angelou, Maya. *Gather Together in My Name*. Random House. 1974. 1st Amer ed. sgn, dj. .... *$75.00–$100.00*

Angelou, Maya. *Heart of a Woman*. NY. (1981). 1st ed. dj. .... *$20.00–$50.00*

Angelou, Maya. *I Shall Not Be Moved*. NY. Random House. 1990. 1st ed. dj. .... *$12.00–$25.00*

Angelou, Maya. *Just Give Me a Cool Drink of Water 'Fore I Die*. NY. Random House. 1971. 1st ed. sgn, dj. .... *$125.00–$200.00*

Angelou, Maya. *Now Sheba Sings the Song*. Dutton. 1987. 1st ed. illus. dj. .... *$15.00–$30.00*

Angelou, Maya. *On the Pulse of the Morning*. Random House. 1993. 1st ed. wrps. inaugural. .... *$25.00–$50.00*

Angelou, Maya. *On the Pulse of the Morning*. NY. Random House. 1993. 1st ed. signed. .... *$50.00–$60.00*

Angelou, Maya. *Singin' and Swingin' and Gettin' Merry Like Christmas*. NY. Random House. 1976. 1st ed. dj, sgn. .... *$60.00–$85.00*

Angione, Genevieve. *All-Bisque and Half-Bisque Dolls*. Thomas Nelson. (1969). .... *$30.00–$45.00*

Angle, Paul M. *Lincoln Reader*. NJ. Rutgers. 1947. .... *$12.00–$18.00*

Anglund, Joan. *Spring Is a New Beginning*. NY. 1963. 1st ed. dj. .... *$14.00–$20.00*

Anglund, Joan Walsh. *A Christmas Book*. NY. (1983). 1st ed. inscr. .... *$25.00–$35.00*

Anglund, Joan Walsh. *In a Pumpkin Shell*. NY. Harcourt. 1960. illus. clr. .... *$22.00–$35.00*

Annesley, George. *Voyages and Travels to India, Ceylon, The Red Sea, Abyssinia and Egypt*. Lon. William Miller. 1809. 3 vols. 1st ed. illus. calf maps. *$1,300.00–$1,500.00*

Anno, Mitsumasa. *Anno's Flea Market*. Philomel Books. 1984. 1st US ed. dj. .... *$15.00–$20.00*

Anno, Mitsumasa. *Anno's Italy*. 1980. 1st ed. dj. .... *$20.00–$30.00*

Anson, Margaret. *Merry Order of St. Bridget: Personal Recollections of the Use of the Rod*. York. private printing. 1857. .... *$60.00–$90.00*

Ansted and Latham. *Channel Islands*. Lon. Allen. 1865. 2nd ed. illus. *$50.00–$80.00*

Anstey, Christopher. *New Bath Guide*. Lon. Biggs. 1804. new ed., teg. .... *$70.00–$100.00*

Antarctic Bibliography, Vol. I. GPO. 1965. .... *$30.00–$40.00*

Anthon, Charles. *Classical Dictionary*. NY. Harper. 1852. 1st ed. ..... *$60.00–$115.00*

Anthony, Gordon. *Russian Ballet*. Lon. Geoffrey Bles. (1939). 1st ed. illus. .... *$50.00–$80.00*

Apes, William. *Son of the Forest*. NY. William Apes. 1831. 2nd rev. ed. .... *$70.00–$100.00*

Apperley, C. J. *Horse & the Hound, Their Various Uses & Treatment Including Practical . . .* Edin. 1863. frontis plates. .... *$60.00–$100.00*

Apperley, C. J. *Hunting Reminescences . . .* Lon. Rudolph Ackerman. 1843. 1st ed. illus. b/w plates. .... *$200.00–$500.00*

Apperley, C. J. *Memoirs of the Life of the Late John Mytton.* Lon. 1851. illus. 18 clr plates by Henry Alken. .... *$800.00–$1,000.00*

Applegate, Frank G. *Indian Stories from Pueblos.* Phila. 1929. illus. in clr. ....
.... *$50.00–$75.00*

Appleton, L H. *Indian Art of the Americas.* NY. (1950). illus. .... *$75.00–$150.00*

Appleton, Victor. *Don Sturdy, The Desert of Mystery.* Grosset & Dunlap. 1925. #1, dj.
.... *$50.00–$75.00*

Appleton, Victor. *Moving Picture Boys.* Grosset & Dunlap. 1913. #1, dj. ....
.... *$15.00–$30.00*

Appleton, Victor. *Tom Swift Among the Fire Fighters.* Grosset & Dunlap. 1921. #24, dj.
.... *$85.00–$115.00*

Appleton, Victor. *Tom Swift and His Air Scout.* Grosset & Dunlap. 1910. no dj. ....
.... *$8.00–$20.00*

Appleton, Victor. *Tom Swift and His Electric Runabout.* Grosset & Dunlap. (1910). 1st ed. # 5, dj. .... *$50.00–$125.00*

Appleton, Victor. *Tom Swift and His Ocean Airport.* Whitman. 1934. #37, dj. ....
.... *$45.00–$90.00*

Appleton, Victor II. *Tom Swift Jr. and His G-Force Inverter.* Grosset & Dunlap. 1968. #30, dj. .... *$75.00–$150.00*

Appleton, Victor II. *Tom Swift Jr., His Repelatron Skyway.* Grosset & Dunlap. 1963. #22. .... *$12.00–$20.00*

Appleton, Victor II. *Tom Swift Jr., His Spectromarine Selector.* Grosset & Dunlap. 1960. #15. .... *$12.00–$25.00*

Appleton, Victor II. *Tom Swift Jr., The Asteroid Pirates.* Grosset & Dunlap. 1963. #21.
....
$10.00–$24.00

Appleton, Victor II. *Tom Swift Jr., The Race to the Moon.* Grosset & Dunlap. 1958. #12.
.... *$12.00–$17.00*

Appleton, Victor II. *Tom Swift Jr. and His Electronic Retroscope.* Grosset & Dunlap. 1959. 1st ed. dj, #14. .... *$15.00–$22.00*

Appleton, Victor II. *Tom Swift Jr., His Jetmarine.* Grosset & Dunlap. 1954. dj. ....
.... *$15.00–$25.00*

Appleton, Victor II. *Tom Swift Jr., His Ultrasonic Cycloplane.* Grosset & Dunlap. 1957. dj, #10. .... *$15.00–$30.00*

Aptheker, Herbert. *Labor Movement in the South During Slavery.* NY. International Pub. wrps. .... *$25.00–$40.00*

Aptheker, Herbert (ed.). *Documentary History of the Negro People in the United States: 1910–1932.* Secaucus. Citadel Press. 1951. 1st ed. dj. .... *$35.00–$50.00*

Arabian Stud Book. Arabian Horse Club. 1959. .... *$20.00–$30.00*

Arbona, Fred. *Mayflies, the Angler and the Trout.* NY. 1980. 1st ed. illus. dj, photos, charts. .... *$45.00–$60.00*

Arbuckle. *Arbuckle's Album of Illustrated Natural History.* np. lithos, 11 plates, chromolitho wrappers. .... *$40.00–$80.00*

Arbuthnot, John. *An Essay Concerning the Effects of Air on Human Bodies.* Lon. 1751. bds paper on spine. .... *$150.00–$200.00*

Archer, Gleason. *Big Business and Radio.* 1939. 1st ed. illus. dj. .... *$45.00–$65.00*

Archer, Jeffrey. *First Among Equals.* NY. Simon & Shuster. 1984. 1st ed. dj. .... *$15.00–$25.00*

Archer, Jeffrey. *Prodigal Daughter.* NY. Simon & Shuster. 1982. 1st ed. dj. .... *$13.00–$30.00*

Archer, T. A. and Charles Lethbridge Kingsford. *Crusades; the Story of the Latin Kingdom of Jerusalem.* Lon. T Fisher Unwin. 1894. illus. calf marbled endpapers, maps. .... *$50.00–$60.00*

Architectural Review Congress Number. Lon. 1906. illus. .... *$40.00–$55.00*

Ardizzone, Edward. *Indian Dairy.* Lon. Bodley Head. 1984. 1st ed. illus. pen and waterclr sketches, dj. .... *$20.00–$35.00*

Ardizzone, Edward. *Ship's Cook Ginger.* Macmillan. 1977. 1st ed. dj. *$10.00–$18.00*

Arizona. Hastings House. 1940. tan cloth. .... *$25.00–$35.00*

Armor, William. *Lives of the Governors of Pennsylvania . . .* Phil. 1872. illus. .... *$45.00–$55.00*

Armour, J. Ogden. *Packers, the Private Car Lines, and the People.* Phila. 1906. 1st ed. illus. .... *$35.00–$225.00*

Armstrong, Benjamin G. *Early Life Among the Indians.* Ashland, WI. 1892. 1st ed. illus. 15 plates. .... *$175.00–$225.00*

Armstrong, Harry G. *Principles and Practice of Aviation Medicine.* Balt. 1939. illus. charts, dj. .... *$100.00–$125.00*

Armstrong, John. *Young Woman's Guide to Virtue, Economy and Happiness . . .* Newcastle. nd. illus. .... *$100.00–$140.00*

Armstrong, John M.D. *Art of Preserving Health: A Poem in Four Books.* Lon. 1744. 1st ed. .... *$185.00–$250.00*

Armstrong, Margaret. *Blue Santo Murder Mystery.* NY. (1941). 1st ed. slipcase, dj. .. .. *$30.00–$75.00*

Army Regulations Adopted for the Use of the Army of the Confederate States. New Orleans. 1861. 198 pp. .... *$400.00–$600.00*

Arnaud de Ronsil, Georges. *Dissertation on Hernias, or Ruptures.* Lon. A Millar. 1748. .... *$200.00–$275.00*

Arnold, Edwin. *Seas & Lands.* NY. 1891. illus. clr plates. .... *$60.00–$90.00*

Arnold, Isaac N. *History of the Life of Abraham Lincoln and the Overthrow of Slavery.* Chi. 1866. 1st ed. illus. .... *$75.00–$95.00*

Arnold, Isaac N. *Sketch of the Life of Abraham Lincoln.* NY. 1869. ..... *$35.00–$40.00*

Arnold, Matthew. *Essays in Criticism.* Lon. Ticknor & Fields. 1865. *$75.00–$125.00*

Arnold, Matthew. *Essays in Criticism.* Lon. 1865. 1st ed. .... *$95.00–$145.00*

Art of Cookery Made Plain & Easy . . . by a Lady. Lon. 1775. .... *$450.00–$350.00*

Art Work of the Mohawk River and Valley, Its Cities & Towns. Chi. 1902. 9 vols. .... *$75.00–$90.00*

Arthur Rackham Fairy Book. Lon. 1933. 1st ed. illus. by author, 8 clr plates. .... *$200.00–$395.00*

Arthur Rackham Fairy Book. NY. Weathervane. 1978. illus. dj. .... *$15.00–$25.00*

Arthur Rackham Fairy Book. Lippincott. 1933. illus. by author, 7 clr plates. .... *$125.00–$350.00*

Arthur, Sir George. *Life of Lord Kitchener: a Great British Life in the Middle East* . . . Lon. Macmillan. 1920. 3 vols. 1st ed. illus. 3/4 green calf maps and photos. .... *$80.00–$100.00*

Artists and Writers Golf Association 1935. 1935. 1st ed. illus. photos, cloth over bds. . ... *$50.00–$80.00*

Artists and Writers Golf Association 1948. 1948. spiral-bound bds. ... *$80.00–$100.00*

Artzybasheff, Boris. *Poor Shaydullah*. NY. 1931. 1st ed. scarce, dj. .. *$50.00–$125.00*

Artzybasheff, Boris. *Poor Shaydullah*. NY. Macmillan. 1931. 1st ed. no dj. .... *$25.00–$70.00*

Ashbery, John. *Can You Hear, Bird*. NY. Farrar Straus & Giroux. (1995). 1st ed. sgn, dj. .... *$30.00–$45.00*

Ashby, Thomas. *Valley Campaigns*. NY. 1914. 1st ed. .... *$50.00–$100.00*

Ashley, Clifford. *Ashley Book of Knots*. NY. Doubleday & Co. (1944). 1st ed. illus. oversized blue cloth pictorial dj, pictorial endpapers. .... *$50.00–$95.00*

Ashley, Clifford W. *Yankee Whaler*. NY. Halcyon House. 1942. illus. .. *$25.00–$50.00*

Ashley, Frederick W. *Vollbehr Incunabula and the Book of Books* . . . Wash. Library of Congress. 1932. 420 cc, slipcase on handmade paper. .... *$35.00–$50.00*

Ashmore, Harry S. *Negro and the Schools*. Chapel Hill. Univ of North Carolina. (1954). 1st ed. .... *$20.00–$30.00*

Ashton, Dorothy Hememway. *Sheldon Vermont, The People Who Lived and Worked There*. privately printed. 1979. red cloth over brown wrps, sgn. .... *$40.00–$50.00*

Ashton, J. *Curious Creatures in Zoology*. Lon. 1890. 1st ed. illus. pictorial cov. .... *$75.00–$100.00*

Ashton, James. *Book of Nature Containing Information for Young People* . . . NY. 1870. flexible cloth. .... *$95.00–$130.00*

Ashton, John. *Chap-Books of the Eighteenth Century*. Lon. 1882. .... *$48.00–$55.00*

Asimov, Isaac. *Asimov's Biographical Encyclopedia of Science & Technology*. Doubleday. 1964. 662 pp, dj. .... *$25.00–$35.00*

Asimov, Isaac. *Choice of Catastrophes*. NY. Simon & Schuster. (1979). 1st ed. dj. .... *$20.00–$30.00*

Asimov, Isaac. *Currents of Space*. NY. Doubleday. 1952. 1st ed. 217 pp, sgn, dj. .... *$175.00–$300.00*

Asimov, Isaac. *Death Dealers*. NY. Avon. 1958. 1st ed. wrps. paperback original. .... *$30.00–$75.00*

Asimov, Isaac. *End of Eternity*. Garden City. 1955. 1st ed. dj. .... *$165.00–$225.00*

Asimov, Isaac. *I, Robot*. NY. Gnome Press. 1950. 1st ed. dj. .... *$350.00–$450.00*

Asimov, Isaac. *In Memory Yet Green*. NY. Doubleday. 1979. 1st ed. dj.. *$17.00–$35.00*

Asimov, Isaac. *In Memory Yet Green*. 1979. 1st ed. inscr....................... *$25.00–$45.00*

Asimov, Isaac. *Murder at the ABA*. Garden City. Doubleday. 1976. 1st ed. dj. ....
.... *$20.00–$45.00*

Asimov, Isaac. *Nemesis*. NY. Doubleday. 1989. 1st ed. dj. .... *$10.00–$15.00*

Asimov, Isaac. *Winds of Change and Other Stories*. Doubleday. 1983. 1st ed. dj...........
.... *$20.00–$30.00*

Askins, Charles. *Game Bird Shooting*. NY. 1931. 1st ed. dj.................... *$37.00–$55.00*

Asquith, Cynthia. *Ghost Book*. NY. Scribner's Sons. 1927. 1st ed......... *$25.00–$40.00*

Assoc of Edison Illuminating Co. *Edisonia*. 1904. 1st ed. illus............. *$55.00–$75.00*

Astaire, Fred. *Steps in Time*. NY. 1959. 1st ed. dj.................................. *$25.00–$85.00*

Astaire, Fred. *Steps in Time*. NY. 1959. 1st ed. wrps. sgn, dj. .... *$325.00–$425.00*

Astor, Gerald. *Operation Iceberg*. NY. 1995. 1st ed. illus. dj................. *$20.00–$25.00*

Atherton, Gertrude. *California; An Intimate History*. NY. 1927. .... *$10.00–$15.00*

Atherton, Gertrude. *The Conqueror*. NY. Macmillan. 1902. 1st ed. ..... *$40.00–$75.00*

Atherton, Gertrude. *The Foghorn*. Bos. 1934. 1st ed. dj....................... *$70.00–$85.00*

Atherton, Gertrude. *The Sophisticates*. Lon. 1931. 1st UK edition, pink cloth bds. ......
.... *$40.00–$50.00*

Atkinson, Joseph. *History of Newark, NJ*. Newark. 1878. 1st ed. illus. by Moran, 334 pp,
plates... *$60.00–$150.00*

Atlas of Cuyahoga County, Ohio. Phil. Titus Simmons & Titus. 1874. folio cloth cvr bds
and lea plates, maps... *$400.00–$500.00*

Attaway, William. *Let Me Breathe Thunder*. NY. Doubleday, Doran. 1939. 1st ed.
author's first book,. .... *$50.00–$100.00*

Atwater, Caleb. *History of the State of Ohio*. Cinc. (1838). 2nd ed. lea........................
.... *$85.00–$150.00*

Atwater, Mary Meigs. *Shuttle-Craft Book of American Hand-Weaving*. NY. Macmillan.
1937. illus. cloth. .... *$25.00–$35.00*

Atwood, Margaret. *Bodily Harm*. Tor. M & S. (1981). 1st ed. inscrb, dj. *$45.00–$60.00*

Atwood, Margaret. *Handmaid's Tale*. Lon. 1986. dj. .... *$28.00–$35.00*

Atwood, Margaret. *Lady Oracle*. Tor. McClelland Steward. (1976). 1st Canadian ed. dj.
.... *$30.00–$45.00*

Atwood, Margaret. *Power Politics*. NY. 1973. 1st ed. dj....................... *$30.00–$35.00*

Atwood, Margaret. *Wilderness Tips*. NY. Doubleday. 1991. 1st ed. dj. . *$10.00–$20.00*

Atwood, Margaret. *Wilderness Tips*. NY. Doubleday. 1991. 1st ed. sgn, dj...................
.... *$25.00–$35.00*

Atwood, Margaret. *Wilderness Tips*. NY. Nan Talese/DD. 1991. 1st ed. ltd. sgn, dj. .....
.... *$45.00–$60.00*

Auchincloss, Louis. *Dark Lady*. Bos. Houghton Mifflin. 1977. 1st ed. dj.....................
.... *$15.00–$20.00*

Auchincloss, Louis. *Honorable Men*. Bos. Houghton Mifflin. 1985. wrps. uncorrected proof. .... *$25.00–$35.00*

Auchincloss, Louis. *Injustice Collectors*. Bos. 1950. 1st ed. dj. .... *$50.00–$150.00*

Auchincloss, Louis. *Watchfires*. Bos. Houghton Mifflin. 1982. 1st ed. dj...................... .... *$15.00–$25.00*

Auchlincloss, Louis. *Injustice Collectors*. Lon. Victor Gollancz. 1951. 1st Brit ed. dj. .. .. *$30.00–$50.00*

Auden, W. H. *A Certain World*. NY. Viking. (1970). 1st ed. dj. .... *$30.00–$50.00*

Auden, W. H. *About the House*. NY. Random House. (1965). 1st ed. dj. *$35.00–$75.00*

Auden, W. H. *Age of Anxiety*. NY. (1947). 1st US ed. dj...................... *$75.00–$125.00*

Auden, W. H. *Age of Anxiety: A Baroque Eclogue*. Lon. Faber & Faber. (1948). 1st Brit ed. dj. .... *$45.00–$95.00*

Auden, W. H. *Collected Poetry of W H Auden*. Random House. 1945. 1st ed. dj........... .... *$100.00–$250.00*

Auden, W. H. *Dance of Death*. (Lon). Faber & Faber. (1933). 1st ed. dj. .... *$165.00–$295.00*

Auden, W. H. *On This Island*. NY. (1937). 1st US ed. dj..................... *$65.00–$100.00*

Auden, W. H. *Poems*. Lon. Faber & Faber. (1930). 1st ed. blue wrps............................ .... *$340.00–$400.00*

Audsley, George A. *Artistic & Decorative Stencilling*. Lon. 1911. illus...................... .... *$95.00–$145.00*

Audsley, W. and G. Audsley. *Guide to Art of Illumination and Missal Painting*. 1862. . ... *$93.00–$125.00*

Audsley, W. and G. Audsley. *Polychromatic Decoration as Applied to Buildings in the Medieval Styles*. Lon. 1882. illus. tall folio 36 plates in gold and clrs............................. .... *$600.00–$975.00*

Audubon, John J. *Birds of America*. NY. 1937. illus. clr plates. .... *$30.00–$45.00*

Audubon, John James. *Quadrupeds of North America*. NY. 1849–51–54. 3 vols. 1st 8vo ed. 155 hand-clr plates, fine binding.. *$6,900.00–$9,000.00*

Audubon, John W. *Audubon's Western Journal 1849–1850*. Cleve. 1906. 1st ed. fldg map, rprnt. .... *$125.00–$200.00*

Audubon, Maria. *Audubon and His Journals*. NY. 1897. 2 vols. .... *$150.00–$250.00*

Auel, Jean. *Clan of the Cave Bear*. NY. Crown. 1980. 1st ed. author's first book, dj...... .... *$50.00–$75.00*

Auel, Jean. *Clan of the Cave Bear*. NY. 1980. 1st ed. author's first book, sgn, dj. .... *$100.00–$200.00*

Auel, Jean. *Mammoth Hunters*. NY. (1985). 1st ed. dj. .... *$5.00–$15.00*

Aurthur, R. A. *Third Marine Division*. Wash. 1948. 1st ed.................... *$50.00–$75.00*

Austen, Jane. *Emma*. Lon. 1816. 3 vols. 1st ed. full brown mor... *$4,312.00–$7,800.00*

Austen, Jane. *Lady Susan . . .* Oxford. 1925. 3 vols. 1st ed. now rprntcd from the manuscript. .... *$50.00–$75.00*

Austen, Jane. *Pride and Prejudice*. NY. Macmillan. illus. gilt peacock cvr, aeg............
.... *$40.00–$60.00*

Auster, Paul. *Ghosts*. LA. Sun and Moon Press. 1986. 1st ed. dj. .... *$40.00–$55.00*

Austin, Gabriel. *Library of Jean Grolier* . . . NY. The Grolier Club. 1971. 1000 cc......
.... *$60.00–$75.00*

Austin, Mary. *American Rhythm*. NY. Harcourt. (1923). 1st ed. 155 pp, dj..................
.... *$150.00–$175.00*

Austin, Mary. *Arrow Maker*. Duffield & Co. 1911. 128 pp.................. *$75.00–$100.00*

Austin, Mary. *Land of Little Rain*. Bos. Houghton Mifflin. 1950. 1st ed. thus, photos by Ansel Adams, dj. .... *$150.00–$195.00*

Austin, Mary. *Land of Little Rain*. Bos/NY. Houghton Mifflin. 1903. 1st ed. author's first book. .... *$125.00–$250.00*

Austin, Stanley. *History of Engraving from Its Inception* . . . Lon. T Werner Laurie. 1908. cloth. .... *$50.00–$60.00*

Avary, Myrta Lockett. *Dixie After the War*. NY. Doubleday. 1906. 1st ed. illus. ....
.... *$45.00–$125.00*

Avedon, Richard and Truman Capote. *Observations*. NY. Simon & Schuster. 1959. 1st ed. illus. photos.. *$80.00–$120.00*

Averill, Charles. *Short Treatise on Operative Surgery, describing the principal operations as they are practised in England and France* . . . Phil. 1823. 1st American ed, 4 fldg plates. .... *$150.00–$200.00*

Avery, Al. *Yankee Flyer in Normandy*. Grosset & Dunlap. 1945. #19, dj. *$18.00–$27.00*

Avery, Al. *Yankee Flyer with the RAF*. Grosset & Dunlap. 1941. Air Combat Stories #8, dj. .... *$15.00–$24.00*

Axe, John. *Effanbee: A Collector's Encyclopedia* . . . Hobby Horse Press. (1983). illus. pictorial bds. .... *$20.00–$30.00*

Ayers, James T. *Diary of James T. Ayers, Civil War Recruiter*. Springfield, IL. 1947. 138 pp. .... *$30.00–$45.00*

Ayling, Augustus D. *Revised Register of the Soldiers and Sailors of New Hampshire in the War of the Rebellion 1861–1866*. Concord. 1895. rev ed. folio, half lea....................
.... *$150.00–$300.00*

Ayres, William S. *Warner Collector's Guide to American Toys*. NY. Main Street Press. (1981). 1st ed. wrps. illus.. *$12.00–$25.00*

Ayton, Laurie, et al. *Golf as Champions Play it*. Chi. Associated Editors. 1925. 1st ed. wrps. illus. .... *$30.00–$50.00*

Babault, Guy. *Chasses et Recherches Zoologiques en Afrique* . . .*1913*. Paris. Librairie Plon. 1917. 1st ed. illus. photos. .... *$80.00–$120.00*

Babbitt, Bruce. *Color and Light*. Flagstaff. Northland Press. 1973. 1st ed. illus. clr plates, ltd 1,750 cc... *$75.00–$110.00*

Babbitt, Bruce. *Grand Canyon*. 1st ed. sgn................................ *$60.00–$80.00*

Babcock, Philip H. *Falling Leaves*. NY. Derrydale. (1937). 1st ed. review copy, 1/950 cc... *$70.00–$100.00*

Babington, S. H. *Navajo Gods and Tom-Toms*. NY. (1950). illus. dj...... *$30.00–$45.00*

Back, Captain. *Narrative of the Arctic Land Expedition to the Mouth of the Great Fish River . . . 1833, 1834, and 1835.* Phila. 1836. 1st Amer ed. rbnd, fldg map, 456 pp.......
.... *$325.00–$650.00*

Bacom, G. *New Large Scale Ordnance Atlas of the British Isles.* 1884. hand-clr maps, full lea... *$175.00–$225.00*

Bacon, Edgar Mayhew. *Narragansett Bay, Its Historic and Romantic Associations and Picturesque Setting.* Putnam. 1904. 1st ed. illus by author, map............. *$50.00–$65.00*

Bacon, Leonard. *Thirteen Historical Discourses . . .* New Haven. Durrie Peck. 1839. 1st ed. illus. .... *$20.00–$30.00*

Badeau, Adam. *Grant in Peace . . . A Personal Memoir.* Phila. 1888. 1st ed. ....
.... *$45.00–$65.00*

Baden-Powell, Lord. *Birds and Beasts in Africa.* Lon. 1938. clr plates. *$30.00–$50.00*

Baden-Powell, Lord. *Handbook for Brownies or Bluebirds.* Lon. (1920). wrps. ....
.... *$30.00–$45.00*

Baden-Powell, Lord. *Indian Memories.* Lon. 1915. 1st ed. illus. clr plates. ....
.... *$85.00–$125.00*

Baden-Powell, Lord. *Paddle Your Own Canoe.* Lon. 1939. dj................ *$50.00–$75.00*

Baden-Powell, Lord. *Scouting for Boys.* np. 1913. 6th ed. wraps. .... *$95.00–$120.00*

Baden-Powell, Robert. *Pigsticking or Hog Hunting.* Lon. 1924. dj...... *$30.00–$40.00*

Baedeker, Karl. *Mediterranean.* 1911. .... *$70.00–$100.00*

Baedeker, Karl. *Belgium and Holland.* Leipzig. 1910. 15th and rev. ..... *$40.00–$60.00*

Baedeker, Karl. *Berlin and Its Environs.* Leipzig. 1908. 3rd ed. .... *$95.00–$125.00*

Baedeker, Karl. *Berlin and Its Environs.* 1923. 6th ed. dj. .... *$14.00–$18.00*

Baedeker, Karl. *Central Italy.* 1914. 14th ed. .... *$15.00–$25.00*

Baedeker, Karl. *Die Rheinlande von der Schweizer bis zur Hollandischen Grenze.* Coblenz. 1864. 358 pp... *$150.00–$250.00*

Baedeker, Karl. *Dominion of Canada.* Leipsic. 1894. 254 pp............. *$95.00–$150.00*

Baedeker, Karl. *Egypt.* 1914. 7th ed... *$47.00–$95.00*

Baedeker, Karl. *Egypt and the Sudan.* Leipzig. 1908. 6th ed. red fabricoid..................
.... *$200.00–$250.00*

Baedeker, Karl. *Etats-Unis.* 1894. .... *$35.00–$50.00*

Baedeker, Karl. *Holland: Handbuch Fur Reisende.* Leipzig. 1927. limp red leatherette, text in German. *$100.00*

Baedeker, Karl. *Italy from the Alps to Naples.* 1909.............................. *$20.00–$30.00*

Baedeker, Karl. *London and Environs.* Leipzig. 1911. 16th edition...... *$50.00–$80.00*

Baedeker, Karl. *London and Its Environs.* Leipzig. 1908. 1st ed........... *$18.00–$25.00*

Baedeker, Karl. *Northern France.* 1889. 1st ed. dj. .... *$35.00–$75.00*

Baedeker, Karl. *Northern Germany.* Leipzig. 1910. 15th ed. .... *$25.00–$65.00*

Baedeker, Karl. *Palatina Und Syrien.* 1900. .... *$125.00–$150.00*

Baedeker, Karl. *Palestine and Syria.* Leipzig. 1912. 5th ed. *$225.00*

Baedeker, Karl. *Paris and Its Environs*. Leipzig. 1891. 10th edition, red cloth. ....
.... *$35.00–$45.00*

Baedeker, Karl. *Rhine from Rottercam to Constance*. Leipzig. 1906. 16th ed. maps, plates.. *$30.00–$35.00*

Baedeker, Karl. *Rhine from Rotterdam to Constance*. Leipsic. 1882. 387 pp. ....
.... *$30.00–$45.00*

Baedeker, Karl. *Southern Germany*. Leipzig. 1914. 12th rev ed. .... *$40.00–$50.00*

Baedeker, Karl. *Southern Germany*. Leipzig. 1907. 10th ed. .... *$15.00–$25.00*

Baedeker, Karl. *Spain and Portugal*. 1908.. *$20.00–$50.00*

Baedeker, Karl. *Switzerland*. Leipzig. 1913. maps. .... *$18.00–$25.00*

Baedeker, Karl. *Switzerland*. 1907. .... *$22.00–$45.00*

Baedeker, Karl. *United States*. 1909. 4th ed. .... *$40.00–$75.00*

Baedeker, Karl. *United States With an Excursion Into Mexico*. Leipzig. 1893. 1st ed. red cloth, 516 pp, 17 maps, 22 plans... *$200.00–$250.00*

Baedeker, Karl. *United States: With an Excursion Into Mexico*. Leipzig. (1904). 3rd rev ed. fldg maps, plans, red fabricoid....................................... *$150.00–$225.00*

Bailey, Alice Cooper. *Katrina and Jan*. Chi. Volland. (1923). illus by Herman Rosse....
.... *$30.00–$100.00*

Bailey, C. W. *Brain and Golf: Some Hints*. Lon. Mills & Boon. (1924). 2nd ed............
.... *$80.00–$100.00*

Bailey, C. W. *Professor on the Golf Links*. Lon. Silas Birch. (1925). 1st ed..................
.... *$100.00–$200.00*

Bailey, Carolyn Sherwin. *Little Reader Series No. 3*. Springfield. (1934). 4 vols. illus by Ruth Hallock. original box, scarce... *$50.00–$65.00*

Bailey, F M. *Birds of New Mexico*. Wash. 1928. illus....................... *$100.00–$150.00*

Bailey, Harold. *Birds of Florida*. Balt. privately published. 1925. illus. fldg map, 76 clr plates.. *$115.00–$160.00*

Bailey, L H. *Standard Cyclopedia of Horticulture*. NY. Macmillan. 1935. 3 vols. illus. 24 clr and 96 b/w. .... *$60.00–$90.00*

Bailey, L. H. *Blackberries of North America*. Ithaca. 1932. illus. .... *$20.00–$32.00*

Bailey, L. H. *Cylopedia of American Horticulture*. NY. 1900–1902. 4 vols. ....
.... *$100.00–$195.00*

Bailey, Pearl. *Talking to Myself*. NY. Harcourt Brace Jovanovich. 1971. 1st ed. 1st prtg, dj. .... *$15.00–$25.00*

Bainbridge, Henry Charles. *Peter Carl Faberge*. Lon. Batsford. 1949. 1st ed. illus. photos, dj. .... *$25.00–$75.00*

Baird, Bill. *Art of the Puppet*. NY. Macmillan. 1965. 1st ed. photos, dj. ....
.... *$70.00–$100.00*

Baird, P. D. *Expeditions to the Canadian Arctic*. 1949. 1st ed. wrps. ...... *$24.00–$32.00*

Baker, C. Alice. *Summer in the Azores With a Glimpse of Madiera*. Bos. Lee and Shepard. 1882. 1st ed. .... *$30.00–$45.00*

Baker, Gen L. C. *History of the U.S. Secret Service.* Phila. 1867. 1st ed.*$40.00–$75.00*

Baker, J. C. *Baptist History of the North Pacific Coast* . . . Phila. 1912. 1st ed. ....
.... *$30.00–$60.00*

Baker, Lillian. *Creative and Collectible.* KY. Collector Books. illus...... *$13.00–$20.00*

Baker, Marcus. *Geographic Dictionary of Alaska.* GPO. 1906. 2nd ed. *$60.00–$80.00*

Baker, Roger. *Dolls & Dolls' Houses* . . . Crescent Books. (1973). illus. dj...................
.... *$15.00–$20.00*

Baker, Samuel W. *Ismailia.* NY. Harper. 1875. 1st Amer ed. illus, plates, 542 pp.........
.... *$100.00–$150.00*

Baker, Samuel W. *Nile Tributaries of Abyssinia.* Lon. Macmillan. 1894. maps..............
.... *$50.00–$60.00*

Bakst, Leon. *Designs of Leon Bakst for the Sleeping Princess.* Lon. 1923. ltd ed. ....
.... *$550.00–$1,200.00*

Balcom, Mary G. *Ketchikan Alaska's Totemland.* Chi. 1961. illus. softcvr, sgn..............
.... *$10.00–$18.00*

Baldacci, David. *Absolute Power.* NY. Warner. 1996. 1st ed. inscr, dj.. *$65.00–$100.00*

Baldwin, Alice M. *New England Clergy & the American Revolution.* NC. 1928. 1st ed.
.... *$15.00–$30.00*

Baldwin, Frederick W. *Biography of the Bar of Orleans County, Vermont.* Montpelier.
1886. illus. 303 pp. .... *$30.00–$40.00*

Baldwin, James. *Fire Next Time.* 1963. 1st ed. dj.................................. *$30.00–$50.00*

Baldwin, James. *Going to Meet the Man.* Dial. 1965. 1st ed. dj............. *$25.00–$50.00*

Baldwin, James. *If Beale Street Could Talk.* NY. 1974. 1st ed. dj. .... *$50.00–$75.00*

Baldwin, James. *Just Above My Head.* NY. Dial Press. (1979). 1st ed. dj......................
.... *$40.00–$50.00*

Baldwin, James. *Little Man, Little Man.* NY. (1976). 1st US prtg. illus by Yoran Cazac.
dj. .... *$40.00–$100.00*

Baldwin, James. *Nobody Knows My Name, More Notes of a Native Son.* NY. Dial Press.
1961. 1st ed. dj. .... *$75.00–$150.00*

Baldwin, James. *Tell Me How Long the Train's Been Gone.* NY. Dial Press. 1968. 1st ed.
dj. .... *$30.00–$65.00*

Baldwin, James. *Un Altro Mondo: Romanzo.* Milan. Feltrinelli. 1963. 1st Italian ed. dj.
.... *$30.00–$50.00*

Baldwin, William C. *African Hunting from Natal to the Zambesi.* NY. 1863. illus. fldg
map. .... *$80.00–$125.00*

Ball, Charles. *History of the Indian Mutiny.* Lon. London Printing & Publ. 1880. 1st ed.
illus. 3/4 dark brown calf steel engrvs. .... *$150.00–$200.00*

Ball, Col. T. A. *Le Golf.* Paris. Editions Paris-Vendome. (1950). 1st ed. illus. in French.
.... *$60.00–$70.00*

Ball, Johnson. *William Caslon 1693–1766, the Ancestry, Life and Connections* . . .
Kineton. The Roundwood Press. 1973. dj................................... *$40.00–$60.00*

Ball, Walter Rouse. *Short Account of the History of Mathematics*. Lon. 1893. 2nd ed. .
.... *$15.00–$30.00*

Ballantine, Stuart. *Radio Telephony for Amateurs*. Mckay. 1923. 2nd ed......................
.... *$15.00–$25.00*

Ballard, Robert D. *Lost Ships of Guadalcanal*. Warner/Madison. 1993. illus. dj. ....
.... *$20.00–$40.00*

Ballinger, Bill. *Chinese Mask*. NY. New American Library. 1965. 1st ed. paperback. ....
.... *$5.00–$11.00*

Balzac, Honore de. *Droll Stories*. Boni & Liveright. 1928. 2 vols. illus. *$20.00–$45.00*

Bamford, Georgia Loring. *Mystery of Jack London*. Oakland. 1931. 1st ed. dj. ....
.... *$95.00–$125.00*

Bancroft, Hubert Howe. *History of Alaska, 1730–1886*. San Francisco. 1886. map......
.... *$150.00–$225.00*

Bancroft, Hubert Howe. *History of British Columbia 1792–1887*. SF. The History Company. 1887. 1st ed. lea, maps...................... *$125.00–$165.00*

Bancroft, Hubert Howe. *History of the Northwest Coast*. San Francisco. 1886. 2 vols.
.... *$75.00–$175.00*

Bancroft, Hubert Howe. *History of Utah*. San Francisco. 1890. 1st ed. illus. clr plates.
.... *$65.00–$135.00*

Bancroft, Hubert Howe. *New Pacific*. NY. 1900. teg, frontis, map........ *$35.00–$65.00*

Bancroft, Laura (L. Frank Baum). *Bandit Jim Crow*. Chi. Reilly & Lee. illus. ....
.... *$50.00–$80.00*

Bancroft, Laura (L. Frank Baum). *Mr. Woodchuck*. Chi. Reilly & Lee. (1906). illus...
.... *$200.00–$250.00*

Bandel, Betty. *Sing the Lord's Song in a Strange Land*. Rutherford, NJ. Associated Univ Presses. 1981. dj. .... *$18.00–$65.00*

Banergi, P. *Snake-Bite with a System of Treatment & Reported Cases & Notes*. Calcutta. 1956. illus. .... *$40.00–$50.00*

Bangay, R. D. *Wireless Telephony*. 1923. 1st cd. illus............................ *$18.00–$25.00*

Bangs, John Kendrick. *Bicyclers and Three Other Forces*. NY. 1896. 1st ed................
.... *$30.00–$50.00*

Bangs, John Kendrick. *Foothills of Parnassus*. NY. 1914. review copy, dj. ....
.... *$50.00–$75.00*

Bangs, John Kendrick. *Ghosts I Have Met*. NY. Harper & Bros. 1898. 1st ed. illus. ....
.... *$50.00–$125.00*

Bangs, John Kendrick. *House-Boat on the Styx*. NY. Harper & Bros. 1896. 1st ed. illus.
.... *$35.00–$75.00*

Bangs, John Kendrick. *Mr. Munchausen*. Bos. Noyes, Platt & Co. 1901. 1st ed. illus. by Peter Newell. .... *$40.00–$60.00*

Bangs, John Kendrick. *Mrs. Raffles*. NY. Harper & Bros. 1905. 1st ed. illus. ....
.... *$75.00–$150.00*

Bangs, John Kendrick. *Olympian Nights*. NY. Harper & Bros. 1902. 1st ed. illus.........
.... *$20.00–$35.00*

Bangs, John Kendrick. *Peeps at People.* NY. Harper & Bros. 1899. 1st ed. illus. by Penfield. presentation copy............ *$120.00–$150.00*

Bangs, John Kendrick. *Pursuit of the House-Boat.* NY. Harper & Bros. 1897. 1st ed. no dj............ *$50.00–$100.00*

Bangs, John Kendrick. *Songs of Cheer.* Bos. 1910. 1st ed. dj............ *$95.00–$125.00*

Bangs, John Kendrick. *The Dreamers.* NY. 1899. 1st ed. illus. by Penfield............ .... *$60.00–$95.00*

Bangs, John Kendrick. *Three Weeks in Politics.* NY. 1894. 1st ed. illus. *$30.00–$45.00*

Bangs, John Kendrick. *Water Ghost and Athens.* NY. 1894. 1st ed. illus............ .... *$25.00–$65.00*

Bank, Arnold. *Calligraphy and Its Influence in the Time of Plantin.* Antwerp. 1955. wrps. inscrb............ *$18.00–$25.00*

Banks, Mike. *Rakaposhi.* Lon. Secker & Warburg. 1959. 1st ed. photos, maps, dj............ .... *$18.00–$30.00*

Banks, Nathaniel P. *Purchase of Alaska.* Wash. 1868. 1st ed............ *$50.00–$75.00*

Banks, Russel. *Relation of My Imprisonment.* Wash. Sun & Moon Press. 1983. 1st trade ed. dj............ *$30.00–$65.00*

Banks, Russell. *Affliction.* NY. Harper & Row. 1989. 1st ed. dj............ *$18.00–$25.00*

Banks, Russell. *Cloudsplitter.* NY. Harper Flamingo. 1998. 1st ed. wrps. advance reading copy............ *$38.00–$45.00*

Banks, Russell. *Continental Draft.* Harper & Row. 1985. 1st ed. dj............ *$20.00–$25.00*

Banks, Russell. *Rule of the Bone.* NY. Harper Collins. 1995. 1st ed. sgn, dj............ .... *$30.00–$75.00*

Banks, Russell. *Searching for Survivors.* NY. Fiction Collective. 1975. 1st ed. author's first collection of short stories, dj............ *$100.00–$300.00*

Banks, Russell. *Sweet Hereafter.* NY. Harper Collins. 1991. 1st ed. sgn, dj............ .... *$20.00–$35.00*

Bannerman, Helen. *Histoire du Petit Negre Sambo.* NY. Stokes. (1921). 1st ed. in French, dj............ *$125.00–$185.00*

Bannerman, Helen. *Little Black Sambo.* Whitman. illus. by Cobb and Shinn, 64 pp, dark brown cloth bds............ *$75.00–$100.00*

Bannerman, Helen. *Little Black Sambo.* NY. Little Golden Book. 1948. *$40.00–$55.00*

Bannerman, Helen. *Little Black Sambo.* Platt & Munk. 1935. dj............ *$165.00–$320.00*

Bannerman, Helen. *Little Black Sambo.* Akron. 1933. illus. by Fern Bisel Peat............ .... *$80.00–$130.00*

Bannerman, Helen. *Little Black Sambo Animated.* DueneWold Printing Corp. (1949). illus. paper bds, 4 moveable plates............ *$150.00–$350.00*

Bannerman, Helen. *Sambo and the Twins.* Phila. 1946. illus. by Helen Bannerman............ .... *$45.00–$60.00*

Bannerman, Helen. *Story of Little Black Sambo.* Lon. 1899. 1st ed. green cloth with dark stripes and lettering............ *$5,000.00–$10,000.00*

Baraka, Amiri. *Home: Social Essays, by LeRoi Jones.* NY. William Morrow. 1966. 1st ed. dJ.. *$55.00–$75.00*

Barbeau, M. *Alaska Beckons.* Caxton. 1947. 1st ed. dj.......................... *$25.00–$35.00*

Barbeau, M. *Haida Myths Illustrated in Argillite Carvings.* Ottawa. 1953. 1st ed. wrps. .... *$90.00–$185.00*

Barbeau, M. *Totem Poles.* Nat'l Museum Canada. 1950. 2 vols. illus. *$110.00–$250.00*

Barbeau, Marius. *Ancient France Lingers.* 1936. illus. softcvr. .... *$20.00–$30.00*

Barbeau, Marius. *Downfall of Temlaham.* Tor. 1928. 1st ed. illus. dj.. *$95.00–$150.00*

Barbeau, Marius. *Jongleur Songs of Old Quebec.* NJ. 1962.................. *$25.00–$35.00*

Barber, Edwin A. *Lead Glazed Pottery.* Phila. 1907. 1st ed. illus. .... *$25.00–$35.00*

Barber, Joel. *Wild Fowl Decoys.* Lyon. Derrydale. 1989. illus. clr and b/w plates, rprnt. ....*$45.00–$85.00*

Barber, Joel. *Wild Fowl Decoys.* NY. 1934. illus. dj.............................. *$75.00–$150.00*

Barber, John (ed.). *History of the Amistad Captives.* New Haven. EL and JW Barber. 1840. 1st ed. 32 pp, plamphlet, fldg plate................................ *$150.00–$250.00*

Barclay, J. T. *City of the Great King . . .* Phil. W H Thompson. 1883. 1st ed. illus. maps, engr. .... *$45.00–$75.00*

Baring-Gould, S. *Family Names & Their Story.* Lon. Seeley & Co. 1910. blue clr. .... *$40.00–$50.00*

Barker, Clive. *Cabal.* Poseidon. 1988. 1st ed. dj, sgn. .... *$30.00–$40.00*

Barker, Clive. *Damnation Game.* NY. Ace-Putnam. (1987). 1st Amer ed. sgn............... .... *$30.00–$55.00*

Barker, Clive. *Great and Secret Show.* NY. Harper & Row. 1989. 1st US ed. dj, sgn..... .... *$35.00–$65.00*

Barker, Clive. *Great and Secret Show.* NY. Harper. 1989. 1st ed. dj. ..... *$10.00–$20.00*

Barker, Clive. *Weaveworld.* Poseidon Press. 1987. 1st US ed. dj. .... *$20.00–$40.00*

Barker, Harold R. *History of the 43rd Division Artillery.* np. John F Greene Co. illus. red cloth, decorated cvr, maps, photos, with dj....................................... *$40.00–$175.00*

Barker, Ralph. *Last Blue Mountain.* NY. Doubleday. 1960. 1st ed. dj. ... *$20.00–$25.00*

Barker, S. Omar. *Songs of the Saddlemen . . .* Denver. Sage Books. 1954. inscrb by author. .... *$20.00–$30.00*

Barley, Joseph A. *Judging Saddle Horses and Roadsters.* Milw. 1945. 1st ed. .... *$32.00–$40.00*

Barn Plans & Outbuildings. NY. 1883. illus. .... *$40.00–$85.00*

Barnard, Charles. *First Steps in Electricity.* NY. 1888. 1st ed. illus. ...... *$40.00–$60.00*

Barnard, Frederick A. P. *Metric System of Weights and Measures.* Bos. 1879. 3rd ed.. .... *$40.00–$55.00*

Barnard, Harry. *Tattered Volunteers: The 27th Alabama Infantry Regiment.* Northport, AL. 1965. scarce, dj. .... *$75.00–$85.00*

Barnard, Lady Anne. *South Africa a Century Ago.* Lon. Smith, Elder. 1901. 2nd impression. original cloth... *$30.00–$40.00*

Barneby, Henry W. *Life and Labour in the Far, Far West* . . . Lon. 1884. 1st ed. map. . ... *$80.00–$175.00*

Barnes, A. R. *South African Household Guide*. Capetown. 1907. 4th ed. *$25.00–$55.00*

Barnes, Henry. *Guerilla Bride*. Bellefontaine. 1858. cloth. privately printed. scarce. .... *$225.00–$300.00*

Barnes, James M. *My Picture Analysis of Gold Strokes*. Phil. 1919. 1st ed. illus. .... *$85.00–$250.00*

Barnes, Linda. *Bitter Finish*. NY. St Martin's. 1983. 1st ed. dj.............. *$65.00–$85.00*

Barnes, R. M. *Military Uniforms of Britain and the Empire*. Lon. 1960. illus............... .... *$35.00–$60.00*

Barnes, Robert. *United States Submarines*. New Haven. 1944. .... *$25.00–$112.00*

Barnes, Will C. *Western Grazing Grounds* . . . *A History of the Live-Stock Industry as Conducted on Open Ranges* . . . Chi. Breeder's Gazette. 1913. 1st ed. illus. 390 pp........ .... *$150.00–$300.00*

Barnum, P. T. *Struggles and Triumphs*. Buffalo. Johnson & Co. 1873. illus. author's ed. .... *$40.00–$55.00*

Barol, B. H. *Treatise on the Marine Boilers of the United States*. Phila. Barnard & Sons. 1851. drawings, embossed cloth.. *$240.00–$300.00*

Baron, Salo. *Social and Religious History of the Jews*. Columbia Univ Press. 1939. 3 vols.. *$30.00–$40.00*

Baron, Stanley. *Benny, King of Swing*. NY. Morrow. 1979. 1st ed. dj.... *$30.00–$45.00*

Baroni, George (ed). *The Pyramiders*. np. nd. 300 pp, photos. .... *$60.00–$75.00*

Barr, Nevada. *Ill Wind*. NY. Putnam. (1997). 1st ed. sgn, dj................... *$55.00–$65.00*

Barrett, Andrea. *Ship Fever*. NY. Norton. 1996. 1st ed. dj.................... *$45.00–$60.00*

Barrett, Edwin S. *What I Saw at Bull Run*. Bos. Beacon Press. 1886. frontis. 48 pp. ....*$125.00–$185.00*

Barrie, J. M. *Little Minister*. Lon. Cassell & Co. 1891. 3 vols. 1st ed. quarter mor slipcase... *$750.00–$1,500.00*

Barrie, J. M. *Peter Pan and Wendy*. NY. 1921. 1st ed. illus. by Mable Lucie Attwell. 9 clr plates, dj. .... *$75.00–$100.00*

Barrie, J. M. *Peter Pan in Kensington Gardens*. Lon. Hodder. 1906. 1st ed. illus. by Arthur Rackham. .... *$375.00–$750.00*

Barrie, J. M. *Peter and Wendy*. Lon. nd. illus. blue cloth, clr frontis, 12 illus............... .... *$150.00–$250.00*

Barrie, J. M. *Peter and Wendy*. Scribner's. 1911. 1st American ed, green cloth............. .... *$85.00–$100.00*

Barrie, J. M. *Peter Pan*. NY. Grosset & Dunlap. photoplay ed. dj...... *$125.00–$200.00*

Barrie, J. M. *Tommy and Grizel*. Scribner's. 1900. 1st ed. illus. by Partridge. .... *$35.00–$45.00*

Barrie, Robert. *Early Days of the Corinthian Yacht Club of Philadelphi*. Phila. private ptg. 1940. illus. photos. .... *$30.00–$40.00*

Barringer, Paul B., J. M. Garnett and Rosewell Page. *University of Virginia . . .* Lewis Pub. 1904. 2 vols. b/w illus. aeg. half lea. .... *$75.00–$100.00*

Barron, Archibald F. *Vines and Vine Culture*. Lon. 1900. illus. 4th ed. *$90.00–$150.00*

Barrows, Anna. *Principles of Cookery*. Chi. American School of Home Economics. 1910. illus. .... *$15.00–$20.00*

Barrows, W. B. *Michigan Bird Life*. Lansing. 1912. illus. .... *$45.00–$75.00*

Barsis, Max. *Ski Whiz! Bottoms Up Old and New*. Daye. 1945. 1st ed. illus. inscribed dj. .... *$25.00–$35.00*

Barth, Henry. *Travels and Discoveries in North Central Africa*. NY. Harper & Bros. 1857. 3 vols. illus. 1st Amer ed. maps. .... *$250.00–$500.00*

Barth, John. *Chimera*. Lon. Andre Deutsch. (1974). 1st ed. dj. .... *$50.00–$65.00*

Barth, John. *End of the Road*. Lon. 1962. 1st UK edition, dj............... *$90.00–$125.00*

Barth, John. *End of the Road*. Doubleday. 1958. 1st ed. dj. .... *$250.00–$500.00*

Barth, John. *Floating Opera*. Garden City. (1956). 1st ed. dj. author's first book. .... *$225.00–$300.00*

Barth, John. *Giles Goat-Boy*. Doubleday. 1966. dj................................. *$30.00–$65.00*

Barth, John. *Lost in the Funhouse*. Garden City. Doubleday. 1968. 1st ed. dj............... .... *$75.00–$100.00*

Barth, John. *Sot-Weed Factor*. Garden City. 1960. 1st ed. dj. .... *$50.00–$200.00*

Barthelme, Donald. *Come Back, Dr. Caligari*. Bos. Little, Brown. 1964. 1st ed. author's first book, dj.. *$150.00–$175.00*

Barthelme, Donald. *Guilty Pleasures*. NY. Farrar, Strauss & Giroux. (1974). 1st ed. dj. .... *$25.00–$40.00*

Barthelme, Donald. *Sixty Stories*. NY. Putnam's Son. (1979). 1st ed. sgn, dj. .... *$24.00–$60.00*

Barthelme, Donald. *Snow White*. NY. Atheneum. 1967. 1st ed. sgn, dj. .... *$135.00–$175.00*

Barthelme, Donald. *Unspeakable Practices, Unnatural Acts*. NY. Farrar, Strauss, Giroux. (1968). 1st ed. dj. .... *$20.00–$40.00*

Bartholomew, Ed. *Wild Bill Longley, a Texas Hard-case*. Houston. 1953. illus.............. .... *$30.00–$40.00*

Bartholow, Roberts. *Practical Treatise on Materia Medica and Therapeutics*. NY. 1884. 5th ed. .... *$25.00–$50.00*

Bartlett, W. *An Elementary Treatise on Optics*. NY. 1839. 1st ed. illus. fldg plates. .... *$30.00–$40.00*

Bartlett, W. H. *Walks About the City and Environs of Jerusalem*. Lon. 1842. frontis 3/4 mor. aeg. .... *$175.00–$225.00*

Barton, Clara. *Red Cross in Peace and War*. 1899. 1st ed.................... *$50.00–$100.00*

Barton, Lucy. *Historic Costume for the Stage*. Lon. 1935. illus. b/w..... *$50.00–$65.00*

Barton, Lucy. *Historic Costume for the Stage*. Bos. 1935. 1st ed. illus. *$50.00–$125.00*

Barton, William E. *Hero in Homespun.* Bos. 1897. 1st ed. illus. by Dan Beard............. .... *$18.00–$25.00*

Bashline, James. *Night Fishing for Trout.* Rockville Centre. 1972. 1st ed. dj. .... *$25.00–$40.00*

Bass, W. W. *Adventures in the Canyons of Colorado . . . Grand Canyon.* 1920. wrps. 38 pp. .... *$95.00–$200.00*

Bassett, Ronald. *Tinfish Run.* NY. Harper and Row. 1977. 1st ed. dj. author's first book. .... *$15.00–$25.00*

Batchelder, Marjorie. *Puppet Theatre Handbook.* NY. 1947. 1st ed. dj. *$15.00–$25.00*

Batchelor, D. *Jack Johnson & His Times.* Lon. 1957. illus. 190 pp, dj. ... *$30.00–$45.00*

Bates, Colonel Charles F. *Custer's Indian Battles.* NY. 1936. illus. folio photos. .... *$35.00–$80.00*

Bates, H. W. *Naturalist on the River Amazons.* Lon. 1873. illus. 3rd ed. .... *$75.00–$150.00*

Bates, Joseph D. *Trout Waters and How to Fish Them.* Bos. 1949. 1st ed..................... .... *$20.00–$27.00*

Bates, Joseph D., Jr. *Atlantic Salmon Flies & Fishing.* Stackpole. 1970. 1st ed. dj. .... *$50.00–$120.00*

Bates, Joseph D., Jr. *Spinning for Game Fish.* Little Brown. (1947). dj. *$20.00–$50.00*

Bates, Joseph D., Jr. *Streamers & Bucktails.* Knopf. 1979. dj. .... *$40.00–$75.00*

Battersby, Col. J. C. *Bridle Bits, a Treatise on Practical Horsemanship.* NY. Orange Judd. 1886. 1st ed. .... *$140.00–$185.00*

Battleground Korea: The Story of the 25th Infantry Division. Arlington. 1951. 1st ed. dj. .... *$50.00–$85.00*

Batty, J. H. *Practical Taxidermy and Home Decoration.* NY. 1880. 1st ed. illus. .... *$30.00–$40.00*

Bauer, Paul. *Himalayan Quest.* Lon. Nicholson & Watson. 1938. 1st ed. photos, maps. .... *$35.00–$40.00*

Baughman, A. J. *History of Huron County, Ohio.* Chi. 1909. 2 vols. 1st ed. illus. .... *$80.00–$100.00*

Baum, Frank. *Land of Oz.* Chi. Reilley & Lee. (1904). red cloth, pictorial pastedown, b/w illus. .... *$40.00–$60.00*

Baum, Frank. *New Wizard of Oz.* Ind. Bobbs-Merrill. (1903). illus. by W W Denslow, green cloth, pictorial pastedown, clr plates. .... *$45.00–$60.00*

Baum, L. Frank. *Dorothy and the Wizard of Oz.* Chi. Reilly & Lee. illus. by John R Neill, rprnt of 1908 ed, b/w drawings, 4 clr paste-on cvr. .... *$60.00–$75.00*

Baum, L. Frank. *John Dough and the Cherub.* Chi. (1906). 1st ed. illus. by John R Neill. rare contest blank present. .... *$500.00–$650.00*

Baum, L. Frank. *Land of Oz — A Sequel to the Wizard.* Chi. (1925). clr frontis............ .... *$40.00–$65.00*

Baum, L. Frank. *Lost Princess of Oz.* Chi. 1939. illus. by J Neill, junior ed................. .... *$18.00–$27.00*

Baum, L. Frank. *Marvelous Land of Oz*. Reilly & Britton. 1904. 1st ed. illus. by J Neill, 2nd state... *$245.00–$575.00*

Baum, L. Frank. *Ozma of Oz*. Chi. Reilly & Britain. 1907. 1st ed. illus. tan cloth. .... *$400.00–$575.00*

Baum, L. Frank. *Patchwork Girl of Oz*. Reilly & Britton. (1913). 1st ed. illus. by Neill, 1st state. .... *$375.00–$425.00*

Baum, L. Frank. *Rinkitink in Oz*. Reilly & Britain. (1916). 1st ed. illus. by J Neill, clr plates... *$675.00–$800.00*

Baum, L. Frank. *Sky Island*. Chi. Reilly & Britton. (1912). 1st ed. illus. by John R Neill. 12 clr plates, red cloth. .... *$385.00–$500.00*

Baum, L. Frank. *Wizard of Oz*. Ind. (1920). 1st ed. b/w illus, 8 clr plates, pictorial cvr. ....*$45.00–$75.00*

Baum, L. Frank. *Wizard of Oz Illustrated*. NY. Grosset & Dunlap. 1939. 1st thus. .... *$50.00–$75.00*

Baum, L. Frank. *Wonderful Wizard of Oz*. West Hatfield, MA. 1985. illus. by Barry Moser, deluxe copy, sgn, #9/50 cc, boxed.................................... *$1,000.00–$1,500.00*

Baumbach, Werner. *Life and Death of the Luftwaffe*. NY. 1960. 1st Amer ed. photos. . ... *$18.00–$25.00*

Baxter, Charles. *South Dakota Guidebook*. NY. Rivers Press. 1974. 1st ed. hardcvr, scarce, sgn, dj. .... *$250.00–$450.00*

Baxter, Gregory. *Calamity Comes of Age*. NY. Macaulay. 1935. 1st ed. dj.................... .... *$20.00–$40.00*

Baxter, John E. *Locker Room Ballads*. NY. Appleton. 1923. 1st ed. illus. .... *$30.00–$50.00*

Bayard, Samuel J. *Sketch of the Life of Commodore Robert F. Stockton*. NY. 1856....... .... *$35.00–$50.00*

Baylor, George. *Bull Run to Bull Run*. Richmond. Johnson. 1900...... *$250.00–$300.00*

Beach, S. A. *Apples of New York*. Alb. 1905. 2 vols. illus. 130 clr plates. .... *$150.00–$375.00*

Beacher, L. *Contact Lens Technique*. self-published. illus. .... *$30.00–$45.00*

Beadle, J. H. *Life in Utah*. Phila. 1870. 1st ed. map, plates. .... *$50.00–$125.00*

Beale, George. *Lieutenant of Cavalry in Lee's Army*. Balt. rprnt, dj. ...... *$20.00–$30.00*

Beale, R. L. T. *History of the Ninth Virginia Cavalry in the War Between the States*. Richmond. B F Johnson Pub Co. 1899. 1st ed. 192 pp. .... *$1,250.00–$1,500.00*

Beale, Reginald. *Practical Greenkeeper*. Lon. Carter. 1936. new ed. illus. green wrps. ....*$80.00–$125.00*

Beamish, Richard. *Boy's Story of Lindbergh*. John C Winston. 1928. illus. green-blue cloth with pictorial paste down. .... *$15.00–$20.00*

Bean, Willard. *ABC History of Palmyry and the Beginning of Mormonism*. Palmyra. 1938. 1st ed. illus. printed wraps, photos... *$25.00–$45.00*

Bear, Greg. *Eon*. NY. Bluejay. 1985. 1st ed. dj sgn............................. *$85.00–$100.00*

Beard, James. *Delights and Prejudices*. NY. 1964. 1st ed. dj................ *$18.00–$25.00*

Beard, James A. *Fireside Cook Book.* NY. Simon & Schuster. 1949. 1st ed. illus. dj..... .... *$20.00–$30.00*

Beard, James B., Harriet J. Beard and David Martin (eds.). *Turfgrass Bibliography from 1672 to 1972.* np. Michigan State Univ. 1977. 1st ed. .... *$70.00–$130.00*

Beard, Mary R. (ed.). *America Through Women's Eyes.* NY. 1933. 1st ed. 558 pp. .... *$30.00–$45.00*

Beattie, Ann. *Alex Katz.* Abrams. 1987. 1st ed. dj................................. *$30.00–$40.00*

Beattie, Ann. *Burning House.* NY. Random House. (1982). review copy, dj sgn. .... *$35.00–$75.00*

Beattie, Ann. *Love Always.* Random House. 1985. 1st ed. dj................. *$18.00–$25.00*

Beattie, Ann. *What Was Mine.* NY. (1991). 1st ed. dj............................. *$18.00–$30.00*

Beatty, Clyde and Earl Wilson. *Jungle Performers.* NY. 1941. 1st ed. sgn, dj.............. .... *$25.00–$90.00*

Beaty, John. *Iron Curtain Over America.* Dallas. Wilkinson Pub Co. 1952. cloth. .... *$50.00–$85.00*

Beaumont, Charles. *Magic Man and Other Science Fantasy Stories.* Greenwich, CT. (1965). 1st ed. pictorial wraps.. *$20.00–$35.00*

Beaver, C. Masten. *Fort Yukon Trader—Three Years in an Alaskan Wilderness.* NY. 1955. 1st ed. illus. dj. .... *$25.00–$40.00*

Bechstein, J. M. *Natural History of Cage Birds.* Lon. 1885. illus. engr. *$30.00–$45.00*

Beck, Alfred. *Hints on Golf for Everyone.* York. private ptg. 1st ed. printed red wrps.... .... *$50.00–$80.00*

Beck, Henry. *Bridge Busters: The 39th Bomb Group (M).* Cleve. 1946. photos, map. ... . *$175.00–$300.00*

Becker, Friedrich. *Breed of the Racehorse.* Lon. British Bloodstock Agency. 1935. 1st ed. .... *$50.00–$85.00*

Beckwith, Edward Griffin. *Reports of Explorations and Surveys . . . for a Railroad from the Mississippi River to the Pacific Ocean.* DC. 1855. Vol. II. illus. hand-tinted plates... .... *$225.00–$300.00*

Beddie, M. K (ed.). *Bibliography of Captain James Cook.* Sydney. 1970. 2nd ed. .... *$40.00–$60.00*

Bedford-Jones, H. B. *Mardi Gras Mystery.* NY. 1921. 1st ed. .... *$18.00–$25.00*

Bedford-Jones, H. B. *Saint Michael's Gold.* NY. 1926. 1st ed. .... *$14.00–$17.00*

Beebe, Lucius. *American West.* 1955. 1st ed... *$30.00–$40.00*

Beebe, William. *Arcturus Adventure.* NY. Putnam. 1926. illus. 1st ed... *$40.00–$60.00*

Beebe, William. *Beneath Tropic Seas.* NY. Putnam. 1928. 1st ed........... *$35.00–$48.00*

Beebe, William. *Nonsuch Land of Water.* 1st ed. sgn, dj........................ *$45.00–$60.00*

Beebe, William. *Pheasant Jungles.* NY. Putnam. 1927. bds..................... *$25.00–$30.00*

Beebe, William. *Pheasants—Their Lives and Homes.* Garden City. 1926. 2 vols. illus. green cloth. .... *$130.00–$175.00*

Beecher, Catherine. *Physiology and Calisthenics for Schools and Families.* NY. 1856. brown cloth. .... *$50.00–$65.00*

Beecher, Catherine E. *Miss Beecher's Domestic Receipt Book.* NY. 1872. 5th ed..........
.... *$30.00–$45.00*

Beecher, Catherine E. *Treatise on Domestic Economy.* NY. 1850. illus. rev ed. ....
.... *$35.00–$65.00*

Beecher, Catherine E. and Harriet Beecher Stowe. *American Woman's Home.* NY. Ford. 1869. 1st ed. illus. 3/4 mor. .... *$80.00–$120.00*

Beecher, Henry W. *Defence of Kansas.* Wash. 1856........................... *$100.00–$150.00*

Beecher, Henry W. *Norwood.* NY. Scribner's. 1868. 1st ed.................... *$35.00–$75.00*

Beecher, Henry W. *Star Papers, Autobiography.* NY. 1855.................... *$25.00–$45.00*

Beecher, John. *All Brave Sailors . . .* NY. Eischer. 1945. dj.................... *$75.00–$90.00*

Beede, A McG. *Sitting Bull—Custer.* Bismark, ND. 1913. 1st ed. illus. *$125.00–$150.00*

Beeding, Francis. *Secret Weapon.* NY. Harper & Bros. 1940. 1st Amer ed. dj. ....
.... *$20.00–$45.00*

Beehler, B. M., T. K. Pratt, and D. A. Zimmerman. *Birds of New Guinea.* Princeton Univ Press. 1986. illus. 56 clr plates, dj... *$50.00–$75.00*

Beehler, W. H. *Cruise of the Brooklyn.* Phila. 1885. illus. maps, plates. *$95.00–$150.00*

Beer, George Louis. *Origins of the British Colonial System 1578–1660.* NY. 1908. ......
.... *$32.00–$47.00*

Beerbohm, Max. *A Survey.* Lon. William Heinemann. 1921. 1st ed. 51 tip-in plates. ....
.... *$100.00–$200.00*

Beerbohm, Max. *A Survey.* NY. 1921. 1st Amer ed. 51 cartoons by Beerbohm. scarce, dj... *$100.00–$150.00*

Beerbohm, Max. *Dreadful Dragon of Hay Hill.* Lon. 1928. 1st ed. clr frontis. ....
.... *$65.00–$80.00*

Beerbohm, Max. *Fifty Caricatures.* NY. Dutton. 1913. illus. 1st Amer ed....................
.... *$100.00–$165.00*

Beerbohm, Max. *Fifty Caricatures.* Lon. Heinemann. 1913. illus. 1st UK ed. tipped-in plates.. *$100.00–$250.00*

Beerbohm, Max. *Happy Hippocrite: A Fairy Tale for Tired Men.* NY. Lane. 1915. ....
.... *$20.00–$25.00*

Beerbohm, Max. *Mainly On the Air.* NY. 1947. 1st ed. dj..................... *$18.00–$50.00*

Beerbohm, Max. *Observations.* Lon. 1925. 1st ed. dj.......................... *$40.00–$150.00*

Beerbohm, Max. *Rossetti and His Circle.* Lon. Heinemann. 1922. 1st ed. illus. 20 clr plates... *$135.00–$175.00*

Beerbohm, Max. *Things New and Old.* Lon. 1923. 1st ed. dj.............. *$50.00–$150.00*

Beerbohm, Max. *Variety of Things.* Knopf. 1928. 1st US ed. ltd 806/2,000 cc, dj. ....
.... *$25.00–$45.00*

Beerbohm, Max. *Zuleika Dobson: An Oxford Love Story.* Lon. William Heinemann. 1911. 1st ed... *$225.00–$300.00*

Beers, D. B. *Atlas of Luzerne County, Pa.* Phila. 1873. illus. hand-clr maps...................
.... *$210.00–$300.00*

Beers, F. W. *Atlas of Delaware County, NY.* 1869. illus. gilt lettering, maps. ....
.... *$125.00–$175.00*

Beers, F. W. *Combination Atlas of Saratoga and Ballston.* NY. Beers. 1876. 1st ed. illus. hand-clr maps. .... *$275.00–$350.00*

Beers, F. W. *History of Mongtomery and Fulton Counties, NY.* NY. 1978. illus. litho, maps, folio. .... *$200.00–$250.00*

Beeton, Isabella. *Book of Household Management.* Lon. 1861. 1st ed. 1/2 lea. ....
.... *$400.00–$800.00*

Begin, Menachem. *Revolt; Story of the Irgun.* NY. Schuman. 1951. ...... *$25.00–$30.00*

Begin, Menachem. *White Nights, the Story of a Prisoner in Russia.* NY. 1977. 1st US ed. dj. .... *$35.00–$45.00*

Behan, Brendan. *Brendan Behan's Island.* NY. Bernard Geiss. 1962. 1st Amer ed. sgn. .... *$85.00–$100.00*

Behan, Brendan. *Confessions of an Irish Rebel.* Lon. 1965. 1st ed. dj. . *$25.00–$35.00*

Behan, Brendan. *Hold Your Hour and Have Another.* Little Brown. 1954. 1st Amer ed. dj. .... *$25.00–$30.00*

Behan, Brendan. *Richard's Cork Leg.* Grove Press. 1974. 1st US ed. dj. *$15.00–$25.00*

Behan, Brendan. *The Scarperer.* NY. 1964. 1st ed. dj. .... *$25.00–$35.00*

Beilis, Mendel. *Story of My Sufferings.* Beilis Pub. 1926. 264 pp. .... *$40.00–$55.00*

Beirne, F. *War of 1812.* NY. 1949. 1st ed. maps. .... *$20.00–$28.00*

Beldam, George W. *Golfing Illustrated.* Lon. Gowans & Gray. 1908. 1st ed. pictorial wrps. .... *$120.00–$250.00*

Belden, George P. *White Chief.* OH. University Press. 1974. rprnt. .... *$25.00–$50.00*

Belknap, Jeremy. *Exeter.* 1831. small, lea. .... *$45.00–$50.00*

Belknap, Jeremy. *Foresters, An American Tale.* Bos. 1796. .... *$75.00–$125.00*

Belknap, Jeremy. *Foresters, An American Tale.* Exeter. S Hardy. 1831. lea. ....
.... *$40.00–$100.00*

Belknap, Jeremy. *Sermon Preached at the Installation of Rev. Jedidiah Morse.* Bos. 1789. 1st ed. wrps. sewn. .... *$75.00–$100.00*

Bell Telephone Laboratories. *History of Engineering and Science in the Bell System.* 1975. 1st ed. illus. dj. .... *$30.00–$45.00*

Bell, Sir Charles. *People of Tibet.* New Delhi. 1991. .... *$35.00–$50.00*

Bell, A. *Spell of the Holy Land.* Bos. 1915. illus. .... *$30.00–$75.00*

Bell, Archie. *Sunset Canada.* Bos. Page. 1918. .... *$35.00–$85.00*

Bell, Charles Dent. *Winter on the Nile in Egypt and in Nubia.* Lon. Hodder & Stoughton. 1889. illus. fold-out map. .... *$80.00–$95.00*

Bell, Edward I. *Political Shame of Mexico.* NY. 1914. 1st ed. .... *$15.00–$45.00*

Bell, Ernest A. *Fighting the Traffic in Young Girls.* np. nd. illus. .... *$20.00–$24.00*

Bell, Gertrude. *Letters of Gertrude Bell.* Lon. Ernest Benn. 1927. 2 vols. 1st ed. illus. green cloth, 32 photos, map of Persia. .... *$75.00–$100.00*

Bell, Gertrude. *Progress in Mountaineering.* Edin. Oliver & Boyd. 1950. 1st ed. illus. maps.. *$25.00–$45.00*

Bell, Landon Covington. *Old Free State.* Rich. Byrd. 1927. 2 vols. illus. maps.............
.... *$60.00–$125.00*

Bell, Louis. *The Telescope.* NY/Lon. 1922. 1st ed. illus......................... *$35.00–$50.00*

Bell, Louise Price. *Kitchen Fun.* Harter. (1932). 1st ed. illus. by Jessie Willcox Smith..
.... *$50.00–$85.00*

Bell, Sir Charles. *Portrait of the Dalai Lama.* Lon. Collins. 1946. 1st ed. illus.............
.... *$50.00–$85.00*

Bell, W. D. M. *Karomojo Safari.* NY. Harcourt Brace. 1949. 1st ed. dj. *$90.00–$150.00*

Bellerive Country Club. St. Louis. BCC 1910. 1st ed. .... *$80.00–$100.00*

Belloc, Hilaire. *Mr Clutterbuck's Election.* Lon. 1908. .... *$75.00–$125.00*

Bellow, Saul. *Adventures of Augie March.* Viking. 1953. 1st ed. dj....... *$90.00–$150.00*

Bellow, Saul. *Dean's December.* NY. Harper and Row. (1982). ltd 500 cc, sgn, slipcase.
.... *$100.00–$135.00*

Bellow, Saul. *Dean's December.* NY. 1982. 1st ed. wrps. dj. .... *$25.00–$35.00*

Bellow, Saul. *Herzog.* NY. 1964. 1st ed. dj, photo on back of jacket. ..... *$40.00–$55.00*

Bellow, Saul. *Last Analysis.* NY. 1965. 1st ed. dj. .... *$40.00–$54.00*

Bellow, Saul. *Mr. Sammler's Planet.* NY. (1970). 1st ed. dj. .... *$45.00–$85.00*

Bellow, Saul. *Seize the Day.* Viking. (1956). 1st ed. dj............................ *$20.00–$75.00*

Bellow, Saul. *The Victim.* NY. Vanguard Press. 1947. 1st ed. dj............ *$60.00–$250.00*

Bellow, Saul. *To Jeruselem and Back.* NY. 1976. 1st ed. dj.................... *$20.00–$60.00*

Bellrose, F. C. and D. J. Holm. *Ecology and Management of the Wood Duck.* Stackpole. 1994. dj.. *$35.00–$54.00*

Belmont, Perry. *An American Democrat.* NY. Columbia University Press. 1940. 1st ed.
.... *$65.00–$115.00*

Bemelmans, L. *Donkey Inside.* Lon. 1947. 1st UK ed. .... *$20.00–$30.00*

Bemelmans, Ludwig. *Blue Danube.* NY. 1945. 1st ed. illus. clr, dj........ *$18.00–$30.00*

Bemelmans, Ludwig. *Castle Number Nine.* NY. 1937. 1st ed. illus. by author..............
.... *$50.00–$65.00*

Bemelmans, Ludwig. *Eye of God.* Viking. 1949. 1st ed. dj. .... *$20.00–$35.00*

Bemelmans, Ludwig. *Hansi.* NY. 1934. 1st ed................................... *$85.00–$175.00*

Bemelmans, Ludwig. *Happy Place.* Bos. Little Brown. 1952. 1st ed. illus...................
.... *$30.00–$50.00*

Bemelmans, Ludwig. *Hotel Bemelmens.* Viking. 1946. 1st ed. dj. .... *$18.00–$25.00*

Bemelmans, Ludwig. *Madeline and the Gypsies.* Viking. 1959. 1st ed.. *$50.00–$65.00*

Bemelmans, Ludwig. *My War With the United States.* NY. Viking. 1937. 1st ed. dj.......
.... *$25.00–$75.00*

Bemelmans, Ludwig. *Now I Lay Me Down to Sleep.* NY. Viking. 1945. illus. ltd 400 cc, sgn, slipcase... *$95.00–$125.00*

Bemelmans, Ludwig. *Parsley*. Harper. 1955. 1st ed. illus..................... *$75.00–$125.00*

Benchley, Nathaniel. *Winter's Tale*. NY. 1964. 1st ed. dj...................... *$25.00–$35.00*

Benchley, Robert. *Benchley or Else*. NY. 1947. 1st ed. .... *$18.00–$25.00*

Benedict, George Grenville. *Vermont in the Civil War* . . . Burlington, VT. 1886–88. 2 vols. 1st ed.. *$75.00–$125.00*

Benet, Stephen V. *Thirteen O'Clock*. NY. 1937. 1st ed. dj..................... *$25.00–$35.00*

Benet, Stephen Vincent. *John Brown's Body*. NY. Doubleday Doran. 1928. 3/4 red mor, teg. .... *$40.00–$75.00*

Benitez, Fernando. *In the Magic Land of Peyote*. Austin. Univ of Texas Press. 1975. 1st ed. scarce, dj. .... *$20.00–$60.00*

Bennett, Colin N. *Guide to Kinematrography*. 1917. 1st ed. illus. .... *$75.00–$85.00*

Bennett, Frank M. *Monitor & the Navy Under Steam*. Bos. Houghton Mifflin. 1900. 1st ed. illus. .... *$50.00–$100.00*

Bennett, Ira C. *History of the Panama Canal* . . . Wash. 1915. 1st ed. illus. plates........ .... *$95.00–$150.00*

Bennett, James. *Overland Journey to California* . . . NY. 1932. wrps. ltd 200 cc, dj. .... *$45.00–$125.00*

Bennett, Russell H. *Complete Rancher*. NY. 1946. 1st ed. illus. by Ross Santee, dj. .... *$120.00–$150.00*

Bennett, William P. *First Baby in Camp*. Salt Lake. 1893. 1st ed. printed pink wraps. . ... *$50.00–$75.00*

Benson E. F. *Colin*. NY. Doran. (1923). 1st Amer ed. 334 pp. .... *$115.00–$150.00*

Benson, A. C. and Weaver, Sir Lawrence, (eds.). *Everybody's Book of the Queen's Dolls' House*. Lon. Daily Telegraph & Meuthen. (1924). 2 vols. illus..... *$60.00–$75.00*

Bent, Arthur Cleveland. *Life Histories of North American Shore Birds*. Dover. 1962. stiff wrps. rprnt. .... *$20.00–$25.00*

Bent, Arthur Cleveland. *Life Histories of North American Thrushes*. Wash. 1949. wrps. plates.. *$28.00–$35.00*

Bentley, E. C. *Trent's Own Case*. NY. Knopf. 1936. 1st ed...................... *$35.00–40.00*

Benton, Frank. *Cowboy Life on the Sidetrack*. Denver. (1903). 1st ed. *$60.00–$125.00*

Benton, Frank. *Honey Bee* . . . GPO. 1896. plates, bds. .... *$35.00–$50.00*

Benton, Josiah Hart. *Voting in the Field*. privately printed. .... *$75.00–$95.00*

Benton, Thomas Hart. *An Artist in America*. McBride. 1937. 1st ed. illus. blue cloth dj. .... *$50.00–$75.00*

Berkeley, Earl of. *Sound Golf by Applying Principles to Practice*. Lon. Seely, Service. (1936). 1st ed.. *$100.00–$120.00*

Berkeley, Edmund Callis. *Giant Brains or Machines That Think*. NY. (1949). 1st ed. 270 pp. dj.. *$100.00–$150.00*

Bermann, Richard A. *Mahdi of Allah* . . . NY. Macmillan. 1932. illus. 1st US ed. red cloth maps... *$40.00–$50.00*

Bernadac, Christian. *Doctors of Mercy*. Geneva. 1977. .... *$30.00–$40.00*

Berndt, R. M. (ed.). *Australian Aboriginal Art.* Sidney. (1964)......... *$250.00–$350.00*

Berners, Dame Juliana. *Treatyse of Fysshynge wyth an Angle.* NY. 1875. 1st American ed, brown cloth. .... *$200.00–$250.00*

Bernheimer, Charles L. *Rainbow Bridge.* Garden City. Doubleday, Doran. 1920. illus. .... *$60.00–$70.00*

Berry, A. J. *Henry Cavendish—His Life and Scientific Work.* Lon. 1960. *$28.00–$40.00*

Berry, F. A., Jr., et al. (eds.). *Handbook of Meteorology.* NY. 1945. 1st ed. dj.............. .... *$35.00–$60.00*

Berryman, John. *Poems.* Norfolk. New Directions. (1942). ltd 1,500 cc stapled wraps, sgn, dj, scarce. .... *$375.00–$475.00*

Berton, Ralph. *Remembering Bix.* Lon. W H Allen. 1974. 1st UK ed. dj. .... *$45.00–$65.00*

Best American Short Stories, 1951. Houghton. 1951. dj........................ *$15.00–$35.00*

Best Short Stories of 1923. Bos. 1924. .... *$45.00–$60.00*

Best, F. *Maori As He Was . . . in Pre-European Days.* New Zealand. 1934. 2nd issue.... .... *$15.00–$20.00*

Bester, Alfred. *Demolished Man.* Chi. Shasta. 1953. dj. .... *$125.00–$175.00*

Betten, H. L. *Upland Game Shooting.* Phila. 1940. 1st ed. illus. by Lynn Bogue Hunt.. .... *$40.00–$60.00*

Betts, Doris. *Gentle Insurrection.* NY. Putnam's Son. 1954. 1st ed. author's first book, dj. .... *$60.00–$150.00*

Beuchner, Thomas S. *Norman Rockwell: Artist and Illustrator.* NY. Abrams. (1970). 1st ed. illus. .... *$40.00–$100.00*

Beveridge, Albert J. *Life of John Marshall.* Bos/NY. Houghton Mifflin Co. 1916–1919. 4 vols. green cloth. .... *$175.00–$225.00*

Bhushan, Jamila Brij. *Indian Jewelry, Ornaments and Decorative Designs.* Bombay. nd. 1st ed. illus... *$75.00–$140.00*

Bianco, Margery Williams. *House That Grew Smaller.* NY. Macmillan. 1931. illus. by Rachel Field, dj... *$35.00–$55.00*

Bianco, Margery Williams. *Poor Cecco.* Ny. Doran. 1925. illus. by Rackham tipped in. .... *$90.00–$150.00*

Bible. *Holy Bible.* Newburyport. William B Allen & Co. 1815. .... *$50.00–$75.00*

Bible. *New Testament.* NH. Justin Hinds. 1825. .... *$25.00–$35.00*

Bible Atlas . . .Phila. American Sunday School Union. 1827. wrps. illus. clred maps, 9 leaves, 135 x 11 cm. .... *$95.00–$115.00*

Bible. *Holy Scriptures, Translated and Corrected by the Spirit of Revelation, By Joseph Smith, Jr., The Seer.* Plano. 1867.. *$400.00–$500.00*

Bible, das ist: die gantze Heilige Schrifft Alten un Newen Testament . . . Martin Luther. Tubingen. 1769. folio, tooled pigskin over wooden bds, metal clasps, woodcut text illus. .... *$220.00–$250.00*

Bickersteth, Rev Edward. *Scripture Help* . . . Bos. S H Parker. 1817. 4 maps. lea........ .... *$40.00–$50.00*

Biddle, Ellen. *Reminiscences of a Soldier's Wife.* Phila. Lippincott. 1907. ....
.... *$125.00–$150.00*

Biddle, Major Charles. *Way of the Eagle.* NY. Scribner's. 1919. 1st ed. illus. photos....
.... *$60.00–$80.00*

Biddle, Major Charles. *Way of the Eagle.* NY. Doubleday. 1968. illus. photos..............
.... *$15.00–$25.00*

Biddulph, John (Colonel). *Pirates of Malabar.* Lon. 1907. .... *$50.00–$75.00*

Bidwel, Percy Wells and John I Falconer. *History of Agriculture in the Northern United States.* DC. Carnegie. 1925. 1st ed. illus................. *$60.00–$90.00*

Bidwell, John. *Echoes of the Past.* Chico, CA. nd. softbound................. *$35.00–$50.00*

Bidwell, John. *Life in California Before the Gold Discovery.* Palo Alto. Lewis Osborne. 1966. .... *$25.00–$35.00*

Bierce, Ambrose. *Cynic's Word Book.* NY. 1906. 1st ed. .... *$65.00–$100.00*

Bierce, Ambrose. *Horseman in the Sky.* San Francisco. 1920. green cloth and bds. ltd. ed. .... *$75.00–$100.00*

Bierce, Ambrose. *Shadow on the Dial and Other Essays.* SF. Robertson. 1909. 1st ed. green buckram, dj. .... *$300.00–$375.00*

Bierce, Ambrose. *Shadow on the Dial and Other Essays.* SF. Robertson. 1909. 1st ed. green buckram, no dj. .... *$55.00–$100.00*

Bierce, Ambrose. *Ten Tales.* Lon. 1925. .... *$50.00–$75.00*

Bierce, Ambrose. *Write It Right. A Little Blacklist of Literary Faults.* NY. Union Library. 1934. dj. .... *$10.00–$45.00*

Bigelow, Jacob. *Useful Arts . . .   with the applications of science.* Bos. Webb & Co. 1842. 396 pp, illus. .... *$60.00–$75.00*

Bigelow, John. *Memoir of the Life & Public Services of John Charles Fremont.* NY. 1856. .... *$40.00–$60.00*

Bigelow, John. *Peach Orchard.* Minn. 1910. 1st ed. illus. fldg maps...... *$55.00–$75.00*

Bigelow, Poultney. *Borderland of Czar & Kaiser.* NY. 1895. 1st ed. illus. by F Remington. .... *$80.00–$100.00*

Bigelow, Poultney. *White Man's Africa.* Harper. 1898. .... *$20.00–$25.00*

Biggers, Earl. *Behind That Curtain.* Bobbs Merrill. 1928. 1st ed. dj.. *$175.00–$200.00*

Biggers, Earl Derr. *Agony Column.* Ind. Bobbs Merrill. 1916. 1st ed. .. *$30.00–$95.00*

Biggers, Earl Derr. *Black Camel.* NY. Grosset & Dunlap. 1929............ *$15.00–$40.00*

Biggers, Earl Derr. *Black Camel.* Ind. Bobbs Merrill. 1929. 1st ed. dj........................
.... *$400.00–$600.00*

Biggers, Earl Derr. *Charlie Chan Carries On.* Ind. 1930. orange cloth dj. ....
.... *$70.00–$125.00*

Biggers, Earl Derr. *Chinese Parrot.* NY. 1926. rprnt, dj......................... *$15.00–$25.00*

Biggers, Earl Derr. *Earl Derr Biggers Tells Ten Stories.* Ind. Bobbs Merrill. (1933). 1st ed. .... *$20.00–$25.00*

Biggers, Earl Derr. *Inside The Lines.* Bobbs Merrill. 1915. 1st ed. .... *$40.00–$50.00*

Biggers, Earl Derr. *Inside the Lines*. Grosset & Dunlap. 1915. rprnt. ... *$15.00–$20.00*

Biggers, Earl Derr. *Keeper of the Keys*. Bobbs Merrill. (1932). 1st ed.. *$30.00–$45.00*

Biggers, Earl Derr. *Love Insurance*. Bobbs Merrill. 1914. 1st ed. .... *$35.00–$75.00*

Billings, John D. *Hardtack and Coffee or the Unwritten Story of Army Life*. Bos. 1887. 1st ed. illus. plates. .... *$200.00–$375.00*

Billings, John D. *Hardtack and Coffee, or The Unwritten Story of Army Life*. Alexandria. 1982. illus. .... *$25.00–$35.00*

Billington, Elizabeth. *Randolph Caldecott Treasury*. NY. Frederick Warne. 1978. 1st ed. dj. .... *$35.00–$60.00*

Bindloss, Harold. *In the Niger Country*. Edin. Blackwood. 1898. original cloth. .... *$100.00–$150.00*

Bingham, Caleb. *Columbian Orator*. Bos. 1817. .... *$40.00–$60.00*

Bingham, Capt. *The Bastille*. NY. James Pott & Co. 1901. 2 vols. illus. .... *$75.00–$100.00*

Bingham, Hiram. *Residence of Twenty-One Years in the Sandwich Islands*. NY. Praeger. (1969). illus. fldg map. .... *$25.00–$40.00*

Bingham, Hiram. *Residence of Twenty-One Years in the Sandwich Islands*. Hartford. Hezekiah Huntington. 1847. 1st ed. illus. fldg map............................ *$250.00–$500.00*

Bingham, John. *Trial of Conspirators . . . Assassination of President Lincoln*. Wash. GPO. 1865. 1st ed. wrps. .... *$200.00–$400.00*

Binkerd, Adam D. *Mammoth Cave and Its Denizens*. Cinc. 1869. 1st ed. wrps. .... *$65.00–$90.00*

Binkley, William C. *Texas Revolution*. Baton Rouge. 1952. 1st ed. dj. ... *$25.00–$50.00*

Bird, H. E. *Chess: A Manual For Beginners*. Lon. nd. illus. .... *$14.00–$20.00*

Bird, Isabella. *Hawaiian Archipelago*. NY. (1882). 5th ed. .... *$60.00–$75.00*

Bird, Isabella. *Hawaiian Archipelago*. Lon. Murray. 1875. 1st ed. green cloth. .... *$150.00–$175.00*

Bird, Isabella. *Lady's Life in the Rocky Mountains*. 1885. illus. 5th ed.. *$65.00–$75.00*

Bird, Isabella L. *Six Months Among the Palm Groves, Coral Reefs, and Volcanoes of the Sandwich Islands*. NY. Putnam. 1882. 5th ed. illus. maps.................. *$150.00–$175.00*

Bird, Isabella L. *Unbeaten Tracks in Japan*. NY. Putnam. 1881. 2 vols. 1st ed. cloth.... .... *$100.00–$150.00*

Birds of New York. The State of New York. 1910–1914. clr plates. ...... *$60.00–$125.00*

Birket-Smith, Kaj. *The Eskimos*. NY. Crown. 1971. illus. 1st Amer ed, dj.................. .... *$40.00–$60.00*

Bishop, Harriet E. *Floral Home*. NY. Sheldon, Blakeman. 1857. 1st ed. illus. 10 plates, 342 pp. .... *$150.00–$225.00*

Bishop, Michael. *Ancient of Days*. NY. Arbor House. (1985). 1st ed. dj. *$20.00–$35.00*

Bishop, Michael. *No Enemy But Time*. NY. Timescape. (1982). 1st ed. dj. .... *$100.00–$125.00*

Bishop, Mrs. J. F. (Isabella Bird). *Yangtze Valley and Beyond*. Lon. Murray. 1899. 1st ed. illus. map. .... *$300.00–$800.00*

Bishop, Mrs. J. F. (Isabella Bird). *Yangste Valley and Beyond*. NY. Putnam. 1900. 2 vols. 1st ed. illus. .... *$195.00–$275.00*

Bishop, Nathaniel H. *Pampas and Andes: A Thousand Miles' Walk Across South America*. Bos. Lee & Shepard. 1869. 1 vol. illus. 14 plates, pictorial gilt orange cloth. .. .. *$110.00–$120.00*

Bishop, Richard E. *Bishop's Wildfowl*. St Paul. Brown & Bigelow. 1948. 1st ed. lea. ... . *$100.00–$200.00*

Bishop, Richard E. *Ways of Wildfowl*. J G Ferguson. 1971. illus. ltd #1096/3000, 64 clr plates, 35 b/w, slipcase. .... *$200.00–$300.00*

Biss, Gerald. *Door of the Unreal*. NY. Putnam. 1920. 1st Amer ed.... *$125.00–$150.00*

Bjist, Robert. *American Flower Garden Directory*. Phil. 1841. .... *$50.00–$75.00*

Black Anti-Semitism and Jewish Racism. NY. Baron. 1969. intro by Nat Hentoff, dj.... .... *$20.00–$25.00*

Black Arrow. Scribner's. 1916. illus. by N C Wyeth, 14 clr plates. .... *$45.00–$65.00*

Black Book: The Nazi Crime Against the Jewish People. NY. Duell Sloan & Pearce. 1946. 1st ed. .... *$60.00–$85.00*

Black, A. P. *End of the Longhorn Trail*. ND. nd. illus. .... *$60.00–$75.00*

Black, William Harman. *If I Were a Jew*. NY. Real Book Co. 1938. 1st ed. cloth. .... *$35.00–$50.00*

Blackburn, I. *Illus. of Gross Morbid Anatomy of the Brain in the Insane*. GPO. 1908. 1st ed. tall book photos. .... *$125.00–$150.00*

Blackford, William Willis. *War Years with Jeb Stuart*. NY. 1945. 1st ed. dj. .... *$35.00–$50.00*

Blackman, William Fremont. *Making of Hawaii* . . . NY/Lon. Macmillan Co. 1899.... .... *$65.00–$85.00*

Blackmore, Howard L. *British Military Firearms 1650–1850*. Lon. 1961. illus. .... *$20.00–$30.00*

Blackwell, Sarah Ellen. *Military Genius* . . . *Life of Anna Ella Carroll of Maryland*. Wash. 1891. 1st ed. .... *$40.00–$50.00*

Blackwood, Algernon. *Day and Night Stories*. NY. Dutton. (1917). 1st Amer ed. 228 pp. .... *$75.00–$125.00*

Blackwood, Algernon. *Doll and One Other*. Arkham House. 1946. 1st ed. dj. .... *$40.00–$90.00*

Blackwood, Algernon. *Incredible Adventures*. NY. 1914. green cloth, 368 pp, 1st Amer ed. .... *$70.00–$80.00*

Blackwood, Algernon. *Strange Stories*. Lon. 1929. 1st ed. bds 750 pp. .... *$45.00–$55.00*

Blackwood, Algernon. *The Centaur*. Macmillan. 1911. 1st ed. .... *$45.00–$60.00*

Blackwood, Algernon. *The Listener*. NY. Vaughn & Gomme. 1914. 1st US ed, ltd. .... *$75.00–$175.00*

Blackwood, Algernon. *The Wave*. NY. E P Dutton & Co. (1916). 1st ed. .... *$25.00–$50.00*

Blades, William F. *Fishing Flies & Fly Tying.* Harrisburg. 1962. 2nd ed. dj. ....
.... *$35.00–$60.00*

Blaikie, William. *How to Get Strong and How to Stay So.* NY. Harper and Bros. 1879.
1st ed. bds. .... *$30.00–$48.00*

Blaikie, Wm G. *Personal Life of David Livingstone.* NY. Harpers. 1881. fldg map........
.... *$35.00–$45.00*

Blaine, John. *Flaming Mountain.* Grosset & Dunlap. 1962. .... *$20.00–$40.00*

Blaine, John. *Rocket's Shadow.* Grosset & Dunlap. 1947. Rick Brant #1, dj. ....
.... *$20.00–$30.00*

Blaine, John. *Veiled Raiders.* Grosset & Dunlap. 1965. #20, map endpapers................
.... *$45.00–$150.00*

Blake, John L. *Farmer's Every Day Book.* Auburn, NY. 1850............. *$75.00–$135.00*

Blake, John L. *Geographical Chronological and Historical Atlas.* NY. 1826. illus.
charts, engr. .... *$75.00–$200.00*

Blake, Rev. J. L. *Conversations on Natural Philosophy . . .* Bos. Lincoln & Edmonds.
1831. illus. Bos stereotype ed. lea frontis. 23 plates in back of book. .... *$50.00–$85.00*

Blake, Sir Henry Arthur. *China.* Lon. A & C. 1909. 1st ed. illus. dark blue cloth. clr
plates. .... *$60.00–$70.00*

Blake, W. O. *History of Slavery and the Slave Trade.* Columbus. 1858. engr.................
.... *$75.00–$125.00*

Blanch, Lesley. *Sabres of Paradise.* Lon. John Murray. 1960. 1st ed. illus. dj maps.......
.... *$75.00–$85.00*

Blanchan, Neltje. *Bird Neighbors.* Doubleday & McClure. 1899........... *$20.00–$35.00*

Blanchan, Neltje. *Birds That Hunt and Are Hunted.* Doubleday & McClure. 1898. 1st
ed. illus. .... *$30.00–$40.00*

Blanchan, Neltje. *Nature Library.* NY. 1926. 5 vols. illus. .... *$32.00–$45.00*

Blanchan, Neltje. *Nature's Garden.* NY. Doubleday Page. 1900. 1st ptg, photos. ....
.... *$25.00–$32.00*

Blanchard, Elizabeth, Amis Cameron and Manly Wade Wellman. *Life and Times of
Sir Archie 1805–1833.* Chapel Hill. UNC Press. 1968. 1st ed. dj............ *$45.00–$55.00*

Blanchard, Rufus. *Discovery and Conquests of the Northwest.* Wheaton. 1880. small..
.... *$125.00–$200.00*

Blanchard, Rufus. *History of Illinois to Accompany and Historical Map of the State.*
Chi. Nat'l School. 1883. 1st ed. 128 pp, fldg map mounted on linen... *$125.00–$175.00*

Blanck, J. *Peter Parley to Penrod.* (Cambridge. 1961). 3rd ptg 25. .... *$20.00–$35.00*

Blanck, Jacob. *Bibliography of American Literature.* New Haven. Yale Univ Press.
(1968). 7 vols. illus... *$300.00–$350.00*

Bland, J. O. and E. Backhouse. *China Under the Empress Dowager.* Phila/Lon. 1912.
....
$25.00–$65.00

Blatty, William. *The Exorcist.* NY. Harper & Row. 1971. 1st ed. scarce, dj..................
.... *$75.00–$125.00*

Blavatsky, Helena Petrovna. *From the Caves and Jungles of Hindostan*. Lon. Theosophical Society. 1908. 1st ed. .... *$50.00–$75.00*

Bleiler, Everett F. *Guide to Supernatural Fiction*. Kent State Univ Press. (1983). .... *$50.00–$60.00*

Bleiler, Everett F. and T. E. Dikty, (eds.). *Best Science Fiction Stories 1950*. NY. Frederick Fell Inc. (1950). 1st ed. dj .... *$15.00–$35.00*

Blesh, Rudi. *Combo USA*. Phila. Chilton. 1971. 1st ed. dj .... *$20.00–$50.00*

Blesh, Rudi. *This Is Jazz*. SF. private ptg. 1943. 1st ed. wrps. inscr.... *$100.00–$475.00*

Blinn, Henry Clay. *Life and Gospel Experience of Mother Ann Lee*. Canterbury. Shakers. 1901. .... *$140.00–$160.00*

Blitzer, Wolf. *Territory of Lies*. NY. Harper & Row. 1989. 1st ed. illus. dj photos.......... .... *$15.00–$25.00*

Bloch, Robert. *Terror*. NY. 1962. 1st ed. paperback. .... *$15.00–$20.00*

Block, Lawrence. *Burglar Who Liked to Quote Kipling*. NY. Random House. 1979. 1st ed. dj. presentation copy sgn. .... *$125.00–$150.00*

Block, Lawrence. *Burglar Who Painted Like Mondrian*. NY. (1983). 1st ed. dj. .... *$50.00–$135.00*

Block, Lawrence. *Burglar Who Studied Spinoza*. NY. Random House. 1980. 1st ed. dj. .... *$35.00–$50.00*

Block, Lawrence. *Dance at the Slaughter House*. NY. (1991). 1st ed. dj...................... .... *$20.00–$40.00*

Block, Lawrence. *Even the Wicked*. NY. (1997). 1st Amer ed. sgn, dj. . *$20.00–$40.00*

Block, Lawrence. *Even the Wicked*. Lon. (1996). 1st ed. ltd, dj.......... *$150.00–$250.00*

Block, Lawrence. *Random Wall*. NY. (1988). 1st ed. dj. .... *$30.00–$35.00*

Block, Lawrence. *Ronald Rabbit Is a Dirty Old Man*. Chi. Bernard Geis. 1971. 1st ed. dj. .... *$150.00–$250.00*

Block, Lawrence. *Sins of the Father*. Arlington Hts. Dark Harvest. 1992. 1st hardcvr ed. intro by Stephen King, dj. .... *$50.00–$65.00*

Block, Lawrence. *Ticket to the Boneyard*. NY. William Morrow. 1990. 1st ed. inscr, dj. .... *$40.00–$50.00*

Block, Lawrence. *Two for Tanner*. Greenwich, CT. (1968). 1st ed. wrps. sgn, dj. .... *$45.00–$65.00*

Block, Lawrence. *When the Sacred Ginmill Closes*. NY. Arbor House. 1986. 1st ed. dj. .... *$35.00–$50.00*

Block, Robert. *Dead Beat*. NY. Simon and Schuster. 1960. 1st ed. dj.... *$60.00–$75.00*

Blot, Pierre. *Hand-Book of Practical Cookery*. NY. Appleton. 1868.. *$125.00–$195.00*

Blot, Pierre. *Hand-Book of Pratical Cookery*. NY. 1868. .... *$18.00–$25.00*

Bly, Robert. *Jumping Out of Bed*. Barre Publishers. 1973. 1st ed. wrps. sgn. .... *$30.00–$45.00*

Bly, Robert. *Light Around the Body*. Lon. 1968. sgn. dj. .... *$50.00–$85.00*

Bly, Robert. *Man in the Black Coat Turns*. Dial. 1981. 1st ed. dj........... *$20.00–$35.00*

Bly, Robert. *Morning Gloria*. SF. 1969. wrps. illus. by Tommie De Paola, 1/800 cc......
.... *$25.00–$30.00*

Bly, Robert. *Silence in the Snowy Fields* . . . Lon. 1967. dj. .... *$40.00–$60.00*

Bly, Robert. *Teeth Mother Naked at Last*. SF. San Francisco City Lights. 1970. sgn by author, dj. .... *$35.00–$50.00*

Bly, Robert. *The Loon*. Minnesota. Ox Head Press. (1977). 1/500 cc, wrps...................
.... *$30.00–$40.00*

Board, John. *Horse and Pencil*. Lon. Johnson. 1950. 1st ed. dj. .... *$15.00–$30.00*

Boas, Franz. *Kathlamet Texts*. DC. GPO. 1901. 1st ed. 261 pp. Bulletin 26. ....
.... *$55.00–$125.00*

Boas, Franz (ed.). *Folk-Tales of Salishan and Sahaptin Tribes*. NY. American Folklore Society. 1917. 1st ed. 201 pp... *$60.00–$75.00*

Bodfish, Capt Hartson. *Chasing the Bowhead*. Harvard Univ Press. 1936. 1st ed. dj....
.... *$28.00–$37.00*

Boerhaave, Hermann. *De Viribus Medicamentorum, The Virtue and Energy of Medicines*. Venice. 1774. illus. 3rd ed.................................... *$150.00–$200.00*

Bogardus. *Field, Cover, and Trap Shooting*. NY. Orange Judd. 1881. frontis.................
.... *$50.00–$80.00*

Bohn, Henry. *Bohn's New Hand Book of Games*. Bos. 1850............. *$100.00–$125.00*

Bohr, Neils. *Theory of Spectra and Atomic Constitution*. Lon. 1922. ..... *$35.00–$45.00*

Bolton, Reginald Pelham. *Washington Heights, Manhattan*. NY. privately printed. 1924. illus. red cloth, photos. .... *$60.00–$75.00*

Bond, Carrie Jacobs. *A Perfect Day and Other Poems*. Joliet. (1926). illus. silhouettes, boxed. .... *$35.00–$50.00*

Bond, Horace Mann. *Education of the Negro in the American Social Order*. NY. Prentice-Hall. 1934. 1st ptg, ex lib.. *$80.00–$95.00*

Bond, J. Wesley. *Minnesota and Its Resources*. NY. Redfield. 1854. 1st ed. illus. clr lithos. .... *$65.00–$75.00*

Bond, James H. *From Out of the Yukon*. Portland, OR. 1948. illus. dj. .. *$35.00–$50.00*

Bondy, Louis W. *Miniature Books: Their History* . . . Lon. Sheppard Press. 1981. 1st ed. dj. .... *$50.00–$150.00*

Boni, M. B. *Fireside Book of Folk Songs*. NY. 1947.............................. *$35.00–$55.00*

Bonner, Mary Graham. *Sir Noble, the Police Horse*. NY. Knopf. 1940. 1st ed. illus. dj.
.... *$35.00–$45.00*

Bonney, Edward. *Banditti of the Prairies* . . . Chi. 1850. wrps. illus. plates.................
.... *$3,000.00–$5,000.00*

Bontemps, Arna. *Chariot in the Sky. A Story of the Jubilee Singers*. Phila. John Winston. 1951. 1st ed. dj. .... *$40.00–$50.00*

Bontemps, Arna and Jack Conroy. *They Seek a City*. Garden City. Doubleday, Doran. 1945. 1st ed. dj. .... *$45.00–$65.00*

Bonwick, James. *Mormons and the Silver Mines*. Lon. 1872............. *$95.00–$125.00*

Book of Baseball. NY. 1911. .... *$150.00–$300.00*

Book of Birds. Nat'l Geo Soc. 1932–39. vols 1 and 2. dj. .... *$20.00–$25.00*

Book of Fishes. NGS. 1924. illus. .... *$18.00–$25.00*

Book of Kalushin. Tel Aviv. 1961. 570 pp, Yiddish, photos. .... *$50.00–$80.00*

Book of Kells. Lon/NY. 1933. illus. 4th ed. tip-in clr plate. .... *$50.00–$65.00*

Book of Pirates by Henry K. Brooke . . . Phila. 1847. illus. .... *$100.00–$175.00*

Boomer and Boschert. *Cider & Wine Presses*. Syracuse, NY. 1876. wrps..................... ....*$65.00–$90.00*

Booth, Mary. *History of the City of New York*. NY. 1867. 2 vols. lea..... *$50.00–$85.00*

Booth, Maud Ballington. *After Prison — What?* NY. 1903. rprnt sgn... *$28.00–$45.00*

Borden, Mary. *Forbidden Zone*. NY. Doubleday. 1930. 1st US ed........ *$25.00–$45.00*

Borden, Mrs. John. *Cruise of the Northern Light*. NY. Macmillan. 1928. 1st ed. illus. map endpapers. .... *$35.00–$75.00*

Borden, W. *Use of the Rontgen Ray by the Medical Dept of the US Army in War with Spain*. Wash. GPO. 1900. illus. plates and text illus............................ *$250.00–$350.00*

Borges, Jorge Luis. *Atlas*. Dutton. (1985). 1st Amer ed. dj.................. *$45.00–$55.00*

Borges, Jorge Luis. *Book of Imaginary Beings*. Dutton. 1969. 1st ed. dj..................... .... *$55.00–$75.00*

Borges, Jorge Luis. *Irish Strategies*. Dublin. Dolmen Press. 1975. #1/350 cc slipcase. .... *$50.00–$75.00*

Borges, Jorge Luis. *Personal Anthology*. NY. Grove Press. (1967). 1st ed. dj. .... *$40.00–$60.00*

Borland, Robert. *Border Raids and Reivers*. Thomas Fraser. 1898........ *$30.00–$50.00*

Born, Max. *Atomic Physics*. NY. 1946. 4th ed. .... *$28.00–$36.00*

Born, Max. *La Constitution de la Matiere*. Paris. 1922. wrps. illus. Nobel Prize winning author. .... *$37.00–$45.00*

Born, Max. *My Life, The Recollections of a Nobel Laureate*. Lon. 1978. 1st Eng ed. dj. .... *$30.00–$40.00*

Bostock, Frank C. *Training of Wild Animals*. NY. 1903. illus............... *$37.00–$45.00*

Botkin, Benjamin Albert. *Civil War Treasury of Tales, Legends and Folklore*. NY. Random House. (1960). 1st ed. dj.. *$25.00–$35.00*

Botkin, Benjamin Albert. *Treasury of Southern Folklore*. 1949............ *$20.00–$30.00*

Botta, Charles. *History of the War of Independence of the U.S.A.* New Haven. Nathan Whiting. 1834. 2 vols. .... *$100.00–$250.00*

Boucher, Jonathan. *Reminiscences of an American Loyalist 1783–1789*. Bos. 1925. bds, 575 cc, boxed.. *$50.00–$100.00*

Boule, Pierre. *Bridge Over the River Kwai*. NY. Vanguard. 1954. 1st Amer ed. adv copy, wrps. .... *$85.00–$100.00*

Bourke, John. *On the Border With Crook*. NY. 1891. 1st ed. bds....... *$300.00–$600.00*

Bourke, John. *Urine Dance of the Zuni Indians of New Mexico*. Ann Arbor. 1885. 1st ed. wrps. .... *$300.00–$400.00*

Bourke, John G. *An Apache Campaign*. Scribner's. (1958). dj. .... *$18.00–$22.00*

Bourke, John G. *Snake Dance of the Moquis of Arizona*. Tucson. 1984. illus. rprnt. .....
.... *$15.00–$22.00*

Bourke, John G. *Scatologic Rites of All Nations*. DC. Lowdermilk. 1891. teg, brown cloth. .... *$125.00–$675.00*

Bourke-White, M. *Dear Fatherland, Rest Quietly*. NY. 1946. 1st ed. sgn. ....
.... *$200.00–$300.00*

Bourke-White, M. *Say, Is This the USA?* NY. Duell, Sloan. 1941. 1st ed. ....
.... *$90.00–$145.00*

Bourke-White, M. *Shooting the Russian War*. NY. Simon & Schuster. 1942. dj. ....
....*30.00–$60.00*

Bourke-White, Margaret. *One Thing Leads to Another*. Bos/NY. Houghton Mifflin. 1936. 1st ed. blue cloth dj. .... *$30.00–$40.00*

Bourke-White, Margaret. *They Called it "Purple Heart Valley." A Combat Chronicle* . . . NY. 1944. illus. 2nd ptg. .... *$20.00–$30.00*

Bouton, Nathaniel. *Mr. Bouton's Centennial Discourses*. Concord. 1830. wrps. fldg map. .... *$35.00–$50.00*

Boutwell, Edna. *Daughter of Liberty*. OH. William Collins+ World Pub Co. ....
.... *$8.00–$12.00*

Bouvier, Jacqueline and Lee. *One Special Summer*. NY. Delacorte Press. 1974. 1st ed. illus. .... *$80.00–$120.00*

Bovey, Martin. *Saga of the Waterfowl*. Wash. 1949. 1st ed. illus. presentation copy, dj. .... *$40.00–$50.00*

Bowditch, Henry I. *Life and Correspondence of Henry I. Bowditch*. Bos. 1902. 2 vols. 1st ed. .... *$75.00–$100.00*

Bowditch, Nathaniel. *American Practical Navigator*. Defense Mapping Agency. 1984. 2 vols. .... *$20.00–$35.00*

Bowditch, Nathaniel. *New American Practical Navigator*. Newburyport. 1802. 1st ed. illus. 7 plates, diagrams, folding map. .... *$900.00–$1,200.00*

Bowen, Elizabeth. *Death of a Heart*. Lon. Victor Gollancz. 1938. 1st ed. dj. ....
.... *$150.00–$200.00*

Bowen, Elizabeth. *Eva Trout*. Lon. Cape. 1968. 1st ed. sgn, dj. .... *$75.00–$100.00*

Bowen, Elizabeth. *House in Paris*. NY. 1936. 1st Amer ed. .... *$150.00–$175.00*

Bowen, Elizabeth. *House in Paris*. Lon. 1935. 1st UK ed. dj. .... *$125.00–$150.00*

Bowen, Elizabeth. *Ivy Gripped the Steps and Other Stories*. NY. Knopf. 1946. 1st ed. dj.
.... *$31.00–$45.00*

Bowen, Elizabeth. *Look at All Those Roses*. NY. Knopf. 1941. 1st ed. dj. ....
.... *$90.00–$125.00*

Bowen, Frank C. *Sea, It's History and Romance*. Eng. McBride. 1927. 4 vols. illus. charts, red cloth, scarce. .... *$145.00–$195.00*

Bowles, Paul. *Little Stone*. Lon. Lehmann. 1950. 1st ed. gilt, dj. .... *$100.00–$150.00*

Bowles, Paul. *Spider's House*. NY. Random House. 1955. 1st ed. dj. . *$120.00–$150.00*

Bowring, John. *Specimens of the Russian Poets.* Bos. 1822. 3/4 lea, mar bds. .... *$50.00–$125.00*

Boy Scouts of America: Handbook for Boys. 1928. wrps. Norman Rockwell cvr. .... *$20.00–$35.00*

Boy's Treasury of Sports, Pastimes and Recreations. NY. 1850. pictorial cloth. .... *$100.00–$125.00*

Boyd, Brendan and Fred Harris. *Great American Baseball Card . . .* 1973. 1st ed. dj. .... *$20.00–$28.00*

Boyd, James. *Drums.* NY. Charles Scribner's Sons. (1925). 1st ed. author's first book... .... *$45.00–$60.00*

Boyd, James. *Drums.* NY. 1928. illus. by N C Wyeth. .... *$35.00–$45.00*

Boyd, William. *An Ice Cream War.* Morrow. 1983. 1st ed. dj. .... *$20.00–$45.00*

Boyd, William. *School Ties.* NY. 1985. 1st Amer ed, dj. .... *$40.00–$50.00*

Boyle, Frederick. *Culture of Greenhouse Orchids.* Lon. 1902. .... *$55.00–$65.00*

Boyle, Kay. *Year Before Last.* NY. Harrison Smith. 1932. 1st ed. dj. ... *$75.00–$100.00*

Boyle, Ray. *Nothing Ever Breaks Except the Heart.* Garden City. Doubleday. 1966. 1st ed. dj. .... *$30.00–$40.00*

Boyle, T. Coraghessan. *Descent of Man.* Bos. Little Brown. 1979. 1st ed. author's first book, dj. .... *$400.00–$475.00*

Boyle, T. Coraghessan. *Descent of Man.* NY. Viking. 1979. 1st ed. dj. .... *$350.00–$425.00*

Boyle, T. Coraghessan. *Water Music.* Bos. Little Brown. (1981). 1st ed. sgn and dated, dj. .... *$60.00–$100.00*

Boys, William F. A. *Practical Treatise on Office & Duties of Coroners.* Tor. 1864. 3/4 calf. .... *$75.00–$125.00*

Brace, Charles Loring. *Short Sermons to News Boys . . .* NY. Scribner's. 1866. inscrb by author. .... *$35.00–$65.00*

Brackenridge, Henry M. *History of the Late War Between the U.S and Great Britain.* Balt. 1817. illus. .... *$100.00–$250.00*

Bradbury, Ray. *Dandelion Wine.* Garden City. Doubleday. 1957. 1st ed. scarce, dj. .... *$360.00–$450.00*

Bradbury, Ray. *Dark Carnival.* Lon. Hamish Hamilton. 1948. 1st English ed. dj. .... *$250.00–$450.00*

Bradbury, Ray. *Dark Carnival.* Arkham House. 1947. ltd 3,000 cc, sgn. .... *$600.00–$900.00*

Bradbury, Ray. *Day It Rained Forever.* Lon. Rupert Hart-Davis. 1959. 1st UK ed. 254 pp, dj. .... *$60.00–$75.00*

Bradbury, Ray. *Halloween Tree.* NY. Knopf. (1972). 1st ed. dj. .... *$75.00–$150.00*

Bradbury, Ray. *Long After Midnight.* NY. 1976. 1st ed. dj. .... *$30.00–$35.00*

Bradbury, Ray. *Martian Chronicles.* Doubleday. 1950. 1st ed. dj. ...... *$275.00–$325.00*

Bradbury, Ray. *Medicine for Melancholy.* Garden City. Doubleday. 1959. 1st ed. sgn, dj. .... *$140.00–$175.00*

Bradbury, Ray. *October Country.* Lon. 1956. dj. .... *$90.00–$100.00*

Bradbury, Ray. *R Is For Rocket.* Garden City. Doubleday. (1962). 1st ed. dj. ....
.... *$125.00–$175.00*

Bradbury, Ray. *S Is for Space.* Doubleday. 1966. 1st ed. dj. .... *$50.00–$75.00*

Bradbury, Ray. *Toynbee Convector.* NY. Knopf. 1988. 1st ed. trade state, dj. ....
.... *$25.00–$35.00*

Bradbury, Ray. *Toynbee Convector.* NY. Knopf. (1988). 1st ed. sgn, dj. *$40.00–$50.00*

Bradbury, Ray. *Where Robot Mice and Robot Men Run Round in Robot Towns.* NY. Knopf. 1977. sgn, dj. .... *$30.00–$50.00*

Bradbury, Ray. *Zen and the Art of Writing.* 1st ed. sgn.......................... *$50.00–$60.00*

Bradford's History of Plimoth Plantation. Bos. 1899. 555 pp. .... *$40.00–$55.00*

Bradford, Richard. *Red Sky at Morning.* Phila. (1968). wrps. advance reading copy. ...
.... *$40.00–$65.00*

Bradford, Roark. *John Henry.* NY. 1931. 1st ed. dj. .... *$22.00–$35.00*

Bradford, Roark. *This Side of Jordan.* NY and Lon. Harper. 1929. dj. *$85.00–$125.00*

Bradley, Marion Zimmer. *House Between the Worlds.* Garden City. 1980. 1st ed. sgn, dj. .... *$35.00–$45.00*

Bradley, Will. *Peter Poodle.* NY. Dodd Mead & Co. 1906. 1st ed. illus. oversize gray pictorial bds. .... *$300.00–$500.00*

Bradley, Will. *Will Bradley, His Chap Book, an account in the words of dean of American* . . . NY. The Typophiles. 1955. 650cc. .... *$45.00–$95.00*

Bradshaw, Gillian. *Hawk of May.* NY. (1980). 1st ed. dj. .... *$20.00–$35.00*

Brady, Cyrus Townsend. *Recollections of a Missionary in the Great West.* NY. Scribner's. 1900. 1st ed. teg. .... *$35.00–$50.00*

Brady, Edwin. *Australia Unlimited.* Melbourne. Geo Robertson. c 1915.......................
.... *$100.00–$275.00*

Brady, Joseph P. *Trial of Aaron Burr.* NY. 1913. 89 pp. .... *$28.00–$35.00*

Braga, Frederic. *Dictionary of the Ojibway Language.* MN. Hist Soc. 1992. wrps. rprnt.
.... *$25.00–$40.00*

Braid, James and Harry Vardon. *How to Play Golf.* NY. nd. illus....... *$45.00–$58.00*

Brain, Belle M. *Transformation of Hawaii.* Revell. (1898). illus. green cloth, decorated frontis. .... *$15.00–$25.00*

Brainerd, Ezra. *Violets of North America.* Burlington. Free Press. 1921. wrps. 24 clr plates. .... *$20.00–$35.00*

Brake, Hezekiah. *On Two Continents.* Kansas. 1896. 1st ed. .... *$85.00–$100.00*

Brand Book for the Montana Grower's Association for 1910. Helena. (1910). red lea.
.... *$800.00–$1,000.00*

Brand Book of Wyoming. Laramie. 1913. 1st ed. lea. .... *$400.00–$700.00*

Brand Book of Wyoming. Laramie. 1919.. *$300.00–$600.00*

Brand, Max. *Hunted Riders.* NY. 1935. 1st ed. dj................................ *$75.00–$125.00*

Brand, Max. *Seventh Man.* NY. 1921. 1st ed. dj. .... *$25.00–$35.00*

Brand, Max. *Streak*. NY. 1937. dj.. *$75.00–$125.00*

Brand, Max. *Valley of Vanishing Men*. NY. 1947. 1st ed. dj. .... *$50.00–$75.00*

Brandt, Clare. *Man in the Mirror*. NY. Randon House. 1994. 1st ed. dj........................
.... *$15.00–$30.00*

Brandt, H. *Alaska Bird Trails*. The Bird Research Foundation. 1943. *$140.00–$170.00*

Brandt, Herbert. *Arizona and Its Bird Life*. Clev. Bird Research Foundation. 1951. illus. clr plates. pictorial green cloth. .... *$60.00–$90.00*

Brant. *True Story of the Lindbergh Kidnapping*. NY. 1932. 1st ed. .... *$30.00–$35.00*

Brant, Rick. *Rocket's Shadow*. Grosset & Dunlap. 1947. dj. .... *$20.00–$25.00*

Braun, Susan Roger. *Miniature Vignettes*. NY. Scribner's. (1975). 1st ed. illus. dj........
.... *$15.00–$25.00*

Brazeal, Brailsford R. *Brotherhood of Sleeping Car Porters*. NY. Harper & Bros. 1946. dj. .... *$75.00–$125.00*

Brazer, Esther Stevens. *Early American Decoration*. Springfield. Pond-Ekbert Cp. 1961. illus. 4th ed. dj. .... *$35.00–$50.00*

Brebner, John B. *North Atlantic Triangle*. New Haven. 1945. maps...... *$28.00–$45.00*

Brehm, Alfred E. *From the North Pole to the Equator*. Lon. 1896. text illus.................
.... *$70.00–$85.00*

Brennan, Joseph Payne. *Nine Horrors and a Dream*. Arkham House. 1958. 1st ed. dj.
.... *$100.00–$200.00*

Bresson, Henri Cartier. *People of Moscow*. NY. 1955. 1st ed. dj........ *$50.00–$135.00*

Brewer, A. T. *History Sixty-first Regiment, Pennsylvania Volunteers, 1861–65*. Pitts. 1911. .... *$100.00–$150.00*

Brewer, Samuel Child. *Every Man His Own Brewer: A Small Treatise* . . . Lon. nd. 3rd ed. half calf. .... *$75.00–$115.00*

Brewster, Charles W. *Rambles About Portsmouth*. Portsmouth. 1859. 1st ed...............
.... *$75.00–$95.00*

Brewster, David. *The Stereoscope*. NY. (1971). facs, dj......................... *$35.00–$45.00*

Brice, Tony. *So Long*. Rand McNally. 1937. 1st ed. illus. bds. .... *$5.00–$12.00*

Brice, Tony. *Tony Brice Picture Book*. Rand McNally. 1944. illus. clr, b/w. ....
.... *$30.00–$45.00*

Bricker, Charles. *Landmarks of Mapmaking*. NY. (1976). illus. maps, dj.....................
.... *$55.00–$100.00*

Brickwork in Italy. Chi. 1925. illus. 298 pp.. *$45.00–$55.00*

Bridges, C. *Thin Air, a Himalayan Interlude*. 1930. 1st ed. .... *$15.00–$20.00*

Brief Exposition of the Established Principles and Regulations of the United Society of Believers Called Shakers. NY. Jenkins. 1851. 30 pp. ....*$95.00–$150.00*

Briggs, Richard. *English Art of Cookery* . . . Lon. 1794. illus. 3rd ed. engr plates.........
.... *$95.00–$150.00*

Bright, Charles. *Story of the Atlantic Cable*. NY. 1903. 1st ed. illus. .... *$20.00–$30.00*

Brin, David. *The Postman*. NY. Bantam. (1985). 1st ed. sgn, dj. .... *$55.00–$80.00*

Brine, Vice-Admiral Lindesay. *Travels Amongst American Indians, Their Ancient Earthworks and Temples* . . . Lon. Sampson Low, Marston. 1894. 1st ed. illus. 429 pp, fldg map... *$150.00–$225.00*

Brininstool, E. A. *Fighting Red Cloud's Warriors: True Tales of Indian Days* . . . NY. 1975. illus. .... *$30.00–$55.00*

Brininstool, E. A. *Trooper with Custer and* . . . *Battle of the Little Bighorn.* Columbus, OH. Hunter, Trader, Trapper. 1925. 1st ed. illus. .... *$100.00–$140.00*

Brisbin, Gen. James. *Belden, the White Chief* . . . *Among the Wild Indians of the Plains.* Cinn. C F Vent. 1870. .... *$50.00–$85.00*

Bristol, Sherlock. *Pioneer Preacher, An Autobiography.* Revell. (1887). 1st ed. .... *$40.00–$50.00*

British Pharmacopeia. Lon. 1885. .... *$35.00–$50.00*

Brittain, Vera. *Rebel Passion.* NY. Fellowship. (1964). 1st US ed. 240 pp. .... *$20.00–$30.00*

Brock, Alan St. H. *History of Fireworks.* Lon. Harrap. 1949. 1st ed. illus. dj................ .... *$70.00–$100.00*

Broder, Patricia Janis. *Bronzes of the American West.* NY. (1974). illus. dj.................. .... *$75.00–$125.00*

Brogile, Louis. *Matter & Light.* NY. 1st Amer ed. dj. .... *$22.00–$35.00*

Bronte, Charlotte. *Jane Eyre: An Autobiography.* Lon. Smith, Elder & Co. 1848. 3 vols. by Currer Bell. 3rd ed. near fine, original cloth............................ *$6,000.00–$9,500.00*

Brooke, Jocelyn. *Wild Orchids of Britain.* Lon. The Bodley Head. 1950. 829/1100 cc. 40 clr plates. dj. slipcase... *$125.00–$175.00*

Brooke, Leslie. *Johnny Crow's Party.* Lon. 1930. illus. by Brooke, 8 clr plates, b/w drawings.. *$35.00–$45.00*

Brooke, Leslie. *Tom Thumb.* Lon/NY. Frederick Warne. nd. illus. pictorial bds. clr plates. .... *$20.00–$40.00*

Brooke, Rupert. *Democracy and the Arts.* Lon. Rupert Hart-Davis. 1946. 1st ed. dj. .... *$35.00–$50.00*

Brooks, E. S. *Under the Allied Flags: A Boy's Adventures* . . . *Against the Boxers in China.* Bos. 1901. 1st ed. illus. .... *$30.00–$45.00*

Brooks, Juanita. *Mountain Meadows Massacre.* Stanford. 1950. 1st ed. illus. map, sgn. .... *$100.00–$150.00*

Brooks, Terry. *Sword of Shannara.* Random House. (1977). 1st ed. so stated. illus. by the Brothers Hilldebrandt. brown cloth, black cloth spine, map frontis, pictorial dj. .... *$100.00–$250.00*

Brooks, Timothy. *Sword of Shannara.* NY. Rinehart. 1977. 1st ed. author's first book, scarce, dj... *$175.00–$225.00*

Brooks, Van Wyck. *New England: Indian Summer, 1865–1915.* NY. 1940. 1st ed. slipcase, #151/997 cc, sgn. .... *$50.00–$65.00*

Broomhall, Marshall (ed.). *Martyred Missionaries of the China Inland Mission.* Lon. nd. illus. fldg maps, photos. .... *$20.00–$30.00*

Brough, Charles Hillman. *Irrigation in Utah*. Balt. 1898. 1st ed. illus. photos, scarce. .... *$25.00–$50.00*

Brown, Bernard. *Amateur Talking Pictures and Recording*. 1933. 1st ed. illus. .... *$18.00–$22.00*

Brown, Capt. Thomas. *Taxidermist's Manual*. Lon. 1874. illus. 25th ed. .... *$25.00–$65.00*

Brown, D. W. *Salt Dishes*. MA. 1937. illus. .... *$30.00–$45.00*

Brown, Dee. *Bury My Heart at Wounded Knee*. (1970). 1st ed. dj. .... *$50.00–$100.00*

Brown, Dee. *Trail Driving Days, The Golden Days of the Old Trail Driving Cattlemen*. NY. 1952. 1st ed. 264 pp, folio, dj. .... *$40.00–$90.00*

Brown, Frederic. *Bloody Moonlight*. NY. 1949. 1st ed. dj .... *$125.00–$265.00*

Brown, Frederic. *Deep End*. NY. Dutton. 1952. 1st ed. dj. .... *$200.00–$275.00*

Brown, Frederic. *Far Cry*. NY. 1951. 1st ed. dj. .... *$150.00–$150.00*

Brown, Frederic. *Mind Thing*. NY. (1961). 1st ed. pictorial wrps. .... *$20.00–$35.00*

Brown, Frederic. *Screaming Mimi*. NY. 1949. 1st ed. dj. .... *$250.00–$300.00*

Brown, Frederic. *Space On My Hands*. Chi. Shasta. (1951). 1st ed. sgn, presentation copy to Fritz Leiber, Leiber's ownership signature, dj. .... *$650.00–$850.00*

Brown, Fredric. *Carnival of Crime*. Carbondale. Southern Illinois Univ. 1985. 1st ed. dj. .... *$40.00–$55.00*

Brown, G. S. *First Steps to Golf*. Bos. Small Maynard. nd. .... *$60.00–$75.00*

Brown, Helen E. *Good Catch; or, Mrs. Emerson's Whaling Cruise*. Phila. 1884. 1st ed. illus. .... *$75.00–$125.00*

Brown, Henry Collins. *City of New York*. NY. Old Colony Press. 1915. 1st ed. illus. limp lea. .... *$35.00–$50.00*

Brown, Hugh Victor. *History of the Education of Negroes in North Carolina*. Raleigh. Irving Swain Press. 1961. 1st ed. sgn. .... *$60.00–$90.00*

Brown, Innis (ed.). *How to Play Golf*. NY. 1930. illus. Spalding's Athletic Library. .... *$45.00–$50.00*

Brown, Jennie Broughton. *Fort Hall on the Oregon Trail* . . . Caldwell. Caxton Printers. 1934. illus. drawings, maps, dj. .... *$45.00–$65.00*

Brown, John Henry. *History of Texas from 1685–1892*. St Louis. (1892-93). 2 vols. .... *$350.00–$700.00*

Brown, L. and D. Amadon. *Eagles, Hawks, and Falcons of the World*. McGraw Hill. 1968. 2 vols. 1st Amer ed. slipcase. .... *$140.00–$200.00*

Brown, Lloyd A. *Story of Maps*. Bos. Little Brown. 1949. 1st ed. illus. bibliography, dj. .... *$20.00–$28.00*

Brown, M. M. *Nature Underground, The Endless Caverns*. New Market. 1921. wrps. illus. .... *$18.00–$25.00*

Brown, Margaret Wise. *Noisy Book*. NY. Harper & Row. 1939. .... *$20.00–$30.00*

Brown, Margaret Wise. *Wait Till the Moon Is Full*. NY. Harper & Row. 1948. illus. by Garth Williams, dj. .... *$30.00–$60.00*

Brown, Paul. *Crazy Quilt Circus Pony*. NY. Scribner's. 1934. rprnt, dj.. *$50.00–$65.00*

Brown, Paul. *Hits and Misses*. NY. Derrydale. 1935. ltd #411/950 cc, sgn, tissue dj. .... *$350.00–$450.00*

Brown, Susan A. *Invalid's Tea Tray*. Bos. 1885..................................... *$30.00–$45.00*

Brown, Thomas. *Elements of Conchology*. Lon. 1816. 1st ed. illus. 9 engr plates.......... .... *$150.00–$250.00*

Brown, Thomas. *Lectures on the Philosophy of the Human Mind*. Phil. 1824. 3 vols. ... . *$225.00–$300.00*

Brown, Warren. *Chicago Cubs*. NY. 1946. illus. .... *$30.00–$40.00*

Brown, William Adams, Jr. *Groping Giant. Revolutionary Russia as Seen by an American Democrat*. New Haven. Yales Univ Press. 1920. 1st ed. .... *$20.00–$50.00*

Brown, William Harvey. *On the South African Frontier*. NY. Scribner's. 1899. fldg maps... *$30.00–$125.00*

Brown, William Symington. *Capability of Women to Practice the Healing Art*. Bos. Ripley. 1859. 1st ed. illus. 15 pp.. *$58.00–$85.00*

Browne, Bellmore H. *Guns and Gunning*. Chicopee Falls. Stevens Arms & Tool. (1908). illus. .... *$70.00–$100.00*

Browne, Halbot K. *Sketches of Young Gentlemen*. Lon. 1838. 1st ed. 6 etched plates by "Phiz," 3/4 crimson mor. .... *$95.00–$120.00*

Browne, J. Ross. *Adventures in Apache Country*. NY. Harper & Co. 1869. illus........... .... *$275.00–$3,325.00*

Brownell, Clarence. *Heart of Japan*. NY. 1903. 1st ed. illus................. *$40.00–$65.00*

Browning, Elizabeth Barrett. *Poems of Elizabeth Browning*. Lon/NY. Warne. 1894..... .... *$25.00–$75.00*

Browning, Robert. *History of Golf*. NY. Dutton. (1955). 1st ed. illus. clr plates. .... *$50.00–$100.00*

Browning, Robert. *Pied Piper of Hamelin*. Phila. (1934). 1st Amer ed. illus by Arthur Rackham. dj.. *$145.00–$175.00*

Browning, Robert. *Saul*. Bos. Prang. 1890. 1st ed. illus. aeg, rare..... *$150.00–$350.00*

Brownlow, W. G. *Sketches of the Rise, Progress & Decline of Secession*. Phila. 1862. 1st ed. illus. .... *$50.00–$175.00*

Bruccoli, Matthew. *F. Scott Fitzgerald: A Descriptive Biography*. Pitt. Univ Pittsburg Press. 1987. rev ed. illus... *$80.00–$100.00*

Bruccoli, Matthew. *Nelson Algren: A Descriptive Biography*. Pitt. Univ Pittsburg Press. 1985. 1st ed. illus. dj. .... *$40.00–$60.00*

Bruce, H. Addington. *Woman in the Making of America*. Bos. Little Brown. 1913. blue pictorial cvr.. *$15.00–$20.00*

Bruce, Lenny. *How to Talk Dirty and Influence People*. Chi. Playboy Press. 1965. 1st ed. cloth, dj... *$35.00–$50.00*

Bruce, Philip A. *Virginia Plutarch*. Univ of NC Press. 1929. 2 vols. 174/200 cc sgn. .... *$45.00–$65.00*

Bruce, William C. *Benjamin Franklin, Self-Revealed*. NY. 1917. 2 vols. *$25.00–$75.00*

Bruette, William. *American Duck, Goose & Brant Shooting*. NY. 1943. *$25.00–$40.00*

Bruette, William. *Cocker Spaniel, Breeding, Breaking & Handling*. NY. 1937. 1st ed. . ... *$25.00–$40.00*

Brummitt, Stella W. *Brother Van*. NY. 1919. 1st ed. .... *$50.00–$75.00*

Bryan, John (ed.). *Notes From Underground*. SF. Underground Press. (1964). wrps. illus. decorated black and gray cvr. .... *$35.00–$50.00*

Bryan, Thomas Conn. *Confederate Georgia*. Athens. 1953. 1st ed. ...... *$48.00–$65.00*

Bryan, W. A. *Key to the Birds of the Hawaiian Group*. Museum Memoirs no 3. 1901. wrps. .... *$35.00–$50.00*

Bryant, W. C. *Picturesque America*. NY. (1872–74). 2 vols. plates.... *$350.00–$500.00*

Bryant, William Cullen. *Flood of Years*. NY. 1878. 1st ed. full mor, raised bands......... .... *$100.00–$145.00*

Bryce, James. *Impressions of South Africa*. Lon. Macmillan. 1897. 1st ed. illus. fldg maps. .... *$45.00–$55.00*

Bryce, Viscount. *Treatment of Armenians in the Ottoman Empire 1915–16*. Lon. 1916. 1st ed. fldg map. .... *$50.00–$75.00*

Bryk, F. *Circumcision in Man and Woman*. 1934. ltd ed. .... *$30.00–$35.00*

Bryk, Felix. *Dark Rapture*. NY. Walden Pub. 1939. illus. dj. .... *$25.00–$45.00*

Bryk, Felix. *Voodoo-Eros*. NY. private ptg. 1933. illus. photos, ltd 500 cc.................... .... *$65.00–$100.00*

Brynner, Irena. *Modern Jewelry: Design and Technique*. NY. 1968. illus. .... *$45.00–$60.00*

Buber, Martin. *Israel and Palestine*. Lon. 1952. dj. .... *$25.00–$45.00*

Buchan, John. *Blanket of the Dark*. Lon. Hodder & Stoughton. 1931. 1st ed. dj........... .... *$200.00–$300.00*

Buchan, John. *Castle Gay*. Lon. Hodder & Stoughton. 1930. 1st ed. dj. .... *$100.00–$350.00*

Buchan, John. *Gap in the Curtain* . . . Bos/NY. 1932. 1st US ed. .... *$35.00–$75.00*

Buchan, John. *Gordon at Khartoum*. Lon. 1934. 1st Eng ed. .... *$16.00–$45.00*

Buchan, John. *Island of Sheep*. Lon. Hodder & Stoughton. 1936. 1st ed. dj. .... *$85.00–$175.00*

Buchan, John. *Power-House*. Lon. Blackwood. 1916. 1st ed. .... *$55.00–$100.00*

Buchan, John. *Witch Wood*. Bos. Houghton Mifflin. 1927. 1st Amer ed. dj.................. .... *$45.00–$75.00*

Buchanan, Edna. *Nobody Lives Forever*. Random House. 1990. 1st ed. First mystery, dj. .... *$20.00–$50.00*

Buchanan, Frederick Stewart. *Emigration of Scottish Mormons to Utah, 1949–1900*. Salt Lake. 1961. sgn. .... *$60.00–$75.00*

Buchanan, James. *Message of the Pres. of the US* . . . *Massacre at Mountain Meadows*. Wash. 1860. softbound. .... *$75.00–$100.00*

Buchanan, Joseph R. *Story of a Labor Agitator*. NY. Outlook. 1903. 1st ed. cloth........ .... *$40.00–$50.00*

Buchanan, Lamont. *Ships of Steam*. NY. 1956. illus. dj. .... *$22.00–$30.00*

Buchanan, Robert Williams. *Saint Abe and His Seven Wives: A Tale of Salt Lake City.* London. 1872. 1st British ed. .... *$50.00–$80.00*

Buck, Frank. *All in a Lifetime.* NY. McBride. 1941. 1st ed. sgn. .... *$65.00–$150.00*

Buck, Frank. *Bring 'em Back Alive.* NY. 1930. 1st ed. illus. photos....... *$30.00–$45.00*

Buck, Franklin. *Yankee Trader in the Gold Rush.* Bos. 1930. dj. .... *$50.00–$65.00*

Buck, M. S. *Book Repair and Restoration.* 1918. illus. .... *$25.00–$30.00*

Buck, Pearl. *China in Black & White.* NY. 1944–1945. 1st ed. illus. woodcuts, 95 pp, dj. .... *$45.00–$95.00*

Buck, Pearl. *Death in the Castle.* NY. (1965). 1st ed. dj...................... *$30.00–$50.00*

Buck, Pearl. *Fighting Angel.* 1936. 1st ed. dj. .... *$24.00–$30.00*

Buck, Pearl S. *Kennedy Women.* NY. 1970. 1st ed. illus. dj, sgn. .... *$16.00–$20.00*

Buckingham, J. S. *Slave States of America.* Lon. (1842). 2 vols. 1st ed. scarce. .... *$150.00–$250.00*

Buckingham, J. S. *Slave States of America.* Negro Univ Press. 1968. rprnt. .... *$30.00–$45.00*

Buckingham, J. E. *Reminiscences and Souvenires of the Assassination of Abraham Lincoln.* Wash. 1894. 1st ed. wrps. illus.................................. *$85.00–$100.00*

Buckingham, Nash. *De Shootinest Gent'man.* Scribner's. 1941. 1st ed. dj. .... *$45.00–$55.00*

Buckingham, Nash. *Game Bag.* NY. 1945. 1st ed. illus. by Hoecker, dj, 1250 cc sgn. .... *$120.00–$170.00*

Buckingham, Nash. *Mark Right!* Derrydale Press. (1936). ltd 1,250 cc, inscrb............. .... *$300.00–$450.00*

Buckingham, Nash. *Tattered Coat.* Putnam. 1944. dj. .... *$45.00–$55.00*

Buckingham, Nash. *Tattered Coat.* Putnam. 1944. #279/995, sgn. .... *$160.00–$300.00*

Buckley, James. *Wrong and Peril of Woman Suffrage.* NY. Revell. 1909. .... *$30.00–$35.00*

Bucknall, Rixon. *Boats, Trains and Channel Packets.* Lon. Stuart. 1957. illus. photos, maps, dj.. *$50.00–$60.00*

Budge, E. A. Wallis. *The Mummy.* Camb Univ Press. 1894. 2nd ed. illus...................... .... *$75.00–$90.00*

Buechner, Thomas S. *Norman Rockwell Artist and Illustrator.* NY. 1970. illus. folio dj. .... *$70.00–$100.00*

Buel, J. W. *Heroes of the Plains.* St Louis. 1883. illus. clr frontis, pictorial cloth. .... *$40.00–$60.00*

Buell, Augustus. *Paul Jones Founder of the American Navy.* NY. Scribner's. 1905. 2 vols. .... *$30.00–$60.00*

Bugbee, Lester. *Slavery in Early Texas.* Political Science Quarterly. 1898. 22 pp......... .... *$65.00–$100.00*

Bugbee, Lester Gladstone. *Texas Frontier.* PA. 1900. .... *$40.00–$65.00*

Builders of Steam Fire Engines, Hose Carriages, Tenders, Etc. Hudson, NY. Clapp & Jones Mfg Co. 1872. purple printed wrps, illus, 60 pp........................ *$225.00–$300.00*

Buist, Robert. *Family Kitchen Gardener*. NY. Saxton. 1850. 1st ed. illus......................
.... *$30.00–$45.00*

Buist, Robert. *Family Kitchen Gardener*. NY. Saxton. 1855. 1st ed. illus..................
.... *$70.00–$115.00*

Buist, Robert. *Rose Manual*. Phila. 1847. 7th ed. .... *$25.00–$35.00*

Bujold, Lois McMaster. *Vor Game*. Norwalk. Easton Press. (1990). 1st ed. full lea, aeg, ribbon bookmark, laid-in Easton bookplate as issued, sgn (not issued in dj)...................
.... *$165.00–$185.00*

Buley, R. Carlyle. *Old Northwest*. Indiana Univ Press. 1951. 2 vols. illus. maps, plates, slipcase... *$30.00–$45.00*

Bulfinch, Thomas. *Age of Chivalry*. Bos. 1859. brown cloth............. *$175.00–$200.00*

Bulfinch, Thomas. *Oregon and Eldorado*. Bos. J E Tilton. 1866. 1st ed. *$60.00–$90.00*

Bulfinch, Thomas. *Oregon and Eldorado*. Bos. 1866. .... *$57.00–$65.00*

Bull, J. *Birds of New York State*. NY. 1974. illus. .... *$45.00–$60.00*

Bull, Rice C. *Soldiering, The Civil War Diary of Rice C. Bull, 123rd Vol. Infantry . . .* CA. San Rafael Presidio. 1978. dj. .... *$25.00–$35.00*

Bullard, Robert L. *Personalities and Reminiscences of the War*. NY. 1925. 1st ed........
.... *$45.00–$50.00*

Bullen, F. T. *Deep-Sea Plunderings*. NY. 1902. 8 illus. .... *$20.00–$25.00*

Bullen, F. T. *Idylls of the Sea*. NY. 1899. (authorized ed). ....' *$20.00–$25.00*

Bullen, Frank. *Back to Sunny Seas*. Lon. 1905. 1st ed. illus. clr plates................
.... *$50.00–$70.00*

Bullen, Frank. *Cruise of the Cachalot*. NY. 1926. illus. by Mead Schaeffer..................
.... *$35.00–$50.00*

Bullen, Frank. *Log of a Sea Wolf . . .* Appleton. 1899. illus. 1st Amer ed. pictorial cloth.
.... *$125.00–$175.00*

Bullen, Frank T. *Apostles of the Southeast*. NY. 1901........................... *$22.00–$32.00*

Bullen, Frank T. *Denizens of the Deep*. NY. 1904. illus........................ *$30.00–$50.00*

Bulletin, Michigan Ornithological Club. Detroit. 1903–1905. 10 bulletins. ....
.... *$20.00–$35.00*

Bullock, James D. *Secret Service of the Confederate States in Europe*. NY/Lon. Thomas Yoseloff. 1959. slipcase rprnt. .... *$45.00–$60.00*

Bulpin, T. V. *Hunter Is Death*. Johannesburg. 1962. 1st ed. illus............ *$22.00–$30.00*

Bumstead, John. *On the Wing*. Bos. 1869. illus. .... *$30.00–$50.00*

Bunyan, John. *Pilgrim's Progress*. Century. 1898. folio, 184 pp........ *$100.00–$105.00*

Bunyan, John. *Pilgrim's Progress*. NY. 1928. .... *$25.00–$40.00*

Bunyan, John. *Pilgrim's Progress . . ., by the Rev. Robert Philip*. Lon. James S Virtue. 1861. illus. 3/4 lea. .... *$50.00–$75.00*

Burbank, Nelson L. *House Construction Details*. NY. 1942. 2nd ed. .... *$22.00–$30.00*

Burch, E. S. and W. Forman. *The Eskimos*. Norman. 1988. dj............. *$25.00–$40.00*

Burch, John P. and Charles W. Burch. *Quantrell: A True History of His Guerrilla Warfare* . . . TX. pub by author. (1923). 1st ed. illus. dj......................... *$50.00–$150.00*

Burckhardt, John Lewis. *Notes on the Bedouins and Wahabys*. Cinc. 1968. rprnt. .... *$20.00–$35.00*

Burder, George. *Welch Indians*. NY. 1922. softbound. .... *$24.00–$35.00*

Burdett, Charles. *Life and Adventures of Christopher Carson*. Phila. 1861. .... *$28.00–$35.00*

Burdett, Charles. *Life of Kit Carson*. NY. Grosset & Dunlap. 1902. .... *$8.00–$15.00*

Burdick, Usher. *Last Battle of the Sioux Nation*. Stevens Point. 1929. 1st ed. dj. .... *$100.00–$150.00*

Burgess, Anthony. *Clockwork Orange*. Lon. 1962. 1st UK ed. dj... *$400.00–$1,200.00*

Burgess, Anthony. *Clockwork Orange*. (1963). 1st Amer ed. purple bds, dj................. .... *$265.00–$400.00*

Burgess, Anthony. *Devil of a State*. Norton. 1962. 1st Amer ed............. *$35.00–$70.00*

Burgess, Anthony. *Devil of a State*. Lon. Heinemann. (1961). 1st ed. dj. .... *$35.00–$100.00*

Burgess, Anthony. *End of the World News*. McGraw-Hill. 1983. 1st US ed. dj............. .... *$12.00–$20.00*

Burgess, Anthony. *Kingdom of the Wicked*. Franklin Library. 1985. 1st ed. illus. .... *$40.00–$60.00*

Burgess, Anthony. *Ninety-Nine Novels*. Lon. Allison & Busby. 1984. dj 1st UK ed. .... *$60.00–$75.00*

Burgess, Gelett. *Bayside Bohemia, Fin de siecle San Francisco & its Little Magazines*. SF. Book Club of California. 1954. 1st ed. ltd 375 cc........................... *$65.00–$100.00*

Burgess, Gelett. *Goop Directory*. Stokes. 1913. 1st ed. illus. paper over bds................. .... *$75.00–$95.00*

Burgess, Gelett. *Goops and How to Be Them*. Stokes. 1900. illus.......... *$50.00–$60.00*

Burgess, Gelett. *Maxims of Methusaleh*. Stokes. (1907)........................ *$25.00–$40.00*

Burgess, Gelett. *More Goops and How Not to Be Them*. NY. Lippincott. 1931. illus. yellow cloth. .... *$25.00–$50.00*

Burgess, Gelett. *Purple Cow and Other Nonsense*. NY. Dover. 1961. illus.................... .... *$25.00–$45.00*

Burgess, Thornton. *Adventures of Reddy Fox*. Bos. Little Brown. 1923. illus. by Harrison Cady.. *$25.00–$50.00*

Burgess, Thornton. *Bedtime Stories*. Grosset & Dunlap. 1974. illus. by Carl and Mary Hauge.. *$25.00–$50.00*

Burgess, Thornton. *Billy Mink*. Little Brown. 1924. 1st ed. illus. by Cady, dj .... *$50.00–$105.00*

Burgess, Thornton. *Book of Nature Lore*. NY. 1965. dj....................... *$25.00–$450.00*

Burgess, Thornton. *Bowser the Hound*. NY. Little Brown. 1920. 1st ed. illus. by Harrison Cady... *$55.00–$175.00*

Burgess, Thornton. *Neatness of Bobby Coon*. Stoll and Edwards. 1927. illus. by Harrison Cady. .... *$50.00–$100.00*

Burgess, Thornton. *While the Story Log Burns*. Bos. 1938. 1st ed. illus. by Lemuel Palmer, green cloth, red lettering, frontis. .... *$50.00–$125.00*

Burgess, Thornton W. *Old Mother Westwind*. Little Brown. 1910. 1st ed. illus. by Kerr, 169 pp, 7 plates. .... *$100.00–$150.00*

Burke, Emma Maxwell. *Perfect Course in Millinery*. NY. 1925. illus... *$30.00–$40.00*

Burke, James Lee. *Neon Rain*. NY. Henry Holt. 1987. 1st ed. sgn, dj. ....
.... *$200.00–$250.00*

Burke, James Lee. *Neon Rain*. Holt. 1987. 1st ed. dj. .... *$95.00–$140.00*

Burke, Jenny and Heard, James (eds.). *Pollock's World of Toys*. Lon. wrps. pamphlet.
.... *$12.00–$15.00*

Burleigh, T. D. *Georgia Birds*. Univ of Oklahoma Press. 1958. dj. ....
.... *$50.00–$100.00*

Burley, W. J. *Wycliffe and the Cycle of Death*. Gollancz. 1990. 1st UK ed. ....
.... *$32.00–$40.00*

Burnaby, Fred. *Ride to Kiva*. NY. Harper. 1877. 1st ed. illus. fldg maps. ....
.... *$100.00–$200.00*

Burnet, J. A. *Treatise on Painting*. Lon. 1850. plates. .... *$85.00–$100.00*

Burnett, Frances Hodgson. *Editha's Burgler*. J Marsh. 1888. blue cloth, 13 plates, 64 pp, illus. by Sandham. .... *$40.00–$50.00*

Burnett, Frances Hodgson. *Giovanni and the Other*. Scribner's. 1892. 1st ed. ....
.... *$50.00–$60.00*

Burnett, Frances Hodgson. *In the Closed Room*. McClure. 1904. 1st ed. illus. by Jessie Wilcox Smith. .... *$30.00–$80.00*

Burnett, Frances Hodgson. *Sara Crewe or What Happened at Miss Minchin's*. NY. 1888. illus. .... *$30.00–$45.00*

Burnett, Frances Hodgson. *Secret Garden*. NY. Stokes. 1911. illus. by Maria Kirk......
.... *$20.00–$50.00*

Burnett, Frances Hodgson. *T. Tembarom*. Century. 1913. 1st ed. illus. by Chapman. ...
.... *$25.00–$30.00*

Burnham, Major Frederick. *Scouting on Two Continents*. Garden City. 1926. 1st ed. sgn. .... *$25.00–$40.00*

Burns, Eugene. *Advanced Fly Fishing*. Harrisburg. 1953. illus. .... *$120.00–$150.00*

Burns, Robert. *The Songs*. Lon. 1903. 1st ed. 536 pp, 4 plates. .... *$50.00–$75.00*

Burns, Walter Noble. *Robin Hood of El Dorado*. NY. (1932). dj. .... *$20.00–$60.00*

Burns, Walter Noble. *Saga of Billy the Kid*. Garden City. (1925–6). dj. *$22.00–$40.00*

Burns, Walter Noble. *Tombstone. An Illiad of the Southwest*. NY. 1927. *$30.00–$45.00*

Burns, Walter Noble. *Year With a Whaler*. NY. Macmillan. 1919. .... *$30.00–$45.00*

Burns, Walter Noble. *Year With a Whaler*. NY. Outing Pub. 1913. 1st ed. illus. ....
.... *$50.00–$85.00*

Burpee, Lawrence J. *Search for the Western Sea* . . . Lon. 1908. 1st ed. illus. 6 maps, 51 plates. .... *$125.00–$200.00*

Burris-Meyer, Elizabeth. *Decorating Livable Houses*. NY. 1937. 1st ed. illus ....
.... *$20.00–$25.00*

Burritt, Elijah H. *Geography of the Heavens and Class Book of Astronomy*. NY. 1860. 345 pp. .... *$75.00–$85.00*

Burritt, Elijah Hinsdale. *Logarithmick Arithmetick Containing a New* . . . *Table of Logarithms* . . . Williamsburgh, MA. 1818. lea, fldg plates, 251 pp. ... *$100.00–$150.00*

Burroughs, Edgar Rice. *At the Earth's Core*. Methuen. 1938. 1st UK ed. ....
.... *$35.00–$45.00*

Burroughs, Edgar Rice. *Bandit of Hell's Bend*. Lon. Methuen. 1926. 1st ed. ....
.... *$35.00–$50.00*

Burroughs, Edgar Rice. *Beasts of Tarzan*. McClurg. 1916. 1st ed. illus. by Allen St John, cloth. .... *$250.00–$500.00*

Burroughs, Edgar Rice. *Beasts of Tarzan*. A L Burt. (1917). dj. .... *$50.00–$75.00*

Burroughs, Edgar Rice. *Beyond Thirty and the Man Eater*. NY. 1957. 1st ed. dj. ....
.... *$65.00–$85.00*

Burroughs, Edgar Rice. *Carson of Venus*. Tarzana. Burroughs, Inc. (1939). 1st ed. fine, dj. .... *$250.00–$600.00*

Burroughs, Edgar Rice. *Cave Girl*. Grosset & Dunlap. 1927. .... *$15.00–$25.00*

Burroughs, Edgar Rice. *Escape on Venus*. Tarzana. (1946). 1st ed. dj. *$90.00–$150.00*

Burroughs, Edgar Rice. *Gods of Mars*. Chi. McClurg. 1918. 1st ed. red cloth, dj. ....
.... *$230.00–$600.00*

Burroughs, Edgar Rice. *Jungle Tales of Tarzan*. Chi. McClurg. 1919. 1st ed. illus. cloth.
.... *$45.00–$60.00*

Burroughs, Edgar Rice. *Land That Time Forgot*. Grosset & Dunlap. 1925. dj. ....
.... *$25.00–$30.00*

Burroughs, Edgar Rice. *Llana of Gathol*. CA. Burroughs. (1948). 1st ed. dj. ....
.... *$95.00–$150.00*

Burroughs, Edgar Rice. *Llana of Gathol*. Tarzana. Burroughs, Inc. (1948). 1st ed. fine, dj. .... *$150.00–$400.00*

Burroughs, Edgar Rice. *Monster Men*. NY. Canaveral Press. 1962. new ed. illus. dj. ...
.... *$30.00–$50.00*

Burroughs, Edgar Rice. *New Adventures of Tarzan "Pop-Up."* Chi. Pleasure Books. (1935). illus. .... *$300.00–$500.00*

Burroughs, Edgar Rice. *Oakdale Affair and the Rider*. Tarzana. Burroughs. 1937. 1st ed. blue cloth, dj. .... *$70.00–$125.00*

Burroughs, Edgar Rice. *Return of Tarzan*. Burt. dj. .... *$45.00–$65.00*

Burroughs, Edgar Rice. *Savage Pellucidar*. NY. Canaveral Press. 1963. 1st thus. dj. ...
.... *$75.00–$85.00*

Burroughs, Edgar Rice. *Tarzan and the Ant Men*. Chi. McClurg. 1924. 1st ed. illus. ...
.... *$75.00–$110.00*

Burroughs, Edgar Rice. *Tarzan and the Forbidden City*. NY. Burroughs. 1938. 1st ed. illus. by John Coleman Burroughs. clr frontis. .... *$125.00–$450.00*

Burroughs, Edgar Rice. *Tarzan and the Foreign Legion*. Tarzana. Burroughs. 1947. 1st ed. dj. .... *$100.00–$125.00*

Burroughs, Edgar Rice. *Tarzan and the Golden Lion*. NY. Grosset & Dunlap. 1923. rprnt. .... *$45.00–$85.00*

Burroughs, Edgar Rice. *Tarzan and the Jewels of Opar*. Grosset & Dunlap. illus. burgundy bds, rprnt, dj. .... *$40.00–$125.00*

Burroughs, Edgar Rice. *Tarzan and the Jewels of Opar*. NY. Grosset & Dunlap. 1918. reprnt.. *$30.00–$75.00*

Burroughs, Edgar Rice. *Tarzan and the Lost Empire*. NY. Metropolitan Books. (1929). 1st ed. orange cloth.. *$50.00–$75.00*

Burroughs, Edgar Rice. *Tarzan Lord of the Jungle*. NY. Grosset & Dunlap. 1928. illus. .... *$30.00–$100.00*

Burroughs, Edgar Rice. *Tarzan of the Apes*. NY. Grosset & Dunlap. 1914. rprnt.......... .... *$10.00–$25.00*

Burroughs, Edgar Rice. *Tarzan of the Apes*. NY. A L Burt. 1915. .... *$25.00–$70.00*

Burroughs, Edgar Rice. *Tarzan the Terrible*. NY. Grosset & Dunlap. (c1940). dj, later ed. .... *$20.00–$35.00*

Burroughs, Edgar Rice. *Tarzan the Untamed*. NY. Grosset & Dunlap. 1920. rprnt....... .... *$45.00–$60.00*

Burroughs, Edgar Rice. *Thuria, Maid of Mars*. Burroughs. dj. .... *$75.00–$85.00*

Burroughs, John. *Bird Stories*. Bos. 1911. 1st ed. illus. by L A Fuertes. *$18.00–$25.00*

Burroughs, John. *Camping & Tramping with Roosevelt*. Bos. 1907. 1st ed. illus. photos. .... *$24.00–$35.00*

Burroughs, John. *In the Catskills*. Bos. Houghton. 1910. 1st ed. 1st prtg. illus. .... *$48.00–$60.00*

Burroughs, Wiliam S. *Exterminator!* NY. Viking Press. 1973. 1st ed. dj sgn. .... *$225.00–$400.00*

Burroughs, William S. *Naked Lunch*. NY. Grove Press. (1959). dj.... *$150.00–$225.00*

Burroughs, William S. *Soft Machine*. NY. Grove Press. 1966. 1st ed. dj...................... .... *$85.00–$95.00*

Burroughs, William S. *Soft Machine*. Lon. 1968. 1st UK ed. .... *$45.00–$65.00*

Burroughs, William S. *Third Mind*. NY. 1978. dj................................. *$35.00–$40.00*

Burroughs, William S. *Tornado Alley*. Cherry Valley Editions. 1989. 1st ed. 1/100 cc.. .... *$75.00–$150.00*

Burroughs, William S. *Western Lands*. NY. Viking. (1987). 1st ed. dj. . *$20.00–$35.00*

Burton, Frederick R. *American Primitive Music . . . Songs of the Ojibways*. NY. 1909. .... *$55.00–$65.00*

Burton, R. *Anatomy of Melancholy . . .* Lon. 1898................................ *$35.00–$75.00*

Burton, Richard. *Lake Regions of Central Africa*. Lon. The Folio Society. 1993. illus.. .... *$60.00–$65.00*

Burton, Richard. *Lake Regions of Central Africa*. NY. Horizon Press. 1961. 2 vols. illus. new ed, djs. .... *$110.00–$150.00*

Burton, Richard F. *City of Saints and Across the Rocky Mts to California*. Lon. 1861. illus. maps plan. .... *$250.00–$500.00*

Burton, Richard F. *City of Saints, and Across the Rocky Mts. to California*. NY. 1862. 1st Amer ed. maps, plates. .... *$125.00–$275.00*

Burton, Richard F. *Land of Midian (Revisited)*. Lon. Kegan Paul. 1879. 2 vols. 1st ed. illus. 6 clr lithos, fldg map. .... *$200.00–$345.00*

Burton, Richard F. *Vikram and the Vampire*. Lon. Longmans, Green. 1870. 1st ed. illus. .... *$650.00–$750.00*

Burton, Richard Francis. *Etruscan Bologna: A Study*. Lon. Smith, Elder. 1876. blue-gray cloth, folding frontis. .... *$225.00–$500.00*

Burton, Richard Francis. *Wanderings in Three Continents*. Lon. Hutchingson & Co. 1901. 1st ed. ed by W H Wilkins, plates. .... *$125.00–$200.00*

Busch, W. *Das Goldene Wilhelm Busch Album*. Hanover. 1966. .... *$45.00–$60.00*

Busch, W. *Max Und Moritz*. NY. illus. b/w. in German. .... *$30.00–$40.00*

Busch, Wilhelm. *Max & Moritz*. Munich. 1939. illus. .... *$25.00–$45.00*

Busch, Wilhelm. *Neues Wilhelm Busch Album*. Leipzig. Weise. 1st ed. dj, slipcase. .... *$100.00–$150.00*

Bushnan, J. S. *Naturalist's Library, Ichthyology*. Edin. 1840. Vol. II. illus. .... *$58.00–$75.00*

Bushnell, Charles I. *Narrative of the Life and Adventures of Levi Hanford . . .* NY. private ptg. (1863). 1st ed. illus. bds. .... *$95.00–$150.00*

Busk, Hans. *Navies of the World*. Lon. 1859. .... *$55.00–$68.00*

Butler, Benjamin F. *Autobiography & Personal Reminiscence of Major-General Benjamin F Butler*. Bos. Thayer. 1892. 1st ed. illus. .... *$85.00–$125.00*

Butler, Benjamin F. *Autobiography . . . of Major General Benjamin F. Butler*. Bos. 1892. 1st ed. illus. .... *$27.00–$35.00*

Butler, Charles. *American Lady*. Phila. Hogan & Thompson. 1836. 1st ed. .... *$85.00–$100.00*

Butler, Maj. W F. *Great Lone Land*. Rutland. Tuttle. (1968). facsimile rprnt. .... *$20.00–$35.00*

Butler, Octavia. *Survivor*. Garden City. Doubleday. 1978. 1st ed. dj.... *$80.00–$125.00*

Butler, Octavia E. *Wild Seed*. Garden City. Doubleday. 1980. 1st ed. dj...................... .... *$85.00–$175.00*

Butler, Robert Olen. *Alleys of Eden*. NY. Horizon. (1981). 1st ed. author's first book, dj, sgn. .... *$100.00–$150.00*

Butler, Samuel. *An Atlas of Antient Geography*. Phila. Carey, Lee & Blanchard. 1838. hand-clr maps. .... *$175.00–$200.00*

Butler, Samuel. *Erewhon*. NY. Limited Editions Club. 1934. illus. by Rockwell Kent, slipcase, 1494/1500 cc. sgn by Kent. .... *$35.00–$50.00*

Butler, T. Harrison. *Cruising Yachts*. Southampton. 1958. 3rd ed. dj..... *$22.00–$35.00*

Butler, Winifred. *Dolls' Dressmaking*. NJ. D Van Nostrand Co. (1962). 1st ed. dj......... .... *$12.00–$20.00*

Buttree, Julia M. *Rhythm of the Redman*. NY. (1930). intro and illus. by E Thomson Seton. .... *$35.00–$45.00*

Butts, I. R. *Merchant and Shipmaster's Manual* . . . Bos. 1867. illus. 4th ed. plates....... .... *$95.00–$135.00*

Butts, I. R. *Tinman's Manual*. Bos. 1861. 205 pp................................... *$50.00–$85.00*

By a Free-Will Baptist. *Church Member's Book . . . In Three Parts*. NH. 1847. .... *$28.00–$30.00*

By a Lady. *Art of Cookery Made Plain and Easy*. Lon. 1770. new addition................... .... *$550.00–$725.00*

By a Lady of Boston. *Stories of Gen. Warren*. 1835. lea. .... *$20.00–$30.00*

By a Practical Housekeeper. *Good Cook*. NY. 1853............................ *$55.00–$65.00*

By-Laws of the Chicago & Rock Island Rail Road Co. NY. 1858. wrps. 10 pp............ .... *$85.00–$100.00*

By-Laws of the Orphan House of Charleston, South Carolina, 4th April 1861.Charleston. Steam Power Press. 1861. 1st ed. wrps. 40 pp. .... *$50.00–$55.00*

Byington, Cyrus. *Dictionary of the Choctaw Language*. Wash. GPO. 1915. .... *$75.00–$85.00*

Byrd, Admiral Richard. *Discovery: The Story of the Second Byrd Antarctic Expedition*. NY. Putnam. 1935. 1st ed. photos, dj..................................... *$35.50–$65.00*

Byrd, Martha. *Chennault: Giving Wings to the Tiger*. Tuscaloosa. Univ of Alabama Press. 1987. 1st ed. illus. photos, dj.. *$20.00–$35.00*

Byrd, Richard E. *Alone*. Putnam. 1938. sgn, dj..................................... *$30.00–$40.00*

Byrd, Richard E. *Intro., The Big Aviation Book for Boys*. Springfield, MA. (1929). dj. .... *$25.00–$35.00*

Byrd, Richard E. *Little America*. NY. Putnam. 1930. 1st ed. illus. maps, dj. .... *$15.00–$25.00*

Byrd, Richard E. *Little America*. NY. 1930. 1st ed. illus. sgn, dj......... *$65.00–$100.00*

Cabell, James Branch. *Ballades of the Hidden Way*. NY. Crosby Gaige. 1928. 1st ed. designs by W A Dwiggins, 831 cc sgn................................... *$60.00–$100.00*

Cabell, James Branch. *Cream of the Jest, A Comedy of Evasions*. NY. 1927................. .... *$35.00–$40.00*

Cable, George. *Creoles of Louisiana*. Lon. 1885. .... *$145.00–$200.00*

Cable, George. *Old Creole Days*. NY. 1879. 1st ed. without ads in rear. .... *$150.00–$175.00*

Cable, George W. *Creoles of Louisiana*. NY. 1884. 1st ed. sgn, slipcase....................... .... *$200.00–$300.00*

Cable, George W. *Gideon's Band*. NY. 1914. 1st ed............................ *$30.00–$40.00*

Cable, George W. *Negro Question*. NY. Doubleday Anchor. 1958......... *$20.00–$30.00*

Cabot, W. B. *In Northern Labrador*. Bos. 1912. 1st ed........................... *$40.00–$80.00*

Cadbury, Betty. *Playthings Past a Collector's Guide to Antique Toys*. NY. Praeger Pub Co. (1976). 1st ed. illus. .... *$12.00–$20.00*

Cady, Daniel. *Rhymes of Vermont Rural Life*. Rutland. 1919. 1st ed. ..... *$15.00–$25.00*

Cady, Harrison. *School Opens on Butternut Hill*. Racine, WI. Whitman. 1929. 1st ed. illus. by author. dj. .... *$75.00–$100.00*

Cady, Jack. *The Well*. NY. Arbor House. (1980). 1st ed. dj. .... *$20.00–$45.00*

Caiger, G. *Dolls on Display*. Tokyo. nd. illus. silk brocade with silk ties, boxed. .... *$95.00–$150.00*

Cain, James M. *Institute*. NY. Mason/Charter. 1976. 1st ed. dj. .... *$25.00–$50.00*

Cain, James M. *Our Government*. NY. Knopf. 1930. 1st ed. author's first book............ .... *$100.00–$175.00*

Cain, James M. *Postman Always Rings Twice*. NY. Grosset & Dunlap. 1934................ .... *$15.00–$35.00*

Cain, James M. *The Moth*. NY. Knopf. 1948. 1st ed. dj. .... *$60.00–$110.00*

Cain, Julien. *Lithographs of Chagall*. Bos. (1969). dj. 2 original lithos by Chagall. .... *$350.00–$800.00*

Calasanctius, M. J. *Voice of Alaska. A Missioner's Memories*. Lachine. 1935. illus. 1st Eng ed. mar bds. .... *$40.00–$50.00*

Caldecott, Randolph. *Last Graphic Pictures*. Lon. 1888. 1st ed. illus. *$85.00–$150.00*

Caldecott, Randolph. *Ride a Cock Horse to Banbury Cross*. Lon. 1884. illus. 6 clr plates. .... *$100.00–$150.00*

Caldecott, Randolph. *Sketchbook of Randolph Caldecott*. Lon/NY. 1883. illus. .... *$70.00–$125.00*

Calderwood, W. L. *Life of the Salmon*. Lon. 1907. illus. .... *$40.00–$50.00*

Caldwell, E. N. *Alaska Trail Dogs*. NY. Richard Smith. 1945. illus. ...... *$35.00–$90.00*

Caldwell, Erskine. *Claudelle Inglish*. Bos. 1958. 1st ed. dj. .... *$20.00–$30.00*

Caldwell, Erskine. *Erskine Caldwell's Gulf Coast Stories*. Bos. Little Brown. 1956. 1st ed. dj. .... *$30.00–$40.00*

Caldwell, Erskine. *God's Little Acre*. Franklin Center. Franklin Library. 1979. ltd, sgn. .... *$85.00–$100.00*

Caldwell, Erskine. *God's Little Acre*. NY. 1933. 1st ed. .... *$800.00–$1,500.00*

Caldwell, Erskine. *Place Called Estherville*. NY. (1949). 1st ed. dj. ..... *$30.00–$40.00*

Caldwell, Erskine. *Southways*. NY. 1938. 1st ed. .... *$25.00–$35.00*

Caldwell, Erskine. *Tenant Farmer*. NY. Phalanx Pres. (c1935). 1st ed. green wrps........ .... *$125.00–$150.00*

Caldwell, Erskine. *The Bastard*. NY. Heron Press. (c1929). 1st ed. illus. by Ty Mahon, 1/1,100 cc, author's first book. .... *$150.00–$200.00*

Caldwell, Erskine. *Tobacco Road*. NY. Scribner's. 1932. red-brown cloth, dj. .... *$125.00–$500.00*

Caldwell, Erskine. *Tobacco Road*. NY. Grosset & Dunlap. (1932). illus. .... *$10.00–$20.00*

Caldwell, Erskine. *Tobacco Road*. NY. 1940. wrps. illus. by Fredenthal, boxed. .... *$45.00–$65.00*

Caldwell, H. R. and J. C. Caldwell. *South China Birds*. Hester May Vanderbugh. 1931. .... *$95.00–$120.00*

Calendar of the American Fur Company's Papers. Wash. 1945. 2 vols. 1st ed. .... *$85.00–$170.00*

California and the Far West.SF. Grabhorn Press. 1948. 1st ed. 217 pp, large folio, plates, ltd 500 cc. .... *$100.00–$200.00*

Calisher, Hortense. *In the Absence of Angelo*. Bos. 1951. 1st ed. dj...... *$30.00–$75.00*

Callaway, Nicholas (ed). *Georgia O'Keefe: 100 Flowers*. NY. 1987. 1st ed. clr plates, folio, dj. .... *$75.00–$100.00*

Calthrop, Dion Clayton. *Charm of Gardens*. Lon. Black. 1910. 1st ed. illus. .... *$80.00–$100.00*

Calvert, Roy E. *Death Penalty Enquiry*. Lon. 1931. softcvr. .... *$14.00–$20.00*

Calvin, Verplanck. *Report of the Superintendant of the State Land Survey* . . . Alb. 1896. 1st ed. maps, photos. .... *$145.00–$200.00*

Calvino, Italo. *Silent Mr. Palomar*. Targ Editions. 1981. 1st ed. 250 cc sgn.................. .... *$150.00–$250.00*

Camehl, A. W. *Blue China Book*. NY. 1916. .... *$20.00–$30.00*

Camp, David. *History of New Britain*. New Britain, CT. 1889. illus. brown cloth.......... .... *$35.00–$45.00*

Camp, John. *Fools Run*. NY. Henry Holt. 1989. 1st ed. sgn, dj.............. *$45.00–$90.00*

Camp, R. *Duck Boats: Blinds, Decoys*. NY. 1952. 1st ed. .... *$40.00–$50.00*

Camp, R. *Game Cookery*. NY. 1958. 1st ed. .... *$20.00–$30.00*

Camp, Samuel G. *Fine Art of Fishing*. Macmillan. 1929 (1911)............ *$50.00–$65.00*

Camp, Samuel G. *Fishing Kits and Equipment*. NY. Outing Publishing. 1910. 1st ed. .. .. *$30.00–$40.00*

Camp, Walter (ed.). *Official Football Rules — 1914*. NY. 1914. wrps. illus.................. .... *$18.00–$25.00*

Campbell, C. A. R. *Bats, Mosquitoes and Dollars*. Bos. 1925. illus. ..... *$30.00–$47.00*

Campbell, Dugald. *Wanderings in Central Africa*. Phila. Lippincott. 1st ed. illus. photo plates... *$50.00–$80.00*

Campbell, Mary Emily. *Attitude of Tennesseans Toward the Union 1847–1861*. NY. 1961. 1st ed.. *$30.00–$45.00*

Campbell, Patrick. *Travels in the Interior Inhabited Parts of North America*. Tor. 1937. ltd 550 cc. .... *$150.00–$300.00*

Campbell, Ruth. *Small Fry and Winged Horse*. Volland. (1927). illus... *$55.00–$85.00*

Campbell, T. J. *Isaac Jogues Discoverer of Lake George*. NY. The America Press. 1911. 1st ed. illus. soft brown wrps. .... *$45.00–$75.00*

Campbell, Wilfred. *Canada*. Lon. A & C Black. 1907. 1st ed. illus. ... *$75.00–$125.00*

Camus, Albert. *Exile and the Kingdom*. NY. 1958. 1st Amer ed, dj.............................. .... *$40.00–$60.00*

Camus, Albert. *L'Homme Revolte*. Paris. Gallimard. (1951). .... *$10.00–$14.00*

Camus, Albert. *Myth of Sisyphus*. NY. 1955. 1st Amer ed. dj. .... *$85.00–$150.00*

Camus, Albert. *Resistance, Rebellion and Death*. 1961. 1st UK ed, dj. ....
.... *$45.00–$50.00*

Camus, Albert. *The Fall*. Kentfield, CA. The Allen Press. 1960. folio 1/140 cc tan-gray and black bds. dj. .... *$400.00–$650.00*

Camus, Albert. *The Plague*. NY. Knopf. 1948. 1st ed. .... *$14.00–$20.00*

Camus, Albert. *The Stranger*. NY. (1946). 1st US ed. dj. .... *$75.00–$125.00*

Candee, Helen C. *Tapestry Book*. NY. 1935.. *$28.00–$40.00*

Candee, Helen C. *Weaves and Draperies*. NY. 1930. 1st ed. illus.......... *$40.00–$55.00*

Canfield, Dorothy. *Home Fires in France*. NY. 1918. 1st ed................. *$20.00–$35.00*

Cannon, Donald J. (ed.). *Heritage of Flames*. NY. Artisan Books. 1977. 1st ed. illus. hist of early Amer firefighting. dj. .... *$60.00–$100.00*

Cannon, George Q. *Delegate From Utah*. Wash. GPO. 1872. wrps. ...... *$45.00–$60.00*

Cannon, George Q. *Physiology of Common Life*. Edin. 1865. Vol. 2. illus. sgn. ....
.... *$100.00–$175.00*

Cannon, George Q. *Writings from the "Western Standard." Published in San Francisco, California*. Liverpool. 1864. 1st ed. .... *$300.00–$650.00*

Canot, Capt. Theodore. *Adventures of an African Slaver*. NY. Albert & Charles Boni. 1928. 1st ed. illus... *$80.00–$120.00*

Canton, Frank M. *Frontier Trails*. Bos. 1930. dj............................... *$100.00–$150.00*

Cantwell, J. C. *Report of the Operations of the US Steamer Nunivak, 1899–1902*. GPO. 1902. 1st ed. illus. 153 photos. green cloth.. *$150.00–$275.00*

Cantwell, Lieut. *Report of the Operations of the US Revenue Steamer Nunivak*. Wash. GPO. 1902. 1st ed. illus. green cloth. .... *$150.00–$250.00*

Capa, R. *Images of War*. NY. (1964). 1st ed. dj..................................... *$75.00–$95.00*

Capa, Robert. *Death in the Making*. NY. Covici-Friede. (1938). 1st ed. dj. ....
.... *$650.00–$750.00*

Capote, Truman. *A Christmas Memory*. NY. (1966). 1st ed. slipcase.. *$80.00–$100.00*

Capote, Truman. *Breakfast at Tiffany's*. NY. (1958). wrps. dj............ *$175.00–$300.00*

Capote, Truman. *Grass Harp, A Play*. NY. (1952). 1st ed. dj............ *$150.00–$300.00*

Capote, Truman. *In Cold Blood*. NY. Random House. (1965). 1st ed. dj. ....
.... *$25.00–$30.00*

Capote, Truman. *Muses Are Heard*. Random House. (1956). 1st ed. dj. ....
.... *$75.00–$125.00*

Capote, Truman. *Other Voices, Other Rooms*. NY. Random House. (1948). 1st ed. dj..
.... *$225.00–$375.00*

Capote, Truman. *Thanksgiving Visitor*. Random House. 1967.............. *$24.00–$35.00*

Capp, Al. *Best of Li'l Abner*. NY. (1978). 1st ed. sgn, dj....................... *$25.00–$35.00*

Capp, Al. *Return of the Schmoo*. NY. 1959. 1st ed. wrps. .... *$28.00–$35.00*

Caputo, Philip. *Rumor of War*. NY. Rinehart & Winston. (1977). 1st ed. dj. ....
.... *$20.00–$30.00*

Caras, Roger. *Monarch of Deadman Bay—The Life and Death of a Kodiak Bear*. Bos. 1969. 1st ed. dj. .... *$10.00–$25.00*

Card, Orson Scott. *Ender's Game*. NY. TOR. 1985. 1st ed. scarce, dj............................
.... *$500.00–$675.00*

Care and Operation of Plows and Cultivators. Moline, IL. John Deere & Co. 1st ed. wrps. illus. .... *$50.00–$65.00*

Carey, A. Merwin. *American Firearms Makers to the End of the 19th Century*. NY. (1953). 1st ed. illus. dj... *$15.00–$25.00*

Carhart, Arthur H. *Fishing in the West*. NY. 1950. 1st ed. dj................. *$10.00–$15.00*

Carleton, Will. *Farm Ballads*. Harper. 1882. illus.................................... *$14.00–$25.00*

Carleton, Will. *Farm Festivals*. NY. 1881. .... *$20.00–$40.00*

Carleton, Will. *Farm Legends*. NY. 1875. .... *$20.00–$45.00*

Carleton, William. *Traits and Stories of the Irish Peasantry*. Dublin. 1843–4. 2 vols.....
.... *$115.00–$150.00*

Carlisle, D. *Belvedere Hounds*. Derrydale Press. 1935. ltd 1,250 cc, pictorial bds, glassine wrapper. .... *$75.00–$125.00*

Carlisle, Lillian Baker. *Vermont Clock and Watch Makers*. VT. 1970. 1st ed. ltd 1,000 cc, dj. .... *$40.00–$50.00*

Carmen, Carl. *French Town*. Pelican Pub. (1968). wrps. illus. presentation copy to Ralph Hill, VT writer. .... *$20.00–$40.00*

Carmer, Carl. *Deep South*. NY. 1930. 1st ed. sgn................................... *$25.00–$50.00*

Carmer, Carl. *Rivers of America: The Hudson*. NY. Farrar & Rinehart. 1939. illus. sgn.
.... *$40.00–$100.00*

Carnegie Endowment Report of the International Commission to Inquire Into the Causes and Conduct of the Balkan Wars. Wash. 1914. illus. maps........ *$15.00–$30.00*

Carnegie, Andrew. *Empire of Business*. NY. Doubleday Page. 1912. .... *$15.00–$25.00*

Carnegie, Andrew. *Round the World*. NY. 1884. 1st Amer trade ed....... *$35.00–$65.00*

Caron, Pierre. *French Dishes for American Tables*. NY. 1886. 1st ed.... *$25.00–$35.00*

Carpenter, Frank. *Alaska Our Northern Wonderland*. NY. 1928. illus. photos 2 fldg maps... *$25.00–$70.00*

Carpenter, Frank. *Mexico*. NY. 1928. illus. photos. .... *$25.00–$45.00*

Carpenter, R. *Game Trails from Alaska to Africa 1938*. private ptg. 1938. ltd 850 cc, sgn.
.... *$125.00–$150.00*

Carpenter, W. *Microscope and Its Revelations*. Phil. Blakiston's. 1901. illus................
.... *$85.00–$150.00*

Carpenter, W. *Microscope and Its Revelations*. Phila. 1856. illus. 1st Amer ed. ....
.... *$125.00–$175.00*

Carpenter, W. *Principles of Human Physiology*. Phila. 1853. 5th Amer ed. ....
.... *$35.00–$45.00*

Carpenter, William. *Microscope & Its Revelations.* Wood. 1883. 2 vols. .... *$90.00–$130.00*

Carr, Harry. *West Is Still Wild.* Bos. 1932. 1st ed. illus. .... *$25.00–$35.00*

Carr, James F. *Mantle Fielding's Dictionary of American Painters, Sculptors and Engravers.* NY. Carr. 1965. rev. .... *$80.00–$120.00*

Carr, John. *Pioneer Days in California: Historical and Personal Sketches.* Eureka. Times Publishing Co. 1891. 1st ed. .... *$125.00–$150.00*

Carr, John Dickson. *Arabian Nights Murder.* NY. 1936. 1st ed. .... *$45.00–$75.00*

Carr, John Dickson. *Death Turns the Tables.* NY. Harper & Bros. 1941. 1st ed. dj. .... *$200.00–$400.00*

Carr, John Dickson. *Third Bullet and Other Stories.* NY. Harper. 1st ed. 231 pp, dj. .... *$30.00–$50.00*

Carrick, Alice Van Leer. *Collector's Luck in England.* Bos. 1926. illus. *$25.00–$30.00*

Carrick, Alice Van Leer. *History of American Silhouettes . . . 1790–1840.* Rutland. (1968). dj. .... *$30.00–$50.00*

Carriker, M. A., Jr. *An Annotated List of the Birds of Costa Rica.* Carnegie Museum of Natural History. 1910. wrps. .... *$45.00–$60.00*

Carrington, Frances C. *Army Life on the Plains.* Phila. 1911. 2nd ed. . *$45.00–$65.00*

Carrington, Herny B. *Indian Question.* Bos. 1884. maps. .... *$225.00–$300.00*

Carroll, Jim. *Basketball Diaries.* Bolinas. (1978). 1st ed. wrps. .... *$280.00–$350.00*

Carroll, Jim. *Book of Nods.* NY. Viking. (1986). 1st ed. hardcvr, scarce, dj. .... *$70.00–$85.00*

Carroll, Jim. *Forced Entries.* NY. Penguin. (1987). 1st ed. wrps. .... *$30.00–$45.00*

Carroll, Jim. *Living at the Movies.* NY. Grossman. 1973. 1st ed. sgn, dj. .... *$175.00–$250.00*

Carroll, Lewis. *Alice in Wonderland.* Lon. Raphael Tuck & Sons. (1910). illus. by Mabel Lucie. 1st thus. scarce, green and gilt binding. .... *$720.00–$800.00*

Carroll, Lewis. *Alice's Adventures in Wonderland.* Bos. Lee and Shepard. 1869. 1st ed. illus. printed in America, 192 pp, green cloth, scarce. .... *$300.00–$500.00*

Carroll, Lewis. *Alice's Adventures in Wonderland.* NY/Lon. Harpers. 1901. illus. by Peter Newell. 1st thus. .... *$130.00–$200.00*

Carroll, Lewis. *Alice's Adventures in Wonderland and Through the Looking Glass.* Rand McNally. 1916. illus. by Milo Winter. clr plates, paste-down on cvr. .... *$35.00–$45.00*

Carroll, Lewis. *Alice's Adventures in Wonderland.* Doubleday. (1907). illus. by Arthur Rackham. .... *$95.00–$165.00*

Carroll, Lewis. *Annotated Alice.* NY. Bramhall House. (1970). illus. rust and buff cvr. pictorial dj. .... *$25.00–$30.00*

Carroll, Lewis. *Hunting of the Snark.* Lon. Macmillan. 1876. 1st ed. illus. by Henry Holiday. pictorial tan cloth. .... *$125.00–$375.00*

Carroll, Lewis. *Sylvie and Bruno.* Lon. 1893. 1st ed. illus. by Harry Furnise. .... *$100.00–$150.00*

Carroll, Lewis. *Through the Looking Glass.* Harper. 1902. illus. by Newell, 40 plates. . ... *$120.00–$130.00*

Carroll, Lewis. *Through the Looking Glass.* Lippincott. (1929). illus. by M Kirk.......... .... *$50.00–$85.00*

Carruth, Hayden. *Adventures of Jones.* NY. Harper. 1895. 1st ed. illus. *$25.00–$35.00*

Carruth, Hayden. *Contra Mortem.* VT. (1967). 1st ed. wrps. 1/250 cc, sgn.................. .... *$85.00–$120.00*

Carruth, Hayden. *Crow and the Heart.* Macmillan. 1959. 1st ed. dj..... *$30.00–$45.00*

Carruth, Haydn. *Mythology of Dark and Light.* NY. 1982. wrps. illus.. *$20.00–$30.00*

Carry, John. *Life of George Washington.* NY. 1807............................ *$95.00–$250.00*

Carson, Rachel. *Edge of the Sea.* Bos. 1955. 1st ed. dj. .... *$30.00–$75.00*

Carson, Rachel. *Silent Spring.* Houghton. 1962. 1st ed. dj.. .... *$55.00–$75.00*

Carson, Rachel. *Under the Sea Wind.* Lon. 1952. 1st ed. 1st thus. dj..... *$30.00–$50.00*

Carson, Rachel. *Under the Sea Wind.* NY. 1941. 1st ed. dj. .... *$100.00–$150.00*

Carter, Jimmy and Rosalynn Carter. *Everything to Gain.* NY. (1987). 1st ed. 2nd ptg, sgn by both. .... *$50.00–$100.00*

Cartier-Bresson, Henri. *Henri Cartier-Bresson Photographer.* Bos. New York Graphics Society. 1979. 1st ed. dj... *$85.00–$150.00*

Cartier-Bresson, Henri. *People of Moscow.* NY. 1955. 1st ed. illus. dj........................ .... *$75.00–$350.00*

Cartier-Brisson, Henri. *From One China to Another.* NY. (1956). 1st ed. dj. .... *$100.00–$125.00*

Cartier-Brisson, Henri. *The Europeans.* NY. (1955). folio pictorial bds. .... *$275.00–$500.00*

Carvalho, S. N. *Incidents of Travel and Adventure in the Far West.* NY. 1857.............. .... *$95.00–$250.00*

Carver, Jonathan. *Travels Through Interior Parts of No. America . . .1766, '67, '68.* Lon. 1781. 3rd ed. lea mor bkd clamshell case, hand-clr maps and plates............................ .... *$900.00–$2,000.00*

Carver, Raymond. *Cathedral.* NY. Knopf. 1983. 1st ed. dj................... *$35.00–$75.00*

Carver, Raymond. *Fires.* Santa Barbara. Capra Press. (1983). wrps...... *$45.00–$55.00*

Carver, Raymond. *New Path to the Waterfall.* NY. Atlantic Monthly Press. 1989. 1st ed. dj. .... *$30.00–$40.00*

Carver, Raymond. *No Heroics, Please.* Lon. Harvill. 1991. 1st ed. dj. *$30.00–$125.00*

Carver, Raymond. *No Heroics, Please.* NY. Vantage. 1992. paperback. *$16.00–$50.00*

Carver, Raymond. *Put Yourself in My Shoes.* NY. 1981. 1st ed. dj. .. *$150.00–$200.00*

Carver, Raymond. *The Toes.* Ewert. 1988. 1st ed. wrps. wrps 26 cc. *$175.00–$125.00*

Carver, Raymond. *This Water.* Concord. Ewert. 1985. wrps. 1/100 sgn cc of an ed of 136 cc... *$135.00–$200.00*

Carver, Raymond. *Ultramarine.* NY. Random House. 1986. 1st ed. dj, sgn.................
.... *$200.00–$300.00*

Carver, Raymond. *Ultramarine.* NY. Random House. 1986. 1st ed. dj. ....
.... *$75.00–$100.00*

Carver, Raymond. *What We Talk About When We Talk About Love.* NY. Knopf. 1981.
1st ed. dj. .... *$95.00–$200.00*

Carver, Raymond. *Where I'm Calling From.* PA. The Franklin Library. 1988. sgn, from
the First Edition Society. .... *$175.00–$200.00*

Carver, Raymond. *Where I'm Calling From.* NY. Atlantic Monthly Press. (1988). 1st ed.
dj. .... *$35.00–$45.00*

Carver, Raymond. *Will You Please Be Quiet, Please.* NY. 1976. 1st ed. dj. ....
.... *$300.00–$450.00*

Cary, Elisabeth Luther. *Works of James McNeill Whistler.* NY. 1907. 1st ed. illus.......
.... *$30.00–$45.00*

Casey, Robert J. *Black Hills and Their Incredible Characters.* Ind. (1949)....................
.... *$20.00–$30.00*

Casey, Robert J. *Texas Border.* Bobbs Merrill. (1950). 1st ed. illus. photos, ltd, sgn, dj.
.... *$25.00–$40.00*

Cassidy, Carl (compiler). *History of the 775th Bombardment Squadron.* IA. 1982. illus.
rprint, 300 cc, sgn. .... *$95.00–$125.00*

Cassill, R. V. *Goss Women.* Doubleday. 1974. 1st ed. dj. .... *$22.00–$27.00*

Cassino, Samuel E., (ed.). *Naturalist's Directory.* Bos. 1884. .... *$20.00–$25.00*

Casson, Herbert N. *Romance of the Reaper.* NY. 1908. illus................ *$18.00–$30.00*

Casson, Herbert N. *Romance of the Reaper.* NY. Doubleday, Page. 1908. 1st ed. illus.
.... *$45.00–$50.00*

Castaneda, Carlos. *Silent Years in Texas History.* Austin. 1934. wrps. sgn.....................
.... *$18.00–$25.00*

Castenada, Carlos. *Teachings of Don Juan.* Berkeley. 1968. 1st ed. dj.........................
.... *$90.00–$150.00*

Castle, Henry A. *Army Mule and Other War Sketches.* Ind. 1898. illus. *$50.00–$75.00*

Castleman, Alfred. *Army of the Potomac.* Milw. 1863........................ *$100.00–$175.00*

Caswell, J. *Sporting Rifles & Rifle Shooting.* 1920. 1st ed. illus. photos. *$24.00–$35.00*

Catalogue and Price List for 1922 of Fireworks . . . Bos. The Masten & Wells Fireworks
Mfg Co. 1922. red printed wrps, 32 pp... *$35.00–$50.00*

Catalogue No. 16. Havana, IL. Havana Metal Wheel Co. nd. wrps. illus......................
$50.00–$65.00

Catalogue No. R-52, Rosettes, Ornaments, . . . Akron, OH. The Enterprise Mfg. Co.
1932. wrps. illus. .... *$30.00–$45.00*

*Catalogue of Drugs Chemicals, Dye Stuffs, Druggists' Sundries, Proprietary
Medicines, Oils, Paints* . . . Burlington, VT. Wells, Richardson & Co. 1878. pebbled
cloth. .... *$95.00–$125.00*

Catalogue of Hardy Fruit Trees and Plants . . . Sioux Falls, Dak Terr. E DeBell. 1884. illus. self-printed wrps, 8 pp.. *$75.00–$100.00*

Catalogue of Microscopes and Accessories. Microtomes. Bacteriological Apparatus. Laboratory Supplies . . . *5th edition*. Phila. Charles Lentz & Sons. 1899. printed wrps, illus, 136 pp. .... *$125.00–$175.00*

Catalogue of Weathervanes, No 9. Waltham, MA. L W Cushing & Sons. 1883. decorative wrps, illus, 20 pp... *$500.00–$750.00*

Catalogues of Birds, Eggs . . . Nat'l Museum of Rhodesia. 1970. stiff wrps scarce........ .... *$50.00–$60.00*

Cate, Wirt Armistead. *Lucius Q.C. Lamar: Secession and Reunion*. Chapel Hill. 1935. 1st ed. illus.. *$30.00–$50.00*

Cather, Willa. *April Twilights*. Bos. Richard G Badger/The Gorham Press. 1903. 1st ed. author's first book, paper cvred bds, paper spine label, uncut, sgn...................... .... *$1,500.00–$2,500.00*

Cather, Willa. *Death Comes for the Archbishop*. Knopf. 1927. 1st ed. dj. .... *$125.00–$200.00*

Cather, Willa. *Death Comes to the Archbishop*. NY. Knopf. 1927. 1st trade, dj, incsrb.. .... *$800.00–$1,000.00*

Cather, Willa. *Gayheart*. NY. 1935. 1/749 cc sgn dj.......................... *$300.00–$400.00*

Cather, Willa. *Lost Lady*. NY. Knopf. 1923. 1st ed................................ *$30.00–$40.00*

Cather, Willa. *My Mortal Enemy*. NY. Knopf. 1926. 1st ed. chipped dj....................... .... *$125.00–$350.00*

Cather, Willa. *Obscure Destiny*. NY. 1932. 1st ed. dj. .... *$40.00–$50.00*

Cather, Willa. *Old Beauty and Others*. NY. 1948. 1st ed. dj................... *$35.00–$65.00*

Cather, Willa. *Professor's House*. NY. 1925. 1st ed. .... *$100.00–$200.00*

Cather, Willa. *Sapphira and the Slave Girl*. NY. 1940. 1st ed. dj.......... *$45.00–$85.00*

Cather, Willa. *Shadows on the Rock*. Knopf. 1931. 1st ed. dj............. *$100.00–$125.00*

Cather, Willa. *Youth and the Bright Medusa*. NY. Knopf. 1920. 1st ed. dj..................... .... *$100.00–$250.00*

Catholic Encyclopedia. NY. Appleton-Encyclopedia Press. 1907–14. 10 vols. ¾ lea. .... *$475.00–$525.00*

Catlin, George. *Illustrations of the Manners, Customs and Condition of the North American Indians: In a Series of Letters and Notes* . . . Lon. Henry G Bohn. 1845. 2 vols. illus. 5th ed. .... *$750.00–$1,250.00*

Catlin, George. *Letters and Notes on the North American Indians*. NY. (1965). 2 vols. illus. .... *$50.00–$75.00*

Catlin, George. *Life Amongst the Indians*. Lon. 1861. 14 plates. .... *$50.00–$125.00*

Catlin, George. *North American Indian Portfolio*. Chi. Swallow Press. (1970). folio, rprnt of earlier ed.. *$700.00–$1,400.00*

Catlin, George. *North American Indians*. Edin. John Grant. 1926. 2 vols...................... .... *$1,200.00–$1,400.00*

Catlin, George. *North American Indians*. Phil. Leary, Stuart & Co. 1913. 2 vols. illus. ex library, red cloth.. *$80.00–$100.00*

Catlin, George. *North American Indians: Being Letters and Notes on Their Manners, Customs, and Conditions*. NY. Dover Pub. 1973. 2 vols. illus. .... *$35.00–$80.00*

Catlin, George. *Story of the Political Philosophers*. NY. 1939. dj.......... *$30.00–$35.00*

Catton, Bruce. *Banners of Shenandoah*. Garden City. 1955. illus. dj..... *$30.00–$40.00*

Catton, Bruce. *Centennial History of the Civil War*. NY. Doubleday. 1961–65. 3 vols. 1st ed. dj, ... *$30.00–$45.00*

Catton, Bruce. *Grant Moves South*. Bos/Tor. 1960. 1st ed. illus. presentation copy, sgn, dj. .... *$30.00–$40.00*

Catton, Bruce. *Terrible Swift Sword*. Garden City. 1963. 1st ed. dj. ...... *$15.00–$22.00*

Caverly, A. M. *History of the Town of Pittsford, Vermont*. Rutland. 1872. illus. rbnd,.... .... *$80.00–$95.00*

Centennial History of Lemhi County, Idaho. Salmon. 1992. Vols 1–3. 1st ed. illus. photos... *$60.00–$75.00*

Century Company War Book. *Battles and Leaders of the Civil War*. NY. 1884–1887. 4 vols.. *$75.00–$100.00*

Cervantes, Miguel de. *History of Don Quixote*. Lon. Gustav Dore. illus. lea bound...... .... *$100.00–$150.00*

Cescinsky, Herbert and Ernest Gribble. *Early English Furniture and Woodwork*. Lon. 1927. 2 vols. illus. folio, lea. .... *$135.00–$200.00*

Chadwick, Lee. *Lighthouses and Lightships*. Lon. 1971. illus. photos, dj...................... .... *$25.00–$33.00*

Chagall, Marc. *Drawings and Watercolors for the Ballet*. NY. (1969). 1st ed. 1 orig litho, dj, slipcase... *$200.00–$250.00*

Chagall, Marc. *Jerusalem Windows*. George Braziller. (1962). 2 orig lithos by Chagall, red cloth, gilt, dj. .... *$1,380.00–$1,500.00*

Chagall, Marc. *Lithographs V*. NY. 1974–1979. 1st Amer ed. .... *$40.00–$60.00*

Chalfant, W. A. *Gold Guns & Ghost Towns*. Stanford. 1947. .... *$25.00–$35.00*

Chamberlain, George A. *African Hunting Among the Thongas*. NY. 1923. 1st ed. illus. .... *$45.00–$65.00*

Chamberlain, Jacob. *Cobra's Den*. Revell. (1900). illus. .... *$22.00–$35.00*

Chamberlain, Samuel. *Open House in New England*. Brattleboro, NH. 1939. sgn........ .... *$18.00–$20.00*

Chamberlain, Samuel. *Rockefeller Center*. 1947. photos, dj................. *$10.00–$18.00*

Chamberlain, Samuel, and Narcissa Chamberlain. *Southern Interiors of Charleston, South Carolina*. NY. Hastings House. (1956). illus. 172 pp. .... *$30.00–$40.00*

Chamberlayne, Churchill Gibson (ed.). *Vestry Book of Bristol Parish . . .* Richmond. private ptg. 1892. 251/500 cc inscribed. .... *$90.00–$100.00*

Chamberlin, Lt. Col. Harry D. *Training Hunters, Jumpers and Hacks*. NY. Derrydale. 1937. ltd #935/950.. *$65.00–$130.00*

Chambers, E. T. D. *Ouananiche and Its Canadian Environment.* Harper & Bros. 1896. 1st ed. .... *$85.00–$120.00*

Chambers, Thomas King. *Renewal of Life.* Phil. Lindsay & Blakiston. 1866. .... *$40.00–$50.00*

Chandler, Raymond. *Backfire: Story for the Screen.* CA. 1984. 1st ed. 1/200 cc, softcvr, sgn, presentation. .... *$85.00–$125.00*

Chandler, Raymond. *Big Sleep.* NY. Knopf. 1939. 1st ed. fine, dj, cloth box. .... *$3,500.00–$75.00*

Chandler, Raymond. *Big Sleep.* 1946. movie ed. .... *$15.00–$25.00*

Chandler, Raymond. *Big Sleep.* Knopf. 1939. 1st ed. no dj. .... *$215.00–$250.00*

Chandler, Raymond. *Big Sleep.* Avon. 1943. pbk #38. .... *$50.00–$65.00*

Chandler, Raymond. *Farewell My Lovely.* NY. Knopf. 1940. 1st ed. no dj. .... *$250.00–$375.00*

Chandler, Raymond. *Farewell My Lovely.* NY. Knopf. 1940. 1st ed. dj. .... *$1,500.00–$2,000.00*

Chandler, Raymond. *High Window.* NY. Knopf. 1942. 1st ed. dj. .... *$85.00–$100.00*

Chandler, Raymond. *Lady in the Lake.* NY. Knopf. 1943. 1st ed. dj. .... *$700.00–$1,500.00*

Chandler, Raymond. *Little Sister.* Houghton Mifflin. 1949. 1st Amer ed. dj. .... *$150.00–$350.00*

Chandler, Raymond. *Long Goodbye.* Bos. Houghton Mifflin. 1954. 1st ed. dj. .... *$275.00–$500.00*

Chandler, Raymond. *Playback.* Lon. Hamish Hamilton. 1958. 1st ed. dj. .... *$250.00–$300.00*

Chandler, Raymond. *Red Wind.* Cleve. World. 1946. 1st ed. dj. .... *$50.00–$100.00*

Chandler, Raymond. *Simple Art of Murder.* NY. Norton. 1968. 1st ed. dj. .... *$50.00–$100.00*

Chandler, Raymond. *Smell of Fear.* Lon. Hamish Hamilton. 1965. 1st ed. dj. .... *$200.00–$300.00*

Channing, William. *Slavery.* Bos. 1835. 1st ed. .... *$75.00–$125.00*

Channing, William Ellery. *Slavery.* Bos. 1835. 1st ed. .... *$50.00–$68.00*

Chanslor, Torrey. *Our First Murder.* Stokes. 1940. 1st ed. dj. .... *$50.00–$75.00*

Chapel, C. E. *Boy's Book of Rifles.* 1948. .... *$18.00–$25.00*

Chapelle, Howard I. *History of American Sailing Ships.* NY. W W Norton. 1935. 1st trade ed. illus, plates, photos, ship drawings. .... *$30.00–$50.00*

Chapelle, Howard I. *History of American Sailing Ships.* NY. 1949. illus. photos, plates, dj. .... *$25.00–$35.00*

Chapelle, Howard I. *Yacht Designing and Plannning.* Norton. (1936). 1st ed. illus. .... *$20.00–$30.00*

Chaplin, R. *Wobbly.* Chi. (1948). presentation copy, dj. .... *$30.00–$50.00*

Chapman, A. *On Safari.* Lon. 1908. illus. photos. .... *$150.00–$300.00*

Chapman, Allen. *Bound to Succeed or Mail Order Franks Chances*. OH. Goldsmith. 1907. cloth. .... *$12.00–$17.00*

Chapman, Allen. *Radio Boys First Wireless*. Grosset & Dunlap. (1922). series #1, dj. ... . *$27.00–$35.00*

Chapman, Allen. *Radio Boys Trailing a Voice*. Grosset & Dunlap. 1922. 1st ed. series #5. .... *$15.00–$35.00*

Chapman, Allen. *Radio Boys with the Flood Fighters*. Grosset & Dunlap. 1925. 1st ed. series #8. .... *$25.00–$30.00*

Chapman, Allen. *Radio Boys with the Forest Rangers*. Grosset & Dunlap. 1923. 1st ed. series #6. .... *$20.00–$25.00*

Chapman, Allen. *Radio Boys with the Iceberg Patrol*. Grosset & Dunlap. 1924. 1st ed. Radio Boys #7, dj. .... *$28.00–$30.00*

Chapman, Charles E. *History of California: The Spanish Period*. NY. 1921. illus. maps. .... *$40.00–$50.00*

Chapman, F. Spencer. *Northern Lights*. NY. 1933. illus. 1st Amer ed. fldg map. .... *$60.00–$75.00*

Chapman, F. M. *Distribution of Bird Life in Ecuador*. NY. 1926. 29 plates, fldg map (Bulletin Amer Museum of Natural History, V 55). .... *$140.00–$170.00*

Chapman, Frank. *Bird Life*. NY. Appleton. 1898. illus. by E S Thompson. pictorial cloth. .... *$60.00–$70.00*

Chapman, Frank. *Warblers of North America*. NY. Appleton. 1907. illus. .... *$30.00–$45.00*

Chapman, Olive Murray. *Across Iceland, the Land of Frost and Fire*. Lon/NY. 1930. 1st ed. illus. .... *$40.00–$95.00*

Chapman, Priscilla. *Hindoo Female Education*. Lon. Seeley & Burnside. 1839. 1st ed. 4 engr illus. .... *$100.00–$150.00*

Chapone, Mary. *Letters on the Improvement of the Mind*. NY. Richard Scott. 1819. small frontis. .... *$50.00–$125.00*

Chappell, Fred. *Dagon*. NY. Harcourt Brace World. (1968). 1st ed. 177 pp, dj. .... *$35.00–$45.00*

Chappelle, Howard I. *Boatbuilding*. NY. Norton. 1941. 1st ed. illus. plans, dj. .... *$35.00–$50.00*

Chapple, H. Barton. *Popular Television*. 1935. 1st ed. illus. dj. .... *$45.00–$60.00*

Chaptal, M. F. A. *Elements of Chemistry*. Buckingham. 1806. 3 vols in. 3rd Amer ed. 612 pp, calf. .... *$100.00–$135.00*

Chardin, Sir John. *Travels in Persia*. Lon. 1927. illus. ltd 975 cc. ..... *$125.00–$225.00*

Charney, Desire. *Ancient Cities of the New World*. NY. Harper & Bros. 1887. illus. 1st US ed. illus. fldg map, 35 plates, text illus, cloth, red lea label. .... *$125.00–$200.00*

Charteris, Leslie. *Call For the Saint*. Garden City. Doubleday Crime Club. (1948). 1st ed. dj. .... *$50.00–$75.00*

Charteris, Leslie. *Last Hero*. Garden City. Doubleday. 1930. 1st ed. dj. *$25.00–$50.00*

Charteris, Leslie. *Saint Goes West*. Garden City. 1943. 1st ed. pictorial dj. .... *$60.00–$85.00*

Charteris, Leslie. *Saint in Miami*. Doubleday. 1940. 1st ed. dj. .... *$100.00–$175.00*

Charteris, Leslie. *Saint Overboard*. NY. Triangle. 1936. dj. .... *$15.00–$45.00*

Charteris, Leslie. *Saint Sees it Through*. Garden City. Doubleday. 1946. 1st ed. dj. ......
.... *$60.00–$75.00*

Charteris, Leslie. *Saint Steps In*. Triangle Books. 1943 .... *$9.00–$15.00*

Charteris, Leslie. *Saint to the Rescue*. Hodder & Stoughton. 1961. 1st UK ed. dj. ....
.... *$50.00–$75.00*

Charteris, Leslie. *Tar Baby*. NY. Holt, Rinehart & Winston. 1973. 1st ed. dj. ....
.... *$40.00–$55.00*

Charteris, Leslie. *Thanks to the Saint*. Lon. Hodder & Stoughton. 1958. 1st ed. dj. ......
.... *$30.00–$125.00*

Charteris, Leslie. *Trust the Saint*. Hodder & Stoughton. 1st UK ed. dj. *$50.00–$75.00*

Charters, Ann. *Kerouac*. (1974). 1st Eng ed. wraps, dj. .... *$30.00–$50.00*

Chase, A. *Dr. Chase's Recipes*. Ann Arbor. 1866. .... *$30.00–$45.00*

Chase, Edward. *Memorial Life of General William Tecumseh Sherman*. Chi. 1891. 1st
ed. .... *$40.00–$85.00*

Chase, J. *California Desert Trails*. Bos. (1919). 1st ed. .... *$25.00–$40.00*

Chase, J. Smeaton. *Yosemite Trails*. Bos. Houghton Mifflin. 1911. map, 16 plates. ....
.... *$30.00–$45.00*

Chase, J. Smeaton. *Yosemite Trails. Camp & Pack-train in the Yosemite Region . . .* Bos.
Houghton Mifflin. 1911. 16 plates. .... *$50.00–$65.00*

Chase, Mary. *Benjamin Lee, 2d: A Record Gathered From Letters, Notebooks, and
Narratives of Friends*. Bos. 1920. photos. .... *$45.00–$65.00*

Chase, Mary Ellen. *Fishing Fleets of New England*. Bos. 1961. illus. .... *$22.00–$35.00*

Chase, Peter S. *Reunion Greeting . . . Complete Description List of the Members of C1
2nd Regt, Vt Vols*. Brattleboro. 1891. .... *$45.00–$80.00*

Chastellux, Francois J. (Marquis de). *Travels in North America in the Years 1780,
1781, and 1782*. Lon. Robinson. 1787. 2 vols. 1st End ed. 2 fldg maps, 3 plates, new ¼
brown calf, marbled bds, red labels. .... *$600.00–$725.00*

Chastellux, Marquis de. *Travels in North America in the Years 1780, 1781, and 1782*.
Chapel Hill. Univ North Carolina Press. 1963. 2 vols. slipcase. .... *$65.00–$85.00*

Chatelain, Verne. *Defenses of Spanish Florida, 1565 to 1763*. Wash. 1941. 1st ed. illus.
fldg maps and plates. .... *$50.00–$75.00*

Chatham, Russell. *Angler's Coast*. Doubleday. 1976. 1st ed. dj. .... *$25.00–$40.00*

Chatterton, E. Keble. *Brotherhood of the Sea*. Lon. Longmans Green. 1927. 1st ed.
illus. endpaper maps. .... *$45.00–$60.00*

Chatterton, E. Keble. *Sailing Models Ancient and Modern*. Lon. 1934. 1st ed. ....
.... *$75.00–$125.00*

Chatwin, Bruce. *On the Black Hills*. NY. Viking. 1983. 1st ed. dj. .... *$30.00–$35.00*

Chavez, Fray Angelico. *Cathedral of the Royal City of the Holy Faith of Saint Francis*.
Santa Fe. 1947. 1st ed. wrps. illus. photos, drawings. .... *$32.00–$40.00*

Chavez, Fray Angelico. *Clothed with the Sun.* Santa Fe. 1939. 1st ed. dj sgn. .... *$125.00–$150.00*

Chavez, Fray Angelico. *Eleven Lady-Lyrics and Other Poems.* Paterson, NJ. 1945. 1st ed. sgn presentation copy, dj. .... *$65.00–$75.00*

Chavez, Fray Angelico. *New Mexico Tryptych.* Paterson, NJ. 1940. 1st ed. illus. by Chavez. dj. .... *$40.00–$50.00*

Chavez, Fray Angelico. *Single Rose. The Rosa Unica and Commentary of Fray Manuel De Santa Clara.* Santa Fe. 1948. 1st ed. stiff wrapper with dj. .... *$25.00–$35.00*

Chavez, Fray Angelico. *Song of Frances.* Flagstaff. (1973). 1st ed. illus. sgn, dj. .... *$30.00–$40.00*

Chayefsky, Paddy. *Altered States.* NY. 1978. 1st ed. dj. .... *$28.00–$35.00*

Cheever, John. *Bridgadier and the Golf Widow.* NY. Harper & Row. (1964). 1st ed. sgn, dj. .... *$95.00–$125.00*

Cheever, John. *Brigadier and the Golf Widow.* NY. (1964). 1st ed. dj. .. *$35.00–$80.00*

Cheever, John. *Bullet Park.* NY. Knopf. 1969. 1st ed. sgn, dj. .... *$85.00–$100.00*

Cheever, John. *Enormous Radio.* NY. 1953. 1st ed. dj. "1" on copyright page.............. .... *$75.00–$200.00*

Cheever, John. *Leaves, the Lion-Fish & the Bear.* Sylvester & Orphanos. 1980. 1/300 cc sgn. .... *$90.00–$130.00*

Cheever, John. *Oh What a Paradise It Seems.* NY. 1982. 1st ed. dj. ...... *$20.00–$25.00*

Cheever, John. *Wapshot Chronicle.* Lon. Gollancz. 1957. 1st ed. dj. ... *$75.00–$100.00*

Cheever, John. *Wapshot Chronicle.* The Franklin Library. (1978). 1st ed. sgn............... .... *$45.00–$125.00*

Cheever, John. *Way Some People Live.* NY. (1943). 1st ed. author's first book............. .... *$850.00–$925.00*

Cheever, John. *World of Apples.* NY. Knopf. 1973. 1st ed. dj. .... *$25.00–$35.00*

Cheiro. *Palmistry For All.* NY. 1916. .... *$10.00–$18.00*

Chekov, Anton. *Cherry Orchard.* Brentanos. 1923. black, red and beige cvr. .... *$75.00–$95.00*

Chekov, Anton. *The Kiss.* NY. 1915. dark green cloth dj. .... *$50.00–$60.00*

Chekov, Anton. *Two Plays: The Cherry Orchard, Three Sisters.* NY. Ltd Ed Club. 1966. illus. 1/1500 cc, sgn by Szalay, slipcase. .... *$40.00–$50.00*

Chekov, Anton. *Uncle Vanya.* NY. Covici Friede. 1930. 1st ed. .... *$75.00–$100.00*

Chennault, Anna. *Chennault and the Flying Tigers.* NY. 1963. photos, maps............... .... *$25.00–$35.00*

Chennault, Claire. *Way of a Fighter: Memoirs of Claire Lee Chennault.* NY. 1949. photos.. *$30.00–$40.00*

Chenu, Charles Maurice. *My Canoe.* Lon. Partridge. 1931. 1st ed. sgn...................... .... *$80.00–$160.00*

Chenu, J. C. *Manuel Conchyliogie et de Paleontologie Conchyliogique.* Paris. 1859–62. 1 vol. illus. ½ mor... *$150.00–$210.00*

Chesterton, G. K. *Ballad of the White Horse.* 1911............................... *$30.00–$37.00*

Chesterton, G. K. *Man Who Knew Too Much.* Lon. Cassell & Co. 1922....................... .... *$25.00–$50.00*

Chicago School of Architecture. Random House. 1964. dj.................... *$25.00–$45.00*

Chichester, Francis. *Lonely Sea and the Sky.* Lon. Hodder & Stoughton. 1967. illus. 352 pp, dj.. *$25.00–$35.00*

Chief Standing Bear. *My People, the Sioux.* Bos. 1928. 2nd ptg, dj. ..... *$35.00–$40.00*

Child's Garden of Verses. Saalfield. 1949. illus. by Fern Bissel Peat. .... *$25.00–$35.00*

Child, Hamilton. *Gazeteer and Business Directory of Bennington County, VT for 1880–1881.* Syracuse. 1880. fldg map, cloth.. *$100.00–$125.00*

Child, Hamilton. *Gazeteer and Business Directory of Cattaraugus County, NY for 1874–1875.* Syracuse. Child. 1874. 1st ed.................................. *$60.00–$75.00*

Child, Hamilton. *Gazeteer and Business Directory of Crawford County, PA for 1874.* Syracuse. 1874. rbnd. .... *$110.00–$125.00*

Child, Hamilton. *Gazeteer and Business Directory of Sullivan County, NY for 1872–1873.* Rock Hill. Fallsburg Printing. 1975. rprnt. #63/1,029 cc. ... *$50.00–$75.00*

Child, Hamilton. *Gazetteer and Business Directory of Rensselaer County, NY, 1870-71.* .... *$55.00–$85.00*

Child, Hamilton. *Gazetteer and Business Directory of Alleghany County, NY for 1875.* Syracuse. Journal Office. 1875. fldg map.................................. *$50.00–$60.00*

Child, Hamilton. *Gazetteer and Business Directory of Orange County, VT 1762-1888.* Syracuse. 1888. illus. spine replaced. .... *$75.00–$85.00*

Child, Hamilton. *Gazetteer and Business Directory of Windham County, VT.* Syracuse. 1884. illus. 624 pp. .... *$75.00–$125.00*

Child, L. Maria. *American Frugal Housewife.* NY. Samuel & William Wood. 1836. 20th ed. bds... *$185.00–$200.00*

Child, L. Maria. *Letters from New York.* NY/Bos. Francis. 1843. 1st ed. 288 pp, 1/1500 cc.. *$75.00–$125.00*

Child, L. Maria. *Letters from New York.* NY. 1849. 10th ed................... *$20.00–$30.00*

Child, L. Maria. *New Flower for Children.* NY. Francis & Co. 1856. 1st ed. cloth. .... *$200.00–$225.00*

Child, L. Maria. *Right Way, the Safe Way . . .* NY. 1860. wrps.............. *$25.00–$35.00*

Child, Maria. *Freedman's Book.* Bos. 1865. 1st ed. green stamped cloth...................... .... *$250.00–$300.00*

Child, Mrs. *American Frugal Housewife.* NY. Wood. 1847.................... *$45.00–$60.00*

Child, Mrs. Lydia M. *An Appeal in Favor of that Class of Americans Called Africans.* MA. Amhurst. 1996. rprnt.. *$8.00–$20.00*

Child, Mrs. Lydia M. *An Appeal in Favor of that Class of Americans Called Africans.* NY. 1836.. *$90.00–$115.00*

Child, William. *History of the Fifth Regiment, N.H. Vol., in Amer. Civ. War.* Bristol. 1893. .... *$100.00–$150.00*

Children and Animals. Wisc. Whitman Pub Co. (1935). 1st ed. illus. oblong pictorial wrps designed by Lotte Schmeil School of Emmy Zweybruck Vienna — art deco. ....
.... *$45.00–$125.00*

Children of God: An American Epic. NY. 1939. 1st ed. map endsheets, dj. ....
.... *$45.00–$50.00*

Children's Picture Book of Birds. NY. Harper. 1861. 1st ed. illus. engrs. blue pebbled cloth. .... *$65.00–$85.00*

Childress, Alice. *A Hero Ain't Nothin' But a Sandwich*. NY. 1973. sgn.. *$45.00–$50.00*

Childress, Alice. *Like One of the Family*. Brooklyn. (1956). 1st ed. dj. *$75.00–$100.00*

Childs, Harold. *Child's Book of Abridged Wisdom*. SF. Paul Elder. (1905). illus. pictorial bds, exposed spine. .... *$75.00–$150.00*

Chilton Automotive Directory. Oct, 1918. clr ads, 770 pp. .... *$45.00–$65.00*

Chiniquy, Father (Charles). *Priest, a Woman, and the Confessional*. Chi. Craig. 1888. 296 pp. .... *$22.00–$35.00*

Chipman, N. P. *Tragedy of Andersonville, Trial of Captain Henry Wirz* . . . Sac. 1911. 2nd ed. .... *$50.00–$65.00*

Chittenden, Hiram. *Yellowstone National Park*. Stanford. 1933. rev. ....
.... *$60.00–$70.00*

Chittenden, Hiram M. *American Fur Trade of the Far West*. NY. Harper. 1902. 3 vols. map plates. .... *$575.00–$900.00*

Chittenden, Hiram M. *History of Early Steamboat Navigation on the Missouri River* . . . NY. 1903. 2 vols. ltd 950 cc. .... *$350.00–$500.00*

Chittenden, Hiram M. *History of the American Fur Trade of the Far West*. Stanford. (1954). 2 vols. rprnt, maps, djs. .... *$75.00–$125.00*

Chittenden, Hiram M. and A. T Richardson. *Life, Letters and Travels of Father Pierre-Jean De Smet*. NY. 1905. 4 vols. .... *$400.00–$850.00*

Chopin, Kate. *Bayou Folk*. Bos. Houghton, Mifflin. 1894. 1st ed. scarce. ....
.... *$300.00–$950.00*

Chopin, Kate. *The Awakening*. Chi & NY. Herbert S Stone. 1899. cx-lib, scarce...........
.... *$500.00–$1,000.00*

Chopin, Kate. *The Awakening*. Chi. Herbert Stone. 1899. 1st ed. decorated cloth, scarce.
.... *$700.00–$1,500.00*

Chrichton, Michael. *Andromeda Strain*. NY. Knopf. 1969. 1st ed. dj.. *$78.00–$135.00*

Chrichton, Michael. *Jurassic Park*. NY. Knopf. 1990. 1st trade ed. dj. *$35.00–$60.00*

Chrichton, Michael (as Michael Douglas). *Dealing or the Berkeley-to-Boston Forty-Brick Lost-Bag Blues*. NY. Knopf. 1971. 1st ed. scarce, dj. .... *$140.00–$150.00*

Chrichton, Michael (as Michael Douglas). *Eaters of the Dead*. NY. Knopf. 1976. 1st ed. dj. .... *$35.00–$45.00*

Christensen, David (ed.). *Peace Corps*. 1966. 10 monographs wrps. ..... *$30.00–$40.00*

Christian Spectator for the Year 1820. New Haven. Howe & Spaulding. Vol 11. ¾ lea and bds. .... *$35.00–$50.00*

Christie, Agatha. *Adventures of the Christmas Pudding*. Lon. Crime Club 1960. dj. .... *$25.00–$35.00*

Christie, Agatha. *And Then There Were None*. NY. Grosset & Dunlap. Photoplay ed. dj. .... *$50.00–$75.00*

Christie, Agatha. *At Bertram's Hotel*. Dodd Mead. 1966. 1st US ed. dj. *$30.00–$50.00*

Christie, Agatha. *At Bertram's Hotel*. Lon. 1965. 1st ed. dj. .... *$35.00–$55.00*

Christie, Agatha. *Big Four*. NY. 1927. 1st Amer ed. dj. .... *$100.00–$125.00*

Christie, Agatha. *Cards on the Table*. Lon. 1936. 1st ed. .... *$200.00–$300.00*

Christie, Agatha. *Cards on the Table*. NY. Dodd Mead. 1937. 1st Amer ed. dj. .... *$300.00–$375.00*

Christie, Agatha. *Caribbean Mystery*. NY. Dodd, Mead. 1965. 1st Amer ed. dj. .... *$20.00–$35.00*

Christie, Agatha. *Death Comes As the End*. Collins. 1945. 1st ed. dj. .... *$125.00–$175.00*

Christie, Agatha. *Easy to Kill*. NY. Dodd Mead. 1939. 1st ed. dj. ..... *$175.00–$250.00*

Christie, Agatha. *Mirror Crack'd From Side to Side*. Lon. Crime Club. (1962). 1st ed. fine, dj. .... *$75.00–$125.00*

Christie, Agatha. *Miss Marple's Final Cases*. Lon. 1979. 1st ed. dj. ..... *$35.00–$45.00*

Christie, Agatha. *Murder in Mesopotamia*. NY. 1936. 1st ed. .... *$45.00–$60.00*

Christie, Agatha. *Pale Horse*. NY. 1962. 1st ed. 1st US ed. dj. .... *$20.00–$30.00*

Christie, Agatha. *Partners in Crime*. NY. Dodd Mead. 1929. 1st ed. dj. *$60.00–$85.00*

Christie, Agatha. *Sleeping Murder*. NY. Dodd, Mead. 1976. 1st US ed. dj. .... *$15.00–$25.00*

Christie, Agatha. *Sleeping Murder*. NY. Dodd, Mead. 1976. 1st ed. dj.. *$10.00–$15.00*

Christie, Agatha. *They Do It With Mirrors*. Lon. Collins Crime Club. 1952. 1st ed. dj.. .... *$75.00–$100.00*

Christie, Agatha. *Thirteen at Dinner*. NY. Dodd Mead. 1933. 1st ed. dj. .... *$295.00–$350.00*

Christie, Agatha. *Towards Zero*. Lon. Crime Club. (1944). 1st ed. fine, scarce, dj......... .... *$350.00–$400.00*

Christmas Carols. Akron. (1937). illus. by Fern Bisel Peat. scarce dj. . *$95.00–$125.00*

Christmas on Stage. Polygraphic Company of America. 1950. 5 pop-ups, spiral bound. .... *$35.00–$55.00*

Christopher, Catherine. *Complete Book of Doll Making and Collecting*. NY. Greystone Press. (1949). 1st ed. illus. .... *$10.00–$25.00*

Christy, Howard Chandler. *Christy Girl*. Bobbs-Merrill. (1906). illus. decorative binding, clr plates. .... *$50.00–$85.00*

Church, James R. *University Football*. NY. 1893. illus. .... *$150.00–$175.00*

Churchill, Frank G. *Practical and Scientific Horseshoeing*. Missouri. Franklin Hudson. 1912. 1st ed.. *$85.00–$95.00*

Churchill, Winston. *Blood Sweat and Tears*. Putnam. 1941. .... *$15.00–$25.00*

Churchill, Winston. *Great Contemporaries*. NY. 1937. 1st US ed......... *$50.00–$85.00*

Churchill, Winston. *History of the English-Speaking Peoples*. Lon. 1956–58. 4 vols. 1st ed. djs... *$175.00–$200.00*

Churchill, Winston. *Liberalism & the Social Problems*. Lon. 1909. 1st UK ed. .... *$400.00–$800.00*

Churchill, Winston. *Second World War*. Lon. 1948–54. 6 vols. 1st ed. djs.................... .... *$125.00–$275.00*

Churchill, Winston. *While England Slept*. NY. 1938. 1st Amer ed. dj... *$60.00–$75.00*

Churchill, Winston. *World Crisis*. NY. 1931. 1st Amer ed. charts, maps and text illus. .... *$70.00–$125.00*

Churchill, Winston S. *Sinews of Peace*. Lon. 1948. 1st ed. dj............. *$75.00–$125.00*

Churchill, Winston Spencer. *Ian Hamilton's March*. Lon/NY. Bombay Longman's Green & Co. 1900. 1st ed. illus. red mor maps and photos................. *$400.00–$600.00*

Chute, Carolyn. *Beans of Egypt Maine*. Lon. (1985). 1st UK ed. dj...... *$45.00–$80.00*

Chute, Carolyn. *Letourneau's Used Auto Parts*. Ticknor & Fields. 1988. 1st ed. dj...... .... *$25.00–$35.00*

Cist, Charles. *Cincinnati in 1841* . . . Cin. by author. 1841. illus. 8 plates. brown cloth. .... *$80.00–$120.00*

Clake, Asia Booth. *Unlocked Book* . . . NY. G P Putnam's Sons. 1938. illus. dj. .... *$35.00–$50.00*

Clancy, P. A. *Birds of Natal and Zululand*. Edin. 1964. illus. .... *$85.00–$135.00*

Clancy, P. A. *Gamebirds of Southern Africa*. NY. 1967. illus................. *$45.00–$60.00*

Clancy, Tom. *Cardinal of the Kremlin*. Putnam. 1988. 1st ed. dj........... *$20.00–$30.00*

Clancy, Tom. *Hunt for Red October*. Annapolis. Naval Institute Press. (1984). 1st ed. author's first book, sgn, dj. .... *$350.00–$800.00*

Clancy, Tom. *Patriot Games*. Putnam. (1987). 1st ed. dj........................ *$25.00–$45.00*

Clancy, Tom. *Red Storm Rising*. Putnam. (1986). 1st ed. dj................... *$30.00–$50.00*

Clark, A. *Lectures on Diseases of the Heart*. Birmingham Medical Library. 1884. 1st ed. .... *$25.00–$50.00*

Clark, Dick. *Murder on Tour: A Rock 'n' Roll Mystery*. NY. Mysterious Press. 1989. 1st ed. with Paul Francis (sgn by Francis)..................................... *$20.00–$35.00*

Clark, Emmons. *History of the Seventh Regiment of New York*. NY. 1890. 2 vols. 1st ed. .... *$75.00–$100.00*

Clark, James. *Shoeing and Blancing the Light Harness Horse*. Buffalo. The Horse World Company. 1916. 1st ed. .... *$125.00–$140.00*

Clark, Mary Higgins. *Cradle Will Fall*. NY. Simon & Schuster. 1980. 1st ed. dj.......... .... *$35.00–$60.00*

Clark, Mary Higgins. *Cry in the Night*. Simon & Schuster. 1982. 1st ed. dj................. .... *$25.00–$30.00*

Clark, Mary Higgins. *Loves Music, Loves to Dance*. NY. Simon & Schuster. 1991. 1st ed. dj. .... *$10.00–$15.00*

Clark, W. P. *Indian Sign Language*. Phila. 1885. 443 pp, map.......... *$100.00–$150.00*

Clark, Walter Van Tilburg. *Track of the Cat*. NY. (1949). 1st ed. dj... *$75.00–$100.00*

Clarke, Arthur. *Exploration of the Moon*. Lon. Frederick Muller. (1954). 1st ed. black cloth. .... *$25.00–$70.00*

Clarke, Arthur C. *2001: A Space Odyssey*. NY. New American Library. 1968. 1st ed. scarce, dj. .... *$300.00–$500.00*

Clarke, Arthur C. *2001: A Space Odyssey*. Lon. 1968. 1st Eng ed. dj. ....
.... *$95.00–$115.00*

Clarke, Arthur C. *2061: Odyssey Three*. Del Rey. 1987. 1st US ed. dj. *$25.00–$30.00*

Clarke, Arthur C. *Childhood's End*. NY. (1953). 1st ed. pictorial wraps, sgn. ....
.... *$50.00–$75.00*

Clarke, Arthur C. *Expedition to Earth*. (1953). 1st ed. printed wraps... *$30.00–$40.00*

Clarke, Arthur C. *Sands of Mars*. NY. Gnome Press. (1952). 1st US ed. dj.................
.... *$90.00–$125.00*

Clarke, Covington. *Mystery Flight of the Q2*. Chi. (1932). 1st ed. dj. ... *$20.00–$40.00*

Clarke, H. T. *Chemistry of Penicillin*. Princeton. 1949. 1st ed. .... *$75.00–$125.00*

Clarke, John Henry. *Dictionary of Practical Materia Medica*. Sussex. 1962. 3 vols. ...
.... *$65.00–$100.00*

Clarke, Lewis. *Narr. of the Sufferings of Lewis and Milton Clarke* . . . Bos. 1846. wrps.
.... *$85.00–$100.00*

Clarke, T. Wood. *Bloody Mohawk*. NY. 1940. 1st ed. dj......................... *$40.00–$65.00*

Clay, John. *My Life on the Range*. Chi. (1924). plates....................... *$100.00–$325.00*

Clay, John. *My Life on the Range*. NY. 1961. rprnt.............................. *$45.00–$75.00*

Clay, R. S. and T. H. Court. *History of the Microscope*. Lon. 1975. rprnt, dj. ....
.... *$60.00–$70.00*

Clay, R. S. and T. H. Court. *History of the Microscope*. Lon. 1932.. *$150.00–$200.00*

Clayton, Victoria V. *White and Black Under the Old Regime*. Milw. (1899). 1st ed. .....
.... *$125.00–$150.00*

Cleater, P. E. *Rockets Through Space*. NY. 1936. illus. 1st Amer ed. . *$100.00–$150.00*

Cleaver, Eldridge. *Eldridge Cleaver: Post Prison Writings and Speeches*. NY. (1969). 1st ed. dj. .... *$25.00–$35.00*

Cleaver, Eldridge. *Idi and the Sultan*. Stanford. C P Times Press. 1984. 1st ed. wrps....
.... *$50.00–$65.00*

Cleaver, Eldridge. *Soul on Ice*. NY. McGraw-Hill. 1968. 1st ed. dj. .... *$75.00–$105.00*

Clemens, Samuel. *Dog's Tale*. NY/Lon. Harper & Bros. 1904. 1st ed. *$75.00–$150.00*

Clemens, Samuel. *Following the Equator*. Hart. Amer Pub Co. 1897. 1st ed. illus. frontis photo. .... *$175.00–$225.00*

Clemens, Samuel. *Life on the Mississippi*. Box. Osgood. 1883. 1st ed. illus. ....
.... *$125.00–$300.00*

Clement, Arthur W. *Our Pioneer Potters*. NY. 1947. illus. ltd 500 cc, slipcase. ....
.... *$45.00–$100.00*

Clerk, Dugald. *Gas Engine*. Lon. 1887. .... *$35.00–$60.00*

Cleveland, Grover. *Fishing & Shooting.* NY. Outing Pub. 1906. 1st ed. *$45.00–$60.00*

Cleveland, Grover. *Fishing and Shooting Sketches.* NY. 1906. illus...... *$20.00–$30.00*

Clifford, F. *Romance of Perfume Lands.* Bos. 1881. .... *$32.00–$45.00*

Clift, Virgil A. (ed.). *Negro Education in America, Its Adequacy, Problems and Needs.* NY. 1962. 1st ed. .... *$28.00–$37.00*

Clougher, T. R. (ed.). *Golf Clubs of the Empire: The Golfing Annual.* Lon. 1931. 5th issue. .... *$45.00–$50.00*

Coan, T. *Life in Hawaii, an Autobiographic Sketch.* NY. 1882. .... *$30.00–$50.00*

Coates, Robert. *Outlaw Years.* NY. 1930. 1st ed. .... *$20.00–$30.00*

Coatsworth, Elizabeth. *Cricket and the Emperor's Son.* NY. 1932. 1st ed. illus. by Weda Yap, dj.. *$35.00–$40.00*

Coatsworth, Elizabeth. *Golden Horshoe.* NY. 1935. 1st ed. illus. by Lawson. .... *$35.00–$50.00*

Cobb, Irvin S. *Roll Call.* Ind. (1942). 1st ed. dj. .... *$17.00–$25.00*

Cobb, Sanford H. *Story of the Palatines.* Putnam. 1897. brown cloth.... *$25.00–$65.00*

Cobb, Ty. *My Life in Baseball.* NY. 1962. 1st ed. dj. .... *$30.00–$40.00*

Cobb, W. Mantague. *First Negro Medical Society . . . Dist. of Columbia, 1884–1939.* Wash. 1939. .... *$35.00–$45.00*

Cobbett, William. *Cottage Economy.* NY. Gould & Son. 1824. 1st Amer ed. .... *$65.00–$100.00*

Cobbett, William. *Letters on the Late War.* NY. J Belden. 1815. 1st ed. bds. .... *$40.00–$60.00*

Coblentz, Stanton A. *Into Plutonian Depths.* NY. (1950). 1st ed. pictorial wrps............ .... *$50.00–$65.00*

Coblentz, Stanton A. *Villains and Vigilantes.* NY. 1936. 1st ed. dj. .... *$35.00–$65.00*

Coburn, Silas. *Across the Ferry.* Mass. 1886. illus. brown cloth frontis. *$30.00–$60.00*

Cochin, Augustin. *Results of Slavery.* Bos. Walker, Wise & Co. 1863. 1st ed................ .... *$40.00–$85.00*

Cochran, D. M. *Frogs of Southeastern Brazil.* Wash. 1955. illus. .... *$25.00–$45.00*

Cochran, D. M and C. J. Goin. *Frogs of Columbia.* Wash. 1970. illus. *$30.00–$45.00*

Cochran, Doris M. *Poisonous Reptiles of the World.* Wash. 1943. wrps. *$40.00–$50.00*

Cock, the Mouse, and the Little Red Hen. Akron. (1931). 1st ed. illus. by Fern Bissel Peat. .... *$95.00–$125.00*

Cody, William. *Adventures of Buffalo Bill.* Harper. 1904. 1st ed. red cloth.................... .... *$20.00–$30.00*

Cody, William. *Buffalo Bill's Life Story.* NY. 1920. .... *$25.00–$40.00*

Cody, William F. *Story of the Wild West & Camp Fire Chats by Buffalo Bill.* Phila. 1889. illus. .... *$35.00–$60.00*

Cody, William F. *True Tales of the Plains.* NY. 1908. .... *$30.00–$100.00*

Coffey, Leora S. *Wilds of Alaska Big-Game Hunting.* NY. (1963). 1st ed. .... *$18.00–$30.00*

Coffin, Albert Isaiah. *Treatise on Midwifery.* Manchester. Medico-Botanic Press. 1849. 184 pp. .... *$100.00–$165.00*

Coffin, Charles "Carleton." *Stories of Our Soldiers.* Bos. 1893. 1st ed. illus. .... *$22.00–$35.00*

Coffin, Charles C. *Boys of 1861.* Bos. 1885. .... *$30.00–$65.00*

Coffin, Charles C. *Life of Abraham Lincoln.* NY. 1893. .... *$40.00–$50.00*

Coffin, Joseph. *Coins of the Popes.* NY. Coward McCann. 1946. illus. inscribed. .... *$30.00–$40.00*

Coffin, Joshua. *Sketch of the History of Newbury, Newburyport, and West Newbury.* Bos. 1845. .... *$40.00–$60.00*

Coffin, Robert Tristram. *Saltwater Farm.* NY. 1937. 1st ed. illus. dj.... *$20.00–$30.00*

Cohen, Octavus R. *Highly Colored.* NY. Dodd, Mead. 1921. 1st ed. dj. *$30.00–$55.00*

Cohen, Octavus Roy. *Bigger and Blacker.* Bos. 1925. 1st ed. sgn. .... *$50.00–$85.00*

Cohen, Octavus Roy. *Townsend Murder Mystery.* Appleton Century. 1933. 1st ed. .... *$25.00–$30.00*

Cohen, Octavus Roy. *Transient Lady.* NY. 1934. 1st ed. dj .... *$40.00–$75.00*

Cohn, Albert M. *George Cruikshank: A Catalogue . . .* Lon. 1924. #34/500 cc, brown cloth, mounted facsimiles, erratum. .... *$250.00–$270.00*

Coigney, Rodolphe L. *Isaak Walton: A New Bibliography, 1653–1987.* NY. 1989. #259/540 cc, sgn. .... *$80.00–$100.00*

Colbert, E. *Chicago and the Great Conflagration.* Cinc. 1872. 1st ed. illus. maps. .... *$28.00–$45.00*

Colby, Merle. *Guide to Alaska.* NY. Macmillan. 1940. blue cloth map in rear pocket.... .... *$20.00–$30.00*

Colby, William and Peter Forbath. *Honorable Men.* NY. Simon & Schuster. 1978. 1st ed. illus. red calf. .... *$19.00–$35.00*

Colcord, Joanna C. *Songs of American Sailormen.* NY. 1938. illus....... *$35.00–$60.00*

Cole, George E. *Early Oregon Jottings . . . of a Pioneer, 1850.* np. (1905). 1st ed. .... *$50.00–$60.00*

Cole, S. W. *American Fruit Book . . .* Bos. 1849. 1st ed. .... *$40.00–$50.00*

Coleman, Elizabeth. *Dolls Makers and Marks Vol 1.* Wash. Hobby House Press. 1966. illus. rev 2nd ed. .... *$15.00–$20.00*

Colenso, John W. *Ten Weeks in Natal.* Camb. Macmillan. 1855. fldg map, plates, original cloth, rbkd. .... *$165.00–$225.00*

Colenso, John W. *Ten Weeks in Natal.* Cam. Macmillan. 1855. fldg map, plates. .... *$275.00–$325.00*

Coleridge, S. T. *Friend: A Series of Essays.* Burlington. Chauncey Goodridge. 1831. 1st Amer ed. 1 vol. .... *$85.00–$150.00*

Colkins Franklin Welles. *Two Wilderness Voyagers.* Revell. 1902......... *$25.00–$35.00*

Colleen Moore's Doll House: The Story of the Most Exquisite Toy in the World. NY. 1935. illus. pamphlet. .... *$15.00–$25.00*

Collier's Photographic History of the European War. NY. Collier. (1916). oblong folio, 144 pp, photos. .... *$30.00–$40.00*

Collier, John. *Presenting Moonshine.* NY. Viking Press. 1941. 1st US ed, dj. ....
.... *$20.00–$40.00*

Collins, A. Frederick. *Experimental Television.* 1932. 1st ed. illus. dj. *$95.00–$175.00*

Collins, Hubert E. *Warpath and Cattle Trail.* NY. 1928. 1st ed. .... *$65.00–$95.00*

Collins, John S. *Across the Plains in '64.* Omaha. 1904. 1st ed. .... *$50.00–$100.00*

Collins, Wilke. *No Name.* NY. 1863. 1st ed. illus. purple cloth. .... *$100.00–$200.00*

Collins, Wilkie. *Armadale.* NY. 1866. 1st Amer ed. .... *$100.00–$300.00*

Collins, Wilkie. *Man and Wife.* NY. Harper & Bros. 1870. 1st Amer ed. illus. lavender pebbled cloth. .... *$95.00–$125.00*

Collins, Wilkie. *The Moonstone.* NY. 1868. illus. 1st Amer ed. .... *$100.00–$225.00*

Collis, Septima M. *Woman's Trip to Alaska.* NY. Cassell. (1890). 1st ed. teg. ....
.... *$75.00–$125.00*

Collodi, Carlo. *Pinnochio.* Phila. (1920). illus. by Maria Kirk. deluxe ed. 14 mounted clr plates, pictorial endpapers, scarce in box. .... *$85.00–$100.00*

Collodi, Carlo. *Pinnochio.* A L Burt. 1930. illus. .... *$20.00–$25.00*

Collodi, Carlo. *Pinocchio.* Winston. illus. by Richardson. pictorial label on cvr. ....
.... *$20.00–$35.00*

Collodi, D. *Pinocchio.* Akron. (1924). illus. by Frances Brundage, pictorial cvr paste-on.
.... *$25.00–$35.00*

Colorado. Hastings House. 1941. tan cloth. .... *$20.00–$30.00*

Colt, Mrs. S. S. *Tourist Guide Through the Empire State.* . . Albany. 1871. 1st ed. ....
.... *$50.00–$60.00*

Colton, Calvin. *Lecture on the Railroad to the Pacific.* NY. 1850. .... *$35.00–$45.00*

Colton, Harold S. *Hopi Kachina Dolls with a Key to the Identification.* Albuquerque. 1949. 1st ed. dj. .... *$50.00–$80.00*

Colton, J. Ferrell. *Last of the Square-Rigged Ships.* NY. Putnam. 1937. 1st ed. illus. dj.
.... *$80.00–$100.00*

Colton, J. H. *Colton's United States Showing the Military Stations* . . . NY. 1862. ....
.... *$95.00–$120.00*

Colton, J. H. *Map of South Carolina.* NY. 1856. in clr. .... *$75.00–$115.00*

Colton, J. H. *Traveler and Tourist's Guide Book Through the United States and the Canadas.* NY. 1850. 2 maps. .... *$100.00–$250.00*

Colton, Walter. *Deck and Port.* NY. Barnes. 1854. .... *$75.00–$155.00*

Colton, Walter. *Three Years in California.* NY. 1850. 1st ed. .... *$95.00–$150.00*

Colum, Padraic. *Frenzied Prince.* Phila. (1943). 1st ed. illus. by Pogany in clr and b/w. decorated endpapers, dj. .... *$75.00–$100.00*

Colum, Padraic. *Girl Who Sat by the Ashes.* NY. 1919. 1st ed. illus. by Dugald Walker.
.... *$40.00–$50.00*

Colum, Padraic (ed.). *Arabian Nights.* NY. 1923. illus. .... *$25.00–$30.00*

Colvin, F. and H. *Aircraft Handbook.* McGraw-Hill. 1929. 4th ed. 690 pp.................... .... *$30.00–$50.00*

Colvin, Verplanck. *Narrative of a Bear Hunt in the Adirondacks.* Albany. Joel Munsell. 1870. wrps. 16 pp. .... *$60.00–$85.00*

Coman, E. T. and H. M. Gibbs. *Time, Tide and Timber.* Stanford. Stanford University Press. 1949. sgn by both authors.................... *$40.00–$60.00*

Combat Digest: 33rd Fighter Group. np. nd. 48 pp, photos, scarce. .. *$125.00–$195.00*

Combat History of 2nd Infantry Division. Baton Rouge. 1946. .... *$55.00–$65.00*

Combe, Andrew. *Principles of Physiology Applied to Preservation of Health.* Edin. 1835. 3rd ed.. *$25.00–$40.00*

Comly, John. *New Spelling Book.* Phil. Solomon W Conrad. 1818. bds........................ .... *$25.00–$45.00*

Commager, Henry Steele. *Blue and the Gray.* NY. (1950). 2 vols. 1st ed. .... *$40.00–$90.00*

Comstock, J. L. *An Introduction to the Study of Botany.* NY. Robinson Pratt & Co. 1843. full lea.. *$30.00–$40.00*

Comstock, J. L. *Elements of Chemistry.* NY. Pratt Woodford & Co. 1853. rev. ed. lea. .... *$24.00–$35.00*

Comstock, J. L. *Manual of Natural Philosophy* . . . Lon. Adam Scott. 1846. .... *$32.00–$50.00*

Comstock, J. L. *System of Natural Philosophy* . . . NY. Pratt Woodford & Co. 1847..... .... *$20.00–$24.00*

Comstock, John H. *Spider Book.* Garden City. 1913............................. *$50.00–$65.00*

Conard, Howard. *Uncle Dick Wootton and the Pioneer Frontiersman.* (Time-Life Books 1980). rprnt of the 1890 ed. .... *$20.00–$35.00*

Conard, Howard. *Uncle Dick Wootton, the Pioneer Frontiersman of the Rocky Mountain Region.* Chi. 1890. 1st ed.................... *$200.00–$300.00*

Conder, Claude Reignier. *Syrian Stone-Lore.* Lon. Palestine Exploration Fund. 1896. illus. fldg maps. .... *$30.00–$45.00*

Condon, E. U. and G. H. Shortly. *Theory of Atomic Spectra.* Macmillan. 1935. 1st ed. .... *$45.00–$65.00*

Condon, R. *Manchurian Candidate.* NY. McGraw-Hill. 1959. 1st ed. dj...................... .... *$75.00–$110.00*

Cone, Mary. *Two Years in California.* Chi. Griggs. 1876. 1st ed. illus. 238 pp............. .... *$95.00–$125.00*

Conkey, W. B. *Official Guide to the Klondyke Country* . . . Chi. 1897. softbound. .... *$200.00–$350.00*

Conklin, E. *Picturesque Arizona.* NY. 1878. .... *$250.00–$300.00*

Conn, Granville. *History of the New Hampshire Surgeons in the War of Rebellion.* Concord. NH Assn of Military Surgeons. 1906. 1st ed. 558 pp. .... *$100.00–$150.00*

Connelley, William. *Wild Bill and His Era. The Life and Adventures of James Hickok.* NY. 1933... *$125.00–$225.00*

Connelley, William E. *Quantrill and the Border Wars.* IA. 1910. 1st ed. illus. maps. .....
.... *$125.00–$250.00*

Connett, E. *Duck Decoys.* VT. 1953. illus. clr and b/w, dj. .... *$14.00–$22.00*

Connett, E. *Wildfowling in the Mississippi Flyway.* Van Nostrand. 1949. 1st ed. illus....
.... *$125.00–$195.00*

Connett, E. (ed.). *Duck Shooting Along the Atlantic Tidewater.* NY. 1947. illus. dj. ......
.... *$55.00–$100.00*

Connett, Eugene V. *My Friend the Trout.* Van Nostrand. (1961). 1st ed. dj. ....
.... *$50.00–$70.00*

Conrad, Joseph. *Conrad Argosy.* NY. 1942. illus. woodcuts, dj. .... *$35.00–$50.00*

Conrad, Joseph. *Lord Jim.* Edin/Lon. William Blackwood. 1900. 1st ed. scarce...........
.... *$600.00–$1,000.00*

Conrad, Joseph. *Lord Jim.* Tor. Gage. 1909. 1st Canadian ed. .... *$150.00–$225.00*

Conrad, Joseph. *Nigger of the Narcissus.* Lon. 1898. 1st ed. .... *$200.00–$450.00*

Conrad, Joseph. *Nigger of the Narcissus: A Tale of the Forecastle.* Garden City.
Doubleday, Page. 1914. gray cloth... *$200.00–$500.00*

Conrad, Joseph. *Tales of Hearsay.* NY. (1925). 1st Amer ed. dj. .... *$50.00–$70.00*

Conrad, Joseph. *Tales of Unrest.* NY. Scribner's Sons. 1898. 1st ed. *$450.00*

Conrad, Joseph. *The Rover.* Doubleday. 1923. 1st ed. dj. .... *$125.00–$150.00*

Conrad, Joseph. *The Rover.* Garden City. Doubleday, Page & Co. 1923. 1st ed. ltd 377,
sgn, tissue guard, dj, original box. .... *$500.00–$875.00*

Conrad, Joseph. *The Sisters.* NY. 1928. marbled bds. ltd 926 cc. .... *$75.00–$100.00*

Conrad, Joseph. *Typhoon and Other Stories.* Lon. Heinemann. 1903. 1st ed. ... *$250.00*

Conroy, Frank. *Stop-Time.* NY. Viking. (1967). 1st ed. author's first book, dj...............
.... *$65.00–$100.00*

Conroy, Frank. *Stop-Time.* NY. Viking. (1967). 1st ed. author's first book....................
.... *$25.00–$40.00*

Conroy, Jack. *The Disinherited.* Lon. (1934). 1st UK ed. rust cloth, ...
.... *$150.00–$200.00*

Conroy, Jack. *Worker-Writer in America.* Chi. (1944). blue cloth dj. .... *$20.00–$25.00*

Conroy, Jack. *World to Win.* Covici Friede. 1st Amer ed. dj................... *$20.00–$35.00*

Conroy, Pat. *Beach Music.* NY. Doubleday. 1995. 1st ed. sgn, dj........... *$40.00–$50.00*

Conroy, Pat. *Great Santini.* Bos. Houghton Mifflin. 1976. 1st ed. sgn, dj......................
.... *$150.00–$200.00*

Conroy, Pat. *Great Santini.* Bos. 1976. 1st ed. sgn, dj. .... *$125.00–$250.00*

Conroy, Pat. *Lords of Discipline.* Bos. Houghton Mifflin. 1980. 1st ed. sgn, dj. ....
.... *$100.00–$225.00*

Conroy, Pat. *Lords of Discipline.* Houghton. 1980. 1st ed. sgn, dj. .... *$90.00–$100.00*

Conroy, Pat. *Prince of Tides.* Bos. 1986. 1st ed. dj. .... *$35.00–$45.00*

Constitution of the State of Deseret . . . Adopted March 2, 1872. Salt Lake. 1872. wrps.
21 pp, scarce. .... *$75.00–$120.00*

Contributions to Medical and Biological Research. NY. 1919. 2 vols. illus. ltd #20/1,600 cc. .... *$75.00–$125.00*

Converse, Florence. *Story of Wellesley*. Bos. 1915. 1st ed. .... *$25.00–$30.00*

Conway, Moncure D. *Life of Thomas Paine*. NY. 1892. 2 vols. .... *$45.00–$85.00*

Conway, W. Martin. *The Alps*. Lon. Adam & Charles Black. 1904. 1st ed. illus. by A D McCormick, 70 clr plates, pictorial blue cloth, teg............................... *$90.00–$110.00*

Conwell, R. H. *History of the Great Boston Fire, Nov. 9th & 10th, 1872*. Bos. 1873. 1st ed. illus. .... *$20.00–$30.00*

Cook, C. *Observations of Fox Hunting and Management of Hounds*. Lon. 1826. .... *$175.00–$250.00*

Cook, C. H. *Among the Pimas*. Albany. 1893. .... *$50.00–$100.00*

Cook, Frederick A. *My Attainment of the Pole*. NY. 1912. illus. .... *$50.00–$100.00*

Cook, Frederick A. *My Attainment of the Pole*. NY. 1911. 1st ed. .... *$75.00–$225.00*

Cook, Frederick A. *To the Top of the Continent*. NY. 1908. 1st ed. ..... *$75.00–$100.00*

Cook, Joel. *America Picturesque and Descriptive*. Phila. 1900. 3 vols. wrps. slipcase... .... *$25.00–$35.00*

Cook, Joel. *Switzerland Picturesque and Descriptive*. Henry Coates. 1904. 1st ed. illus. tissued photos, dj. .... *$30.00–$45.00*

Cook, John A. *Pursuing the Whale*. Bos. Houghton Mifflin. 1926. 1st ed. gray cloth. ... . *$20.00–$80.00*

Cook, Roy Bird. *Family and Early Life of Stonewall Jackson*. VA. 1925. 1st ed. .... *$50.00–$75.00*

Cooke, Philip St. George. *Scenes and Adventures in the Army*. Phila. 1859. 2nd ed...... .... *$100.00–$250.00*

Cooke, Philip St. George. *Scenes and Adventures in the Army*. Phila. 1857................. .... *$250.00–$500.00*

Cooke, T. G. *Finger Prints, Secret Service, Crime Detection*. Chi. 1936. illus............... .... *$20.00–$30.00*

Coon, Carlton S. *Story of Man*. NY. Knopf. 1954. 1st ed...................... *$25.00–$30.00*

Cooper, A. *Complete Distiller* . . . Lon. 1757. .... *$225.00–$300.00*

Cooper, Alonzo. *In & Out of Rebel Prisons*. NY. Oliphant. 1888. 1st ed. .... *$125.00–$150.00*

Cooper, Frederic Tabor. *An Argosy of Fables*. NY. Stoles. (1921). 1st ed. illus. clr plates.. *$70.00–$100.00*

Cooper, J Wesley. *Louisiana: A Treasure of Plantation Homes*. Natchez. Southern Historical Pub. 1961. illus. dj... *$30.00–$40.00*

Cooper, J. W. *Experienced Botanist or Indian Physician*. PA. 1840. . *$175.00–$215.00*

Cooper, James Fenimore. *The Deerslayer*. Scribner's. 1925. 1st ed. illus. by N C Wyeth, dj. .... *$425.00–$500.00*

Cooper, James Fennimore. *Last of the Mohicans*. NY. 1919. illus. by N C Wyeth. 1st Wyeth ed. .... *$75.00–$140.00*

Cooper, James Fennimore. *The Deerslayer.* Phil. 1841. 1st ed. purple cloth. ....
.... *$150.00–$350.00*

Cooper, James Fennimore. *The Pathfinder.* Lon. Bentley. 1840. 3 vols. 1st ed. 1st UK ed. .... *$500.00–$2,000.00*

Cooper, James Fennimore. *The Pathfinder.* Phila. Lea & Blanchard. 1840. 2 vols. 1st Amer ed. .... *$350.00–$550.00*

Cooper, James Fennimore. *The Prairie.* Phila. 1832. 2 vols. 5th ed...... *$40.00–$60.00*

Cooper, John M. *Analytical & Critical Biblio. of Tribes of Tierra Del Fuego.* GPO. 1917. fldg map... *$35.00–$50.00*

Cooper, Lt. A. *In & Out of Rebel Prisons.* Oswego, NY. 1888. illus.... *$75.00–$115.00*

Coover, Robert. *Universal Baseball Associaton, Inc.* Lon. 1970. 1st ed. dj...................
.... *$45.00–$65.00*

Coppard, A E. *Fishmonger's Fiddle.* Lon. 1925..................... *$20.00–$30.00*

Coppard, A. E. *Fearful Pleasures.* Arkham House. 1946. 1st US ed. dj. ....
.... *$80.00–$100.00*

Coppinger, Joseph. *American Practical Brewer and Tanner.* NY. 1815. 1st ed. plates...
.... *$300.00–$450.00*

Copway, George. *Life, History and Travels of Kah-Ge-Ga-Gak-Bowk . . . Ojibway . . .* PA. 1847. 2nd ed. presentation copy, sgn.............................. *$200.00–$225.00*

Corbett, Jim. *Man-Eaters of Kumaon.* NY/Bombay. (1946). 1st US ed. dj. ....
.... *$25.00–$35.00*

Corbett, Jim. *Man-Eating Leopard of Rudrapravag.* Oxford University Press. 1948. 1st Amer ed. rust cloth. .... *$25.00–$100.00*

Corcoran, A. P. *Boy Scouts in Africa.* Barse & Hopkins. 1923. .... *$10.00–$15.00*

Corder, E. M. *Deer Hunter.* NY. Exeter. (1979). 1st ed. dj.................... *$25.00–$30.00*

Cornelius, Mrs. *Young Housekeeper's Friend.* Bos/NY. 1859. rev ed..................
.... *$20.00–$30.00*

Cornelius, Mrs. *Young Housekeeper's Friend.* Bos/NY. 1846............. *$100.00–$175.00*

Cornish, Dudley Taylor. *Sable Arm, Negro Troops in the Union Army, 1861–1865.* NY. 1956. 1st ed.. *$40.00–$65.00*

Cornwallis, Caroline Francis. *An Introduction to Practical Organic Chemistry.* Lon. Pickering. 1843.. *$100.00–$170.00*

Cornwell, Bernard. *Sharpe's Eagle.* NY. Viking. (1981). 1st ed. dj....... *$45.00–$65.00*

Cornwell, Bernard. *Sharpe's Eagle.* NY. Viking Press. (1981). 1st ed. dj.....................
.... *$40.00–$65.00*

Correll and Gosden. *All About Amos 'n' Andy and Their Creators Correll & Gosden.* NY. 1930. illus. 2nd ed.. *$22.00–$35.00*

Correspondence Between the Rev Samuel H Cox of Brooklyn . . . NY. Office of the American Anti-Slavery Society. 1846. wrps. .... *$50.00–$75.00*

Corso, Gregory. *Bomb.* City Lights. 1958....................... *$85.00–$100.00*

Corso, Gregory. *Happy Birthday of Death.* New Directions. (1960). 1st ed. wrps. ....
.... *$35.00–$45.00*

Cory, David. *Iceberg Express.* NY. (1922). 1st ed. illus. by P H Webb. scarce dj. .... *$25.00–$35.00*

Cossley-Batt, Jill. *Last of the California Rangers.* NY/Lon. Funk & Wagnalls. 1928. 1st ed. .... *$90.00–$120.00*

Cossley-Batt, Jill. *Last of the California Rangers.* NY/Lon. Funk & Wagnalls. (1928). illus. 2nd ptg. .... *$25.00–$75.00*

Cotton, Bruce. *Reflections on the Civil War.* CT. 1981. .... *$35.00–$45.00*

Couch, Jonathan F. L. S. *History of the Fishes of the British Isles.* Lon. George Bell & Sons. 1879. 4 vols. illus. with 252 tissue-guarded full-clr chromoliths, pictorial design of fish on front cvr. .... *$900.00–$1,000.00*

Coues, Elliott. *Birds of the Northwest.* Bos. 1877. .... *$50.00–$80.00*

Coues, Elliott. *Expeditions of Zebulon Montgomery Pike to Headwaters . . .* Minn. 1965. 3 vols. rprnt, ltd 2000 cc. .... *$100.00–$200.00*

Coues, Elliott. *Key to North American Birds.* 1890. 4th ed. illus. 1 clr plate, cloth......... .... *$50.00–$75.00*

Coues, Elliott. *Key to North American Birds.* Salem. 1972. illus. 6 plates. .... *$30.00–$40.00*

Coues, Elliott (ed.). *New Light on the Early History of the Greater Northwest . . .* NY. 1895. 3 vols. maps, ltd 500 cc. .... *$250.00–$300.00*

Coulter, Ellis Merton. *Civil War and Readjustment in Kentucky.* Chapel Hill. 1926. 1st ed. .... *$65.00–$90.00*

Coulter, Ellis Merton. *William G. Brownlow, Fighting Parson of the Southern Highlands.* Chapel Hill. 1937. 1st ed. .... *$30.00–$60.00*

Courlander, Harold. *Negro Folk Music, USA.* NY. 1963. dj................... *$30.00–$45.00*

Couture, Richard T. *Powhatan: A Bicentennial History.* Dietz. 1980. b/w illus. inscrb dj. .... *$40.00–$50.00*

Covarrubias, Miguel. *Island of Bali.* NY. Knopf. 1937. 1st ed. illus. by Covarrubias, photos, pictorial cloth, dj. .... *$75.00–$90.00*

Coward, Noel. *Bitter Sweet and Other Plays.* NY. 1929. 1st Amer ed. ltd 1000 cc, nbr, sgn. .... *$200.00–$250.00*

Coward, Noel. *Private Lives.* Lon. 1930. dj. .... *$100.00–$300.00*

Coward, Noel. *Quadrille, a Play in Three Acts.* Lon. 1952. dj. .... *$25.00–$40.00*

Cox, Earnest Sevier. *White America.* Richmond, VA. White American Society. 1923. 1st ed. dj, scarce. .... *$100.00–$200.00*

Cox, Ernest. *White America.* Richmond, VA. White American Society. (1925). Congress ed, dj. .... *$35.00–$75.00*

Cox, Jacob D. *Military Reminiscences of the Civil War.* NY. 1900. 2 vols.................... .... *$195.00–$250.00*

Cox, Palmer. *Brownies at Home.* Century. 1893. illus. b/w. .... *$50.00–$75.00*

Cox, Palmer. *Brownies. Their Book.* NY. (1887). 1st ed. illustrated bds. .... *$200.00–$300.00*

Cox, Palmer. *Rhyme & Reason*. Clark's O.N.T. Thread. illus. booklet pictorial. clr paper wrps. .... *$50.00–$75.00*

Cox, Warren. *Chinese Ivory Sculpture*. NY. 1946. 1st ed. folio.............. *$38.00–$50.00*

Crafts, W. A. *Southern Rebellion*. Bos. Walker. 1862. 1st ed. illus. steel engr. ....
....*$200.00–$225.00*

Craig, Maurice. *Irish Book Bindings 1600–1800*. Lon. (1954). illus. dj.........................
.... *$275.00–$350.00*

Craig, Maurice. *Psychological Medicine*. Lon. 1905. plates.................. *$20.00–$27.00*

Craighead, John J., Jay Sumner and John A. Mitchell. *Grizzly Bears of Yellowstone*. Island Press. 1995. 1st ed. 1st ptg. illus. with clr and b/w photos. gray cloth, dj. ....
.... *$90.00–$115.00*

Cram's Universal Atlas. Chi. 1889. ¾ lea... *$95.00–$125.00*

Cram, Mildred. *Old Seaport Towns of the South*. NY. Dodd Mead. 1917. 1st ed. pictorial cloth. .... *$25.00–$35.00*

Cramer, Zadok. *Navigator, Containing Directions for Navigating the Monongahela, Allegheny, Ohio and Mississippi Rivers*. Pitt. 1817. 9th ed. maps....... *$280.00–$300.00*

Crane, Frances. *Coral Princess Murders*. NY. (1954). 1st ed. dj. .... *$20.00–$30.00*

Crane, Frances. *Murder on the Purple Water*. NY. (1947). 1st ed. dj. ... *$40.00–$75.00*

Crane, Hart. *Seven Lyrics*. Camb. The Ibex Press. (c1966). 1st ed. 1/250 cc...................
....*$75.00–$145.00*

Crane, Stephen. *Monster and Other Stories*. NY/Lon. Harper & Bros. 1899. 1st ed. ....
.... *$150.00–$200.00*

Crane, Stephen. *O'Ruddy*. NY. Stokes. 1903. 1st ed............................ *$45.00–$125.00*

Crane, Stephen. *Open Boat and Other Stories*. Lon. 1898. 1st ed. green cloth. ....
.... *$195.00–$225.00*

Crane, Stephen. *Red Badge of Courage*. NY. Appleton & Co. 1896. tan cloth..............
.... *$75.00–$145.00*

Crane, Stephen. *Red Badge of Courage*. NY. Appleton. 1896. 1st ed. ....
.... *$125.00–$200.00*

Crane, Stephen. *Works of Stephen Crane*. Knopf. 1925. 12 vols. ltd ed, boxed..............
.... *$250.00–$300.00*

Crane, Walter. *Absurd ABC*. Lon. Routledge & Sons. 1st ed. red lea. *$275.00–$350.00*

Crane, Walter. *Flora's Feast of Flowers*. Lon. 1889. 1st ed. illus. 40 pp, pictorial bds..
.... *$90.00–$150.00*

Crane, Walter. *Masque of Days*. Lon/Paris/NY/Melbourne. Cassell & Co. 1901. illus. by Crane. pictorial bds. .... *$120.00–$180.00*

Crane, Walter. *Queen Summer*. Lon/Paris/Melbourne. Cassell & Co. 1891. 1st ed. pictorial bds. .... *$120.00–$180.00*

Crane, Walter. *Walter Crane's Picture Book*. Lon. (1874). 1st ed. 64 clr plates, aeg.
.... *$475.00–$600.00*

Crapo, Capt. Thomas and Wife. *Strange But True*. New Bedford. 1893. 1st ed. brown cloth. .... *$25.00–$65.00*

Crapo, W. W. *New Bedford Centennial Address.* New Bedford. 1876. 1st ed............... .... *$15.00–$25.00*

Craven, Avery. *Edmund Ruffin Southerner.* NY. Appleton. 1932............ *$45.00–$50.00*

Crawford, Mary Caroline. *Romance of Old New England Churches.* Bos. L C Page. (1903). illus.. *$15.00–$30.00*

Crawford, Samuel W. *Genesis of the Civil War. The Story of Sumter, 1860–1861.* NY. 1887. .... *$100.00–$125.00*

Creighton, Helen. *Maritime Folk Songs.* NY. Folklorica. 1979. dj........ *$25.00–$35.00*

*Creole Cookery Book.*New Orleans. T H Thomason. 1885. 1st ed. by Christian Woman's Exchange. .... *$100.00–$150.00*

Crews, Harry. *A Childhood . . .* Harper. 1978. 1st ed. dj...................... *$75.00–$200.00*

Crews, Harry. *All We Need of Hell.* NY. 1987. 1st ed. dj. .... *$40.00–$50.00*

Crews, Harry. *Blood and Grits.* NY. (1979). 1st ed. dj...................... *$40.00–$50.00*

Crews, Harry. *Feast of Snakes.* Lon. (1977). 1st UK ed. dj................. *$75.00–$125.00*

Crews, Harry. *Gospel Singer.* NY. Morrow. (1968). 1st ed. author's first book, dj......... .... *$400.00–$900.00*

Crews, Harry. *Gypsie's Curse.* NY. (1974). 1st ed. dj. .... *$80.00–$125.00*

Crews, Harry. *Karate Is a Thing of the Spirit.* NY. 1971. 1st ed. dj... *$100.00–$150.00*

Crews, Harry. *Knockout Artist.* NY. (1988). 1st ed. dj. .... *$25.00–$40.00*

Crews, Harry. *Madonna at Ringside.* Lord John. 1992. 1/275 cc, sgn... *$75.00–$90.00*

Crews, Harry. *Naked in Garden Hills.* NY. 1969. 1st ed. dj................. *$75.00–$200.00*

Crews, Harry. *Scar Lover.* NY. (1992). dj. .... *$20.00–$30.00*

Crews, Harry. *This Thing Don't Lead to Heaven.* NY. 1970. 1st ed. dj. .... *$125.00–$250.00*

Crichton, Michael. *Andromeda Strain.* NY. Knopf. 1969. 1st ed. dj...... *$50.00–$65.00*

Crichton, Michael. *Great Train Robbery.* Knopf. 1975. 1st ed. dj. .... *$35.00–$65.00*

Crichton, Michael. *Jurassic Park.* NY. 1990. 1st ed. dj......................... *$35.00–$75.00*

Crichton, Michael. *Rising Sun.* NY. 1992. sgn, dj. .... *$25.00–$40.00*

Crichton, Michael. *Sphere.* NY. Knopf. 1987. 1st ed. dj. .... *$20.00–$40.00*

Crichton, Michael. *Terminal Man.* NY. 1972. 1st ed. dj....................... *$45.00–$60.00*

Crockett, Walter Hill. *History of Lake Champlain.* Burlington, VT. Hobart & Shanley. 1909. illus. .... *$95.00–$120.00*

Croff, G. B. *Progressive American Architecture.* Wash. 1875. illus. folio, plates. .... *$1,200.00–$1,450.00*

Croffut, W. A., et al. *Military and Civil History of Conn . . . During War of 1861–65.* NY. 1868.. *$75.00–$150.00*

Croly, Mrs. J. C. *Jennie June's American Cookery Book.* NY. 1870. ..... *$45.00–$62.00*

Cromie, R. *Dillinger: A Short & Violent Life.* NY. 1962. 1st ed. sgn, dj. *$22.00–$28.00*

Cron, Gretchen. *Roaring Veldt.* NY. Putnam. 1930. 1st Amer ed. illus. plates. .... *$30.00–$50.00*

Cronau, Rudolf. *Amerika*. Leipzig. 1892. illus. photos, maps............ *$125.00–$375.00*

Cronin, A. J. *Grand Canary*. Lon. 1933. dj... *$25.00–$40.00*

Cronyn, George W. (ed.). *Path of the Rainbow*. NY. Boni and Liveright. 1918. 1st ed. 2nd ptg. rare... *$50.00–$110.00*

Cross, Ida. *History of the Labor Movement in California*. Berkeley. Univ of California. (1974). rprnt.. *$25.00–$50.00*

Cross, Robert. *Auvergne: Its Thermo-Mineral Springs* . . . Lon. Robert Hardwicke. 1867. 1st ed. illus. clr litho plates. .... *$40.00–$50.00*

Cross, Wilbur. *History of Henry Fielding*. Yale. 1918. 3 vols. 1st ed..... *$50.00–$75.00*

Crossman, E. C. *Military & Sporting Rifle Shooting*. NC. (1932). .... *$30.00–$40.00*

Crosswaith, Frank B. *Negro and Socialism*. NY. United Colored Socialists of Amer. 4 pp, brochure... *$45.00–$65.00*

Crosswaith, Frank R. and Alfred B. Lewis. *True Freedom for Negro and White Labor*. NY. Negro Labor News Service. wrps. .... *$30.00–$65.00*

Crothers, Samuel McChord. *Children of Dickens*. Scribner's. 1925. 1st ed. illus..........
.... *$30.00–$75.00*

Crothers, Samuel McChord. *Children of Dickens*. NY. 1925. 1st ed. illus. by Jessie Willcox Smith. scarce dj. .... *$200.00–$350.00*

Crowe, Philip K. *Sport Is Where You Find It*. NY. Van Nostrand. (1953). 1st ed. sgn.....
.... *$30.00–$50.00*

Crowninshield, Mary Bradford. *All Among the Lighthouses*. Bos. 1886....................
.... *$42.00–$50.00*

Cruise of the Revenue Steamer Corwin in Alaska. Wash. GPO. 1883. illus. clr and b/w plates, 165.. *$135.00–$300.00*

Crump, Paul. *Grille, Assassin, Grille!*. Paris. Presses de la Cite. 1963. 1st French ed. dj.
.... *$15.00–$25.00*

Culff, Robert. *World of Toys*. Lon. Paul Hamlyn. (1969). 1st ed. illus. b/w photos. ....
.... *$20.00–$35.00*

Cullen, Countee. *Black Christ*. Harper. 1929. 1st ed. illus. by Charles Cullen...............
.... *$50.00–$325.00*

Cullen, Countee. *Color*. NY. Harper. 1925. 1st ed. author's first book,dj.....................
.... *$600.00–$2,000.00*

Cullen, Countee. *Copper Sun*. NY. 1927. 1st ed. mar bds, dj.............. *$75.00–$300.00*

Cullen, William. *Synopsis of Methodical Nosolog*, . . . *with the Synonimous of Those from Savages*. Phila. Parry Hall. 1793. enlarged, translated by Henry Wilkins, 8 pp, bds.
.... *$350.00–$500.00*

Culmsee, Carlton. *Utah's Black Hawk War*. Logan. 1973. 1st ed. wrps. scarce.............
.... *$35.00–$40.00*

Culver, Henry B. *Book of Old Ships*. NY. 1928. illus. drawings, mor, mar bds. ....
.... *$35.00–$55.00*

Culverwell, Robert J. *How to Live 100 Years*. Lon. 1847. stiff paper. ... *$30.00–$45.00*

Cummings, Byron. *Discovery of Rainbow Bridge: The Natural Bridges of Utah and the Discovery of Betatakin*. Cummings Publication Council. 1959. wrps. Bulletin No 1, photos, map... *$15.00–$25.00*

Cummings, Byron. *First Inhabitants of Arizona and the Southwest*. Tucson. 1953. wrps. pictorial dj, map endpapers, clr photos, fldg map..................................... *$70.00–$85.00*

cummings, e e. *eimi*. NY. 1933. 1/1381 cc, sgn. .... *$175.00–$250.00*

cummings, e e. *Him*. NY. 1927. 1st ed. dj... *$150.00–$175.00*

cummings, e e. *Tulips and Chimneys*. NY. 1923. 1st ed. .... *$300.00–$500.00*

cummings, e e. *W*. NY. 1931. 1st ed. brown paper bds....................... *$125.00–$200.00*

Cuneo, John. *Winged Mars: Volume 1, The German Air Weapon 1870–1914*. Harrisburg. 1942. illus. .... *$60.00–$100.00*

Cunningham, Albert B. *Old Black Bass*. NY/Chi. (1922). illus. dj. ...... *$22.00–$32.00*

Cunningham, Eugene. *Famous in the West*. El Paso. 1926. wrps. illus. 25 pp, scarce. .. .. *$275.00–$450.00*

Cunningham, Peter. *Hand-Book of London*. Lon. 1850........................ *$45.00–$60.00*

Cunningham, Will M. *Cross Masonic Text-Book*. Phila. 1864. illus. rev ed. .... *$12.00–$20.00*

Curran and Kauffeld. *Snakes and Their Ways*. 1937. 1st ed.................. *$20.00–$25.00*

Currey, L. W. *Science Fiction and Fantasy Authors* . . . Bos. (1979). 1st ed. dj............ .... *$100.00–$125.00*

Currier & Ives Prints: The Red Indian. Lon/NY. 1931. intro by W S Hall, sgn by Hall, dj.. *$35.00–$45.00*

Currier, John J. *History of Newbury, Mass. 1635–1902*. Bos. 1902. cloth. .... *$30.00–$40.00*

Curry, Manfred. *Yacht Racing* . . . NY. 1927... *$25.00–$35.00*

Curtis, Edward S. *Portraits from North American Indian Life*. NY. Promontory Press. (1972). 1st ed. thus, oblong folio, sepia portraits.................................. *$60.00–$100.00*

Curtis, George W. *Horses, Cattle, Sheep and Swine*. NY. Rural Publishing. 1893. 2nd rev ed. illus. .... *$50.00–$65.00*

Curtis, George William. *Howadji in Syria*. NY. 1856. 1st ed. maps...... *$30.00–$45.00*

Curtis, John. *Harvey's Views on the Circulation of the Blood*. NY. 1915....................... .... *$60.00–$75.00*

Curtis, John H. *An Essay on the Deaf and Dumb*. Lon. 1834. 2nd ed. 2 plates.............. .... *$40.00–$50.00*

Curtis, Mattoon. *Story of Snuff and Snuff Boxes*. NY. 1935. illus. dj..... *$25.00–$35.00*

Curtis, Natalie (ed and compiler). *Indians' Book*. NY. Harper & Bros. 1907. 1st ed. illus. .... *$235.00–$250.00*

Curtis, Newton. *From Bull Run to Chancellorsville*. NY. 1906. .... *$85.00–$95.00*

Curtis, Paul A. *Sportsmen All*. Derrydale Press. (1938). 1/950, illus. .... *$80.00–$95.00*

Curtis, Paul A., Jr. *American Game Shooting*. NY. 1927. dj................. *$48.00–$62.00*

Curtis, W. H. *Elements of Wood Ship Construction.* NY. 1919. 1st ed. illus. ....
.... *$65.00–$95.00*

Curtis, William E. *Children of the Sun.* Chi. 1833. inscr.................... *$175.00–$225.00*

Curtiss, Ursula. *Hours to Kill.* NY. (1961). 1st ed. dj............................ *$10.00–$35.00*

Curtiss, Ursula. *Voice Out of Darkness.* NY. (1948). 1st ed. dj.............. *$12.00–$45.00*

Curwood, James. *Danger Trail.* Bobbs Merrill. (1910). 1st ed. .... *$20.00–$30.00*

Curwood, James. *Plains of Abraham.* NY. 1928. 1st ed. dj.................... *$20.00–$25.00*

Cushing, Caleb. *Reminiscences of Spain.* Bos. 1833. 2 vols in one........ *$35.00–$45.00*

Cushing, Caleb. *Reply to the Letter of J Fenimore Cooper . . .* Bos. 1834. 1st ed. printed wrps, sewn, 76 pp, inscrb. .... *$95.00–$125.00*

Cushing, Harvey. *Consecratio Medici.* 1928. 1st ed............................ *$40.00–$150.00*

Cushing, Harvey. *From a Surgeon's Journal 1915–1918.* Bos. 1936. 1st ed. ....
.... *$50.00–$75.00*

Cushing, Harvey. *Harvey Cushing's Seventieth Birthday Party, April 8, 1939.* np. Thomas. 1939. 1st ed. illus. dj. .... *$60.00–$100.00*

Cushing, Harvey. *Life of Sir William Osler.* Oxford. Clarendon Press. 1925. 2 vols. 1st ed. illus. 4th impression.. *$90.00–$375.00*

Cushing, Harvey. *Life of Sir William Osler.* Ox. 1940............................ *$30.00–$40.00*

Cushman, H. B. *History of the Choctaw, Chickasaw and Natchez Indians.* Greenville. 1899. .... *$160.00–$250.00*

Cussans, John E. *Handbook of Heraldry.* Lon. Chatto & Windus. 1893. 4th ed. ....
.... *$30.00–$45.00*

Custead, E. Rose and Elza Custead. *Songs and Stories of Bygone Days in Fayette County.* NY. 1882. 1st ed.. *$20.00–$30.00*

Custer, Carl. *Story of the American Clipper.* NY. (1930). illus. .... *$40.00–$55.00*

Custer, Elizabeth. *Boots and Saddles.* NY. 1885. 1st ed. 2nd issue, map and portrait....
.... *$45.00–$85.00*

Custer, Elizabeth. *Following the Guidon.* NY. 1890. 1st ed. .... *$45.00–$85.00*

Custer, Elizabeth. *Tenting On the Plains.* Norman, OK. (1971). 3 vols. new ed. boxed.
.... *$35.00–$55.00*

Custer, Elizabeth. *Tenting On the Plains.* NY. 1895...................... *$45.00–$75.00*

Custer, Gen. G. A. *Life on the Plains.* NY. 1874. 1st ed. illus. .... *$100.00–$250.00*

Cutler, Carl C. *Greyhounds of the Sea.* NY. 1930................................ *$50.00–$100.00*

Cutler, Carl C. *Queens of the Western Ocean.* US Naval Institute. 1967. illus. ....
.... *$30.00–$40.00*

D'Aulaire, Ingri and Edgar Parin. *Leif the Lucky.* Doubleday. (1941). illus. pictorial bds, map endpapers, dj. .... *$25.00–$35.00*

D'Ewes, J. *Sporting in Both Hemispheres.* Lon. 1858. 2nd ed............. *$95.00–$125.00*

Dabney, R. L. *Life & Campaigns of Lieut-Gen. T. J. Jackson.* NY. 1866. 1st ed. fldg map.
.... *$75.00–$125.00*

Dahl, Roald. *Ah, Sweet Mysteries of Life*. Knopf. 1989. illus. 1st US ed. dj. ....
.... *$30.00–$40.00*

Dahl, Roald. *Charlie and the Chocolate Factory*. NY. 1963. 1st ed. dj. . *$45.00–$65.00*

Dahl, Roald. *Fantastic Mr. Fox*. NY. 1970. 1st ed. dj. .... *$16.00–$20.00*

Dahl, Roald. *Gremlins*. NY. Random House. (1943). 1st US ed. author' first book. ......
.... *$600.00–$975.00*

Dahl, Roald. *Switch Bitch*. NY. 1974. 1st ed. dj. .... *$30.00–$50.00*

Daiken, Leslie. *Children's Toys Throughout the Ages*. NY. Frederick A Praiger. (1953). 1st ed. illus. dj. b/w photos... *$12.00–$40.00*

Daiken, Leslie. *World of Toys*. Lon. Lambarde Press. 1963. 1st UK ed, b/w photos......
.... *$15.00–$30.00*

Dale, Harrison C. (ed.). *Ashley-Smith Explor. & Disc. of Route to Pacific 1822–1829*. Cleve. 1918. 1st ed. maps, plates. .... *$175.00–$250.00*

Dalgliesh, Alice. *Enchanted Book*. 1947. 1st ed. dj. .... *$20.00–$35.00*

Dalgliesh, Alice. *Long Live the King*. NY. 1937. illus. 77 pp, pictorial endpapers. ....
.... *$25.00–$35.00*

Dali, Salvador. *Hidden Faces*. 1944. illus. 1st US ed. dj. .... *$65.00–$75.00*

Dali, Salvador. *Les Diners De Gala*. NY. Felicie. (1973). illus. pictorial cloth. gold foil pictorial dj.. *$60.00–$90.00*

Dali, Salvador. *Secret Life of Salvador Dali*. NY. 1942. 1st Amer ed. dj. ....
.... *$125.00–$250.00*

Dana James D. *Manual of Mineralogy*. New Haven. Durrie & Peck. 1855. 7th ed. ....
.... *$25.00–$40.00*

Dana, Charles. *Eastern Journeys*. NY. 1898. teg. .... *$30.00–$40.00*

Dana, Charles. *Life of Ulysses S. Grant*. 1868. .... *$25.00–$40.00*

Dana, Charles L. *Peaks of Medical History: Outline of Evolution of Medicine*. NY. 1926. 1st ed. illus. plates. .... *$75.00–$100.00*

Dana, E. S. *Textbook of Mineralogy*. NY. 1926. 4th rev ed. ....:........ *$25.00–$35.00*

Dana, James D. *Manual of Mineralogy and Lithology Containing the Elements of the Science of Minerals and Rocks*. Lon. 1882. 4th ed. .... *$40.00–$60.00*

Dana, Richard Henry. *To Cuba and Back*. Bos. 1859. 1st ed. 288 pp. ....
.... *$100.00–$125.00*

Dana, Richard Henry, Jr. *Two Years Before the Mast*. Chi. Lakeside. 1930. slipcase. ..
.... *$60.00–$80.00*

Dance of the Hours. NY. Disney. (1940). 1st ed. stiff pictorial paper bds, illus, dj. ....
.... *$80.00–$95.00*

Daniele, Joseph. *Building Colonial Furnishings, Miniatures & Folk Art*. Pa. Stackpole Books. (1976). 1st ed.. *$25.00–$30.00*

Daniels, Elam. *An Exposure of Father Divine* . . . Fairfield. 1946. wrps. illus. ....
.... *$25.00–$45.00*

Darby, Charles. *Bacchanalia. Or, A Description of a Drunken Club*. Lon. 1680. folio, calf. .... *$325.00–$425.00*

Darrow, Clarence. *Open Shop*. Chi. Charles H Kerr. nd, c1920. wrps. 32 pp, rprnt.......
.... *$40.00–$45.00*

Darrow, Clarence. *Story of My Life*. NY. Scribner's. 1932. 1st ed. sgn dj......................
.... *$400.00–$700.00*

Darwin, Charles. *Descent of Man*. Lon. 1888. 2 vols. 2nd rev ed. gray-green cloth. .....
.... *$125.00–$225.00*

Darwin, Charles. *Descent of Man* . . . NY. 1871. 2 vols. 1st Amer ed. *$350.00–$550.00*

Darwin, Charles. *Descent of Man and Selection in Relation to Sex*. NY. P F Collier. 1902. 2 vols. .... *$12.00–$24.00*

Darwin, Charles. *Descent of Man and Selection in Relation to Sex*. Lon. John Murray. 1871. 2 vols. 1st ed. 2nd issue... *$100.00–$1,250.00*

Darwin, Charles. *Effects of Cross- and Self-Fertilization* . . . NY. 1889. *$38.00–$45.00*

Darwin, Charles. *Expression of the Emotions: Man & Animals*. Appleton. 1873..........
.... *$75.00–$125.00*

Darwin, Charles. *Insectivorous Plants*. NY. 1875. 1st US ed............. *$125.00–$175.00*

Darwin, Charles. *Journal of Researches* . . . *Countries Visited by HMS Beagle*. Hafner. (1901). 26 plates.. *$40.00–$50.00*

Darwin, Charles. *Naturalist's Voyage* . . . *of HMS Beagle*. Lon. John Murray. 1890. 500 pp. .... *$60.00–$75.00*

Darwin, Charles. *On the Origin of Species By Means of Natural Selection*. Appleton. 1871. 5th ed. .... *$90.00–$150.00*

Darwin, Charles. *On the Origin of Species By Means of Natural Selection*. Lon. 1859. 3rd issue.. *$8,000.00–$10,000.00*

Darwin, Charles. *On the Origin of Species By Means of Natural Selection*. NY. 1860. 1st Amer ed. fldg diagram. brown cloth.. *$1,000.00–$2,500.00*

Darwin, Charles. *Various Contrivances By Which Orchids Are Fertilized*. Univ of Chi Press. 1984. wrps. facs of 1877 ed.. *$25.00–$35.00*

Darwin, Charles. *Works*. NY. Appleton. 1873–1883. 11 vols............. *$150.00–$250.00*

Darwin, G. H. *Evolution of Satellites*. GPO. 1898. pamphlet................. *$20.00–$35.00*

Das Plakat. *Vol 12, #4*. Berlin. April, 1921. wrps. illus. .... *$125.00–$175.00*

Daumas, M. *Scientific Instruments Of The 17th &18th Centuries*. Lon. 1972. dj. ....
.... *$30.00–$50.00*

Davenport, Alfred. *Camp and Field Life of the Fifth New York Volunteer Infantry*. NY. 1879. .... *$175.00–$250.00*

Davenport, Cyril. *Royal English Book Bindings*. Lon. 1896. 1st ed. illus......................
.... *$45.00–$65.00*

Davenport, John. *Aphrodisiacs and Anti-Aphrodisiacs*. Lon. 1869. 1st ed. illus. ....
.... *$75.00–$125.00*

Davenport-Hill, Florence. *Children of the State*. Lon. Macmillan. 1889. 2nd ed. 46 pp.
.... *$46.00–$100.00*

Davidson, Ellis. *Practical Manual of House Painting*. Lon. 1884. .... *$45.00–$50.00*

Davidson, Gordon Charles. *North West Company*. Berkeley. 1918. 1st ed. illus. maps, plates. .... *$95.00–$145.00*

Davidson, J. N. *Muh-he-ka-ne-ok. A History of the Stockbridge Nation*. Milwaukee. 1893. .... *$45.00–$55.00*

Davie, Oliver. *Nests and Eggs of North American Birds*. OH. Landon Press. 1898. illus. .... *$45.00–$60.00*

Davie, Oliver. *Reveries and Recollections of a Naturalist*. Columbus. private ptg. 1898. 1st ed. illus. plates, teg, #50/200 cc. .... *$60.00–$90.00*

Davies, Thomas. *Preparation and Mounting of Microscopic Objects*. NY. 1876. 2nd ed, illus, 214 pp. .... *$30.00–$45.00*

Davies, Thomas. *Preparation and Mounting of Microscopic Objects*. Lon. 1864. 1st ed. .... *$40.00–$50.00*

Davis, Angela Y. *Women Culture and Politics*. NY. Random House. 1989. 1st ed. .... *$15.00–$25.00*

Davis, Brian L. *German Army Uniforms & Insignia, 1933–1940*. NY. 1972. wrps. .... *$25.00–$35.00*

Davis, Burke. *Grey Fox: Robert E. Lee and the Civil War*. NY. 1956. illus. maps, dj. .... *$25.00–$35.00*

Davis, Daniel. *An Address to Inhabitants . . . Maine . . .* Portland. 1791. .... *$50.00–$100.00*

Davis, Henry P. *Training Your Own Bird Dog*. Putnam's Sons. 1948. 1st ed. dj. .... *$30.00–$40.00*

Davis, Jefferson. *Purchase of Camels for Military Transportation*. Wash. 1857. illus. .... *$150.00–$200.00*

Davis, Jefferson. *Rise and Fall of the Confederate Government*. NY. 1881. 2 vols. 1st ed. 808 pp. .... *$150.00–$275.00*

Davis, Jerome. *Capitalism and Its Culture*. NY. Farrar & Rinehart. 1941. 3rd ed. cloth inscrb. .... *$30.00–$45.00*

Davis, Jodie. *Teach Yourself to Make Angels & Fairies*. NY. Friedman/Fairfax Pub. 1996. dj. .... *$12.00–$20.00*

Davis, M. L. *Memoirs of Aaron Burr*. NY. 1836. 2 vols. .... *$100.00–$300.00*

Davis, Mary Lee. *Uncle Sam's Attic, the Intimate Story of Alaska*. Bos. 1930. 1st ed. ... . *$35.00–$50.00*

Davis, Ossie. *Escape to Freedom*. NY. Viking. 1976. 2nd ptg. sgn, dj. *$75.00–$100.00*

Davis, Paris M. *An Authentick History of the late War Between the United States and Great Britain*. Ithaca. Davis & Saunders. 1829. 1st ed. original sheep, black label. .... *$100.00–$120.00*

Davis, Rear-Admiral C. H. (ed.). *Narrative of the North Polar Expedition. US Ship Polaris*. Wash. GPO. 1878. 2nd ptg, engr, lithos, maps, decorative red cloth. .... *$60.00–$75.00*

Davis, Reg S. and Steiner. *Mona Lisa Philipine Orchids*. NY. 1952. .... *$50.00–$65.00*

Davis, Richard Harding. *About Paris*. NY. Harper. 1895. 1st ed. illus. by Dana Gibson. .... *$20.00–$35.00*

Davis, Richard Harding. *Bar Sinister*. NY. 1903. 1st ed........................ *$30.00–$50.00*

Davis, Richard Harding. *Cuban and Porto Rican Campaigns*. NY. 1898. 1st ed. illus..
.... *$30.00–$75.00*

Davis, Richard Harding. *Van Bibber and Others*. NY. 1892. 1st ed...... *$35.00–$40.00*

Davis, Richard Harding. *Vera the Medium*. Scribner's. 1908. 1st ed. purple binding. ...
.... *$25.00–$40.00*

Davis, Richard Harding. *West From a Car Window*. NY/Lon. 1892. 1st ed. illus. by Frederick Remington. .... *$50.00–$65.00*

Davis, Susan Lawrence. *Authentic History of the Ku Klux Klan 1865–1877*. NY. Private ptg. 1924. .... *$140.00–$225.00*

Davis, W. *El Gringo, or New Mexico and Her People*. NY. 1857. .... *$75.00–$300.00*

Davis, W. W. H. *History of Doylestown Old and New*. Doylestown, PA. Intelligencer Print. (1905). illus. green cloth... *$60.00–$85.00*

Davis, W. W. H. *History of Doylestown, Old and New*. Doylestown. 1900. 1st ed. illus. green cloth gold lettering on front cvr and spine................................... *$65.00–$75.00*

Davis, W. W. H. *Spanish Conquest of New Mexico*. Doylestown, PA. private ptg. 1886. 1st ed. inscr, pullout map.. *$350.00–$600.00*

Davis, William W. *History of Bucks County Pennsylvania*. NY/Chi. Lewis Pub Co. 1905. 3 vols. illus. 2nd ed, rev and enlarged lea and marbled bds. marbled endpapers. presentation copy sgn by author. .... *$200.00–$300.00*

Dawson, Mrs. Nelson (Edith B.). *Enamels*. Chi. 1910. illus.................. *$25.00–$35.00*

Dawson, Sarah M. *Confederate Girl's Diary*. Bos. 1913. 1st ed. .... *$75.00–$125.00*

Dawson, Simon J. *Report of the Exploration of the Country Between Lake Superior and the Red River Settlement . . .* Tor. Legislative Assembly. 1859. 3 large fldg maps. ....
.... *$285.00–$300.00*

Dawson, W. F. *Christmas: Its Origin and Associations*. Lon. Stock. 1902. 1st ed. illus. teg. .... *$100.00–$150.00*

Day, Jeremiah. *Introducton to Algebra*. New Haven. 1814. 1st ed. .... *$45.00–$65.00*

Day, L. W. *Story of the One Hundred and First Ohio Infantry*. Cleve. 1894. 1st ed. illus.
.... *$150.00–$250.00*

Day, Lal Behari. *Bengal Peasant Life*. Lon. 1892.................................. *$22.00–$30.00*

Dayan, Moshe. *Story of My Life*. NY. 1976. 1st ed. illus. photos, sgn, dj.....................
.... *$30.00–$45.00*

Dayton, Fred Erving. *Steamboat Days*. NY. 1925. 1st ed. illus. by John Wolcott Adams.
.... *$40.00–$60.00*

De Angel, Marguerite. *Book of Nursery & Mother Goose Rhymes*. Garden City. Doubleday. 1954. illus. Caldecott Honor book, dj................................... *$35.00–$50.00*

De Beauvoir, Simone. *Long March*. Cleve/NY. 1958. 1st ed. dj............. *$47.00–$60.00*

De Beauvoir, Simone. *The Mandarins*. NY. 1956. 1st Amer ed. dj. .... *$22.00–$30.00*

De Bothezat, George. *Back to Newton*. NY. 1936. 1st ed. 152 pp, dj..... *$30.00–$35.00*

De Brunhoff, Jean. *Babar and Father Christmas*. NY. (1940). 1st ed. illus. dj. ....
.... *$80.00–$90.00*

De Brunhoff, Jean. *Babar and His Children*. NY. (1938). 1st Amer, illus, folio. ....
.... *$100.00–$175.00*

De Brunhoff, Jean. *Babar the King*. NY. Random House. 1986. folio, printed in France, dj. .... *$35.00–$50.00*

De Brunhoff, Jean. *Babar the King*. Smith/Haas. 1935. 1st Amer ed. folio.................
.... *$125.00–$150.00*

De Brunhoff, Jean. *Travels of Babar*. Smith Haas. 1934. 1st ed. illus. ....
.... *$250.00–$300.00*

De Camp, Etta. *Return of Frank Stockton*. NY. 1913. 1st ed.................. *$75.00–$85.00*

De Chastellux, Marquis. *Travels in North America in the Years 1780, 1781,1782*. Lon. G G J and J Robinson. 1788. 2 vols. contemporary calf binding. raised bands, black and red labels on spine. 2 folding maps... *$750.00–$850.00*

De Clifford, N. F. *Egypt the Cradle of Ancient Masonry*. NY. 1907. 2 vols..................
.... *$65.00–$85.00*

De Fontelle, M. *Conversations on the Plurality of Worlds*. Dublin. Wilson. 1761. illus..
.... *$50.00–$100.00*

De Groat, Robert W. *Totem Poles—A Happy Hobby for Boys*. NY. Boy Scouts of America. 1930. 1st ed. wrps. illus... *$28.00–$35.00*

De La Mare, Walter. *Eight Tales*. Sauk City. 1971. 1st ed. 2,992 cc, dj. *$35.00–$45.00*

De La Mare, Walter. *Memoirs of a Midget*. Lon. (1921). 1st ed. dj...... *$35.00–$50.00*

De La Mare, Walter. *Mr. Bumps and His Monkey*. Chi. 1942. 1st ed. illus. ....
.... *$95.00–$135.00*

De La Mare, Walter. *Riddle and Other Stories*. Lon. (1923). 1st ed. blue clr, dj. ....
.... *$120.00–$150.00*

De Leon, T. C., (ed.). *South Songs: From the Lays of Later Days*. NY. 1866. 1st ed. .....
.... *$95.00–$125.00*

De Marinis, Rick. *Coming Triumph of the Free World*. NY. Viking. 1988. 1st ed. dj. ....
.... *$15.00–$25.00*

De Maupassant, Guy. *Odd Number*. Lon. 1891. 1st Eng ed. .... *$50.00–$75.00*

De Poncins, Gontran. *From a Chinese City*. Garden City. 1957. 1st ed. dj...................
.... *$50.00–$65.00*

De Quille, Dan. *History of the Big Bonanza*. Hartford. 1876............. *$100.00–$250.00*

De Quille, Dan. *History of the Comstock Silver Lode*. Nev. (1889). wrps. ....
....*$100.00–$250.00*

De Quincey, Thomas. *Essays on the Poets and Other English Writers*. Bos. Ticknor & Fields. 1859. .... *$50.00–$80.00*

De Roos, Frederick. *Personal Narrative of Travels in the U.S. and Canada in 1826*. Lon. 1827. illus. 2nd ed. lithos, maps.. *$165.00–$250.00*

De Segur, Philip. *History of the Expedition to Russia*. Lon. Treuttel & Wurtz. 1825. 2 vols in one. folding map rev and corrected. .... *$60.00–$90.00*

De Shields, James T. *Border Wars of Texas*. Tioga, TX. 1912. 1st ed. illus. ....
.... *$175.00–$250.00*

De Smet, P. J. *Western Missions and Missionaries.* NY. 1859. 1st ed. *$105.00–$195.00*

De Smet, Pierre-Jean. *Oregon Missions and Travels Over the Rocky Mountains.* NY. 1847. 1st ed. wrps. plates, fldg map.. *$350.00–$900.00*

De Voto, Bernard. *Across the Wide Missouri.* Bos. 1947. illus.............. *$40.00–$90.00*

De Voto, Bernard. *Mark Twain at Work.* 1942. 1st ed. dj. .... *$22.00–$35.00*

De Voto, Bernard. *Year of Decision 1846.* Bos. 1943. 1st ed. dj. .... *$24.00–$32.00*

De Vries, Hugo. *Species and Varieties. Their Origin by Mutation.* Chi. 1906. 2nd ed. ... . *$75.00–$95.00*

De Vries, Peter. *I Hear America Singing.* Little Brown. 1976. 1st ed. dj. .... *$24.00–$30.00*

De Vries, Peter. *Into Your Tent I'll Creep.* Bos. 1971. 1st Amer ed. dj. .. *$20.00–$30.00*

De Vries, Peter. *Slouching Towards Kalamazoo.* Bos. (1983). 1st ed. sgn, dj. .... *$20.00–$30.00*

De Vries, Peter. *Vale of Laughter.* Bos. 1967. sgn, presentation copy, dj...................... .... *$35.00–$45.00*

Deane, Samuel. *History of Scituate, Massachusetts.* Bos. 1831. 1st ed. 406 pp............. .... *$200.00–$225.00*

Dearborn, R. F. *Saratoga Illustrated.* Troy, NY. 1872. 1st ed. illus. fldg map, clr lithos. .... *$96.00–$125.00*

Death, J. *Beer of the Bible with a Visit to an Arab Brewery.* Lon. 1887. 179 pp............ ....*$90.00–$250.00*

Debs, Eugene. *His Life, Writings and Speeches.* Girard. 1908. sgn. ... *$100.00–$135.00*

Decker, Amelia Stickney. *That Ancient Trail.* pub by author. (1942). illus. 3rd ed......... .... *$20.00–$30.00*

Decker, John W. *Cheese Making.* WI. 1909... *$30.00–$45.00*

Decter, Midge. *Liberated Woman and Other Americans.* NY. Coward McCann. [1971]. 256 pp, dj.. *$30.00–$40.00*

Deere, John & Co. *How to Keep Your Farm Equipment in the Fight.* illus. .... *$15.00–$25.00*

Deere, John & Co. *Operation, Care and Repair of Farm Machinery.* 1957. illus........... .... *$25.00–$45.00*

Deering Ideals. Chi. Deering Harvester Co. 1902. illus. pictorial wrps. .... *$40.00–$50.00*

Defoe, Daniel. *Adventures of Robinson Crusoe.* Lon. (1867). illus. gilt cloth................ .... *$90.00–$115.00*

Defoe, Daniel. *Journal of the Plague Year.* 1968. illus. LEC 1/1500 cc sgn. dj. glassine slipcase.. *$50.00–$85.00*

Defoe, Daniel. *Life and Strange Surprising Adventures of Robinson Crusoe.* NY/Lon. Harper & Bros. (1900). illus. by Louis and Frederick Rhead. black cloth, pictorial pastedown. .... *$20.00–$30.00*

Defoe, Daniel. *Memoirs of a Cavalier.* Lon. (1720). 1st ed. calf......... *$175.00–$250.00*

Defoe, Daniel. *Moll Flanders.* Lane. 1929. illus...................................... *$40.00–$75.00*

Defoe, Daniel. *Robinson Crusoe*. NY. Cosmo. 1920. illus. with clr plate by N C Wyeth.
.... *$90.00–$190.00*

Defoe, Daniel. *Robinson Crusoe*. Worcester, MA. 1795. illus. wood-engr frontis. ....
.... *$60.00–$90.00*

Deighton, Len. *Bomber*. NY. Harper & Row. 1970. 1st ed. dj. .... *$44.00–$55.00*

Deighton, Len. *Funeral in Berlin*. Putnam. 1965. 1st US ed. dj. .... *$60.00–$70.00*

Deighton, Len. *Ipcress File*. NY. Simon & Schuster. 1963. 1st US ed. dj. ....
.... *$75.00–$140.00*

Deighton, Len. *Only When I Laugh*. NY. 1987. ltd 250 cc, sgn, slipcase. ....
.... *$95.00–$125.00*

Deite, C. *Practical Treatise on Manufacture of Perfumery*. Phila. 1892. illus. 1st Amer
ed. .... *$40.00–$55.00*

Del Rey, Lester. *Attack from Atlantis*. Phila. Winston. (1953). 207 pp, dj. ....
.... *$50.00–$65.00*

Delany, Samuel R. *Dhalgren*. Bantam Books. (1975). 1st ed. pictorial wrps. ....
.... *$20.00–$25.00*

Dellenbaugh, Frederick S. *Romance of the Colorado River*. Putnam. 1903. 2nd ptg.
illus. photos, drawings. .... *$70.00–$100.00*

Dellenbaugh, Frederick S. *Romance of the Colorado River*. NY. P. Putnam's Sons.
1903. illus. 399 pp. .... *$75.00–$90.00*

Dempsey, Hugh. *History in Their Blood, The Indian Portraits of N. Grandmaison*.
Hudson Hills, NY. 1982. 1st Amer ed. dj. .... *$40.00–$50.00*

Dempsey, Jack. *Dempsey: By the Man Himself*. 1960. 1st ed. sgn. .... *$50.00–$65.00*

Dempsey, Jack. *Round by Round*. 1940. 1st ed. wrps. .... *$28.00–$35.00*

Denham, Major Dixon. *Narrative of Travels & Discoveries in Northern & Central
Africa*. 1826. .... *$650.00–$700.00*

Denhardt, Robert Moorman. *King Ranch Quarter Horses*. Norman. Univ Oklahoma
Press. 1970. 1st ed. dj. .... *$50.00–$65.00*

Denhardt, Robert Moorman. *Quarter Horses*. Norman. Univ Oklahoma Press. 1967.
1st ed. sgn, dj. .... *$40.00–$65.00*

Denliger, Milo. *Complete Cocker Spaniel*. DC. Denlinger. 1946. 1st ed. *$35.00–$40.00*

Dennis, Morgan. *Morgan Dennis Dog Book*. NY. 1946. 1st ed. illus. dj. ....
.... *$25.00–$35.00*

Denslow, W. W. *Denslow's Scarecrow and the Tin Man*. 1903. 1st ed. illus. linen..........
.... *$300.00–$600.00*

Denslow, W. W. *Mother Goose*. NY. McClure. 1901. illus. paper bds. ....
.... *$100.00–$500.00*

Denslow, W. W. *Pearl and the Pumpkin*. NY. Dillingham Co. 1904. 1st ed. illus. green
cloth. .... *$100.00–$200.00*

Denslow, W. W. *Scarecrow and the Tin-Man*. Dillingham. (1904)...... *$150.00–$300.00*

Denslow, W. W. *When I Grow Up*. Century. 1909. 1st ed. illus. 24 clr plates................
.... *$100.00–$150.00*

Denslow, William. *Freemasony & the American Indian*. Missouri Lodge of Research. 1972. illus. photos. .... *$25.00–$45.00*

Densmore, Frances. *Chippewa Music II*. DC. GPO. 1913. 1st ed. 341pp. Bulletin 53.. .... *$50.00–$90.00*

Densmore, Frances. *Papago Music*. Wash. GPO. 1929. illus. .... *$35.00–$60.00*

Derby, W. L. A. *Tall Ships*. NY. Scribner's. 1937. 1st ed. illus. photos, plates................ .... *$50.00–$100.00*

Derby, W. L. A. *Tall Ships Pass*. Lon. 1937. illus................................... *$75.00–$110.00*

Derleth, August. *Bright Journey*. NY. Scribner's. 1940. 1st ed. inscr...... *$50.00–$65.00*

Derleth, August. *Casebook of Solar Pons*. Sauk City. 1965. 1st ed. dj... *$35.00–$45.00*

Derleth, August. *Dark Mind, Dark Heart*. Sauk City. Arkham House. 1962. dj inscrb and sgn.. *$80.00–$120.00*

Derleth, August. *Fell Purpose*. NY. Arcadia House. 1953. 1st ed. dj...... *$45.00–$50.00*

Derleth, August. *Not Long For This World*. Sauk City. 1948. 1st ed. ltd, dj. ....*$150.00–$175.00*

Derleth, August. *Over the Edge*. Arkham House. 1964. 1st ed. dj.......... *$30.00–$45.00*

Derleth, August. *Over the Edge*. Sauk City. Arkham House. 1964. 1st ed. dj. sgn. .... *$50.00–$75.00*

Derleth, August. *Restless Is the River*. Scribner's. 1939. 1st ed. dj...... *$50.00–$100.00*

Derleth, August. *Something Near*. Sauk City. Arkham House. 1945. 1st ed. 274 pp, inscrb..:.................................. *$75.00–$95.00*

Derleth, August. *Thirty Years of Arkham House*. Sauk City. 1970. 1st ed. dj. .... *$50.00–$85.00*

Derry, Joseph. *Story of the Confederate States*. Richmond. 1895. 1st ed. illus.............. .... *$50.00–$100.00*

Descharnes, Robert. *World of Salvador Dali*. Atide Books. nd. dj......... *$50.00–$80.00*

Description and Rules for the Management of the U.S. Magazine Rifle Model of 1903, caliber .30. DC. GPO. 1909. rev. .... *$20.00–$35.00*

Description of the New York Central Park. NY. 1869........................ *$250.00–$700.00*

Descriptive Catalogue of School Supplies. Chi. Central School Supply House. c 1897-98. illus. pictorial wrps, 88 pp... *$95.00–$125.00*

Desio, Ardito. *Ascent of K2*. Lon. 1955. 1st ed. photos, maps. .... *$45.00–$58.00*

Desmond, Kay. *All Color Book of Dolls*. Lon. Octopus Books Ltd. 1974. 1st ed. illus. photos... *$10.00–$25.00*

Desmond, Ray. *Bibliography of British Gardens*. London. St. Paul's Bibliographies. (1988). 1st ed. illus.. *$50.00–$80.00*

Deutsch, Babette. *Take Them, Stranger*. NY. (1944). 1st ed. sgn. .... *$44.00–$60.00*

Development of the Locomotive. OH. Central Steel Co. (1925). illus. buff and brown clr. .... *$15.00–$20.00*

Dewees, F. P. *Molly Maguires*. Phila. 1877. map................................... *$95.00–$150.00*

Dewees, William. *Compendious System of Midwifery*. Phila. Carey & Lea. 1832. 5th ed. engr, 636 pp. .... *$130.00–$150.00*

Dewees, William. *Compendious System of Midwifery*. Phila. 1847. illus. lea................... .... *$75.00–$120.00*

Dewees, William. *Treatise on the Diseases of Females*. Phila. 1840. illus. 7th ed. calf, steel plates. .... *$75.00–$125.00*

Dewey, John. *Experience and Education*. 1938. 1st ed. sgn. .... *$55.00–$75.00*

Dewitt, David Miller. *Judicial Murder of Mary E. Surratt*. Balt. 1895. 1st ed................ .... *$185.00–$250.00*

Dick & Jane: Our New Friends. 1946. .... *$65.00–$70.00*

Dick and Jane: Before We Read. 1965. softcvr. .... *$50.00–$75.00*

Dick and Jane: Fun Wherever We Are. 1962. softcvr. .... *$35.00–$85.00*

Dick and Jane: Fun With Dick & Jane. 1940. .... *$70.00–$120.00*

Dick and Jane: Now We Read. 1965. softcvr. .... *$75.00–$165.00*

Dick and Jane: We Look and See. 1946–47. softcvr. .... *$40.00–$120.00*

Dick and Jane: We Talk, Spell and Write. 1951. softcvr. .... *$75.00–$195.00*

Dick, Philip. *Counter Clock World*. NY. Berkley. (1967). wrps. .... *$40.00–$50.00*

Dick, Philip. *Game Players of Titan*. Ace Pub. (1963). wrps. .... *$20.00–$25.00*

Dick, Philip. *Time Out of Joint*. Lon. 1961. 1st UK ed. blue cloth. .... *$120.00–$150.00*

Dick, Philip K. *Broken Bubble*. NY. Arbor House. (1988). 1st ed. dj. .... *$30.00–$40.00*

Dick, Philip K. *Cosmic Puppets*. Severn House. (1986). 1st ed. dj. .... *$35.00–$45.00*

Dick, Philip K. *Crack in Space*. Wallington. Severn House. (1989). 1st separate hardcvr ed, dj. .... *$25.00–$45.00*

Dick, Philip K. *Golden Man*. Berkeley. (1980). 1st ed. paperback. .... *$30.00–$35.00*

Dick, Philip K. *I Hope I Shall Arrive Soon*. NY. 1985. dj....................... *$25.00–$35.00*

Dick, Philip K. *Our Friends from Frolix 8*. Lon. Kinnell. 1989. 1st hardcvr ed, dj......... ....*$25.00–$65.00*

Dick, Philip K. *Scanner Darkly*. Garden City. 1977. 1st ed. dj............. *$75.00–$125.00*

Dick, William B. *Dick's Hand Book of Cribbage*. NY. 1885................... *$18.00–$25.00*

Dicke and Jane: Fun With Dick & Jane. 1946. .... *$150.00–$180.00*

Dickens, Charles. *A Christmas Carol*. Lon. Chapman & Hall. 1843. 1st ed. reddish-brown ribbed cloth.. *$5,750.00–$10,000.00*

Dickens, Charles. *A Christmas Carol*. Phil. 1844. illus. by John Leech, 4 clr plates, 4 woodcuts, dark blue binding, 158 pp. .... *$600.00–$900.00*

Dickens, Charles. *Battle of Life*. Lon. Bradbury and Evans. 1846. 30 vols. 1st ed. cloth aeg.. *$200.00–$350.00*

Dickens, Charles. *Dombey & Son*. NY. 1847. wrps. .... *$100.00–$210.00*

Dickens, Charles. *Life and Adventures of Martin Chuzzlewit*. Lon. Chapman and Hall. 1844. 1st ed. illus. original bds. .... *$75.00–$150.00*

Dickens, Charles. *Life and Adventures of Nicholas Nickelby.* Chapman & Hall. 1839. 1st ed in book form. .... *$150.00–$200.00*

Dickens, Charles. *Little Dorrit.* Lon. 1857. illus. 1st ed in book form, engr, ½ calf, mar bds .... *$185.00–$285.00*

Dickens, Charles. *Martin Chuzzlewit.* Ticknor & Fields. 1867. illus. ...... *$50.00–$85.00*

Dickens, Charles. *Our Mutual Friend.* Lon. 1865. 2 vols. 1st ed in book form. .... *$150.00–$250.00*

Dickens, Charles. *The Chimes.* Lon. Limited Ed Club. 1931. 1st thus. ltd 1,500 cc sgn by Arthur Rackham, cvr design by Rackham, teg, illus. .... *$400.00–$500.00*

Dickens, Charles. *Works of . . .* NY. Scribner's. 1899. 36 vols. illus. .... *$1,000.00–$3,000.00*

Dickens, Charles. *Works of . . .* Lon. Folio Society. 1981–88. 16 vols. illus. cloth backed bds. slipcases. .... *$200.00–$300.00*

Dickey, James. *Deliverance.* Bos. 1970. 1st ed. 1st ptg, dj. .... *$35.00–$55.00*

Dickey, James. *To the White Sea.* Houghton. 1993. 1st ed. sgn, dj. .... *$45.00–$50.00*

Dickey, James. *Tucky the Hunter.* NY. Crown Pub Co. 1978. 1st ed. ..... *$25.00–$35.00*

Dickinson, Emily. *Bolts of Melody.* NY. 1945. 1st ed. Todd & Bingham (eds). .... *$25.00–$40.00*

Dickinson, Emily. *Poems.* Bos. Roberts. 1891. 1st ed. ed by T W Higginson and Mabel Loomis Todd, second series, 8vo, 230 pp, teg, gray-green cloth. .... *$350.00–$800.00*

Dickinson, Emily. *Poems.* Bos. Roberts Bros. 1892. 9th ed. dec cloth. .... *$90.00–$120.00*

Dickinson, Emily. *Single Hound.* Bos. 1914. .... *$300.00–$400.00*

Dickinson, S. N. *Boston Almanac for the Year 1843.* Bos. illus. .... *$35.00–$45.00*

Dickson, Walter. *Japan.* Peter Fenelon Collier. 1898. illus. red cloth. ... *$22.00–$30.00*

Didion, Joan. *Run River.* Obolensky. 1963. 1st ed. dj. .... *$75.00–$125.00*

Didion, Joan. *Slouching Towards Bethlehem.* NY. 1968. dj. .... *$40.00–$60.00*

Dietz, August. *Postal Service of the Confederate States of America.* Richmond. 1929. 1st ed. sgn. .... *$200.00–$350.00*

Digges, Jeremiah. *Cape Cod Pilot.* Provincetown/NY. WPA. 1937. 2nd ptg dj. .... *$25.00–$35.00*

Dillard, Annie. *An American Childhood.* Harper. 1987. 1st ed. dj. .... *$25.00–$30.00*

Dillard, Annie. *Holy the Firm.* NY. Harper & Row. (1977). 1st ed. dj. .. *$30.00–$75.00*

Dillon, Richard. *Images of Chinatown: Louis J. Stellman's Chinatown Photographs.* SF. Book Club of California. 1976. 1st ed. .... *$75.00–$140.00*

Dillon, Richard H. *Hatchet Men.* NY. (1962). illus. .... *$10.00–$20.00*

Dimsdale, Thomas J. *Vigilantes of Montana.* Helena. nd. 4th ed. .... *$50.00–$75.00*

Dinesen, Isak. *Anecdotes of Destiny.* NY. Random House. (1958). 1st ed. dj. .... *$30.00–$60.00*

Dinesen, Isak. *Last Tales.* NY. 1959. 1st ed. dj. .... *$15.00–$25.00*

Dinesen, Isak. *Out of Africa.* NY. 1938. 1st ed. dj.............................. *$100.00–$175.00*

Dinesen, Isak. *Seven Gothic Tales.* NY. 1934. 1st ed. dj. .... *$35.00–$85.00*

Directory of the City of New Brunswick 1855–56. J Terhune. 1855... *$100.00–$135.00*

Dirigibles Captifs Spheriques; Parachutes; Treuils & Tenders D'Aerostation. Paris. Zodiac, Anciens Establissements Aeronautiques. 1918. illus. pictorial wrps, 32 pp........ .... *$175.00–$250.00*

Dismond, Binga. *We Who Would Die.* NY. Wendell Malliet and Co. 1943. 1st ed. illus. by E Simms Campbell. inscr, dj... *$100.00–$300.00*

Disney. *Mickey Mouse Story Book.* Phila. (1931). orange pictorial cloth...................... .... *$140.00–$750.00*

Disney. *Mickey Mouse Waddle Book.* NY. 1934. bds. .... *$300.00–$800.00*

Disney. *Pop-up Mickey Mouse.* Blue Ribbon Books. 1933. illus. 3 pop-ups.................. .... *$125.00–$600.00*

Disney. *Pop-Up Minnie Mouse.* 1933. illus. 3 pop-ups...................... *$200.00–$350.00*

Disney, Alfred N. *Origin and Development of the Microscope.* Lon. 1928. illus. plates. .... *$140.00–$150.00*

Disney, Walt. *Bambi.* NY. Grosset & Dunlap. (1942). illus. yellow pictorial bds dj........ .... *$65.00–$85.00*

Disney, Walt. *Fantasia Program.* 1940. 1st ed. wrps. illus. clr............. *$40.00–$200.00*

Disney, Walt. *Life of Donald Duck.* NY. Random House. (1941). 1st ed. pictorial bds. .... *$75.00–$125.00*

Disney, Walt. *Mickey Mouse Stories, Book #2.* Phila. David McKay. 1934. wrps. illus. .... *$100.00–$175.00*

Disney, Walt. *Pop-Up Mickey Mouse.* NY. Blue Ribbon. 1933. 1st ed. illus. 3 pop-ups. .... *$300.00–$600.00*

Disney, Walt. *Snow White and the Seven Dwarfs.* Walt Disney Enterprises. 1938. 1st ed. wrps. illus. clr pictures from the movie. .... *$75.00–$80.00*

Disney, Walt. *Stories from Fantasia.* Random House. (1940). 1st ed. dj...................... .... *$75.00–$100.00*

Disney, Walt. *Three Little Pigs.* NY. Blue Ribbon. (1933). illus. dj.... *$200.00–$250.00*

Ditmars, R. *Reptiles of the World.* Lon. 1946. illus. rev ed.................... *$25.00–$35.00*

Ditmars, R. L. *Snakes of the World.* NY. (1931). .... *$25.00–$35.00*

Diving . . . Attempt to Describe Method of Supplying Diver With Air. Hartford. 1813. 1st ed. wrps. pamphlet... *$200.00–$375.00*

Dix, Dorothea. *Memorial to the Legislature of Massachusetts.* Salem. Gazette Office. 1843. 1st ed. wrps. unopened, 15 pp.................................... *$200.00–$375.00*

Dixon, Franklin. *Brushing The Mountain Top.* Grosset & Dunlap. 1934. *$10.00–$15.00*

Dixon, Franklin. *Hardy Boys A Figure in Hiding.* Grosset & Dunlap. 1937. ....*$7.00–$15.00*

Dixon, Franklin. *Hidden Harbor Mystery.* Grosset & Dunlap. 1935. Hardy Boys #14.. .... *$14.00–$25.00*

Dixon, Franklin. *Hooded Hawk Mystery*. Grosset & Dunlap. 1971. Hardy Boys #34, dj.
.... *$20.00–$25.00*

Dixon, Franklin. *House on the Cliff*. Grosset & Dunlap. 1927. Hardy Boys #2, dj. ....
.... *$20.00–$25.00*

Dixon, Franklin. *House on the Cliff*. Grosset & Dunlap. (1959). Hardy Boys #2, dj. ....
.... *$20.00–$25.00*

Dixon, Franklin. *Hunting for Hidden Gold*. Grosset & Dunlap. illus. ... *$12.00–$15.00*

Dixon, Franklin. *Mark On the Door*. Grosset & Dunlap. dj................... *$15.00–$20.00*

Dixon, Franklin. *Missing Chums*. Grosset & Dunlap. (1957). dj. .... *$15.00–$20.00*

Dixon, Franklin. *Missing Chums*. Grosset & Dunlap. (1957). Hardy Boys, dj. ....
.... *$12.00–$15.00*

Dixon, Franklin. *Mystery of Cabin Island*. Grosset & Dunlap. 1929. Hardy Boys #8, dj.
.... *$19.00–$25.00*

Dixon, Franklin. *Mystery of Cabin Island*. Grosset & Dunlap. 1929. Hardy Boys #8....
.... *$9.00–$12.00*

Dixon, Franklin. *Shore Road Mystery*. Grosset & Dunlap....................... *$8.00–$10.00*

Dixon, Franklin. *Short Wave Mystery*. Grosset & Dunlap. (1945). Hardy Boys #24, dj.
.... *$18.00–$25.00*

Dixon, Franklin. *Sign of the Crooked Arrow*. Grosset & Dunlap. (1934). Hardy Boys #28, dj... *$18.00–$25.00*

Dixon, Franklin. *While the Clock Ticked*. Grosset & Dunlap. 1941. tan cloth. ....
.... *$15.00–$20.00*

Dixon, H. *John Howard & the Prison World of Europe*. 1852. .... *$35.00–$50.00*

Dixon, Joseph K. *Vanishing Race, The Last Great Indian Council* . . . NY. 1914. illus..
.... *$85.00–$125.00*

Dixon, Peter. *Bobby Benson in the Tunnel of Gold*. 1936. 1st ed. wrps. illus..............
.... *$12.00–$15.00*

Dixon, Sam Houston. *Romance and Tragedy of Texas History*. Houston. 1924. 1st ed. inscrb and sgn. .... *$15.00–$25.00*

Dixon, William Scarth. *Fox-Hunting in the 20th Century*. 1925. .... *$25.00–$35.00*

Dobell, Horace. *On the Nature, Cause, and Treatment of Tuberculosis*. Lon. 1866. ....
.... *$20.00–$25.00*

Dobie, Frank. *Tales of Old Time Texas*. Bos. 1955. dj. .... *$45.00–$55.00*

Dobie, J Frank. *Man Bird and Beast*. Austin. 1930. 1st ed. cloth. .... *$35.00–$45.00*

Dobie, J. Frank. *Apache Gold & Yanqui Silver*. Little Brown. 1939. 1st ed. dj. ....
.... *$30.00–$75.00*

Dobie, J. Frank. *As the Moving Finger Writ*. np. (1955). wrps. 12 pp. .. *$25.00–$40.00*

Dobie, J. Frank. *Ben Lilly Legend*. 1950. 1st ed. dj. .... *$30.00–$60.00*

Dobie, J. Frank. *Life and Literature of the South West*. Austin. 1943. 1st ed. illus. by Peter Hurd. .... *$50.00–$90.00*

Dobie, J. Frank. *The Longhorns*. Bos. 1941. 1st ed. dj........................... *$40.00–$50.00*

Dobie, J. Frank. *The Mustangs*. Bos. Little Brown. (1952). 1st ed. dj. ... *$40.00–$70.00*

Dobie, J. Frank. *The Mustangs*. Bos. Little Brown. (1952). 1st ed. .... *$25.00–$40.00*

Dobie, J. Frank. *Voice of the Coyote*. Little Brown. 1949. 1st ed. dj. .... *$50.00–$90.00*

Dobie, J. Frank. *Wild and Wily*. Flagstaff. Northland Press. 1980. 1st ed. dj................
.... *$30.00–$45.00*

Dobson, William. *Kunopaedia, a Practical Essay on Breaking or Training the English Spaniel or Pointer*. Lon. 1817. 2nd ed. .... *$100.00–$200.00*

Dobyns, Henry F. and Robert C. Euler. *Ghost Dance of 1889*. Ariz. Prescott College Press. 1967. illus. photos, dj... *$45.00–$60.00*

Docstader, Frederick. *Kachina and the White Man*. Cranbrook Inst. 1954. 1st ed. dj....
.... *$30.00–$40.00*

Doctorow, E. L. *Billy Bathgate*. Random House. (1989). 1st ed. ltd 300 cc, sgn, slipcase.
.... *$85.00–$125.00*

Doctorow, E. L. *Lives of the Poets*. NY. Random House. (1984). 1st ed. dj...................
.... *$25.00–$30.00*

Doctorow, E. L. *Loon Lake*. NY. Random House. (1980). 1st ed. 1/350 cc, sgn, slipcase.
.... *$100.00–$120.00*

Doctorow, E. L. *Loon Lake*. NY. Random House. 1980. 1st ed. dj........ *$20.00–$30.00*

Doctorow, E. L. *Ragtime*. NY. (1975). 1st ed. sgn, dj. .... *$50.00–$65.00*

Doctorow, E. L. *Welcome to Hard Times*. NY. 1960. 1st ed. dj.............. *$60.00–$75.00*

Documents Concerning German-Polish Relations and the Outbreak of Hostilities Between Great Britain and Germany on September 3, 1939. Lon. Secretary of State, Foreign Affairs. 1939. 1st ed. wrps. .... *$50.00–$80.00*

Dodge, Col. Richard I. *Our Wild Indians*. Hartford. 1882................... *$50.00–$100.00*

Dodge, Grenville. *Battle of Atlanta and Other Campaign Addresses, etc*. Monarch. 1910. 1st ed. illus.. *$65.00–$175.00*

Dodge, Mary M. *Hans Brinker*. Scribner's. 1926. illus. clr plates. .... *$22.00–$30.00*

Dodge, Mary M. *When Life Is Young*. Century. 1894. 1st ed. illus. .... *$30.00–$40.00*

Dodge, Richard I. *Plains of the Great West & Their Inhabitants*. NY. 1877. 1st ed. illus. fldg map.. *$95.00–$125.00*

Doig, Ivan. *Sea Runners*. NY. Atheneum. 1982. 1st ed. dj. .... *$125.00–$150.00*

Dolbear, A. E. *The Telephone*. 1877. 1st ed. illus. cloth....................... *$95.00–$150.00*

Doll's House. Viking Press & Kestrel Books. 1981. oblong, facsimile of antique pop-up book, illus. by Meggendorfer. .... *$30.00–$40.00*

Domenech, Emmanuel. *Seven Years' Residence in the Great Deserts of North America*. Lon. Longman, Green, Logman and Roberts. 1860. 2 vols. 1st ed. illus. fldg map, plates.
.... *$600.00–$850.00*

Donaldson, Alfred L. *History of the Adirondacks*. NY. 1921. 2 vols. 1st ed. ....
.... *$110.00–$200.00*

Donne, John. *The Sermons*. Berkeley. Univ of CA. 1962. 10 vols. .... *$195.00–$250.00*

Donnelly, Ned. *Self-Defense; or, The Art of Boxing*. Lon. Weldon. 1879. 1st ed............
.... *$150.00–$250.00*

Dore Bible Gallery. Phila. 1883. illus. .... *$45.00–$65.00*

Dore, J. R. *Old Bibles or An Account of the Various Versions of the English Bible*. Lon. 1876. .... *$45.00–$60.00*

Dorsett, Helen. *Cabinetmaker's Guide for Dollhouse Furniture*. privately printed. 1964. spiral bound, pamphlet. .... *$20.00–$25.00*

Dorsey, James Owen and John R. Swanton. *Dictionary of the Biloxi and Ofo Languages*. DC. GPO. 1912. 1st ed. .... *$50.00–$125.00*

Dorsey, Sarah A. *Recollections of Henry Watkins Allen . . . Confederate Army*. NY. 1866. 1st ed. lea. .... *$125.00–$200.00*

Dos Passos John. *State of the Nation*. NY. Houghton Mifflin. 1944. 1st ed. dj. .... *$25.00–$45.00*

Dos Passos, John. *42nd Parallel*. NY/Lon. 1930. 1st ed. dj. .... *$60.00–$85.00*

Dossenbach, Monique and Hans. *Great Stud Farms of the World*. NY. William Morrow. 1978. 1st US ed. illus. dj. .... *$95.00–$150.00*

Douet, Valerie Jackson. *Dollhouses, the Collector's Guide*. Chartwell Books. (1994). folio. .... *$10.00–$15.00*

Doughty, Charles M. *Wanderings in Arabia*. Lon. Duckworth & Co. [1923]. 2 vols. maps. .... *$60.00–$75.00*

Douglas, Norman. *In the Beginning*. NY. 1928. 1st Amer ed. dj. .... *$50.00–$80.00*

Douglass, Frederick. *Frederick Douglass on Women's Rights*. Westport. Greenwood Press. (1976). 190 pp. .... *$20.00–$35.00*

Douglass, Frederick. *Life and Times*. Hartford. 1881. 1st ed. illus. ..... *$350.00–$700.00*

Douglass, Frederick. *My Bondage and My Freedom*. NY/Auburn. 1855. 1st ed. .... *$90.00–$130.00*

Dow, George Francis. *Slave Ships and Slaving*. Salem. Marine Research Society. 1927. 1st ed. .... *$145.00–$250.00*

Dow, George Francis. *Slave Ships and Slaving*. Mass. Marine Res Soc. 1927. illus. .... *$135.00–$225.00*

Dow, George Francis. *Whale Ships and Whaling, a Pictorial History . . .* Salem. Marine Research Society. 1925. 1st ed. illus. with b/w plates. .... *$100.00–$140.00*

Downing, A. *Treatise on the Theory and Practice of Landscape Gardening*. NY. Putnam. 1852. illus. .... *$165.00–$185.00*

Downing, A. G. *Architectural Heritage of Newport, RI*. NY. 1967. 2nd ed. dj. .... *$50.00–$75.00*

Downing, A. J. *Fruit and Fruit Trees of America*. NY. John Wiley. 1866. illus. .... *$60.00–$100.00*

Downing, A. J. *Fruits and Fruit Trees of America*. NY. 1846. cloth. .. *$100.00–$300.00*

Downing, A. J. *Fruits and Fruit Trees of America . . .* NY. 1858. illus. .... *$125.00–$200.00*

Downing, A. J. *Rural Essays*. NY. 1853. illus. .... *$75.00–$150.00*

Downing, A. J. *Treatise on the Theory and Practice of Landscape Gardening*. NY. 1859. 6th ed. illus. .... *$125.00–$150.00*

Dowsett, H. M. *Wireless Telephony and Broadcasting.* 1924. 1st ed. illus. ....
.... *$75.00–$100.00*

Doyle, Arthur Conan. *Adventures of Sherlock Holmes.* NY. (1892). 1st Amer ed..........
.... *$300.00–$500.00*

Doyle, Arthur Conan. *Adventures of Sherlock Holmes.* Lon. 1892. 1st ed. blue cloth. ..
.... *$1,750.00–$2,000.00*

Doyle, Arthur Conan. *Case-book of Sherlock Holmes.* Lon. Murray. 1927. 1st ed. ....
.... *$300.00–$350.00*

Doyle, Arthur Conan. *Croxley Master.* NY. Doran. (1925). 1st Amer ed. dj..................
.... *$80.00–$150.00*

Doyle, Arthur Conan. *Danger and Other Stories.* Lon. 1918. 1st ed. brown cloth. ....
.... *$60.00–$195.00*

Doyle, Arthur Conan. *Desert Drama.* Phil. 1898. illus. by Pazet. 1st US ed..................
.... *$100.00–$125.00*

Doyle, Arthur Conan. *Green Flag.* NY. 1900. 1st Amer ed. .... *$65.00–$125.00*

Doyle, Arthur Conan. *Hound of the Baskervilles.* Lon. 1927. rprnt dj. . *$60.00–$75.00*

Doyle, Arthur Conan. *Hound of the Baskervilles.* Lon. 1902. 1st ed. first issue, aeg, frontis, illus.. *$750.00–$1,500.00*

Doyle, Arthur Conan. *Hound of the Baskervilles.* Lon. Newnes. 1902. 1st ed. 1st state with "you" for "your" on page 13, line 3...................................... *$1,200.00–$2,000.00*

Doyle, Arthur Conan. *Hound of the Baskervilles.* NY. 1902. 1st Amer ed. 249 pp. 8 pp of ads. .... *$600.00–$1,000.00*

Doyle, Arthur Conan. *Lost World.* Lon. Hodder & Stoughton. (1912). 1st ed. illus. 319 pp. .... *$150.00–$225.00*

Doyle, Arthur Conan. *Lost World.* NY. (1912). 1st Amer ed.................. *$65.00–$75.00*

Doyle, Arthur Conan. *New Revelation.* NY. (1918). .... *$35.00–$45.00*

Doyle, Arthur Conan. *Sign of Four.* Lon. George Newnes. 1893. 3rd ed. red pictorial cvrs... *$375.00–$400.00*

Doyle, Arthur Conan. *Sir Nigel.* NY. 1906. 1st Amer ed. .... *$30.00–$45.00*

Doyle, Arthur Conan. *The Parasite.* Lon. Constable. 1894. 1st ed. .... *$65.00–$90.00*

Doyle, Arthur Conan. *Through the Magic Door.* Lon. 1907. illus....... *$65.00–$135.00*

Doyle, Arthur Conan. *Valley of Fear.* Doran. 1914. 1st ed................. *$140.00–$175.00*

Doyle, Arthur Conan. *White Company.* NY. 1922. illus. by N C Wyeth, dj. ....
.... *$60.00–$100.00*

Drago, H. *Wild, Woolly & Wicked.* NY. 1960. 1st ed. dj. .... *$30.00–$40.00*

Dragoo, Don. *Mounds for the Dead.* Pitts. Carnegie Museum. 1963. illus. 315 pp..........
.... *$30.00–$40.00*

Drake, Benjamin. *Life of Tecumseh and of His Brother the Prophet . . .* Cinc. 1855......
.... *$90.00–$200.00*

Drake, D. *Dr. Daniel Drake's Letters on Slavery.* NY. 1940. 1st ed. ltd 250 cc, dj. ....
.... *$65.00–$75.00*

Drake, Ensg. Robert. *Boy Allies Under the Sea, or the Vanishing Submarine*. NY. 1916. illus. .... $25.00–$45.00

Drake, Francis. *Indian History for Young Folks*. NY/Lon. Harper & Bros. 1919. illus. red dec cloth. .... $20.00–$35.00

Drane, Maude Johnston. *History of Henry County, Kentucky*. 1948. 1st ed.................. .... $50.00–$60.00

Draper, John William. *Intellectual Development of Europe*. NY. Harper & Bros. 1876. 2 vols. rev ed.................. $40.00–$50.00

Dream of the Red Chamber. (NY). Pantheon Books. (1958). pictorial cvr dj.................. .... $18.00–$35.00

Dreiser, Theodore. *Gallery of Women*. NY. Liverwright. 1929. 2 vols. 1st ed. djs.................. .... $150.00–$300.00

Driggs, Howard. *Westward America*. NY. (1942). dj. .... $30.00–$40.00

Driggs, Howard R. *Pony Express Goes Through*. NY. 1935.................. $35.00–$45.00

Drinker, Frederick E. and James G. Lewis. *Radio, Miracle of the 20th Century*. 1922. 1st ed. illus.................. $20.00–$25.00

Drummond, H. *Tropical Africa*. NY. 1890. .... $50.00–$60.00

Drury, John. *Old Illinois Houses*. Illinois State Historical Society. 1948. 1st ed. illus. 21 plates.................. $75.00–$125.00

Du Bois, Theodora. *Murder Strikes an Atomic Unit*. NY. 1946. 1st ed. dj.................. .... $20.00–$30.00

Du Bois, W. E. B. *Darkwater*. NY. Harcourt, Brace and Howe. 1920. 1st ed. dark blue cloth. .... $100.00–$125.00

Du Bois, W. E. B. *In Battle for Peace*. NY. 1952. 1st ed. dj.................. $30.00–$40.00

Du Bois, W. E. B. *World and Africa*. NY. (1947).................. $35.00–$50.00

Du Chaillu, Paul. *Land of the Midnight Sun*. NY. Harper. (1881). 2 vols. illus. wood engrs. pocket map.................. $40.00–$60.00

Du Chaillu, Paul. *Lost in the Jungle*. NY. 1869. 1st ed.................. $40.00–$50.00

Du Chaillu, Paul. *Midnight Sun*. NY. 1881. 2 vols. illus. fldg map.... $100.00–$200.00

Du Chaillu, Paul. *Stories of the Gorilla Country*. NY. 1868. 1st ed. illus.................. .... $275.00–$350.00

Du Maurier, Daphne. *Scapegoat*. NY. 1957. 1st ed. dj.................. $18.00–$25.00

Du Puy, William Atherton. *Hawaii and Its Race Problem*. Wash. GPO. 1932. illus...... .... $20.00–$40.00

Dubois, Abbe J. *Hindu Manner, Customs & Ceremonies*. Oxford. Clarendon. 1899. 2nd rev, corrected and enlarged ed. 732 pp.................. $60.00–$75.00

Dubois, Donald. *Fisherman's Handbood of Trout Flies*. NY. 1960. 1st ed. illus. clr plates dj. .... $45.00–$55.00

Dubois, W. E. B. *Dark Princess*. NY. Harcourt. 1928. 1st ed. near fine. .... $135.00–$150.00

Dubourg, George. *The Violin*. Lon. 1852. 4th ed. .... $30.00–$40.00

Dubus, Andre. *All the Time in the World*. NY. Knopf. 1996. 1st ed........ $35.00–$50.00

Dubus, Andre. *Finding a Girl in America*. Bos. Godine. 1980. 1st ed. inscr, dj. ....
.... *$150.00–$200.00*

Dubus, Andre. *The Lieutenant*. NY. Dial. 1967. 1st ed. author's first book, dj. ....
.... *$65.00–$175.00*

Duchaussois, P. *Mid Snow and Ice: The Apostles of the North-West*. Lon. 1923. 1st ed. illus. .... *$60.00–$85.00*

Duckworth, C. L. D. and G. E. Langmuir. *West Highland Steamers*. Lon. 1935. illus. 239 pp with index, pictorial bds. .... *$60.00–$100.00*

Duffus, R. L. *Santa Fe Trail*. NY. 1930. 1st ed. illus. sgn. .... *$30.00–$40.00*

Dufresne, Frank. *Alaska's Animals and Fishes*. NY. Barnes. 1946. 1st ed. illus. dj. ....
.... *$20.00–$35.00*

Dufur, S. M. *Over the Deadline or Tracked by Bloodlines*. Burlington, VT. 1902. ....
.... *$55.00–$75.00*

Dulac, Edmund. *Daughters of the Stars*. Lon. 1939. dj. .... *$35.00–$50.00*

Dulac, Edmund. *Edmund Dulac's Fairy Book*. Doran. (1916). 1st ed. illus. ....
.... *$160.00–$230.00*

Dulac, Edmund. *Edmund Dulac's Picture Book*. Lon. Hodder & Stoughton. 1915. 1st ed. wrps. illus. 19 plates. .... *$125.00–$150.00*

Dulac, Edmund. *Stories for the Arabian Nights*. Hodder & Stoughton. nd. illus. by Dulac. .... *$75.00–$160.00*

Dulac, Edmund. *Stories from Hans Anderson*. Doran. nd. 1st ed. illus. by Dulac, clr plates. .... *$100.00–$135.00*

Dulles, Allen. *Germany's Underground*. NY. Macmillan. 1947. 1st ed. sgn, dj. ....
.... *$50.00–$75.00*

Dumas, Lt-Gen. M. *Memoirs of His Own Time Including the Revolution*. Phila. 1839. 2 vols. .... *$175.00–$250.00*

Dumond, Dwight L. *Secession Movement*. NY. Macmillan. 1931. 1st ed. dj. ....
.... *$30.00–$50.00*

Dumont Henrietta. *Lady's Oracle*. Phila. Peck & Bliss. 1853. 270 pp, aeg. ....
.... *$60.00–$75.00*

Dunaway, W. F. *Reminiscences of a Rebel*. NY. 1913. .... *$175.00–$250.00*

Dunbar, Alice Moore. *Masterpieces of Negro Eloquence*. NY. 1914.. *$140.00–$180.00*

Dunbar, Paul Laurence. *Candle-Lightin' Time*. NY. 1901. 1st ed. photos by Hampton Camera Club, 127 pp. .... *$125.00–$200.00*

Dunbar, Paul Laurence. *Folks From Dixie*. NY. 1926. illus. by Kemble. ....
.... *$45.00–$55.00*

Dunbar, Paul Laurence. *Howdy Honey Howdy*. NY. 1905. 1st ed. illus. photos. ....
.... *$175.00–$375.00*

Dunbar, Paul Laurence. *Li'l Gal*. NY. 1904. 1st ed. photos. .... *$100.00–$150.00*

Dunbar, Paul Laurence. *Lyrics of Love and Laughter*. Dodd Mead. 1903. 1st ed. ....
.... *$40.00–$115.00*

Dunbar, Paul Laurence. *Lyrics of Lowly Life*. NY. Dodd, Mead. 1896. 1st ed. author's first book published by major company. .... *$195.00–$300.00*

Dunbar, Paul Laurence. *Lyrics of Lowly Life*. NY. 1909. .... *$65.00–$80.00*

Dunbar, Paul Laurence. *Poems of Cabin and Field*. NY. Dodd, Mead. 1902. illus. photos, decorative cvr. .... *$125.00–$150.00*

Dunbar, Paul Laurence. *Poems of Cabin and Field*. NY. 1899. 1st ed. illus. by Hampton Institute. .... *$125.00–$250.00*

Dunbar, Paul Laurence. *When Malindy Sings*. NY. Dodd Mead & Co. 1903. illus. photos, brown decorated cloth, frontis. .... *$175.00–$250.00*

Duncan Brothers. *United States Homeopathic Pharmacopoeia*. Chi. 1878. 1st ed. 281 pp. .... *$50.00–$60.00*

Duncan, Isadore. *My Life*. NY. 1927. illus. ltd #105/650 cc. .... *$40.00–$50.00*

Dunlop, William. *History of the American Theatre*. NY. 1832. .... *$200.00–$350.00*

Dunn, Finley Peter. *Mr. Dooley in Peace and in War*. Bos. Small, Maynard. 1898. 1st ed. green cloth. .... *$75.00–$90.00*

Dunn, Robert W. *Labor and Automobiles*. NY. International. 1929. 1st ed. dj. .... *$30.00–$40.00*

Dunn, Robert W. (ed.). *Palmer Raids*. NY. International. 1948. 1st ed. wrps. .... *$20.00–$30.00*

Dunn, William Edward. *Spanish and French Rivalry in the Gulf Region of the United States 1678–1702*. Austin. 1917. wrps. 238 pp, 5 maps (1 fldg). .... *$95.00–$125.00*

Dunne, Burt. *Play Ball!* NY. 1947. 1st ed. wrps. illus. .... *$25.00–$50.00*

Dunne, Peter M. *Early Jesuit Missions in Tarahumara*. Berkeley, CA. 1948. 1st ed. illus. fldg map. .... *$40.00–$75.00*

Dunning, John. *Booked to Die*. NY. Scribner's. 1992. 1st ed. sgn, dj. *$750.00–$900.00*

Dunning, John. *Booked to Die*. NY. Scribner's. 1992. 1st ed. dj. .... *$450.00–$600.00*

Dunning, John. *Bookman's Wake*. NY. Scribner's. 1995. 1st ed. dj .... *$40.00–$65.00*

Dunning, John. *Bookman's Wake*. NY. Scribner's. 1995. 1st ed. sgn, dj. .... *$85.00–$100.00*

Dunning, John. *Deadline*. Huntington Beach. James Cahill. 1995. 1st Amer ed. sgn, dj. .... *$75.00–$100.00*

Dunsany, Lord. *Blessing of Pan*. NY. Putnam. 1928. 1st Amer ed. 277 pp. .... *$30.00–$40.00*

Dunsany, Lord. *Chronicles of Rodriquez*. NY. Putnam. 1922. 1st ed. .... *$10.00–$35.00*

Dunsany, Lord. *Fourth Book of Jorkens*. Arkham House. 1948. 1st ed. dj. .... *$80.00–$100.00*

Dunsany, Lord. *His Fellow Man*. Lon. 1952. 1st ed. dj. .... *$65.00–$85.00*

Dunsany, Lord. *Rory and Bran*. Putnam. 1937. 1st ed. green cloth. ...... *$25.00–$75.00*

Dunsany, Lord. *Selections from the Writings*. Churchtown, Dundrum. Cuala Press. 1912. 1st ed. 1/250 cc. .... *$200.00–$225.00*

Dunsany, Lord. *Sword of Welleran*. Bos. 1916. 1st Amer. ed. .... *$25.00–$45.00*

Dunsany, Lord. *Sword of Welleran*. Lon. 1908. 1st ed. illus. by Sidney Sime. ....
.... *$95.00–$150.00*

Dunsany, Lord. *Tales of War*. Dub. Talbot. 1918. 1st ed. dj............... *$200.00–$225.00*

Dunsany, Lord. *Time and the Gods*. Lon. Heinemann. 1906. 1st ed. 1st issue, 179 pp, illus. .... *$100.00–$150.00*

Dunton, W. Herbert. *Rigging of a Texan*. Austin. The Texas State Historical Asso. 1943. illus. .... *$25.00–$40.00*

DuPont, J. E. *Philippine Birds*. Delaware Museum of Natural History. 1971. dj............
.... *$35.00–$45.00*

Durant, Will. *Philosophy and the Social Problem*. NY. 1917. .... *$35.00–$45.00*

Durrell, Lawrence. *Clea*. NY. Dutton. 1960. 1st ed. dj.......................... *$20.00–$30.00*

Durrell, Lawrence. *Livia*. Lon. Faber & Faber. (1978). 1st ed. dj......... *$25.00–$40.00*

Durrell, Lawrence. *Numquam*. Lon. Faber. (1970). 1st ed. dj. .... *$25.00–$45.00*

Durrell, Lawrence. *Prospero's Cell and Reflections on a Marine Venus*. Dutton. 1960. 1st ed. dj. .... *$35.00–$45.00*

Durrell, Lawrence. *Zero & Asylum in the Snow; Two Excursions Into Reality*. Berkeley, CA. 1947. 1st ed. dj. .... *$30.00–$75.00*

Durso, Joseph. *DiMaggio, The Last American Knight*. Little Brown & Co. 1995. 1st ed. dj. .... *$15.00–$20.00*

Dussauce, H. *General Treatise on the Manufacture of Vinegar*. Phila. 1871. 1st ed. ....
.... *$35.00–$45.00*

Dustin, Fred. *Custer Tragedy*. Ann Arbor. 1939. 200 cc, maps. .... *$150.00–$250.00*

Dustin, Fred. *Saginaw Treaty of 1819 between Gen. Louis Cass and Chippewa Indians*. Saginaw. 1919.. *$50.00–$75.00*

Duvoisin, Roger. *All Aboard*. NY. Grosset & Dunlap. (1935). 1st ed. illus. pictorial bds, decorated endpapers, pictorial dj... *$60.00–$275.00*

Dwiggins, W. A. *Crew of the Ship Earth*. Hingham. 1944. wrps. 1500 cc. ....
....*$25.00–$35.00*

Dwiggins, W. A. *Technique for Dealing with Artists*. NY. Press of the Woolly Whale. 1941. wrps. illus. 954 cc... *$30.00–$40.00*

Dwight, N. *Lives of the Signers of the Declaration of Independence*. NY. 1851. 1st ed.. .... *$35.00–$60.00*

Dwight, S. E. *Hebrew Wife*. Glasgow. Gallie. 1837. 1st Glasgow ed. 148 pp. ....
....*$90.00–$150.00*

Dwight, Theodore. *History of the Hartford Convention*. NY. White. 1833. 1st ed. original cloth and paper label.. *$100.00–$125.00*

Dyke, A. L. *Dyke's Automobile & Gasoline Engine Encyclopedia*. Chi. 1924. illus. dj...
.... *$45.00–$85.00*

Dylan, Thomas. *Adventures in the Skin Trade*. Lon. Putnam. (1955). 1st ed. dj. ....
.... *$75.00–$100.00*

Dylan, Thomas. *Portrait of the Artist as a Young Dog*. Norfolk, CT. New Directions. (c1940). 1st Amer ed. dj.. *$250.00–$275.00*

Eames, Wilberforce. *Early New England Catechisms.* Worcester. Hamilton. 1898. 1st ed. wrps. presentation copy. .... *$75.00–$115.00*

Earhart, Amelia. *Last Flight.* NY. 1937. 1st ed. illus. dj. .... *$40.00–$65.00*

Earle, Alice Morse. *Child Life in the Colonial Days.* NY. Macmillan. 1899. 1st ed. illus. .... *$40.00–$55.00*

Earle, Alice Morse. *Sun Dials and Roses of Yesterday.* NY. 1902. 1st ed. illus. .... *$75.00–$120.00*

Earle, Alice Morse. *Two Centuries of Costume in America.* NY. 1903. 2 vols. 1st ed. illus. .... *$40.00–$125.00*

East of Antelope Island. Bountiful. Daughters of Utah Pioneers. 1961. 1st ed. .... *$35.00–$50.00*

East of the Sun and West of the Moon. NY. 1922. illus. by Kay Nielsen, tip-in clr plates, dj. .... *$150.00–$300.00*

Eastlake, William. *Child's Garden of Verses for the Revolution.* NY. Grove Press. 1970. 1st ed. dj. .... *$25.00–$40.00*

Eastlake, William. *Go in Beauty.* NY. (1956). 1st ed. author's first book, dj. .... *$100.00–$200.00*

Eastman, Charles A. *Indian Boyhood.* NY. 1902. illus. .... *$70.00–$85.00*

Eastman, Charles G. *Poems of . . .* Montpelier. 1848. .... *$45.00–$55.00*

Eastman, F. *History of the State of New York.* NY. 1830. lea. .... *$55.00–$65.00*

Eastman, M. E. *East of the White Hills.* N Conway, NH. (1900). 1st ed. illus. .... *$40.00–$60.00*

Eastman, Mrs. Mary H. *Aunt Phillis's Cabin or Southern Life as It Is.* Phil. Lippincott. 1852. .... *$75.00–$125.00*

Eastman, Mrs. Mary. *American Aboriginal Portfolio.* Phila. 1853. 84 pp, 26 engr, large 4to, aeg, gold-stamped bds, rare. .... *$750.00–$1,500.00*

Eaton, Allen H. *Handicrafts of the Southern Highlanders.* illus. 2nd ptg, dj. .... *$50.00–$65.00*

Eaton, Eldon Howard. *Birds of New York.* Albany. 1914. 2nd ed. ex lib. ....*$40.00–$50.00*

Eaton, Elon Howard. *Birds of New York.* Albany. 1910. 2 vols. illus. clr plates. .... *$100.00–$200.00*

Eaton, Faith. *Classic Dolls' Houses.* Lon. Artus Books. (1994). rprnt, dj. .... *$15.00–$30.00*

Eaton, Faith. *Dolls in Color.* NY. Macmillan Pub. (1975). illus. 1st US ed, clr photos. ....*$15.00–$25.00*

Eaton, Faith. *Miniature House.* NY. Harry H Abrams. (1991). illus. 1st US ed. .... *$45.00–$65.00*

Eaton, John H. *Life of Andrew Jackson.* Phila. 1824. 2nd ed. ....: *$50.00–$100.00*

Eaton, John P. and Charles A. Haas. *Titanic.* NY. 1986. illus. dj. .... *$30.00–$45.00*

Eaton, Seymour. *Traveling Bears in Outdoor Sports.* Barse & Hopkins. 1915. illus. .... *$135.00–$185.00*

Eaton, Walter P. *Skyline Camps*. Wilde. 1922. pictorial paste label....... *$35.00–$40.00*

Eckert, A. and Karalus. *Owls of North America*. Doubleday. 1974. 1st ed. illus. dj......
.... *$35.00–$55.00*

Eckert, Allan W. *Sorrow in Our Heart*. NY. 1992. 1st ed. dj. .... *$30.00–$40.00*

Eckert, Allan W. *Great Auk*. Bos. Little Brown & Co. 1963. dj............ *$50.00–$75.00*

Economy Cream Separator. Chi. Sears, Roebuck & Co. 1907. illus. pictorial wrps.......
.... *$35.00–$45.00*

Eddington, A. S. *Space Time & Gravitation*. Camb. 1921. 1st ed. .... *$40.00–$60.00*

Eddy, Clyde. *Down the World's Most Dangerous River*. NY. Frederick A Stokes Co. 1929. illus. .... *$170.00–$230.00*

Edison Swan Co. *Pageant of the Lamp*. 1948. 1st ed. illus..................... *$50.00–$65.00*

Edison, Judith. *Dolls From Kewpie to Barbie and Beyond*. NY. Smithmark. (1994). 1st ed. illus. clr and b/w, dj. .... *$20.00–$30.00*

Edmonds, Walter. *Chad Hanna*. Bos. Little Brown. (1940). 1st ed. dj.. *$25.00–$50.00*

Edmonds, Walter. *Drums Along the Mohawk*. Bos. 1936. 1st ed........... *$25.00–$50.00*

Edmonds, Walter. *In the Hands of the Senecas*. Bos. Little Brown. (1947). 1st ed. dj...
.... *$30.00–$50.00*

Education of a French Model. NY. Boar's Head Books. 1950. 186 pp, illus, photos by Man Ray, rprnt, dj.. *$75.00–$100.00*

Edward and Miriam: A Tale of Iceland. Phil. American Sunday School Union. 1836. illus. frontis lea and bds woodcuts. .... *$14.00–$20.00*

Edward, Ruth Dudley. *Victor Gollancz: A Biography*. Lon. Gollancz. 1987. 1st ed. dj.
.... *$30.00–$40.00*

Edwards, Amelia. *Pharaohs, Fellahs and Explorers*. NY. Harper & Bros. 1891. 1st Amer ed. illus. .... *$50.00–$70.00*

Edwards, Amelia. *Thousand Miles Up the Nile*. NY. 2nd ed. cloth cvr.........................
.... *$30.00–$85.00*

Edwards, E. and J. Rattray. *Whale Off*. NY. 1932. 1st ed. illus............ *$27.00–$40.00*

Edwards, Gladys Brown. A*natomy and Conformation of the Horse*. Croton-on-Hudson. Dreenan. 1980. wrps. illus. photos and drawings. .... *$35.00–$40.00*

Edwards, John E. *Life of Rev. John Wesley Childs* . . . Early. 1852. 1st ed....................
.... *$90.00–$125.00*

Edwards, Jonathan. *Freedom of the Will*. NY. 1858............................... *$35.00–$50.00*

Edwards, Jonathan. *Treatise on Religious Affections*. American Tract Society. ....
.... *$20.00–$35.00*

Edwards, Lionel. *Getting to Know Your Pony*. NY. (1948). 1st US ed. illus................
....*$30.00–$35.00*

Edwards, Lionel. *The Fox*. NY. Scribner's. nd. illus............................. *$50.00–$150.00*

Edwards, President. *Life of Rev. David Brainerd*. American Tract Society. nd. lea and bds.. *$30.00–$35.00*

Edwards, William B. *Civil War Guns*. Harrisburg. 1962. illus. dj.......... *$35.00–$75.00*

Edwards, William B. *Story of Colts Revolver*. 1953. 1st ed. dj............ *$65.00–$100.00*

Eickemeyer, Carl. *Among the Pueblo Indians*. NY. 1895. .... *$50.00–$65.00*

Eidinoff, Maxwell Leigh and Hyman Ruchlis. *Atomics for the Millions*. NY/Lon. 1947. 1st ed. illus. by Maurice Sendak. .... *$100.00–$120.00*

Einstein, Albert. *Out of My Later Years*. NY. (1950). 1st ed. dj. .... *$15.00–$35.00*

Einstein, Albert. *Relativity, The Special and General Theory*. Lon. (1920). ....
.... *$75.00–$150.00*

Einstein, Albert. *Uber Die Spezielle Und Die Allgemeine Relativitatstheorie*. wrps. 4th ed. .... *$50.00–$65.00*

Einstein, Albert and Leopold Infeld. *Evolution of Physics*. NY. Simon & Schuster. 1938. 1st ed.. *$55.00–$100.00*

Einstein, Albert and Leopold Infeld. *New Physics*. Palestine. 1947. 1st Hebrew ed. sgn, dj. .... *$85.00–$125.00*

Eisenschiml, Otto. *Story of Shiloh*. Chi. 1946. .... *$40.00–$50.00*

Elder, Paul. *California the Beautiful*. SF. 1911. .... *$75.00–$80.00*

Elder, Paul. *Old Spanish Missions of California*. SF. Elder. 1913. 50 illus. 1.4 buckram, pictorial paste label.. *$65.00–$70.00*

Eldridge, Charlotte. *Godey Lady Doll Book*. NY. Hastings House. (1953). illus. ....
.... *$15.00–$25.00*

Eldridge, Eleanor. *Slave Narrative*. Prov. 1842. .... *$125.00–$150.00*

Eldridge, S. *Heroic Life of U.S. Grant*. Bos. (1902). illus. 4 chromo, b/w illus. ....
.... *$35.00–$50.00*

Electric Gas Lighting. Bos. Boston Electric Co. 1880. illus. 12 pp. .... *$40.00–$50.00*

Electric Railway Dictionary. CA. 1972. rprnt of 1911 ed. dj. .... *$125.00–$250.00*

***Electric Signals for Passenger and Freight Elevators* . . . .** NY. Elevator Supply and Repair Co. 1913. 48 pp. .... *$90.00–$100.00*

Eliot, George. *Mill on the Floss*. Edin/Lon. William Blackwood. 1869. 3 vols. 1st ed...
.... *$500.00*

Eliot, George. *Mill on the Floss*. Phil. 1860. purple cloth...................... *$75.00–$100.00*

Eliot, George. *Romola*. Lon. 1863. 3 vols. 1st ed................................... *$450.00*

Eliot, George. *Romola*. NY. 1863. 1st Amer cd................................... *$115.00–$275.00*

Eliot, George. *Silas Marner*. Edin/Lon. 1861. 1st ed. .... *$850.00–$2,000.00*

Eliot, George. *Silas Marner, the Weaver of Raveloe*. Edin/Lon. 27 March, 1861. 1st ed. cloth. .... *$3,000.00–$5,000.00*

Eliot, George. *The Works*. Edin. 1878–80. 20 vols. .... *$95.00–$125.00*

Eliot, T. S. *Confidential Clerk*. NY. (1954). 1st ed. dj. .... *$25.00–$50.00*

Eliot, T. S. *Dante*. Lon. Faber & Faber. (1929). 1st ed. dj. .... *$100.00–$250.00*

Eliot, T. S. *Elder Statesman*. NY. 1959. 1st Amer ed. dj...................... *$55.00–$65.00*

Eliot, T. S. *Film of Murder in the Cathedral*. NY. Harcourt. 1952. 1st US ed. dj. ....
.... *$25.00–$35.00*

Eliot, T. S. *Four Quartets.* Lon. Faber & Faber. (1944). 1st Brit. ed. dj. ....
....*$200.00–$400.00*

Eliot, T. S. *Old Possum's Book of Practical Cats.* Lon. 1939. 1st ed. dj. ....
.... *$350.00–$400.00*

Elkins, Aaron. *Deceptive Clarity.* Walker. 1987. 1st ed. dj. .... *$125.00–$150.00*

Elkins, Aaron. *Murder in the Queen's Armes.* Walker. 1985. 1st ed. dj. *$125.00–$225.00*

Ellett, Charles, Jr. *Mississippi and the Ohio Rivers.* Phila. 1853. inscrb, illus, 366 pp..
.... *$125.00–$175.00*

Elliot, Daniel Giraud. *North American Shore Birds.* NY. Harper. 1895. illus. ....
.... *$40.00–$75.00*

Elliot, George H. *Report on a Tour of Inspection of European Light-house Establishments Made in 1873.* GPO. 1874. 1st ed. illus. .... *$100.00–$150.00*

Elliot, William. *Washington Guide.* Wash. Franck Taylor. 1837. illus. fldg maps. ....
.... *$60.00–$90.00*

Elliotson, John. *Numerous Cases of Surgical Operations Without Pain in the Mesmeric State.* Phila. Lea and Blanchard. 1843. 1st Amer ed. .... *$750.00–$1,500.00*

Elliott, Henry W. *Report upon the Condition of Affairs in the Territory of Alaska.* Wash. GPO. 1875. 277 pp. .... *$85.00–$95.00*

Ellis, Havelock. *Study in the Psychology of Sex.* Phila. 1928. 7 vols. ... *$75.00–$125.00*

Ellis, Havelock. *World of Dreams.* Bos. 1915. .... *$35.00–$85.00*

Ellison, Harlan. *Alone Against Tomorrow.* NY. 1971. 1st ed. sgn, dj. .... *$35.00–$60.00*

Ellison, Harlan. *Approaching Oblivion.* NY. 1974. 1st ed. sgn, dj. .... *$40.00–$75.00*

Ellison, Harlan. *Spider Kiss.* NY. Armchair Detective Library. (1991). 1st ed. ltd 26 lettered and sgn cc, slipcase. *$225.00*

Ellison, Harlan. *Stalking the Nightmare.* Phantasia Press. 1st trade ed. . *$25.00–$35.00*

Ellison, Harlan. *Stalking the Nightmare.* Phantasia Press. 1982. 1st ed. ltd 750 cc, sgn.
.... *$75.00–$90.00*

Ellison, Harlan. *Strange Wine.* NY. Harper & Row. (1978). 1st ed. dj. ... *$55.00–$85.00*

Ellison, Harlan. *Strange Wine.* Harper. 1978. 1st ed. dj. .... *$60.00–$70.00*

Ellison, Harlan, Terry Dowling, Richard Delap and Gil Lamont (eds.). *Essential Ellison: A 35-Year Retrospective.* Omaha. Nemo Press. 1987. 1st ed. ltd 26 lettered and sgn cc, laid-in sgn bookplate, dj. .... *$450.00–$500.00*

Ellison, Ralph. *Going to the Territory.* NY. 1986. 1st ed. dj. .... *$45.00–$75.00*

Ellison, Ralph. *Invisible Man.* NY. 1952. 1st ed. dj. .... *$650.00–$750.00*

Ellison, Ralph. *Shadow and Act.* Lon. 1967. 1st UK ed. black paper covered bds. dj. ...
.... *$25.00–$90.00*

Ellwanger, George H. *In Gold and Silver.* NY. Appleton. 1892. 1st ed. illus. #99/200 cc.
.... *$70.00–$100.00*

Ellwanger, H. B. *The Rose.* Lon. William Heinemann. 1893. rev, 310 pp. ....
.... *$65.00–$85.00*

Ellyson's Business Directory and Almanac for the Year 1845. H K Ellyson. ....
.... *$125.00–$200.00*

Elwes, H. J. *Memoirs of Travel, Sport and Natural History.* Lon. 1930. 317 pp. ....
.... *$22.00–$35.00*

Elzas, Barnett. *Jews of South Carolina.* Phila. 1905. #104/175 cc. .... *$55.00–$65.00*

Emanuel, Walter. *Dog's Day.* Lon. Heinemann. 1902. illus. by Cecil Aldin. ....
.... *$225.00–$250.00*

Embick, Milton. *Military History of the Third Division, 9th Corp. Army Potomac.* np.
1913. 1st ed. illus.. *$48.00–$60.00*

Emerson, Adaline E. *Ralph Emerson, Jr.: Life and Letters. Edited by his Mother.*
Rockford, IL. 1891. 1st ed. illus. .... *$90.00–$125.00*

Emerson, Alice B. *Ruth Fielding at Snow Camp.* Cupples & Leon. 1913. Fielding #3, dj.
.... *$15.00–$20.00*

Emerson, Jill. *I Am Curious.* NY. (1970). 1st ed. wrps. sgn. .... *$150.00–$200.00*

Emerson, Nathaniel B. *Unwritten Literature of Hawaii: The Sacred Songs of the Hul.*
Rutland. Tuttle. 1965. rprnt, 288 pp. Bulletin 38..................... *$35.00–$45.00*

Emerson, Ralph Waldo. *Complete Works of . . .* Bos. Houghton Mifflin. 1903. 12 vols.
illus. Concord ed.. *$70.00–$100.00*

Emerson, Ralph Waldo. *Essays.* Bos. 1844. 1st ed. 2nd series......... *$200.00–$500.00*

Emerson, Ralph Waldo. *Essays . . .* Bos. 1841, 1844. 2 vols. 1st ed. 1st and 2nd series.
.... *$950.00–$1,500.00*

Emerson, Ralph Waldo. *Letters and Social Aims.* Bos. Osgood. 1876. 1st ed. ....
.... *$195.00–$225.00*

Emerson, Ralph Waldo. *Letters and Social Aims.* Bos. Osgood. 1876. 1st ed. ....
.... *$60.00–$85.00*

Emerson, Ralph Waldo. *Society and Solitude.* Bos. 1870. 1st ed. sm 8vo....................
.... *$50.00–$75.00*

Emory, William. *Lieutenant Emory Reports.* Albuquerque. Univ. of New Mexico Press.
(1951). illus. rprnt of 1848 ed. .... *$50.00–$80.00*

Emory, William. *Report on the United States and Mexican Boundary Survey.* Austin.
Texas State Historical Assoc. (1987). facsimile. copiously illus. .... *$150.00–$200.00*

Encyclopaedia Britannica — Facsimile of First Edition Printed in 1768 to 1771. 3
vols. illus. 160 copper plates. .... *$150.00–$175.00*

Encyclopaedia Britannica, 11th Edition. NY. 1910. 20 vols. .... *$150.00–$300.00*

Encylopedia Britannica. Cambridge. Univ Press. 1911. 20 vols. 11th ed. illus..............
.... *$150.00–$250.00*

Endell, Fritz. *Old Tavern Signs.* Houghton Mifflin. 1916. illus. ltd #327/550 cc............
.... *$40.00–$65.00*

Endell, Fritz. *Old Tavern Signs, An Excursion in the History of Hospitality.* Houghton
Mifflin. 1916. 1st ed. illus. ltd #327/500. .... *$45.00–$55.00*

Endicott, Wendell. *Adventures in Alaska and Along the Trail.* NY. Frederick Stokes.
1928. illus. green cloth, decorated cvr, frontis, map endpapers............... *$50.00–$60.00*

Endicott, Wendell. *Adventures with Rod and Harpoon Along the Florida Keys.* NY.
Stokes. 1925. 1st ed. 1st ptg. illus...................................... *$65.00–$125.00*

Endicott, William. *Wrecked Among Cannibals in the Fijis*. Marine Research Soc. 1923.
.... *$50.00–$95.00*

Engen, Rodney K. *Kate Greenaway*. Lon/NY. Academy Editions Harmony Books. (1976). illus. green cloth with pictorial dj.. *$15.00–$25.00*

Engineers, Architects and Builders in Iron and Steel. East Berlin, CT. The Berlin Iron Bridge Co. c 1890–95. printed wrps, illus, 302 pp. .... *$125.00–$250.00*

English, L. E. F. *Newfoundland Past and Present*. Tor. Thomas Nelson & Sons. nd. illus. red stiff wrps.. *$15.00–$20.00*

Ensko, Stephen. *American Silversmiths*. (1989). 1st ed. illus. dj............. *$35.00–$40.00*

Epstein, Geo. J. *Strabismus, A Clinical Handbook*. Phila. 1948. illus.... *$35.00–$48.00*

EROS Magazine, Vol 1, #1. .... *$50.00–$75.00*

Erskine, Albert Russel. *History of the Studebaker Corporation*. The Studebaker Corporation. 1924.. *$35.00–$65.00*

Erskine, Laurie York. *Renfrew Rides North*. Grosset & Dunlap. 1931. Renfrew Books #3, dj.. *$22.00–$25.00*

Esdaile, James. *Mesmerism in India*. (1902). Amer ed. .... *$55.00–$70.00*

Esposito, Colonel Vincent, Jr. *West Point Atlas of American Wars*. NY. Praeger. 1960. 2 vols. 1st ed. illus. maps, oblong. .... *$70.00–$145.00*

Esquirel, Laura. *Like Water for Chocolate*. Doubleday. 1989. 1st ed. dj. ....
.... *$35.00–$60.00*

Eustis, Celestine. *Cooking in Old Creole Days*. NY. 1903. 1st ed. .... *$25.00–$40.00*

Eustis, Helen. *Fool Killer*. Garden City. Doubleday. 1954. 1st ed. dj... *$85.00–$100.00*

Euwe, Max. *Judgment and Planning in Chess*. NY. Scribner's Sons. 1955. ....
.... *$35.00–$45.00*

Evangelical Lutheran Church: a Liturgy . . . Balt. Lutheran Church. 1847. ....
.... *$100.00–$125.00*

Evans, Augusta Inez. *Tale of the Alamo*. NY. 1888. .... *$55.00–$68.00*

Evans, C. S. *Sleeping Beauty*. Lon. (1920). 1st ed. illus. by Arthur Rackham. dj. ....
.... *$375.00–$1,250.00*

Evans, Clement Anselm (ed.). *Confederate Military History*. Atlanta. Confederate Publishing Co. 1899. 12 vols. 1st ed. illus. plates, maps...................... *$485.00–$800.00*

Evans, Eli N. *Provincials: A Personal History of Jews in the South*. Atheneum. 1973. 2nd ptg. dj.. *$25.00–$35.00*

Evans, Frederick William. *Egyptian Sphinx*. Mt Lebanon. nd. wrps... *$87.00–$110.00*

Evans, Joan. *History of Jewelry, 1100–1870*. NY. (1953). illus. dj..... *$100.00–$125.00*

Evans, John. *Ancient Bronze Implements, Weapons* . . . *Great Britain & Ireland*. NY. 1881. .... *$65.00–$85.00*

Evans, John. *Ancient Stone Implements* . . . NY. 1872. 1st ed. 640 pp. *$75.00–$100.00*

Evans, Nicholas. *Horse Whisperer*. Delacorte. 1995. 1st ed. author's first book, sgn, dj.
.... *$65.00–$125.00*

Evarts, Jeremiah, et al. *Essays on the Present Crisis in the Condition of the American Indians*. Bos. (1829). 1st ed. .... *$125.00–$225.00*

Everett, Fred. *Fun With Trout.* Harrisburg. Stackpole. 1952. 1st ed. illus. ....
.... *$70.00–$100.00*

Everitt, Graham. *English Caricaturists and Graphic Humanists of the Nineteenth Century.* 1886. illus. plates, ¾ mor and cloth. .... *$110.00–$125.00*

Ewards, A. Cecil. *Persian Carpet.* Lon. Duckworth. (1967). 3rd ed. illus. dj. ....
.... *$60.00–$90.00*

Ewart, John S. *Kingdom of Canada: Imperial Federation: Colonial Conferences: Alaska Boundary and Other Essays.* Tor. 1908. 1st ed. illus. 2 maps, sgn. ....
.... *$35.00–$45.00*

Ewing, Juliana Horatia. *Lob-Lie-By-the-Fire.* NY. E & J B Young. illus. pictorial cloth.
.... *$25.00–$35.00*

Examples of Church Furnishings. NY. J & R Lamb Co. 1886. stiff wrps, illus, 72 pp..
....*$75.00–$100.00*

Eyre, John. *European Stranger in America.* NY. 1839. 1st ed. 84 pp... *$75.00–$100.00*

Faber, Eduard. *Nobel Prize Winners in Chemistry 1901–1961.* Abelard-Schuman. 1963. rev. .... *$25.00–$35.00*

Faber, J. Henri. *Life of the Grasshopper.* NY. 1917. dj. .... *$35.00–$50.00*

Fabre, H. *Fabre's Book of Insects.* NY. 1935. .... *$45.00–$50.00*

Fagg, William P. *Afro-Portuguese Ivories.* Lon. dj. .... *$65.00–$90.00*

Fahnestock, W. P. *Artificial Somnambulism, Called Mesmerism; or Animal Magnetism.* Phila. 1869. .... *$95.00–$125.00*

Fairbridge, Dorothea. *Historic Farms of South Africa.* Lon. 1931. 1st ed. illus. dj........
.... *$125.00–$150.00*

Fairchild, David. *Garden Islands of the Great East.* NY. Scribner's. 1943. illus. endpaper maps. .... *$25.00–$30.00*

Fairchild, David. *World Was My Garden.* Scribner's. 1938. 1st ed. illus. *$35.00–$45.00*

Fairchild, David and Marian. *Book of Monsters.* Wash. 1914. .... *$100.00–$150.00*

Fairchild, T. B. *History of the Town of Cuyahoga Falls, Summit County, Ohio.* Cleve. 1876. 1st ed. .... *$65.00–$75.00*

Fairy Tales of Charles Perrault. Dodge. illus. by Harry Clarke, intro by Bodkin. ....
.... *$150.00–$250.00*

Faithfull, Emily. *Three Visits to America.* NY. Fowler & Wells. (1884). 1st US ed. 400 pp. .... *$95.00–$125.00*

Falk, Kathryn. *Miniature Needlepoint and Sewing Projects for Dollhouses.* NY. Hawthorn Books. (1977). 1st ed. dj. .... *$18.00–$30.00*

Fall, Bernard. *Hell in a Very Small Place.* Phila. 1966. 1st ed. dj. .... *$40.00–$50.00*

Fall, Bernard. *Street Without Joy.* Harrisburg. (1964). 4th ed. dj........... *$30.00–$35.00*

Fall, Bernard. *Street Without Joy.* Harrisburg. 1961. 1st ed. dj........... *$425.00–$500.00*

Fall, Bernard. *Vietnam in the Balance.* 1966. wrps................................. *$25.00–$35.00*

Falls of Niagara. Tor. 1866. illus. 12 chromolitho scenes. maroon cloth. ....
.... *$60.00–$75.00*

Family Cabinet Atlas. Phila. Carey & Lea. 1932. 1st Amer ed. rev, clred maps, bds. .... *$60.00–$100.00*

Family Circle's Guide to Trout Flies & How to Tie Them. (1954). illus. 48 pp, boxed. .... *$25.00–$45.00*

Faris, John T. *Roaming the Rockies* . . . Farrar & Rinehart. 1930. illus. *$35.00–$45.00*

Farley, Walter. *Son of the Black Stallion*. 1947. 1st ed. dj..................... *$25.00–$35.00*

Farlie, Barbara. *All About Doll Houses*. IN. Bobbs Merrill. 1st ed. illus. 2nd ptg, dj.... .... *$15.00–$25.00*

Farm Receipt Book of John and Jane Longstreth of Phoenixville, Pennsylvania, 1764–1811. folio, parchment, 272 pp. .... *$400.00–$525.00*

Farmer's and Horsemen's True Guide. Rochester, NY. Fisher & Co. 1841. illus........... .... *$125.00–$150.00*

Farmer, Fannie Merritt. *Chafing Dish Possibilities*. Bos. Little Brown. 1898. 1st ed. .. .. *$50.00–$80.00*

Farmer, Philip Jose. *Dare*. NY. (1965). 1st ed. pictorial wrps............... *$15.00–$25.00*

Farmer, Philip Jose. *Day World Breakup*. NY. (1990). 1st ed. dj........... *$20.00–$25.00*

Farmer, Philip Jose. *Feast Unknown*. Essex House. (1969). 1st ed...... *$50.00–$100.00*

Farmer, Philip Jose. *Love Song*. Macmillan. 1983. 1st ed. ltd 500 cc, dj....................... .... *$65.00–$75.00*

Farmer, Philip Jose. *Magic Labyrinth*. Berkley Putnam. 1980. 1st ed. sgn, dj. .... *$20.00–$30.00*

Farmer, Philip Jose. *Tarzan Alive*. Garden City. 1972. 1st ed. dj......... *$65.00–$100.00*

Farnham, Eliza. *Life in Prairie Land*. NY. 1847..................................... *$65.00–$85.00*

Farnol, Jeffrey. *The Shadow*. Bos. Little Brown. 1929. 1st Amer ed. 306 pp. .... *$25.00–$35.00*

Farquhar, Roger Brooke. *Historic Montgomery County Old Homes & History*. 1952. sgn... *$35.00–$50.00*

Farrar, Emmie Ferguson and Emilee Hines. *Old Virginia Houses*. Delmar. illus. b/w photos. dj. .... *$40.00–$55.00*

Farrel, James T. *Tutto, Ma Non Un Cuore*. Arnoldo Mondadori Editore. 1957. 1st Italian ed of Gas-House McGinty, inscrb, dj.. *$75.00–$100.00*

Farrell, James T. *Father and Son*. Vanguard. 1940. 1st ed. dj........... *$125.00–$140.00*

Farrell, James T. *My Baseball Diary*. NY. (1957). 1st ed. dj. .... *$45.00–$55.00*

Farrell, James T. *My Days of Anger*. Vanguard. 1943. 1st ed. dj. ...... *$100.00–$120.00*

Farrell, James T. *Yet Other Waters*. Vanguard. 1952. 1st ed. dj............. *$50.00–$60.00*

Farrington, S. Kip. *Atlantic Game Fishing*. NY. 1937. illus. sgn....... *$145.00–$185.00*

Farrington, S. Kip. *Atlantic Game Fishing*. 1939.................................... *$28.00–$35.00*

Farrington, S. Kip, Jr. *Ducks Came Back*. NY. Coward McCann. 1945. 1st ed. illus. by Lynne Bogue Hunt, 138 pp. .... *$30.00–$40.00*

Fast, Howard. *Passion of Sacco and Vanzetti*. Lon. 1954. 1st ed. dj. ..... *$20.00–$30.00*

Faubion, Nina Lane. *Some Edible Mushrooms and How to Know Them*. OR. 1938. illus.
.... *$14.00–$20.00*

Faulkner, Georgene. *White Elephant*. Volland. 1929. illus. by Richardson.....................
.... *$25.00–$45.00*

Faulkner, William. *A Fable*. NY. Random House. (1954). 1st ed. dj.. *$100.00–$150.00*

Faulkner, William. *Absalom Absalom*. NY. 1936. 1st ed. diagram at rear, dj.................
.... *$150.00–$450.00*

Faulkner, William. *As I Lay Dying*. Lon. Jonathan Cape. 1935. 1st ed. dj.....................
.... *$360.00–$650.00*

Faulkner, William. *Big Woods*. Random House. 1955. 1st ed. .... *$85.00–$95.00*

Faulkner, William. *Doctor Martino and Other Stories*. NY. Harrison Smith & Robert
Haas. (1934). dj. .... *$350.00–$1,300.00*

Faulkner, William. *Faulkner Reader*. NY. 1959..................................... *$30.00–$45.00*

Faulkner, William. *Go Down Moses and Other Stories*. NY. Random House. (c1942).
1st ed. dj. .... *$700.00–$900.00*

Faulkner, William. *Intruder in the Dust*. NY. (1948). 1st ed. dj......... *$125.00–$225.00*

Faulkner, William. *Light in August*. NY. The Modern Library. (1950). dj. ....
.... *$12.00–$20.00*

Faulkner, William. *Light in August*. NY. Smith & Haas. (1932). 1st ed. dj...................
.... *$200.00–$900.00*

Faulkner, William. *Pylon*. Smith. 1935. 1st ed. dj. .... *$350.00–$500.00*

Faulkner, William. *Requiem for a Nun*. Chatto & Windus. 1953. 1st UK ed. dj............
.... *$35.00–$65.00*

Faulkner, William. *Requiem for a Nun*. Random House. (1951). 1st ed. dj.................
.... *$75.00–$125.00*

Faulkner, William. *Sanctuary*. NY. Jonathan Cape and Harrison Smith. (1931). 1st ed.
gray cloth over maroon bds, patterned endpapers, dj. .... *$1,800.00–$2,500.00*

Faulkner, William. *Sanctuary*. NY. Jonathan Cape and Harrison Smith. (1931). 1st ed.
dj. .... *$350.00–$750.00*

Faulkner, William. *Sartoris*. NY. (1929). 1st ed. dj. .... *$1,300.00–$2,600.00*

Faulkner, William. *The Mansion*. NY. Random House. (1959). 1st ed. cloth dj. ....
.... *$95.00–$200.00*

Faulkner, William. *The Reivers*. NY. Random House. 1962. 1st ed. dj......................
.... *$75.00–$100.00*

Faulkner, William. *The Town*. Random House. (1957). 1st ed. dj........ *$65.00–$100.00*

Faulkner, William. *The Town*. Chatto & Windus. 1958. 1st Eng ed. dj.. *$50.00–$75.00*

Faulkner, William. *Wild Palms*. NY. Random House. 1939. 1st ptg. cloth, ex-lib, dj....
.... *$50.00–$75.00*

Faulkner, William. *Wild Palms*. NY. (1939). 1st ed. dj..................... *$400.00–$750.00*

Fawcett, Benjamin. *Saints Everlasting Rest*. NY. American Tract Society....................
.... *$10.00–$20.00*

Fawcett, Clara Hallard. *Dolls: A Guide for Collectors*. NY. Lindquist Pub. (1947). 1st ed. .... *$25.00–$65.00*

Fawcett, Clara Hallard. *On Making & Dressing Dolls*. Wash. Hobby House Press. (1963). reissue ed. .... *$25.00–$35.00*

Fawcett, Col. P. H. *Lost Trails, Lost Cities*. Funk & Wagnalls. 1953. illus. green cvr, dj. .... *$15.00–$25.00*

Feagans, Raymond. *Railroad That Ran by the Tide*. Howell-North Berkeley. 1972. illus. dj, scarce. .... *$60.00–$80.00*

Feather, Leonard. *Pleasures of Jazz*. NY. Horizon. 1976. 1st ed. dj. ..... *$30.00–$40.00*

Federal Writers' Project. *New Hampshire*. 1st ed................................. *$20.00–$40.00*

Federal Writers' Project. *New Jersey*. 1st ed. map. .... *$35.00–$40.00*

Fedo, Michael W. *They Was Just Niggers*. Ontario, CA. Brasch & Brasch. 1979. wrps. .... *$25.00–$60.00*

Feek, Andrew J. *Every Man His Own Trainer or How to Develop . . . Trotter or Pacer*. NY. 1889. 1st ed. .... *$68.00–$85.00*

Feiffer, Jules. *Little Murders*. NY. 1968. 1st ed. dj................................ *$50.00–$75.00*

Feiffer, Jules. *Sick Sick Sick*. NY. McGraw-Hill. (1958). 1st ed. author's first book, paperback, inscrb, dj... *$100.00–$125.00*

Feiffer, Jules. *The Explainers*. NY. McGraw-Hill. (1960). wrps. inscrb........................ ....*$85.00–$100.00*

Felix S. Cohen's Handbook of Federal Indian Law. Albuquerque. 1958. .... *$28.00–$35.00*

Fellows, M. H. *Land of Little Rain*. Chi. 1946. illus. dj. .... *$45.00–$65.00*

Felt, E. P. *Insects Affecting Park and Woodland Trees*. Albany. 1905. illus. .... *$45.00–$60.00*

Ferber, Edna. *Giant*. Garden City. 1952. 1st ed. dj................................ *$35.00–$45.00*

Ferber, Edna. *Saratoga Trunk*. Garden City. 1941. 1st ed. dj. .... *$18.00–$25.00*

Ferlinghetti, Lawrence. *A Coney Island of the Mind*. New Directions. 1968. 1st ed. green cloth. .... *$50.00–$75.00*

Ferlinghetti, Lawrence. *Mexican Night*. New Directions. 1970. 1st ed. wrps................ .... *$25.00–$45.00*

Ferlinghetti, Lawrence. *Secret Meaning of Things*. 1968. dj. .... *$30.00–$40.00*

Ferlinghetti, Lawrence. *Trip to Italy and France*. 1979. ltd 250 cc, sgn........................ .... *$75.00–$100.00*

Fermi, Enrico. *Thermodynamics*. Prentice-Hall. 1937. 1st ed. .... *$300.00–$500.00*

Ferris, Benjamin G. *Utah and the Mormons*. NY. 1854. illus........... *$100.00–$250.00*

Ferris, Warren Angus. *Life in the Rocky Mountains 1830–1825*. Salt Lake. 1940. 1st ed. fldg map... *$150.00–$250.00*

Fessenden, T. *New American Gardener*. NY. 1828. 1st ed. lea. .... *$75.00–$100.00*

Fessenden, Thomas G. *Compete Farmer*. Bos. Russell, Odiorne. 1825. *$65.00–$75.00*

Fessenden, Thomas (ed.). *New England Farmer.* Bos. 1833–35. Vol. XI–XIII. ....
.... *$175.00–$200.00*

Fewkes, Jesse Walter. *Preliminary Report on a Visit to the Navaho National Monument Arizona.* DC. GPO. 1911. 1st ed. .... *$50.00–$125.00*

Ficklen, Bessie A. *Handbook of Fist Puppets.* Phil. Lippincott. (1935). 1st ed. dj. ....
.... *$20.00–$35.00*

Ficklen, John Rose. *History of Reconstruction in Louisiana.* Balt. 1910. 1st ed. wrps...
.... *$55.00–$100.00*

Field, Eugene. *Echoes From the Sabine Farm.* Chi. 1893. 1st ed. 294/500 cc...............
.... *$50.00–$75.00*

Field, Eugene. *Gingham Dog and the Calico Cat.* Newark. (1926). dj. *$100.00–$150.00*

Field, Eugene. *Lullaby-Land.* Scribner's. 1897. 1st ed. illus. by Charles Robinson. ....
.... *$50.00–$125.00*

Field, Eugene. *Poems of Childhood.* Scribner's. 1904. 1st ed. illus. by Parrish, black cloth clr paste-on. .... *$75.00–$175.00*

Field, Eugene. *Poems of Childhood.* NY. Scribner's. 1904. illus. by Maxfield Parrish....
.... *$90.00–$100.00*

Field, Eugene. *Songs of Childhood.* Scribner's. 1895. blue cloth. .... *$25.00–$50.00*

Field, Eugene. *Winken, Blynken and Nod.* Saalfield. 1930. illus. .... *$25.00–$45.00*

Field, Eugene. *Writings in Prose and Verse.* NY. Scribner's. 1896. 10 vols. 1st ed. gray green cl aeg... *$60.00–$80.00*

Field, Henry M. *Bright Skies and Dark Shadows.* NY. 1890. 1st ed. maps, sgn. ....
.... *$20.00–$35.00*

Field, Henry M. *History of the Atlantic Telegraph.* NY. 1866. 1st ed. illus....................
.... *$55.00–$90.00*

Field, M. *City Architecture.* NY. Putnam. 1853. 1st ed. illus.............. *$120.00–$200.00*

Field, M. *City Architecture: or, Designs for Dwellings, Houses, Stores, Hotels, etc.* NY. Putnam. 1853. 1st ed. illus. .... *$80.00–$120.00*

Field, Rachel. *Calico Bush.* NY. Macmillan. 1931. 1st ed. 213 pp, inscrb. ....
.... *$60.00–$80.00*

Fielde, Adele. *A Corner of Cathay.* NY. Macmillan. 1894. 11 clr plates, pictorial cloth, teg. .... *$30.00–$45.00*

Fielde, Adele M. *Pagoda Shadows, Studies from Life in China.* Bos. Corthell. 1884. illus. frontis... *$30.00–$40.00*

Fielding, Mantle. *Gilbert Stuarts Portraits of George Washington.* Phil. 1923. 350 cc sgn by author. .... *$75.00–$95.00*

Fifth Over the Southwest Pacific. LA. AAF Publications (Fifth Air Force). nd. wrps. illus. .... *$95.00–$125.00*

Fifth Report of Senate Fact Finding Comm. on Un-American Activities. Sac. 1949. wrps. illus. .... *$15.00–$25.00*

Figuier. *Mammalia, Popularly Described by Typical Species.* Lon. 1870. illus..............
.... *$35.00–$45.00*

Figuier, Louis. *Human Race.* NY. Appleton. 1872. 1st Amer ed. illus............................
.... *$150.00–$250.00*

Findlay, Frederick Roderick Noble. *Big Game Shooting and Travel in South East Africa.* Camden. 1990. rprnt of 1903 ed. illus. .... *$50.00–$140.00*

Findlay, Palmer. *Story of Childbirth.* NY. 1934. 1st ed. .... *$50.00–$75.00*

Findley, Palmer. *Priests of Lucina: Story of Obstetrics.* Bos. 1939. 1st ed.....................
.... *$22.00–$35.00*

Finger, Charles J. *Frontier Ballads Heard and Gathered By.* NY. 1927. 1st ed. illus. woodcuts, #29/201 cc, sgn. .... *$25.00–$45.00*

Finger, Charles J. *Romantic Rascals.* NY. McBride. 1927. illus. black cloth. ....
.... *$20.00–$25.00*

Finley, Rev. James B. *History of the Wyandott Missions.* OH. 1840. 1st ed. 432 pp.......
.... *$200.00–$300.00*

Finley, Ruth. *Old Patchwork Quilts and the Women Who Made Them.* Phila. 1929. 1st ed. .... *$60.00–$75.00*

Firbank, Ronald. *Inclinations.* Lon. Grant Richards. 1916. illus. by Albert Rutherston. dj.. *$190.00 –$250.00*

Firebough, Ellen. *Physician's Wife and the Things That Pertain to Her Life.* Phila. 1894. 1st ed. 186 pp. .... *$75.00–$125.00*

Fireman, Janet. *Spanish Royal Corps of Engineers . . .* Glendale. Arthur H Clark. 1977. 1st ed. illus. facs maps and plans. .... *$35.00–$50.00*

First Annual Report of the Board of Pharmacy of the State of Washington. Olympia. 1892. 1st ed. wrps.. *$40.00–$50.00*

First Annual Sports and Bicycle Races. PA. 1896. wrps. 8 pp. .... *$19.00–$30.00*

Fish, Hamilton. *Challenge of World Communism.* Milwaukee. 1946. 1st ed. cloth. ....
.... *$30.00–$50.00*

Fishbein, M., et al. *Bibliography of Infantile Paralysis, 1789–1944.* Phila. 1946. 1st ed.
.... *$50.00–$65.00*

Fisher, A. K. *Hawks and Owls of the United States.* DC. GPO. 1893. brown cloth, clr plates, tissue guards. .... *$100.00–$160.00*

Fisher, A. K. *Hawks and Owls of the United States.* US Dept of Agriculture. 1893. illus. 25 clr lithos. .... *$140.00–$160.00*

Fisher, Angela. *Africa Adorned.* NY. Abrams. (1984). 1st ed. illus. clr plates...............
.... *$80.00–$120.00*

Fisher, Dorothy Canfield. *Vermont Tradition.* Bos. 1953. 1st ed. .... *$18.00–$25.00*

Fisher, Harrison. *American Beauties.* Ind. (1909). 1st ed. illus. by Fisher...................
.... *$400.00–$575.00*

Fisher, Harrison. *Dream of Fair Women.* NY. 1907. illus.................... *$140.00–$225.00*

Fisher, Harrison. *Harrison Fisher Book.* NY. Scribner's. 1907. 1st ed. intro by James Carrington.. *$80.00–$120.00*

Fisher, Harrison. *Harrison Fisher's American Girls in Miniature.* NY. 1912. illus. clr plates.. *$75.00–$125.00*

Fisher, Harrison. *Hiawatha*. Ind. 1906. 1st ed. .... *$50.00–$150.00*

Fisher, Harrison. *Little Gift Book*. Ind. 1913. 1st ed. original box. ..... *$100.00–$125.00*

Fisher, James. *Spring Day*. NY. George Lindsay. 1813. illus. 4 woodcuts. ....
.... *$40.00–$75.00*

Fisher, Rev. H. D. *Gun and the Gospel*. Chi. 1896. 1st ed. .... *$50.00–$75.00*

Fisher, Rudolph. *Walls of Jericho*. NY. Knopf. 1928. 1st ed. .... *$45.00–$90.00*

Fisher, Vardis. *Darkness and the Deep*. NY. (1943). dj. .... *$40.00–$50.00*

Fiske. *Dutch & Quaker Colonies in America*. Bos. 1899. 2 vols. .... *$30.00–$40.00*

Fiske, John. *American Revolution*. Bos/NY. 1896. 2 vols. green cloth. ....
.... *$100.00–$125.00*

Fiske, John. *John Fiske's Historical Writings*. Bos. 1902. 12 vols. .... *$50.00–$65.00*

Fite, Emerson D. *Book of Old Maps*. Camb. 1926. 1st ed. folio, maps. ....
.... *$150.00–$195.00*

Fitz-Adam, Adam. *The World*. Lon. Dodsley. 1772. 4 vols. 1st ed. copper engr, rare. ...
.... *$175.00–$300.00*

Fitzgerald, F. Scott. *Flappers and Philosophers*. NY. Scribner's. 1920. 1st ed. green
cloth. .... *$50.00–$75.00*

Fitzgerald, F. Scott. *All the Sad Young Men*. NY. Scribner's. 1926. 1st ed. dj. ....
.... *$100.00–$120.00*

Fitzgerald, F. Scott. *All the Sad Young Men*. NY. 1926. 1st ed. no dj. ..... *$50.00–$60.00*

Fitzgerald, F. Scott. *Beautiful and Damned*. Scribner's. 1922. 1st ed. .... *$65.00–$90.00*

Fitzgerald, F. Scott. *Great Gatsby*. NY. Scribner's. 1925. 1st ed. 1st ptg. ....
.... *$400.00–$675.00*

Fitzgerald, F. Scott. *Stories of F. Scott Fitzgerald*. NY. Scribner's Sons. 1951. 1st ed. dj.
.... *$75.00–$85.00*

Fitzgerald, F. Scott. *Tales of the Jazz Age*. Tor. Copp Clark. 1922. 1st Canadian ed. .....
.... *$200.00–$350.00*

Fitzgerald, F. Scott. *Tales of the Jazz Age*. NY. 1922. no dj. .... *$75.00–$90.00*

Fitzgerald, F. Scott. *Tender Is the Night*. NY. Scribner's. 1932. 1st ed. ....
.... *$200.00–$300.00*

Fitzgerald, Rugh Coder. *A Different Story*. Unicorn. illus. .... *$50.00–$65.00*

Flagg, Fannie. *Fried Green Tomatoes at the Whistlestop Cafe*. NY. Random House.
1987. 1st ed. sgn, dj. .... *$50.00–$60.00*

Flagg, Wilson. *Birds and Seasons of New England*. Bos. Osgood. 1875. 1st ed. illus. aeg.
.... *$55.00–$80.00*

Flags of Army of U.S. During the War of Rebellion 1861–65. Phila. 1887. 1st ed. illus.
clr lithos, folio. .... *$275.00–$450.00*

Flammarion, Camille. *Death and Its Mystery*. Century. 1922. 1st US ed. cloth............
.... *$50.00–$60.00*

Flammarion, Camille. *The Atmosphere*. NY. 1873. illus. lithos woodcuts.....................
.... *$75.00–$90.00*

Flammarion, Camille. *Wonders of the Heavens*. NY. Scribner's. 1907. illus. cloth. .... *$40.00–$50.00*

Fleischer, Nat. *50 Years at Ringside*. NY. 1958. 1st ed. wrps.................. *$35.00–$50.00*

Fleischman, Sid. *Whipping Boy*. NY. Greenwillow Books. (1986). dj. .. *$18.00–$45.00*

Fleming, Alexander (ed.). *Penicillin, Its Practical Application*. Lon. Butterworth. 1946. 1st ed... *$55.00–$65.00*

Fleming, Ian. *Chitty Chitty Bang Bang*. NY. Random House. (1964). 1st ed. illus. red cvr dj.. *$20.00–$25.00*

Fleming, Ian. *Diamond Smugglers*. Lon. (1957). 1st ed. black cloth dj.......................... .... *$150.00–$175.00*

Fleming, Ian. *Dr. No*. Lon. Jonathan Cape. 1958. 1st ed. dj. .... *$500.00–$1,300.00*

Fleming, Ian. *From Russia With Love*. Lon. Jonathan Cape. 1957. 1st ed. dj................. .... *$1,500.00–$1,750.00*

Fleming, Ian. *Goldfinger*. Lon. 1959. 1st ed. dj. .... *$500.00–$625.00*

Fleming, Ian. *Goldfinger*. NY. Macmillan. 1959. 1st Amer ed. dj. .... *$90.00–$250.00*

Fleming, Ian. *Man With the Golden Gun*. Lon. Jonathan Cape. (1965). 1st ed. dj. .... *$100.00–$125.00*

Fleming, Ian. *Octopussy and the Living Daylights*. Lon. Jonathan Cape. 1966. 1st ed. dj. .... *$50.00–$100.00*

Fleming, Ian. *Spy Who Loved Me*. Lon. Jonathan Cape. (1962). 1st ed. cloth, dj. .... *$125.00–$230.00*

Fleming, Ian. *You Only Live Twice*. Lon. Jonathan Cape. (1964). 1st ed. dj.................. .... *$90.00–$125.00*

Fleming, John Ambrose. *Electrons, Electric Waves and Wireless Telephony*. 1923. 1st ed. illus. .... *$45.00–$65.00*

Fleming, Thomas. *Now We Are Enemies*. NY. St Martin's Press. 1960. 1st ed. dj. black cloth and red paper cvred bds.. *$25.00–$50.00*

Flint, Austin. *Medical Ethics and Etiquette*. NY. Appleton. 1883. 1st ed. 97 pp. .... *$60.00–$95.00*

Flint, Austin. *Physical Exploration and Diagnosis of Diseases Affecting Respiratory Organs*. Phila. 1856. 1st ed. 636 pp. .... *$75.00–$100.00*

Flint, Sir William Russell. *Drawings*. Lon. Collins. (19500. 1st ed. illus...................... .... *$100.00–$150.00*

Flint, Timothy. *Life and Adventures of Daniel Boone*. Cinc. 1868. maps, illus. .... *$100.00–$250.00*

Flint, Timothy. *Recollections of the Last Ten Years . . . Journeys in the Valley of the Mississippi . . .* Bos. Cummings, Hilliard. 1826. 1st ed...................... *$125.00–$225.00*

Fluge, Friederich. *Der Seekrieg: The German Navy's Story, 1939–1945*. Annap. Naval Inst. 1965. maps, dj. .... *$15.00–$20.00*

Foley, Dan. *Toys Through the Ages*. Phil/NY. Chilton Books. 1962. 1st ed. illus. dj. .... *$20.00–$45.00*

Foley, Edwin. *Book of Decorative Furniture*. NY. 1911. 2 vols. 1st ed. 100 tip-in clr plates. .... *$175.00–$250.00*

Foley, Rae. *Back Door to Death*. NY. Dodd, Mead. 1963. 1st ed. inscrb, dj................... .... *$35.00–$45.00*

Folig, Fred. *Lucy Boston on Women's Rights and Spiritualism*. NY. 1855. 1st ed. illus. . ... *$50.00–$65.00*

Foran, W. *Kill or to Be Killed*. NY. 1988. 1st ed. dj. .... *$25.00–$35.00*

Forbes, Alexander. *California, a History of Upper and Lower California*. Lon. 1839. 1st ed. illus. map. .... *$925.00–$1,200.00*

Forbes, Allan and Ralph E. Eastman. *Yankee Sailing Cards*. Bos. State Street Trust. (1948–1952). 3 vols. wrps. illus. .... *$45.00–$80.00*

Forbes, Esther. *America's Paul Revere*. Bos. 1946. 1st ed. illus. by Lynd Ward. dj. .... *$45.00–$60.00*

Forbes, Esther. *Johnny Tremain*. Bos. Houghton Mifflin. (1943). dec green cloth. .... *$20.00–$30.00*

Forbes-Lindsay, C. H. *India Past and Present*. Phila. 1903. 2 vols. illus. fldg map. .... *$50.00–$75.00*

Forbush, Edward Howe. *Birds of Massachusetts . . .* 1929. 3 vols. illus. folio clr plates by Fuertes, et al. .... *$100.00–$150.00*

Forbush, Edward Howe. *Domestic Cat*. Bos. 1916. 1st ed. wrps. illus. *$65.00–$75.00*

Forbush, Edward Howe. *Game Birds, Wild Fowl & Shore Birds*. 1912. illus................. .... *$45.00–$60.00*

Forbush, Edward Howe. *History of Game Birds . . . of Massachusetts*. 1912. illus. plates. .... *$45.00–$50.00*

Forbush, Edward Howe. *Portraits of New England Birds*. MA. 1932. illus................. .... *$50.00–$75.00*

Force, Manning Ferguson. *General Sherman*. NY. 1899. 1st ed. .... *$50.00–$125.00*

Ford, Ford Maddox. *Great Trade Routes*. Unwin. 1937. 1st ed. wrps... *$30.00–$45.00*

Ford, Paul. *Great K. & A. Train Robbery*. Dodd Mead. 1897. 1st ed. ..... *$20.00–$30.00*

Ford, Richard. *Piece of My Heart*. NY. Harper & Row. (1976). 1st ed. author's first book, sgn, dj. .... *$225.00–$450.00*

Ford, Richard. *Rock Springs*. NY. Atlantic Monthly. (1987). 1st ed. sgn, dj................... .... *$30.00–$75.00*

Ford, Robert. *Thistledown*. Paisley. Gardner. 1913. 1st ed. illus. by John Duncan. teg. . ... *$60.00–$90.00*

Forder, Nick. *Victorian Dollhouses*. NJ. Chartwell Books. (1966). dj.... *$14.00–$18.00*

Foreman, Grant. *Indian Justice: A Cherokee Murder Trial at Tahlequah in 1840*. Oklahoma City. 1934. .... *$75.00–$85.00*

Forester, C. S. *African Queen*. Bos. 1935. 1st Amer ed. dj. .... *$375.00–$500.00*

Forester, C. S. *Captain from Connecticut*. Bos. Little/Brown. 1942. dj. . *$30.00–$35.00*

Forester, C. S. *Captain Horatio Hornblower*. Bos. 1939. 1st Amer ed. illus by Wyeth, dj. .... *$30.00–$50.00*

Forester, C. S. *Hornblower Companion.* Bos. Little Brown. (1964). 1st ed. red cloth, bds, dj. .... *$170.00–$350.00*

Forester, C. S. *Lord Hornblower.* Bos. Little Brown. 1946. 1st ed. .... *$20.00–$30.00*

Forester, C. S. *Randall and the River of Time.* Little Brown. 1950. 1st ed. dj. .... *$30.00–$38.00*

Forester, C. S. *Sky and the Forest.* Lon. Michael Joseph. (1948). 1st UK ed. dj. .... *$16.00–$40.00*

Forester, C. S. *The Commodore.* Lon. Michael Joseph LTD. (1945). 1st UK ed. dj........ .... *$25.00–$100.00*

Forester, C. S. *The Gun.* Bos. Little Brown. 1933............... *$125.00–$155.00*

Forester, C. S. *The Ship.* Bos. Little Brown & Co. (1943). red cloth bds...................... .... *$20.00–$30.00*

Forester, C. S. *To the Indies.* Bos. Little Brown & Co. 1940. dj............ *$60.00–$85.00*

Forester, Frank. *Fishing with Hook and Line.* Hurst & Co. 1858. illus. *$50.00–$60.00*

Forester, Frank. *Hints to Horse-Keepers.* NY. 1859. .... *$48.00–$75.00*

Forman, Samuel Engle. *Life and Writings of Thomas Jefferson . . .* Bowen Merrill. 1900. 2nd ed. .... *$50.00–$65.00*

Formby, John. *American Civil War . . .* NY. 1910. 2 vols. illus. maps. *$95.00–$125.00*

Forster, E. M. *Passage to India.* Arnold. 1924. 1st ed. dj. .... *$600.00–$800.00*

Forster, E. M. *Room With a View.* Lon. 1908. .... *$150.00–$250.00*

Forster, Frank J. *Country Houses.* NY. 1931. 1st ed............... *$125.00–$175.00*

Forsyth, Frederick. *Biafra Story.* Lon. Penguin. 1969. 1st ed. paperback original......... .... *$125.00–$150.00*

Forsyth, William. *An Epitome of Mr. Forsyth's Treatise on the Culture and Management of Fruit-Trees.* Phila. Poyntell. 1804. illus. .... *$50.00–$100.00*

Forsythe, Frederick. *Odessa File.* Viking. 1972. 1st US ed. dj. .... *$20.00–$30.00*

Fossett, Frank. *Colorado: Its Gold and Silver Mines.* NY. 1879. 1st thus. illus. maps, plates............... *$100.00–$300.00*

Fossett, Frank. *Colorado: Its Gold and Silver Mines.* NY. 1880. illus. 2nd ed. fldg maps. .... *$75.00–$125.00*

Foster, Sophie Lee. *Revolutionary Reader, Reminiscences and Indian Legends.* Atlanta, GA. Byrd. 1913. illus. red cloth, gilt lettering. .... *$30.00–$50.00*

Four Gospels of the Lord Jesus Christ/According to the Authorized Version of King James. Waltham St Laurence. The Golden Cockerel Press. 1931. illus. with 65 wood engrs by Eric Gill, #20/500 cc, tan cloth, white pigskin spine and corner, teg, by Sangorski and Sutcliffe, slipcase................. *$2,000.00–$7,500.00*

Fourth Report on Un-American Activities in California. Sacramento. 1948. 1st ed. .... *$60.00–$75.00*

Fowke, Gerard. *Archaeological History of Ohio . . .* Columbus. Ohio State Archaeological & Hist Society. (1902). illus. fldg plate........................ *$75.00–$100.00*

Fowler, H. W. *Dictionary of Modern English Usage.* Ox. 1926. 1st ed.. *$50.00–$75.00*

Fowler, Harlan D. *Camels to California.* Stanford Univ Press. 1950. illus. dj...............
.... *$25.00–$35.00*

Fowler, Jacob. *Journal of Jacob Fowler . . .* NY. Francis P Harper. 1898. 1st ed. 790/950 cc, blue cloth.. *$100.00–$135.00*

Fowler, L. N. *Principles of Phrenology & Physiology . . .* NY. 1842. 1st ed. ....
.... *$55.00–$65.00*

Fowler, O. S. *A Home for All. Or the Gravel Wall & Octagon Mode of Building.* NY. 1877. illus. .... *$45.00–$60.00*

Fowler, O. S. *Fowler's Practical Phrenology.* NY. 1853......................... *$35.00–$50.00*

Fowles, J. *The Aristos.* Bos. Little Brown. (1964). 1st ed. dj. .... *$135.00–$150.00*

Fowles, John. *A Maggot.* Lon. Jonathan Cape. 1985. 1/500 cc, sgn. ... *$125.00–$150.00*

Fowles, John. *The Collector.* 1963. 1st ed. 1st state, author's first book.........................
.... *$100.00–$150.00*

Fox, Carl. *The Doll.* NY. Harry N Abrams. illus. dj, clr and b/w plates.....................
.... *$100.00–$225.00*

Fox, Carl. *The Doll: New Shorter Edition.* NY. Harry N Abrams. wrps. *$20.00–$35.00*

Fox, John. *Little Shepherd of Kingdom Come.* NY. 1931. 1st ed. illus. by Wyeth..........
.... *$150.00–$225.00*

Fox, John R. *In Happy Valley.* Scribner's. 1917. illus............................ *$20.00–$30.00*

Foxcraft, Thomas. *Observations, Historical and Practical, on the Rise and Primitive State of New-England . . .: A Sermon.* Bos. S Kneeland and T Green, for S Gerrish. 1730. 1st ed. 46 pp. .... *$600.00–$1,500.00*

Frame, Janet. *Face in the Water.* NY. 1961. 1st ed. dj.......................... *$30.00–$40.00*

France, Anatole. *Gods Are Athirst.* Lon. (1927). dj. .... *$35.00–$45.00*

Franchere, Gabriel. *Narr. of a Voyage to the Northwest Coast of America 1811, 1812, 1813, 1814.* NY. 1854. 1st ed in Eng. .... *$250.00–$350.00*

Francis, Dick. *10-lb. Penalty.* Lon. Michael Joseph. 1997. 1st ed. sgn, dj.......................
.... *$55.00–$85.00*

Francis, Dick. *Driving Force.* Lon. Michael Joseph. 1992. 1st ed. dj..... *$50.00–$65.00*

Francis, Dick. *Enquiry.* NY. Harper & Row. 1969. 1st Amer ed. dj. ..... *$75.00–$90.00*

Francis, Dick. *Flying Finish.* Lon. Michael Joseph. 1966. 1st ed. dj.. *$400.00–$450.00*

Francis, Dick. *For Kicks.* Lon. Michael Joseph. 1965. 1st ed. dj.................... *$1,250.00*

Francis, Dick. *High Stakes.* NY. 1976. 1st Amer ed. dj........................... *$30.00–$40.00*

Francis, Dick. *High Stakes.* Lon. 1975. 1st ed. dj. .... *$85.00–$100.00*

Francis, Dick. *Hot Money.* Lon. Michael Joseph. 1987. 1st ed. dj......... *$45.00–$50.00*

Francis, Dick. *In the Frame.* NY. 1977. 1st Amer ed. dj...................... *$30.00–$40.00*

Francis, Dick. *In the Frame.* Lon. 1976. 1st ed. dj................................ *$50.00–$65.00*

Francis, Dick. *Knock Down.* Lon. Michael Joseph. 1974. 1st ed. dj... *$125.00–$135.00*

Francis, Dick. *The Danger.* Lon. Michael Joseph. 1983. 1st ed. dj........ *$45.00–$50.00*

Francis, Jean. *Dolls I Have Known and Loved*. Canada. privately printed. 1980. illus. pictorial bds, ltd ed 1000 cc sgn by author. .... *$25.00–$40.00*

Francis, John W. *Old New York or Reminiscences of the Past Sixty Years*. NY. 1858. 1st ed. .... *$30.00–$50.00*

Francis, Peter. *I Worked in a Soviet Factory*. Lon. Jarrolds. 1939. illus. *$20.00–$35.00*

Frank Leslie's Illustrated History of the Civil War. NY. 1895. 1st ed. small folio. ....
.... *$60.00–$125.00*

Frank, Larry. *Indian Silver Jewelry. 1868–1930*. Bos. 1978. 1st ed...... *$45.00–$75.00*

Frank, P. *Alas, Babylon*. Phila. Lippincott. 1959. 1st ed. scarce, dj. .. *$200.00–$250.00*

Franklin, Colin and Charlotte. *Catalogue of Early Colour Printing* . . . Oxford. 1977. illus. clr plates... *$50.00–$70.00*

Franklin, John. *Narrative of a Journey to the Shores of the Polar Sea, 1819–22*. Lon. 1823. 1st ed. illus. maps, plates... *$400.00–$885.00*

Fraser, Antonia. *History of Toys*. Delacorte Press. (1966). illus. dj,....... *$30.00–$45.00*

Fraser, Chelsea. *Heroes of the Air*. Crowell. 1928. illus. rev, 550 pp,.... *$25.00–$35.00*

Fraser, George MacDonald. *Flashman and the Angel of the Lord*. NY. Knopf. (1994). 1st ed. dj. .... *$35.00–$50.00*

Fraser, George MacDonald. *Flashman and the Dragon*. NY. Knopf. (1986). 1st Amer ed. dj. .... *$35.00–$75.00*

Fraser, George MacDonald. *Flashman and the Mountain of Light*. Lon. Collins Harvill. (1990). 1st UK ed. dj.. *$50.00–$90.00*

Fraser, George MacDonald. *Flashman and the Redskins*. NY. Knopf. (1982). 1st US ed dj. .... *$35.00–$50.00*

Fraser, George MacDonald. *General Danced at Dawn*. NY. Knopf. (1973). 1st US ed. white-cloth cvred bds, dj, scarce. .... *$75.00–$100.00*

Fraser, George MacDonald. *The Pyrates*. NY. Knopf. (1984). dj........... *$25.00–$45.00*

Fraser, J. Baillie. *Mesopotamia and Assyria, from the Earliest Ages to the Present*. NY. Harper. 1842. 1st Amer ed. fldg map frontis, 336 pp. .... *$30.00–$40.00*

Frazier, Don. *Recognizing Derrydale Press Books*. np. privately printed. 1983. illus. 22 clr plates, #55/347 cc, brown lea... *$210.00–$250.00*

Frederick Remington: The American West. Kent, OH. Volair Ltd. 1978. ed by Philip St Claire, plates, boxed. .... *$80.00–$120.00*

Freece, Hans P. *Letters of an Apostate Mormon to His Son*. NY. private ptg. 1908. ......
....*$65.00–$85.00*

Freeman, Douglas Southall. *Lee's Lieutenants*. NY. Scribner's. 1942. 3 vols. 1st ed. illus. cloth. .... *$50.00–$75.00*

Freeman, Douglas Southall. *Lee's Lieutenants: A Study in Command*. Scribner's. 3 vols. illus. b/w illus maps.. *$100.00–$125.00*

Freeman, Douglas Southall. *Robert E. Lee, A Biography*. NY. 1934–5. 4 vols. illus.....
.... *$95.00–$250.00*

Freeman, Harry C. *Brief History of Butte, Montana*. Shepard. 1900. 1st ed.................
.... *$75.00–$125.00*

Freeman, Joseph. *Discourse of the Proper Training of Children*. Ludlow, VT. 1862. wrps. .... *$25.00–$40.00*

Freese, Ernest Irving. *Perspective Projection*. NY. The Pencil Points Press. 1930. 1st ed. illus. light brown paper bds. .... *$15.00–$30.00*

Freligh, Martin. *Homeopathic Practice of Medicine*. NY. Lamport, Blakeman & Law. 1854. 2nd ed. .... *$90.00–$150.00*

Fremont, Capt. J. C. *Report of the Exploring Expedition to the Rocky Mountains . . .* Wash. 1842. maps. .... *$125.00–$250.00*

Fremont, John. *Life of Col Fremont*. (NY). 1856. 1st ed. 32 pp, sewn, portrait, 2 full-page illus. .... *$85.00–$100.00*

French, John C. *Passenger Pidgeon in Pennsylvania*. Altoona. Altoona Tribune. 1919. 1st ed. wrps. illus. .... *$100.00–$150.00*

Freud, Sigmund. *Interpretation of Dreams*. NY. 1937. dj. .... *$30.00–$40.00*

Freud, Sigmund. *Introductory Lectures on Psycho-Analysis*. Lon. 1929. ....
.... *$50.00–$80.00*

Freud, Sigmund. *Modern Sexual Morality and Modern Nervousness*. NY. Eugenics Pub Co. 1931. boards. .... *$50.00–$75.00*

Freud, Sigmund. *Note on the Unconscious in PsychoAnalysis*. Lon. 1912. wrps. ....
.... *$25.00–$35.00*

Freud, Sigmund. *Problem of Lay-Analyses*. NY. 1927. 1st Amer ed. dj. *$65.00–$85.00*

Friedan, Betty. *Feminine Mystique*. NY. 1963. 1st ed. dj. .... *$100.00–$150.00*

Friede, Adele M. *Pagoda Shadows*. Bos. 18814. .... *$35.00–$45.00*

Friedman, Bruce Jay. *Black Angels*. NY. (1966). 1st ed. dj. .... *$35.00–$45.00*

Friedman, Bruce Jay. *Stern*. NY. 1962. 1st ed. dj. .... *$50.00–$60.00*

Friedmann, H. *The Cowbirds*. Charles C Thomas. 1929. dj. presentation copy. ....
.... *$45.00–$60.00*

Frignet, Ernest. *La Californie: Histoire des Progres de l'un Etats-Unis . . .* Paris. Schlesinger Freres. 1867. printed wrps, 2nd ed,. .... *$50.00–$75.00*

Froiseth, Jennie Anderson. *Women of Mormonism*. Detroit. 1887. illus. ....
.... *$90.00–$100.00*

Frost Robert. *West Running Brook*. NY. Henry Holt. 1928. 1st ed. no dj. ....
.... *$65.00–$95.00*

Frost, A. B. *Stuff and Nonsense*. NY. Scribner's. (1884). illus. orig pictorial bds. ....
.... *$60.00–$110.00*

Frost, John. *American Naval Biography*. Phila. 1844. illus. 3/4 mor.... *$87.00–$185.00*

Frost, John. *Book of Travels in Africa*. NY/Phila. 1848. illus. .... *$50.00–$85.00*

Frost, John. *Pictorial History of Mexico and the Mexican War*. Phila. 1849. maps. ....
.... *$35.00–$50.00*

Frost, Robert. *A Boy's Will*. Lon. 1913. 1st ed. author's first book. cream paper wrps with 8-petaled flower ornament. .... *$850.00–$1,500.00*

Frost, Robert. *Collected Poems of Robert Frost*. NY. Henry Holt. 1939. sgn and dated, dj. .... *$450.00–$750.00*

Frost, Robert. *Complete Poems.* NY. Holt, Rinehart & Winston. (1962). 1st ed. dj........
.... *$25.00–$45.00*

Frost, Robert. *Complete Poems of Robert Frost.* Lon. (1951). dj........... *$40.00–$50.00*

Frost, Robert. *Further Range.* NY. 1936. ltd 803 cc, sgn. .... *$275.00–$500.00*

Frost, Robert. *In the Clearing.* NY. (1962). 1st ed. dj. .... *$45.00–$75.00*

Frost, Robert. *Masque of Mercy.* NY. 1947. 1st ed. .... *$15.00–$85.00*

Frost, Robert. *Masque of Reason.* NY. Henry Holt. (1945). 1st ed. dj. ... *$35.00–$75.00*

Frost, Robert. *New Hampshire.* NY. 1923. 1st ed. .... *$100.00–$150.00*

Frost, Robert. *Steeple Bush.* NY. Henry Holt. 1947. 1st ed. ltd 750 cc, sgn, dj. ....
.... *$125.00–$350.00*

Frost, Robert. *Witness Tree.* NY. Henry Holt. 1942. 1st ed. ltd, sgn. . *$475.00–$500.00*

Frost, Robert. *Witness Tree.* NY. (1942). 1st ed. dj. .... *$35.00–$100.00*

Frost, Stanley. *Challenge of the Klan.* Ind. 1924. 1st ed. .... *$40.00–$55.00*

Fry, Christopher. *Lady's Not for Burning.* Lon. 1949. dj. .... *$30.00–$40.00*

Fry, J. Reese. *Life of Gen. Zachary Taylor.* Phila. 1848. illus. .... *$37.00–$45.00*

Fryer, Jane E. *Mary Frances Cook Book.* Phil. Winston. 1912. 1st ed. illus. ....
.... *$95.00–$185.00*

Fryer, Jane E. *Mary Frances Sewing Book.* Phila. 1913. 1st ed. illus. patterns present. .
.... *$150.00–$225.00*

Fryer, Mary Ann. *John Fryer of the Bounty.* Lon. Golden Cockerel Press. 1939. illus.
ltd #226/300 cc, sgn, colophon. .... *$325.00–$375.00*

Fuentes, Carlos. *Aura.* NY. 1965. 1st Eng ed. dj. .... *$75.00–$100.00*

Fuentes, Carlos. *Old Gringo.* NY. 1985. 1st ed. 2nd ptg, dj. .... *$20.00–$45.00*

Fuentes, Carlos. *Where the Air is Clear.* NY. Ivan Obolensky. 1960. 1st ed. dj.............
.... *$20.00–$35.00*

Fugitives. *The Story of Clyde Barrow and Bonnie Parker.* Dallas. 1934. 1st ed. ....
.... *$47.00–$65.00*

Fuhrer, Charles. *Mysteries of Montreal . . .* Montreal. 1881. 245 pp... *$85.00–$100.00*

Fulghum, David. *Vietnam Experience.* Boston Pub Co. (1981–1988). 21 vols. ....
.... *$150.00–$200.00*

Fuller, Claud E. and Richard D. Steuart. *Firearms of the Confederacy, the Shoulder
Arms, Pistols and Revolvers of the Confederate Soldier.* Huntington, WV. Standard
Publications. 1944. 1st ed. scarce dj. .... *$200.00–$350.00*

Fuller, J. F. C. *Generalship of Ulysses S. Grant.* NY. 1929.................... *$37.00–$45.00*

Fuller, Metta. *Fresh Leaves From Western Woods.* Buffalo. 1852. 2 vols. 1st ed. ....
.... *$15.00–$25.00*

Fuller, R. Buckminster. *Nine Chains to the Moon.* Phila. 1938. 1st ed. authors first
book, dj. .... *$75.00–$95.00*

Fuller, R. Buckminster. *Utopia or Oblivion.* Penguin Press. 1970. 1st UK ed. dj.........
.... *$30.00–$50.00*

Fulton, Frances. *To and Through Nebraska.* Lincoln. 1884. 1st ed. 273 pp....................
.... *$100.00–$145.00*

Fulton, James A. *Peach Culture.* NY. 1905. .... *$25.00–$50.00*

Furlong, Charles W. *Let 'Er Buck.* NY. 1921. 1st ed. sgn. .... *$55.00–$65.00*

Furneaux, W. *British Butterflies and Moths.* Lon. 1911. plates............. *$45.00–$55.00*

Furst, Peter T. and Jill L. Furst. *North American Indian Art.* NY. Rizzoli. illus. photos, dj. .... *$40.00–$65.00*

Fuzzlebug, Fritz (John J. Dunkle). *Prison Life During the Rebellion.* Singer's Glen, VA. 1869. 1st ed. wrps. .... *$125.00–$150.00*

Gabler, James M. *Wine into Words.* Baltimore. Bacchus Press. 1985. 1st ed. dj............
.... *$35.00–$50.00*

Gade, John A. *Book Plates — Old and New.* NY. 1898. illus. .... *$25.00–$30.00*

Gaelic Fairy Tales. Glasgow. 1908. illus. by Katherine Cameron. .... *$30.00–$40.00*

Gage, S. H. *The Microscope.* Ithaca. Comstock Publishing. 1936. .... *$40.00–$50.00*

Gage, W. L. *Palestine: Historical and Descriptive.* Bos. 1883. illus....... *$55.00–$95.00*

Gallant, Mavis. *Across the Bridge.* NY. (1993). 1st ed. dj. .... *$18.00–$25.00*

Gallant, Mavis. *Other Paris.* Bos. Houghton Mifflin. 1956. 1st ed. author's first book, dj. .... *$75.00–$85.00*

Gallaudet, Thomas. *Plan of a Seminary for the Education of Instructers of Youth.* Bos. Cummings, Hilliard & Co. 1825. 1st ed. illus. 39 pp. .... *$50.00–$75.00*

Gallico, Paul. *Snow Goose.* 1941. 1st ed. dj. .... *$225.00–$250.00*

Galsworthy, John. *Forsythe Saga.* Lon. Heinemann. 1922. 1st ed. lea, aeg. ....
.... *$200.00–$400.00*

Galsworthy, John. *Loyalties.* Scribner's. 1922. 1st US ed. dj. .... *$60.00–$70.00*

Galsworthy, John. *Maid in Waiting.* Lon. 1931. 1st ed. dj..................... *$25.00–$50.00*

Galsworthy, John. *Memories.* NY. 1914. illus. .... *$30.00–$40.00*

Galsworthy, John. *Swan Song.* NY. Scribner's. 1928. 1st US ed. dj....... *$40.00–$50.00*

Galsworthy, John. *Swan Song.* Lon. 1928... *$50.00–$75.00*

Gambling World by Rouge et Noir. Dodd Mead. 1898. .... *$50.00–$65.00*

Gambling, Gaming Supplies. Chi. H C Evans Co. 1929. wrps............. *$85.00–$125.00*

Gammons, Rev. John G. *Third Massachusetts Regiment Volunteer . . . 1861–1863.* Prov. 1906. 1st ed. illus. .... *$75.00–$100.00*

Garces, Francisco. *Record of Travels in Arizona and California, 1175–1776.* SF. John Howell-Books. trans by John Galvin. ltd 1250 cc. .... *$50.00–$80.00*

Garcia Marquez, Gabriel. *In Evil Hour.* NY. Harper & Row. (1979). 1st Amer ed, dj..
.... *$60.00–$100.00*

Gard, Wayne. *Rawhide Texas.* Norman. 1965. 1st ed. illus. cloth, dj. .... *$22.00–$30.00*

Gardiner, Howard C. *In Pursuit of the Golden Dream: Reminiscences of San Francisco* . . . MA. Western Hemisphere. 1970. 1st ed. illus. 8 plates 2 maps, 1 fldg....................
.... *$60.00–$90.00*

Gardner, Erle Stanley. *Case of the Grinning Gorilla.* Morrow. 1952. 1st ed. dj............
.... *$25.00–$35.00*

Gardner, Erle Stanley. *Case of the Screaming Woman.* NY. 1957. 1st ed. dj................
.... *$35.00–$45.00*

Gardner, Erle Stanley. *Case of the Substitute Face.* NY. William Morrow. 1938. 1st ed.
dj. .... *$350.00–$400.00*

Gardner, Erle Stanley. *Case of the Careless Cupid.* NY. William Morrow. 1968. 1st ed.
dj. .... *$45.00–$50.00*

Gardner, Erle Stanley. *Case of the Ice-Cold Hands.* NY. William Morrow. 1962. 1st ed.
dj. .... *$50.00–$60.00*

Gardner, Erle Stanley. *DA Breaks an Egg.* NY. William Morrow. 1949. 1st ed. dj........
.... *$40.00–$50.00*

Gardner, John. *In the Suicide Mountains.* NY. Knopf. 1977. 1st ed. dj. *$30.00–$35.00*

Gardner, John. *King's Indian: Stories and Tales.* NY. Knopf. 1974. 1st ed. dj..............
.... *$35.00–$60.00*

Gardner, John. *Life and Times of Chaucer.* NY. Knopf. 1977. 1st ed. dj......................
.... *$35.00–$45.00*

Gardner, John. *October Light.* Knopf. 1976. 1st ed. dj. .... *$45.00–$50.00*

Gardner, John. *Sunlight Dialogues.* NY. 1972. 1st ed. dj....................... *$60.00–$70.00*

Garfield, James R. *Report of the Commissioner of Corporations on the Beef Industry.* Wash. GPO. 1905. .... *$75.00–$100.00*

Garis, Howard. *Uncle Wiggily on the Farm.* NY. Platt & Munk Co. 1939. illus. green cloth dj. .... *$15.00–$25.00*

Garland, H. *Life of John Randolph of Roanoke.* NY. 1851. 2 vols. .... *$30.00–$40.00*

Garland, Hamlin. *Trail-makers of the Middle Border.* Macmillan. 1926. 1st ed. dj. ......
.... *$25.00–$35.00*

Garner, Elvira. *Ezekiel.* Henry Holt. illus. paper over boards. .... *$50.00–$65.00*

Garner, T. and A. Stratton. *Domestic Architecture of England During the Tudor Period.* NY. (1929). 2 vols. 2nd ed. 210 plates................................... *$150.00–$300.00*

Garnett, David. *First "Hippy" Revolution.* Cerrillos, NM. 1970. 1st ed. wrps. sgn. ....
.... *$40.00–$50.00*

Garnett, Porter (ed.). *Papers of San Francisco Vigilance Committee of 1851.* Berkeley. Univ of Calif Press. 1910. wrps. .... *$40.00–$70.00*

Garnett, Theodore Stanford. *J E B Stuart (Major General) Commander of the Cavalry Corps.* NY and DC. Neale Publishing Co. 1907. 1st ed. illus. plates............................
.... *$200.00–$250.00*

Garrard, Lewis H. *Wah-To-Yah and the Taos Trail.* SF. Grabhorn Press. 1936. illus. ltd 550 cc.. *$125.00–$140.00*

Garrison, Fielding H. *An Introduction to the History of Medicine.* Saunders. 1914. 763 pp. .... *$75.00–$100.00*

Garwood, Darrell. *Artist in Iowa: A Life of Grant Wood.* NY. WW Norton. 1944. 1st ed. illus. photos, dj. .... *$25.00–$30.00*

Gask, Norman. *Old Silver Spoons of England.* Lon. 1926. illus. rbnd, ¼ lea. .... *$75.00–$125.00*

Gass, Patrick. *Gass's Journal of the Lewis & Clark Expedition.* Chi. McClurg. 1904. illus. two-tone cloth, spine lettered in gilt, teg..................................... *$350.00–$500.00*

Gass, Patrick. *Journal of the Voyages and Travels of a Corps of Discovery under the Command of Capt Lewis . . .* Minn. Ross & Haines. 1958. illus. photos. fldg endpaper map. clr 1,109/2,000 cc. .... *$50.00–$100.00*

Gass, William. *Omensetter's Luck.* (NY). New American Library. (1966). 1st ed. author's first novel, dj.. *$60.00–$125.00*

Gass, William. *Omensetter's Luck.* (NY). New American Library. (1966). 1st ed. author's first novel, sgn, dj. .... *$225.00–$300.00*

Gass, William. *The Tunnel.* NY. Knopf. 1995. 1st ed. dj......................... *$35.00–$45.00*

Gass, William. *World Within the World.* NY. Knopf. 1978. 1st ed. dj..... *$34.00–$45.00*

Gaster, M. *Hebrew Illuminated Bibles of the 9th and 10th Centuries.* Lon. 1901. folio, plates.. *$85.00–$125.00*

Gasthoff's Parade Floats & Decorations. Tampa, FL. Gastoff's Display Service, Inc. 1937–38. pictorial wrps, illus, 24 pp... *$40.00–$50.00*

Gatty, Mrs. A. *Book of Sun Dials.* Lon. 1872. 1st ed. illus. plates...... *$100.00–$200.00*

Gay, John. *Beggar's Opera.* Paris. 1937. illus. ltd #162/1,500 cc, slipcase..................... .... *$65.00–$75.00*

Gay, Joseph R. *Progress and Achievements of the Colored People . . .* Wash. 1913. 1st ed. 434 pp. .... *$50.00–$60.00*

Gay, Wanda. *Growing Pains.* Coward. 1940. 1st ed. illus. author's first book, 15 pp, dj. .... *$200.00–$300.00*

Gay, Wanda. *Millions of Cats.* Coward. 1928. 1st ed. illus. by author, 15 pp, dj. .... *$200.00–$300.00*

Gee, Ernest R. *Early American Sporting Books 1734-1844.* NY. Derrydale Press. 1928. illus. 500 cc, sgn... *$85.00–$100.00*

Gee, Hugh and Sally Gee. *Belinda and the Magic Journey.* NY. Chanticleer Press. 1948. dj.. *$35.00–$45.00*

Geer, John. *Beyond the Lines: or a Yankee Prisoner Loose in Dixie.* Phila. 1863. 1st ed. illus. .... *$50.00–$125.00*

Geer, Walter. *Campaigns of the Civil War.* 1926. 1st ed....................... *$75.00–$130.00*

Genet, Jean. *Book of the Dance.* Bos. 1920. dj. .... *$40.00–$55.00*

Genthe, Arnold. *Old Chinatown.* NY. 1908. 2nd ed............................. *$80.00–$100.00*

Genthe, Arnold. *Pictures of Old Chinatown.* NY. 1908. 1st ed. illus. scarce. .... *$200.00–$259.00*

Georgia Scenes by a Native Georgian. NY. 1840. illus. 2nd ed.......... *$100.00–$195.00*

Gerard, Max (ed.). *Dali.* NY. Abradale/Abrams. 1968. 1st ed. illus. trans by Eleanor Morse... *$75.00–$125.00*

Gerhard, Peter. *Pirates on the West Coast of New Spain*. Glendale. Arthur H Clark. 1960. 1st ed. illus. repro maps and engr.. *$35.00–$45.00*

Gerken, Jo Elizabeth. *Wonderful Dolls of War*. NE. Doll Research Asso. (1964). illus. sgn... *$30.00–$60.00*

Gernsbach, Hugo. *Radio for All*. 1922. 1st ed. illus. .... *$30.00–$40.00*

Gernsbach, Hugo. *Ralph 124C41+ A Romance of the Year 2660*. 1925. 1st ed............. .... *$175.00–$245.00*

Gersheim, Helmut. *Origins of Photography*. NY. (1982). 1st Amer ed. illus. dj, slipcase.. *$40.00–$50.00*

Gerstaecker, Frederick. *Wanderings and Fortunes of Some German Immigrants*. NY. 1948. .... *$95.00–$250.00*

Gerstaecker, Frederick. *Wild Sports of the Far West*. NY. 1884. .... *$35.00–$55.00*

Gibrain, Kahlil. *The Prophet*. NY. Knopf. 1923. 1st ed. dj. .... *$40.00–$95.00*

Gibson, Charles Dana. *Gibson Book*. NY. 1907. 2 vols. .... *$125.00–$175.00*

Gibson, Charles Dana. *Pictures of People*. NY. Russell. 1901. 1st ed. illus. oblong folio... *$80.00–$95.00*

Gibson, W. B. *Book of Secrets*. 1927. 1st ed. dj................................. *$175.00–$200.00*

Gibson, W. H. *Our Edible Toadstools and Mushroom*. NY. 1895. illus. *$85.00–$125.00*

Gibson, William Hamilton. *Our Native Orchids*. NY. 1905................... *$50.00–$65.00*

Gide, Charles. *Communist and Co-Operative Colonies*. NY. Crowell. 1930. dj. .... *$50.00–$75.00*

Gielow, Martha S. *Mammy's Reminiscences and Other Sketches*. NY. A S Barnes. (1898). illus. blue-green decorated cloth.. *$85.00–$125.00*

Gilbert, Bil. *The Trailblazers*. NY. Time-Life Books. (1973). illus. decorated imitation lea with pictorial paste-down. .... *$10.00–$15.00*

Gilbert, Bil. *The Trailblazers*. NY. Time-Life Books. 1973. illus. pictorial leatherette cvr. .... *$15.00–$20.00*

Gilbert, William. *On the Magnet*. NY. (1958). rprnt, illus..................... *$75.00–$95.00*

Giles, Herbert A. *Chinese English Dictionary*. 1912. 2nd ed. revised........................... .... *$120.00–$160.00*

Giles, Rosean A. *Shasta County California*. CA. 1949. 1st ed. illus. map, ltd 1,000 cc.. .... *$50.00–$60.00*

Gilham, Major William. *Manual of Instruction for the Volunteers and Militia of the United States*. Phila. De Silver. 1861. .... *$225.00–$250.00*

Gill, Evan. *Eric Gill: A Bibliography*. Winchester & Detroit. St Paul's Bibliographies. 1991. rev ed. illus. .... *$80.00–$120.00*

Gill, Sir William. *Pompeiana: The Topography, Edifices & Ornaments of Pompeii*. Lon. 1835. 2 vols. illus. .... *$300.00–$400.00*

Gillespie, W. Bro. Nelson. *History of Apollo Lodge No.13 . . . Troy, N.Y*. NY. 1886. illus. plates... *$30.00–$40.00*

Gillette, Mrs. F. L. *White House Cook Book*. Chi. 1889........................ *$65.00–$85.00*

Gillian, Arthur J. *Menace of Chemical Warfare to Civilian Populations*. Lon. Chemical Workers Union. 1932. wrps. 20 pp, pictorial cvr. .... *$25.00–$35.00*

Gillies, Rev. John. *Memoirs of the Life and Character of the Late George Whitefield*. Bos. Samuel Armstrong. 1813. lea. .... *$18.00–$25.00*

Gillis, Charles J. *Another Summer*. NY. Little & Co. 1893. blue cloth. . *$60.00–$80.00*

Gillmore, Parker. *Prairie and Forest*. Lon. Chapman & Hall. 1874. 1st ed. illus. wood-engr. plates. .... *$50.00–$80.00*

Gilman, Caroline. *Recollections of a Southern Matron*. NY. Harper. 1838. 272 pp. .... *$125.00–$200.00*

Gilmore, Parker. *Accessible Field Sports*. Lon. Chapman & Hall. 1869. 1st ed. illus.... .... *$45.00–$80.00*

Ginsberg, Allen. *Bixby Canyon, Ocean Path, Word Breeze*. Botham. 1972. 1st ed. wrps. .... *$35.00–$40.00*

Ginsberg, Allen. *Fall of America*. SF. 1972. wrps. .... *$20.00–$45.00*

Ginsberg, Allen. *Journals Mid-fifties, 1954–1958*. NY. Harper Collins. (1995). 1st ed. wrps. .... *$18.00–$45.00*

Ginsberg, Allen. *Planet News*. CA. City Lights. 1968. wrps. 1st US ed. dj. .... *$25.00–$35.00*

Ginsberg, Allen. *Reality Sandwiches*. (1963). 1st ed. wrps. .... *$35.00–$45.00*

Ginsberg, Allen. *White Shroud: Poems 1980–1985*. NY. Harper. (1986). 1st ed. dj 1/200 sgn boxed. .... *$150.00–$225.00*

Ginzburg, R. *An Unhurried View of Erotica*. NY. 1958. slipcase. .... *$10.00–$25.00*

Giovanni, Nikki. *Cotton Candy on a Rainy Day*. NY. Morrow. 1978. 1st ed. sgn, dj. .... *$45.00–$90.00*

Glacier National Park Montana . . .1920. illus. 32 pp pictorial wrps, brochure. .... *$75.00–$100.00*

Gladstone, J. H. *Michael Farada*. Lon. 1874. 2nd ed. repairs. .... *$22.00–$35.00*

Glasfurd, A. *Musings of an Old Shikari*. Lon. John Lane. (1928). illus. green cloth. .... *$75.00–$100.00*

Glasgow, Ellen. *Descendant*. NY. Harper. 1897. 1st ed. author's first book. .... *$200.00–$235.00*

Glasgow, Ellen. *Freeman and Other Poems*. NY. Doubleday Page. 1902. 1st ed. .... *$225.00–$250.00*

Glasser, Otto. *Dr. Wilhelm C. Roentgen*. 1934. 1st Eng ed. dj. .... *$45.00–$60.00*

Glazier, Capt. Willard. *Down the Great River*. Phila. 1893. .... *$25.00–$35.00*

Glazier, Capt. Willard. *Headwaters of the Mississippi*. NY. 1893. .... *$35.00–$50.00*

Gleason, Prof. Oscar R. F. *Gleason's Horse Book*. Chi. Donohue. 1892. .... *$65.00–$80.00*

Glenister, A. G. *Birds of the Malay Peninsula*. Oxford Univ Press. 1951. illus. dj. .... *$35.00–$55.00*

Gloucester Directory 1899–1900. MA. 1899. bds. .... *$45.00–$55.00*

Goaman, Muriel. *Judy's & Andrew's Puppet Book*. Bos. Plays, Inc. (1967). 1st US ed. .... *$15.00–$20.00*

Goddard, Henry Herbert. *Kallikak Family*. NY. 1916........................... *$25.00–$35.00*

Godman, John D. *American Natural History*. Phil. Stoddart & Atherton. 1831. 3vols. . ... *$140.00–$250.00*

Godspeed, Charles. *Yankee Bookseller*. Bos. Houghton Mifflin. 1937. 1st ed. ltd 310 cc, sgn, slipcase.. *$125.00–$175.00*

Godspeed, Charles. *Yankee Bookseller*. Bos. Houghton Mifflin. 1937. 1st ed. dj........... .... *$35.00–$75.00*

Godwin, Gail. *Glass People*. NY. 1972. 1st ed. dj.................................. *$45.00–$60.00*

Goebbels, Joseph. *Kampf um Berlin*. Munchen. 1938. illus. .... *$24.00–$30.00*

Goff, Kenneth. *Strange Fire*. Col. 1954. 1st ed. illus. cloth. .... *$20.00–$30.00*

Goines, Donald. *Black Gangster*. LA. Holloway House. 1972. 1st ed. paperback original... *$15.00–$35.00*

Gold, Herbert. *Fathers*. NY. 1966. 1st ed. dj. .... *$18.00–$28.00*

Gold, Herbert. *Love & Like*. NY. 1960. 1st ed. sgn, presentation copy, dj...................... .... *$40.00–$65.00*

Goldberg, R. *Rube Goldberg's Guide to Europe*. NY. 1954. 1st ed. presentation copy, sgn... *$30.00–$45.00*

Golden, Arthur. *Memoirs of a Geisha*. NY. Knopf. 1997. 1st ed. 1st state. author's first novel. dj. .... *$50.00–$60.00*

Goldenberg, Samuel. *Lace: Its Origin and History*. NY. 1904. 1st ed. illus. presentation copy... *$50.00–$85.00*

Golding, William. *An Egyptian Journal*. Faber. 1985. 1st ed. dj. .... *$30.00–$40.00*

Golding, William. *Lord of the Flies*. NY. Coward-McCann. 1955. 1st ed. dj................. .... *$300.00–$1,100.00*

Golding, William. *Lord of the Flies*. Lon. Faber & Faber. (1954). dj, red cloth............. .... *$100.00–$150.00*

Golding, William. *Lord of the Flies*. Lon. Faber & Faber. (1954). 1st ed. 1st UK ed. dj. .... *$1,500.00–$2,000.00*

Golding, William. *The Pyramid*. Lon. Faber & Faber. (1967). 1st ed. sgn, dj................. .... *$240.00–$300.00*

Goldman, Emma. *My Dissillusionment in Russia*. Lon. 1925. 1st UK ed. 263 pp, red cloth, paper label, sgn.. *$150.00–$250.00*

Goldman, Emma. *Place of the Individual in Society*. Chi. Free Society Forum. nd. wrps. .... *$35.00–$45.00*

Goldman, Emma. *Social Significance of the Modern Drama*. Bos. 1914. .... *$30.00–$67.00*

Goldman, William. *Marathon Man*. NY. Delacorte. 1974. 1st ed. dj. .... *$25.00–$65.00*

Goldschmidt, Lucien: naef, J. Weston. *Truthful Lens . . .1844–1914*. NY. Grolier Club. 1980. 1st ed. illus. ltd 1,000 cc, slipcase.. *$300.00–$350.00*

Goldsmith, Alfred N. *Radio Telephony.* NY. Wireless Press. (1918). 1st ed. 247 pp, illus. .... *$50.00–$75.00*

Goldsmith, Oliver. *History of the Earth and Animated Nature.* Lon. Blackie and Son. 1854. Vol 11 only. .... *$40.00–$50.00*

Goldsmith, Oliver. *Vicar of Wakefield.* Lon. J M Dent. (c1910). illus. aeg, bound by Sangorski & Sutcliffe. .... *$100.00–$150.00*

Goldsmith, Oliver. *Vicar of Wakefield.* Lon. Harrap. (1929). 1st ed thus. illus by Arthur Rackham. .... *$100.00–$150.00*

Goldsmith, Oliver. *Vicar of Wakefield.* McKay. 1929. illus. by Arthur Rackham, clr plates. .... *$75.00–$125.00*

Goldstrom, John. *Narrative History of Aviation.* NY. 1930. 1st ed. illus. .... *$65.00–$85.00*

Goldwater, Barry. *Arizona.* 1978. 1st ed. dj. .... *$28.00–$35.00*

Goldwater, Barry. *Face of Arizona.* np. 1964. 1st ed. ltd #769/1,000 cc, sgn. .... *$125.00–$180.00*

Goldwater, Barry. *Journey Down the Green & Colorado Rivers.* Tempe. 1970. illus. photos, dj. .... *$35.00–$45.00*

Gommez, R. *Cake Decoration: Flower and Classic Piping.* Lon. 1899. *$65.00–$90.00*

Goode, George Brown. *Smithsonian Institution 1846–1896 A History . . .* Wash. 1897. .... *$50.00–$75.00*

Goodison, N. *English Barometers 1680–1860 . . .* Lon. 1969. illus. 1st UK ed. plates. .. .. *$50.00–$60.00*

Goodman, Paul. *Break Up of Our Camp.* NY. 1949. dj. .... *$25.00–$35.00*

Goodman, Paul. *Compulsory Mis-Education.* NY. 1964. dj. .... *$20.00–$25.00*

Goodman, Paul. *Growing Up Absurd . . .* NY. Random House. 1960. 1st ed. dj cloth. .. .. *$40.00–$50.00*

Goodman, Paul. *Hawkweed.* Random House. 1967. 1st ed. dj. .... *$16.00–$20.00*

Goodman, Richard M. *Genetic Disorders Among the Jewish People.* Balt. Johns Hopkins. 1979. 1st ed. dj cloth. .... *$85.00–$100.00*

Goodrich, Charles. *Lives of the Signers of the Declaration of Independence.* Hartford. R Huntington. 1841. illus. frontis. .... *$20.00–$35.00*

Goodrich, Charles A. *History of the United States of America.* Bos. Amer Stationers. (1834). .... *$20.00–$30.00*

Goodrich, Samuel. *Second Book of History . . .* Bos. Hendee. 1836. sheep backed printed boards 16 maps. .... *$50.00–$75.00*

Goodrich, Samuel Griswold. *History of the Indians of North & South America.* NY. 1844. 1st ed. illus. .... *$45.00–$60.00*

Goodrich, Samuel Griswold. *Recollections of a Lifetime.* NY. 1851. 2 vols. .... *$95.00–$250.00*

Goodrich, Ward L. *Modern Clock.* Chi. 1905. 1st ed. illus. .... *$40.00–$55.00*

Goodrich-Freer, A. *Things Seen in Palestine.* NY. 1913. .... *$45.00–$65.00*

Goodspeed, Charles. *Yankee Bookseller*. Bos. Houghton Mifflin. 1937. 1st ed. 1/310 cc. sgn slipcase. .... *$125.00–$175.00*

Goodspeed, Charles. *Yankee Bookseller*. Bos. Houghton Mifflin. 1937. 1st ed. dj.........
.... *$35.00–$75.00*

Goodwin, C. C. *Wedge of Gold*. Salt Lake City. 1893. 1st ed. .... *$50.00–$65.00*

Goodwin, D. *Pigeons and Doves of the World*. Cornell University. 1983. dj................
.... *$40.00–$55.00*

Goodwin, Grace Duffield. *Anti-Suffrage*. NY. 1913. .... *$25.00–$35.00*

Goodyear, W. A. *Coal Mines of the Western Coast of the United States*. SF. 1877. 1st ed. 153 pp. .... *$75.00–$125.00*

Gorbachev, Mikhail. *Perestroika Is the Concern of All Soviet Peoples*. Moscow. 1989. wrps. 1st Eng ed. .... *$40.00–$50.00*

Gordeon, William S. *Recollections of the Old Quarter*. Lynchburg. Moose Bros. 1902. 1st ed. illus. b/w photos. .... *$75.00–$100.00*

Gordimer, Nadine. *House Gun*. Lon. Bloomsbury. (1998). 1st Brit ed. sgn, dj. ....
.... *$75.00–$85.00*

Gordimer, Nadine. *Lying Days*. NY. Simon and Schuster. 1953. 1st ed. author's first novel, dj. .... *$50.00–$65.00*

Gordimer, Nadine. *Occasion for Loving*. NY. (1963). 1st Amer ed. dj. . *$25.00–$35.00*

Gordimer, Nadine. *Soft Voice of the Serpent*. NY. Simon & Schuster. 1952. 1st Amer ed. author's first book, dj. .... *$55.00–$100.00*

Gordimer, Nadine. *Something Out There*. NY. Viking. 1984. 1st US ed. sgn, dj. ....
.... *$50.00–$65.00*

Gordon, A. C and Page Thomas Nelson. *Befo' De War — Echoes in Negro Dialect*. NY. 1888. .... *$40.00–$50.00*

Gordon, Armistead Churchill. *Jefferson Davis*. Scribner's. 1918. 1st ed. ....
.... *$40.00–$50.00*

Gordon, Elizabeth. *Bird Children*. Volland. (1912). illus. .... *$85.00–$95.00*

Gordon, Elizabeth. *Buddy Jim*. NY. Wise-Parslow Co. (1935). illus. pictorial cloth cvr. .... *$15.00–$40.00*

Gordon, Elizabeth. *Flower Children*. Volland. (1910). illus. bds. .... *$75.00–$95.00*

Gordon, Elizabeth. *I Wonder Why?*. Chi. (1916). 1st ed. illus. in clr and b/w. ....
.... *$15.00–$25.00*

Gordon, Elizabeth. *Loraine and the Little People of the Ocean*. Chi/NY. (1922). 1st ed. illus. in clr and b/w. .... *$35.00–$40.00*

Gordon, Elizabeth. *Really-So Stories*. Joliet. (1924). 1st ed. illus.......... *$40.00–$50.00*

Gordon, John B. *Reminiscences of the Civil War*. NY. 1904. .... *$80.00–$125.00*

Gordon, Mary. *Company of Women*. NY. 1980. 1st ed. dj, sgn. .... *$30.00–$40.00*

Gordon, Sarah. *Hitler, Germans, and the Jewish Question*. Princeton. Princeton Univ Press. 1984. 1st ed. dj. .... *$20.00–$30.00*

Gordon, T. *Gazetteer of the State of Pennsylvania*. Phila. 1832. 1st ed. lea. ....
.... *$65.00–$85.00*

Gordon, T. F. *Gazetteer of the State of New Jersey.* Trenton. 1834. 2 vols in one. map.
.... *$175.00–$250.00*

Goren, Charles. *Sports Illustrated Book of Bridge.* NY. 1961. illus. dj, slipcase. ....
.... *$50.00–$70.00*

Gorey, Edward. *Black Doll.* NY. Gotham Book Mart. 1973. 1st ed. black wraps...........
.... *$60.00–$125.00*

Gorey, Edward. *Blue Aspic.* Meredith Press. 1968. 1st ed. dj. .... *$65.00–$100.00*

Gorey, Edward. *Broken Spoke.* NY. Dodd. 1976. 1st ed. dj..................... *$45.00–$65.00*

Gorey, Edward. *Dancing Cats & Neglected Murderesses.* NY. Workman Publishing. (1980). 1st trade ed. pictorial glossy wraps, sgn..................................... *$45.00–$65.00*

Gorey, Edward. *Doubtful Guest.* Lon. (1958). 1st Brit ed. dj.............. *$75.00–$125.00*

Gorey, Edward. *Dracula. A Toy Theatre.* Scribner's. 1979. folio, spiral bound..............
.... *$150.00–$200.00*

Gorey, Edward. *Eclectic Abecedarium.* NY. Adams. (1983). 1st trade ed. glossy bds, sgn.. *$45.00–$50.00*

Gorey, Edward. *Epileptic Bicycle.* NY. Dodd Mead. (1969). 5th ptg dj...........................
.... *$20.00–$30.00*

Gorey, Edward. *Fatal Lozenge.* Ivan Oblelinsky 1960. wrps. .... *$40.00–$65.00*

Gorey, Edward. *Gilded Bat.* NY. Simon Shuster. (1966). 1st ed. dj..... *$75.00–$100.00*

Gorey, Edward. *The Listing Attic.* NY. Duell Sloan Pearce. (1954). 1st ed. dj. ....
....*$165.00–$235.00*

Gorey, Edward. *Unstrung Harp.* Duell. 1953. 1st ed. author's first book, dj. ....
.... *$150.00–$300.00*

Gorey, Edward. *Utter Zoo Alphabet.* NY. Meredith Press. (1967). 1st ed. dj. ....
.... *$40.00–$65.00*

Gorey, Edward. *Vinegar Works.* NY. 1963. 3 vols. 1st ed................... *$135.00–$250.00*

Gorey, Edward. *Water Flowers.* NY. Congdon and Weed. (1982). 1st ed. sgn, dj. ....
.... *$35.00–$50.00*

Gorey, Edward. *Willowdale Handcar.* NY. Dodd, Mead. (1979). 1st hardcvr ed. dj. .....
.... *$25.00–$45.00*

Gorky, Maxim. *The Judge.* McBride. 1924. 1st ed. .... *$30.00–$40.00*

Gotham's Pageant of Games and Toys. NY. Gotham Pressed Steel Corp. illus. pictorial wrps, 36 pp. .... *$75.00–$100.00*

Goudy, Frederic W. *Italian Old Style . . .* Phil. 1924. black boards....... *$35.00–$50.00*

Goulart, Ron. *Skyrocket Steele Conquers the Universe and Other Media Tale.* Eugene, OR. (1990). 1st ed. 300 cc, sgn, dj.. *$20.00–$30.00*

Gould, J. *Birds of Great Britian.* Lon. 1873. 5 vols. illus. large folio, 367 clr plates. .....
.... *$50,000.00–$75,000.00*

Gould, J. *Century of Birds from the Himalaya Mountains.* Lon. 1832. 1st ed. illus. large folio, 80 hand-clr plates.. *$7,800.00–$10,000.00*

Gould, J. *Handbook to the Birds of Australia.* Lon. 1865. 2 vols. ...... *$200.00–$300.00*

Gould, Jean. *Young Mariner Melville*. NY. Dodd, Mead. 1956. 1st ed. dj. .... *$25.00–$35.00*

Gould, John. *Toucans*. Lon. 1852–54. folio, 51 hand-clr plates. *$25,000.00–$30,000.00*

Gould, Marcus. *Report of the Trial of Friends*. Phila. 1829. ¼ mor. ..... *$95.00–$150.00*

Gould, R. T. *Case For the Sea Serpent*. Lon. 1930. illus. .... *$55.00–$95.00*

Grady, James. *Six Days of the Condor*. NY. Norton. 1974. 1st ed. dj. . *$75.00–$250.00*

Graebner, Theodore. *Church Bells in the Forest, A Story of Lutheran Pioneer Work on the Michigan Frontier, 1840–1850*. St Louis. Concordia. 1944. wrps. illus. 98 pp.......... .... *$28.00–$40.00*

Graffagnino, J. K. *Shaping of Vermont*. Rutland. 1983. illus. 147 pp, dj...................... .... *$40.00–$50.00*

Grafton, C. C. The Right Rev. *Lineage from Apostolic Times of the American Catholic Church* . . . Milwaukee. The Young Churchman Co. (1911). 1st ed. illus. pictorial cvr. .. .. *$25.00–$35.00*

Grafton, Sue. *"A" Is For Alibi*. NY. Holt. 1982. dj................................. *$50.00–$70.00*

Grafton, Sue. *"A" Is for Alibi*. NY. Holt. 1982. 1st ed. dj. .... *$900.00–$1,300.00*

Grafton, Sue. *"B" Is for Burglar*. Lon. Macmillan. 1986. 1st ed. inscrb, dj. ....*$200.00–$250.00*

Grafton, Sue. *"C" Is for Corpse*. NY. 1986. 1st ed. dj. .... *$625.00–$700.00*

Grafton, Sue. *"E" Is for Evidence*. NY. Holt. 1988. 1st ed. dj. .... *$75.00–$150.00*

Grafton, Sue. *"E" Is for Evidence*. NY. Holt. 1988. 1st ed. sgn, dj..... *$175.00–$250.00*

Grafton, Sue. *"F" Is for Fugitive*. NY. Holt. 1989. 1st ed. sgn, dj........ *$75.00–$125.00*

Grafton, Sue. *"F" Is for Fugitive*. NY. Holt. 1989. 1st ed. dj. .... *$45.00–$60.00*

Grafton, Sue. *"H" Is for Homicide*. NY. Holt. 1991. 1st ed. inscrb, dj... *$35.00–$70.00*

Grafton, Sue. *"H" Is for Homicide*. NY. Holt. 1991. 1st ed. dj............. *$15.00–$50.00*

Grafton, Sue. *"I" Is for Innocent*. NY. Holt. 1993. 1st ed. sgn, dj......... *$35.00–$75.00*

Grafton, Sue. *"J" Is for Judgment*. NY. Holt. (1993). 1st ed. dj. .... *$15.00–$25.00*

Grafton, Sue. *"J" Is for Judgment*. NY. Holt. 1993. 1st ed. inscrb, dj. ... *$40.00–$50.00*

Grafton, Sue. *"K" Is for Killer*. NY. Holt. (1994). 1st ed. dj.................. *$14.00–$28.00*

Grafton, Sue. *Keziah Dane*. NY. Macmillan. 1967. 1st ed. author's first non-mystery, dj. .... *$300.00–$700.00*

Graham, Col. W. A. *Custer Myth*. Harrisburg. (1953). 1st ed. illus. dj. . *$50.00–$65.00*

Graham, Frank. *Brooklyn Dodgers*. NY. Putnam' s Series. 1947. illus. dj. .... *$32.00–$40.00*

Graham, Stephen. *Through Russian Central Asia*. Lon. 1916. illus. fldg map, photos. . ... *$30.00–$40.00*

Grahame, Kenneth. *Dream Days*. Lon. 1902. illus. by Maxfield Parrish, 2,228 pp. .... *$95.00–$130.00*

Grahame, Kenneth. *Golden Age*. Lon/NY. 1900. illus. by Maxfield Parrish. .... *$85.00–$100.00*

Grahame, Kenneth. *Wind in the Willows*. Lon. Methuen and Co. (1908). 1st ed. near fine, ¼ mor slipcase.. *$2,200.00–$8,000.00*

Grahame, Kenneth. *Wind in the Willows*. Scribner's. 1908. 1st Amer ed......................
.... *$150.00–$250.00*

Grainge, William. *Daemonologia. Discourse on Witchcraft*. Harrogate. 1882...............
.... *$30.00–$40.00*

Grand Union Grille Works. Chi. 1911. wrps. architectural cat. .... *$38.00–$45.00*

Grand, Gordon. *Old Man and Other Colonel Weatherford Stories*. Derrydale. 1934. 1st Amer ed. .... *$45.00–$60.00*

Grand, Gordon. *Silver Horn*. NY. 1932. illus. 1/950 cc. .... *$75.00–$130.00*

Grant, B. C. *Taos Today*. Taos. 1925. photos. .... *$75.00–$150.00*

Grant, Blanche C. (ed.). *Kit Carson's Own Story of His Life*. Taos. 1926. softbound....
.... *$75.00–$125.00*

Grant, Douglas. *Fortunate Slave, An Illustration of African Slavery . . .* Lon. 1968. 1st ed. dj. .... *$33.00–$45.00*

Grant, George Monro (ed). *Picturesque Canada: The Country As It Was and Is*. Tor. 1882. 1st ed. mor, engr. .... *$125.00–$200.00*

Grant, James J. *Single Shot Rifles*. NY. 1947. illus. photos, plates........ *$30.00–$40.00*

Grant, Madison. *Passing of the Great Race or Racial Basis of European History*. Scribner's. 1923. 4th rev ed. 476 pp,... *$35.00–$50.00*

Grant, Ulysses S. *Personal Memoirs of U.S. Grant*. NY. 1885. 2 vols. 1st ed. ....
.... *$50.00–$85.00*

Grant, Ulysses S. *Report of Lt-General U.S. Grant . . . 1864-65*. NY. 1865. wrps. ....
.... *$100.00–$150.00*

Gras, Gunter. *Dog Years*. NY. 1965. 1st ed. dj. .... *$25.00–$35.00*

Grau, Shirley Ann. *Black Prince*. NY. Knopf. 1955. 1st ed. author's first book, sgn, dj.
.... *$75.00–$100.00*

Graumont, Raoul and John Hensel. *Encyclopedia of Knots and Fancy Rope Work*. Camb. Cornell Maritime Press. 1972. 4th ed. illus. dj............................ *$35.00–$40.00*

Graves, Jackson A. *My Seventy Years in California 1857–1927*. LA. Times-Mirror. 1927. .... *$60.00–$85.00*

Graves, John. *Frontier Guns*. Fort Worth. 1964. illus. photos, pict wrps.......................
.... *$15.00–$25.00*

Graves, Robert. *Islands of Unwisdom*. Garden City. Doubleday. 1949. 1st ed. dj. ....
.... *$50.00–$75.00*

Graves, Robert. *On English Poetry*. Lon. Heinemann. 1922. 1st ed. . *$150.00–$160.00*

Graves, Robert. *Sergeant Lamb's America*. NY. Random House. (1940). 1st ed. dj red cloth. .... *$90.00–$125.00*

Graves, Robert. *The Shout*. Lon. Elkin Matthews & Marrot. 1929. 1st ed. ltd #341/530cc, dj. .... *$225.00–$250.00*

Graves, Robert J. *Clinical Lectures on the Practice of Medicine*. Lon. 1884. 2 vols.....
.... *$20.00–$35.00*

Gray, Asa. *First Lessons in Botany & Vegetable Physiology*. Ivison & Phinney. 1857. 236 pp. .... *$100.00–$135.00*

Gray, Asa. *Gray's Botanical Text-Book (6th Ed)*. American Book Co. 1879. 2 vols. .... *$60.00–$85.00*

Gray, Asa. *Introduction to Structural and Systematic Botany*. NY. 1860. 5th ed............. .... *$25.00–$32.00*

Gray, Asa. *Introduction to Structural and Systematic Botany and Vegatable Physiology*. NY. Ivison Phinney & So. 1862. 5th rev ed... *$30.00–$60.00*

Gray, Harold. *Little Orphan Annie and Jumbo the Circus Elephant*. Chi. Pleasure Books. (1935). 1st ed. 3 pop-ups. .... *$150.00–$500.00*

Gray, Harold. *Little Orphan Annie and Sandy*. Racine. Whitman. 1933. 1st ed. pictorial boards.. *$35.00–$45.00*

Gray, W. H. *History of Oregon, 1792–1849, . . .* Portland. 1870. 1st ed......................... .... *$175.00–$225.00*

Gray, William C. *Camp-Fire Musings*. NY. Randolph. 1894. 1st ed. illus. .... *$40.00–$60.00*

Great Northwest: A Guide Book and Itinerary. St Paul. 1889. illus. fldg map, engr....... .... *$37.00–$45.00*

Greco, James. *Story of Englewood Cliffs*. NJ. (1964). tan and brown cvr. pictorial dj.... .... *$20.00–$25.00*

Greeley, Horace. *History of the Struggles for Slavery*. NY. 1856. 1st ed. wrps. .... *$75.00–$100.00*

Greely, Adophus W. *Three Years of Arctic Service*. NY. Scribner's. 1886. 2 vols. 1st ed. illus. 428 pp, illus, pocket maps, frontis, full lea................................. *$175.00–$250.00*

Green, Anna Katharine. *Leavenworth Case*. NY. Putnam. 1878. 1st ed. cloth. .... *$400.00–$450.00*

Green, Arthur R. *Sundials, Incised Dials, or Mass Clocks*. NY/Tor. 1926. 1st ed. illus. *$35.00–$45.00*

Green, Ben K. *Thousand Miles of Mustangin'*. Flagstaff. Northland Press. 1972. 1st ed. brown cloth dj sgn. .... *$100.00–$150.00*

Green, Calvin and Seth Y. Wells. *Brief Exposition of . . . the Shakers*. NY. 1851. .... *$115.00–$150.00*

Green, Edwin L. *Indians of South Carolina*. Columbia, SC. (1904). 1st ed................... .... *$55.00–$75.00*

Green, Gil. *Portugal's Revolution*. NY. International. 1976. wrps. sgn... *$45.00–$55.00*

Green, Gil. *Young Communists and Unity of the Youth*. NY. Youth Publishers. 1935. wrps. sgn.. *$50.00–$65.00*

Green, Nelson Winch. *Fifteen Years Among the Mormons: Being the Narrative of Mrs. Mary Ettie V. Smith, Late of Great Salt Lake City*. NY. 1858................. *$60.00–$145.00*

Green, Richard Lancelyn. *Bibliography of A Conan Doyle*. Oxford. Clarendon Press. 1983. illus. dj.. *$70.00–$80.00*

Greenaway, Kate. *A Apple Pie*. Lon. Routledge. 1886. .... *$95.00–$300.00*

Greenaway, Kate. *A Apple Pie*. Lon. Frederick Warne. .... *$18.00–$25.00*

Greenaway, Kate. *Mother Goose*. Lon. Frederick Warne. (1881). ..... *$100.00–$200.00*

Greene, Graham. *Human Factor*. Lon. 1978. 1st UK ed......................... *$35.00–$65.00*

Greene, Graham. *Our Man in Havana*. Lon. 1958. dj. .... *$85.00–$100.00*

Greene, Graham. *Our Man in Havana*. NY. 1958. 1st US ed. dj........... *$45.00–$75.00*

Greene, Graham. *Potting Shed*. Lon. 1958. dj.................................... *$27.00–$100.00*

Greene, Graham. *Third Man and The Fallen Idol*. Lon. Heinemann. 1950. dj..............
.... *$50.00–$60.00*

Greene, Graham. *This Gun Is for Hire*. NY. Doubleday Doran. 1936. 1st Amer ed. no
dj... *$100.00–$125.00*

Greene, Graham. *Travels With My Aunt*. NY. 1970. 1st ed. 1st Amer ed. dj...................
.... *$25.00–$35.00*

Greene, Graham. *Travels With My Aunt*. 1969. 1st UK ed. dj............... *$20.00–$30.00*

Greene, Vivien. *English Dolls' Houses of the Eighteenth and Nineteenth Centuries*. Lon.
B T Batsford Ltd. (1955). 1st ed. illus... *$80.00–$100.00*

Greenhowe, Jean. *Making a Victorian Dolls' House*. NY. Taplinger Pub. (1979). 1st ed.
dj... *$15.00–$20.00*

Greenough, Ruth Hornblower. *Bible for My Grandchildren*. Bos. private ptg. 1950. 2
vols. illus. ltd 1,000 sets... *$85.00–$175.00*

Greenwood, Grace. *New Life in New Lands*. NY. 1873. 413 pp............. *$30.00–$45.00*

Greenwood, Grace. *New Life in New Lands: Notes of Travel*. NY. J B Ford & Co. 1873.
.... *$75.00–$140.00*

Greer, James K. *Texas Ranger and Frontiersman* . . . Dallas. 1932. sgn. ....
.... *$100.00–$300.00*

Gregory, Dick. *Shadow That Scares Me*. Garden City. Doubleday. 1968. 1st ed. sgn, dj.
.... *$45.00–$60.00*

Gregory, Samuel. *Gregory's History of Mexico*. Bos. 1847. illus. rbnd, 100 pp. ....
.... *$275.00–$290.00*

Gregory, W. K. and H. C. Raven. *In Quest of Gorillas*. New Bedford. 1937. illus. with
b/w photos, map. .... *$35.00–$60.00*

Gremillion, Nelson. *Company G, 1st Regiment, Louisiana Cavalry, CSA*. np. private ptg.
1986. 1st ed.. *$35.00–$65.00*

Grenfell, Wilfred. *40 Years For Labrador*. NY. 1932. presentation copy, sgn, dj...........
.... *$45.00–$60.00*

Grenfell, Wilfred. *Adrift on an Ice-Pan*. Bos. (1909). 1st ed. 69 pp, sgn. ....
.... *$50.00–$60.00*

Grenfell, Wilfred. *Adrift on an Ice-Pan*. Bos. Houghton Mifflin. 1909. 1st ed. illus. .....
.... *$45.00–$100.00*

Grenfell, Wilfred. *Down North on Labrador*. Chi. 1911. 1st ed. illus.... *$20.00–$30.00*

Grenfell, Wilfred. *Labrador*. NY. 1922... *$35.00–$45.00*

Grenfell, Wilfred. *Labrador Doctor*. NY. 1919. illus. original sketch on flyleaf by
author. .... *$65.00–$95.00*

Grenfell, Wilfred. *Labrador Doctor: The Autobiography.* Bos/NY. Houghton Mifflin. (1910). 1st ed. illus. green cloth photos. an original drawing and signature by Grenfell on front endpaper. .... *$75.00–$125.00*

Grew, Joseph. *Report From Tokyo.* Simon & Schuster. 1942. dj. .... *$15.00–$30.00*

Grey, Zane. *Arizona Ames.* Grosset & Dunlap. 1932. rprnt, dj. .... *$12.00–$15.00*

Grey, Zane. *Black Mesa.* Harper & Bros. 1955. 1st ed. dj. .... *$65.00–$175.00*

Grey, Zane. *Border Legion.* NY. Harper & Bros. 1916. illus. dark green cloth. ....
.... *$40.00–$50.00*

Grey, Zane. *Desert of Wheat.* Grosset & Dunlap. 1919. rprnt, dj. .... *$10.00–$15.00*

Grey, Zane. *Forlorn River.* Grosset & Dunlap. 1927. rprnt, dj. .... *$20.00–$35.00*

Grey, Zane. *Knights of the Range.* NY/Lon. Harper. 1939. 1st ed. dj. *$175.00–$250.00*

Grey, Zane. *Lost Wagon Train.* NY. Harper & Bros. 1936. 1st ed. dj. *$250.00–$400.00*

Grey, Zane. *Majesty's Rancho.* NY/Lon. Harper. (1938). 1st ed. dj.... *$100.00–$250.00*

Grey, Zane. *Rainbow Trail.* NY. Harper. 1915. green cloth. .... *$20.00–$35.00*

Grey, Zane. *Red Headed Outfield.* NY. 1915. dj. .... *$14.00–$18.00*

Grey, Zane. *Riders of the Purple Sage.* Grosset & Dunlap. 1940. rprnt, dj. ....
.... *$10.00–$14.00*

Grey, Zane. *Roping Lions in the Grand Canyon.* NY. G & D. 1924. illus. reprint, pictorial dj. .... *$20.00–$45.00*

Grey, Zane. *Roping Lions in the Grand Canyon.* NY. Harper & Bros. 1924. 1st ed. ......
.... *$250.00–$300.00*

Grey, Zane. *Shepherd of Guadaloupe.* NY. Harper. 1930. 1st ed. dj... *$100.00–$200.00*

Grey, Zane. *Sunset Pass.* NY/LON. Harper & Bros. 1931. 1st ed. rust cvr with blue lettering. decorated endpapers. .... *$35.00–$60.00*

Grey, Zane. *Tales of Fishing Virgin Seas.* Harper. (1925). 1st ed. illus... *$70.00–$95.00*

Grey, Zane. *Tales of Fresh-Water Fishing.* NY. 1928. 1st ed. .... *$125.00–$200.00*

Grey, Zane. *Tales of Southern Rivers.* NY. Harper. 1924. 1st ed. green cloth, 249 pp. ...
.... *$125.00–$200.00*

Grey, Zane. *Tales of the Angler's Eldorado.* NY. Grosset & Dunlap. 1926. illus. photos, dj. .... *$45.00–$75.00*

Grey, Zane. *Thundering Herd.* NY. 1925. 1st ed. dj. .... *$35.00–$100.00*

Grey, Zane. *Vanishing American.* NY/Lon. Harper. 1925. 1st ed. dj. . *$150.00–$200.00*

Grey, Zane. *West of the Pecos.* NY. Harper. 1937. 1st ed. dj .... *$75.00–$85.00*

Grey, Zane. *Wild Horse Mesa.* NY/Lon. Harper. 1928. 1st ed. blue cloth dj ....
.... *$50.00–$75.00*

Gridley, A. D. *History of the Town of Kirkland.* NY. 1874. sgn. .... *$45.00–$55.00*

Griffin, J. H. *Church and the Black Man.* 1969. wrps. illus .... *$20.00–$25.00*

Griffin, S. G. *History of the Town of Keene from 1732 to 1874.* Keene. 1904. half lea, 3 fldg maps, plates. .... *$50.00–$70.00*

Griffis, William Elliot. *Corea the Hermit Nation*. NY. 1882. illus. map. ....
.... *$75.00–$150.00*

Grimble, Augustus. *Salmon Rivers of England and Wales*. Lon. Kegan Paul. 1913. 2nd
ed. illus. .... *$100.00–$115.00*

Grimes, Martha. *Help the Poor Struggler*. Bos. (1985). 1st ed. dj......... *$30.00–$40.00*

Grimes, Martha. *Man with a Load of Mischief*. Bos. Little Brown. (1981). 1st ed. map
frontis, scarce, dj. .... *$150.00–$250.00*

Grimm Brothers. *Little Brother & Little Sister*. Lon. (1917). 1st ed. illus. by Arthur
Rackham. scarce dj... *$500.00–$900.00*

Grimm, Herbert L. and Paul L. Roy. *Human Interest Stories of . . . at Gettysburg*.
Times & News Pub. 1927. illus. b/w photos. wrps. .... *$45.00–$65.00*

Grimm, Wilhelm. *Dear Mili*. NY. Farrar, Straus and Giroux. (1988). 1st ed. illus. green
cloth pictorial dj... *$20.00–$35.00*

Grimwood, V. R. *American Ship Models . . .* NY. W W Norton & Co. (1942). illus. pull-
out plans.. *$35.00–$40.00*

Grinnel, J. , H. C. Bryant and T. I. Storer. *Game Birds of California*. Berkeley. 1918.
illus. dj. .... *$175.00–$350.00*

Grinnell, G. *American Duck Shooting*. NY. 1901.................................. *$45.00–$65.00*

Grinnell, George Bird. *Blackfoot Lodge Tales*. NY. 1913. .... *$30.00–$45.00*

Grinnell, George Bird. *Blackfoot Lodge Tales*. NY. 1892. 1st ed........... *$50.00–$85.00*

Grinnell, George Bird. *Indians of Today*. NY. 1915. 3rd ptg, plates...... *$45.00–$75.00*

Griscom, John H. *Use of Tobacco and the Evils, Physical, Mental, Moral and Social
Resulting Therefrom*. NY. Putnam. 1868. 1st ed. wrps. 37 pp, scarce.... *$80.00–$100.00*

Grisham, John. *Chamber*. NY. Doubleday. 1994. 1st ed. dj.................. *$20.00–$25.00*

Grisham, John. *Chamber*. NY. Doubleday. (1994). 1/350 cc, sgn, nbr, slipcase.............
.... *$100.00–$150.00*

Grisham, John. *Pelican Brief*. NY. Doubleday. (1992). 1st ed. dj. .... *$15.00–$50.00*

Grisham, John. *Rainmaker*. NY. Doubleday. 1995. 1st ed. dj. .... *$15.00–$30.00*

Grisham, John. *The Client*. NY. Doubleday. (1993). 1st ed. dj. .... *$25.00–$35.00*

Grisham, John. *The Firm*. NY. Doubleday. 1991. 1st ed. sgn, dj. ...... *$175.00–$250.00*

Grisham, John. *The Firm*. NY. Doubleday. 1991. 1st ed. dj................. *$75.00–$100.00*

Grisham, John. *Time to Kill*. Tarrytown. Wynwood Press. 1989. 1st ed. author's first
book, dj... *$1,200.00–$1,500.00*

Grocer's Companion. Bos. New England Grocer Office. (1883). brown cloth..............
.... *$20.00–$50.00*

Gromme, O. J. *Birds of Wisconsin*. University of Wisconsin. 1963. dj. . *$45.00–$60.00*

Gross, H. I. *Antique & Classic Cameras*. NY. 1965. 1st ed. illus. dj...... *$35.00–$50.00*

Grover, Eulalie Osgood. *Overall Boys*. Rand McNally. (1905). 1st ed. illus. ....
.... *$60.00–$80.00*

Grover, Eulalie Osgood. *Sunbonnet Babies Book*. NY. 1902. .... *$50.00–$70.00*

Grover, Eulalie Osgood. *Sunbonnet Babies' Book*. Rand McNally. 1928. illus. .... *$25.00–$35.00*

Gruelle, Johnny. *Friendly Fairies*. Volland. (1919). illus. by author. ..... *$50.00–$75.00*

Gruelle, Johnny. *Little Sunny Stories*. Chi. Volland. 1919. illus. in clr by Gruelle. dj.... .... *$100.00–$200.00*

Gruelle, Johnny. *Raggedy Ann Stories*. Volland. (1918). 1st ed. illus. ... *$50.00–$70.00*

Gruelle, Johnny. *Raggedy Ann's Alphabet Book*. NY. Volland. 1925. illus. by Gruelle.. .... *$45.00–$50.00*

Gruelle, Johnny. *Raggedy Ann's Magical Wishes*. Chi. Donohue. 1928. illus. 1st thus. full clr... *$35.00–$45.00*

Guide to the Birds of South America. Wynnewood. 1970. dj. .... *$75.00–$100.00*

Guide to the City of Moscow . . . Moscow. Cooperative Pub Society of Foreign Workers. 1937. 1st ed. cloth. .... *$35.00–$45.00*

Guillemin, Amedee. *Heavens: An Illustrated Handbook of Popular Astronomy*. Lon. Bently. 1868. 3rd ed. 503 pp, clr litho. .... *$60.00–$85.00*

Guillet, Edwin. *Early Life in Upper Canada*. Tor. 1933. illus. b/w and clr. .... *$65.00–$75.00*

Guernsey, Charles A. *Wyoming Cowboy Days*. NY. 1936.................... *$85.00–$145.00*

Gun Cotton and Its Uses. Lon. illus... *$25.00–$45.00*

Gunnison, J. W. *The Mormons*. Phila. 1852. 1st ed............................ *$150.00–$200.00*

Gunther, R. T. *Historic Instruments for the Advancement of Science*. Humphrey Milford. 1925. glassine wrps... *$25.00–$45.00*

Gurganus, Allan. *Oldest Living Confederate Widow Tells All*. NY. Knopf. (1989). 1st ed. dj.. *$65.00–$75.00*

Gussow, H. T. and W. S. Odell. *Mushrooms and Toadstools*. Ottawa. 1927. 1st ed. illus. .... *$27.00–$38.00*

Guthrie, A. B. *Blue Hen's Chick*. (1965). 1st ed. dj................................ *$25.00–$35.00*

Guthrie, Jr. A. B. *These Thousand Hills*. Bos. Houghton Mifflin. (1956). 1st ed. dj red orange cloth. .... *$35.00–$75.00*

Gutman, Israel. *Encyclopedia of the Holocaust*. NY. Yad Vashem/Macmillan. 1990. 4 vols. 1st ed. djs. photos. .... *$150.00–$250.00*

Gutstein, Morris. *Story of the Jews of Newport*. NY. Block Pub Co. 1936. 1st ed. illus. blue cloth. .... *$50.00–$65.00*

H. L. R. and M. L. R. *Talks on Graphology*. Bos. Lee and Shepard Pub. 1900. gray oblong bds. .... *$20.00–$40.00*

Hadassah, The Jewish Orphan. Phil. American Sunday School Union. (1834). marbled bds, lea backed. .... *$50.00–$75.00*

Haddock, J. *Souvenir of the Thousand Islands on the St. Lawrence River*. NY. 1896. illus. .... *$30.00–$50.00*

Hafen, LeRoy and Ann W. *Handcarts to Zion*. Glendale. 1960. "Pioneers" ed. illus. maps, photos, dj.. *$50.00–$85.00*

Hafen, Leroy R (ed.). *Mountain Men* . . . Glendale. Arthur H Clark. 1965–72. 10 vols. 1st ed. illus. photos, paintings, brown cloth. .... *$1,000.00–$1,600.00*

Haggard, H. Rider. *Ayesha.* NY. 1905. 1st Amer ed. .... *$50.00–$70.00*

Haggard, H. Rider. *Dr. Therne.* Lon. 1898. 1st ed. .... *$50.00–$75.00*

Haggard, H. Rider. *Lysbeth: A Tale of the Dutch.* NY/Lon/Bombay. 1901. illus. .... *$65.00–$125.00*

Haggard, H. Rider. *Regeneration.* Lon. Longmans Green & Co. 1910. 1st ed. scarce... .... *$100.00–$150.00*

Haggard, H. Rider. *Stella Fregulius, a Tale of Three Destinies.* Longmans Green. 1904. blue cloth. .... *$65.00–$75.00*

Haggard, H. Rider. *Stella Frigelius, a Tale of Three Destinies.* Longmans Green. 1904. blue cloth. .... *$35.00–$125.00*

Haggard, H. Rider. *Virgin of the Sun.* NY. Doubleday. 1922. 1st ed. .... *$40.00–$50.00*

Haggard, H. Rider. *When the World Shook.* Longmans Green. 1919. 1st ed. .... *$30.00–$95.00*

Haggard, Howard W. *Lame, the Halt, and the Blind.* Lon. 1932. 1st ed. illus. .... *$25.00–$35.00*

Haggard, Howard W. *Mystery, Magic, and Medicine.* Garden City. 1933. 1st ed. illus. .... *$25.00–$35.00*

Haig-Brown, Roderick. *Western Angler.* Morrow. 1947. .... *$25.00–$35.00*

Haight, Austin D. *Biography of a Sportsman.* NY. Crowell. 1939. 1st ed. illus. slipcase. .... *$30.00–$50.00*

Haines, Elijah M. *American Indian (Uh-Nish-In-Na-Ba).* Chi. The Ma-sin-na'-gan Co. 1888. 1st ed. illus. .... *$75.00–$125.00*

Haines, Francis. *Nez Percees.* Univ of OK Press. (1955). 1st ed. dj. ...... *$50.00–$75.00*

Hakluyt, Richard. *Principal Navigations, Voyages, Traffiques and Discoveries of the English Nation.* Lon. Dutton. 1927. 8 vols. cloth. .... *$145.00–$200.00*

Hale, Edward Everett. *Man Without a Country.* Bos. Roberts Bros. 1889. illus. by F T Merrill. .... *$35.00–$40.00*

Hale, Edwin M. *Systematic Treatise on Abortion.* Chi. 1866. illus. clr plates. .... *$65.00–$95.00*

Haley, Alex. *Roots.* Doubleday. 1976. 1st ed. dj. .... *$40.00–$100.00*

Hall, Albert Neely. *Wonderful Hill.* Chi. Rand McNally. (1914). 1st ed. illus. by Norman Hall. .... *$100.00–$135.00*

Hall, Capt. Charles Francis. *Narrative of the North Polar Expedition.* Wash. GPO. 1876. 1st ed. illus. maps. .... *$120.00–$150.00*

Hall, Charles F. and C. H. Davis, Rear Adm., USN. *North Polar Expedition 1871–1872.* DC. GPO. 1876. 1st ed. illus. .... *$200.00–$450.00*

Hall, Charles F. and J. E. Nourse. *Narrative of the Second Arctic Expedition Made by Chas F. Hall.* DC. GPO. 1879. illus. maps. .... *$85.00–$100.00*

Hall, Donald. *Life Work.* Bos. Beacon Press. (1993). 1st ed. dj. .... *$24.00–$30.00*

Hall, Donald. *Yellow Room.* NY. Harper & Row. (1971). 1st ed. sgn, dj. *$40.00–$50.00*

Hall, Ester Greenacre. *College on Horseback*. NY. Harrison Smith & Robert Haas. 1933. 1st ed............ *$38.00–$45.00*

Hall, Fred S. *Sympathetic Strikes and Sympathetic Lockouts*. NY. 1898. softbound. .... *$35.00–$45.00*

Hall, Henry. *Ethan Allen: The Robin Hood of Vermont*. NY. Appleton. 1897. .... *$20.00–$35.00*

Hall, Henry Marion. *Woodcock Ways*. NY. Oxford Univ. Press. 1946. 1st ed. illus. .... *$30.00–$45.00*

Hall, Hiland. *History of Vermont*. Albany. 1868. 1st ed. inscrb........... *$100.00–$125.00*

Hall, Radclyff. *Well of Loneliness*. NY. Covici Friede. 1929. 2 vols. Victory ed. #157/201 cc, sgn, publisher's box, rare. .... *$400.00–$600.00*

Hall, Radclyffe. *Well of Lonliness*. Lon. 1928. 1st ed. dj. .... *$250.00–$350.00*

Hall, Sharlot M. *Cactus and Pine*. private publ. 1924. 2nd ed. rev., enlarged, sgn........ .... *$30.00–$65.00*

Hall, Thomas F. *Has the North Pole Been Discovered?* Bos. Richard G Badger. 1st ed. photos, charts, maps, dj. .... *$70.00–$90.00*

Halliday, Brett. *Michael Shayne Takes Over*. NY. Henry Holt. 1941. 1st ed. inscrb, dj.. .... *$30.00–$45.00*

Halliday, Brett. *Murder Is My Business*. NY. Dodd, Mead. 1945. 1st ed. dj................. .... *$65.00–$80.00*

Halliday, Brett. *She Woke to Darkness*. NY. Torquil. 1954. 1st ed. dj. .... *$45.00–$70.00*

Hallock, Charles. *Camp Life in Florida, A Handbook for Sportsmen and Settlers*. NY. 1876. .... *$35.00–$50.00*

Hallowell, A. Irving. *Role of Conjuring in Saulteaux Society*. Univ of PA Press. 1942. 1st ed. waxine dj............ *$25.00–$35.00*

Halpin, Warren T. *Hoofbeats: Drawings and Comments*. Phila. Lippincott. 1938. 1st ed. illus. .... *$70.00–$100.00*

Halsey, F. W. *Pioneers of Unadilla Village*. Unadilla, NY. 1902. ltd 650 cc.................. .... *$45.00–$55.00*

Halsey, Margaret. *Color Blind: A White Woman Looks at the Negro*. NY. 1946. .... *$20.00–$30.00*

Halsey, Rosalie V. *Forgotten Books of the American Nursery* . . . Bos. Charles E Goodspeed. 1911. 700 cc. .... *$60.00–$80.00*

Halstead, W. C. *Brain & Intelligence: A Quantitative Study of Frontal Lobes*. Chi. 1947. 1st ed. dj. .... *$100.00–$125.00*

Haluck, Paul. *Harness Making*. Phila. 1904............ *$35.00–$40.00*

Hamerton, Philip G. *Saone. A Summer Voyage*. Lon. 1887. illus. maps. *$50.00–$65.00*

Hamilton, Robert. *Gospel Among the Redmen*. Nashville. 1930. wrps.. *$50.00–$65.00*

Hamilton, William T. *My Sixty Years on the Plains*. NY. 1905. 1st ed. illus.................. .... *$150.00–$175.00*

Hamley Cowboy Catalogue 32. Oregon. (1932). wrps. illus. .... *$175.00–$225.00*

Hammerton, Philip. *Etcher's Handbook*. Lon. 1875. illus. 2nd ed......... *$50.00–$75.00*

Hammett, Dashiel. *Thin Man*. NY. Grosset & Dunlap. rprnt, dj............ *$10.00–$20.00*

Hammett, Dashiell. *Adventures of Sam Spade*. Cleve. World Pub. (1945). 1st ed. dj. ....
.... *$60.00–$75.00*

Hammett, Dashiell. *Big Knockover*. NY. Random House. (1966). 1st ed. dj. ....
.... *$40.00–$60.00*

Hammett, Dashiell. *Blood Money*. Cleve. World Pub. 1943. 1st ed. dj. . *$75.00–$85.00*

Hammett, Dashiell. *Glass Key*. NY. 1931. 1st ed............................. *$150.00–$250.00*

Hammett, Dashiell. *Maltese Falcon*. NY. Knopf. 1930. 1st ed. tan cloth.......................
.... *$350.00–$500.00*

Hammett, Dashiell. *Thin Man*. NY. 1934. 1st ed. .... *$195.00–$350.00*

Hammett, Dashiell. *Dain Curse*. NY. Knopf. 1929. 1st ed. yellow cvr. skull and bones stamped in red on cvr. .... *$350.00–$400.00*

Hammond, Harriot Milton. *Aunt Bet, the Story of a Long Life*. Winchester. The Handley Library. (1927). illus. b/w photos. .... *$50.00–$75.00*

Hanaford, Mrs. P. A. *Young Captain; A Memorial of Capt. Richard C. Berby* . . . Bos. 1865. .... *$25.00–$35.00*

Hanaford, Phebe. *Daughters of America*. Augusta. True and Co. 1882. illus. ....
.... *$20.00–$30.00*

Handbook for European and Oriental Travelers. United States Express Co. 1896. traveller's guide, brown cloth. .... *$15.00–$20.00*

Handbook for Scout Masters-Boy Scouts of America. NY. 1914. 1st ed. illus. ....
.... *$25.00–$35.00*

Handbook for Travellers to Niagra Falls . . . Buffalo/Rochester. Ontario and St Lawrence Steamboat Co. 1854. 175 pp, fldg map.................................... *$55.00–$70.00*

Handbook of Informaton for Passengers and Skippers. Nippon Yuse Kaisha. 1896. map in pocket. .... *$40.00–$65.00*

Handbook of the Benet-Mercie Machine Rifle . . . Wash. GPO. 1917. 31 plates. wrps.
.... *$50.00–$75.00*

Handbook of the Colt Automatic . . . Wash. GPO. 1917. illus. 16 plates. wrps..............
.... *$50.00–$75.00*

Handbook of the Gatling Gun . . . Wash. GPO. 1917. 7 fldg plates. wrps......................
.... *$50.00–$75.00*

Handbook of the Maxim Automatic Machine Gun . . . Wash. GPO. 1917. 17 plates. wrps. .... *$50.00–$75.00*

Handbook of the Oneida Society. Oneida, NY. Office of Oneida Circular. 1875. 48 pp. .... *$65.00–$85.00*

Handbook of the Vickers Machine Gun . . . Wash. GPO. 1917. 16 plates. wrps..............
.... *$50.00–$75.00*

Handbook of Tobacco Culture for Planters in So. Rhodesia. Salisbury. 1913. 1st ed. illus. .... *$75.00–$115.00*

Handy, W. C. *Father of the Blues*. NY. Macmillan. 1941. 1st ed. dj... *$125.00–$275.00*

Handy, W. C. (ed.). *Blues: An Anthology.* NY. Albert & Charles Boni. 1926. illus. by Covarrubias. 1st ptg of author's first book, intro by Abbe Niles, scarce. .... *$140.00–$275.00*

Hann, Julius. *Handbook of Climatology, Pt I: General Climatology.* Macmillan. 1903. .... *$30.00–$65.00*

Hanna, A. J. *Flight into Oblivion.* Johnson Pub Co. 1938. 1st ed. .... *$35.00–$50.00*

Hannah, Barry. *Airships.* Knopf. 1978. 1st ed. dj, sgn............................ *$75.00–$95.00*

Hannah, Barry. *Geronimo Rex.* Viking. 1972. 1st ed. dj, sgn............. *$150.00–$175.00*

Hannah, Barry. *Nightwatchmen.* NY. Viking. (1973). 1st ed. dj. .... *$100.00–$200.00*

Hannay, James. *History of the War of 1812.* New Brunswick. 1901. 9 maps printed in text, original cloth... *$120.00–$135.00*

Hansard, George Agar. *Book of Archery.* Lon. 1840. illus. rbnd. .... *$75.00–$125.00*

Hansberry, Lorraine. *Raisin in the Sun.* NY. !959. wrps. .... *$50.00–$85.00*

Hansen, Ron. *Desperadoes.* NY. Knopf. 1979. 1st ed. author's first book, dj. .... *$25.00–$35.00*

Hanson, F. A. L. *Counterpoint in Maori Culture.* Lon. 1983. illus........ *$55.00–$70.00*

Harbaugh, H. *Birds of the Bible.* Phila. Lindsay & Blackiston. 1854. 1st ed. illus. aeg. .... *$70.00–$100.00*

Hardee, W. J. *Rifle and Light Infantry Tactics.* Phila. 1861. Vol. 1. illus. lea and cloth bds.. *$125.00–$140.00*

Hardee, William. *Rifle and Light Infantry Tactics.* Phil. 1861. 2 vols. *$125.00–$275.00*

Harding, A. *Wolf and Coyote Trapping.* OH. 1939. illus......................... *$50.00–$75.00*

Harding, A. R. *Fur Farming.* OH. Harding Pub. 1916. 2nd ed.............. *$14.00–$20.00*

Harding, A. R. *Ginseng and Other Medicinal Plants.* Columbus. illus. photos, rev. .... *$25.00–$40.00*

Harding, A. R. *Mink Trapping.* Columbus. 1906. illus. .... *$20.00–$28.00*

Hardware. NY/New Haven, CT. Sargent & Co. 1888. 1,090 pp. .... *$195.00–$250.00*

Hardy, Thomas. *Group of Noble Dames.* Lon. 1891. 1st ed................. *$75.00–$115.00*

Hardy, Thomas. *Human Shows, Far Fantasies, Songs and Trifles.* Lon. 1925. 1st ed. dj. .... *$65.00–$100.00*

Hardy, Thomas. *Jude the Obscure.* NY. Limited Editions Club. 1932. illus. wood engr by Agnes Parker, 932/1,500 cc sgn, slipcase... *$40.00–$50.00*

Hardy, Thomas. *Jude the Obscure.* NY. 1896. 1st Amer ed. .... *$50.00–$95.00*

Hardy, Thomas. *Tess of the D'Urbervilles.* NY. 1892. 1st Amer ed. ...... *$60.00–$80.00*

Hardy, Thomas. *Well-Beloved.* Harpers. 1897. 1st Amer ed.................. *$75.00–$95.00*

Hardy, Thomas. *Woodlanders.* Lon. Macmillan. 1887. 3 vols. 1st ed. green cloth. .... *$1,200.00–$2,000.00*

Harland, Marion. *Some Colonial Homesteads and Their Stories.* Putnam. 1897. 3rd ed. b/w photos. .... *$30.00–$45.00*

Harlow, Alvin. *Old Waybills.* NY. 1934. dj. .... *$40.00–$60.00*

Harman, Dolly Stearns. *Beach Fires*. Bos. Christopher Pub. 1934. scarce.....................
.... *$25.00–$40.00*

Harold, Childe. *Child's Book of Abridged Wisdom*. SF. Paul Elder. (1905). 1st ed. illus.
pictorial boards, exposed spine double pages. .... *$75.00–$100.00*

Harpham Brothers Company Catalogue No. 36, Saddlery Accessories. NE. nd. wrps.
.... *$30.00–$40.00*

Harris, Joel Chandler. *Aaron in the Wildwood*. Bos. 1897. 1st ed. .... *$55.00–$95.00*

Harris, Joel Chandler. *Gabriel Tolliver*. NY. 1902. 1st ed. 448 pp. .... *$85.00–$225.00*

Harris, Joel Chandler. *Little Union Scout*. NY. McClure. 1904. 1st ed. illus. by Gibbs
green cloth. .... *$65.00–$300.00*

Harris, Joel Chandler. *Nights With Uncle Remus: Myths and Legends of the Old
Plantation*. Bos. 1883. 1st published ed. pictorial cloth, 416 pp............ *$80.00–$120.00*

Harris, Joel Chandler. *On the Wings of Occasion*. NY. 1900. 1st ed. ... *$50.00–$80.00*

Harris, Joel Chandler. *Tar Baby and Other Rhymes of Uncle Remus*. NY. Appleton.
1904. 1st ed. illus. orange cloth. .... *$100.00–$250.00*

Harris, Joel Chandler. *Told By Uncle Remus, New Stories of the Old Plantation*. NY.
McClure Phillips & Co. 1905. 1st ed. 3rd imp. illus. .... *$150.00–$175.00*

Harris, Joel Chandler. *Uncle Remus Returns*. Bos. Houghton Mifflin. 1918. 1st ed.
illus. by A B Frost and Conde. .... *$65.00–$300.00*

Harris, Joel Chandler. *Wally Wanderoon and His Story Telling Machine*. NY. 1903. 1st
ed. illus. 294 pp. .... *$85.00–$125.00*

Harris, Nathaniel. *Gesellschaft fur Chemische Industrie in Basel*. np. 1934. illus. clr
plates, large orange cloth, dj, slipcase.. *$30.00–$45.00*

Harris, T. W. *Treatise on Insects Injurious to Vegetation*. Bos. 1862. illus. 640 pp, plates.
.... *$125.00–$200.00*

Harris, Thomas. *Silence of the Lambs*. NY. 1988. 1st ed. dj. .... *$45.00–$60.00*

Harris, Thomas L. *Lyric of the Golden Age*. NY. 1856. 1st ed. 381 pp. ....
.... *$100.00–$150.00*

Harris, W. R. *Catholic Church in Utah*. Salt Lake City. (1909). 1st ed. map.................
.... *$50.00–$75.00*

Harrison, Donald C. *Distant Patrol*. Dept of Historic Resources. illus. b/w and clr
photo, maps, dj. .... *$20.00–$25.00*

Harrison, Percival T. *Bungalow Residences: A Handbook*. Lon. Crosby, Lockwood.
1909. pictorial green cloth, plates, 79 pp. .... *$75.00–$135.00*

Hart, B. H. Liddell. *Sherman* . . . NY. Dodd Mead. 1929. 1st ed. dj. maps..................
.... *$50.00–$75.00*

Hart, B. H. Liddell. *Tanks*. Lon. Cassell. (1959). 2 vols. 1st ed. illus. cloth djs plates and
fldg maps. .... *$60.00–$90.00*

Hart, George. *Violin and Its Music*. Lon. 1875. illus. .... *$50.00–$80.00*

Harte, Bret. *Bell-Ringer of the Angel's and Other Stories*. Bos. Houghton Mifflin. 1894.
1st ed.. *$20.00–$40.00*

Harte, Bret. *Crusade of the Excelsior*. Bos. Houghton Mifflin. 1887. 1st ed. 1/300 cc.. .... *$40.00–$60.00*

Harte, Bret. *Maruja*. NY. Houghton Mifflin. 1885. 1st ed..................... *$40.00–$60.00*

Harte, Bret. *Poems*. Bos. Fields & Osgood. 1871. 1st ed. brown cloth gold lettering..... .... *$40.00–$50.00*

Harte, Bret. *Salomy Jane*. Bos. Houghton Mifflin. 1910. 1st ed. dj. .... *$50.00–$250.00*

Harting, James Edmund. *Sketches of Bird Life from Twenty Years' Observation of Their Haunts and Habits*. Lon. Allen. 1883. 1st ed. illus................................ *$80.00–$120.00*

Hartley, Florence. *Ladie's Handbook of Fancy and Ornamental Work*. Phila. 1859....... .... *$75.00–$95.00*

Hartshorne, A. *Old English Drinking Glasses*. Lon. 1897. folio, plates, 499 pp. .... *$150.00–$250.00*

Harvey, Fred. *Grand Canyon National Park*. LA. 1914. wrps. photo album. .... *$25.00–$35.00*

Harvey, Rev. M. *Newfoundland in 1897*. Lon. 1897. illus. .... *$25.00–$40.00*

Harvey, William Fryer. *Arm of Mrs. Egan*. NY. Dutton. 1952. 1st ed. 256 pp, dj. .... *$50.00–$65.00*

Harwell, Richard. *Colorado Volunteers in New Mexico*. Chi. Lakeside. 1962. reprint... .... *$25.00–$35.00*

Haskell, Frank Aretas. *Battle of Gettysburg*. WI. 1908. 1st ed. illus..... *$50.00–$75.00*

Hatcher, Edmund N. *Last Four Weeks of the War*. Columbus. Cooperative Pub. 1892. illus. .... *$50.00–$80.00*

Haupt, Herman. *General Theory of Bridge Construction*. NY. 1856..... *$45.00–$60.00*

Hauser, Thomas. *Muhammad Ali. His Life and Times*. NY. Simon & Schuster. 1991. sgn. .... *$65.00–$85.00*

Hausman, Leon A. *Book of Songbirds*. NY. (1956). 1st ed. illus. clr and b/w, 78 RPM record included. .... *$22.00–$30.00*

Haviland, Laura S. *Woman's Life Work*. MI. 1881. illus. .... *$50.00–$75.00*

Hawk Eye Camera. Bos. Blair Camera Company. 1889. illus, wrps....... *$50.00–$75.00*

Hawker, George. *An English Woman's 25 Years in Tropical Africa*. Lon. 1911. .... *$75.00–$90.00*

Hawker, P. *Instructions to Young Sportsmen . . . Guns & Shooting*. 1858...................... .... *$45.00–$50.00*

Hawley, Walter. *Oriental Rugs, Antique and Modern*. Tudor Publishing. 1937. 11 clr plates. .... *$60.00–$90.00*

Hawley, Walter A. *Early Days of Santa Barbara, California*. Santa Barbara. 1910. wrps. plates. .... *$100.00–$135.00*

Hawthorne, Nathaniel. *Doctor Grimshawe's Secret*. Osgood. 1883. 1st ed.................. .... *$50.00–$125.00*

Hawthorne, Nathaniel. *House of Seven Gables*. Bos. Tichnor, Reed, and Fields. 1851. 1st ed. brown cloth. .... *$600.00–$2,000.00*

Hawthorne, Nathaniel. *Marble Faun*. Bos. 1860. 2 vols. 1st ed. 1st Amer ed...............
.... *$400.00–$700.00*

Hawthorne, Nathaniel. *Our Old Home*. Ticknor & Fields. 1863. 1st ed. 1st state. ....
.... *$150.00–$285.00*

Hawthorne, Nathaniel. *Scarlet Letter*. Bos. Ticknor, Reed, & Fields. 1850. ....
.... *$300.00–$400.00*

Hawthorne, Nathaniel. *Scarlet Letter*. NY. Grosset & Dunlap. illus. dj, illus from photoplay. .... *$30.00–$50.00*

Hawthorne, Nathaniel. *True Stories From History and Biography*. Bos. Ticknor & Reed and Fields. 1851. 1st ed. cloth.. *$150.00–$200.00*

Hawthorne, Nathaniel. *Wonder Book*. Doran. (1922). illus. by Arthur Rackham. ....
.... *$150.00–$200.00*

Hawthorne, Nathaniel. *Wonderbook for Girls and Boys*. Houghton. 1893. 1st ed. illus. by Walter Crane.. *$100.00–$150.00*

Hay, John. *Pike County Ballads*. Bos. Houghton Mifflin. (1912). 1st ed. illus. by N C Wyeth. pictorial paste-down on cvr.................................. *$100.00–$150.00*

Hay, William Howard. *New Health Era*. NY. Hay System. (1934). 1st ed. 5th ptg,........
.... *$40.00–$55.00*

Hayden, A. *Spode and His Successors*. Lon. 1925. .... *$60.00–$75.00*

Hayden, A. S. *Early History of the Disciples in the Western Reserve, Ohio* . . . Cinc. 1876. 1st ed.. *$50.00–$125.00*

Hayden, F. V. *Report of the US Geological Survey of the Territories*. Wash. 1979. clr plates.. *$65.00–$100.00*

Hayden, F. V. *Bulletin of the Geological and Geographical Survey of the Territories, Vol II, No 1*. Wash. 1876. wrps. 63 pp, 29 plates. .... *$95.00–$110.00*

Hayes, Albert H. *Medical Treatise on Nervous Affections*. Bos. Peabody Medical Inst. (1870). 137 pp. .... *$50.00–$75.00*

Hayes, Isaac. *An Arctic Boat Journey*. Bos. 1860. 1st ed. 375 pp, maps. *$40.00–$50.00*

Hayes, J. Gordon. *Conquest of the South Pole*. NY. Macmillan. 1933. 1st Amer ed. illus, maps.. *$60.00–$75.00*

Haynes, Warden G. *Pictures From Prison Life and Suggestions on Discipline*. 1869....
.... *$50.00–$65.00*

Hayward, John. *Gazetteer of Vermont* . . . Bos. 1849. illus. 216 pp....... *$65.00–$95.00*

Hazelton, John Adams. *Hazelton Letters: A Contribution to Western Americana*. Stockton. College of the Pacific. 1958. 1st ed. bds................................. *$35.00–$50.00*

Head, Sir Francis B. *A Narrative*. Lon. Murray. 1839. 2nd ed. ½ calf, marbled boards.
.... *$100.00–$120.00*

Headland, Isaac T. *Chinese Mother Goose Rhymes*. NY. Fleming Revell. (1900). 1st ed. illus. .... *$75.00–$125.00*

Headland, Isaac Taylor. *Court Life in China*. NY. (1909). illus. 2nd ed. photos...........
.... *$30.00–$40.00*

Headley, J. T. *Adirondacks or Life in the Woods*. NY. 1849. 1st ed. 288 pp.................
.... *$95.00–$115.00*

Headley, Joel Tyler. *Second War with England*. NY. Scribner's. 1853. 2 vols. 10 plates (1 fldg), pictorial brown cloth. .... *$135.00–$150.00*

Healy, Capt. M. A. *Report of the Cruise of the Revenue Marine Steamer . . .* Wash. 1889. illus. cloth 128 pp. .... *$150.00–$200.00*

Healy, M. A. *Report of the Cruise of the Revenue Marine Steamer Corwin in the Arctic Ocean in the Year 1885*. DC. GPO. 1887. 1st ed. illus. 38 wood-engr plates, 4 lithos, 2 fldg charts. .... *$125.00–$150.00*

Heaney, Seamus. *Door Into the Dark*. Faber. 1969. 1st ed. dj. .... *$100.00–$150.00*

Heaney, Seamus. *Poems 1965–1975*. NY. Farrar Straus Giroux. (1980). 1st ed. dj. ....
.... *$30.00–$40.00*

Heaney, Seamus. *Station Island*. Lon. 1984. 1st ed. dj. .... *$50.00–$75.00*

Hearn, Lafcadio. *Boy Who Drew Cats*. Tokyo. 1898. printed and hand clr in handmade crepe paper, 18 pp. .... *$120.00–$300.00*

Hearn, Lafcadio. *Chita: A Memory of Last Island*. NY. 1889. 1st ed. 204 pp. ....
.... *$200.00–$300.00*

Hearn, Lafcadio. *In Ghostly Japan*. Bos. 1899. 1st ed. illus. photos, teg, Hearn's last book. .... *$115.00–$150.00*

Hearn, Lafcadio. *Japan*. NY. 1904. 1st ed. 1st issue, teg, dj. .... *$95.00–$325.00*

Hearn, Lafcadio. *Karma*. NY. 1918. 1st ed. .... *$100.00–$150.00*

Hearn, Lafcadio. *Kokaro*. Bos. 1896. 1st ed. .... *$50.00–$75.00*

Hearn, Lafcadio. *Kwaidan*. Tokyo. 1932. illus. ltd 1,500 cc, sgn, silk case. ....
.... *$150.00–$225.00*

Hearn, Lafcadio. *Out of the East*. Bos. (1895). 1st ed. .... *$35.00–$50.00*

Hearn, Lafcadio. *Romance of the Milky Way*. Lon. 1905. 1st Eng ed. ... *$45.00–$55.00*

Hearn, Lafcadio. *Romance of the Milky Way and Other Studies and Stories*. Bos. Houghton Mifflin. 1905. 1st ed. .... *$75.00–$150.00*

Hearst, Mrs. William Randolph, Jr. *Horses of San Simeon*. San Simeon. San Simeon Press. 1985. sgn, slipcase. .... *$225.00–$295.00*

Heathcote, J. M. *Skating and Figure Skating*. Lon. 1892. illus. .... *$60.00–$85.00*

Hebert, Frank. *40 Years Prospecting & Mining in the Black Hills of So. Dakota*. Rapid City. 1921. 1st ed. sgn. .... *$35.00–$45.00*

Heckewelder, John. *History, Manners and Customs of the Indian Nations Who Once Inhabited Pennsylvania and the Neighboring States*. NY. Arno Press. 1971. reprint. dj.
.... *$22.00–$30.00*

Heckewelder, John. *Narr. of United Brethren Among Delaware & Mohegan Indians*. Cleve. 1907. large paper copy. .... *$140.00–$275.00*

Hedges, Isaac A. *Sugar Canes and Their Products, Culture and Manufacture*. St Louis. 1881. illus. .... *$28.00–$35.00*

Hedin, Sven. *A Conquest of Tibet*. Garden City. Halcyon House. 1934. illus. ....
.... *$50.00–$75.00*

Hedin, Sven. *Through Asia*. NY. Harper & Bros. 1899. 2 vols. 1st ed. 300 photos and sketches, fldg map at rear, decorative cloth, teg. .... *$250.00–$400.00*

Hedrick, U P. *Plums of New York.* Albany. J B Lyon. 1911. illus. 97 clr plates. ....
.... *$75.00–$100.00*

Hedrick, U. P. *Cherries of New York.* Albany. 1915. clr plates. .... *$150.00–$175.00*

Hedrick, U. P. *Peaches of New York.* Albany. 1917. illus. clr plates. .. *$100.00–$295.00*

Hedrick, U. P. *Pears of New York.* Albany. 1921. illus. .... *$180.00–$225.00*

Hedrick, U. P. *Plums of New York.* Albany. 1911. clr plates. .... *$125.00–$165.00*

Hedrick, U. P. (ed.). *Sturtevant's Notes on Edible Plants.* Alb. Lyon. 1919. 1st ed. ....
.... *$60.00–$85.00*

Hedrick, U. P. *Peaches of New York.* Albany. J B Lyon. 1917. illus. 92 clr plates. ....
.... *$75.00–$100.00*

Heffernan, J. W. *New York Fire Department Examination Questions.* NY. Duffield. 1929. Vol. 1. pullouts. .... *$35.00–$50.00*

Heffernan, J. W. *New York Fire Department Examination Questions.* NY. Duffield. 1929. Vol. 1. illus. photos, pullouts. .... *$25.00–$50.00*

Heilman, G. *Origins of Birds.* NY. 1927. 2 clr plates, dj .... *$65.00–$75.00*

Heilner, Van Campen. *Adventures in Angling.* Stewart Kidd. (1922). 1st ed. illus. ....
.... *$50.00–$85.00*

Heilner, Van Campen. *Our American Game Birds.* Garden City. Doubleday Doran. 1941. 1st ed. illus. with clr paintings by Lynn Bogue Hunt, dj. .... *$60.00–$85.00*

Heilprin, Angelo. *Alaska and the Klondike.* NY. 1899. illus. inscrb. ...... *$35.00–$45.00*

Heilprin, Angelo. *Town Geology.* Phila. 1885. 1st ed. 142 pp, illus. ...... *$65.00–$75.00*

Heindel, Max. *Astro-Diagnosis: A Guide to Healing.* Lon. (1929). 3rd ed. ....
.... *$15.00–$25.00*

Heindel, Max and Augusta F. Heindel. *Astro-Diagnosis . . .* Oceanside, CA/Lon. The Rosicrucian Fellowship. (1929). 2nd ed. illus. ...., *$60.00–$85.00*

Heiner, Dr. Henry. *Gesundheits Schatzkammer.* Lancaster, PA. (1831). *$30.00–$40.00*

Heinl, Lt. Col. Robert. *Marines of Midway.* Wash. 1948. maps, soft cvrs. ....
.... *$75.00–$95.00*

Heinlein, Robert. *Door Into Summer.* Garden City. Doubleday. 1957. 1st ed. scarce, dj.
.... *$300.00–$450.00*

Heinlein, Robert A. *Assignment in Eternity.* Fantasy Press. (1953). 1st ed. dj ....
.... *$175.00–$350.00*

Heinlein, Robert A. *Cat Who Walks Through Walls.* NY. 1985. 1st ed. dj ....
.... *$25.00–$30.00*

Heinlein, Robert A. *Farmer in the Sky.* Scribner's. 1950. 1st ed. dj... *$150.00–$225.00*

Heinlein, Robert A. *Number of the Beast.* Lon. 1980. 1st ed. dj .... *$30.00–$40.00*

Heinlein, Robert A. *Orphans of the Sky.* Putnam. (1964). 1st ed. .... *$50.00–$75.00*

Heinlein, Robert A. *Orphans of the Sky.* Lon. Gollancz. 1963. 1st ed. 1st UK ed. dj.....
.... *$300.00–$525.00*

Heinlein, Robert A. *Space Cadet.* NY. Scribner's. 1948. 1st ed. dj. ... *$400.00–$500.00*

Heinlein, Robert A. *Stranger in a Strange Land*. NY. Putnam. (1961). 1st ed. dj...........
.... *$500.00–$950.00*

Heinlein, Robert A. *Waldo and Magic, Inc*. Garden City. 1950. 1st ed. dj.....................
.... *$200.00–$300.00*

Heisler Automotive Works. *Heisler Geared Locomotives*. Erie. Heisler Locomotive Works. 1908. wrps. illus. 47 pp, cat.. *$60.00–$75.00*

Heitler, W. *Quantum Theory of Radiation*. Oxford Univ Pr. 1950. 2nd ed. 272 pp, dj....
.... *$50.00–$60.00*

Heller, Joseph. *Catch-22*. NY. 1961. 1st ed. author's first book, dj..... *$400.00–$500.00*

Heller, Joseph. *God Knows*. NY. 1984. 1st ed. sgn, dj. .... *$35.00–$40.00*

Heller, Joseph. *Good As Gold*. Simon. (1979). 1st ed. .... *$35.00–$45.00*

Heller, Joseph. *We Bombed in New Haven*. NY. Knopf. 1968. 1st ed. dj.......................
.... *$60.00–$75.00*

Hellman, Lillian. *Children's Hour*. NY. 19134. 1st ed. dj.................. *$250.00–$300.00*

Hellman, Lillian. *Little Foxes*. NY. 1939. 1st ed. dj. .... *$30.00–$45.00*

Helms, Herman (ed.). *Book of the New York International Chess Tournament 1924*. NY. Amer Chess Bulletin. 1925. 1st ed. scarce... *$85.00–$95.00*

Helper, Hinton Rowan. *Impending Crisis of the South*. NY. 1857......... *$40.00–$60.00*

Helprin, Mark. *Ellis Island and Other Stories*. NY. Delacorte Press. (1981). 1st ed. dj.
.... *$50.00–$60.00*

Hemenway, Abby M. *Clarke Papers; Mrs. Meech and Her Family* . . . Burlington. 1878. 312 pp. .... *$42.00–$50.00*

Hemenway, Abby Maria. *Vermont Historical Gazetteer* . . . *Vol III*. NH. 1877. illus. hard to find. .... *$300.00–$425.00*

Hemenway, Abby Maria. *Vermont Historical Gazetteer* . . . *Vol IV*. Montpelier. 1882. illus. rbnd. .... *$130.00–$165.00*

Hemenway, Abby Maria. *Vermont Historical Gazetteer* . . . *Vol V*. Brandon. 1891. illus.
.... *$425.00–$475.00*

Hemenway, Abby Maria. *Vermont Historical Gazetteer* . . . *Vols. I & II*. Burlington. 1867, 1871. illus. .... *$200.00–$300.00*

Hemenway, Abby Maria. *Vermont Historical Gazetteer* . . . *Vol IV*. Monpelier. 1882. illus. 1,200 pp. .... *$165.00–$175.00*

Hemingway, Ernest. *Across the River and into the Trees*. NY. Scribner's. 1950. 1st ed. dj. .... *$100.00–$185.00*

Hemingway, Ernest. *Death in the Afternoon*. NY. 1932. 1st ed. dj. ....
.... *$750.00–$1,250.00*

Hemingway, Ernest. *Farewell to Arms*. Scribner's. 1929. 1st ed. dj. *$800.00–$1,400.00*

Hemingway, Ernest. *For Whom the Bell Tolls*. Scribner's. 1940. no dj. *$34.00–$40.00*

Hemingway, Ernest. *For Whom the Bell Tolls*. NY. Scribner's. 1940. 1st ed. dj. ....
.... *$200.00–$650.00*

Hemingway, Ernest. *Islands in the Stream*. NY. Scribner's. 1970. 1st ed. dj. ....
.... *$50.00–$75.00*

Hemingway, Ernest. *Marlin, Big Fish.* 1992. ltd 1,000 cc of 1st hardcvr appearance, dj. .... *$175.00–$250.00*

Hemingway, Ernest. *Moveable Feast.* NY. (1964). 1st ed. dj. .... *$60.00–$100.00*

Hemingway, Ernest. *Old Man and the Sea.* Lon. Jonathan Cape. (1952). 1st Eng ed. dj. .... *$100.00–$225.00*

Hemingway, Ernest. *Old Man and the Sea.* NY. Scribner's. 1952. 1st ed. dj. ....
.... *$180.00–$400.00*

Hemingway, Ernest. *Old Man and the Sea.* NY. Scribner's. 1952. 1st ed. *$15.00–$25.00*

Hemingway, Ernest. *Three Stories & Ten Poems.* Paris. Contact Publishing Co. 1923. 1st ed. author's first book, 1/300 cc printed, grayish-blue printed paper wrps, uncut, slipcase... *$10,000.00–$15,000.00*

Hemingway, Ernest. *To Have and Have Not.* NY. Scribner's. 1937. 1st ed. ....
.... *$850.00–$1,000.00*

Hemingway, Ernest. *Winner Take Nothing.* NY. (1933). 1st ed. dj.. *$450.00–$1,250.00*

Hempel, J. *Homeopathic Domestic Physician.* 1846. illus. .... *$20.00–$30.00*

Henderson, Alice P. *Rainbow's End: Alaska.* NY. Herbert Stone & Co. 1898. 1st ed. ...
.... *$125.00–$150.00*

Henderson, Mrs. Mary. *Diet for the Sick.* NY. 1885. illus. 234 pp, green decorated cloth. .... *$25.00–$35.00*

Henderson, Mrs. Mary F. *Practical Cooking and Dinner Giving.* NY. Harper. 1881. 1st ed. .... *$70.00–$100.00*

Henderson, Peter. *Henderson's Handbook of Plants and General Horticulture.* NY. 1910. 2nd ed. illus. .... *$50.00–$65.00*

Henderson, W. A. *Modern Domestic Cookery and Useful Receipt Book.* Bos. 1844. .....
.... *$135.00–$170.00*

Henely, Louise Miller. *Letters from the Yellowstone.* Iowa. 1914. 1st ed. illus. inscrb....
.... *$50.00–$100.00*

Hening, Mrs. E. F. *History of the African Mission of the Episcopal Church in the United States* . . . NY. Stanford & Swords. 1850. 1st ed. fldg map, 300 pp. ....
.... *$40.00–$50.00*

Hennessy, Max. *Dangerous Years.* NY. Atheneum. (1977). 1st US ed dj.......................
.... *$17.00–$45.00*

Henry, Alice. *Women and the Labor Movement.* NY. Doran. (1923). 1st ed. 241 pp.......
.... *$45.00–$65.00*

Henry, Capt. W. S. *Campaign Sketches of the War with Mexico.* NY. 1847. 1st ed. illus.
.... *$190.00–$250.00*

Henry, Marguerite. *Album of Horses.* Chi. Rand McNally. 1951. illus. dj. ....
.... *$32.00–$45.00*

Henry, Marguerite. *Birds at Home.* Chi. Donohue. 1942. 1st ed. illus. scarce, dj.........
.... *$45.00–$58.00*

Henry, Marguerite. *Black Gold.* Chi. Rand McNally. 1957. illus. by Wesley Dennis, presentation copy, sgn by Henry and Dennis, dj.................................... *$85.00–$125.00*

Henry, Marguerite. *Brighty of the Grand Canyon*. Chi. Rand McNally. 1953. 1st ed. illus. by Wesley Dennis, dj. .... *$50.00–$65.00*

Henry, Marguerite. *Justin Morgan Had a Horse*. Chi. Wilcox & Follett. 1945. 1st ed.. .... *$25.00–$45.00*

Henry, Marguerite. *King of the Wind*. NY. Rand McNally & Co. (1951). illus. red cloth. .... *$10.00–$20.00*

Henry, Marguerite. *King of the Wind*. Chi. Rand McNally. 1948. 1st ed. illus. by Wesley Dennis, dj. .... *$50.00–$95.00*

Henry, Marguerite and Wesley Dennis. *Benjamin West and His Cat Grimalkin*. Ind. Bobbs Merrill. 1947. dj. .... *$58.00–$65.00*

Henry, O. *Cabbages and Kings*. NY. 1904. 1st ed. .... *$100.00–$150.00*

Henry, O. *Heart of the West*. McClure. 1907. 1st ed. .... *$60.00–$85.00*

Henry, O. *Whirlygigs*. NY. 1910. 1st ed. 1st Amer ed. .... *$60.00–$80.00*

Henry, Robert Mitchell. *Evolution of Sinn Fein*. Dublin. 1920. 1st ed. sgn by Sean Cullen. .... *$35.00–$95.00*

Henry, Robert Selph. *Story of the Confederacy*. Ind. (1931). .... *$30.00–$40.00*

Henry, Will. *Alias Butch Cassidy*. NY. (1967). 1st ed. dj. .... *$50.00–$75.00*

Henry, Will. *To Follow a Flag*. NY. Random House. (1953). 1st ed. dj. *$65.00–$100.00*

Henry, Will. *Who Rides With Wyatt*. Random House. (1955). 1st ed. dj. *$30.00–$40.00*

Henson, Josiah. *Truth Stranger Than Fiction*. MA. Corner House Pub. 1973. dj. .... *$14.00–$20.00*

Hentoff, Nat. *Peace Agitator*. NY. Macmillan. 1963. 1st ed. author's first book, dj. .... *$10.00–$20.00*

Henty, G. A. *Beric the Briton*. Scribner's. 1895. illus. by Parkinson. 1st US ed. brown cloth. .... *$30.00–$45.00*

Henty, G. A. *Both Sides of the Border*. Lon. 1899. 1st ed. illus. .... *$50.00–$70.00*

Henty, G. A. *By Pike & Dyke*. Lon. (1890). .... *$25.00–$30.00*

Henty, G. A. *In the Irish Brigade*. Scribner's. 1900. 1st ed. .... *$30.00–$35.00*

Henty, G. A. *Maori and Settler . . .* NY. .... *$12.00–$25.00*

Henty, G. A. *On the Irrawoddy*. Scribner's. 1896. blue decorated cvr. .... *$40.00–$45.00*

Henty, G. A. *Out With Garibaldi*. NY. 1900. 1st Amer ed. illus. .... *$40.00–$75.00*

Henty, G. A. *Redskins and Colonists*. NY. (1905). dj. .... *$25.00–$30.00*

Henty, G. A. *Through Russian Snows*. NY. Scribner's. 1895. illus. by Overend. maps. .... *$40.00–$60.00*

Henty, G. A. *With Buller in Natal*. Lon. nd. 1st Eng ed. .... *$35.00–$55.00*

Henty, G. A. *With Cochrane the Dauntless*. NY. 1896. 1st Amer ed....... *$30.00–$45.00*

Henty, G. A. *With Lee in Virginia*. NY. illus. by Gordon Browne. .... *$15.00–$40.00*

Henty, G. A. *With Wolfe in Canada*. Lon. illus. by Gordon Browne, green pictorial bds. .... *$20.00–$25.00*

Henty, G. A. *Young Franc-Tireurs and Their Adventures in the Franco-Prussian War.* The Federal Book Co. nd. illus. .... *$15.00–$30.00*

Herbert, Frank. *Charterhouse Dune.* NY. (1985). 1st ed. ltd 750 cc, sgn, dj. ....
.... *$50.00–$70.00*

Herbert, Frank. *God Emperor of Dune.* NY. Putnam. 1981. 1st ed. dj.. *$25.00–$85.00*

Herbert, Frank. *God Emperor of Dune.* NY. 1981. 1st ed. sgn, dj......... *$50.00–$75.00*

Herbert, Frank. *Heretics of Dune.* NY. (1984). 1st Amer ed. 1,500 cc, sgn, slipcase. ...
.... *$50.00–$100.00*

Herbert, Frank. *White Plague.* NY. (1982). 1st ed. 1/500 cc, sgn......... *$40.00–$50.00*

Herbert, George R. *South Sea Bubbles.* Lon. Bentley. 1872. illus. .... *$40.00–$65.00*

Herbert, H. *First Principles of Evolution.* NY. Appleton. 1896. .... *$18.00–$25.00*

Herbert, Henry William. *American Game in Its Seasons.* NY. Scribner's. 1853. 1st ed. illus. .... *$145.00–$250.00*

Herbert, Henry William. *Frank Forester's Field Sports.* NY. Stringer & Townshend. 1849. 2 vols. illus. 1st Amer ed. .... *$125.00–$200.00*

Herbert, Henry William. *Frank Forester's Fish and Fishing.* NY. Stringer & Townshend. 1850. 1st ed. illus. .... *$75.00–$100.00*

Herbert, Henry William. *Hints to Horsekeepers.* NY. Orange Judd. (1859). 1st ed. illus.
.... *$60.00–$100.00*

Herbert, Henry William (Frank Forester). *American Game in Its Seasons.* NY. Scribner's. 1853. 1st ed. .... *$125.00–$250.00*

Herford, Oliver. *An Alphabet of Celebrities.* Bos. 1899. 1st ed. .... *$50.00–$75.00*

Heriot, George. *Travels Through the Canadas.* Rutland. Chas E Tuttle Co. (1971). reprint, illus, fldg map, dj... *$60.00–$75.00*

Herndon, Angelo. *Let Me Live.* NY. Random House. (1937). cloth frontis. ....
.... *$50.00–$75.00*

Herrick, F. H. *American Eagle.* Appleton Century. 1934...................... *$30.00–$45.00*

Herrick, F. H. *Flower Poems.* Lon. Routledge. illus. by Castle reg. .... *$50.00–$80.00*

Herrigel, Eugen. *Zen in the Art of Archery.* NY. Pantheon. (1953). 1st ed. dj...............
.... *$30.00–$40.00*

Hersey, John. *Hiroshima.* NY. Knopf. 1946. 1st ed. dj.......................... *$10.00–$20.00*

Hersey, John. *Key West Tales.* NY. 1994. 1st ed. dj............................... *$18.00–$25.00*

Hersey, John. *The Wall.* NY. Limited Editions Club. 1957. illus. aquatints and drawings, 727/1,500 cc sgn by artist... *$25.00–$40.00*

Hersey, John. *The Wall.* NY. 1950. 1st ed. dj. .... *$25.00–$35.00*

Hersey, John. *War Lover.* Knopf. 1959. 1st ed. dj................................. *$15.00–$25.00*

Hertz, Louis. *Handbook of Old American Toys.* Wetherfield. 1947. 1st ed.....................
.... *$25.00–$50.00*

Hervey, John. *American Trotter.* NY. Cower McCann. 1947. 1st ed. dj. ....
.... *$85.00–$150.00*

Hesse, Hermann. *Siddhartha.* NY. New Directions. 1951. 1st Amer ed. dj. ....
.... *$85.00–$100.00*

Hewiit, Edward R. *Trout and Salmon Fisherman for Seventy-five Years.* Scribner's.
1948. .... *$40.00–$65.00*

Hewitt, Abram S. *On the Statistics and Geography of the Production of Iron.* NY. 1856.
wrps. .... *$45.00–$70.00*

Hewlett, John. *Harlem Story.* NY. 1948. 1st ed. dj. .... *$50.00–$75.00*

Heyde, Albert. *Der Schachwettkampfzwischen Dr S Tarrasch und M Tschigorin Ende
1893.* Berlin. Bruer. 1893. 1st ed. .... *$150.00–$198.00*

Heydecker, Joe J. and J. Leeb. *Nuremberg Trial: A History of Nazi Germany.* Cleve.
1962. 1st ed. .... *$30.00–$40.00*

Heyerdahl, Thor. *American Indians in the Pacific.* Lon. Allen & Unwin. (1952). 1st Eng
ed. illus. dj. .... *$70.00–$90.00*

Heyward, DuBose. *Half Pint Flask.* NY. 1929. 1st ed. dj. .... *$40.00–$60.00*

Heyward, DuBose. *Half Pint Flask.* Farrar & Rinehart. 1929. 1st ed. black cloth. ....
.... *$20.00–$40.00*

Hiaasen, Carl. *Stormy Weather.* NY. Knopf. 1995. 1st ed. sgn, dj. .... *$30.00–$45.00*

Hiaasen, Carl and William D. Montalbano. *Powder Burns.* NY. Atheneum. 1981. 1st
ed. dj. .... *$350.00–$425.00*

Hibben, Frank. *Prehistoric Man in Europe.* Univ of OK Press. 1958. 1st ed. illus. ....
.... *$22.00–$27.00*

Hibbert, Shirley. *Field Flowers.* Lon. 1878. illus. .... *$35.00–$45.00*

Hibbert, Shirley. *Wild Flower.* Lon. 1878. 2nd ed. illus. .... *$25.00–$40.00*

Higbee, Elias and Robert Thompson. *Latter Day Saints, Alias Mormons.* DC. 1840.
second oldest US document to mention Mormons, 13 pp. *$350.00*

Higgins, Jack. *Day of Judgment.* Lon. Collins. 1978. 1st ed. dj. .... *$25.00–$65.00*

Higgins, Jack. *Eagle Has Landed.* Collins. 1975. 1st UK ed. dj. .... *$100.00–$250.00*

Higgins, Jack. *Eye of the Storm.* Lon. Chapmans. 1992. 1st ed. dj. .... *$15.00–$45.00*

Higgins, Jack. *Last Place God Made.* Lon. Collins. 1971. 1st ed. dj.. *$225.00–$250.00*

Higgins, Jack. *Savage Day.* Lon. Collins. 1972. 1st ed. dj. .... *$65.00–$100.00*

Higginson, Ella. *Alaska.* NY. Macmillan Co. 1926. illus. new ed. .... *$20.00–$35.00*

Hildreth, Richard. *White Slave.* Lon. 1852. 1st UK ed. .... *$45.00–$65.00*

Hill, B. L. *An Epitome of the Homoeopathic Healing Arts.* Detroit. 1869. ....
.... *$45.00–$55.00*

Hill, Charles T. *Fighting a Fire.* NY. 1898. illus. pictorial red cloth. ..... *$50.00–$90.00*

Hill, Frank Pierce. *American Plays Printed 1714–1830.* Stanford Univ Press. (1934). dj.
.... *$30.00–$50.00*

Hill, Grace Livingston. *Through These Fires.* Phila. 1943. 1st ed. dj. ... *$35.00–$47.00*

Hill, John Wesley. *If Lincoln Were Here.* NY/Lon. Putnam. 1925. blue decorated cloth.
.... *$18.00–$25.00*

Hill, L. *Meteorological & Chronological Register, 1806 to 1869.* Plymouth, MA. 1869. 1st ed............... *$30.00–$45.00*

Hill, Ralph Nading. *Sidewheeler Saga.* Rinehart. 1953. 1st ed. illus. dj. *$22.00–$35.00*

Hill, Ralph Nading. *Voyages of Brian Sea Worthy.* Montpelier. Vermont Life Magazine. 1971. 151 pp, dj............... *$16.00–$25.00*

Hill, Robin. *Australian Birds.* NY. 1967. 1st ed. illus. clr plates, dj........ *$35.00–$45.00*

Hill, W. Henry, et al. *Antonio Stradivari, His Life and Work (1644–1737).* Lon. Macmillan and Co. 1909. illus............... *$75.00–$150.00*

Hillary, Sir Edmund. *Schoolhouse in the Clouds.* Garden City. Doubleday. 1964. 1st ed. clr photos, dj............... *$15.00–$30.00*

Hillary, William. *Observations on the Changes of the Air . . . Yellow Fever.* Lon. 1766. 2nd ed. bds............... *$235.00–$400.00*

Hillerman, Tony. *Talking God.* Harper. (1989). 1st ed. dj............... *$20.00–$35.00*

Hillerman, Tony. *Coyote Waits.* NY. (1990). 1st ed. .... *$55.00–$75.00*

Hillerman, Tony. *Dance Hall of the Dead.* NY. (1973). 1st ed. 100 cc inscrb and sgn slipcase............... *$100.00–$125.00*

Hillerman, Tony. *Dark Wind.* NY. (1982). 1st ed. sgn, dj............... *$100.00–$175.00*

Hillerman, Tony. *Fly on the Wall.* NY. Harper & Row. 1971. 1st ed. dj...............
.... *$300.00–$500.00*

Hillerman, Tony. *Great Taos Bank Robbery and Other Indian Country Affairs.* Albuquerque. (1973). 1st ed. sgn, dj............... *$325.00–$450.00*

Hillerman, Tony. *Listening Woman.* NY. (1978). 1st ed. sgn, dj, slipcase. ....
.... *$295.00–$375.00*

Hillerman, Tony. *New Mexico, Rio Grande and Other Essays.* Portland. Graphic Arts Center. (1989). 1st ed. dj............... *$35.00–$45.00*

Hillerman, Tony. *People of Darkness.* NY. Harper & Row. 1980. 1st ed. dj...............
.... *$250.00–$325.00*

Hillerman, Tony. *People of Darkness.* Lon. 1982. 1st Eng ed. dj.......... *$60.00–$75.00*

Hillerman, Tony. *Sacred Clowns.* NY. Harper Collins. (1993). wrps. .... *$30.00–$45.00*

Hillerman, Tony. *Thief of Time.* NY. Harper & Row. 1988. 1st ed. dj.... *$25.00–$50.00*

Hillerman, Tony. *Thief of Time.* NY. Harper & Row. 1988. 1st ed. dj, sgn. ....
.... *$60.00–$75.00*

Hillier, Mary. *Automata & Mechanical Toys.* Lon. Bloomsbury Books. 1988. illus. 2nd ed. .... *$15.00–$30.00*

Hillier, Mary. *Dolls and Dollmakers.* NY. Putnam. (1968). 1st ed. .... *$40.00–$50.00*

Hillier, Mary. *History of Wax Dolls.* MD. Hobby House Press. (1985). 1st ed. dj. ....
.... *$18.00–$35.00*

Hills, Margaret T. (ed). *English Bible in America: A Bibliography . . .* NY. 1961.........
.... *$50.00–$80.00*

Hilton, James. *Goodbye, Mr. Chips.* Bos. Little Brown. 1935. 1st illus ed. dj. ....
.... *$22.00–$35.00*

Himes, Chester. *Case of Rape.* NY. Targ Editions. (1980). 1st ed. dj... *$90.00–$125.00*

Hinds, William. *American Communities*. . . Oneida. Office of the American Socialist. 1878. 176 pp. .... *$100.00–$150.00*

Hines, Millie. *Most Wonderful Dollhouse Book*. NY. Butterick Pub. (1979). dj............... .... *$8.00–$12.00*

Hingston, R. W. G. *Problems of Instinct and Intelligence*. Lon. 1928. 1st ed. cloth....... .... *$25.00–$35.00*

Hinton, S. E. *Tex*. NY. Delacorte. (1979). 1st ed. dj. .... *$25.00–$50.00*

Hinton, S. E. *That Was Then This Is Now*. NY. (1971). 1st ed. dj. .... *$60.00–$95.00*

Hinton, S E. *The Outsiders*. NY. 1967. 1st ed. dj. .... *$100.00–$250.00*

Hipkins, A. J. *Musical Instruments* . . . Lon. 1945. illus. .... *$65.00–$75.00*

Hiss Case. A Lesson for the American People. Wash. GPO. 1950. Nixon speech. .... *$35.00–$40.00*

Hiss, Alger. *In the Court of Public Opinion*. NY. Knopf. 1957. dj.......... *$15.00–$25.00*

Historic Illustrations of the Bible. Lon. Fisher. (1841). illus. 30 engr plates, ¾ mor...... ....*$100.00–$180.00*

History of Bluebeard. Windsor, VT. Cochran. nd. wrps. illus. 31 pp. .... *$75.00–$100.00*

History of Golf in Southern California. LA. 1925. 1st ed. .... *$75.00–$115.00*

History of Kane County. Salt Lake. Daughters of Utah Pioneers. 1970. 1st ed. illus. photos, maps, scarce. .... *$60.00–$75.00*

History of Los Angeles County. CA. Berkeley. 1959. reprint map........ *$95.00–$150.00*

History of Medicine and Surgery and Physicians and Surgeons of Chicago. Chi. 1922. 1st ed. .... *$150.00–$200.00*

History of Rock County, Wisconsin. Chi. 1879. ¾ lea. .... *$100.00–$125.00*

History of the 121st Regiment Pennsylvania Volunteers. Phil. 1906...... *$50.00–$80.00*

History of the 14th Armored Division. Atlanta. nd. .... *$55.00–$65.00*

History of the 157th Infantry Regiment, 4 June, '43–8 May, '45. Baton Rouge. 1946. 1st ed. illus. photos, fldg maps. .... *$95.00–$130.00*

History of the Connecticut Valley in Massachusetts. Phil. 1879. 2 vols. *$60.00–$80.00*

History of the Fifth Massachusetts Battery. Bos. 1902. .... *$175.00–$250.00*

History of the Fire & Police Depts of Paterson, NJ. Paterson. 1893. 1st ed. illus. plates. .... *$48.00–$60.00*

History of the Town of Johnson, VT. Burlington. 1907. .... *$20.00–$30.00*

History of the Translations or rather Versions of the English Bible Anno Domini 1380 to 1611. Alhambra. Braun. 1948. 1st facs ed. .... *$50.00–$80.00*

Hitchcock, Edward. *Elementary Geology*. NY. 1845. 3rd ed. .... *$50.00–$65.00*

Hitchcock, Edward, et al. *Report on the Geology of Vermont* . . . Claremont, NH. 1861. 2 vols. illus. fldg maps. .... *$60.00–$100.00*

Hitchens, Robert. *Black Spaniel*. NY. F A Stokes. (1905). 1st Amer ed. 380 pp. .... *$25.00–$35.00*

Hitchens, Robert. *Near East*. Century. 1913. 1st ed. 268 pp, plates....... *$60.00–$75.00*

Hitler, Adolph. *My New Order*. NY. (1941). 1st Amer ed. dj............... *$75.00–$100.00*

Hitt, Thomas. *Treatise on Fruit Trees*. Dublin. 1758. fldg copperplate engr, rbnd,.........
.... *$250.00–$325.00*

Hively, William (ed.) *Nine California Photographers*. Berkeley. Friends of the Bancroft Lib. 1980. illus. photos. black wrps. .... *$20.00–$30.00*

Hoare, H. W. *Evolution of the English Bible . . . from 1382 to 1885*. Lon. Murray. 1902. rev. 2nd ed. illus. .... *$30.00–$40.00*

Hoban, Russell. *Kleinzeit*. NY. 1974. 1st ed. dj...................................... *$25.00–$40.00*

Hobbs, William H. *Characteristics of Existing Glaciers*. NY. Macmillan. 1911. 1st ed. illus. ...., *$40.00–$60.00*

Hobley, C. W. *Bantu Beliefs and Magic*. Lon. 1922. illus...................... *$75.00–$125.00*

Hobson, R. L. *Chinese Art*. Macmillan. 1927. illus. clr plates, rbnd, ex-lib. ....
.... *$25.00–$50.00*

Hobson, R. L. *Chinese Pottery & Porcelain . . .* NY. Funk & Wagnalls. 1915. 2 vols. illus. 1,500cc, teg, 40 clr plates... *$150.00–$200.00*

Hochbaum, H. Albert. *Travels and Traditions of Waterfowl*. MN. 1955. 1st ed. illus. dj.. *$18.00–$30.00*

Hodge, Frederick Webb. *Handbook of American Indians North of Mexico*. GPO. 1907-10. 2 vols. illus. .... *$95.00–$150.00*

Hodge, Hirim. *Arizona . . .* NY. 1877. 1st ed. sgn............................. *$175.00–$225.00*

Hodgkin, A. E. *Archers Craft*. NY. Barnes. nd. illus. dj........................ *$30.00–$45.00*

Hoegh, Leo A. and Howard Doyle. *Timberwolf Tracks*. Wash. 1946. 1st ed. illus. photos, maps... *$80.00–$100.00*

Hoffa, Jimmy. *Name Is Hoffa*. Detroit. Teamsters. nd. wrps. illus. photos, 40 pp..........
.... *$15.00–$25.00*

Hoffer, Eric. *True Believer*. Secker. 1952. 1st UK ed dj. .... *$25.00–$35.00*

Hoffman, Abbie. *Best of Abbie Hoffman*. NY. Four Walls Eight Windows. 1989. 1st ed. dj.. *$18.00–$30.00*

Hoffman, Abbie. *Square Dancing in the Ice Age*. NY. Putnam. (1982). 1st ed ....
.... *$25.00–$45.00*

Hoffman, Abbie. *Steal This Book*. NY. Grove Press. 1971. 1st ed. illus. sgn. ....
.... *$100.00–$160.00*

Hoffman, Alice. *Property Of*. NY. Farrar, Straus & Giroux. (1977). 1st ed. author's first book, inscrb, dj. .... *$125.00–$175.00*

Hoffman, E. *The Nutcracker*. NY. 1984. 1st ed. dj................................ *$20.00–$45.00*

Hoffman, Heinrich. *Slovenly Peter*. NY. 1935. #138/1,500 cc. .... *$400.00–$600.00*

Hoffman, Professor. *King Ko Ko*. Lon. 1904. 1st ed. illus. .... *$50.00–$85.00*

Hoffman, Professor. *Later Magic*. Routledge...................................... *$40.00–$64.00*

Hoffman, Professor. *Modern Magic, A Practical Treatise on the Art of Conjuring*. Phila. nd. illus. 563 pp... *$60.00–$75.00*

Hoffman, William. *The Monitor*. NY. Carleton Pub. 1863. 1st ed. illus.......................
.... *$100.00–$125.00*

Holbrook, Florence. *Hiawatha Alphabet*. Chi. Rand McNally & Co. (1910). 1st ed. illus. by H D Pohl. bds. pictorial paste-down. .... *$45.00–$100.00*

Holbrook, Stewart. *The Columbia*. NY. 1956. 1st ed. sgn, dj. .... *$30.00–$50.00*

Holbrook, Stewart H. *Story of American Railroads*. NY. 1947. 1st ed. illus. dj. ....
.... *$20.00–$25.00*

Holden, C. F. *Louis Agassiz; His Life and Work*. NY. Putnam. 1893. 1st ed. illus. plates cloth. .... *$40.00–$60.00*

Holden, Edith. *Country Diary of an Edwardian Lady*. 1978. illus. a facsimile reproduction dj .... *$20.00–$35.00*

Holden, William Curry. *Spur Ranch*. Bos. (1934). 1st ed. map endpapers. ....
.... *$200.00–$300.00*

Holder, C. *Life in the Open*. NY. 1906. 1st ed. .... *$40.00–$50.00*

Holder, Charles Frederick. *Adventures of Torqua*. Bos. Little Brown. 1902. 1st ed. red pictorial. cloth. .... *$100.00–$140.00*

Holder, Charles Frederick. *All About Pasadena and Its Vicinity*. Bos. Lee & Shepard. 1889. 1st ed. illus. .... *$90.00–$180.00*

Holder, Charles Frederick. *Along the Forida Reef*. NY. Appleton. 1892. 1st ed. illus...
.... *$60.00–$100.00*

Holder, Charles Frederick. *Big Game at Sea*. Lon. 1908. 1st UK ed.... *$25.00–$40.00*

Holder, Charles Frederick. *Cannel Islands of California*. Chi. McClurg. 1910. 1st ed. illus. .... *$90.00–$180.00*

Holder, Charles Frederick. *Game Fishes of the World*. Lon. Hodder & Stoughton. (1913). illus. .... *$120.00–$200.00*

Holder, Charles Frederick. *Santa Catalina, an Isle of Summer*. SF. Murdock. 1895. 1st ed. illus. .... *$120.00–$500.00*

Hole, S. Reynolds. *Book About Roses*. Lon. Blackwood. 1887. clr frontis. ....
.... *$35.00–$65.00*

Holiday, Billie. *Lady Sings the Blues*. NY. Doubleday. 1956. 1st ed. 250 pp, dj. ....
.... *$65.00–$120.00*

Holland, Bob, Dan and Ray. *Good Shot*. NY. Knopf. 1946. 1st ed. illus. ....
.... *$25.00–$50.00*

Holland, W. J. *Moth Book*. NY. Doubleday Page & Co. 1904. illus. .... *$45.00–$75.00*

Hollander, Annette. *Bookcraft: How to Construct Note Pad Covers*. Lon. (1974). 1st ed. illus. .... *$20.00–$30.00*

Holley, Marietta. *Samantha at Saratoga*. Phila. 1887. illus. .... *$18.00–$25.00*

Holley, Marietta. *Samantha at the World's Fair*. NY. Funk & Wagnalls. 1893. 1st ed. illus. by Baron C DeGrimm, large 8vo, 694 pp, by Josiah Allen's Wife.. *$18.00–$40.00*

Holley, Marietta. *Samantha on the Race Problem*. NY. Dodd Mead Co. 1892. illus. ......
.... *$75.00–$100.00*

Holley, Marietta. *Samantha on the Woman Question*. Urbana. Univ. of Illinois Press. 1983. .... *$15.00–$30.00*

Holley, Mary Austin. *Texas Diary 1835–1838*. Austin. Texas Quarterly. 1965. wrps. illus. .... *$28.00–$35.00*

Holliday, Carl. *History of Southern Literature*. NY. 1906...................... *$30.00–$68.00*

Holling, H. C. *Book of Indians*. NY. Platt & Munk. (1935). illus. .... *$25.00–$40.00*

Holling, Holling C. *Claws of the Thunderbird*. Joliet. Volland. (1928). illus. by Holling. .... *$40.00–$55.00*

Hollis, A. C. *The Masai*. Oxford. 1905. illus. scarce. .... *$125.00–$225.00*

Hollon, W. Eugene. *Beyond the Cross Timbers*. Univ of OK Press. 1955. 1st ed. dj. .... *$30.00–$40.00*

Holloway, Mark. *Heavens on Earth*. Lon. 1951. 1st ed. dj.................... *$25.00–$40.00*

Holloway, W. R. *Indiana (Directory)*. Ind. 1870. 1st ed. illus. maps, lithos, cloth. .... *$150.00–$175.00*

Holme, C. G. *Children's Toys of Yesterday*. NY. Studio Ltd. 1932. illus. *$15.00–$25.00*

Holmes, Maurice. *From New Spain by Sea to the Californias*. Glendale. Arthur H Clark. 1963. illus. charts and plates, red cloth..................................... *$35.00–$50.00*

Holmes, O. W. *Common Law*. Bos. Little Brown. 1923...................... *$25.00–$35.00*

Holmes, Oliver Wendell. *Autocrat at the Breakfast Table*. Bos. 1894. 2 vols. illus. by Howard Pyle. .... *$25.00–$40.00*

Holmes, Oliver Wendell. *Complete Poetical Works of Oliver Wendell Holmes*. Bos. Houghton. 1895. illus. teg. .... *$30.00–$65.00*

Holmes, W. H. *Aboriginal Pottery of the Eastern United States*. DC. GPO. 1903. dark green cloth, clr plates. .... *$90.00–$175.00*

Holmstrom, J. G. *Modern Blacksmithing, Rational Horse Shoeing and Waggon Making*. Lon. 1913. illus. cloth... *$30.00–$50.00*

Holsinger, John B. *Descriptions of Virginia Caves*. VA Div of Mineral Resources. 1975. illus. b/w photos. maps of caves. 7 fldg maps of cave systems.............. *$40.00–$50.00*

Holy Bible. NY. Amer Bible Society. 1838, 1839. 26th ed. .... *$30.00–$40.00*

Holy Bible. Hartford. 1845. steel engr, 2 maps. .... *$50.00–$75.00*

Holy Bible. Phila. Berriman & Co. (1796). folio, calf. .... *$100.00–$150.00*

Holy Bible. Bos. 1812. lea. .... *$150.00–$175.00*

Holy Bible Contained in the Old and New Testaments and the Apocrypha. Bos. (1904). 14 vols. illus. full lea. .... *$250.00–$300.00*

Holy Bible Explained. Balt. Keatinge. 1808. illus. lea. .... *$50.00–$75.00*

Holzworth, John M. *Wild Grizzlies of Alaska*. NY. 1930. 1st ed. illus. dj..................... .... *$37.00–$60.00*

Homans, James E. *Self-propelled Vehicles*. . . NY. 1907. .... *$20.00–$35.00*

Homeopathic Domestic Medicine. NY. 1848................................... *$15.00–$25.00*

Honey, W. B. *German Porcelain*. Lon. Faber & Faber. 1947. 1st ed. folio. .... *$30.00–$40.00*

Honey, W. B. *Wedgewood Ware*. Lon. Faber & Faber. (1948). dj........... *$40.00–$50.00*

Hood, Grant. *Modern Methods in Horology*. Bradley Polytechnic Institute. 1944. illus.
.... *$22.00–$30.00*

Hood, Jennings and Charles J. Young. *American Orders & Societies and Their Decorations*. Phila. 1917. illus. clr plates. .... *$30.00–$45.00*

Hood, Thomas. *Epping Hunt*. NY. Derrydale Press. 1930. #229/490 cc, bds. ....
.... *$75.00–$100.00*

Hook, Sidney. *Reason, Social Myths and Democracy*. NY. 1940. 1st ed. dj. ....
.... *$25.00–$35.00*

Hook, Sidney, et al. *Meaning of Marx*. NY. Farrar. 1934. wrps. reprint. *$18.00–$25.00*

Hooker, William F. *Prairie Schooner*. Chi. 1918. 1st ed. illus............... *$60.00–$100.00*

Hooper, Lucy. *Lady's Book of Flowers and Poetry*. Phila. 1863. illus. clr plates. ....
.... *$40.00–$95.00*

Hoover, Herbert. *A Boyhood in Iowa*. NY. 1931. ltd ed. sgn.............. *$125.00–$150.00*

Hope, Bob. *They Got Me Covered*. Hollywood. 1941. 1st ed. wrps........ *$20.00–$30.00*

Hope, Laura Lee. *Bobbsey Twins and Their Schoolmates*. Grosset & Dunlap. 1928. dj.
.... *$20.00–$30.00*

Hope, Laura Lee. *Bobbsey Twins at Meadowbrook*. Grosset & Dunlap. 1915. Bobbsey Twins #7, dj. .... *$22.00–$27.00*

Hope, Laura Lee. *Bobbsey Twins in Cedar Camp*. Grosset & Dunlap. 1921. dj............
.... *$20.00–$25.00*

Hope, Laura Lee. *Bobbsey Twins of Lakeport*. Grosset & Dunlap. 1961. #1................
.... *$7.00–$10.00*

Hope, Laura Lee. *Bobbsey Twins on Blueberry Island*. Grosset & Dunlap. 1917. Bobbsey Twins #10, dj. .... *$25.00–$37.00*

Hope, Laura Lee. *Bunny Brown and His Sister Sue Playing Circus*. Grosset & Dunlap. 1916. dj. .... *$12.00–$18.00*

Hope, Laura Lee. *In the Land of Cotton*. Grosset & Dunlap. 1942. #35........................
.... *$12.00–$22.00*

Hope, Laura Lee. *Outdoor Girls of Cape Cod*. Grosset & Dunlap. 1924. dj.................
.... *$25.00–$35.00*

Hopkins, Gen. Frederick W. *Eulogy at Norwich, Vt., Feb.22, 1848 . . . Truman R. Ransom . . .* Hanover. 1848. 1st ed. wrps.. *$45.00–$75.00*

Hopkins, John Henry. *Two Discourses on the Second Advent of the Redeemer*. Burlington, VT. Goodrich. 1843. 3rd ed. wraps.................................... *$95.00–$125.00*

Hopkins, Rev. Samuel. *Historical Memoirs Relating to the Housatonic Indians*. NY. 1911. rprnt. .... *$60.00–$85.00*

Hopkins, William F. *Air-Ship Dragon-Fly*. NY. Doubleday. 1906. 1st ed. illus. by Ruth M Hallock... *$22.00–$27.50*

Hopkinson, E. *Records of Birds Bred in Captivity*. Lon. 1926............... *$45.00–$60.00*

Hopkinson, F. *Pathetic . . . Narrative of Miss Perrine*. Phila. 1841. *$900.00–$2,500.00*

Hoppe, Willie. *20 Years of Billiards*. NY. 1925. 1st ed. illus................. *$30.00–$45.00*

Horan, Jack. *Burnt Leather*. Mon. 1937. wrps. .... *$30.00–$40.00*

Horan, James D. *Confederate Agent*. Crown. (1960). 3rd ptg, dj, illus.. *$25.00–$35.00*

Horan, James D. *McKenney-Hall Portrait Gallery of American Indians*. NY. Crown. (1972). 1st ed. illus. in clr...................... *$90.00–$125.00*

Horgan, Paul. *Great River: The Rio Grande*. NY/Tor. Rinehart & Co. 1954. 2 vols. slipcase.................................. *$20.00–$40.00*

Horgan, Paul. *Lamy of Santa Fe*. Farrar, Straus & Giroux. (1975). 1st ed. dj................ .... *$30.00–$50.00*

Horgan, Paul. *No Quarter Given*. NY. Harper. 1935. 1st ed. green cloth...................... .... *$25.00–$35.00*

Horgan, Paul. *Peach Stone*. NY. Farrar, Straus & Giroux. (1967). 1st ed. dj. .... *$20.00–$65.00*

Horn, Stanley. *Robert E. Lee Reader*. Ind/NY. (1949). 1st ed. red cloth...................... .... *$20.00–$35.00*

Horn, Stanley F. *Invisible Empire. The Story of the Ku Klux Klan*. Bos. 1939. 1st ed. illus. dj.................................. *$45.00–$60.00*

Horn, Stanley Fitzgerald. *Decisive Battle of Nashville*. Baton Rouge. 1956. 1st ed. presentation copy, dj.................... *$25.00–$35.00*

Hornaday, W. T. *Our Vanishing Wildlife*. NY. Zoological Society. 1913. 1st ed. illus.... .... *$20.00–$40.00*

Hornaday, William T. *Campfires in the Canadian Rockies*. NY. Scribner's. 1906. 1st issue, maps.................... *$125.00–$150.00*

Hornbein, Thomas F. *Everest: The West Ridge*. SF. The Sierra Club. 1966. 201 pp, frontis, clr photos, map.................... *$60.00–$75.00*

Horne, Charles F. *Great Men and Famous Women*. NY. Selmar Hess Pub. (1894). 8 vols. 1st ed. illus. ¾ lea and pebbled cloth. .... *$250.00–$350.00*

Horne, Charles F (ed.) *Great Men and Famous Women*. NY. Selmar Hess Pub. (1894). 4 vols. 1st ed. illus. ¾ lea and pebbled cloth with gold lettering on cvr and spine. raised bands. marbleized endpapers................ *$90.00–$200.00*

Horne, George. *Pheasant Keeping for Amateurs*. Lon. illus................... *$55.00–$95.00*

Hornung, Ernest William. *Camera Fiend*. NY. Scribner's. 1911. 1st ed. illus............... .... *$90.00–$125.00*

Hornung, Ernest William. *Mr. Justice Raffles*. NY. 1909. 1st Amer ed....................... .... *$20.00–$40.00*

Hornung, Ernest William. *Stingaree*. NY. Scribner's. 1905. 1st ed. illus. .... *$30.00–$75.00*

Horst, Claude W. *Model Sail & Power Boats*. NY. Bruce Pub. 1939. illus. photos and plans (6 fold out), scarce. .... *$100.00–$135.00*

Horwich, Frances R. *Ding Dong School Book*. NY. Rand McNally & Co. 1953. 1st ed. illus. pictorial wrps.................... *$15.00–$25.00*

Hosaka, Edward Y. *Sport Fishing in Hawaii*. Honolulu. 1944. illus. dj. *$15.00–$25.00*

Houdini, Harry. *Miracle Mongers and Their Methods*. NY. Dutton. (1920). 1st ed. brown cloth. .... *$50.00–$60.00*

Hough, Franklin B. *History of Jefferson County in the State of New York . . .* Alb. 1854. 1st ed. 601 pp, illus. .... *$50.00–$100.00*

House, Edward J. *A Hunter's Camp-Fires.* 1909. .... *$35.00–$55.00*

House, Homer D. *Wildflowers of New York.* Albany. 1918. 2 vols. illus. folio, plates..... .... *$75.00–$150.00*

House, Homer D. *Wildflowers of New York.* Albany. Univ of State of New York. 1921. illus. folder with plates. .... *$50.00–$80.00*

Houseman, A. E. *Shropshire Lad.* Lon. (1907). 1st ed. sgn. .... *$225.00–$600.00*

Housman, Clemence. *Were-Wolf.* Lon. John Lane. 1896. 1st ed. illus............................ .... *$150.00–$225.00*

Houston, Henry C. *Thirty-second Maine Regiment of Infantry Volunteers.* Portland. Press of the Southworth Bros. 1903. .... *$35.00–$50.00*

Houston, John W. *Address On the Hist. of the Boundaries of the St. of Delaware.* Wilmington, DE. 1879. 1st ed. wrps. .... *$35.00–$50.00*

Houston, Julie. *Woman's Day Book of Best Loved Toys & Dolls.* NY. Sedgewood Press. (1982). dj. .... *$10.00–$15.00*

Hovey, C. M. *Magazine of Horticulture.* Bos. Hovey. 1893. Vol. 29...... *$25.00–$50.00*

Howard, Clark. *Zebra.* NY. Marek. 1979. dj. .... *$20.00–$25.00*

Howard, F. E. *English Church Woodwork.* Lon. Batsford. 1917. illus.... *$50.00–$80.00*

Howard, Joseph Kinsey. *Strange Empire.* NY. William Morrow & Co. 1952. illus. dj.. .... *$15.00–$40.00*

Howard, Oliver O. *Nez Perce Joseph. An Account of . . .* Bos. 1881. 1st ed. illus. plates, fldg maps. .... *$150.00–$500.00*

Howard, Robert. *Conan the Barbarian.* NY. Gnome Press. 1954. 1st ed. .... *$65.00–$125.00*

Howard, Robert. *King Conan.* Gnome Press. (1953). 1st ed. dj. .... *$75.00–$200.00*

Howard, Robert. *Singers in the Shadows.* Donald M Grant. 1970. 1st ed. dj. .... *$95.00–$150.00*

Howard, Robert. *Sword of Conan.* Gnome Press. 1952. 1st ed. dj..... *$125.00–$175.00*

Howe, Julia Ward. *World's Own.* Bos. Ticknor & Fields. 1857. 1st ed......................... .... *$175.00–$250.00*

Howell, A. H. *Birds of Alabama.* Montgomery. Dept of Game & Fisheries. 1924. illus.. .... *$20.00–$45.00*

Howells, W. D. *Boy's Town.* Harper. 1890. 1st ed. illus. .... *$20.00–$30.00*

Hower, Ralph Merle. *History of an Advertising Agency.* Cambridge. 1949. rev ed........ .... *$20.00–$45.00*

Howitt, William. *Boy's Adventures in the Wilds of Australia.* Bos. 1855. 1st US ed. illus. .... *$50.00–$65.00*

Howlett, E. *Driving Lessons.* NY. Russell & Son. 1894. 1st ed. illus. .. *$70.00–$110.00*

Hoyland, John. *Historical Survey of the Customs, Habits & Present Stae of the Gypsies.* York. 1816. 1st ed. 265 pp. .... *$225.00–$500.00*

Hrdlicka, Ales. *Early Man in South America.* Wash. GPO. 1912. wrps. *$40.00–$50.00*

Hrdlicka, Ales. *Skeletal Remains Suggesting or Attributed to Early Man in North America*. Wash. 1907. illus. bds. .... *$28.00–$40.00*

Hrdlicka, Ales. *Tuberculosis Among Certain Tribes*. Wash. GPO. 1909. wrps. illus. ......
.... *$25.00–$50.00*

Hubback, T. R. *To Far Western Alaska for Big Game*. Lon. Rowland Ward. 1929. 1st ed. illus. decorated green cloth. photos. clr map in pocket........................ *$115.00–$250.00*

Hubbard, Clifford L. *Dogs in Britain*. Lon. Macmillan. 1948. 1st ed. illus. dj. ....
.... *$35.00–$65.00*

Hubbard, Elbert. *In the Spotlight*. East Aurora. Roycrofters. 1917. illus. ....
.... *$20.00–$30.00*

Hubbard, Henry V., and Theodora Kimball. *An Introduction to the Study of Landscape Design*. Bos. Hubbard Educatonal Trust. 1967. rev ed. dj. .... *$22.00–$35.00*

Hubbard, L. Ron. *Battlefield Earth: A Saga of the Year 3000*. St Martin's Press. (1982). 1st ed. dj. .... *$35.00–$45.00*

Hubbard, L. Ron. *Dianetics: The Modern Science of Mental Health*. NY. Hermitage House. (1950). 1st ed. dj. .... *$95.00–$125.00*

Hubbard, L. Ron. *Slaves of Sleep*. Chi. Shasta Pub. 1948. 1st ed. dj...........................
.... *$300.00–$400.00*

Hubbard, L. Ron. *The Kingslayer*. LA. Fantasy Publishing Co. 1949. 1st ed. dj.........
.... *$85.00–$200.00*

Hubbard, L. Ron. *Triton and Battle of Wizards*. LA. Fantasy Publishing Co. 1949. 1st ed. dj.. *$150.00–$200.00*

Hubbard, L. Ron. *Typewriter in the Sky/Fear*. Gnome. 1951. 1st ed. *$175.00–$275.00*

Hubbard, W. *Narrative of the Troubles with the Indians in New England* . . . Bos. 1677. illus. map. .... *$22,000.00–$45,000.00*

Huddle, David. *High Spirits*. Bos. David R Godine. 1989. 1st ed. dj. .... *$20.00–$25.00*

Huddle, David. *Intimates*. Bos. David R Godine. 1993. 1st ed. dj.......... *$20.00–$25.00*

Huddle, David. *Only the Little Bone*. Bos. David R Godine. 1986. 1st ed. dj. ....
.... *$20.00–$25.00*

Hudson, Alvin. *Streetcars of Birmingham*. Birmingham. pub by author. wrps. spiral bound, scarce. .... *$100.00–$135.00*

Hudson, Derek. *Arthur Rackham: His Life and Work*. Lon. William Heinemann. 1960. 1st ed. illus. tipped-in clr plates. .... *$50.00–$75.00*

Hudson, W. H. *Afoot in England*. Lon. 1909. 1st ed. .... *$40.00–$60.00*

Hudson, W. H. *Crystal Age*. NY. Dutton. 1917. .... *$30.00–$35.00*

Hudson, W. H. *Far Away and Long Ago*. NY. Dutton. 1918. 1st Amer ed. ....
.... *$20.00–$35.00*

Hudson, W. H. *Green Mansions*. Lon. Duckworth. 1926. illus. aeg, bound by Bayntun.
.... *$100.00–$150.00*

Hudson, W. H. *Green Mansions*. Phila. 1935. 1,500 cc, sgn by illus.... *$75.00–$100.00*

Hudson, W. H. *Lost British Birds*. Lon. 1894. wrps. .... *$30.00–$50.00*

Huey, Pennock. *True Hist. of the Charge of 8th Pa. Cavalry at Chancelorsville*. Phila. 1883. 1st ed. illus... *$115.00–$145.00*

Huffaker, Clair. *One Time, I Saw Morning Come Home*. NY. 1974. dj, scarce. .... *$25.00–$45.00*

Hughes, Dorothy. *Davidian Report*. NY. (1952). 1st ed. sj................... *$25.00–$35.00*

Hughes, Dorothy. *Pueblo on the Mesa, the First Fifty Years of the University of New Mexico*. Albuquerque. 1939. 1st ed. illus. photos. .... *$50.00–$60.00*

Hughes, Dorothy. *Ride the Pink Horse*. NY. (1946). 1st ed. dj. .... *$75.00–$100.00*

Hughes, Elizabeth and Marion Lester. *Big Book of Buttons*. MA. 1991. illus. rprnt.... .... *$95.00–$125.00*

Hughes, G. B. *Horse Brasses*. Country Life. 1956. 1st ed. dj. .... *$30.00–$40.00*

Hughes, G. B. *Small Antique Silverware*. Batsford. 1957. illus. .... *$25.00–$50.00*

Hughes, Langston. *Book of Negro Humor*. NY. Dodd Mead. 1966. 1st ed. dj. .... *$50.00–$75.00*

Hughes, Langston. *Fields of Wonder*. NY. Knopf. 1947. 1st ed. dj. .... *$195.00–$250.00*

Hughes, Langston. *Poems From Black Africa*. Bloomington. 1963. 1st ed. dj............... .... *$55.00–$85.00*

Hughes, Langston. *Simple Stakes of Claim*. NY. Rinehart. 1957. 1st ed. dj................. .... *$75.00–$175.00*

Hughes, Richard B. *Pioneer Years in the Black Hills* . . . Glendale. Arthur H Clark. 1957. 1st ed. illus. photos. red cloth. .... *$75.00–$100.00*

Hult, Ruby E. *Steamboats in the Timber*. Caldwell. Caxton. 1953. 1st ed. illus. photos, dj. .... *$35.00–$50.00*

Hume, H. H. *Citrus Fruits and Their Culture*. Jacksonville. 1904. 1st ed. illus. .... *$35.00–$45.00*

Humphrey Maude. *Babes of the Year*. Stokes. 1888. illus. by author. *$150.00–$250.00*

Humphrey, Maude. *Treasury of Stories, Jingles and Rhymes*. Stokes. 1894. illus. clr plates.. *$135.00–$160.00*

Humphreys, Frederick. *Humphreys' Mentor and Medical Advisor*. NY. 1926. rev. ed. . ... *$15.00–$25.00*

Humphreys, G. R. *List of Irish Birds*. Dublin. 1939. 5th ed................... *$30.00–$45.00*

Humphries, Sydney. *Oriental Carpets*. Lon. Black. 1910. cloth, teg, 24 clr plates........ .... *$60.00–$80.00*

Hunt, Blanche Seale. *Little Brown Koko*. American Clrtype. (1940). 1st ed.................. .... *$50.00–$75.00*

Hunt, Lynne Bogue. *Our American Game Birds*. NY. Doubleday Doran. 1941. illus. dj. .... *$35.00–$65.00*

Hunt, Maj. Elvid. *History of Fort Leavenworth, 1827–1927*. Ft. Leavenworth, KS. 1926. illus. sgn... *$25.00–$40.00*

Hunt, Wilson Price. *Overland Diary of Wilson Price Hunt*. Ashland. The Oregon Book Society. 1973. illus. 600 cc.. *$40.00–$60.00*

Hunter, Alexander. *Women of the Debateable Land*. DC. Corden Publishing. 1912. 1st ed. illus. plates, fldg map, scarce. .... *$295.00–$350.00*

Hunter, Dard. *My Life With Paper*. NY. Knopf. 1858. dj................... *$100.00–$200.00*

Hunter, Dard. *Papermaking Through Eighteen Centuries*. NY. William Edwin Rudge. 1930. 1st ed. illus... *$40.00–$60.00*

Hunter, Dard. *Papermaking: The History and Technique of an Ancient Craft*. NY. Knopf. 1947. 2nd ed. .... *$90.00–$100.00*

Hunter, George L. *Decorative Furniture*. Phila. 1923. 1st ed. illus. ...... *$75.00–$95.00*

Hunter, J. A. and Daniel P. Mannix. *Tales of the African Frontier*. NY. Harper. (1954). 1st ed. illus. photo plates, dj.. *$45.00–$75.00*

Huntington, Dwight W. *Our Big Game*. NY. Scribner's. 1904. 1st ed. ... *$40.00–$50.00*

Huntington, Emily. *Cooking Garden*. np. (1885). 1st ed. illus. by Jessie Shepherd. .... *$80.00–$120.00*

Huntington, R. Gen. *Grant's Arabian Horses*. Phil. Lippincott. 1885. 1st ed. illus. plates.. *$225.00–$250.00*

Hurd, D. H. *Town and City Atlas of the State of New Hampshire*. Bos. 1892. folio........ .... *$150.00–$250.00*

Hurn, Ethel A. *Wisconsin Women in the War Between the States*. WI. (1911). .... *$40.00–$60.00*

Huse, Caleb. *Supplies For the Confederate Army* . . . Bos. 1904. 1st ed. wrps. .... *$85.00–$125.00*

Hussey, John A, (ed.) *Voyage of the Raccoon: A Secret Journal of a Visit to Oregon, California and Hawaii*. SF. Book Club of Calif. 1958. illus. drawings, cloth-backed mar bds... *$50.00–$75.00*

Hutchings, James Mason. *Seeking the Elephant* . . . Glendale. Arthur H Clark. 1980. 1st ed. 1/750 cc, red cloth. .... *$50.00–$80.00*

Hutchins, Samuel. *Theory of the Universe*. NY. 1868. .... *$60.00–$75.00*

Hutchinson, Francis. *An Historical Essay Concerning Witchcraft*. Lon. 1718. 1st ed. ¾ calf. .... *$325.00–$400.00*

Hutchinson, Horace G. *Golf*. Lon. 1898. illus. 6th ed........................... *$45.00–$50.00*

Hutchinson, Horace G. *Golfing: The Oval Series of Games*. Lon. Rutledge. 1903. 7th ed. .... *$60.00–$75.00*

Hutchinson, Rev. H. N. *Prehistoric Man and Beast*. NY. 1897. illus. by Cecil Aldin, 298 pp. .... *$35.00–$55.00*

Huxley, Aldous. *Along the Road*. NY. Doran. (1925). bds. lea spine. label. 162/250 cc. sgn.. *$50.00–$75.00*

Huxley, Aldous. *Brave New World*. Lon. Chatto & Windus. 1932. 1st ed. dj. .... *$600.00–$1,500.00*

Huxley, Aldous. *Brave New World Revisited*. NY. 1958. 1st ed. dj. .... *$20.00–$50.00*

Huxley, Aldous. *Brief Candles: Stories*. NY. 1930. 1st Amer ed. .... *$50.00–$75.00*

Huxley, Aldous. *Defeat of Youth & Other Poems*. Oxford. B H Blackwell. 1918. 1st ed. stiff wrps. .... *$175.00–$225.00*

Huxley, Aldous. *Eyeless in Gaza*. Lon. Chatto & Windus. 1936. 1st ed. dj..................... .... *$75.00–$150.00*

Huxley, Aldous. *Leda*. NY. George Doran. 1920. 1st ed. .... *$25.00–$50.00*

Huxley, Aldous. *Point, Counterpoint*. Lon. 1928. 1st UK ed. dj............ *$60.00–$90.00*

Huxley, Aldous. *Themes and Variations*. Lon. 1932. 1st ed. dj........... *$100.00–$300.00*

Huxley, Aldous. *Time Must Have a Stop*. NY. Harper. 1944. 1st ed. dj. *$45.00–$150.00*

Huxley, Julian. *Huxley's Diary of the Voyage of H.M.S. Rattlesnake*. NY. Doubleday. 1936. 1st Amer ed... *$40.00–$50.00*

Huxley, Julian. *Science and Social Needs*. NY. Harper & Brothers. 1935. inscrb........... .... *$30.00–$60.00*

Huxley, Leonard. *Life and Letters of Thomas Henry Huxley*. Lon. 1903. 3 vols. 2nd ed. .... *$40.00–$50.00*

Huxley, Thomas. *American Address with a Lecture on the Study of Biology*. NY. 1877. 1st ed. illus... *$50.00–$75.00*

Huxley, Thomas. *Evidence as to Man's Place in Nature*. Lon. Norgate. 1863. 1st ed. ... . *$300.00–$600.00*

Huxley, Thomas. *Evidence as to Man's Place in Nature*. NY. Appleton. 1863. 1st Amer ed. .... *$120.00–$400.00*

Huxley, Thomas. *Lay Sermons, Addresses & Reviews*. Lon. 1870. .... *$30.00–$45.00*

Huxley, Thomas. *Manual of the Anatomy of Invertebrate Animals*. Appleton. 1888....... .... *$30.00–$50.00*

Huxley, Thomas. *Yoga*. Lon. 1902. 1st ed. wrps. 43 pp. .... *$75.00–$100.00*

Hyatt, Arthur H. (ed.). *Book of Sundial Mottoes*. Lon/NY. 1903. 1st ed. aeg. .... *$60.00–$90.00*

Hyatt, Rebecca Dougherty. *"Marthy Law's Kiverlid."* pub by author. (1937)............... .... *$25.00–$35.00*

Hyde, H. Montgomery (ed.). *Trials of Oscar Wilde*. Lon/Edin/Glas. William Hodge & Co. (1952). illus. 4th reprnt... *$15.00–$30.00*

Hyer, J. K., W. Starring and A. Hann. *Dictionary of the Sioux Language*. New Haven. 1968. ltd 300 cc. .... *$75.00–$100.00*

Ibsen, Henrik. *Doll's House*. NY. 1889. 1st Amer ed............................ *$25.00–$35.00*

Ibsen, Henrik. *Peer Gynt*. Garden City. 1929. 1st ed. .... *$50.00–$75.00*

Illingworth, Frank. *North of the Circle*. NY. Philosophical Library. (1951). 1st ed. illus. dj. .... *$15.00–$30.00*

Illustrated Catalogue of Iron Toys. Fullerton, PA. Dent Hardware Co. c 1900. pictorial wrps, 39 pp. .... *$75.00–$100.00*

Illustrated Catalogue of Lightning Conductors. Nottingham, England. Blackburn, Starling & Co, Ltd. 1924. pictorial wrps, 8 pp. .... *$50.00–$75.00*

Illustrated Catalogue of School Merchandise. Bos. J L Hammett Co. 1872–73. printed wrps, illus. .... *$150.00–$125.00*

Illustrated Catalogue of US Cartridge Company's Collection of Firearms. MA. (c1903). illus. 140 pp.. *$50.00–$75.00*

Illustrated List of Bride Cakes. Chester, England. Bolland & Sons. c1893. beige wrps, 44 pp. .... *$50.00–$75.00*

Illustrated Memoir of the World War. Conn. National Pub Co. 1930. 1st ed. illus. folio presentation copy. .... *$12.00–$25.00*

Ilustrated Catalogue of Railway and Contractors Supplies. Buda Foundry & Mfg Co. 1902. illus. cat. .... *$75.00–$125.00*

Imray, James. *Sailing Directions for the English Channel, the Bristol Channel, and South & South West Coasts of Ireland.* Lon. Imray. 1850. illus. .... *$50.00–$80.00*

Indian Narratives. *Containing a Correct and Interesting History of the Indian Wars.* Claremont. 1854. .... *$55.00–$75.00*

Ingalls, Albert G. (ed.). *Amateur Telescope Making.* NY. Scientific America Inc. 1970. 3 vols. .... *$50.00–$75.00*

Inge, William. *Dark at the Top of the Stairs.* NY. (1958). 1st ed. dj. ...... *$30.00–$40.00*

Inge, William. *Dark at the Top of the Stairs.* NY. Random House. (1958). 1st ed. dj. .... *$75.00–$125.00*

Ingersoll, C. J. *Discourse Concerning the Influence of America on the Mind.* Phila. 1823. .... *$50.00–$75.00*

Ingersoll, Ernest. *Crest of the Continent.* Chi. 1885. 1st ed. frontis, engr. .... *$25.00–$40.00*

Ingersoll, Ernest. *Goldfields of the Klondike and the Wonders of Alaska.* Edgewood. ... . *$45.00–$60.00*

Ingham, George Thomas. *Digging Gold Among the Rockies.* Phila. 1888. illus. .... *$100.00–$250.00*

Ingraham, I. (ed.). *Sunny South or Southerner at Home.* 1860. 1st ed. .... *$100.00–$250.00*

Inman, Col. Henry. *Old Santa Fe Trail, Story of a Great Highway.* Topeka. 1916. illus. .... *$25.00–$35.00*

Inman, Henry. *Great Salt Lake Trail.* NY. 1898. 1st ed. illus. 529 pp, plates. .... *$75.00–$100.00*

Inn, Henry. *Chinese Houses and Gardens.* Honolulu. 1940. illus. ltd 2,000 cc, sgn....... .... *$50.00–$85.00*

Instructions for Voluntary Observers of the Signal Service, United States Army. Wash. GPO. 1882. illus. 108 pp. .... *$35.00–$55.00*

Investigation of the Fur-Seal and Other Fisheries of Alaska. DC. GPO. 1889. illus. photos, maps. .... *$40.00–$80.00*

Ipsen, Ludvig S. *Book Plates.* Bos. 1904. illus. .... *$75.00–$100.00*

Iron Toys. PA. Dent Hardware. wrps. illus. cat. .... *$48.00–$55.00*

Irving, John. *158-Pound Marriage.* NY. Random House. (1974). 1st ed. inscrb with full-page self-caricature in wrestling mode, dj. .... *$350.00–$800.00*

Irving, John. *Hotel New Hampshire.* 1981. 1st ed. dj. .... *$35.00–$45.00*

Irving, John. *Widow for One Year.* NY. Randon House. (1998). 1st ed. dj. .... *$20.00–$40.00*

Irving, John. *World According to Garp*. NY. Dutton. 1978. 1st ed. dj.... *$45.00–$85.00*

Irving, John Treat. *Indian Sketches Taken During an Expedition to the Pawnee . . .* Phila. 1835. 2 vols. ½ mor................... *$150.00–$235.00*

Irving, Washington. *Astoria or Anecdotes of an Enterprise Beyond Rocky Mountains*. Phila. 1836. 2 vols. 1st Amer ed. .... *$350.00–$500.00*

Irving, Washington. *Legends of the Alhambra*. Phil/Lon. Lippincott. 1909. illus. George Hood. blue cloth, pictorial pastedown................. *$25.00–$50.00*

Irving, Washington. *Rip Van Winkle*. Phil. David McKay. (1921). illus. front cvr pastedown by Wyeth, 8 clr plates. .... *$100.00–$150.00*

Irving, Washington. *Works of Washington Irving*. NY. Putnam. (1895). 40 vols. lea marb bds.................... *$1,000.00–$2,000.00*

Irwin, W. *Highlights of Manhattan*. NY. (1927). 1st ed. illus. .... *$20.00–$40.00*

Isaacs, Edith J. R. *Negro in the American Theatre*. NY. Theatre Arts, Inc. 1947. illus. photos, 143 pp. .... *$35.00–$50.00*

Isadora Duncan, Twenty-four Studies by Arnold Genthe. NY. Mitchell Kennerly. 1929. 1st ed. teg.................. *$125.00–$175.00*

Isherwood, Christopher. *Berlin of Sally Bowles*. Lon. Hogarth. 1975. 1st collected ed. dj................... *$50.00–$75.00*

Isherwood, Christopher. *Condor and the Cows*. NY. 1949. 1st Amer ed..................... .... *$40.00–$55.00*

Isherwood, Christopher. *Exhumations*. NY. 1966. 1st ed. dj................. *$25.00–$40.00*

Isherwood, Christopher. *Prater Violet*. Lon. Methuen & Co. 1946. 1st ed. dj.............. .... *$50.00–$75.00*

Isherwood, Christopher. *Single Man*. NY. 1964. 1st ed. dj. .... *$25.00–$35.00*

***J. S. Lothrop's Champaign County Directory 1870–71* . . .**Chi. 1871. illus. fldg map... .... *$55.00–$75.00*

Jackson, C. *Foreign Bodies in the Air and Food Passages*. MA. 1924. .. *$50.00–$75.00*

Jackson, Frederick G. *Thousand Days in the Arctic*. NY. 1899. 1st ed. illus. fldg maps. .... *$85.00–$140.00*

Jackson, Helen Hunt. *Glimpses of California and the Missions*. Bos. Little Brown. 1914. plates................... *$35.00–$40.00*

Jackson, Helen Hunt (H. H.). *Ramona*. Roberts Bros. 1884. 1st ed. green cloth. .... *$350.00–$500.00*

Jackson, Helen Hunt. *Sonnets & Lyrics*. Bos. 1886. 1st ed. cloth. .... *$30.00–$75.00*

Jackson, Jesse. *Tessie*. NY. Harper & Row. 1968. 1st ed. dj. .... *$25.00–$35.00*

Jackson, Leroy F. *Peter Patter Book*. Chi. Rand McNally & Co. 1918. 1st ed. illus. green bds with pictorial paste-down................... *$35.00–$95.00*

Jackson, Sheldon. *Alaska and the Missions on the North Pacific Coast*. NY. 1880. engr, 400 pp, map. .... *$50.00–$125.00*

Jackson, Shirley. *Bird's Nest*. NY. Farrar, Straus, Young. (1954). 1st ed. 276 pp, dj. .... *$50.00–$100.00*

Jackson, Shirley. *Haunting of Hill House*. NY. 1959. 1st ed. dj. .... *$150.00–$475.00*

Jackson, Shirley. *Road Through the Wall*. NY. Farrar, Straus. 1948. 1st ed. dj, author's scarce first book... *$200.00–$375.00*

Jackson, Shirley. *The Lottery*. 1949. 1st ed. dj. .... *$150.00–$225.00*

Jackson, Shirley. *The Sundial*. NY. Farrar, Straus & Cudahy. (1958). 1st ed. dj............ .... *$65.00–$100.00*

Jackson, Shirley. *We Have Always Lived in the Castle*. NY. Viking. (1962). 1st ed. dj. . ... *$85.00–$155.00*

Jacobs, Flora Gill. *Dolls' Houses in America*. NY. Scribner's. (1974). 1st ed. illus. dj... .... *$35.00–$60.00*

Jacobs, Flora Gill. *History of Doll's Houses Four: Centuries of the Domestic World in Miniature*. NY. Scribner's. 1953. 1st ed. dj................................. *$40.00–$50.00*

Jacobs, Laura. *Barbie, What a Doll!*. NY. Artabras. (1994). 1st ed. illus. dj. .... *$15.00–$25.00*

Jacobs, Michael. *Rebel Invasion of Maryland, Penn. & Battle of Gettysburg*. Gettysburg. 1909. wrps. .... *$35.00–$40.00*

Jacobsen, Carol L. *Past and Present Portrait of Dolls*. CA. Mandarin Pub. sgn, dj...... .... *$20.00–$25.00*

James, Cyril Lionel Robert. *History of Negro Revolt*. Lon. Fact. 1938. 1st ed. wrps. ... . *$75.00–$125.00*

James, Edgar. *Allen Outlaws and Their Career of Crime* . . . Balt. 1912. 1st ed. wrps. illus. .... *$45.00–$55.00*

James, G. W. *Practical Basket Making*. Pasadena. nd. illus. .... *$100.00–$125.00*

James, George W. *Through Ramona's Country*. Bos. 1909. 1st ed. .... *$55.00–$65.00*

James, George W. *What the White Race May Learn from the Indian*. Chi. Forbes & Co. 1908. illus. .... *$85.00–$100.00*

James, George Wharton. *Grand Canyon of Arizona*. Bos. Little Brown. 1910. fldg map. .... *$65.00–$175.00*

James, George Wharton. *Indian Basketry*. The Rio Grande Press. (1970). 3rd ed. .... *$25.00–$35.00*

James, George Wharton. *Indian Blankets and Their Makers*. NY. 1937. new ed. .... *$75.00–$100.00*

James, George Wharton. *Utah the Land of Blossoming Valleys*. Bos. 1922. 1st ed. illus. clr. .... *$65.00–$115.00*

James, Henry. *Bostonians*. Lon/NY. Macmillan. (1886). 1st Amer ed. 1 vol................. .... *$150.00–$250.00*

James, Henry. *Bostonians*. Lon. 1886. 3 vols. boxed. .... *$900.00–$1,500.00*

James, Henry. *Daisy Miller*. Lon. Macmillan. 1879. 2 vols. 1st UK ed...................... .... *$300.00–$400.00*

James, Henry. *Ghostly Tales of Henry James*. New Brunswick. Rutgers Univ Press. 1948. dj.. *$35.00–$45.00*

James, Henry. *Letters of Henry James*. NY. Scribner's. 1920. 1st Amer ed. illus......... .... *$25.00–$40.00*

James, Henry. *Notebooks of Henry James*. NY. 1947. 1st ed. cloth, dj. . *$45.00–$50.00*

James, Henry. *Roderick Hudson*. Bos. James Osgood. 1876. 1st ed. green cloth. author's first novel. .... *$60.00–$90.00*

James, Henry. *Siege of London*. Bos. Osgood. 1883. 1st ed. green cloth. .... *$225.00–$300.00*

James, Henry. *The Ambassadors*. NY. 1903. 1st Amer ed. dj............ *$100.00–$300.00*

James, Henry. *Washington Square*. NY. Harper. 1881. 1st ed. illus. by George Du Maurier... *$100.00–$275.00*

James, Henry. *What Maisie Knew*. Chi/NY. Herbert S Stone. 1897. 1st Amer ed. .... *$100.00–$200.00*

James, Jesse, Jr. *Jesse James, My Father.* Missouri. 1899. wrps........ *$100.00–$300.00*

James, P. D. *A Certain Justice*. NY. Knopf. 1997. 1st ed. sgn, dj. .... *$30.00–$45.00*

James, P. D. *Children of Men*. NY. Knopf. 1993. 1st Amer ed. sng, dj.. *$30.00–$50.00*

James, P. D. *Death of an Expert Witness*. Lon. Faber and Faber. 1977. 1st ed. sgn, dj. .. .. *$100.00–$150.00*

James, P. D. *Innocent Blood*. Lon. Faber and Faber. 1980. 1st ed. sgn, dj...................... .... *$50.00–$125.00*

James, P. D. *Innocent Blood*. Lon. Faber and Faber. 1980. 1st ed. sgn, dj...................... .... *$50.00–$85.00*

James, P. D. *Innocent Blood*. NY. Scribner's. 1980. 1st ed. 1st Amer ed. dj.................. .... *$20.00–$35.00*

James, P. D. *Skull Beneath the Skin*. NY. 1982. 1st ed. dj....................... *$40.00–$50.00*

James, P. D. *Taste for Death*. Lon. 1986. 1st ed. sgn, dj. .... *$75.00–$100.00*

James, P. D. and T. A. Critchley. *Maul and the Pear Tree: the Ratcliff Murders 1811*. NY. Mysterious Press. 1986. dj... *$15.00–$20.00*

James, Weldon Johnson. *God's Trombones*. NY. Viking Press. (1927). illus. no dj........ .... *$30.00–$60.00*

James, Will. *Dark Horse*. NY. Scribner's. 1939. 1st ed. illus. cloth, clr frontis. .... *$100.00–$175.00*

James, Will. *Lone Cowboy: My Life Story*. NY. Scribner's. 1930. 1st ed. illus. by author, dj... *$150.00–$250.00*

James, Will. *Three Mustangeers*. NY. 1933. 1st ed. .... *$45.00–$65.00*

James, William. *Will to Believe*. NY. 1897. 1st ed. .... *$200.00–$300.00*

Jane's Fighting Ships. 1920. .... *$85.00–$100.00*

Jane's Fighting Ships. 1971. .... *$20.00–$30.00*

Jane, Fred T. *Imperial Russian Navy.* Lon. 1899. illus....................... *$125.00–$200.00*

Jansen, Murk. *Feebleness of Growth & Congenital Dwarfism . . .* Lon. 1921. 1st ed. .... *$60.00–$80.00*

Janvier, T. A. *Aztec Treasure-House*. NY. 1890. 1st ed. .... *$50.00–$75.00*

Janvier, Thomas A. *In the Sargasso Sea*. NY. Harper. 1898. 1st ed. ...... *$30.00–$45.00*

Japan Imperial Government Railways Guide. Tokyo. 1915. 62 pp, maps, illus..............
.... *$40.00–$45.00*

Jarrell, Randall. *Pictures from an Institution*. NY. Knopf. 1954. 1st ed. dj. ....
.... *$35.00–$75.00*

Jarrell, Randall. *Third Book of Criticism*. NY. Farrar, Straus & Giroux. (1969). 1st ed.
dj. .... *$45.00–$60.00*

Jay, William. *Inquiry Into Character & Tendency of American Anti-Slavery Soc*. 1838.
6th ed. .... *$40.00–$50.00*

Jay, William. *Review of the Causes and Consequences of the Mexican War*. Fos.
Benjamin B Murray & Co. 1849. 1st ed. inscrb. .... *$140.00–$200.00*

Jay, William. *View of the Action of the Federal Government, In Behalf of Slavery*. NY.
1839. green cloth, 217 pp. .... *$75.00–$175.00*

Jeans, James. *New Background of Science*. NY. Macmillan. 1933. .... *$15.00–$25.00*

Jeans, James. *Through Space and Time*. NY. Macmillan. 1934. .... *$15.00–$40.00*

Jeffers, Robinson. *Dear Judas and Other Poems*. NY. Horace Liveright. 1929. 1st ed.
1/375 cc, sgn, slipcase. .... *$250.00–$300.00*

Jefferson, Joseph. *Autobiography of Joseph Jefferson*. NY. 1890. .... *$20.00–$30.00*

Jefferson, Joseph. *Life and Morals of Jesus of Nazareth*. Wash. GPO. 1904. facs.........
.... *$70.00–$150.00*

Jeffrey, William H. *Richmond Prisons 1861–62*. VT. nd. 1st ed. .... *$75.00–$100.00*

Jeffries, Richard. *Gamekeeper at Home*. Lon. Smith, Elder. 1892. new ed. illus.........
.... *$35.00–$60.00*

Jeffries, Richard. *Gamekeeper at Home*. Bos. 1880. aeg, illus. .... *$40.00–$50.00*

Jehl, Francis. *Menlo Park: Reminiscences*. Dearborn, Mich. Edison Insitute. 1937.
3 vols. 1st complete ed. stiff wrps... *$95.00–$150.00*

Jehl, Francis. *Menlo Park: Reminiscences*. Dearborn, Mich. Edison Institute. 1936.
2 parts in one vol, 430 pp, dj... *$60.00–$85.00*

Jekyll, Gertrude. *Children and Gardens*. Lon. 1908. .... *$35.00–$50.00*

Jekyll, Gertrude. *Gardener's Testament*. Lon. Country Life. (1937). 1st ed. illus. ....
.... *$75.00–$90.00*

Jekyll, Gertrude. *Home and Garden*. Lon. Longmans, Green. 1901. illus. new ed. ....
.... *$50.00–$90.00*

Jekyll, Gertrude. *Lilys for English Gardens*. Covent Garden. 1901. 1st ed. ....
.... *$60.00–$75.00*

Jekyll, Gertrude. *Old West Surrey*. Lon. 1904. 1st ed. photos. .... *$100.00–$150.00*

Jekyll, Gertrude. *Wood and Garden*. Lon. Longmans, Green. 1899. illus. 4th
impression.. *$100.00–$150.00*

Jellicoe, Viscount. *Crisis of the Naval War*. NY/Lon. 1920. illus. plates, pocket charts..
.... *$40.00–$65.00*

Jenkins, C. Francis. *Boyhood of an Inventor*. Wash. 1931. inscrb. ..... *$85.00–$110.00*

Jenkins, Dan. *Best 18 Golf Holes in America*. NY. 1966. 1st ed. dj. ...... *$22.00–$32.00*

Jenness, Diamond. *Indians of Canada*. Ottawa. Nat'l Museum of Canada. 1955. illus. red cloth. .... *$35.00–$65.00*

Jennett, Sean. *Making of Books*. Lon. Faber & Faber. 1951. illus. .... *$30.00–$50.00*

Jennings, John. *Salem Frigate*. NY. Doubleday & Co. (1946). 1st ed. gray-green cloth, dj. .... *$15.00–$25.00*

Jennings, John. *Shadow and the Glory*. NY. Reynal & Hitchcock. (1943). 1st ed. blue decorated cloth, dj. .... *$15.00–$25.00*

Jennings, N. A. *Texas Ranger*. NY. Scribner's. 1899. 1st ed. 321 pp, glassine dj. .... *$150.00–$500.00*

Jennings, Preston J. *Book of Trout Flies*. Crown. 1935. 1st trade ed. ..... *$20.00–$45.00*

Jennings, Preston J. *Book of Trout Flies*. Derrydale Press. 1935. ltd 850, numbered..... .... *$250.00–$375.00*

Jennings, Robert. *Horse and His Diseases*. Phila. 1860. 1st ed. illus. ... *$25.00–$35.00*

Jensen, Gerald E. *Early American Dollhouse Miniatures*. PA. Chilton Book Co. (1981). 1st ed. dj. .... *$20.00–$25.00*

Jenson, Andrew. *Historical Record, a Monthly Periodical*. Salt Lake. vols 7-9. 1st ed.. .... *$100.00–$150.00*

Jessee, Dean C. (comp. & ed.). *Personal Writings of Joseph Smith*. Salt Lake. 1985. illus. photos, dj. .... *$50.00–$65.00*

Jessup, Henry Harris. *Women of the Arabs*. NY. Dodd Mead. (1973). illus. green decorated cloth. .... *$75.00–$125.00*

Jewett, Charles. *Speeches, Poems and Miscellaneous Writings on. . .Temperance and Liquor Traffic*. Bos. Jewett. 1849. 1st ed. illus. 200 pp. .... *$75.00–$100.00*

Jewett, Paul. *New England Farrier*. Exeter. 1826. 4th ed. .... *$130.00–$165.00*

Jewett, Sarah Orne. *Country By-Ways*. Bos. Houghton Mifflin. 1881. 1st ed. 249 pp, green cloth, 2,000 cc printed. .... *$125.00–$150.00*

Jewett, Sarah Orne. *Country of the Pointed Firs*. Bos. Houghton Mifflin. 1896. 1st ed. 1/984cc .... *$120.00–$155.00*

Jewett, Sarah Orne. *Deephaven*. Bos. 1877. 1st ed. cloth. .... *$30.00–$45.00*

Jillson, Willard R. *Coal Industry in Kentucky: An Historical Sketch*. Frankfort. 1922. 1st ed. illus. .... *$35.00–$50.00*

Jobe, Joseph. *Great Age of Sail*. Switzerland. Lausanne. (1976). illus. trans. by Michael Kelly, slipcase. .... *$50.00–$100.00*

Jobe, Joseph. *Great Tapestries*. Lausanne. 1965. large folio, dj, slipcase. .... *$50.00–$60.00*

Jocelyn, Stephen Perry. *Mostly Alkali: A Biography*. Caldwell. Caxton Printers. 1953. 1st ed. illus. photos, map. .... *$35.00–$50.00*

Johl, Janet Pagter. *Still More About Dolls*. NY. H L Lindquist. (1950). 1st ed. illus. dj. .... *$25.00–$75.00*

Johl, Janet Pagter. *Your Dolls and Mine*. NY. H L Lindquist. 1952. 1st ed. illus. dj, sgn. .... *$45.00–$60.00*

John F Kennedy Memorial Miniature.... NY. Random House. (1966). 4 vols. 1st ed. illus. by Jan Menting, cloth, slipcase. .... ***$60.00–$100.00***

John, Erica. *Fear of Flying.* NY. Holt, Rinehart. 1973. 1st ed. sgn, dj. ***$95.00–$125.00***

Johns, Henry T. *Life with the Forty-ninth Massachusetts Volunteers.* Pittsfield, MA. Alvord. 1864. .... ***$125.00–$150.00***

Johns, Rowland. *Our Friend the Scottish Terrier.* NY. (1933). 1st ed. dj. .... ***$15.00–$22.00***

Johnson's Illustrated Family Atlas. NY. 1863. folio. .... ***$385.00–$425.00***

Johnson's New Illustrated Family Atlas of the World. NY. 1865. folio, mor, maps........ .... ***$600.00–$750.00***

Johnson, Audrey. *Furnishing Dolls' Houses.* Long. G Bell & Sons Ltd. 1972. 1st ed. illus. dj. .... ***$25.00–$50.00***

Johnson, Burges. *Lost Art of Profanity.* Bobbs Merrill. 1948. 1st ed. dj. ***$30.00–$40.00***

Johnson, Clifton. *Picturesque Hudson.* NY. 1909. 1st ed. illus. .... ***$25.00–$35.00***

Johnson, Edward, M.D. *Hydropathy.* Lon. 1843. illus. .... ***$60.00–$80.00***

Johnson, G. *Ante-Bellum North Carolina.* 1937. .... ***$60.00–$75.00***

Johnson, Harold. *Who's Who in the American League.* 1935. .... ***$27.00–$35.00***

Johnson, Harry H. *British Central Africa.* NY. Edward Arnold. 1897. fldg maps, illus, pictorial cloth. .... ***$150.00–$350.00***

Johnson, Haynes. *Bay of Pigs.* NY. Norton. 1964. illus. maps, dj. .... ***$20.00–$30.00***

Johnson, Helen Kendrick. *Woman and the Republlic.* NY. 1897. 1st ed. 327 pp. .... ***$65.00–$75.00***

Johnson, Ithiel. *Story of My Life.* VT. Free Press. 1912. illus. green cloth. .... ***$15.00–$20.00***

Johnson, J. H. *Great Western Gun Works.* 1873. cat. .... ***$95.00–$150.00***

Johnson, James R. *Treatise on the Medicinal Leech.* Lon. Longman, Hurst, Rees, Orme, and Brown. 1816. 1st ed. library stamps, 147 pp, scarce...................... ***$225.00–$450.00***

Johnson, James Weldon. *God's Trombones.* NY. 1927. 1st ed. .... ***$50.00–$70.00***

Johnson, James Weldon (ed.). *Book of American Negro Spirituals.* NY. 1925.............. .... ***$50.00–$70.00***

Johnson, Martin. *Safari.* NY. 1928. illus. .... ***$35.00–$40.00***

Johnson, Merle. *American First Editions.* NY. 1936. 3rd ed. .... ***$25.00–$30.00***

Johnson, Merle. *Bibliography of the Works of Mark Twain.* NY. 1935. rev ed. dj. .... ***$60.00–$80.00***

Johnson, Richard M. *Biographical Sketch of Col Richard M Johnson of Kentucky. By a Kentuckian.* NY. 1843. 1st ed. pictorial wrps, sewn, 46 pp. .... ***$150.00–$200.00***

Johnson, Samuel. *The Idler.* Lon. Davis. 1767. 2 vols. 3rd ed. 1st ed in book form. .... ***$200.00–$250.00***

Johnson, Sir Harry H. and K. C. B. *British Central Africa.* Lon. Methuen. 1897. 1st ed. maps, illus. .... ***$300.00–$350.00***

Johnson, W. Fletcher. *Life of Sitting Bull and History of the Indian War of 1890-91*. Edgewood Publishing Co. 1891. 1st ed. illus... *$40.00–$50.00*

Johnson, Walter R. *Report to the Navy Dept. of the U.S. on American Coals . . .* GPO. 1844. 1st ed... *$60.00–$75.00*

Johnston, Carol. *Thomas Wolfe: A Descriptive Biography*. Pitt. Univ Pittsburgh Press. 1987. 1st ed. illus... *$60.00–$75.00*

Johnston, F. B. and T. T Waterman. *Early Architecture of North Carolina*. Univ of NC. 1947. 2nd ptg, folio, plates.. *$150.00–$200.00*

Johnston, Harry H. *Uganda Protectorate*. NY. Dodd Mead. 1904. 2 vols. 2nd enlarged ed. illus. 48 clr plates, 9 maps, ½ red mor, teg. .... *$300.00–$375.00*

Johnston, Mary. *The Witch*. Houghton. 1914. dj.................................... *$30.00–$40.00*

Johnston, Mary. *To Have and To Hold*. Bos. Houghton Mifflin. 1900. 1st ed. illus...... .... *$45.00–$60.00*

Johnston, Sir Harry. *British Central Africa*. NY. Edward Arnold. 1897. illus. 1st Amer ed, maps.. *$200.00–$400.00*

Johnstone, Annie Fellows. *Ole Mammy's Torment*. Bos. 1897. .... *$25.00–$45.00*

Jolly Jump-ups and Their New House. MA. McLoughlin Bros. 1939. 6 pop-ups.......... .... *$30.00–$40.00*

Jolly Jump-Ups Favorite Nursery Stories. McLoughlin Bros. 1942. pictorial bds, pop-up stories.. *$45.00–$95.00*

Jolly, Ellen Ryan. *Nuns of the Battlefield*. Providence, RI. Providence Visitor Press. 1927. 1st ed. 336 pp. .... *$45.00–$65.00*

Jones, Bobby. *Golf Is My Game*. NY. 1960. 1st ed. dj. .... *$30.00–$40.00*

Jones, Charles C., Jr. *Negro Myths from the Georgia Coast Told in the Vernacular*. Bos. Houghton Mifflin. 1888. 1st ed. 171 pp... *$150.00–$250.00*

Jones, Howard. *Key For the Identification of Nests and Eggs of Common Birds*. OH. 1927. wrps. .... *$25.00–$30.00*

Jones, J. William. *Christ in the Camp or Religion in Lee's Army*. B F Johnston. 1887. illus. b/w illus. .... *$60.00–$75.00*

Jones, James. *From Here to Eternity*. NY. 1951. 1st ed. author's first book, dj............. .... *$130.00–$150.00*

Jones, James. *Some Came Running*. NY. Scribner's. (1957). 1st ed. dj. . *$45.00–$85.00*

Jones, Laurence Clifton. *Piney Woods and Its Story*. Revell. 1922. 1st ed. illus. .... *$35.00–$50.00*

Jones, LeRoi. *Dutchman and the Stone*. NY. Morrow. 1964. 1st ed. dj. . *$30.00–$50.00*

Jones, LeRoi (aka Imamu Amiri Baraka). *Raise: Essays Since 1965*. Random House. 1971. 1st ed. dj. .... *$25.00–$35.00*

Jones, N. E. *Squirrel Hunters of Ohio . . .* Cinc. 1898. 1st ed. illus. .... *$70.00–$85.00*

Jones, P. *Annals and Recollections of Oneida County*. Rome, NY. 1851....................... .... *$60.00–$80.00*

Jones, Robert Edmond. *Drawings for the Theatre*. NY. 1925. .... *$60.00–$80.00*

Jones, Thomas. *Experience of Thomas Jones . . . a Slave For Forty-Three Years*. Bos. 1850. wrps. 2nd ed. .... *$50.00–$85.00*

Jones, Virgil Carrington. *Ranger Mosby*. Chapel Hill. (1944). 1st ed... *$40.00–$85.00*

Jones, William A. *Report Upon the Reconnaissance of Northwestern Wyoming . . .* Wash. GPO. 1874. illus. 56 fldg litho plates.................................... *$100.00–$140.00*

Jones, Winfield. *Story of the Ku Klux Klan*. DC. (1921). ex-lib, 107 pp. ....
.... *$50.00–$100.00*

Jones, Winfield. *Story of the Ku Klux Klan*. Wash. (1921). 107 pp. .... *$150.00–$175.00*

Jong, Erica. *At the Edge of the Body*. NY. Holt, Rinehart & Winston. 1979. 1st ed. dj. .
.... *$9.00–$20.00*

Jong, Erica. *Fear of Flying*. NY. 1973. dj................................. *$35.00–$45.00*

Jong, Erica. *Loveroot*. NY. 1975. 1st ed. dj. .... *$35.00–$45.00*

Jordan, David Starr and Barton Warren Evermann. *American Food and Game Fishes . . .* NY. Doubleday, Page. 1903. illus. chromo plates,. .... *$40.00–$60.00*

Jordan, J. *Elephants & Ivory*. NY. Rinehart & Co. 1956. 1st ed. illus. dj.....................
.... *$30.00–$85.00*

Jordan, Nina. *Homemade Dolls in Foreign Dress*. NY. (1939). 1st ed. illus. by author. dj... *$45.00–$60.00*

Jordan, Nina R. *Homemade Dolls in Foreign Dress*. NY. Harcourt Brace & Co. (1939). 1st ed. illus. 2nd ptg, dj. .... *$18.00–$30.00*

Jordan, Weymouth T. *Hugh Davis and His Alabama Plantation*. Univ of Ala Press. 1948. 1st ed. dj. .... *$30.00–$40.00*

Josephus, Ben Gorion. *Wonderful & Most Deplorable Hist. of Latter Times of Jews*. Bellows Falls, VT. 1819. calf over bds....................................... *$45.00–$75.00*

Journal of a Prisoner of War in Richmond. NY. 1862. .... *$40.00–$50.00*

Journal of a Young Lady of Virginia, 1782. Balt. 1871. .... *$20.00–$25.00*

Joyce, James. *Cat and the Devil*. Lon. Faber & Faber. (1965). 1st ed. cloth, dj.............
.... *$50.00–$60.00*

Joyce, James. *Chamber Music*. NY. 1923................................. *$75.00–$95.00*

Joyce, James. *Exiles, a Play*. NY. Huebsch. 1918. 1st US ed. .... *$150.00–$200.00*

Joyce, James. *Haveth Childers Everywhere*. Lon. Faber & Faber. (1931). 1st Eng ed. stiff wrps. .... *$65.00–$75.00*

Joyce, James. *Portrait of the Artist as a Young Man*. NY. (1948). wrps. *$40.00–$50.00*

Joyce, James. *Stephen Hero*. np. New Directions. 1944. 1st Amer ed. dj.....................
.... *$30.00–$90.00*

Joyce, James. *Ulysses*. Paris. Shakespeare and Company. 1922. 1st ed. #443/750 cc in handmade paper... *$5,000.00–$7,000.00*

Judd, Mary. *Wigwam Stories*. Bos. 1901. illus. .... *$20.00–$45.00*

Judd, S. D. *Bobwhite & Other Quails of US*. Wash. 1905. illus. wrps.... *$20.00–$30.00*

Jung, Carl G. *Contributions to Analytical Psychology*. Harcourt. 1928. 1st Amer ed. ...
.... *$50.00–$60.00*

Junkin, D. *Life of Winfield Scott Hancock.* NY. 1880. illus..................... *$35.00–$48.00*

Kafka, Franz. *Parables.* NY. (1947). 1st ed. dj. .... *$35.00–$45.00*

Kahn, David. *Code Breakers.* Lon. Weidenfield & Nicholson. (1966). dj. ....
.... *$40.00–$55.00*

Kahn, David. *Code Breakers.* NY. Macmillan. (1967). 1st ed. illus. dj. . *$60.00–$75.00*

Kalvern, Harry. *Negro and the First Amendment.* 1965. 1st ed. dj cloth. ....
.... *$30.00–$45.00*

Kane, Elisha Kent. *Arctic Explorations: . . . in Search of Sir John Franklin.* Phila. 1856.
2 vols. maps.. *$100.00–$175.00*

Kane, Elisha Kent. *US Grinnell Expedition in Search of Sir John Franklin.* NY. 1854.
1st ed. 552 pp, maps, illus.. *$75.00–$100.00*

Kantor, MacKinlay. *Andersonville.* NY. 1955. .... *$40.00–$50.00*

Kantor, MacKinlay. *Wicked Water.* NY. (1949). 1st ed. dj. .... *$50.00–$60.00*

Kaplan, Sidney. *Black Presence in the Era of the American Revolution, 1770–1800.* DC.
Smithsonian. 1973. dj... *$35.00–$50.00*

Kargau, F. D. *St. Louis in Fruhren Dahren.* St. Louis, MO. 1893. cloth, decorated
endpapers, gold on spine.. *$50.00–$60.00*

Karloff, Boris (ed.). *And the Darkness Falls.* Cleve. 1946. 1st ed......... *$20.00–$25.00*

Katayev, Valentin. *White Sail Gleams.* Moscow. 1954. illus. .... *$22.00–$35.00*

Katzenbach, Lois and William. *Practical Book of American Wallpaper.* Phila. (1951).
inscrb, dj... *$45.00–$55.00*

Kay, S. *Travels & Researches in Caffaria.* NY. 1834. fldg map............. *$30.00–$45.00*

Kearfott, Clarence Baker. *Highland Mills.* Vantage Press. illus. b/w photos, map,
endpapers, dj.. *$50.00–$65.00*

Keene, Caroline. *Haunted Bridge.* Grosset & Dunlap. 1937. dj. .... *$20.00–$30.00*

Keene, Caroline. *Message in the Hollow Oak.* Grosset & Dunlap. 1935–36. #12. ....
.... *$125.00–$150.00*

Keene, Carolyn. *In the Shadow of the Tower.* Grosset & Dunlap. 1934. illus. dj............
.... *$20.00–$50.00*

Keene, Carolyn. *Password to Larkspur Lane.* Grosset & Dunlap. wartime ed. no dj. ....
.... *$10.00–$15.00*

Keene, Carolyn. *Ringmaster's Secret.* Grosset & Dunlap. 1959. Cameo ed of Nancy
Drew #31, dj. .... *$25.00–$35.00*

Keene, Carolyn. *Secret of the Golden Pavilion.* Grosset & Dunlap. (1959). ....
.... *$8.00–$12.00*

Keene, Carolyn. *Secret of the Old Clock.* Grosset & Dunlap. 1959. Nancy Drew #1, dj.
.... *$25.00–$50.00*

Keene, Carolyn. *Three Cornered Mystery.* Grosset & Dunlap. 1935. Dana Girls, dj......
.... *$20.00–$35.00*

Keene, Carolyn. *Witch Tree Symbol.* Grosset & Dunlap. 1955. Nancy Drew #33..........
.... *$10.00–$20.00*

Keillor, Garrison. *Lake Wobegone Days.* Viking. 1985. 1st ed. dj......... *$30.00–$50.00*

Keith, Thomas. *New Treatise on the Use of Globes*. Longman, Hurst. 1805. 4 fldg plates, original sheep.. *$75.00–$150.00*

Keithahn, Edward. *Monuments in Cedar*. Ketchikan. 1945. 1st ed. illus. ....
.... *$40.00–$95.00*

Kelemen, P. *Medieval American Art*. NY. 1943. 2 vols. 1st ed. .... *$75.00–$150.00*

Kelland, Clarence Budington. *Death Keeps a Secret*. NY. (1953). 1st ed. dj................
.... *$25.00–$40.00*

Keller, Helen. *Our Duties to the Blind*. Bos. 1904. 1st ed. wrps. author's first book.......
.... *$75.00–$125.00*

Keller, Helen. *Story of My Life*. NY. Doubleday. 1903. 1st ed. 441 pp... *$35.00–$50.00*

Kellerman, Faye. *Sacred and Profane*. NY. Arbor House. 1987. 1st ed. dj.....................
.... *$35.00–$50.00*

Kellerman, Jonathan. *Butcher's Theater*. NY. Bantam. 1988. 1st ed. dj.........................
.... *$18.00–$25.00*

Kellerman, Jonathan. *Time Bomb*. NY. Bantam. 1990. 1st ed. dj.......... *$10.00–$20.00*

Kellog, Vernon. *Nuova the New Bee*. NY. (1920). illus. by Milo Winter. scarce dj........
.... *$30.00–$45.00*

Kelly's Hand Forged Bits and Spurs. El Paso, TX. Kelly Bros Mfg. nd. wrps. catalogue #22. .... *$65.00–$95.00*

Kelly, Charles. *Outlaw Trail*. NY. 1959. .... *$30.00–$45.00*

Kelly, Charles. *Outlaw Trail: A History of Butch Cassidy* . . . Salt Lake City. printed by author. 1938. 1st ed. illus. photo plates, brown cloth, lettered in gilt... *$150.00–$200.00*

Kelly, Emmet. *Clown*. NY. 1954. 1st ed. wrps. .... *$40.00–$55.00*

Kelly, Fanny. *Narrative of My Captivity Among the Sioux Indians*. Hartford. 1871. illus. .... *$50.00–$100.00*

Kelly, H. *Medical Gynecology*. NY/Lon. 1908. 1st ed. illus................. *$75.00–$120.00*

Kelly, H. A. *Snakes of Maryland*. Balt. 1936. wrps. illus. .... *$15.00–$25.00*

Kelly, L. V. *Range of Men: The Story of the Ranchers and Indians of Alberta*. Tor. William Briggs. 1913. 1st ed. illus, teg... *$750.00–$800.00*

Kelly, Robert. *Cruise of the Pnyx*. NY. (1979). 1st ed. wrps. 1/500 cc... *$35.00–$45.00*

Kelly, Walt. *Equal Time for Pogo*. NY. Simon & Schuster. 1968. 1st ed. hard cvr. ....
.... *$80.00–$85.00*

Kelly, Walt. *Incomplete Pogo*. NY. (1954). 1st ed. wrps.......................... *$18.00–$25.00*

Kelly, Walt. *Pogo*. 1961. wrps. .... *$65.00–$75.00*

Kelly, Walt. *Pogo Peek-A-Book*. NY. 1955. 1st ed. wrps. illus. .... *$27.00–$30.00*

Kelly, Walt. *Positively Pogo*. NY. 1957. 1st ed. wrps............................. *$18.00–$25.00*

Kelly, Walt. *Song of the Pogo*. Simon & Schuster. 1956. 1st ed. illus..... *$35.00–$60.00*

Kelly, Walt. *Uncle Pogo So-So Stories*. NY. 1953. 1st ed. wrps............. *$18.00–$25.00*

Kelso, Isaac. *Stars and Bars; Or, The Reign of Terror in Missouri*. Bos. 1863. 1st ed.....
.... *$50.00–$75.00*

Kemelman, Harry. *Nine Mile Walk*. NY. Putnam. 1967. 1st ed. dj. .... *$55.00–$75.00*

Kemelman, Harry. *One Fine Day the Rabbi Bought a Cross*. NY. William Morrow. 1987. 1st ed. dj. .... *$20.00–$30.00*

Kemelman, Harry. *Saturday the Rabbi Went Hungry*. NY. Crown. 1966. Book Club ed. dj. .... *$9.00–$15.00*

Kemelman, Harry. *Sunday the Rabbi Stayed Home*. NY. 1969. 1st ed. dj...................... .... *$25.00–$30.00*

Kemelman, Harry. *Tuesday the Rabbi Saw Red*. NY. Arthur Fields. 1973. 1st ed. dj. .... *$22.00–$36.00*

Kemelman, Harry. *Wednesday the Rabbi Got Wet*. NY. William Morrow. 1976. 1st ed. dj. .... *$30.00–$40.00*

Kemp, John R. *New Orleans*. Preservation Resource Center. (1981). 1st ed. photos and maps.. *$20.00–$40.00*

Kendall, J. B. *Treatise on the Horse and His Diseases*. VT. 1891. .... *$25.00–$40.00*

Kennan, George. *Siberia and the Exile System*. NY. Century. 1891. 2vols. 1st ed. illus. maps, woodcuts, 409 pp, 575 pp.. *$90.00–$125.00*

Kennan, George. *Tent Life in Siberia*. NY. Putnam. 1882. .... *$75.00–$90.00*

Kennedy, Edward. *Our Day and Generation*. 1979. sgn, dj.................. *$30.00–$40.00*

Kennedy, John. *History of Steam Navigation*. Liverpool. 1903. illus... *$90.00–$110.00*

Kennedy, John F. *Profiles in Courage*. NY. Harper & Row. 1964. Memorial ed. dj. .... *$25.00–$45.00*

Kennedy, John F. *Profiles in Courage*. NY. 1961. Inaugural ed. dj........ *$60.00–$65.00*

Kennedy, Joseph P. *I'm for Roosevelt*. NY. 1936.............................. *$95.00–$125.00*

Kennedy, Michael S. (ed.). *Red Man's West . . .* NY. Hastings House. 1965. 1st ed. illus. 194/199 cc buckskin with silkscreen Indian shield on front cvr........... *$100.00–$130.00*

Kennedy, Sen. John F. *Strategy of Peace*. NY. 1960. 1st ed................. *$35.00–$40.00*

Kennedy, William. *Quinn's Book*. Lon. Jonathan Cape. 1988. 1st Brit ed. dj, sgn......... .... *$15.00–$20.00*

Kenrick, William. *American Silk Grower's Guide*. Bos. 1839. 2nd ed. illus................ .... *$80.00–$95.00*

Kent, Alexander. *Inshore Squadron*. NY. G P Putnam. 1979. 1st US ed. dj.................. .... *$30.00–$65.00*

Kent, Rockwell. *N by E*. Brewer & Warren. 1930. 1st ed. illus. dj. .... *$25.00–$35.00*

Kent, Rockwell. *Northern Christmas*. NY. (1941). dj. .... *$50.00–$70.00*

Kent, Rockwell. *Rockwell Kentiana*. NY. 1933. 1st ed...................... *$40.00–$50.00*

Kent, Rockwell. *Salomina*. NY. 1935. 1st ed. dj. .... *$35.00–$50.00*

Kephart, Horace. *Camping and Woodcraft*. Outing Publishing Co. 1916–1917. 2 vols. .... *$25.00–$35.00*

Kercheville, F. M. *Preliminary Glossary of New Mexican Spanish*. Albuquerque. 1934. wrps. .... *$30.00–$45.00*

Kerouac, Jack. *Book of Dreams*. City Lights. (1961). 1st ed. wrps.... *$150.00–$200.00*

Kerouac, Jack. *Dharma Bums*. NY. 1958. 1st ed. dj........................ *$125.00–$200.00*

Kerouac, Jack. *Lonesome Traveler.* NY. (1960). 1st ed. dj. .... *$75.00–$125.00*

Kerouac, Jack. *Maggie Cassidy.* NY. Avon. 1925. 1st ed. paperback original ....
.... *$28.00–$35.00*

Kerouac, Jack. *On the Road.* Viking. 1957. 1st ed. dj. .... *$1,000.00–$1,500.00*

Kerouac, Jack. *Pull My Daisy.* Grove Press. (1961). 1st ed. dj. .... *$95.00–$150.00*

Kerouac, Jack. *Satori in Paris.* NY. Grove Press. (1966). 1st ed. dj... *$200.00–$275.00*

Kerouac, Jack. *Tristessa.* NY. 1960. 1st ed. wrps. .... *$40.00–$60.00*

Kerouac, Jack. *Visions of Cody.* McGraw Hill. (1972). 1st ed. dj. .... *$65.00–$85.00*

Kerouac, John. *Town and the City.* NY. Harcourt. (1950). 1st ed. dj. *$160.00–$270.00*

Kerr, Donald I. *African Adventure.* Harrisburg, PA. Stackpole. (1957). 1st ed. illus. photos, dj. .... *$70.00–$100.00*

Kerr, Evor Samuel, Jr. *United States Coast Guard.* NY. Kelly Pub. 1935. illus. green pictorial cloth. .... *$36.00–$45.00*

Kerr, J. Lennox. *Wilfred Grenfell.* NY. Dodd Mead. 1959. illus. 259 pp, dj. ....
.... *$22.00–$35.00*

Kerr, Philip. *German Requiem.* Lon. Viking. 1991. 1st ed. dj. .... *$50.00–$100.00*

Kerr, Walter. *Silent Clowns.* NY. Knopf. 1975. 1st ed. illus. dj.............. *$35.00–$50.00*

Kersh, Gerald. *Song of the Flea.* Garden City. 1948. dj. .... *$45.00–$55.00*

Kesey, Ken. *Demon Box.* NY. Viking. 1986. 1st ed. dj, sgn. .... *$45.00–$65.00*

Kesey, Ken. *Kesey's Garage Sale.* NY. Viking. 1973. simultaneous issue, 1st ed. in wrps, sgn. .... *$45.00–$180.00*

Kesey, Ken. *Kesey's Garage Sale.* NY. Viking. 1973. 1st ed. dj, sgn... *$115.00–$210.00*

Kesey, Ken. *Sometimes a Great Notion.* (1964). 1st ed. dj. .... *$150.00–$200.00*

Kesey, Ken. *Wavy Gravy.* NY. (1974). wrps... *$50.00–$75.00*

Ketchum, Milo S. *Designs of Steel Mills Buildings and the Calculation of Stresses in Framed Structures.* NY. 1905. 1st ed. .... *$40.00–$60.00*

Keynes, J. M. *Treatise on Money.* NY. (1930). 2 vols. 1st ed. dj. .... *$100.00–$200.00*

Khayyam, Omar. *The Rubaiyat.* NY. (1930). illus. by Pogany, 500 cc. ....
.... *$200.00–$350.00*

Kidder, Daniel P. *Mormonism and the Mormons.* NY. 1844. 2nd ed. 342 pp. ....
.... *$75.00–$125.00*

Kieran, John W. *American Sporting Scene.* NY. 1941. 1st ed. dj. .... *$30.00–$45.00*

Kiernan, Dr. P. F. *Hints on Horse-Shoeing.* GPO. 1871. 1st ed. 11 pp. ....
.... *$75.00–$100.00*

Killikelley, Sarah H. *History of Pittsburgh.* Pitts. 1906. 1st ed. illus. 568 pp. ....
.... *$35.00–$45.00*

Kimball, Edward L. and Andrew E. *Spencer W. Kimball, Twelfth President of the Church.* Salt Lake. 1978. illus. photos, sgn, dj. .... *$110.00–$135.00*

Kincaid, Jamaica. *Autobiography of My Mother.* Farrar, Straus & Giroux. 1996. 1st ed. sgn, dj. .... *$30.00–$35.00*

Kincaid, Jamaica. *Small Place*. NY. (1988). 1st ed. dj. .... *$35.00–$45.00*

King, Clarence. *Mountaineering in the Sierra Nevada*. Bos. 1872. 1st ed. ....
.... *$125.00–$200.00*

King, Constance Eileen. *Collector's History of Dolls*. Lon. (1983). dj. . *$40.00–$60.00*

King, Coretta Scott. *My Life With Martin Luther King, Jr.* NY. 1969. 1st ed. dj, sgn. ...
.... *$50.00–$75.00*

King, Martin Luther. *Triumph of Conscience*. NY. (1968). 1st ed. dj. ... *$75.00–$50.00*

King, Martin Luther, Jr. *Where Do We Go From Here?* NY. 1967). 1st ed. dj. ....
.... *$125.00–$95.00*

King, Martin Luther, Jr. *Where Do We Go From Here: Chaos or Community?*. NY. (1967). 1st ed. dj. .... *$75.00–$125.00*

King, Stephen. *Christine*. NY. Viking. 1983. 1st ed. red cloth, dj. .... *$65.00–$85.00*

King, Stephen. *Cycle of the Werewolf*. 1985. 1st ed. dj. .... *$65.00–$80.00*

King, Stephen. *Dark Half*. Hodder & Stoughton. 1989. 1st UK dj. .... *$50.00–$65.00*

King, Stephen. *Dark Tower*. RI. Grant. 1982. 1st ed. scarce, dj. .... *$350.00–$550.00*

King, Stephen. *Dead Zone*. Viking. 1979. 1st ed. dj. .... *$65.00–$75.00*

King, Stephen. *Different Seasons*. Viking. 1982. 1st ed. dj. .... *$30.00–$45.00*

King, Stephen. *Dolores Claiborne*. Hodder & Stoughton. 1992. 1st UK ed dj. ....
.... *$40.00–$50.00*

King, Stephen. *Eyes of the Dragon*. NY. Viking. 1987. 1st ed. illus. dj. . *$12.00–$25.00*

King, Stephen. *It*. Viking. 1986. 1st ed. dj. .... *$30.00–$45.00*

King, Stephen. *The Shining*. Doubleday. 1977. 1st ed. dj. .... *$100.00–$150.00*

King, Stephen. *The Stand*. Garden City. Doubleday. 1978. 1st ed. dj. *$145.00–$275.00*

King, Stephen and Peter Straub. *The Talisman*. West Kingston. Donald M Grant. 1984. 2 vols. 1st ed. slipcase. .... *$100.00–$125.00*

Kinglsey, Charles. *Water Babies*. NY. nd. illus. by G Sopher. .... *$45.00–$50.00*

Kingsford, Anna Bonus. *Ideal in Diet*. Lon. 1898. .... *$24.00–$35.00*

Kingsley, Charles. *Westward Ho!* NY. (1920). illus. by N C Wyeth. .... *$45.00–$65.00*

Kingston, W. H. G. *Henricks the Hunter*. NY. Armstrong. 1880. illus. engr plates.........
.... *$40.00–$60.00*

Kinietz, Vernon. *Chippewa Village*. Bloomfield Hills, MI. Cranbrook. 1947. 1st ed. illus. 259 pp, dj. .... *$35.00–$45.00*

Kinnell, Galway. *Black Light*. Bos. 1966. 1st ed. dj, sgn. .... *$35.00–$45.00*

Kinnell, Galway. *What a Kingdom It Was*. Bos. 1960. 3rd ptg, sgn, dj. ....
.... *$60.00–$75.00*

Kinnell, Galway and Claire Van Vliet. *Two Poems*. Newark, VT. Janus Press. 1979. 1st ed. ltd ed, 185 cc, sgn by author and artist. .... *$100.00–$150.00*

Kinney, Henry W. *Manchuria Today*. Darien. 1930. illus. 100 pp. .... *$15.00–$25.00*

Kinsey, A. C. *Gall Wasp Genus Cynips*. Bloomington. 1929. .... *$24.00–$35.00*

Kinsey, Alfred C., et al. *Sexual Behavior in the Human Female*. Phila/Lon. Saunders. 1953. 1st ed.. *$95.00–$125.00*

Kinsey, Alfred C., et al. *Sexual Behavior in the Human Male*. Phila/Lon. Saunders. 1948. 1st ed.. *$95.00–$125.00*

Kip, William I. *Early Jesuit Missions in North America*. NY. 1846. 2 vols in one, map. .... *$150.00–$225.00*

Kipling, Rudyard. *Barrack Room Ballads*. 1892. 1st ed. illus. .... *$100.00–$130.00*

Kipling, Rudyard. *Brushwood Boy*. NY. 18991. illus......................... *$85.00–$100.00*

Kipling, Rudyard. *Captains Courageous*. NY. Century. 1897. 1st Amer ed. green cloth, teg. .... *$75.00–$100.00*

Kipling, Rudyard. *Collected Dog Stories*. Lon. 1934. lea, teg. .... *$125.00–$200.00*

Kipling, Rudyard. *Just So Stories*. Lon. 1902. 1st ed........................ *$300.00–$500.00*

Kipling, Rudyard. *Kim*. NY. 1901. 1st Amer ed. .... *$75.00–$100.00*

Kipling, Rudyard. *Many Inventions*. NY. Macmillan. 1893. 1st ed........ *$20.00–$30.00*

Kipling, Rudyard. *Puck of Pook's Hill*. NY. 1906. illus. by Arthur Rackham, 4 clr plates, teg. .... *$45.00–$75.00*

Kipling, Rudyard. *Second Jungle Book*. Lon. 1895. 1st ed. .... *$75.00–$100.00*

Kipling, Rudyard. *Song of the English*. NY. Doubleday Page. (1909). illus. by W Heath Robinson. 16 tipped-in clr plates. drawings, tissue guards.................. *$120.00–$150.00*

Kipling, Rudyard. *Songs of the Sea*. Lon. Macmillan. 1927. illus. .... *$40.00–$80.00*

Kipling, Rudyard. *Works of Rudyard Kipling*. Doubleday & McClure. 1898. 14 vols. ¾ lea, bds, teg. .... *$150.00–$175.00*

Kirby, Georgiana B. *Years of Experience, An Autobiographical Narrative*. NY. 1887. 1st ed. .... *$120.00–$200.00*

Kirby, Percival R. *Musical Instruments of the Native Races of South Africa*. Johannesburg. 1965. illus. 2nd ed, dj... *$50.00–$125.00*

Kirby, Percival R. *Musical Instruments of the Native Races of South Africa*. Lon. Oxford Univ Press. 1934. .... *$50.00–$75.00*

Kirkland, Mrs. (Caroline Matilda). *Evening Book: or Fireside Talk on Morals and Manners*. NY. Scribner's. 1852. 1st ed. red cloth, stamped, aeg, 312 pp. ....*$150.00–$200.00*

Kirkland, Thomas, and Robert Kennedy. *Historic Camden*. Columbia, SC. The State Co. 1905-26. 2 vols. 1st ed. 486 pp, illus, maps.................................... *$175.00–$250.00*

Kitchin, Thomas. *Map of New York* . . . Lon. R Baldwin. 1778. .... *$60.00–$80.00*

Kitto, John. *Palestine: Physical Geography, Natural History* . . . Lon. 1841. illus. ¾ calf. .... *$45.00–$75.00*

Kittredge, George Lyman. *Witchcraft in Old and New England*. Harvard. 1929. 1st ed. .... *$105.00–$200.00*

Kittredge, George Lyman. *Witchcraft in Old and New England*. NY. Russell & Russell. (1956)... *$20.00–$45.00*

Kittredge, Henry. *Shipmasters of Cape Cod*. 1935. 1st ed. dj............... *$25.00–$35.00*

Kitzmiller, Helen H. *One Hundred Years of Western Reserve*. OH. 1926. photos. .... *$20.00–$30.00*

Klansman's Manual. Atlanta. 1924. 1st ed. wrps. .... *$75.00–$125.00*

Klein, Frederic Shriver (ed.). *Just South of Gettysburg, Carroll County, Md, in the Civil War*. MD. 1963. 1st ed. sgn, dj .... *$42.00–$50.00*

Klein, H. *Mushrooms and Other Fungi*. Garden City. 1962. 1st Amer ed. photos, dj. .... *$30.00–$40.00*

Klingberg, Frank. *An Appraisal of the Negro in Colonial S.C*. Wash. 1941. 1st ed. .... *$35.00–$45.00*

Kluckhohn, C. and K. Spencer. *Bibliography of the Navaho Indians*. NY. 1940. .... *$75.00–$100.00*

Knee, Ernest. *Santa Fe, New Mexico*. NY. Hastings House. 1942. 1st ed. photos........... .... *$20.00–$35.00*

Knight, Charles, (ed.). *Old England: A Pictorial Museum of Regal . . .* Lon. James Sangster. (c1880's). 2 vols. illus. chromo plates, red cloth. aeg. .... *$80.00–$125.00*

Knight, Damon. *In Search of Wonder: Essays on Modern Science Fiction*. Chi. 1956. 1st ed. dj. .... *$20.00–$25.00*

Knight, Mrs. Helen C. *Hannah More . . .* NY. American Tract Society. (1862). rev ed. ....

Knights of the Ku Klux Klan . . .Atlanta. 1926. wrps. .... *$55.00–$75.00*

Knipe, Emilie Benson. *Story of Old Ironsides*. NY. Dodd Mead. (1928). 1st ed. .... *$40.00–$65.00*

Knowles, James D. *Memoir of Mrs. Ann H. Judson*. Bos. 1829. fldg map, calf.............. .... *$50.00–$60.00*

Knowlton, Charles. *Fruits of Philosophy . . .* Mount Vernon. Peter Pauper Press. 1937. rprnt. dj. decorated paper bds.. *$30.00–$40.00*

Knox, Dudley W. *Naval Genius of George Washington*. Bos. 1932. 1st ed. ltd 550 cc. .... *$65.00–$85.00*

Knox, Thomas. *Travels of Marco Polo for Boys and Girls*. NY. 1885.... *$50.00–$95.00*

Knox, Thomas W. *Adventures of Two Youths in a Journey to Egypt and Holy Land*. NY. 1883. illus. .... *$20.00–$30.00*

Koch, Rudolph. *Little ABC Book of*. Bos. David R Godine. 1976. 1st ed thus, ltd 2,500 cc... *$15.00–$25.00*

Kolb, Ellsworth L. *Through the Grand Canyon from Wyoming to Mexico*. NY. 1958. 1st ed. illus. blue cloth. .... *$25.00–$35.00*

Koontz, Dean R. *Coldfire*. Putnam. 1991. ltd 750 cc, dj, slipcase. .... *$75.00–$125.00*

Koontz, Dean R. *Dragon Tears*. Putnam. 1993. 1st ed. dj sgn............... *$30.00–$45.00*

Koontz, Dean R. *Night Chills*. NY. Atheneum. 1976. 334 pp, dj........ *$185.00–$225.00*

Koontz, Dean R. *Servants of Twilight*. Illinois. 1988. 1st US ed. dj. ...... *$35.00–$45.00*

Kopp, Marie. *Birth Control in Practice*. NY. 1934. 1st ed. dj. .... *$40.00–$50.00*

Korn, Bertram Wallace. *American Jewry and the Civil War*. Phila. 1951. 1st ed. illus. .... *$50.00–$75.00*

Kornbluth, C. M. *Mile Beyond the Moon.* Garden City. 1958. 1st ed. dj. ....
.... *$75.00–$85.00*

Kornbluth, Jesse. *Pre-Pop Warhol.* NY. 1988. 1st ed. .... *$58.00–$70.00*

Koros, Alexander Cosma De. *Dictionary of Tibetan English.* New Delhi. Cosmo Publications. 1978. reprint. .... *$30.00–$45.00*

Korson, George (ed.). *Pennsylvania Songs and Legends.* Phila. Univ of Penn. 1949. 1st ed. dj. .... *$8.00–$30.00*

Kouwenhoven, John. *Columbia Historical Portrait of New York.* NY. 1953. dj. ....
.... *$40.00–$60.00*

Kovacs, Ernie. *Zoomar.* Doubleday. 1957. 1st ed. dj. .... *$45.00–$60.00*

Krauss, Ruth. *A Hole Is to Dig.* NY. 1952. 1st ed. illus. by Maurice Sendak, dj. ....
.... *$125.00–$200.00*

Krauss, Ruth. *Charlotte and the White Horse.* NY. Harper & Brothers. illus. by Maurice Sendak in clr pictorial bds. dj. .... *$50.00–$75.00*

Krider, John. *Forty Years Notes of a Field Ornithologist.* Phila. 1879. .. *$30.00–$50.00*

Krige, E. J. *Social System of the Zulus.* Lon. 1957. illus. 3rd ed. .... *$35.00–$45.00*

Kroeber, A. L. *Handbook of the Indians of California.* Wash. GPO. 1925. illus. maps plates. .... *$200.00–$300.00*

Krug, J A. *Columbia River.* Wash. 1947. illus. folio. pocket maps. .... *$50.00–$75.00*

Krug, J. A. *Colorado River.* DC. GPO. 1946. wrps. .... *$65.00–$100.00*

Kunitz, Stanley. *Intellectual Things.* NY. Doubleday Doran. 1930. 1st ed. author's first book, 63 pp, dj. .... *$125.00–$195.00*

Kunitz, Stanley. *Passport to the War.* NY. Holt. (1944). 1st ed. 60 pp, dj. ....
.... *$40.00–$85.00*

Kunz, George Frederick. *Curious Lore of Precious Stones.* Phila. 1913. illus. ....
.... *$125.00–$150.00*

Kuppuram, G. and Kumdamani K. *History and Science and Technology in India.* Delhi. Sundeep Prakashan. 1990. .... *$150.00–$185.00*

Kuran, Aptullah. *Mosque in Early Ottoman Architecture.* Chi. 1968. illus. ....
.... *$35.00–$50.00*

Kurtz and Erlich. *Art of the Toy Soldier.* NY. 1987. illus. folio. .... *$40.00–$60.00*

Kylie, Hieronymus and Hall. *CCC Forestry.* Wash. GPO. 1937. 335 pp, photos. ....
.... *$18.00–$25.00*

L'Amour, Louis. *Bendigo Shafter.* NY. (1979). 1st ed. dj. .... *$75.00–$100.00*

L'Amour, Louis. *Frontier.* Bantam. (1984). 1st ed. photos, dj. .... *$40.00–$60.00*

L'Amour, Louis. *Hopalong Cassidy and the Trail to Seven Pines.* Garden City. Doubleday. 1951. 1st ed. author's first Western novel, dj. .... *$375.00–$500.00*

L'Amour, Louis. *Last of the Breed.* Bantam Books. 1986. dj. .... *$12.00–$20.00*

L'Amour, Louis. *Lonesome Gods.* Bantam Books. 1983. 1st ed. dj. ...... *$12.00–$28.00*

L'Amour, Louis. *Over on the Dry Side.* NY. (1975). 1st ed. dj. .... *$100.00–$150.00*

L'Amour, Louis. *Rivers West.* NY. 1975. 1st ed. dj. .... *$100.00–$150.00*

L'Amour, Louis. *Sackett's Land*. NY. 1974. 1st ed. dj. .... *$140.00–$165.00*

L'Engle, Madeleine. *Ladder of Angels*. Seabury. 1979. 1st ed. illus. dj. *$25.00–$35.00*

L'Engle, Madeleine. *Wrinkle in Time*. NY. 1987. 1st ed. dj.................... *$65.00–$75.00*

La Farge, Oliver. *As Long as the Grass Shall Grow*. NY. Alliance Book Corp. 1940. 1st ed. sgn.. *$50.00–$65.00*

La Farge, Oliver. *Higher Life in Art*. NY. 1908. 1st ed. .... *$45.00–$50.00*

La Farge, Oliver. *Laughing Boy*. Houghton. 1929. 1st ed. dj.............. *$75.00–$125.00*

La Farge, Oliver (ed.). *Changing Indian*. Norman. Univ of Oklahoma. 1942. 1st ed dj. .... *$25.00–$35.00*

La Fayette, Gen. *Memoirs of Embracing Details of Public and Private Life*. Hartford. 1825. 1st ed. lea.. *$50.00–$100.00*

La Fontaine, Jean de. *Fables in Rhyme*. Volland. (1918). illus. by Rae. *$35.00–$50.00*

La Monte, Francesca. *North American Games Fishes*. NY. 1945. 1st ed. illus. limp lea, clr plates... *$25.00–$35.00*

Lacroix, Paul. *Arts in the Middle Ages*. NY. 1875. illus. .... *$22.00–$30.00*

Ladie's Indispensable Assistant. Being a Companion for the Sister, Mother, and Wife. NY. 1851. orig blue cloth. .... *$75.00–$100.00*

Lafever, Minard. *Beauties of Modern Architecture*. NY. Appleton. 1855. illus. new ed. .... *$80.00–$120.00*

Lahee, Henry C. *Famous Violinists of Today and Yesterday*. Bos. 1906. illus............... .... *$25.00–$35.00*

Lake, Simon. *Submarine in War and Peace*. Phila. 1918. 1st ed. illus. photos, presentation copy, sgn. .... *$50.00–$75.00*

Lama Anagarika Govinda. *Foundations of Tibetan Mysticism*. Lon. Rider. (1959). illus. photos, 1st ed. in Eng, sgn. .... *$50.00–$70.00*

Lamb, Charles and Mary Lamb. *Tales from Shakespeare*. Lon/NY. 1909. illus. with 12 clr plates by Arthur Rackham, red lea................................. *$100.00–$150.00*

Lamb, Frank W. *Indian Baskets of North America*. Riverside, CA. 1972. illus. dj........ .... *$45.00–$75.00*

Lamb, M. *Homes of America*. NY. 1879. illus. 256 pp, aeg............... *$100.00–$150.00*

Lamb, Mrs. Martha. *History of the City of New York; It's Origin, Rise and Progress*. NY. Barnes. 1877. 2 vols. illus. maps, plates........................... *$50.00–$65.00*

Lamb, Wallace E. *Lake Champlain and Lake George Valleys*. NY. 1940. 3 vols. illus. maps... *$100.00–$165.00*

Lamon and Slocum. *Mating and Breeding of Poultry*. NY. 1920. illus.. *$40.00–$60.00*

Lamson, David. *Two Years Experience Among the Shakers; Being a Description of . . .* West Boylston. 1848. 212 pp. .... *$140.00–$185.00*

Landor, A. Henry Savage. *In the Forbidden Land*. NY. Harper & Bros. 1899. fldg map, clr plates... *$125.00–$200.00*

Landor, A. Henry Savage. *Across Wildest Africa*. Lon. Hurst & Blackett. 1907. 2 vols. illus. .... *$195.00–$260.00*

Landor, A. Henry Savage. *China and Allies.* Lon. Heinemann. 1901. 2 vol. illus. 8 maps, 53 plates, text illus. dark blue cloth, red lea labels..................... *$175.00–$225.00*

Lands in Alabama . . . GPO. 1828. 1st ed.. *$18.00–$25.00*

Landseer and Herring. *Aunt Louisa's Choice Present* . . . Lon. Frederick Warne. (c1860s). illus. chromos, blue cloth. .... *$100.00–$175.00*

Lane, C. K. *Rabbits, Cats and Cavies.* Lon. J M Dent. 1903. illus. gilt decoration and lettered green cloth. .... *$40.00–$60.00*

Lane, Carl D. *American Paddle Steamboats.* NY. Coward McCann. 1943. illus. decorated endpapers, dj. .... *$45.00–$55.00*

Lane, Frank. *Kingdom of the Octopus.* NY. Sheridan House. 1960. dj. . *$15.00–$30.00*

Lane, Margaret. *Tale of Beatrix Potter, A Biography.* NY. (1946). 1st ed...................... .... *$35.00–$50.00*

Lang, Andrew. *Animal Story Book.* Lon. 1896. illus. 1st UK ed. .... *$100.00–$150.00*

Lang, Andrew. *Blue Poetry Book.* Lon. 1891. 1st Eng ed. illus........... *$75.00–$100.00*

Lang, Andrew. *Book of Dreams and Ghosts.* Lon/NY/Bombay. Longmans, Green & Co. 1897. 1st ed. pict cloth. .... *$45.00–$125.00*

Lang, Andrew. *Book of Romance.* Lon. 1902. 1st Eng ed. illus. .... *$50.00–$80.00*

Lang, Andrew. *Green Fairy Book.* Lon. 1924. illus. .... *$30.00–$40.00*

Lang, Andrew. *True Story Book.* Lon. 1893. illus. 1st UK ed. .... *$100.00–$135.00*

Lanier, Charles D. *We Go Foxhunting Abroad.* np. private ptg. 1924. 1st ed. sgn. .... *$32.00–$45.00*

Lankes, J. J. *Woodcut Manual.* NY. Crown. 1932. rprnt....................... *$12.00–$25.00*

Lardner, Rev. Dionysius. *Cabinet Cyclopaedia.* Phila. 1832. illus. ...... *$50.00–$65.00*

Lardner, Ring. *Bib Ballads.* Chi. (1915). 1st ed. author's first book, illus,1/1500 cc, boxed. .... *$275.00–$350.00*

Lardner, Ring. *Big Town.* Ind. 1921. 1st ed. .... *$50.00–$65.00*

Lardner, Ring. *Gullible's Travels.* Ind. (1917). 1st ed........................... *$50.00–$70.00*

Lardner, Ring. *My Four Weeks in France.* Ind. (1918). 1st ed. illus....... *$60.00–$70.00*

Lardner, Ring. *You Know Me Al.* NY. (1916). 1st ed............................. *$30.00–$37.00*

Larned, Linda H. *New Hostess To-Day.* NY. 1917............................... *$14.00–$21.00*

Larsen, Kenneth. *Flying Saucer Designs.* LA. 1965. 1st ed. illus. three-ring binder...... .... *$50.00–$80.00*

Last Journals of David L. Livingstone. Hartford. 1875. illus. maps....... *$35.00–$40.00*

Lathrop, Dorothy C. *Sung Under the Umbrella Tree.* NY. 1935. 1st ed. scarce dj......... .... *$35.00–$50.00*

Lathrop, Elise. *Early American Inns and Taverns.* NY. 1926. 1st ed. .... *$25.00–$30.00*

Lathrop, Elise. *Historic Houses of Early America.* NY. 1936. rprnt, 464 pp, photos, dj. .... *$15.00–$25.00*

Lathrop, S. K. *Treasures of Ancient America* . . . Geneva. Albert Skira. illus. cloth, dj, wrp-around band... *$50.00–$80.00*

Lattimore, Owen. *Inner Asian Frontiers of China.* NY. 1940. illus........ *$25.00–$35.00*

Laura Bancroft. *Prairie Dog Town.* Chi. Reilly & Britton. (1906). 1st ed. illus. 16 clr plates. an L Frank Baum pseudonym book... *$350.00–$500.00*

Laura Bancroft. *Sugar-Loaf Mountain.* Chi. Reilly & Britton. (1906). 1st ed. illus. 16 clr plates. an L Frank Baum pseudonym book. .... *$275.00–$350.00*

Laurie, J. and R. S. Gutteridge. *Homeopathic Domestic Medicine* . . . Lon. 1888. ......
.... *$45.00–$55.00*

Laut, Agnes C. *Blazed Trail of the Old Frontier.* NY. 1926. 1st ed. illus. 271 pp. ....
.... *$60.00–$125.00*

Laut, Agnes C. *Conquest of Our Western Empire.* NY. 1927. 1st ed. dj. *$50.00–$80.00*

Laut, Agnes C. *Conquest of the Great Northwest* . . . NY. 1908. 2 vols. 1st ed. illus. ....
.... *$65.00–$85.00*

Laut, Agnes C. *Pathfinders of the West.* NY. 1904. 1st ed........................ *$40.00–$50.00*

Laut, Agnes C. *Story of the Trapper.* NY. 1902. 1st ed. author's first book...................
.... *$35.00–$50.00*

Laut, Agnes C. *Vikings of the Pacific.* NY. Macmillan. (1905). illus. maps...................
.... *$18.00–$25.00*

Lavin, Mary. *House in Clewe Street.* Bos. 1945. 1st ed. dj...................... *$50.00–$65.00*

LaWall, Charles H. *Four Thousand Years of Pharmacy.* Lippincott. 1927. 665 pp, prentation copy. .... *$65.00–$85.00*

Lawrence, D. H. *Amores.* NY. 1916. 1st Amer ed................................. *$80.00–$100.00*

Lawrence, D. H. *David.* Knopf. 1926. dj. .... *$35.00–$65.00*

Lawrence, D. H. *Lady Chatterly's Lover.* Knopf. 1932. 1st Amer ed.... *$75.00–$125.00*

Lawrence, D. H. *Ladybird, the Fox, the Captain's Doll.* Lon. Martin Secker. (1923). 1st ed. dj. .... *$125.00–$350.00*

Lawrence, D. H. *Lovely Lady.* NY. Viking. 1933. 1st US ed. dj. .... *$30.00–$50.00*

Lawrence, D. H. *Mornings in Mexico.* Lon. Martin Secker. 1927. 1st ed. dj...................
.... *$300.00–$500.00*

Lawrence, D. H. *Pansies.* NY. 1929. 1st Amer ed. dj............................. *$30.00–$50.00*

Lawrence, D. H. *Pansies: Poems.* np. (1929). pink wraps, sgn. .... *$125.00–$400.00*

Lawrence, D. H. *Pornography & Obscenity.* Faber & Faber. 1929. 1st Eng ed. ....
.... *$25.00–$50.00*

Lawrence, D. H. *Touch and Go: A Play in Three Acts.* Lon. C W Daniel. 1920. 1st ed. wrps. .... *$300.00–$400.00*

Lawrence, D. H. *Virgin and the Gypsy.* Lon. Martin Secker. (1930). 1st English ed. dj.
.... *$100.00–$250.00*

Lawrence, D. H. *Women in Love.* Lon. Martin Seeker. 1921. 1st trade ed......................
.... *$125.00–$300.00*

Lawrence, Robert M. *Magic of the Horseshoe.* Bos/NY. 1898. 1st ed. . *$50.00–$75.00*

Lawrence, T. E. *Revolt in the Desert.* NY. 1927. illus. 1st US ed. fldg map, dj. ....
.... *$75.00–$100.00*

Lawrence, T. E. *Seven Pillars of Wisdom.* Doubleday Doran. 1935. 1st ed. #3/750 cc, dj. .... *$300.00–$400.00*

Laws of the State of Vermont. Rutland. Josiah Fay. 1798. lea............ *$115.00–$135.00*

Lawson, Charles. *Lawson's Switcher Guide on the Game of Checkers.* Worcester, MA. 1899. 1st ed.. *$22.00–$35.00*

Lawson, John. *History of North Carolina.* Raleigh. 1860. 1st ed....... *$115.00–$150.00*

Lawson, Robert. *Ben and Me.* Little Brown. 1944. dj. .... *$50.00–$60.00*

Lawson, Robert. *Rabbit Hill.* NY. 1944. 1st ed. dj. .... *$40.00–$60.00*

Layard, Austen H. *Discoveries in the Ruins of Nineveh and Babylon.* NY. 1853. 1st ed. illus. maps, lithos, 686 pp.. *$75.00–$100.00*

Layard, Austen Henry. *Nineveh and Its Remains.* NY. Putnam. 1849. 2 vols. illus. 1st Amer ed. litho, map,.. *$195.00–$300.00*

Lazarus, Emma. *Songs of a Semite.* NY. 1882. 1st ed........................... *$65.00–$90.00*

Le Blanc, Maurice. *From Midnight to Morning.* Macaulay. 1933. 1st ed. dj. .... *$75.00–$100.00*

Le Carre, John. *Call For the Dead.* 1962. 1st Amer ed. dj.............. *$600.00–$900.00*

Le Carre, John. *Honourable Schoolboy.* Lon. Hodder & Stoughton. 1977. 1st US ed dj. .... *$25.00–$45.00*

Le Carre, John. *Little Drummer Girl.* Knopf. 1983. 1st US ed. dj......... *$15.00–$25.00*

Le Carre, John. *Little Drummer Girl.* Lon. Hodder & Stoughton. 1983. 1st UK ed. dj. .... *$45.00–$60.00*

Le Carre, John. *Looking-Glass War.* Lon. Heinemann. 1965. 1st ed. dj. *$45.00–$50.00*

Le Carre, John. *Our Game.* Lon. Hodder & Stoughton. 1995. 1st Eng ed. dj.............. .... *$150.00–$300.00*

Le Carre, John. *Perfect Spy.* NY. Knopf. 1986. 1st Amer ed. sgn, dj. *$50.00–$150.00*

Le Carre, John. *Russia House.* NY. Knopf. 1989. 1st ed. dj. .... *$10.00–$20.00*

Le Carre, John. *Russia House.* Lon. Hodder & Stoughton. 1989. 1st Eng ed. dj. .... *$20.00–$50.00*

Le Carre, John. *Secret Pilgrim.* NY. 1991. 1st Amer ed. sgn, dj......... *$85.00–$100.00*

Le Carre, John. *Small Town in Germany.* NY. Coward-McCann. 1968. 1st Amer ed. dj. .... *$50.00–$80.00*

Le Carre, John. *Smiley's People.* NY. Knopf. 1980. 1st Amer ed. dj. .... *$35.00–$65.00*

Le Carre, John. *Spy Who Came in From the Cold.* Lon. Gollancz. 1963. 1st ed. dj....... .... *$750.00–$950.00*

Le Carre, John. *Tinker, Tailor, Soldier, Spy.* Lon. 1974. 1st UK ed. sgn, dj. .... *$75.00–$100.00*

Le Gallienne, Eva. *At 33.* NY. Longmans. 1940. rprnt, dj. .... *$25.00–$45.00*

Le Gallienne, Richard. *Romance of Perfume.* NY. 1928. 1st ed. illus. by George Barbier, clr plates, Richard Hudnut brochure in rear pocket, dj........................ *$100.00–$185.00*

Le Guin, Ursula. *Dispossessed.* NY. (1974). 1st ed. dj........................... *$50.00–$60.00*

Le Guin, Ursula. *Lathe of Heaven.* Lon. 1972. 1st UK ed. dj. .... *$30.00–$85.00*

Le Guin, Ursula. *Word for World Is Forest*. NY. Putnam. 1976. 1st Amer ed. dj. .... *$95.00–$125.00*

Le May, Curtis. *Mission with LeMay: My Story*. NY. 1965. photos. ...... *$15.00–$25.00*

Le Moine, J. M. *Picturesque Quebec*. Montreal. 1882. softcvr. .... *$24.00–$30.00*

Lea, Elizabeth E. *Domestic Cookery, Useful Receipts*. Balt. 1853. 5th ed. .... *$50.00–$85.00*

Lea, Isaac. *Descriptions of the Soft Parts . . . of Unionidae of the U.S*. Phila. 1863. 1st ed. wrps. illus. folio. .... *$75.00–$100.00*

Lea, Tom. *Bullfight Manual for Spectators*. Mexico. 1949. 1st ed. wrps. *$30.00–$40.00*

Lea, Tom. *Hands of Cantu*. Bos. Little Brown. (1964). 1st ed. dj. .... *$32.00–$45.00*

Lea, Tom. *King Ranch*. Little Brown. (1957). 2 vols. 1st ed. .... *$75.00–$100.00*

Lea, Tom. *Wonderful Country*. Bos. (1952). 1st ed. dj. .... *$25.00–$35.00*

Leach, David G. *Rhododendrons of the World*. NY. Scribner's. 1st ed. illus. fldg clr plates, folio, dj. .... *$50.00–$65.00*

Leadbeater, C. W. *Some Glimpses of Ocultism*. Lon. 1903. .... *$20.00–$30.00*

Leaf, Munro. *Story of Ferdinand*. Lon. Hamish Hamilton. (1937). illus. by Robert Lawson. 1st UK ed. .... *$40.00–$60.00*

Leaf, Munro. *Wee Gillis*. NY. 1938. 1st ed. illus. dj. .... *$100.00–$150.00*

Leary, Timothy. *High Priest*. NY. 1968. 1st ed. .... *$35.00–$45.00*

Lederer, William and Eugene Burdick. *Ugly American*. 1958. 1st ed. dj. .... *$25.00–$35.00*

Ledger, Edmund. *Sun: Its Planets and Their Satellites*. Lon. Edward Stanford. 1882. illus. 3 Woodbury types, 1 clr litho, wood engrs in text. .... *$100.00–$150.00*

Lee, Amy Freeman. *Hobby Horses*. NY. Derrydale. 1940. ltd #105/250, sgn. .... *$125.00–$250.00*

Lee, Art. *Fishing Dry Flies for Trout on Rivers and Streams*. NY. 1982. 1st ed. dj. .... *$30.00–$50.00*

Lee, Harper. *To Kill a Mockingbird*. Lon. 1960. 1st Brit ed. dj. .... *$200.00–$300.00*

Lee, Irvin H. *Negro Medal of Honor Men*. NY. Dodd Mead. (1969). dj. *$14.00–$35.00*

Lee, Robert. *Clinical Midwifery*. Phila. 1849. 1st Amer ed. .... *$125.00–$150.00*

Leeds, Joseph. *Let My People Know . . .* pub by Manny's Friends. 1943. wrps. 2nd print. .... *$75.00–$100.00*

Lees, Willis T. *Stories in Stone*. NY. Chautauqua Press. 1927. illus. photos, dj. .... *$35.00–$40.00*

Leeson, F. *Identification of Snakes of the Gold Coast*. Lon. 1950. illus. .... *$65.00–$100.00*

Leffingwell, William Bruce. *Art of Wing Shooting*. Rand McNally. 1895. 1st ed. slipcase. .... *$95.00–$125.00*

Leffingwell, William Bruce. *Shooting on Upland, Marsh, and Stream*. Rand McNally. 1890. 1st ed. .... *$75.00–$125.00*

Leffingwell, William Bruce. *Wild Fowl Shooting.* Rand McNally. 1890. 1st ed. ....
.... *$75.00–$95.00*

Legend of the Shasta Spring of California. SF. nd. 1st ed. wrps. .... *$50.00–$75.00*

Leger, Jacques Nicolas. *Haiti, Her History and Her Detractors.* NY/Wash. 1907. 1st ed.
.... *$95.00–$150.00*

Leiber, Fritz. *Bazaar of the Bizarre.* Kingston. 1st ed. 1300 cc, dj......... *$25.00–$35.00*

Leiber, Fritz. *Heroes and Horrors.* Whispers Press. 1978. 1st ed. dj..... *$25.00–$35.00*

Leiber, Fritz. *Two Sought Adventure.* NY. Gnome. 1957. 1st ed. 1st binding, dj. ....
.... *$45.00–$60.00*

Leibovitch, J. *Ancient Egypt.* Cairo. 1938. 1st ed. wrps. illus................ *$25.00–$40.00*

Leighton, Clare. *Four Hedges.* NY. 1935. illus. sgn, dj. .... *$75.00–$100.00*

Leighton, Clare. *Growing New Roots: An Essay with Fourteen Wood Engravings.* Book
Club of California. 1979. 1st ed. thus, #264/500 cc, sgn........................... *$45.00–$60.00*

Leighton, Clare. *Southern Harvest.* Macmillan. 1942. 1st ed. 1st ptg, sgn, dj. ....
.... *$45.00–$60.00*

Leighton, Clare. *Where Land Meets Sea.* NY. Rinehart. 1954. 1st ed. illus. dj. ....
.... *$65.00–$80.00*

Leighton, Clare. *Where Land Meets Sea.* NY. (1954). illus. by Leighton, dj. ....
.... *$20.00–$30.00*

Leland, E. H. *Farm Homes.* NY. 1881. illus... *$30.00–$67.00*

Lennon, John. *In His Own Write.* Lon. 1964. 1st ed............................... *$50.00–$60.00*

Lennon, John. *Spaniard in the Works.* Lon. 1965. .... *$85.00–$125.00*

Lenski, Lois. *Little Fire Engine.* 1946. 1st ed.. *$30.00–$50.00*

Lenski, Lois. *Skipping Village.* NY. 1927. 1st ed. illus. by author......... *$35.00–$100.00*

Lenski, Lois. *Strawberry Girl.* Lippincott. 1945. 1st ed. illus................ *$25.00–$35.00*

Lensky, Lois. *Jack Horner's Pie.* Harper. 1927. 1st ed. illus.................. *$20.00–$35.00*

Lenton, H. T. *Warships of W W II.* Lon. 1968. illus. .... *$35.00–$50.00*

Lentz, Harold. *Pop-Up Pinnochio.* NY. 1932..................................... *$95.00–$125.00*

Leonard, Elmore. *City Primeval.* NY. Arbor House. 1980. 1st ed. dj. ... *$50.00–$65.00*

Leonard, Elmore. *City Primeval.* Lon. W H Allen. 1981. 1st Eng ed. dj......................
.... *$70.00–$85.00*

Leonard, Elmore. *Killshot.* NY. Arbor House/William Morrow. 1989. 1st ed. dj. ....
.... *$35.00–$45.00*

Leonard, Elmore. *Moonshine War.* Garden City. Doubleday. 1969. 1st ed. dj...............
.... *$145.00–$290.00*

Leonard, Elmore. *Stick.* NY. Arbor House. 1983. 1st ed. dj, sgn. .... *$50.00–$65.00*

Leonard, Elmore. *Swag.* NY. Delacorte. 1976. 1st ed. dj. .... *$95.00–$125.00*

Leonard, Elmore. *Touch.* NY. Arbor House. 1987. 1st ed. dj. .... *$10.00–$35.00*

Leonhardt, Olive. *New Orleans Drawn and Quartered.* Richmond. The Dale Press.
1938. illus. .... *$35.00–$50.00*

Leopold, Aldo. *Report on a Game Survey of the North Central States*. Madison. Amer Game Assoc. 1931. 1st ed. illus. .... *$35.00–$70.00*

Lerner, Max. *America as a Civilization*. NY. Simon & Schuster. 1957. 3rd ptg cloth. .... *$15.00–$25.00*

Lesley, J. P. *Geological Hand Atlas of the Sixty-Seven Counties of Pennsylvania. . .1874 to 1884*. Harrisburg. 1885. maps. .... *$65.00–$85.00*

Leslie, Frank. *Famous Leaders and Battle Scenes of the Civil War*. NY. 1896. 1st ed. folio .... *$135.00–$160.00*

Leslie, Frank. *Illustrated History of the Civil War*. NY. (1895). illus. repaired. .... *$40.00–$60.00*

Leslie, Frank. *Leslie's Famous War Pictures: Portfolio of War and Nation — Civil War*. DC. War Dept. 1906. illus. 582 pp, rebound, folio. .... *$150.00–$175.00*

Leslie, J., et al. *Narrative of Discovery and Adventure in the Polar Seas and Regions*. Edin. Oliver & Boyd. 1830. fldg map, ½ lea. .... *$65.00–$100.00*

Leslie, Miss. *75 Receipts for Pastry, Cakes, and Sweetmeats*. Bos. nd. *$145.00–$185.00*

Leslie, Miss. *Directions for Cookery*. Phila. 1863. 59th ed .... *$18.00–$25.00*

Leslie, Miss. *Miss Leslie's New Recipes for Cooking*. Phila. 1854. ...... *$120.00–$150.00*

Lessing, Do(is. *African Stories*. Simon. 1965. 1st US ed. dj. .... *$25.00–$35.00*

Lessing, Doris. *Fifth Child*. NY. 1988. 1st ed. dj .... *$20.00–$25.00*

Lessing, Doris. *Real Thing*. Harper Collins. (1992). 1st ed. 214 pp, dj. . *$12.00–$25.00*

Lester, Chadwick. *Baseball Joe Around the World*. Cupples & Leon. 1918. Baseball Joe #8, dj .... *$42.00–$75.00*

Lester, J. C. and D. L. Wilson. *Ku Klux Klan*. Nashville. 1884. wrps. ....*$700.00–$750.00*

Letters of John James Audubon, 1826–1840. 1930. 2 vols. ltd 225 cc, slipcase. .... *$250.00–$275.00*

Letts, W. M. and M. F. S. Letts. *Helmet and Cowl*. NY. Stokes. nd. illus. by Stephen Reid .... *$45.00–$50.00*

Lever, John. *Practical Treatise on Organic Diseases of the Uterus*. Newburgh, NY. Proudfit. 1845. 1st Amer ed. .... *$100.00–$175.00*

Levi, Wendell M. *The Pigeon*. Sumter, SC. 1963. illus. sgn. .... *$50.00–$65.00*

Levi-Strauss, Claude. *Introduction to a Science of Mythology: The Raw and the Cooked and From Honey to Ashes*. NY. Harper & Row. 1969. 2 vols. 1st Amer ed. dj .... *$100.00–$133.00*

Levin, Ira. *Rosemary's Baby*. NY. Rinehart. 1967. 1st ed. dj .... *$75.00–$100.00*

Levine, Philip. *New Season*. WA. Graywolf Press. (1975). 1st ed. 225 letterpress copies not sgn. .... *$100.00–$145.00*

Levine, Philip. *Walk With Tom Jefferson*. NY. 1988. 1st ed. sgn, dj .... *$55.00–$72.00*

Lewis, Alfred Henry. *Wolfville*. NY. Stokes. 1902. 1st ed. .... *$70.00–$90.00*

Lewis, G. Griffin. *Practical Book of Oriental Rugs*. NY. 1945. illus. rev ed. .... *$50.00–$65.00*

Lewis, G. Griffin. *Practical Book of Oriental Rugs*. Phila. 1920. map, illus. .... *$75.00–$95.00*

Lewis, Jan. *Pursuit of Happiness* . . . Camb Univ. 1983. dj. .... *$20.00–$25.00*

Lewis, John. *Printed Ephemera*. Ipswich. (1962). 1st ed. illus. dj. .... *$40.00–$60.00*

Lewis, Sinclair. *Ann Vickers*. NY. Doubleday. (1933). dj. .... *$150.00–$250.00*

Lewis, Sinclair. *Arrowsmith*. NY. 1925. .... *$45.00–$55.00*

Lewis, Sinclair. *Dodsworth*. NY. Grosset & Dunlap. (1929). dj. .... *$35.00–$45.00*

Lewis, Sinclair. *Elmer Gantry*. NY. 1927. 1st ed. dj. .... *$50.00–$80.00*

Lewis, Sinclair. *Elmer Gantry*. NY. Harcourt, Brace & World. (1927). 1st ed. 1st binding with "G" on spine resembling "C", dj. .... *$200.00–$250.00*

Lewis, Sinclair. *Free Air*. NY. 1919. 1st ed. dj. .... *$45.00–$55.00*

Lewis, Sinclair. *Prodigal Parents*. Doubleday. 1938. 1st ed. dj. .... *$45.00–$60.00*

Lewisohn, Ludwig. *Island Within*. NY. Harper & Bros. 1928. inscribed. *$30.00–$45.00*

Leyner, Mark. *Et Tu, Babe*. NY. Harmony. 1992. 1st ed. dj. .... *$22.00–$30.00*

Lichten, Frances. *Folk Art of Rural Pennsylvania*. NY. Scribner's. (1946). illus............. .... *$35.00–$65.00*

Lichtenstein, Gaston. *George Washington's Birthday* . . . Wm. Byrd. 1924. dj. .... *$30.00–$45.00*

Liddle, Hart B. H. *Sherman, The Genius of the Civil War*. Ernest Benn Ltd. 1930........ .... *$30.00–$45.00*

Lieber, Fritz. *Specter is Hauntin Texas*. NY. Walker. (1968). 1st ed. 245 pp, dj. .... *$30.00–$45.00*

Liebetrau, Preben. *Oriental Rugs in Color*. NY. 1963. illus. dj. .... *$40.00–$50.00*

Liebig, Justus. *Natural Laws of Husbandry*. Lon. Walton & Maberly. 1863. 416 pp. .... *$125.00–$175.00*

Life & Adventures of Sam Bass the Notorious . . . *Train Robber*. Dallas. 1878. wrps. . ... *$75.00–$100.00*

Life of Fremont. NY. 1856. 1st ed. illus. .... *$32.00–$40.00*

Life of General Putnam. NY. Nofis & Cornish. 1847. illus. with woodcuts, small......... .... *$20.00–$75.00*

Life of Miss Anne Catley: Celebrated Singing Performer . . . Lon. 1888...................... .... *$30.00–$40.00*

Life of Sergeant I. W. Ambler. Bos. Lea & Shepard. 1883. illus. red-brown decorated cloth gold lettering on spine. .... *$45.00–$50.00*

Likins, W. M. *Patriotism Capitalized or Religion Turned Into Gold*. PA. The Watchman Pub Co. 1925. 1st ed. wrps. .... *$60.00–$75.00*

Lilienthal, Howard. *Imperative Surgery for the General Practioner* . . . NY. Macmillan. 1901. rprnt. .... *$50.00–$60.00*

Lincoln, Abraham. *Abraham Lincoln, President of the United States*. Worcester. Achille J St Onge. 1950. 1st ed. illus. miniature book 2 x 3 inches, calf, bound by Sangorski & Sutcliffe of Lon, ltd 1500 cc. .... *$125.00–$175.00*

Lincoln, Almira. *Familiar Lectures on Botany . . . For the Use of Schools and Academics*. Hartford. Huntington. 1832. 3rd ed. 440 pp. .... *$25.00–$40.00*

Lincoln, Mrs. D. A. *Boston School Kitchen Text-Book*. Bos. Little Brown. 1905............ .... *$15.00–$30.00*

Lind, Andrew W., *Hawaii's Japanese: An Experiment in Democracy*. Princeton. Princeton Univ Press. 1946. 1st ed.. *$35.00–$50.00*

Lindberg, Anne Morrow. *Dearly Beloved*. Harcourt. 1962. sgn, dj....... *$35.00–$45.00*

Lindberg, Anne Morrow. *Flower and the Nettle, Diaries and Letters of . . .1936–39*. NY. Harcourt Brace. (1976). 1st ed. dj.. *$10.00–$25.00*

Lindberg, Anne Morrow. *Gift From the Sea*. 1955. 1st ed. illus. slipcase...................... .... *$35.00–$50.00*

Lindberg, Anne Morrow. *North to the Orient*. Harcourt Brace. 1935. 1st ed. dj. .... *$25.00–$35.00*

Lindberg, Charles A. *Of Flight and Life*. NY. Scribner's. 1948. 1st ed. dj. .... *$50.00–$60.00*

Lindberg, Charles A. *Spirit of St. Louis*. NY. Scribner's. 1953. dj. .... *$50.00–$90.00*

Lindbergh in Paris, All the Photos. Paris. Edison Nilsson. wrps. photo paste-down on cvr. .... *$25.00–$40.00*

Lindbergh, Charles. *Of Flight and Life*. NY. Scribner's. 1948. 1st ed. dj...................... .... *$50.00–$60.00*

Lindbergh, Charles. *Spirit of St Louis*. NY. Scribner's. 1953. 1st ed. illus. decorated endpapers. blue cloth dj.. *$45.00–$100.00*

Lindbergh, Charles A. *We*. NY. Putnam. 1927. 1st ed. dj. .... *$100.00–$125.00*

Lindley and Widney. *California of the South*. NY. 1888. 1st ed. illus... *$32.00–$45.00*

Lindsay, David Moore. *Voyage to the Arctic in the Whaler "Aurora"*. Bos. 1911. 1st ed. illus. .... *$60.00–$75.00*

Lindsay, Maud and Emilie Poulsson. *Joyous Guests*. Bos. Lothrop Lee & Shepard Co. (1921). illus. pictorial cvr. .... *$40.00–$55.00*

Linsley, D. C. *Morgan Horses*. NY. Saxton. 1857. 1st ed.................... *$450.00–$535.00*

Lipton, Lawrence. *Holy Barbarians*. NY. 1959. 1st ed. dj. .... *$45.00–$65.00*

Lipton, Lawrence. *Holy Barbarians*. NY. Julian Messner. 1959. 1st ed. dj. .... *$25.00–$40.00*

Littauer, Capt. Vladimir. *Common Sense Horsemanship*. NY. Van Nostrand. 1951. 1st ed. dj. .... *$45.00–$58.00*

Littauer, Captain V. S. *Jumping the Horse*. NY. Derrydale. 1931. 1st ed. *$32.00–$60.00*

Little Childs A B C Home Book. NY. McLoughlin Bros Publishers. wrps. chromolithos. .... *$50.00–$75.00*

Littlejohn, F. J. *Legends of Michigan and the Old Northwest*. Mich. 1875.................... .... *$40.00–$60.00*

Livermore, Mary. *My Story of the War*. Hartford. 1889. illus. .... *$50.00–$75.00*

Lives of Distinguished Shoemakers. Portland. 1849. 1st ed. brown cloth. ....
.... *$50.00–$100.00*

Lives of the Holy Evangelists, and Apostles, With their Martyrdoms, . . . Barnard, VT. 1813. 120 pp. .... *$20.00–$25.00*

Livingston, John. *Birds of the Northern Forest*. Houghton Mifflin. 1956. 1st ed. dj. .....
.... *$20.00–$35.00*

Livingstone, David. *Missionary Travels and Researches in South Africa*. Lon. John Murray. 1857. 1st ed. 687 pp, map.. *$200.00–$350.00*

Livingstone, David. *Missionary Travels and Researches in South Africa*. NY. 1858. illus. 1st Amer ed. maps. .... *$125.00–$200.00*

Livingstone, David. *Narrative of an Expedition to the Zambese and Its Tributaries*. Lon. John Murray. 1865. 1st ed. fldg map. tan cloth. .... *$250.00–$375.00*

Livingtons, David and Charles. *Narrative of an Expedition to the Zambesi & Its Tributaries; 1858–1864*. NY. Harper & Bros. 1866. 1st Amer ed. illus, fldg map. ....
.... *$110.00–$125.00*

Llewellyn, Karl. *Cheyenne Way*. Norman. Univ of OK. 1941. 1st ed. illus. scarce.........
....*$50.00–$65.00*

Llewellyn, Sam. *Blood Orange*. NY. Summit. 1989. 1st ed. dj. .... *$15.00–$25.00*

Lloyd, A. B. *In Dwarf Land and Cannibal Country*. Lon. Fisher Unwin. 1899. 1st ed. illus. photos.. *$69.00–$100.00*

Lloyd, Freeman. *All Spaniels*. NY. nd. illus. .... *$15.00–$25.00*

Lobel, Arnold. *Fables*. Harper Collins Pub. (1980). illus. pictorial dj. ... *$10.00–$15.00*

Lobel, Arnold. *Frog and Toad All Year*. NY. Harper & Row. 1976. 1st ed. sgn with original Lobel Frog character. .... *$48.00–$60.00*

Locke, David Ross. *Hannah Jane*. Lee and Shepard. 1882. 1st ed. ...... *$65.00–$125.00*

Locke, David Ross. *Ekkoes from Kentucky by Petroleum B Nasby*. Bos. 1868. 1st ed. illus. by Thomas Nast.. *$100.00–$150.00*

Lockett, Hattie Greene. *Unwritten Literature of the Hopi*. Tucson. 1933. wrps. illus. photos. Bulletin No 2, Vol IV, No 4. .... *$28.00–$40.00*

Lockwood, Luke V. *Colonial Furniture in America*. NY. 1926. 2 vols. 3rd ed...............
.... *$95.00–$125.00*

Lockwood, Thomas D. *Electricity, Magnetism, and Electric Telegraphy*. 1883. 1st ed. illus. .... *$45.00–$65.00*

Lodge, Sir Oliver. *Electrons*. Lon. 1907. 2nd ed................................... *$40.00–$50.00*

Lodge, Sir Oliver. *Ether and Reality*. Lon. 1925. 1st ed........................ *$30.00–$40.00*

Loewy, Raymond. *Locomotive*. Lon/NY. The Studio. (1937). 1st ed. illus. tan cloth. lettering in dark brown. .... *$65.00–$100.00*

Lofting, Hugh. *Doctor Dolittle and the Secret Lake*. Lippincott. (1948). 1st ed. illus. dj. .... *$75.00–$100.00*

Lofting, Hugh. *Doctor Dolittle in the Moon*. NY. Frederick Stokes. (1928). 1st ed........
.... *$30.00–$45.00*

Lofting, Hugh. *Doctor Dolittle's Circus*. NY. (1924). 1st ed. .... *$40.00–$50.00*

Lofting, Hugh. *Doctor Dolittle's Zoo*. NY. (1925). 1st ed..................... *$45.00–$50.00*

Lofting, Hugh. *Doctor Doolittle's Zoo*. NY. Frederick Stokes. (1925). 1st ed................
.... *$30.00–$50.00*

Lofting, Hugh. *Voyages of Doctor Dolittle*. NY. Frederick A Stokes. 1922. illus. 2nd ptg.
.... *$60.00–$90.00*

Logan, H. and L. C. Cosper. *Orchids Are Easy to Grow*. Englewood Cliffs, NJ. 1949.
dj. .... *$25.00–$35.00*

Logan, James and R. R. McIan. *Clans of the Scottish Highlands*. Lon. Ackerman & Co.
1845–47. 2 vols. 1st ed. illus. 72 hand-clr plates, folio, 2 clr armorial frontises. ....
.... *$5,000.00–$7,000.00*

Logan, Mrs. John. *Reminiscences of a Soldier's Wife*. NY. Scribner's. 1913. 1st ed. illus.
inscribed and signed. .... *$40.00–$60.00*

Logan, Mrs. John A. *Thirty Years in Washington*. Hartford. 1901. 1st ed. illus. ¾ lea and
red cloth. .... *$35.00–$75.00*

Logue, Roscoe. *Tumbleweeds and Barb Wire Fences*. Amarillo. 1936. 1st ed. illus. ....
.... *$30.00–$45.00*

Logue, Roscoe. *Under Texas and Border Skies*. Amarillo. 1935. wrps. 2nd ptg. ....
.... *$45.00–$65.00*

Lomax, Alan. *Folk Songs of North America*. Garden City. (1960). .... *$25.00–$35.00*

Lomax, John A. *Adventures of a Ballad Hunter*. NY. 1947. 1st ed. dj. .. *$30.00–$60.00*

Lomax, John A. *Cowboy Songs and Other Frontier Ballads*. NY. 1911. 1st ed. 2nd ptg.
dj. .... *$65.00–$115.00*

Lomax, John A. and Alan Lomax. *American Ballads and Folk Songs*. NY. 1934. 1st ed.
.... *$20.00–$35.00*

Lommel, A. *Masks, Their Meaning and Function*. Zurich. 1970. photos.....................
.... *$100.00–$135.00*

London, Jack. *Burning Daylight*. Macmillan. 1910. 1st ed. .... *$100.00–$125.00*

London, Jack. *Daughter of Snows*. NY. 1902. 2nd ed. .... *$22.00–$35.00*

London, Jack. *Jerry of the Islands*. Macmillan. 1917. 1st ed. .... *$85.00–$100.00*

London, Jack. *Love of Life*. 1st ed.. *$100.00–$115.00*

London, Jack. *Martin Eden*. NY. Macmillan. 1909. 1st ed. blue decorated cloth. ....
.... *$175.00–$250.00*

London, Jack. *Scarlet Plague*. Macmillan. 1915. 1st ed.................... *$150.00–$200.00*

London, Jack. *Sea Wolf*. NY. Macmillan. 1904. 1st ed. illus. teg. blue decorated cloth..
.... *$120.00–$150.00*

London, Jack. *Smoke Bellew*. NY. Century. 1912. 1st ed.................... *$150.00–$250.00*

London, Jack. *Star Rover*. NY. Grosset & Dunlap. 1917. frontis. .... *$15.00–$20.00*

London, Jack. *Star Rover*. NY. 1915. 1st ed. blue decorated cloth..... *$200.00–$300.00*

London, Jack. *Tales of the Fish Control*. NY. Macmillan. 1st ed. illus. blue decorated
cloth teg. .... *$175.00–$200.00*

London, Jack. *Tales of the Fish Patrol*. NY. Grosset & Dunlap. 1905.... *$20.00–$25.00*

London, Jack. *War of the Classes*. NY. 1905. 1st ed................................ *$55.00–$70.00*

London, Jack. *When God Laughs*. NY. 1911. 1st ed. illus. decorated cloth. ....
....*$175.00–$250.00*

London, Jack. *White Fang*. NY. 1906. 1st ed. .... *$75.00–$85.00*

Lonfellow, Henry Wadsworth. *Poetical Works*. Lon. illus. 6 mounted albumen photos
mor, aeg. .... *$50.00–$90.00*

Long, E. *History of Pathology*. Balt. 1928. 1st ed................................... *$40.00–$50.00*

Long, Haniel. *Children, Students, and a Few Adults*. Santa Fe. 1942. 2nd ed. wraps. ...
.... *$20.00–$35.00*

Long, Haniel. *Grist Mill*. NM. Rydal Press. 1946. 1st ed. dj. .... *$50.00–$65.00*

Long, Haniel. *Interliner to Cabeza de Vaca*. Santa Fe. 1936. 1st ed. dj..........................
.... *$175.00–$250.00*

Long, Haniel. *Notes for a New Mythology*. Chi. 1926. 1st ed. ltd 450 cc, sgn. ....
.... *$55.00–$150.00*

Long, Haniel. *Pinon Country*. NY. (1941). 1st ed. dj. .... *$40.00–$85.00*

Long, Haniel. *Spring Returns*. NY. (1958). 1st ed. dj.............................. *$15.00–$35.00*

Long, Huey. *My First Days in the White House*. Telegraph Press. 1935. 1st ed. ....
.... *$45.00–$50.00*

Long, John Luther. *Billy Boy*. NY. 1906. 1st ed. illus. in clr and b/w by Jesse Willcox
Smith. scarce. .... *$95.00–$135.00*

Long, Major A. W. *Irish Sport of Yesterday*. Bos. Houghton Mifflin. 1923. 1st ed. illus.
.... *$40.00–$100.00*

Long, William J. *Following the Deer*. Ginn & Co. 1903. 1st ed. .... *$25.00–$40.00*

Longfellow, Henry Wadsworth. *Courtship of Miles Standish*. Ind. 1903. 1st thus. clr
and b/w illus. .... *$50.00–$85.00*

Longfellow, Henry Wadsworth. *Courtship of Miles Standish and Other Poems*. Bos.
Ticknor & Fields. 1858. 1st ed... *$80.00–$150.00*

Longfellow, Henry Wadsworth. *Divine Tragedy*. Bos. James R Osgood. 1871. 1st ed..
.... *$75.00–$175.00*

Longfellow, Henry Wadsworth. *Longfellow's Poetical Works*. Bos. Houghton &
Mifflin. 1886. 4 vols.. *$60.00–$75.00*

Longfellow, Henry Wadsworth. *Song of Hiawatha*. Bos. Ticknor and Fields. 1855. 1st
Amer ed. points of issue include "Dove" instead of "Dived" in line 7, p 95. ....
.... *$300.00–$500.00*

Longfellow, Henry Wadsworth. *Song of Hiawatha*. Platt and Monk. 1963. 1st ed. thus.
gold illus cloth. .... *$35.00–$50.00*

Longfellow, Henry Wadsworth. *Tales of a Wayside Inn*. Bos. 1863. 1st ed. ....
.... *$60.00–$145.00*

Longman, E. D. *Pins & Pincushions*. Lon. Longmans & Green. 1911. 1st ed. illus. cloth.
.... *$45.00–$175.00*

Longstreet, Augustus B. *Georgia Scenes*. NY. 1860. 2nd ed. 214 pp, illus....................
.... *$65.00–$85.00*

Longstreet, Helen D. *Lee and Longstreet at High Tide: Gettysburg* . . . Gainesville, GA. 1905. illus. 2nd ed. .... *$50.00–$100.00*

Longstreet, Stephen. *Real Jazz Old and New*. Baton Rouge. Louisianna State Univ Press. 1956. 1st ed. illus. dj. .... *$50.00–$95.00*

Longstreet, Stephen. *Sportin' House*. LA. Sherbourne Press. 1965. 1st ed. illus. dj. .... *$50.00–$75.00*

Longstreth, T. Morris. *Understanding the Weather*. NY. 1953. rev ed, dj, 10 illus, 118 pp. .... *$10.00–$14.00*

Lonn, Ella. *Reconstruction in Louisiana After 1868*. NY/Lon. 1918. 1st ed. maps. .... *$125.00–$150.00*

Lonn, Ella. *Salt as a Factor in the Confederacy*. NY. 1933. 1st ed. ..... *$125.00–$175.00*

Loomis, Frederic. *Hunting Extinct Animals in Patagonian Pampas*. NY. 1913. 141 pp, illus. .... *$65.00–$85.00*

Loos, Anita. *Gentlemen Prefer Blondes*. NY. 1925. 1st ed. dj. .... *$65.00–$95.00*

Lopez, Barry. *Crossing Open Ground*. NY. Scribner's. 1988. 1st ed. dj. *$30.00–$40.00*

Lopez, Barry. *Of Wolves and Men*. NY. Scribner's. 1978. 1st ed. dj. ..... *$95.00–$125.00*

Loque, Roscoe. *Tumbleweeds and Barb Wire Fences*. Amarillo. 1936. 1st ed. wrps. .... *$50.00–$85.00*

Lord, Eliot, John Trenor and Samuel Barrows. *Italian in America*. NY. BF Buck & Co. 1905. illus. red cloth, frontis. .... *$40.00–$70.00*

Lorentz, H. A. *Theory of Electrons* . . . Leipzig. 1916. 2nd ed. .... *$30.00–$40.00*

Loring, Charles G. *Neutral Relations of England & the United States*. NY. 1863. wrps. .... *$30.00–$60.00*

Loss of the United States Steamer Oneida. US GovDoc, HED#236. 1870. fldg map..... .... *$25.00–$35.00*

Lossing, Benson J. *History of the Civil War, 1861–1865*. NY. 1912. illus. .... *$65.00–$90.00*

Lossing, Benson J. *Pictorial Field Book of the American Revolution*. Freeport, NY. 1969. 2 vols. rprnt. .... *$35.00–$55.00*

Lossing, Benson J. *Pictorial Field-Book of the War of 1812*. NY. Harper & Bros. 1869. clr frontis, gilt red calf, rbkd. .... *$150.00–$225.00*

Lossing, Benson J. *Pictorial History of the Civil War in the United States* . . . Phila. 1866. 3 vols. ½ lea. .... *$85.00–$100.00*

Lossing, J. G. *Biographical Sketches of Signers of the Declaration of American Independence*. 1848. .... *$45.00–$50.00*

Lothrop, Jason. *Juvenile Philospher: or, Youth's Manual of Philosophy, Natural Experimental & Analytical*. Bogert. 1823. 312 pp. .... *$125.00–$150.00*

Love, Robertus. *Rise and Fall of Jesse James*. NY. (1939). .... *$22.00–$33.00*

Lovecraft, H. P. *At the Mountains of Madness and Other Novels*. Sauk City. Arkham House. 1964. 1st ed. dj. .... *$100.00–$250.00*

Lovecraft, H. P. *Dagon and Other Macabre Tales*. Sauk City. Arkham House. 1965. 1st ed. dj. .... *$85.00–$150.00*

Lovecraft, H. P. *Dark Brotherwood.* Arkham House. 1966. 1st ed. dj. *$95.00–$125.00*

Lovecraft, H. P. *Dunwich Horror & Others.* Arkham House. 1963. 1st ed....................
.... *$30.00–$45.00*

Lovecraft, H. P. *Dunwich Horror and Others.* Sauk City. Arkham House. 1963. 1st ed. dj. .... *$85.00–$100.00*

Lovecraft, H. P. *Horror in the Museum and Other Revisions.* Sauk City. Arkham House. 1970. 1st ed. dj. .... *$50.00–$150.00*

Lovecraft, H. P. *Something About Cats.* Arkham House. 1949. 1st ed. dj......................
.... *$125.00–$200.00*

Lovecraft, H. P and August Derleth. *Lurker at the Threshold.* Sauk City. Arkham House. 1945. 1st ed. dj. .... *$85.00–$175.00*

Lovecraft, H. P and Diverse Hands. *Dark Brotherhood and Other Pieces.* Sauk City. Arkham House. 1966. 1st ed. dj.. *$50.00–$125.00*

Lovecraft, H. P. and August Derleth. *Watchers Out of Time.* Arkham House. 1974. 1st ed. dj. .... *$30.00–$45.00*

Lovell, Mrs. F. S. and L. C. Lovell. *History of the Town of Rockingham, Vt.* Bellows Falls. 1958. illus. .... *$45.00–$55.00*

Lovett, Sarah. *Dangerous Attachments.* NY. (1995). 1st ed. dj. .... *$25.00–$35.00*

Lowel, G. *More Small Italian Villas and Farmhouses.* NY. 1920. folio. . *$70.00–$85.00*

Lowell Offering. Lowell, MA. Misses Curtis & Farley. May, 1845. wrps. rare...............
.... *$35.00–$50.00*

Lowell, James Russell. *Biglow Papers.* Bos. Ticknor & Fields. 1867. 1st Amer ed........
.... *$75.00–$150.00*

Lowell, James Russell. *The Courtin'.* Bos. 1874. illus. by Winslow Homer...................
.... *$75.00–$125.00*

Lowell, James Russell. *The Rose.* Bos. 1878. .... *$20.00–$30.00*

Lowell, Percival. *Mars and Its Canals.* NY. Macmillan. 1906. 1st ed. illus. green cloth.
.... *$180.00–$240.00*

Lowell, Robert. *For the Union Dead.* NY. Farrar, Straus Giroux. (c1964). 1st ed. dj. ....
.... *$35.00–$50.00*

Lowell, Robert. *Lord Weary's Castle.* NY. (1946). 1st ed. dj. .... *$175.00–$200.00*

Lowell, Robert. *Mils of the Kavanaughs.* NY. 1951. 1st ed. .... *$100.00–$125.00*

Lowell, Robert. *Oresteia of Aeschylus.* NY. Farrar, Straus & Giroux. (1978). 1st ed. dj, blue cloth. .... *$45.00–$55.00*

Lowell, Robert. *The Dolphin.* NY. (1973). 1st ed. dj. .... *$25.00–$35.00*

Lower Colorado River Land Use Plan. DC. GPO. 1964. wrps. illus. clr maps. ....
.... *$25.00–$50.00*

Lowie, Robert H. *Primitive Religion.* Lon. Routledge. 1925. 1st Eng ed.......................
.... *$95.00–$125.00*

Lubbock, Basil. *China Clippers.* Glasgow. 1946.................................. *$50.00–$80.00*

Lubbock, Basil. *Last of the Windjammers.* Bos. Lauriat. 1927. 1st Amer ed. 2 vols. illus. blue cloth. .... *$75.00–$125.00*

Lubbock, Basil. *Log of the Cutty Sark*. Charles Lauriat. 1924. 1st ed. illus. dj............... .... *$50.00–$80.00*

Lubbock, Basil. *Log of the Cutty Sark*. Glasgow. Brownison & Ferguson. 1974. rprnt, dj. .... *$25.00–$40.00*

Lubbock, Sir John. *Ants, Bees and Wasps*. NY. 1890............................ *$37.00–$40.00*

Lubbock, Sir John. *Origin of Civilisation and the Primitive Condition of Man*. NY. Appleton. 1895. illus. green cloth, frontis... *$35.00–$50.00*

Lubbock, Sir John. *Origin of Civilization & the Primitive Condition of Man*. NY. Appleton. 1875. 3rd ed. plates. .... *$55.00–$60.00*

Ludlow, Fitz Hugh. *Heart of the Continent, A Record of Travel Across the Plains* . . . NY. 1870.. *$100.00–$150.00*

Ludlum, Robert. *Bourne Ultimatum*. NY. Random House. 1990. 1st ed. dj................... .... *$20.00–$30.00*

Ludlum, Robert. *Icarus Agenda*. NY. Random House. 1988. 1st ed. dj. *$10.00–$30.00*

Ludlum, Robert. *Osterman Weekend*. NY. 1972. 1st ed. dj. ....*$40.00–$60.00*

Ludlum, Robert. *Road to Gandolfo*. Dial. 1975. 1st ed. 3 dj's. .... *$60.00–$85.00*

Ludlum, Robert. *Scarlatti Inheritance*. NY. World Pub. (1971). 1st ed. dj.................... .... *$35.00–$75.00*

Lumholtz, Carl. *Among Cannibals*. NY. 1889. portrait maps, chromo-liths, decorative cloth, 395 pp. .... *$175.00–$225.00*

Lumley, Brian. *Beneath the Moors*. WI. Arkham House. 1974. 1st ed. dj. .... *$30.00–$85.00*

Lummis, Charles F. *King of the Broncos & Other Stories of New Mexico*. NY. 1897. .. .. *$40.00–$55.00*

Lummis, Charles F. *Mesa, Canon and Pueblo*. Century. (1925). illus. . *$22.00–$35.00*

Lutz, Alma. *Created Equal*. John Day. (1940). 1st ed. sgn, dj. .... *$40.00–$50.00*

Lutz, Frank. *Fieldbook of Insects*. NY. 1921. illus. clr plates................. *$18.00–$25.00*

Lydenberg, Harry. *Care and Repair of Books*. NY. R R Bowker Co. 1931. 1st ed........ .... *$25.00–$40.00*

Lyell, Charles. *Elements of Geology*. Lon. 1839. 1st ed. 543 pp. .... *$200.00–$300.00*

Lyell, Sir Charles. *Travels in North America, Canada, and Nova Scotia with Geological Observations*. Lon. John Murray. 1855. 2nd ed. fldg map, plates.................................... .... *$250.00–$325.00*

Lymon, Henry and Frank Woolner. *Complete Book of Striped Bass Fishing*. NY. (1954). dj. .... *$15.00–$25.00*

Lynch, Bohun. *Collecting*. Lon. Jarrolds. 1928. 1st ed. presentation copy signed. .... *$20.00–$45.00*

Lynch, Jeremiah. *Egyptian Sketches*. Lon. 1890. illus........................... *$40.00–$75.00*

Lynch, W. F. *Narrative of the US Expedition to the River Jordan & Dead Sea*. Phila. 1849. illus. .... *$50.00–$100.00*

Lynk, Miles. *Black Troopers* . . . TN. 1971. rprnt................................. *$30.00–$45.00*

Lynk, Miles. *Black Troopers* . . . TN. M V Lynk Pub House. 1899. illus. red cloth. ....
.... *$750.00–$900.00*

Lyons, Nick. *Confessions of a Fly Fishing Addict*. Simon & Schuster. 1989. 1st ed. dj. .
.... *$25.00–$40.00*

M'Clintock. *Voyage of the Fox in the Arctic Seas*. Bos. Ticknor & Fields. 1860. illus. 4 maps, 3 fldg. .... *$40.00–$60.00*

M'Clintock, Capt. *Narrative of the Discovery of the Fate of Sir John Franklin* . . . Lon. 1860. illus. maps... *$50.00–$75.00*

M'Clintock, Francis L. *Voyage of the "Fox" in the Arctic Seas*. Bos. Ticknor & Fields. 1860. author's ed. small 8vo, frontis, illus, fldg maps. .... *$100.00–$130.00*

Mabie, Hamilton Wright. *Under the Trees & Elsewhere*. NY. Dodd, Mead. 1902. illus. 1st illus ed... *$30.00–$60.00*

MacDiarmid, Hugh. *Sangshaw*. Blackwood. 1925. 1st ed. dj............ *$150.00–$300.00*

MacDonald, Alexander. *Design for Angling, The Dry Fly on Western Trout Streams*. Bos. 1947.. *$65.00–$100.00*

MacDonald, John D. *Pale Gray for Guilt*. NY. Gold Medal Books. 1968. 1st ed. wrps. .... *$35.00–$55.00*

MacFall, Haldane. *Aubrey Beardsley, The Man and His Work*. Lon. 1928. illus............
.... *$75.00–$100.00*

MacGillivray, D. *Mandarin-Romanized Dictionary of Chinese*. Shanghai. 1918. 4th ed. .... *$25.00–$35.00*

MacGillvray. *History of British Quadrapeds*. Edin. 1838. 1st ed. 310 pp......................
.... *$100.00–$140.00*

Machen, Arthur. *Far Off Things*. NY. 1923. 1st ed. .... *$75.00–$85.00*

Machen, Arthur. *Great God Pan and the Inmost Light*. Lon. 1894. 1st ed. dj...............
.... *$25.00–$65.00*

Machen, Arthur. *London Adventure*. Lon. Martin Secker. (1924). dj. ... *$65.00–$75.00*

Machen, Arthur. *Rose Garden*. NY. 1932. wrps. 50 cc privately printed......................
.... *$30.00–$40.00*

Machen, Arthur. *The Terror*. Lon. (1917). 1st ed. .... *$35.00–$45.00*

Machen, Arthur. *Things Near and Far*. NY. (1923). 1st Amer.............. *$20.00–$30.00*

Mack, Arthur C. *Palisades of the Hudson*. NJ. The Palisade Press. (1909). 1st ed. illus. red pictorial cvr. pull-out map.. *$35.00–$95.00*

Mack, Connie. *My 66 Years in the Big Leagues*. Phila. 1950. 1st ed. ..... *$25.00–$35.00*

MacKay, Douglas. *Honourable Company—A History of the Hudson's Bay Company*. IN. (1936). 1st ed. dj. .... *$25.00–$50.00*

Macken, Arthur. *Dog and Duck*. NY. 1924. 1st ed................................ *$22.00–$30.00*

Mackenzie, A. L. *Clarence Milton, the Heroic Fireman* . . . Cleveland. United Printing Co. 1900. 1st ed. illus. blue cloth... *$50.00–$75.00*

Mackenzie, Alexander. *Voyages from Montreal on River St Lawrence* . . . *Preliminary Account of the Rise and Progress of the Present Fur Trade*. Tor. Master Works of Canadian Authors. 1927. illus. .... *$35.00–$55.00*

Mackenzie, Jean Kenyon. *Black Sheep: Adventures in West Africa*. Bos. Houghton Mifflin. 1916. 1st ed. illus. photos. .... *$80.00–$100.00*

MacLean, Alistair. *Guns of Navarone*. NY. Doubleday. 1957. 1st ed. dj. ....
.... *$50.00–$125.00*

MacLean, Alistair. *HMS Ulysses*. Lon. Collins. (1955). 1st UK ed. author's first book, dj. .... *$95.00–$250.00*

MacLean, Alistair. *Ice Station Zebra*. Lon. Collins. 1963. 1st ed. dj. ..... *$30.00–$45.00*

MacLean, Alistair. *Lonely Sea*. Garden City. Doubleday. 1986. 1st ed. green cloth dj. .
.... *$15.00–$35.00*

MacLean, Alistair. *South by Java Head*. Lon. Collins. 1958. 1st ed. dj. *$50.00–$75.00*

MacLean, Norman. *River Runs Through It*. Chi. 1976. 1st ed. illus. dj. *$35.00–$75.00*

MacLeish, Archibald. *Conquistador*. Bos/NY. Houghton Mifflin. 1932. 1st ed. no dj...
.... *$20.00–$35.00*

MacLeish, Archibald. *Herakles*. Bos. 1967. 1st ed. dj. .... *$20.00–$25.00*

MacLeish, Archibald. *Irresponsibles*. Duell. 1944. 1st ed. dj. .... *$50.00–$65.00*

MacLeish, Archibald. *Public Speech*. NY. Farrar & Rinhart. (1936). 1st ed. sgn. ....
.... *$80.00–$120.00*

MacLeod, G. *Treatment of Horses by Homeopathy*. Walden, Eng. Daniel Co, Ltd. 1983. dj. .... *$18.00–$25.00*

MacManus, Seaumas. *Red Poocher*. 1903. 1st US ed. .... *$25.00–$35.00*

MacMillan, Donald B. *Four Years in the White North*. Bos. 1925. illus. *$50.00–$65.00*

MacPhail, Christian. *Kitchen Adventures. . .or Experiments in Diet Changes*. Edin. 1933. 1st ed... *$15.00–$22.00*

Maeterlinck, Maurice. *Blue Bird*. NY. 1913. illus. .... *$125.00–$145.00*

Maeterlinck, Maurice. *Blue Bird*. NY. Souvenir Book. 1910. illus. pictorial cvrs..........
.... *$30.00–$40.00*

Maeterlinck, Maurice. *Blue Bird*. NY. 1911. illus. with 25 clr plates by Robinson. ......
.... *$125.00–$150.00*

Maeterlinck, Maurice. *Life of the White Ant*. 1939. illus. sgn by von Hagen. ....
.... *$20.00–$25.00*

Maeterlinck, Maurice. *Intelligence of the Flowers*. NY. (1907). 1st Amer ed. decorated bds... *$30.00–$40.00*

Magalever, Jacob. *Death to Traitors*. 1960. 1st ed. dj........................... *$20.00–$25.00*

Magician's Own Book . . . NY. 1857. 1st ed...................................... *$150.00–$200.00*

Magner, D. *Standard Horse and Stock Book*. Akron. Standard. 1903..... *$60.00–$85.00*

Mahan, A. T. *Gulf and Inland Waters*. NY. Scribner's Sons. 1883. 1st ed. maps and plans.
.... *$85.00–$125.00*

Mahan, A. T. *Influence of Sea Power Upon History*. Lon. 1890. illus. 1st Eng ed. 557 pp. .... *$10.00–$125.00*

Mahan, A. T. *Life of Nelson*. Bos. Little Brown. 1900. 2 vols. 2nd ed. revised, illus, 20 maps and plans, teg. .... *$120.00–$150.00*

Mahan, A. T. *Sea Power in Its Relation to the War of 1812*. Lon. 1905. 2 vols. dj........ .... *$78.00–$95.00*

Mahan, A. T. *Types of Naval Officers*. Lon. 1902. illus. plates.............. *$55.00–$74.00*

Mahan, D. H. *An Elementary Course of Civil Engineering* . . . NY. 1838. 2nd ed. fldg plates.. *$75.00–$220.00*

Mahan, D. H. *Treatise on Field Fortification*. NY. 1861. 3rd rev ed....... *$30.00–$50.00*

Maidment, James (ed.). *Scottish Ballads and Songs*. Edin. 1868. 2 vols.................... .... *$35.00–$45.00*

Mailer, Norman. *Advertisements For Myself*. NY. Putnam. 1959. 1st ed. dj.................. .... *$35.00–$45.00*

Mailer, Norman. *An American Dream*. Dial. 1971. 1st ed. dj................ *$28.00–$35.00*

Mailer, Norman. *Barbara Shore*. NY. Rinehart & Co. (1951). 1st ed. dj...................... .... *$75.00–$100.00*

Mailer, Norman. *Last Night. A Story of Armageddon*. NY. 1984. ltd 250 cc, sgn.......... .... *$95.00–$130.00*

Mailer, Norman. *Marilyn, A Biography*. NY. 1973. 1st ed. dj.............. *$35.00–$50.00*

Mailer, Norman. *Naked and the Dead*. NY. Rinehart. (1948). 1st ed. sgn, dj............... .... *$150.00–$300.00*

Mailer, Norman. *Prisoner of Sex*. NY. 1971. dj. .... *$20.00–$30.00*

Maine, a Guide Down East. Houghton Mifflin. 1937. illus. map in rear pocket, dj........ .... *$25.00–$35.00*

Major, John (ed.). *Complete Angler*. Lon. D Bogue. 1844. illus. 12 plates. woodcuts. large paper copy.. *$100.00–$150.00*

Malamud, Bernard. *Dubin's Lives*. NY. 1979. 750 cc.......................... *$45.00–$60.00*

Malamud, Bernard. *Magic Barrel*. Chatto & Windus. 1979. 1st UK ed dj. .... *$18.00–$35.00*

Malamud, Bernard. *Magic Barrel*. NY. Farrar, Straus. 1958. 1st ed. dj. .... *$125.00–$150.00*

Malamud, Bernard. *Pictures of Fidelman*. Farrar. 1969. 1st ed. dj........ *$32.00–$40.00*

Malamud, Bernard. *The Fixer*. NY. 1966. 1st ed. dj............................ *$50.00–$100.00*

Malamud, Bernard. *The Natural*. NY. (1952). 1st ed. of author's first book. .... *$125.00–$250.00*

Malamud, Bernard. *The Tenants*. Farrar. (1971). 1st ed. dj. .... *$45.00–$65.00*

Malls, Thom E. *People Called Apache*. NJ. 1974. dj. .... *$75.00–$125.00*

Mammals of Utah. Univ of Kansas Pub. wrps 1/50 cc. .... *$50.00–$65.00*

Manfacturers of Military, Sporting, Hunting, and Target Breech-Loading Rifles, Shotguns and Pistols. NY. E Remington & Sons. 1883. printed wrps, 48 pp. .... *$175.00–$250.00*

Mann, A. *History of the Forty-Fifth Regiment (Mass.)*. 1908. .... *$100.00–$150.00*

Mann, F. W. *Bullet's Flight from Powder to Target*. Huntington, WV. 1942. illus. photos, 2d ed. .... *$50.00–$95.00*

Mann, H. *Historical Annals of Dedham, MA, to 1847*. Dedham, MA. 1847. .... *$65.00–$85.00*

Mann, Horace. *Speech of Hon Horace Mann of Mass on Slavery & the Slave Trade* . . . Phila. 1849. 48 pp, unbound...................... *$60.00–$85.00*

Mann, Kathleen. *Peasant Costume in Europe*. Lon. 1931. illus. clr plates. .... *$35.00–$60.00*

Mann, Mrs. Horace. *Christianity in the Kitchen* . . . Bos. 1861............ *$50.00–$72.00*

Mann, Thomas. *Joseph and His Brothers*. NY. 1938. 6th ptg of Amer ed. sgn............... .... *$125.00–$150.00*

Mann, Thomas. *Magic Mountain*. NY. 1962. 2 vols. 1st ed. 1500 cc. *$125.00–$150.00*

Mann, Thomas. *Tales of Jacob*. Lon. 1934. 1st ed. dj............................ *$75.00–$100.00*

Mann, Thomas. *This War*. NY. 1940. 1st Amer ed. 69 pp, dj. .... *$50.00–$65.00*

Mann, Thomas. *Transposed Heads*. NY. Knopf. 1941. 1st Amer ed. dj. *$40.00–$65.00*

Manners, Customs, and Antiquities of the Indians of North and South America. Bos. 1844. 1st ed................... *$125.00–$150.00*

Manni, Pietro. *Manuale Pratico per la Cura degli Apparentemente Morti*. Napoli. 1835. 4th ed. plates.................... *$200.00–$300.00*

Manning, Samuel. *Palestine Illustrated by Pen and Pencil*. NY. Hurst & Co. nd. illus. folio pictorial cloth. .... *$50.00–$75.00*

Mansfield, Katherine. *Doves Nest and Other Stories*. Lon. Constable. (1923). 1st ed... .... *$40.00–$50.00*

Mansfield, Katherine. *Novels and Novelists*. Lon. Constable. 1930. 1st ed. ed by J Middleton Murray, dj. .... *$120.00–$150.00*

Mansfield, Katherine. *Poems*. NY. Knopf. 1924. 1st ed. .... *$35.00–$45.00*

Mansfield, Katherine. *Short Stories of* . . . NY. Knopf. 1937. .... *$25.00–$35.00*

Mansfield, Katherine. *The Aloe*. NY. 1930. 1st Amer ed. 750 cc. .... *$50.00–$100.00*

Manson, F. L. *Wright to 1910: The First Golden Age*. Reinhold. 1958. dj..................... .... *$120.00–$150.00*

Mantle, Mickey and Phil Pepe. *My Favorite Summer*. NY. Doubleday. 1991. 1st ed. dj. .... *$20.00–$25.00*

Manual of Homeopathic Veterinary Practice* . . . *Domestic Animals. NY. 1874. ½ lea. .... *$45.00–$55.00*

Manual of Pack Transportation. Wash. GPO. 1917. illus...................... *$30.00–$40.00*

Manuel, Frank. *Portrait of Isaac Newton*. Belknap Press. 1968. dj. ...... *$40.00–$50.00*

Manufacturers of Bells and Toys Catalogue No 40. East Hampton, CT. The N N Hill Brass Co. 1921. printed wrps, 31 pp........................ *$50.00–$75.00*

Manufacturers of Every Description of Aircraft, Balloons, Parachutes, Airships & Aeronautical Apparatus . . . Lon. C G Spencer & Sons, Ltd. 1919. illus. pictorial wrps, 12 pp. .... *$125.00–$200.00*

Manufacturers of Horse Clothing, Harness and Saddlery. Phila. Blair & Letts. 1888-89. illus. printed wrps, 16 pp. .... *$50.00–$75.00*

Manwaring, Christopher. *Essays, Historical, Moral, Political and Agricultural*. New London, CT. 1829. 1st ed. bds. .... *$85.00–$125.00*

March, Joseph. *Mancure*. NY. 1928. 6th ptg. .... *$18.00–$22.00*

March, Joseph Moncure. *The Set-Up*. NY. Covici Friede. 1928 .... *$25.00–$60.00*

Marcus, Jacob. *Rise and Destiny of the German Jew*. Cinc. Union of Amer Hebrew Congregations. 1934. black cloth. .... *$15.00–$22.00*

Marcy, Randolph. *Prairie Traveler*. NY. Harper. 1859. 1st ed. illus. fldg map .... *$500.00–$700.00*

Marie Burroughs Art Portfolio of Stage Celebrities. Chi. 1894. 14 parts, bound. .... *$50.00–$75.00*

Maritime History of New York. NY. WPA Writers Project. 1941. illus. dj. .... *$35.00–$50.00*

Marks, David. *Life Of . . . ME*. 1831 .... *$50.00–$100.00*

Marquand, John P. *Stopover: Tokyo*. Bos. 1957. 1st ed. dj .... *$27.00–$35.00*

Marquis, Don. *Archie's Life of Mehitabel*. 1933. 1st ed. dj .... *$50.00–$85.00*

Marquis, Don. *Danny's Own Story*. Garden City. 1912. 1st ed .... *$55.00–$65.00*

Marquis, Don. *Revolt of the Oyster*. NY. 1922. dj .... *$30.00–$45.00*

Marriott, Alice. *Maria, The Potter of San Idelfonso*. Norman. 1948. 1st ed. dj. .... *$50.00–$100.00*

Marryat, Capt. *Children of the New Forest*. NY. Harper Bros. 1864. 279 pp. .... *$25.00–$35.00*

Marryat, Capt. Frederick. *Settlers in Canada*. Lon. 1844. 2 vols. 1st ed. mor, mar bds. .... *$100.00–$150.00*

Marryat, Frank. *Mountains and Molehills or Recollections of a Burnt Journal*. NY. 1855. illus. Amer ed. .... *$75.00–$125.00*

Marryatt, Frank. *Mountains and Molehills or Recollections of a Burnt Journal*. NY. Harper & Bros. 1855. 1st Amer ed. illus. .... *$100.00–$300.00*

Marsh, Ngaio. *Death of a Peer*. Bos. Little, Brown. 1940. 1st ed. dj. .. *$75.00–$100.00*

Marsh, Ngaio. *Swing, Brother, Swing*. Lon. Collins Crime Club. 1949. 1st ed. dj. .... *$60.00–$75.00*

Marsh, Othniel Charles. *Dinocerata: A Monograph of an Extinct Order of Gigantic Mammals*. Wash. GPO. 1886. illus. plates. .... *$125.00–$175.00*

Marshall, A. J. *Bower Birds*. Clarendon Press. 1954. dj. .... *$60.00–$85.00*

Marshall, Albert O. *Army Life from a Soldier's Journal*. IL. self-published. 1893 .... *$60.00–$90.00*

Marshall, J. *History of the Colonies Planted by the English*. Phila. 1824. .... *$40.00–$55.00*

Marshall, John. *Life of George Washington . . .* Phila. 1836. 2 vols .... *$50.00–$90.00*

Marshall, Logan. *Sinking of the Titanic and Great Sea Disasters*. Myers. 1912. illus. photos, rbnd. .... *$35.00–$45.00*

Marshall, Logan. *Sinking of the Titanic and Great Sea Distasters*. Meyers. 1912. illus. red cl, pictorial paste-down. .... *$95.00–$125.00*

Martin and Martin. *Harness, Sadlery, Horse Clothing*. NY/Phila. 1890s cat. .... *$45.00–$60.00*

Martin, Charles-Noel. *The Atom: Friend or Foe*. Franklin Watts. (1962). dj................ .... *$14.00–$25.00*

Martin, L. C. *Optical Measuring Instruments*. Glasgow. 1924. illus. ex lib, 270 pp. .... *$30.00–$45.00*

Martin, Sadie E. *Life and Professional Career of Emma Abbott*. Minn. 1891. illus. photos.. *$25.00–$35.00*

Martineau, Harriet. *Retrospect of Western Travel*. NY. Harper. 1838. 1st US ed. 2 vols. 276 pp and 239 pp. .... *$100.00–$250.00*

Martyn, Charles. *William Ward Genealogy . . .* NY. Artemus Ward. 1925. illus............. .... *$45.00–$65.00*

Martyn, Mrs. S. T. *Women of the Bible*. NY. Amer Tract Society. 1868. illus.............. .... *$20.00–$30.00*

Marvin, Edwin E. *Fifth Regiment, Connecticut Volunteers*. Hartford. Wiley, Waterman & Eaton. 1889. 1st ed. .... *$200.00–$275.00*

Marx, Groucho. *Memoirs of a Lousy Lover*. NY. 1963. 1st ed. wrps..... *$25.00–$35.00*

Marx, Karl. *World Without Jews*. NY. Philosophical Lib. 1959. 1st ed. dj. .... *$30.00–$40.00*

Marx, Karl and Frederick Engles. *Civil War in the United States*. NY. International Pub Co. 1937. 1st ed. .... *$40.00–$55.00*

Mary Rose, Rev. Mother. *Mission Tour in the Southwest Pacific*. Bos. (1942). illus.... .... *$15.00–$22.00*

Masefield, John. *Midnight Folk*. Lon. 1927. 1st UK ed. dj.................... *$75.00–$95.00*

Masefield, John. *Selected Poems*. Lon. Heinemann. 1922. 341/500 cc. . *$50.00–$60.00*

Masefield, John. *Taking of the Gry*. NY. Macmillan Co. (1934). 1st ed. red cloth dj. .... *$25.00–$45.00*

Masefield, John. *Wanderer of Liverpool*. NY. 1930. 1st ed. 350 cc.... *$100.00–$135.00*

Mason, Amelia. *Women of the French Salons*. The Century Co. 1891. green cloth, frontis.. *$35.00–$45.00*

Mason, Bobbie Ann. *In Country*. NY. Harper & Row. (1985). 1st ed. dj .... *$30.00–$40.00*

Mason, Bobbie Ann. *Shiloh*. NY. Harper & Row. 1982. 1st ed. dj........ *$45.00–$60.00*

Mason, Charles F. *Medical Electricity*. 1887. 1st ed............................ *$30.00–$45.00*

Mason, F. Van Wyck. *Our Valiant Few*. Bos. Little Brown. 1956. 1st ed. gray cloth dj.. .... *$25.00–$55.00*

Mason, F. Van Wyck. *Young Titan*. Garden City. Doubleday. (1959). 1st ed. dj dark blue cloth. .... *$16.00–$40.00*

Mason, F. Van Wyck. *Rascal's Heaven*. Bos. Little Brown. (1980). 1st ed. dj............... .... *$20.00–$30.00*

Mason, Michael H. *Where the River Runs Dry*. Lon. 1934. illus. dj ..... *$20.00–$30.00*

Mason, Otis Tufton. *Aboriginal American Harpoons*. Wash. 1900. illus. ....
.... *$35.00–$65.00*

Masters, Edgar Lee. *Golden Fleece of California*. NY. (1936). 1st ed. . *$25.00–$35.00*

Masters, Edgar Lee. *Spoon River Anthology*. NY. 1915. 1st ed. .... *$250.00–$350.00*

Matheson, R. *Handbook of the Mosquitoes of North America*. Ithaca. 1944. ....
.... *$25.00–$35.00*

Mathews. *Writing Table of the 20th Century*. NY. 1900. illus. .... *$35.00–$40.00*

Mathews, John Joseph. *Wah'Kon-Tah: The Osage and the White Man's Road*. Univ of OK. 1932. 1st ed. illus. fldg map. .... *$25.00–$45.00*

Matsuo, Kinoaki. *How Japan Plans to Win*. Bos. Little Brown. 1942. trans by Haan. ...
.... *$35.00–$50.00*

Matthews, B. *Tales of Fantasy and Fact*. NY. 1896. 1st ed. .... *$35.00–$50.00*

Matthiessen, Peter. *African Silences*. NY. Random House. 1991. 1st ed. dj. ....
.... *$15.00–$20.00*

Matthiessen, Peter. *Cloud Forest*. NY. Viking. 1961. 1st ed. dj. .... *$20.00–$75.00*

Matthiessen, Peter. *Indian Country*. NY. Viking. 1984. 1st ed. dj. .... *$45.00–$75.00*

Matthiessen, Peter. *Lost Man's River*. NY. Random House. 1997. 1st ed. sgn, dj. ....
.... *$40.00–$50.00*

Matthiessen, Peter. *Midnight Turning Gray*. Bristol. Ampersand Press. 1984. 1st ed. wrps. author's first collection, sgn. .... *$65.00–$85.00*

Matthiessen, Peter. *Midnight Turning Gray*. Bristol, RI. Ampersand Press. 1984. 1st ed. wrps. author's first collection. .... *$35.00–$40.00*

Matthiessen, Peter. *Oomingmak*. NY. Hastings House. 1967. 1st ed. dj, sgn. ....
.... *$85.00–$100.00*

Matthiessen, Peter. *Oomingmak*. NY. Hastings House. 1967. 1st ed. dj. *$45.00–$50.00*

Matthiessen, Peter. *Partisans*. NY. Viking. 1955. 1st ed. sgn, dj. .... *$300.00–$450.00*

Matthiessen, Peter. *Sal Si Puedes*. NY. Random House. 1969. 1st ed. deep red dj. ....
.... *$35.00–$200.00*

Matthiessen, Peter. *Shore Birds of North America*. NY. Viking. 1967. 1st ed. dj. ....
.... *$55.00–$75.00*

Matthiessen, Peter. *Under the Mountain Wall*. NY. Viking. 1962. 1st ed. illus. dj. ....
.... *$25.00–$55.00*

Matthiessen, Peter. *Wildlife in America*. NY. (1959). 1st ed. illus. drawings, dj.............
.... *$150.00–$175.00*

Matthiessen, Peter. *Wind Birds*. NY. Viking. 1973. 1st ed. dj. .... *$75.00–$85.00*

Maugham, W. Somerset. *Cakes and Ale*. Lon. (1930). 1st ed. dj. ...... *$200.00–$300.00*

Maugham, W. Somerset. *Making of a Saint*. Lon. T Fisher Unwin. (1898). 1st ed. green bds. .... *$90.00–$125.00*

Maugham, W. Somerset. *Moon and Sixpence*. Doran. 1919. 1st Amer ed. ....
.... *$50.00–$75.00*

Maugham, W. Somerset. *Of Human Bondage*. Doran. 1915. 1st ed. dj.......................
.... *$250.00–$800.00*

Maugham, W. Somerset. *Summing Up.* Garden City. Doubleday, Duran. 1938. 1st ed. black cloth, dj. .... *$25.00–$75.00*

Maugham, W. Somerset. *Theatre.* NY. Doubleday. 1937. 1st ed. dj. *$125.00–$200.00*

Maugham, W. Somerset. *Then and Now.* Lon. (1946). 1st ed. dj. .... *$30.00–$60.00*

Maugham, W. Somerset. *Writer's Notebook.* Lon. (1949). 1st ed. dj.... *$40.00–$50.00*

Mauldin, Bill. *This Damn Tree Leaks: A Collection of War Cartoons.* Stars & Stripes. 1945. 1st ed. wrps. .... *$20.00–$30.00*

Mauldin, Bill. *Up Front.* NY. 1945. 1st ed. .... *$10.00–$20.00*

Maunsell, Henry. *Dublin Practice of Midwifery.* NY. William LeBlanc. 1842. 1st Amer ed. 292 pp. .... *$200.00–$275.00*

Maurice, Sir Frederick. *Statesmen and Soldiers of the Civil War.* Bos. 1926. 1st ed..... .... *$35.00–$50.00*

Mauriceau, A. M. *Married Woman's Private Medical Companion.* NY. 1852. .... *$100.00–$175.00*

Mauriceau, A. M. *Married Woman's Private Medical Companion.* NY. 1848. cloth. .... *$150.00–$250.00*

Maury, M. F. *Physical Geography of the Sea.* NY. Harper & Bros. 1856. 6th ed. 13 fold-out plates. .... *$65.00–$75.00*

Mawson, Sir Douglas. *Home of the Blizzard . . .* Phila. Lippincott. (1915). 2 vols. illus. 1st Amer ed. blue cloth, fldg map in rear pocket. .... *$200.00–$300.00*

Mawterlinck, Maurice. *Life of the Bee.* Lon. George Allen. (1911). 1st ed. illus.......... .... *$150.00–$200.00*

Maxim, Sir Hiram. *Artificial and Natural Flight.* NY. 1908. 1st ed. illus. .... *$50.00–$100.00*

Maxwell, Aymer. *Pheasants & Covert Shooting.* 1913. illus. clr plates. *$60.00–$85.00*

May, J. B. *Hawks of North America.* NY. 1935. .... *$75.00–$85.00*

Maydon, Major H. C. *Big Game Shooting in Africa.* Lon. Seeley, Service. 1951. .... *$60.00–$75.00*

Mayer, John. *Sportsman's Director.* Simkin Marshall. 1845. 7th ed. ..... *$45.00–$55.00*

Mayer, Robert. *Super-folks.* NY. 1977. 1st ed. dj. .... *$25.00–$40.00*

Mayer, Tom. *Climbing for the Evening Star.* Bos. 1974. 1st ed. dj. .... *$30.00–$40.00*

McAdie, Alexander. *FOG.* MacMillan. 1934. 23 pp, plates. .... *$30.00–$50.00*

McAllester, David P. *Enemy Way Music.* Cambridge, MA. 1954. wrps. 96 pp. .... *$50.00–$65.00*

McAllister, Agnes. *Lone Woman in Africa.* NY. 1896. illus. .... *$60.00–$85.00*

McBain, Ed. *Ax.* NY. Simon & Schuster. 1964. 1st ed. dj. .... *$150.00–$200.00*

McBain, Ed. *Blood Relatives.* NY. Random House. 1975. 1st ed. dj. ...... *$50.00–$60.00*

McBain, Ed. *Poison.* NY. Arbor House. 1987. 1st ed. dj. .... *$25.00–$45.00*

McBain, Ed. *Sadie When She Died.* Garden City. Doubleday. 1972. 1st ed. dj. .... *$50.00–$60.00*

McCaffrey, Anne. *White Dragon.* Del Rey Books. 1978. 1st ed. dj. ...... *$45.00–$55.00*

McCaleb, Walter. *Conquest of the West*. NY. Prentice-Hall. (1947). 1st ed. dj............... *$20.00–$25.00*

McCann, E. Armitage. *Ship Model Making*. NY. Henley Pub. 1927. illus. 129 pp, plans (in back pocket)..................... *$25.00–$45.00*

McCarthy, Cormac. *All the Pretty Horses*. NY. Knopf. 1992. wrps. uncorrected proof copy.............. *$300.00–$400.00*

McCarthy, Cormac. *All the Pretty Horses*. NY. 1992. 1st ed. illus.... *$100.00–$275.00*

McCarthy, Cormac. *Blood Meridian*. NY. Random House. 1985. 1st ed. dj................. *$675.00–$975.00*

McCarthy, Cormac. *Blood Meridian*. NY. Random House. 1985. 1st ed. dj................. *$650.00–$850.00*

McCarthy, Cormac. *Stone Mason*. NJ. Ecco Press. 1994. 1st ed. dj...... *$65.00–$75.00*

McCarthy, Cormac. *Stonemason*. Ecco Preso. 1994. 1st ed................... *$40.00–$50.00*

McCarthy, Cormac. *Suttree*. NY. Random House. 1979. 1st ed. dj............... *$500.00–$1,000.00*

McCarthy, Cormac. *The Crossing*. NY. Knopf. 1994. ltd ed, sgn, dj. *$375.00–$450.00*

McCarthy, Cormac. *The Crossing*. NY. 1994. 1st ed. dj....................... *$30.00–$50.00*

McCarthy, John J. *Science of Fighting Fire*. NY. 1943. 1st ed. illus. .... *$45.00–$55.00*

McCarthy, Mary. *Cannibals and Missionaries*. NY. 1970. 1st ed. dj. ... *$10.00–$20.00*

McCarthy, Mary. *The Group*. NY. 1963. 1st ed. dj. .... *$25.00–$30.00*

McCarthy, Mary. *Vietnam*. NY. 1967. wrps........................... *$30.00–$45.00*

McClane, A. J. *Practical Fly Fisherman*. NY. 1953. dj........................... *$25.00–$35.00*

McClellan, Elisabeth. *History of American Costume*. NY. 1937........... *$30.00–$45.00*

McClellan, George B. *Report of the Secretary of War*. Wash. GPO. 1864..................... *$85.00–$100.00*

McClellan, George B. *Rept. on the Organization & Campaigns . . . Army of the Potomac*. NY. 1864. 1st ed. illus. maps..................... *$35.00–$60.00*

McClintock, James H. *Mormon Settlement in Arizona*. Phoenix. 1921. illus. photos, fldg map, biblio. .... *$60.00–$85.00*

McClintock, John S. *Pioneer Days in the Black Hills*. Deadwood. 1939. 1st ed........... *$100.00–$145.00*

McClure, J. B. *Edison and His Inventions*. 1879. 1st ed. illus.............. *$65.00–$100.00*

McCormick, A. *Tinker Gypsies of Caloway*. Dumfries. 1906. illus. sgn. *$25.00–$38.00*

McCormick, John. *Complete Oficionado*. 1967. 1st ed. dj..................... *$20.00–$25.00*

McCracken, H. *Alaska Bear Trails*. NY. 1931. 1st ed............................ *$40.00–$50.00*

McCracken, H. *Charles M. Russell Book*. Garden City. 1957. 1st ed. dj. .... *$45.00–$60.00*

McCracken, Harold. *Flaming Bear*. Phila/NY. 1951. 1st ed. presentation copy, sgn..... *$55.00–$75.00*

McCracken, Harold. *Frank Tenny Johnson Book*. NY. 1974. 1st ed. folio, dj. .... *$48.00–$65.00*

McCracken, Harold. *George Catlin and the Old Frontier.* NY. 1959. 1st ed. illus. sgn, dj. .... *$50.00–$70.00*

McCracken, Harold. *Portrait of the Old West.* NY. McGraw-Hill. (1952). 1st ed. illus. dj. .... *$50.00–$95.00*

McCullagh, Rev. Joseph H. *Sunday-School Man of the South* . . . Phila. 1889. 1st ed. illus. .... *$55.00–$75.00*

McCullers, Carson. *Clock Without Hands.* Bos. Houghton Mifflin. 1961. 1st ed. dj .... *$50.00–$85.00*

McCullers, Carson. *Member of the Wedding.* Bos. Houghton Mifflin. 1946. 1st ed. dj. .... *$50.00–$125.00*

McCullock, J. R. *Dictionary, Practical, Theoretical, and Historical, of Commerce and Commercial Navigation.* Phila. Thomas Wardle. 1840. 2 vols. 1st Amer ed.................... .... *$200.00–$275.00*

McCullough, Colleen. *Creed For the Third Millennium.* Harper. 1985. 1st ed. sgn, dj... .... *$35.00–$45.00*

McCullough, Colleen. *Square Root of Wonderful.* Lon. 1958. 1st Eng ed. dj. .... *$20.00–$35.00*

McCullough, Colleen. *Tim.* NY. Harper & Row. 1974. 1st ed. author's first book, dj..... .... *$70.00–$100.00*

McCurdy, Edward. *Mind of Leonardo Da Vinci.* Lon. Jonathan Cape. 1928. illus. calf with marbled end papers. .... *$60.00–$80.00*

McCutchan, Philip. *Halfyde on the Amazon.* NY. St Martin's Press. (1988). 1st US ed. dj. .... *$15.00–$25.00*

McCutcheon, John T. *In Africa: Hunting Adventures in the Big Game Country.* Ind. Bobbs, Merrill. (1910). 1st trade ed. illus. photos, plates.................. *$115.00–$150.00*

McDiarmid, Hugh. *Fire of the Spirit.* Glasgow. 1965. wrps.................. *$30.00–$45.00*

McDougall, John. *Forest, Lake and Prairie: Twenty Years of Frontier Life in Western Canada 1842–62.* Tor. Briggs. 1895. 1st ed. 267 pp, plates and drawings...................... .... *$22.00–$30.00*

McDuddie, Franklin. *History of the Town of Rochester, NH.* Manchester. 1892. 2 vols. 1st ed. illus.. *$50.00–$65.00*

McEwan, Ian. *In Between the Sheets.* Lon. 1978. 1st ed. dj. .... *$175.00–$250.00*

McFee, William. *Pilgrims of Adversity.* Doubleday Doran. 1928. 1st ed. dj. .... *$45.00–$50.00*

McGahern, John. *Collected Stories.* NY. 1993. 1st Amer ed. dj. .... *$18.00–$25.00*

McGlashan, C. F. *History of the Donner Party: A Tragedy of the Sierra.* SF. A Carlisle & Co. 1929. 15th ed. inscrb by McGlashan.. *$70.00–$100.00*

McGlashan, C. F. *History of the Donner Party: A Tragedy of the Sierra.* SF. AL Bancroft & Co. 1881. 4th ed. insrb by McGlashan. .... *$125.00–$200.00*

McGowan, Archibald. *Prisoners of War, A Reminiscence of the Rebellion.* NY. 1901. 1st ed. .... *$75.00–$125.00*

McGuire, Hunter and George L. Christian. *Confederate Cause and Conduct in the War Between the States*. Richmond. Jenkins. 1907. 1st ed..................... *$75.00–$125.00*

McGuire, J. *Diary of a Southern Refugee During the War*. NY. 1867. 1st ed. ....
.... *$60.00–$75.00*

McGuire, Walter P. and Franklin K. Mathiews (eds.). *Boy Scouts' Year Book*. NY/Lon. Appleton and Co. 1915. illus. red cloth. .... *$100.00–$150.00*

McHugh, Tom. *Time of the Buffalo*. NY. 1972. 1st ed. illus. cloth dj. .... *$15.00–$30.00*

McKay, Claude. *Banjo*. NY. 1929. 1st ed. dj. .... *$110.00–$300.00*

McKay, Claude. *Harlem Shadows*. NY. (1922). 1st ed. blue cloth dj...........................
.... *$700.00–$2,000.00*

McKay, Claude. *Harlem Shadows*. NY. (1922). 1st ed. .... *$200.00–$250.00*

McKay, David O. *Statements on Communism and the Constitution of the United States*. Salt Lake. 1964. 1st ed. wrps. .... *$65.00–$85.00*

McKay, G. L. and C. Larsen. *Princples and Practices of Butter-Making*. NY. (1922). 3rd ed. 405 pp, illus... *$20.00–$35.00*

McKee, Edwin D. *Environment and History of the Toroweap and Kaibgab Formations of Northern Arizona and Southern Utah*. DC. Carnegie Inst. 1938. illus. foldouts, plates. .... *$75.00–$125.00*

McKee, Ruth K. *Mary Richardson Walker*. Caldwell, ID. Caxton Printers. 1945. dj......
.... *$50.00–$75.00*

McKenney, Thomas L. and James Hall. *History of the Indian Tribes of North America with Biographical Sketches and Anecdotes of the Pricipal Chiefs* . . . Phila. Bowen. 1848–1850. 3 vols. 120 handclred plates. .... *$15,000.00–$18,000.00*

McKenney, Thomas L. and Jason Hall. *Indian Tribes of North America*. Ohio. 1978. 2 vols. illus. 120 plates, 1st ed thus, lea, slipcase. .... *$400.00–$450.00*

McKenny, Margaret. *Birds in the Garden and How to Attract Them*. NY. Reynal & Hitchcock. 1939... *$27.00–$40.00*

McLaughlin, James. *My Friend the Indian*. Bos. 1910. illus. 16 plates. *$50.00–$75.00*

McLean, John, MA, PhD. *Indians of Canada, Their Manner & Customs*. Lon. Kelly. 1892. illus. 3rd ed.. *$95.00–$125.00*

McMullen, Joseph V. *Islamic Carpets*. NY. 1965............................... *$150.00–$200.00*

McMullen, Thomas. *Handbook of Wines*. NY. 1852. 1st ed. .... *$28.00–$40.00*

McMurtrie, Douglas C. *Early Printing in Tennessee*. Chi. 1933. .... *$50.00–$60.00*

McMurtrie, Wm. *Report Upon an Examination of Wool and Other Animal Fibers*. DC. GPO. 1886. illus. .... *$70.00–$85.00*

McMurtry, Larry. *Anything for Billy*. Simon & Schuster. (1988). 1st ed. dj.................
.... *$30.00–$45.00*

McMurtry, Larry. *Desert Rose*. NY. Simon & Schuster. 1983. 1st ltd ed. 1/250 cc, sgn, slipcase.. *$100.00–$300.00*

McMurtry, Larry. *Last Picture Show*. Dial Press. 1966. 1st ed. dj.... *$225.00–$300.00*

McMurtry, Larry. *Lonesome Dove*. NY. Simon & Schuster. 1985. 1st ed. paper-cvred boards, dj. .... *$150.00–$250.00*

McMurtry, Larry. *Moving On*. NY. Simon & Schuster. 1970. 1st ed. dj. .... *$100.00–$125.00*

McMurtry, Larry. *Terms of Endearment*. NY. Simon & Schuster. (1975). 1st ed. dj, sgn. .... *$50.00–$75.00*

McNally, Georgia. *Babyhood of Wild Beasts*. Doran. (1917). illus. photos, frontis......... .... *$15.00–$30.00*

McNemar, Richard. *Concise Answer . . . Who, or What Are the Shakers*. Stockbridge. 1826. 1st ed... *$200.00–$250.00*

McPhee, John. *Coming into the Country*. Lon. 1978. 1st ed. dj. .... *$30.00–$45.00*

McPhee, John. *Deltoid Pumpkin Seed*. Farrar. 1973. 1st ed. dj. .... *$24.00–$35.00*

McPhee, John. *Encounters with the Archdruid*. NY. FSG. (1971). 1st ed. dj. .... *$125.00–$150.00*

McPhee, John. *Giving Good Weight*. NY. Farrar Straus Giroux. (1979). 1st ed. dj......... .... *$25.00–$40.00*

McPhee, John. *Headmaster. Frank L Boyden . . .* NY. Farrar, Strauss & Giroux. 1966. 1st ed. illus. photos, dj.. *$50.00–$100.00*

McPhee, John. *Looking For a Ship*. NY. Farrar, Strauss & Giroux. 1990. 1st ed. dj....... .... *$10.00–$20.00*

McPhee, John. *Looking for a Ship*. NY. Farrar, Straus & Giroux. (1990). 1st ed. sgn, dj. .... *$50.00–$60.00*

McPhee, John. *Pine Barrens*. Farrar, Straus & Giroux. 1968. dj. .... *$75.00–$95.00*

McPhee, John. *Roomful of Hovings*. NY. 1968. dj. .... *$85.00–$100.00*

McPherson, Edward. *Handbook of Politics for 1878*. Wash. 1878. large 8vo. .... *$40.00–$50.00*

McQuade, James. *Cruise of the Montauk to Bermuda, the West Indies & Florida*. NY. Thos R Knox. 1885. 1st ed. illus... *$62.00–$75.00*

McRae, D. G. W. *Arts and Crafts of Canada*. Tor. 1944. illus. dj. .... *$25.00–$35.00*

Mead, Margaret. *An Anthropoligist at Work: The Writings of Ruth Benedict*. Bos. Houghton-Mifflin. 1959. 1st ed. dj. .... *$20.00–$30.00*

Mead, Margaret. *An Anthropologist at Work: Writings of Ruth Benedict*. Bos. Houghton Mifflin. 1959. 2nd ed. sgn and dated by Mead. .... *$40.00–$55.00*

Mead, Margaret. *Male and Female*. NY. 1st ed. dj............................... *$45.00–$65.00*

Mead, Margaret. *Sex and Temperament in Three Primitive Societies*. NY. Morrow. 1935. 1st ed. 335 pp. .... *$25.00–$35.00*

Mead, Margaret. *Twentieth Century Faith Hope & Survival*. NY. 1972. 1st ed. dj. .... *$28.00–$45.00*

Mead, Margaret and Ruth L. Bunzel (eds.). *Golden Age of American Anthropology*. NY. George Braziller. 1960. 1st ed... *$20.00–$60.00*

Mead, McKim and White. *Monograph of. . .in Two Volumes*. NY. Architectural Book Pub Co. 1925. folders with string ties, students ed.............................. *$200.00–$300.00*

Meade, Robert D. *Judah P. Benjamin, Confederate Statesman*. NY. 1943. illus. 4th ptg, presentation copy, dj... *$20.00–$35.00*

Meany, Tom. *Babe Ruth*. 1947. 1st ed. .... *$20.00–$25.00*

Meany, Tom. *Boston Red Sox*. 1956. 1st ed. dj... *$22.00–$30.00*

Medical Directory for Scotland 1853. Lon. John Churchill. .... *$45.00–$65.00*

Medical Society of VA. *Confederate Medicine 1861–1865*. np. 1961. wrps...................
.... *$54.00–$75.00*

Meignan, Victor. *From Paris to Peking Over Siberian Snows*. Lon. 1889. illus. 2nd ed.
.... *$125.00–$245.00*

Meigs, Charles D. *Complete Treatise on Midwifery*. Phila. 1852. illus. 4th Amer ed. calf,
steel plates. .... *$60.00–$75.00*

Meigs, Charles D. *Woman: Her Diseases and Remedies*. Phila. 1851.... *$25.00–$50.00*

Meigs, Cornelia. *Mother Makes Christmas*. NY. (1940). 1st ed. illus. by Lenski in clr
and b/w. dj. .... *$30.00–$50.00*

Meigs, Cornelia. *Railroad West*. Little Brown. 1944............................... *$18.00–$20.00*

Meikle, James. *The Traveller*. Albany. E Torrey & W Seaver. 1812. lea. *$45.00–$85.00*

Meinertzhagen, Richard. *Birds of Arabia*. Edin. Oliver & Boyd. (1954). 1st ed. illus. 19
clr plates. fldg pocket map. .... *$200.00–$300.00*

Meinertzhagen, Richard. *Birds of Arabia*. Edin. Oliver & Boyd. (1954). 1st ed. illus. clr
plates maps and folding pocket map.. *$200.00–$300.00*

Mellon, James. *African Hunter*. NY. Harcourt Brace Jovanovich. (1975). 1st ed. photos,
dj. .... *$150.00–$250.00*

Melville, Herman. *Journal of a Visit to London and the Continent*. Lon. 1949. dj.........
.... *$20.00–$35.00*

Melville, Herman. *Journal Up the Straits*. NY. The Colophon. 1935. 1st ed. 182 pp,
paper bds with lea label, 650 copies printed...................................... *$50.00–$100.00*

Mencken, H. L. *Minority Report—Notebooks*. NY. 1956. 1st ed. dj....... *$30.00–$40.00*

Mencken, H. L. *Philosophy of Friedrich Nietzsche*. Bos. 1913. 3rd ed.. *$35.00–$50.00*

Mencken, H. L. *Treatise on Right and Wrong*. NY. 1934. 1st ed. dj....... *$30.00–$50.00*

Mencken, H. L. *Book of Burlesques*. Lon. 1923. 1st Eng ed. .... *$24.00–$32.00*

Mencken, H. L. *Europe After 8:15*. NY. John Lane. 1914. .... *$80.00–$125.00*

Mencken, H. L. *Happy Days*. NY. 1940. 1st ed. dj. .... *$25.00–$35.00*

Mencken, H. L. *Notes on Democracy*. NY. Knopf. (1926). 1st ed........ *$60.00–$125.00*

Menefee, Josephine T. *Virginia Housekeeper's Guide*. Roanoke. Stone Printing. 1935.
.... *$50.00–$80.00*

Menninger, Karl A. *Man Against Himself*. NY. 1938. sgn. .... *$65.00–$95.00*

Menocal, A. G. *Report of the US Nicaragua Surveying Party 1885*. Wash. GPO. 1886.
fldg maps. .... *$200.00–$250.00*

Merril, George P. *Contributions to the History of Geology*. Wash. GPO. 1906. illus. 780
pp. .... *$85.00–$100.00*

Merryman, Richard. *Andrew Wyeth*. Bos. 1968. 1st trade ed. clr plates, oblong, dj. .....
.... *$100.00–$200.00*

Merryweather, James C. *Fire Protection of Mansions*. Lon. 1899. 3rd ed...................
.... *$60.00–$110.00*

Mertins, Louis and Esther. *Intervals of Robert Frost*. Berkeley. 1947. wrps................
.... *$50.00–$65.00*

Merton, H. W. *Descriptive Mentality From the Head, Face and Hand*. Phila. 1899. 1st ed. illus. .... *$65.00–$75.00*

Merton, Thomas. *Ascent to Truth*. NY. Harcourt Brace. (1951). 1st ed. dj. ....
.... *$40.00–$60.00*

Merton, Thomas. *Waters of Siloe*. Harcourt. 1949. 1st ed. dj. .... *$50.00–$75.00*

Merwin, Samuel. *Silk*. Bos. 1923. 1st ed. illus. by N C Wyeth.............. *$30.00–$75.00*

Meyer De Schauensee, R. M. *Birds of China*. Smithsonian Inst Press. 1984. illus. 38 clr plates and 30 wash drawings. dj.. *$70.00–$90.00*

Meyrick, F. J. *Life in the Bush*. Lon. Thomas Nelson. (1939). 1st ed. illus. dj...............
.... *$30.00–$40.00*

Michael Robartes and the Dancer. Dublin. Cuala Press. 1920. ltd 400 cc....................
.... *$100.00–$145.00*

Michaux, Henri. *Selected Writings*. NY. New Directions. nd. 1st Amer ed. trans by Richard Ellman. dj... *$30.00–$45.00*

Michelet, Jules. *The Bird*. Lon. T Nelson & Sons. 1869. 1st ed. illus. by Giacomelli, aeg... *$40.00–$50.00*

Michelson, Truman. *Owl Sacred Pack of the Fox Indians*. DC. GPO. 1921. 1st ed........
.... *$50.00–$120.00*

Michener, James A. *Floating World*. NY. 1954. 1st ed. dj..................... *$70.00–$85.00*

Michener, James A. *Hawaii*. NY. Random House. (1959). 1st ed. genealogical charts, dj.. *$85.00–$200.00*

Michener, James A. *Hawaii*. NY. Random House. 1959. dj. .... *$35.00–$50.00*

Michener, James A. *Heirs of the Incas*. NY. 1924. 1st ed. dj. .... *$10.00–$20.00*

Michener, James A. *Sayonara*. NY. 1954. 1st ed. dj............................ *$95.00–$125.00*

Michener, James A. *Space*. 1982. wrps. uncorrected proof. .... *$75.00–$95.00*

Michener, James A. *The Drifters*. NY. Random House. (1971). 1st ed. dj......................
.... *$40.00–$70.00*

Michener, James A. *The Source*. NY. 1965. 1st ed. dj. .... *$25.00–$40.00*

Michener, James A. *Unit in the Social Studies*. Camb. (1940). 1st ed. wrps. author's first book. .... *$300.00–$500.00*

Michener, James A and A. Grove Day. *Rascals in Paradise*. Lon. Secker & Warburg. 1957. 1st UK ed. dj. .... *$100.00–$125.00*

Michigan in Summer. Grand Rapids & Indiana Railroad. 1898. wrps. illus. 22 pp, brochure, fldg maps... *$30.00–$50.00*

Middleton, W. E. Knowles. *History of the Thermometer and Its Use in Meteorology*. Balt. Johns Hopkins Press. 1946. dj... *$18.00–$24.00*

Milburn, George. *Hobo's Hornbook*. NY. Ives Washburn. 1930. 1st ed. dj...................
.... *$125.00–$175.00*

Miles, John E. *Railroads, Their Employees and the Public*. Farrar, Straus and Cudahy. 1956. 1st ed. dj. .... *$14.00–$25.00*

Milfort, Louis Le Clerc. *Memoirs or a Quick Glance at My Various Travels* . . . GA. The Beehive Press. (1972). brown cloth. orange endpapers. pictorial dj......... *$23.00–$45.00*

Mill, John Stuart. *Autobiography*. NY. 1874. 1st Amer ed..................... *$60.00–$85.00*

Mill, John Stuart. *Subjection of Women*. NY. Appleton. 1870. 2nd US ed. 188 pp. ....
.... *$150.00–$200.00*

Mill, John Stuart. *Subjection of Women*. Phila. 1869. 1st US ed. 174 pp. ....
.... *$250.00–$400.00*

Mill, John Stuart. *Subjection of Women*. Phil. Lippincott. 1869. 1st Amer ed,...............
.... *$175.00–$500.00*

Millais, J. G., et al. *British Deer & Ground Game, Dogs, Guns & Rifles*. The London & Counties Press Association. 1913. ltd 950 cc, numbered, full lea........ *$500.00–$650.00*

Millay, Edna St. Vincent. *Buck in the Snow*. Harper. 1928. 1st ed. dj. .. *$45.00–$60.00*

Millay, Edna St. Vincent. *Fatal Interview*. Harper. 1931. 1st ed. dj...... *$25.00–$35.00*

Millay, Edna St. Vincent. *Harp Weaver*. NY. Harper & Bros. 1923. 1st ed. dj...............
.... *$50.00–$90.00*

Millay, Edna St. Vincent. *Mine the Harvest*. NY. 1954. 1st ed. dj......... *$27.00–$35.00*

Millay, Edna St. Vincent. *Princess Marries the Page*. Harper & Bros. 1932. 1st ed. dj.
.... *$22.00–$35.00*

Millburn, William Henry. *Rifle, Axe, and Saddlebags and Other Lectures*. NY. 1857. .
.... *$35.00–$75.00*

Miller. *World in the Air: Story of Flying in Pictures*. NY. 1930. 2 vols.. *$75.00–$95.00*

Miller, Arthur. *Collected Plays*. NY. 1957. 1st ed. dj............................. *$38.00–$50.00*

Miller, Arthur. *Death of a Salesman*. NY. 1949. 1st ed. dj................... *$75.00–$125.00*

Miller, Arthur. *Focus*. Reynal & Hitchcock. 1945. 1st ed. dj. .... *$38.00–$60.00*

Miller, Arthur. *The Misfits*. NY. (1964). 1st ed. dj.,............................. *$95.00–$125.00*

Miller, Arthur. *The Price: A Play*. NY. Viking. (1968). 1st ed. dj......... *$20.00–$65.00*

Miller, Francis Trevelyan. *Byrd's Great Adventure*. Phila. Winston. (1930). 1st ed. maps.. *$18.00–$25.00*

Miller, Francis Trevelyan (ed). *Photographic History of the Civil War*. NY. 1911. 10 vols. illus. decorated blue cloth... *$350.00–$500.00*

Miller, Henry. *Black Spring*. NY. Grove Press. 1963. 1st US ed. dj....... *$35.00–$50.00*

Miller, Henry. *Tropic of Cancer*. NY. Grove Press. 1961. 1st authorized US ed............
.... *$20.00–$60.00*

Miller, Henry. *Tropic of Cancer*. Grove. 1961. dj. .... *$30.00–$55.00*

Miller, Henry. *Tropic of Capricorn*. Lon. (1964). 1st ed. dj. .... *$35.00–$60.00*

Miller, Henry. *Tropic of Capricorn*. NY. Grove Press. 1961. 1st US ptg. dj. ....
.... *$20.00–$50.00*

Miller, Henry. *Wisdom of the Heart*. Lon. 1947.................................... *$15.00–$25.00*

Miller, O. B. *Little Pictures of Japan*. (1925). .... *$25.00–$40.00*

Miller, Olive Beaupre. *My Book House*. Chi. 1971. 12 vols................. *$60.00–$150.00*

Miller, Olive Beaupre. *My Book House*. Chi. (1937)............................ *$100.00–$150.00*

Miller, Olive Beaupre. *My Book House: The Latchkey*. Chi. 1921......... *$25.00–$30.00*

Miller, Olive Beaupre. *My Book House: The Treasure Chest*. Chi. 1920. illus. .... *$20.00–$25.00*

Miller, Olive Beaupre. *Nursery Friends From France*. 1927. illus. .... *$20.00–$35.00*

Miller, Olive Beaupre. *Tales Told in Holland*. 1926. .... *$25.00–$35.00*

Miller, Olive Beaupre. *Tales Told in Holland*. The Bookhouse for Children. (1952)...... .... *$20.00–$30.00*

Miller, Olive Thorne. *Little People of Asia*. NY. E P Dutton. 1888. 1st ed. illus. wood engrs.. *$40.00–$50.00*

Miller, W. *Structure of the Lung*. Bos. 1893. sgn. .... *$25.00–$32.00*

Miller, William. *Evidence from Scripture and History of the Second Coming of Christ About the Year 1843*. Troy, NY. Elias Gates. 1838. 2nd ed. cloth-backed boards............ .... *$360.00–$425.00*

Milligan, Robert H. *Jungle Folk of Africa*. Revell. (1908). 2nd ed. decorative cvrs. .... *$25.00–$35.00*

Mills, Anson. *My Story*. Wash. 1918. 1st ed. illus. limp cloth illus. ..... *$110.00–$235.00*

Mills, John. *Life of a Foxhound*. Lon. Philip Allan. (1921). 5th ed. illus............................. .... *$30.00–$50.00*

Milmine, Georgine. *Life of Mary Baker G. Eddy and the History of Christian Science*. NY. Doubleday, Page & Co. 1909. 1st ed. edited and largely written by Willa Cather. ... . *$195.00–$500.00*

Milne, A. *By Way of Introduction*. NY. 1929. 1st Amer ed. ltd 166 cc, sgn, slipcase....... .... *$150.00–$300.00*

Milne, A. A. *Christopher Robin Birthday Book*. Lon. Methuen. (1930). decorations by Shepard. .... *$100.00–$200.00*

Milne, A. A. *Four Days' Wonder*. Lon. 1933. 1st ed. dj. .... *$35.00–$45.00*

Milne, A. A. *Fourteen Songs From When We Were Very Young*. Dutton. (1926). bds and cloth spine.. *$20.00–$50.00*

Milne, A. A. *Gallery of Children*. McKay. (1925). 1st Amer ed............ *$75.00–$125.00*

Milne, A. A. *House at Pooh Corner*. NY. Dutton. (1928). illus............. *$85.00–$175.00*

Milne, A. A. *King's Breakfast*. Lon. Methuen. (1925). illus. pictorial boards dj. .... *$95.00–$175.00*

Milne, A. A. *Michael and Mary*. Lon. 1930. 1st ed. dj. .... *$50.00–$80.00*

Milne, A. A. *Now We Are Six*. Lon. 1927. 1st ed. illus. teg.................. *$150.00–$275.00*

Milne, A. A. *Now We Are Six*. Dutton. (1927). 1st Amer ed. illus by Shepard. .... *$100.00–$140.00*

Milne, A. A. *Teddy Bear and Other Songs*. Dutton. (1926). bds and cloth spine. .... *$25.00–$60.00*

Milne, A. A. *Toad of Toad Hall*. Lon. 1929. 1st ed. dj............................ *$65.00–$115.00*

Milne, A. A. *When We Were Very Young*. NY. Dutton. 1924. illus. 1st Amer ed. red cloth. .... *$250.00–$350.00*

Milne, A. A. *Winnie the Pooh and the Bees.* Dutton. 1952. 4 pop-ups, spiral bound. ......
.... *$40.00–$55.00*

Milne, A. A. *Winnie-the-Pooh.* Lon. (1926). 1st ed. illus. green pictorial cloth. ....
.... *$600.00–$1,000.00*

Minarik, Else. *Little Bear.* Harper & Row. (1960). illus. by Maurice Sendak................
.... *$15.00–$20.00*

Mingtao, Zhang, et al. *Roof of the World.* NY/Beijing. Abrams/Foreign Language Press.
(1982). 1st Amer ed. illus, dj.. *$30.00–$45.00*

Miniatures from Paris, Showing the Leading Designs by the Great Parisian Modistes
... Bos. Wm S Butler & Co. 1898-99. pictorial wrps, 32 pp. .... *$50.00–$75.00*

Minkoff, George R. *Bibliography of the Black Sun Press.* Great Neck. 1970. ....
.... *$50.00–$95.00*

Minqgue, Anna C. *Loretto Annals of the Century.* NY. 1912. 1st ed. illus. 252 pp. ....
.... *$18.00–$25.00*

Miscellany of Arms & Armor. Presented to Bashford Dean. np. 1927. illus. ltd #127/150
cc, presentation copy from Hugh Smiley. .... *$125.00–$200.00*

Miss Beecher's Domestic Receipt-Book. NY. 1867. 5th ed..................... *$30.00–$45.00*

Miss Leslie. *Directions for Cookery.* Phila. 1839. 468 pp, 7th ed. .... *$75.00–$100.00*

Mitchell's Modern Geography of the World. Phila. 1856. illus. woodcuts. ....
.... *$25.00–$35.00*

Mitchell's New General Atlas. Phila. 1864. folio, maps..................... *$300.00–$400.00*

Mitchell, Elyne. *Silver Brumby's Daughter.* Lon. Hutchinson. 1960. 1st ed. dj. ....
.... *$25.00–$50.00*

Mitchell, John D. *Lost Mines & Buried Treasures . . .* CA. Desert Magazine Press.
(1953). illus. 2nd ptg. .... *$10.00–$20.00*

Mitchell, Joseph. *Up in the Old Hotel and Other Stories.* NY. Pantheon Books. (1922).
1st ed. dj, bds.. *$45.00–$60.00*

Mitchell, Leonard Jan. *Luchow's German Cookbook.* NY. Doubleday & Co. 1953. 1st
ed. illus. rcd cloth. .... *$18.00–$25.00*

Mitchell, Margaret. *Gone With the Wind.* NY. Macmillan. 1936. 1st ed. 2nd ptg...........
.... *$85.00–$100.00*

Mitchell, Margaret. *Gone With the Wind.* NY. 1936. 2nd ptg, dj. .... *$40.00–$60.00*

Mitchell, Margaret. *Gone With the Wind.* NY. 1936. 1st ed. inscrb, sgn, gray cloth,
"Published May 1936" appears on copyright page, pictorial dj...... *$2,450.00–$5,000.00*

Mitchell, S. A. *Mitchell's New Atlas of the United States.* Phila. 1874. illus. hand-clr
maps.. *$115.00–$135.00*

Mitchell, S. Weir. *Autobiography of a Quack.* NY. Century Co. 1900. 1st ed. illus........
.... *$45.00–$60.00*

Mitchell, William Ansel. *Linn County Kansas. A History.* Kansas City. 1928...............
.... *$50.00–$100.00*

Mitchener, C. H. (ed.). *Historic Events in the Tuscarawas and Muskingham Valleys.*
Dayton. 1876. .... *$40.00–$65.00*

Mitford, Mary Russell. *Our Village*. Lon. Macmillan. 1893. illus. by Hugh Thompson, 1/475 cc, printed Dec 1883. .... *$150.00–$300.00*

Mitford, William. *History of Greece*. Lon. Cadell. 1822. 10 vols. ¾ calf, mar bds. .... *$125.00–$220.00*

Mivart, St. George. *On Genesis of Species*. NY. 1871. 1st ed. illus. 1st Amer ed. .... *$26.00–$35.00*

Moberg, Vilhelm. *Utvanderarna*. Stockholm. Albert Bonniers Foerlag. 1949. 1st ed. sgn, scarce.. *$250.00–$300.00*

Moffat, Robert. *Missionary Labours and Scenes in Southern Africa*. NY. Robert Carter. 1843. 1st Amer ed.. *$75.00–$95.00*

Molnar, John Edgar. *Author-Title Index to Joseph Sabin's Dictionary of Books Relating to America*. Metuchen. 1974. .... *$100.00–$140.00*

Molyneux, Edwin. *Chrysanthemums and Their Culture*. Lon. 1881. 1st ed.................. .... *$30.00–$40.00*

Monroe, James. *Message From the President*. Wash. 1821. 1st ed. wrps. sewn.............. .... *$75.00–$95.00*

Monroe, Marilyn. *My Story*. NY. 1974. 1st ed. dj.................................. *$30.00–$35.00*

Monsarrat, Nicholas. *Fair Day's Work*. Lon. Cassell. (1964). 1st UK ed. blue cloth dj. .... *$10.00–$20.00*

Montagu M. F. Ashley (ed.). *Studies and Essays in the History of Science and Learning . . .* NY. Henry Schuman. 1944... *$35.00–$75.00*

Monteath, Robert. *Forester's Guide and Profitable Planter*. Edin. Stirling & Kennedy. 1824. 2nd ed. 15 plates.. *$100.00–$125.00*

Montessori, Maria. *Dr. Montessori's Own Handbook*. NY. Stokes. (1914). 1st ed......... .... *$35.00–$40.00*

Montessori, Maria. *Montessori Method*. NY. Stokes. 1912. illus. 1st US ed. author's first book, 377 pp, scarce... *$125.00–$150.00*

Montgomery, Frances. *Billy Whiskers Tourist*. Saalfield. 1929. illus..... *$20.00–$35.00*

Montgomery, Frances Trego. *On a Lark to the Planets*. Akron. 1904. 1st ed. illus. by Winifred Elrod... *$50.00–$60.00*

Montgomery, L. M. *Anne of Avonlea*. Grosset & Dunlap. dj.................. *$10.00–$22.00*

Montgomery, L. M. *Anne of the Island*. Grosset & Dunlap. dj. .... *$12.00–$15.00*

Montgomery, L. M. *Anne's House of Dreams*. A L Burt. dj................... *$25.00–$37.00*

Montgomery, L. M. *Chronicles of Avonlea*. NY. Grosset & Dunlap. 1976. dj............... .... *$14.00–$20.00*

Montgomery, L. M. *Golden Road*. 1913. 1st ed. .... *$9.00–$25.00*

Montgomery, L. M. *Jane of Lantern Hill*. Grosset & Dunlap. 1937. dj. *$10.00–$18.00*

Montgomery, L. M. *Jane of Lantern Hill*. Tor. McClelland & Stewart. 1937. 1st ed. inscrb... *$150.00–$175.00*

Montgomery, L. M. *Rainbow Valley*. NY. 1919. wrps. rprnt. .... *$30.00–$40.00*

Moore, Albert B. *Conscription & Conflict in the Confederacy*. NY. Macmillan. 1924. dj.. *$40.00–$70.00*

Moore, Brian. *Cold Heaven*. NY. Holt Rinehart Winston. (1983). 1st ed. dj..................
.... *$20.00–$25.00*

Moore, Brian. *Great Victorian Collection*. NY. Farrar, Straus & Giroux. (1975). 1st ed.
dj. .... *$25.00–$45.00*

Moore, Brian. *Lonely Passion of Judith Hearne*. Bos. Little Brown. 1955. 1st Amer
ed. .... *$100.00–$125.00*

Moore, Clement C. *Night Before Christmas*. Chi. 1908. illus. by J R Neill...................
.... *$40.00–$50.00*

Moore, Clement C. *Poems*. NY. 1844. 1st ed. presentation copy.. *$3,000.00–$6,500.00*

Moore, Elaine T. *Winning Your Spurs*. Bos. Little Brown. 1954. 1st ed. dj...................
.... *$30.00–$45.00*

Moore, Frank. *Rebel Rhymes and Rhapsodies*. NY. 1864. 1st ed. calf spine, bds...........
.... *$55.00–$100.00*

Moore, Frank. *Women of the War*. Hartford. 1866. 1st ed. 9 steel engr, illus.................
.... *$35.00–$45.00*

Moore, George Henry. *Notes on the History of Slavery in Massachusetts*. NY. 1866. 1st
ed. .... *$150.00–$175.00*

Moore, John Hamilton. *Seaman's Complete Daily Assistant & New Mariner's
Compass*. Lon. 1796. 5th ed. sailcloth over calf. .... *$190.00–$235.00*

Moore, Joseph. *Penicillin in Syphilis*. Chas Thomas. 1946. 1st ed. dj.... *$22.00–$25.00*

Moore, Marianne. *Arctic Ox*. Lon. Faber & Faber. 1964. 1st ed. dj....... *$35.00–$45.00*

Moore, Marianne. *Collected Poems*. Lon. Faber and Faber. 1951. 1st ed. 1st UK ed. dj.
.... *$55.00–$85.00*

Moore, Marianne. *Collected Poems*. NY. Macmillan. 1951. 1st ed. 1st trade ed. dj......
.... *$90.00–$100.00*

Moore, Marianne. *Complete Poems*. NY. Macmillan. (1967). 1st ed. dj......................
.... *$55.00–$100.00*

Moore, Marianne. *Marianne Moore Reader*. NY. Viking. 1961. 1st ed. orange cloth....
.... *$22.00–$35.00*

Moore, Marianne. *O to Be a Dragon*. NY. Viking. 1959. 1st ed. dj....... *$35.00–$65.00*

Moore, Marianne. *Poems*. Lon. Egoist Press. 1921. 1st ed. wrps. author's first book,
decorative wraps. .... *$500.00–$1,000.00*

Moore, Marianne. *Tell Me, Tell Me*. NY. Viking. 1966. 1st ed. dj.......... *$45.00–$90.00*

Moore, William. *Indian Wars of the United States. . .with Accounts of the Origin,
Manners, Superstitions, Etc. of the Aborigines*. Phila. Leary. 1850. 1st ed. illus. rbnd. ...
.... *$80.00–$120.00*

Moorehead, Warren King. *Report of the Susquehanna River Expedition*. Andover, MA.
1938. 1st ed. wrps. illus. photos, maps. .... *$110.00–$130.00*

Moorman, Donald R. and Gene A. Sessions. *Camp Floyd and the Mormons*. Salt Lake.
1992. illus. photos, maps, dj... *$35.00–$45.00*

Moravian Tiles. Doylestown, PA. Moravian Pottery and Tile Works. early 20th century.
printed wrps, illus, 16 pp.. *$40.00–$50.00*

More, Hannah. *Strictures on the Modern System of Female Education*. Phila. Budd and Bartram. 1800. 2 vols. 1st ed.. *$125.00–$225.00*

More, Jedidiah. *Sermon*. Charlestown. 1799. rprnt by Hudson and Goodwin. ....
.... *$150.00–$175.00*

Morell, David. *Fifth Profession*. NY. (1990). 1st ed. dj........................... *$15.00–$25.00*

Morell, David. *Fraternity of the Stone*. NY. (1985). 1st ed. dj. .... *$15.00–$25.00*

Morgan, Lewis H. *House and House-Life of the American Aborigines*. Wash. GPO. 1881. illus. litho and photo plates. .... *$95.00–$125.00*

Morley, Christopher. *Christmas Tobacco*. 1960. illus. 300 cc. .... *$25.00–$35.00*

Morley, Christopher. *Haunted Bookshop*. Garden City. Doubleday, Page. 1919. 1st ed. 2nd issue. no # on p 76, sgn... *$700.00–$1,000.00*

Morley, Christopher. *Old Mandarin*. NY. 1947. 1st ed.......................... *$22.00–$30.00*

Morley, Christopher. *Seacoast of Bohemia*. 1929. 1st ed. wrps.............. *$15.00–$20.00*

Mormon Conflict, 1850–1859. New Haven. 1960. 1st ed. ex lib............. *$30.00–$40.00*

Morrell, L. A. *American Shepherd*. NY. Harper. 1857. .... *$35.00–$45.00*

Morris, E. P. *Fore-and-Aft Rig in America*. New Haven. Yale Univ Press. 1927. illus. photo plates, cloth, 1/1000 cc.. *$40.00–$50.00*

Morris, Frank and E. A. Eames. *Our Wild Orchids*. NY. 1929. 1st ed. illus. dj. ....
.... *$28.00–$35.00*

Morris, Malcolm Alexander. *Diseases of the Skin*. Phil. 1894. illus. 17 woodcuts, 8 chromolithos, dj.. *$20.00–$40.00*

Morris, Robert. *Freemasonry in the Holy Land*. NY. Masonic Publishing. 1872. 1st ed. illus. .... *$60.00–$70.00*

Morrison, Toni. *Beloved*. NY. (1987). 1st ed. sgn, dj......................... *$200.00–$600.00*

Morrison, Toni. *Beloved*. NY. Knopf. (1987). 1st ed. dj. .... *$30.00–$85.00*

Morrison, Toni. *Bluest Eye*. Lon. 1979. 1st ed. dj................................. *$65.00–$75.00*

Morrison, Toni. *Jazz*. NY. Knopf. 1992. 1st ed. dj sgn. .... *$95.00–$125.00*

Morrison, Toni. *Paradise*. NY. Knopf. 1997. 1st ed. dj........................... *$18.00–$30.00*

Morrison, Toni. *Song of Solomon*. NY. Knopf. 1977. 1st ed. dj. .... *$75.00–$125.00*

Morrison, Toni. *Tar Baby*. NY. Knopf. 1981. 1st ed. dj......................... *$30.00–$75.00*

Morse, A. H. *Radio: Beam and Broadcast*. 1925. 1st ed. illus............... *$70.00–$90.00*

Morse, Edward Lind. *Samuel F. B. Morse: His Letters and Journals*. 1914. 2 vols. 1st ed. illus. .... *$65.00–$115.00*

Morse, Frances. *Furniture of Olden Time*. Macmillan. (1941). illus. ...... *$35.00–$45.00*

Morse, J. *Geography Made Easy*. Utica, NY. 1819................................ *$30.00–$50.00*

Morse, J. and E. Parish. *Compendious History of New England*. Charlestown. 1820. .
.... *$20.00–$30.00*

Morse, Jedidiah. *American Gazeteer*. Bos. 1797. 7 maps. .... *$100.00–$250.00*

Morse, Jedidiah. *American Gazetteer*. Bos. 1810. rev, 2 maps. .... *$50.00–$100.00*

Morse, Jedidiah. *Annals of the American Revolution* . . . Hartford. 1824. illus. .... *$85.00–$100.00*

Morse, Jedidiah. *Geography Made Easy.* Bos. Thomas & Andrews. 1818. 19th ed. 2 pull-out maps in clr. .... *$75.00–$100.00*

Morse, Jedidiah. *Traveller's Guide.* New Haven. 1823 lea, fldg map. .. *$60.00–$75.00*

Morse, Samuel F. B. *Examination of the Telegraphic Apparatus.* GPO. 1869. Vol 4. .... *$30.00–$40.00*

Mortensen, William. *Mortensen on the Negative.* NY. 1940. 1st ed. illus. .... *$25.00–$35.00*

Morton, Rosalie Slaughter. *Woman Surgeon.* Stokes. 1937. 3rd ptg. .... *$20.00–$40.00*

Mosby, John Singleton. *Mosby's War Reminiscences and Stuart's Cavalry Campaigns.* Boston. Geo A Jones & Co. 1887. .... *$25.00–$50.00*

Mother Goose. Saalfield. 1933. illus. by Fern Bissel Peat. .... *$30.00–$40.00*

Moton, Robert Russa. *What the Negro Thinks.* Garden City. Doubleday Doran. 1929. 1st ed. .... *$50.00–$150.00*

Moxon, Joseph. *Tutor to Astronomy and Geography.* Lon. S Roycroft. 1686. 4th ed, enlarged, lea, drawings, diagrams, 271 pp. .... *$500.00–$700.00*

Mr. Dooley in Peace and War. Bos. Maynard. 1898. 1st ed. author's 1st book. .... *$75.00–$125.00*

Mrs. Putnam's Receipt Book. Bos. 1858. .... *$33.00–$40.00*

Muenscher, W. C. and M. A. Rice. *Garden Spice and Wild Pot Herbs.* Ithaca. 1955. illus. .... *$40.00–$50.00*

Muir, John. *My First Summer in the Sierra.* Bos. 1911. 1st ed. .... *$95.00–$125.00*

Muir, John. *Our National Parks.* Bos. 1902. 2nd ptg. .... *$25.00–$45.00*

Muir, John. *Our National Parks.* Bos. Houghton Mifflin. 1909. 1st enlarged ed. fldg map, 31 plates. .... *$125.00–$200.00*

Muir, John. *Travels in Alaska.* Bos. 1915. 1st ed. illus. .... *$35.00–$80.00*

Muir, John. *Yosemite and the Sierra Nevada.* Bos. Houghton Mifflin. (1948). 1st ed later ptg, photographs by Ansel Adams, dj. .... *$65.00–$130.00*

Muir, John (ed.). *Picturesque California* . . . NY. 1894. illus. folio. .. *$140.00–$180.00*

Muir, Leo J. *Century of Mormon Activities in Calfornia.* Salt Lake. nd, 1951. Vols 1 and 2. illus. photos, sgn. .... *$125.00–$150.00*

Muir, Percy. *English Children's Books 1600 to 1900.* Lon. Batsford. (1985). 3rd impression, dj. .... *$30.00–$75.00*

Muir, Percy. *Victorian Illustrated Books.* NY. (1971). 1st ed. dj. .... *$40.00–$50.00*

Mulford, Clarence. *Hopalong Cassidy and Lucky at the Double X Ranch.* NY. 1950. 1st ed. illus. by Jack Crowe, 2 pop-ups. .... *$140.00–$160.00*

Mulford, Isaac S. *Civil and Political History of New Jersey.* Phila. 1851. 500 pp. .... *$48.00–$60.00*

Mulfurd, Clarence. *Hopalong Cassidy's Coloring Book.* NY. 1951. wrps. .... *$15.00–$20.00*

Mullins, Michael A. *Fremont Rifles: A Hist. of 37th Ill. Vet. Vol. Infantry.* NC. 1990. illus. sgn, dj. .... *$35.00–$50.00*

Mulock, Dinah Maria. *Woman's Kingdom.* NY. 1869. 1st ed. illus........ *$33.00–$40.00*

Mulvaney, Charles Pelham. *History of the Northwest Rebellion of 1885.* Tor. 1886. 440 pp, maps.. *$40.00–$50.00*

Mumford, John Kimberly. *Oriental Rugs.* NY. 1923. 4th ed. .... *$35.00–$50.00*

Mumford, John Kimberly. *Oriental Rugs.* NY. 1902. .... *$50.00–$75.00*

Mundy, Talbot. *Ivory Trail.* Bobbs Merrill. 1919. 1st ed. .... *$15.00–$22.00*

Mundy, Talbot. *Purple Pirate.* Gnome. 1959. dj.................................. *$30.00–$50.00*

Munford, Beverly B. *Virginia's Attitude Toward Slavery and Secession.* L H Jenkins. 1909. 1st ed... *$25.00–$45.00*

Munn, Robert F. *Coal Industry in America.* Morgantown. West Virginia Univ Library. 1977. 2nd ed. .... *$20.00–$30.00*

Munro, Alice. *Who Do You Think You Are?* Macmillan of Canada. 1978. 1st ed. dj. .... *$35.00–$45.00*

Munro, Hector Hugh ("Saki"). *Toys of Peace.* Lon. John Lane. 1919. 1st ed. 303 pp.. .... *$60.00–$75.00*

Munson, John W. *Reminiscences of a Mosby Guerilla.* NY. 1906. 1st ed. illus. .... *$75.00–$100.00*

Munson, Loveland. *Early History of Manchester, VT.* Manchester. 1876. .... *$35.00–$55.00*

Munson, R. W. *Hemerocallis, the Day Lily.* Portland. Timber Press. (1989). 1st ed. illus. dj. .... *$30.00–$40.00*

Murdoch, Iris. *The Unicorn.* Lon. 1963. 1st ed. dj. .... *$35.00–$45.00*

Murphy, E. Jefferson. *Understanding Africa.* NY. (1969). illus. by Louise Jefferson, sgn, dj. .... *$15.00–$20.00*

Murphy, Matthew M. *Snake Dance People and Their Country.* np. nd. illus. soft decorated cvr... *$30.00–$40.00*

Murphy, Robert Cushman. *Oceanic Birds of So. America.* NY. 1936. 2 vols. illus. boxed. .... *$80.00–$125.00*

Murray, W. H. H. *Daylight Land.* 1888. illus. .... *$28.00–$37.00*

Murray, W. H. H. *Daylight Land.* Bos. Cupples & Hurd. 1888. 1st ed. pictorial cloth.. .... *$25.00–$35.00*

Murray, W. H. H. *How John Norton the Trapper Kept His Christmas.* private ptg. 1885. .... *$25.00–$30.00*

Mussolini, Benito. *Cardinal's Mistress.* NY. 1928. 1st ed. in English. ... *$45.00–$65.00*

My Cave Life in Vicksburg. NY. Appleton. 1864. 1st ed. .... *$150.00–$225.00*

Myers, Frank. *Soldiering in Dakota Among the Indians.* SD. 1936. wrps. .... *$20.00–$35.00*

Myler, L. S. *Jewels of Masonic Oratory.* Akron. 1898. 1st ed................. *$25.00–$35.00*

Myrick, Herbert. *Cache La Poudre, the Romance of a Tenderfoot in the Days of Custer.* NY. Orange Judd. 1905. 1st ed.. *$125.00–$225.00*

Mytinger, Caroline. *Headhunting in the Solomon Island*. Macmillan. 1942. 1st ed. illus. dj. .... *$18.00–$25.00*

Nabokov, Vladimir. *Invitation to a Beheading*. Putnam. 1959. 1st US ed. dj. .... *$45.00–$75.00*

Nabokov, Vladimir. *King, Queen, Knave*. McGraw-Hill. 1968. 1st US ed. dj. .... *$25.00–$30.00*

Nabokov, Vladimir. *Lectures on Russian Literature*. 1981. 1st ed. .... *$25.00–$30.00*

Nabokov, Vladimir. *Lolita*. Paris. 1955. 2 vols. 1st ed. wrps. 1st issue. .... *$275.00–$400.00*

Nabokov, Vladimir. *Look at the Harlequins!* McGraw-Hill. 1974. 1st ed. dj. .... *$25.00–$30.00*

Nabokov, Vladimir. *Nabokov's Quartet*. NY. 1966. 1st ed. .... *$35.00–$55.00*

Nabokov, Vladimir. *Notes on Prosody*. NY. 1964. dj. .... *$50.00–$75.00*

Nabokov, Vladimir. *Pale Fire*. Putnam. 1962. 1st US ed. dj. .... *$95.00–$125.00*

Nabokov, Vladimir. *Real Life of Sebastian Knight*. Norfolk. New Directions. (1941). 1st Amer ed. .... *$60.00–$100.00*

Nabokov, Vladimir. *The Defense*. NY. Putnam. 1964. 1st ed in English, dj.................. .... *$40.00–$125.00*

Naipaul, V. S. *Loss of El Dorado*. Lon. Andre Deutsch. 1960. 1st ed. dj....................... .... *$80.00–$100.00*

Naipaul, V. S. *Loss of El Dorado*. NY. Knopf. 1970. 1st US ed. dj. .... *$30.00–$75.00*

Nansen, Dr. Fridtjof. *Farthest North. . .1893–96*. NY. Harper & Bros. 1897. 2 vols. 1st Amer ed. 4 fldg maps, 16 clr plates, pictorial cloth, teg........................ *$95.00–$120.00*

Nansen, Fridtjof. *Eskimo Life*. Lon. Longmans, Green. 1893. frontis, plates, woodcuts. ....*$130.00–$175.00*

Nansen, Fridtjof. *First Crossing of Greenland*. Lon. 1892. illus. fldg map.................... .... *$45.00–$65.00*

Nansen, Fridtjof. *Through Siberia the Land of the Future*. NY. Stokes. 1914. 1st Amer ed. illus, maps.. *$175.00–$250.00*

Napheys, Geo. H. *Physical Life of a Woman*. Phila. George Maclean. 1870. .... *$28.00–$38.00*

Narrative of Capt. James Cook's Voyages Round the World. Lon. 1848.*$58.00–$70.00*

Narrative of Five Youths From the Sandwich Islands . . . NY. 1816. wrps................... .... *$50.00–$100.00*

Nash, E. B. *Leaders in Homeopathic Therapeutics*. Phila. 1901. 2nd ed. *$35.00–$40.00*

Nash, Ogden. *Moon Is Shining Bright As Day*. Lippincott. 1953. 1st ed. *$25.00–$35.00*

Nash, Ogden. *Private Dining Room*. Bos. Little & Brown. 1953. dj. ..... *$15.00–$30.00*

Nash, Wallis. *Two Years in Oregon*. Appleton. 1882. 2nd ed.................. *$60.00–$75.00*

Nasmyth, James and James Carpenter. *The Moon: Considered as a Planet, A World, and A Satellite*. Lon. 1885. illus. 3rd ed................................. *$75.00–$150.00*

Nathan, George Jean. *Art of the Night*. NY. 1928. 1st ed. ltd #192/200 cc, sgn............ .... *$45.00–$75.00*

Nation, Carry A. *Use and Need of the Life of Carry A. Nation* . . . Topeka. 1905. wrps. illus. .... *$85.00–$125.00*

Natural History of the Whale. NY. Columbia Univ Press. 1978. 1st ed. dj. .... *$16.00–$20.00*

Nature Library. Doubleday. 1904. 10 vols. .... *$200.00–$280.00*

Nature's Romance "Over the Loop." Denver. 1903. wrps. souvenir picture book. .... *$65.00–$75.00*

Nautical Almanac and Astronomical Ephemeris for the Year 1837. Lon. John Murray. 1835. 526 pp. .... *$35.00–$45.00*

Near, I. W. *History of Steuben County, NY, and Its People*. Chi. 1911. 2 vols. .... *$100.00–$135.00*

Nearing, Scott. *Black America*. Shocken Books. 1969. illus. rprnt. .... *$22.00–$30.00*

Nearing, Scott. *Black America*. NY. Vanguard. 1929. 1st ed. illus. dj. . *$85.00–$125.00*

Nearing, Scott. *British General Strike*. NY. Vanguard. 1926. 1st ed. ...... *$20.00–$30.00*

Nearing, Scott. *Conscience of a Radical*. MA. 1965. 1st ed. dj. .... *$22.00–$30.00*

Nearing, Scott. *Europe—West and East*. NY. Vanguard. 1934. 1st ed. wrps. .... *$25.00–$40.00*

Nearing, Scott. *From Capitalism to Communism*. DC. World Events. nd. wrps. 24 pp... .... *$18.00–$25.00*

Nearing, Scott. *Maple Sugar Book*. 2nd ed. dj. .... *$10.00–$20.00*

Nearing, Scott. *Rise and Decline of Christian Civilization*. Ridgewood. pub by author. 1940. wrps. 24 pp. .... *$20.00–$25.00*

Nearing, Scott. *Victory Without Peace*. DC. World Events. nd. wrps. 16 pp. .... *$18.00–$25.00*

Nearing, Scott. *Warless World*. NY. Vanguard Press. nd. wrps. 32 pp. .... *$25.00–$35.00*

Nearing, Scott and Ward Percy. *Would the Practice of Christ's Teachings Make For Social Progress*. KS. Haldeman Julius Co. nd. pamphlet. wrps. .... *$20.00–$25.00*

Neff, Jackob. *Army and Navy of America from the French & Indian Wars* . . . Phila. 1845. fldg plates. .... *$52.00–$60.00*

Neill, Edward. *History of Minnesota* . . . Phila. 1858. 1st ed. fldg map. *$50.00–$95.00*

Neill, Miss E. *Every-Day Cook-Book and Encyclopedia of Practical Recipes*. NY. 1888. .... *$25.00–$35.00*

Neiman, LeRoy. *LeRoy Neiman on Safari*. Ny. Abrams. 1997. 1st ed. illus. dj. .... *$45.00–$60.00*

Nelson, E. W. *Report Upon the Natural History of Collections* . . . *Alaska*. Wash. 1887. illus. .... *$85.00–$125.00*

Nelson, Henry Loomis and H. A. Ogden. *Uniforms of the United States Army*. NY. 1959. illus. .... *$40.00–$50.00*

Neltje, Blanchan. *American Flower Garden*. NY. Doubleday, Page. 1909. illus. .... *$20.00–$75.00*

Nevins, Rev. William. *Thoughts on Popery*. Amer Tract Society. (1836). .... *$20.00–$30.00*

Nevins, W. S. *Witchcraft in Salem Village.* Salem/Bos. 1892. illus. .... *$60.00–$85.00*

New American Pocket Farrier and Farmer's Guide. Phila. Perry. nd. illus....................
.... *$35.00–$47.00*

New England Primer. Dodd Mead. 1899. 2nd rprnt............................. *$75.00–$175.00*

New Mexico. Hastings House. 1940. orange cloth. .... *$35.00–$60.00*

New System of Domestic Cookery . . . by a Lady. Edin. 1843. illus. rbnd, ¾ calf, mar bds.. *$95.00–$110.00*

New Treatise on Surveying and Navigation. NY. 1864. .... *$18.00–$25.00*

Newcombe, Rexford. *Old Kentucky Architecture.* NY. 1940. 1st ed. plates....................
.... *$35.00–$45.00*

Newell, Peter. *Hole Book.* NY. 1908. 1st ed. illus. .... *$70.00–$125.00*

Newell, Peter. *Slant Book.* NY. (1910). 1st ed. illus. .... *$150.00–$300.00*

Newhall, Walter S. *A Memoir.* Phila. 1864. 1st ed. regimental.............. *$60.00–$75.00*

Newhouse, S. *Trapper's Guide; A Manual . . .* NY. 1869. illus. 3rd ed... *$35.00–$47.00*

Newton, Edward A. *Amenities of Book Collecting.* Bos. Atlantic Monthly Press. 1918. 1st ed. illus. scarce errata slip present.. *$40.00–$50.00*

Newton, Helmut. *White Women.* 1976. 1st ed. presentation copy, dj.... *$75.00–$150.00*

Newton, Isaac. *Opticks or a Treatise of the Reflections, Refractions, Inflections & Colours of Light.* Lon. G Bell & Sons. 1931. rprnt. .... *$65.00–$100.00*

Newton, Robert R. *Ancient Planetary Observations and the Validity of Ephemeris Time.* Balt. 1976. .... *$15.00–$25.00*

Nichols, Frederick. *Early Architecture of Georgia.* Chapel Hill. UNC Press. 1957. 1st ed. illus. 292 pp, slipcase. .... *$150.00–$200.00*

Nidever, George. *Life and Adventures of George Nidever.* Berkeley. Univ. of Calif. Press. 1937. illus. plates. .... *$50.00–$70.00*

Nikoleyev, B. A. *Thermodynumic Assessment of Rocket Engines.* NY. 1963. trans by W E G Jones, 150 pp... *$30.00–$40.00*

Nimoy, Leonard. *I Am Not Spock.* Millbrae. 1975. 1st ed. softbound, photos................
.... *$30.00–$40.00*

Nimrod. *The Chace, the Turf and the Road.* Lon. Murray. 1843. 2nd ed. illus..............
.... *$70.00–$100.00*

Nin, Anais. *Children of the Albatross.* Dutton. 1947. 1st US ed. dj. .... *$50.00–$95.00*

Nin, Anais. *Four Chambered Heart.* 1950. dj. .... *$85.00–$250.00*

Nin, Anais. *Four Chambered Heart.* NY. Duell, Sloan and Pearce. (1950). 1st ed. dj.....
.... *$40.00–$50.00*

Nin, Anais. *Ladders to Fire.* Dutton. 1946. 1st ed. dj. .... *$50.00–$110.00*

Nin, Anais. *Novel of the Future.* NY. Macmillan. 1968. 1st ed. dj. .... *$30.00–$55.00*

Nin, Anais. *Spy in the House of Love.* NY. British Book Centre. 1954. 1st Amer ed. dj. .... *$35.00–$75.00*

Ninth Air Force Service Command in the Eropean Theatre of Operations. NY. 1945. 1st ed. photos.. *$75.00–$95.00*

Niven, Larry. *Integral Trees*. NY. Ballantine. 1984. 1st ed. dj, presentation copy........... .... *$25.00–$35.00*

Nixon, Richard. *Memoirs of Richard Nixon*. NY. Grosset. 1978. 1st ed. boxed, sgn. .... *$145.00–$175.00*

Nixon, Richard. *No More Vietnams*. sgn. .... *$45.00–$75.00*

Noah's Ark A B C. NY. 1884. pictorial wrps lithos. .... *$30.00–$50.00*

Noah, Mordecai M. *Discourse. . .Consecration of the Synogogue of K.K. She'erith Yilra'el. . .on Friday, the 10th of Nisan, 5578*. NY. CS Van Winkle. 1818. 1st ed. .... *$125.00–$250.00*

Nobel, Alfred. *Les Explosifs Modernes*. Paris. 1876. 1st ed. .... *$200.00–$230.00*

Noebel, David A. *Marxist Minstrels*. Tulsa. 1974. 1st ed. paperback...... *$60.00–$70.00*

Nordenskjold, N. Otto G. and John Gunnar Anderssen. *Antarctica*. Lon. 1905. 1st ed. illus. clr plates, pictorial green cloth, ex lib. .... *$185.00–$210.00*

Nordhoff, Charles. *Communistic Societies of the United States* . . . NY. Harper & Brothers. 1875. 439 pp. .... *$100.00–$200.00*

Norman, Dorothy. *Alfred Stieglitz, an American Seer*. NY. 1973. 1st ed. illus. dj. .... *$75.00–$90.00*

Norris, Frank. *McTeague, A Story of San Francisco*. NY. 1899. 1st ed. .... *$100.00–$245.00*

Norris, Frank. *Octopus, a Story of California*. NY. 1901. 1st ed. claret cloth, leaded, decorated in gilt. .... *$100.00–$150.00*

Norris, Frank. *The Pit*. NY. 1903. 1st ed. .... *$50.00–$80.00*

Norris, Frank. *The Pit*. NY. Doubleday and Page. 1903. 1st ed. .... *$25.00–$45.00*

Norris, Frank. *The Pit, a Story of Chicago*. NY. Doubleday. 1903. 1st ed...................... .... *$50.00–$75.00*

Norris, Mary Harriott. *Golden Age of Vassar*. NY. Vassar College. 1915. 1st ed. mar. 1/800 cc. endpapers. .... *$80.00–$100.00*

North, Arthur Walbridge. *Mother of California* . . . SF. Paul Elder. (1908). 1st ed. illus. photos. cloth. .... *$35.00–$60.00*

Northrup, H. D. *Chinese Horrors & Persecutions of Christians* . . . Phila. 1900. 1st ed. illus. engr, photos. .... *$135.00–$225.00*

Northrup, Solomon. *Narr. of a Citizen of N.Y. Kidnapped* . . . *in 1841, Rescued in 1853*. Derby & Miller. 1853. .... *$75.00–$150.00*

Northrup, Solomon. *Twelve Years a Slave*. Baton Rouge. Louisiana State Univ Press. 1968. republication, dj... *$20.00–$30.00*

Norton, A. Tiffany. *History of Sullivan's Campaign Against Iroquois*. Lima, NY. 1879. fldg map... *$65.00–$70.00*

Norton, Andre. *Cats Eye*. Harcourt. 1961. 1st ed. dj. .... *$30.00–$45.00*

Norton, Andre. *Night of Masks*. Harcourt. 1964. 1st ed. dj.................... *$65.00–$85.00*

Norton, Andre. *Sword Is Drawn*. Bos. Houghton Mifflin. 1944. 1st ed. 180 pp. .... *$30.00–$45.00*

Norton, Andre. *Ware Hawk*. NY. Atheneum. 1983. 1st ed. dj................. *$25.00–$35.00*

Norton, Andre. *Wraiths of Time.* NY. 1976. 1st ed. dj. .... *$50.00–$65.00*

Norton, Caroline T. *Rocky Mountain Cook Book.* Denver. 1903 .... *$30.00–$40.00*

Norton, John P. *Elements of Scientific Agriculture.* Pease. 1859. 1st ed. 208 pp. .... *$60.00–$75.00*

Noyes, A. J. *In the Land of Chinook, or the Story of Blaine County.* Helena. 1917. 1st ed. illus. .... *$75.00–$145.00*

Noyes, Katherine M. *Jesse Macy: An Autobiography.* Springfield, IL. 1933. 1st ed. illus. .... *$50.00–$75.00*

Noyes, Stanley. *Los Comanches. The Horse People.* Albuquerque. (1993). 1st ed. dj .... *$35.00–$45.00*

Noyes, Stanley. *No Flowers for a Clown.* NY. 1961. 1st ed. dj .... *$15.00–$30.00*

Nutt, Frederick. *Complete Confectioner . . .* Lon. 1809. illus. plates, calf. .... *$150.00–$225.00*

Nuttall, T. *Manual of Ornithology.* Bos. 1834 .... *$45.00–$75.00*

Nutting, Wallace. *American Windsors.* Wallace Nutting. (1917). .... *$65.00–$75.00*

Nutting, Wallace. *Clock Book.* Old America. 1924. 1st ed. .... *$55.00–$67.00*

Nutting, Wallace. *Furniture of the Pilgrim Century 1620–1720.* Bos. 1921. 1st ed. illus. .... *$40.00–$90.00*

Nutting, Wallace. *Massachusetts Beautiful.* NY. 1923. 1st cd. .... *$18.00–$40.00*

Nutting, Wallace. *New Hampshire Beautiful.* 1923. 1st ed. .... *$20.00–$40.00*

Nutting, Wallace. *Photographic Art Secrets.* NY. 1927. 1st ed. illus. ...... *$60.00–$75.00*

Nutting, Wallace. *Vermont Beautiful.* 1st ed. .... *$20.00–$35.00*

Nutting, Wallace. *Windsor Handbook.* Saugus, MA. (1917). tan cloth. . *$40.00–$60.00*

Nutting, Wallace. *Windsor Handbook.* Rutland. Charles Tuttle. 1978. paperback. .... *$10.00–$15.00*

Nutting, Walllace. *Furniture of the Pilgrim Century.* Framingham. Old America Co. (1924). rprnt .... *$75.00–$125.00*

O'Brian, Patrick. *H.M.S. Surprise.* Phil. Lippincott. (1973). 1st US ed dj. .... *$125.00–$225.00*

O'Brien, Edward J. (ed.). *Best Short Stories of 1922.* NY. 1922. includes Fitzgerald, Hecht, Lardner. .... *$75.00–$100.00*

O'Brien, Edward J. (ed.). *Best Short Stories of 1923.* Bos. (1924). first ptg of Ernest Hemingway, mispelled "Hemenway." .... *$125.00–$400.00*

O'Brien, Frederick. *Atolls of the Sun.* NY. 1922. 1st ed. photos, map... *$45.00–$70.00*

O'Brien, Patrick. *Clarissa Oakes.* Lon. Harper Collins. (1992). 1sr UK ed. dj .... *$80.00–$100.00*

O'Brien, Patrick. *HMS Surprise.* Phila. Lippincott. (1973). 1st US ed. dj, third novel in Aubrey-Maturin series .... *$275.00–$350.00*

O'Brien, Patrick. *Reverse of the Medal.* Lon. Collins. 1986. 1st ed. dj. .... *$100.00–$160.00*

O'Brien, Patrick. *The Truelove.* NY. Norton. (1992). 1st Amer ed. dj. .. *$35.00–$50.00*

O'Brien, Tim. *Things They Carried*. 1990. 1st ed. dj. .... *$40.00–$70.00*

O'Cathasaigh, P. *Story of the Irish Citizen Army*. Dublin. 1919. 1st ed. wrps. ....
.... *$175.00–$300.00*

O'Connor, Flannery. *Good Man Is Hard to Find*. NY. Harcourt Brace. (1955). 1st ed. 251 pp, dj. .... *$400.00–$600.00*

O'Connor, Flannery. *Habit of Being*. NY. Farrar, Straus & Giroux. 1979. 1st ed. dj. ....
.... *$25.00–$65.00*

O'Connor, Flannery. *Mysteries and Manners*. NY. 1969. 1st ed. dj. ..... *$45.00–$60.00*

O'Connor, Flannery. *Wise Blood*. NY. 1952. 1st ed. dj. .... *$350.00–$725.00*

O'Connor, Frank. *Lords and Commons: Translations from the Irish*. Dublin. Cuala Press. 1938. 1st ed. 1/250 cc, dj. .... *$150.00–$300.00*

O'Connor, J. *Big Game Animals of North America*. NY. 1961. folio, dj. *$45.00–$60.00*

O'Connor, Jack. *Art of Hunting Big Game in North America*. NY. 1967. 1st ed. illus. dj.
.... *$35.00–$50.00*

O'Connor, Jack. *Big Game Rifle*. NY. 1952. 1st ed. dj. .... *$60.00–$100.00*

O'Connor, Jack. *Jack O'Connor's Big Game Hunts*. NY. 1963. illus. .... *$60.00–$75.00*

O'Connor, Kathryn. *Presidio La Bahia Del Espritu . . .* 1966. 1st ed. illus. cloth. ....
.... *$35.00–$50.00*

O'Faolain, Sean. *Come Back to Erin*. Viking. 1940. 1st US ed. dj. .... *$45.00–$50.00*

O'Faolain, Sean. *Life Story of Eamon De Valera*. Dublin. 1933. 1st ed. *$60.00–$75.00*

O'Hara, Frank. *Lunch Poems*. San Francisco. City Lights Books. (1964). 1st ed. wrps.
.... *$25.00–$35.00*

O'Hara, John. *And Other Stories: A Collection of 12 New Stories*. NY. Random House. (1968). 1st trade ed. sgn. .... *$35.00–$50.00*

O'Hara, John. *Cape Cod Lighter*. NY. Ramdom House. 1962. 1st ed. dj. ....
.... *$20.00–$30.00*

O'Hara, John. *Farmers Hotel*. Random House. 1951. 1st ed. dj. .... *$30.00–$40.00*

O'Hara, John. *From the Terrace*. NY. Random House. 1958. 1st ed. dj........................
.... *$30.00–$60.00*

O'Hara, John. *Instrument*. NY. Random House. (1967). 1st ed. ltd 300 cc, teg, sgn, slipcase.. *$90.00–$100.00*

O'Hara, John. *Lovey Childs: A Philadelphian's Story*. NY. Random House. (1969). 1st ed. ltd 200 cc, sgn, slipcase. .... *$40.00–$80.00*

O'Hara, John. *Rage to Live*. NY. Random House. (1949). 1st ed. dj. .... *$75.00–$90.00*

O'Hara, John. *Ten North Frederick*. NY. Random House. (1955). 1st ed. dj. ....
.... *$30.00–$45.00*

O'Hara, John. *Waiting for Winter*. NY. Random House. (1966). 1st ed. ltd 300 cc, teg, sgn, slipcase. .... *$50.00–$80.00*

O'Hara, John. *Waiting for Winter*. NY. 1966. 1st ed. dj........................ *$18.00–$45.00*

O'Keefe, Georgia. *Georgia O'Keefe*. NY. 1976. 1st ed. folio, dj. .... *$75.00–$100.00*

O'Neill, Eugene. *Ah, Wilderness*. NY. Limited Editions Club. 1972. illus. clr plates by Shannon Stirnweis, slipcase, 932/1500 cc. .... *$20.00–$30.00*

O'Neill, Eugene. *Ah, Wilderness*. Random House. 1933. 1st ed. dj. ..... *$55.00–$100.00*

O'Neill, Eugene. *Anna Christie*. NY. 1930. illus. 775 cc, sgn. .... *$95.00–$200.00*

O'Neill, Eugene. *Dynamo*. NY. Horace Liveright. 1929. 1st ed. dj. .... *$65.00–$75.00*

O'Neill, Eugene. *Iceman Cometh*. NY. Random House. 1946. dj. .... *$25.00–$75.00*

O'Neill, Eugene. *Lazarus Laughed*. NY. 1927. 1st ed. dj. .... *$75.00–$150.00*

O'Neill, Eugene. *Mourning Becomes Electra*. Boni & Liveright. 1931. 1st ed. dj. ....
.... *$60.00–$100.00*

O'Neill, Eugene. *Strange Interlude*. NY. Boni & Liveright. 1928. 1st ed. dj. ....
.... *$35.00–$95.00*

Oates, Joyce Carol. *Angel of Light*. Dutton. 1981. 1st ed. dj. .... *$20.00–$25.00*

Oates, Joyce Carol. *Goddess and Other Women*. Vanguard. 1974. 1st ed. dj. ....
.... *$25.00–$30.00*

Oates, Joyce Carol. *Marriage and Infidelities*. Vanguard. 1972. 1st ed. dj. ....
.... *$25.00–$30.00*

Oates, Joyce Carol. *On Boxing*. NY. 1987. illus. sgn, dj. .... *$45.00–$55.00*

Oates, Joyce Carol. *Triumph of the Spider Monkey*. ltd 350 cc, presentation copy, sgn.
.... *$75.00–$85.00*

Oberholser, Harry. *Bird Life of Texas*. Austin & Lon. Univ of Texas. (1974). 1st ed. illus. by Fuertes 36 clr plates. full-page maps. slipcase........................ *$100.00–$150.00*

Ocker, William. *Blind Flight in Theory and Practice*. The Naylor Co. 1932. 3rd ptg. illus. frontis, cloth... *$18.00–$22.00*

Odets, Clifford. *Clash by Night*. NY. Random House. (c1942). 1st ed. dj......................
.... *$50.00–$60.00*

Odets, Clifford. *Golden Boy*. NY. 1937. 1st ed. sgn. .... *$135.00–$150.00*

Odets, Clifford. *Paradise Lost: A Play in Three Acts*. NY. Random House. (c1936). 1st ed. dj. .... *$125.00–$175.00*

Odum, Howard. *Rainbow Round My Shoulder: The Blue Trail of Black Ulysses*. Bobbs Merrill. 1928. 1st ed. dj. .... *$37.00–$65.00*

Odum, Howard W. *Cold Blue Moon*. Ind. Bobbs Merril. 1931. 1st ed.........................
.... *$50.00–$65.00*

Odum, Howard W. and Guy B. Johnson. *Negro and His Songs*. Hatboro, PA. Folklore Associates. 1964. rprnt, dj.. *$65.00–$75.00*

Odum, Howard W. and Guy B. Johnson. *Negro and His Songs*. Chapel Hill. Univ of North Carolina Press. 1925. 1st ed... *$65.00–$125.00*

Official Guide of The National Association of Professional Baseball Leagues. NY. Spalding. 1903. wrps. illus. photos. .... *$100.00–$125.00*

Official Horse Show Blue Book. Vol. 30. events of 1936, lea, aeg. .... *$30.00–$50.00*

Official Horse Show Blue Book. Vol. 23. events of 1929, lea, aeg. .... *$45.00–$80.00*

Official Horse Show Blue Book. Vol. 27. events of 1933, lea, aeg. .... *$40.00–$65.00*

Official Railway and Steamboat Traveler's Guide . . .Tourists in Japan. Yokahama. 1889. map in pocket. .... *$40.00–$55.00*

Ogden, Ruth. *Little Pierre and Big Peter.* Stokes. (1915). illus. by Maria Kirk. green cloth with paste-down endpapers, dj. .... *$50.00–$60.00*

Ogg, Frederick Austin. *Opening of the Mississippi.* NY. 1904. 1st ed. illus. maps. .... *$37.00–$50.00*

Okaura, Kakuzo. *Book of Tea.* NY. 1912.................................. *$20.00–$45.00*

Olcott, Charles S. *Lure of the Camera.* Bos. 1914. 1st ed. 301 pp......... *$20.00–$35.00*

Old Dame Trot and Her Comical Cat. Lon. nd. illus. .... *$350.00–$450.00*

Oldrin, John. *Round Meadow.* NY. Viking. 1951. 1st ed. illus. by Kurt Weise.............. .... *$18.00–$35.00*

Oliphant, Pat. *An Informal Gathering.* Simon & Schuster. 1978. 1st ed. dj................... .... *$15.00–$25.00*

Oliver, Mary. *No Voyage and Other Poems.* Bos. Houghton Mifflin. 1965. wrps. sgn author's first book. .... *$75.00–$100.00*

Oliver, W. R. B. *Maoris of New Zealand and Australia.* Wellington. 1949.................... .... *$50.00–$65.00*

Oliver, W. R. B. *New Zealand Birds.* Wellington. 1955. 2nd ed. clr plates.................... .... *$67.00–$75.00*

Olympia 1936. Germany. 1936. 2 vols. illus. photos 350 tipped-in photos. .... *$200.00–$450.00*

Omwake, John. *Conestoga Six-Horse Bell Teams.* Cinn. Ebert & Richardson. 1930. 1st ed. illus. .... *$150.00–$165.00*

Ondaatje, Michael. *English Patient.* NY. Knopf. 1992. 1st Amer ed. dj....................... .... *$65.00–$275.00*

Operation, Care and Repair of Farm Machinery. Moline, IL. John Deere & Co. illus. 22nd ed. .... *$25.00–$30.00*

Oppenheimer, J. Robert. *Lectures on Electrodynamics.* NY. Gordon & Breach. 1970.. .... *$20.00–$35.00*

Oppenheimer, J. Robert. *Open Mind.* NY. Simon & Schuster. 1955. 1st ed. dj............ .... *$20.00–$35.00*

Oppenheimer, J. Robert. *Science and the Common Understanding.* NY. 1954. 1st ed.. .... *$25.00–$30.00*

Oration Delivered in Wallingford . . . Before Republicans of Ct. New Haven. 1801. .... *$32.00–$45.00*

Orcutt, Samuel. *Indians of the Housatonic & Naugatuck Valleys.* Hartford. 1882. illus. .... *$90.00–$135.00*

Orton, Job. *Religious Exercises Recommended: Or Discourses . . .* Bridgeport. 1809. 1st Amer ed. .... *$25.00–$40.00*

Orwell Reader, George Orwell. NY. 1956. 1st ed. wrps. .... *$50.00–$75.00*

Orwell, George. *Animal Farm.* Tor. Saunders. 1946. 1st Canadian ed. dj...................... .... *$100.00–$150.00*

Orwell, George. *Animal Farm*. Harcourt Brace. (1946). green cloth, dj. *$30.00–$40.00*

Orwell, George. *Animal Farm*. NY. Harcourt. 1946. 1st US ed. dj....... *$75.00–$175.00*

Orwell, George. *Animal Farm*. Lon. 1945. 1st ed. .... *$75.00–$125.00*

Orwell, George. *England Your England, and Other Essays*. Lon. Secker & Warburg. 1953. 1st ed. dj. .... *$50.00–$95.00*

Orwell, George. *Nineteen Eighty Four*. NY. 1949. 1st Amer ed. red dj. *$45.00–$150.00*

Osborne, Russell. *Journal of a Trapper*. Boise. 1921. .... *$37.00–$50.00*

Osgood, C. *Ingalik Material Culture*. New Haven. 1940. illus................ *$60.00–$80.00*

Osgood, Samuel. *Thomas Crawford and Art in America*. NY. John F Trow & Son. 1875. wrps. inscribed by author. .... *$25.00–$35.00*

Osler, Sir William. *Student Life*. Bos/NY. 1931. red cloth...................... *$55.00–$75.00*

Osler, William. *Aeguanimitas*. Phila. 1906. 2nd ed. 475 pp................... *$60.00–$75.00*

Osler, William. *An Alabama Student and Other Biographical Essays*. Oxford. 1908. .... *$75.00–$150.00*

Osler, William. *Biblioteca Osleriana: A Catalogue of Books Illustrating the History of Medicine & Science*. McGill-Queens Univ Pr. 1969. 2nd ed. 792 pp.. *$250.00–$375.00*

Osler, William. *Lectures on the Diagnosis of Abdominal Tumors*. NY. 1895. .... *$75.00–$125.00*

Osler, William. *Old Humanities and the New Science*. Bos. 1920. dj... *$75.00–$140.00*

Osler, William. *Principles and Practice of Medicine*. NY. Appleton. 1918.................... .... *$25.00–$40.00*

Osler, William. *Principles and Practice of Medicine*. NY. Appleton. 1899................... .... *$90.00–$125.00*

Osler, William. *Science & Immortality: Ingersoll Lecture*. Bos. 1904. 1st ed. .... *$60.00–$95.00*

Ossian. *Poems of Ossian*. Lon. Cadell & Davies. 1807. 2 vols. trans by James McPherson. mor.. *$55.00–$100.00*

Ossoll, Margaret Fuller. *Woman in the 19th Century*. Jewett. 1955. ...... *$30.00–$40.00*

Oswald, John Clyde. *Printing in the Americas*. NY. Gregg. (1937). 1st ed. illus. .... *$70.00–$100.00*

Oswald, John Clyde. *Printing in the Americas*. NY/Lon. 1937. 1st ed. illus. dj............. .... *$45.00–$85.00*

Otero, Miguel A. *Report of the Governor of New Mexico*. Wash. 1903. illus. fldg map. .... *$140.00–$175.00*

Otis, James. *Toby Tyler or Ten Weeks with a Circus*. NY. Harper & Bros. 1881. 1st ed. illus. .... *$135.00–$195.00*

Otis, James. *Toby Tyler or Ten Weeks with a Circus*. NY. Harper. 1881. 1st ed. scarce... .... *$150.00–$300.00*

Otis, Raymond. *Fire in the Night*. NY. 1934. 1st ed. dj. .... *$85.00–$300.00*

Otis, Raymond. *Little Valley*. Lon. (1937). 1st ed. dj........................ *$135.00–$200.00*

Ottley, Roi. *New World A-Coming*. Bos. Houghton Mifflin. 1943. 1st ed. dj...................
.... *$30.00–$45.00*

Ottley, Roi. *New World A-Coming: Inside Black America*. Bos. (1943). illus. 364 pp. ...
.... *$9.50–$14.00*

Oudemans, A. C. *Great Sea-Serpent*. Lon. 1892. illus......................... *$55.00–$150.00*

Our New Friends. Dick & Jane Reader. 1946. .... *$25.00–$30.00*

Ovid. *Art of Love*. NY. Limited Editions Club. 1971. illus. by Eric Fraser, 932/1,500 cc, sgn slipcase.. *$20.00–$30.00*

Owen, Catherine. *Choice Cookery*. NY. 1889. .... *$30.00–$45.00*

Owen, Catherine. *Culture and Cooking*. NY. 1881............................... *$30.00–$45.00*

Owen, Mabel. *Morgan Horse*. np. 1971. illus. by Toni Card. ltd #29/135, sgn. ....
.... *$95.00–$135.00*

Owen, Sir R. *Memoir on the Gorilla*. Lon. 1865................................. *$500.00–$750.00*

Ozick, Cynthia. *Messiah of Stockholm*. NY. Knopf. 1987. 1st ed. dj. .... *$15.00–$25.00*

Ozick, Cynthia. *Puttermesser Papers*. NY. Knopf. 1997. 1st ed. National Book Award Finalist, dj... *$20.00–$35.00*

Packer, Eleanor. *Charlie McCarthy . . . So Help Me, Mr Bergen*. NY. Grosset & Dunlap. 1938. 1st ed. illus. photos and drawings, pictorial bds. .... *$25.00–$35.00*

Paddock, Mrs. A. G. *Fate of Madame La Tour, A Tale of Great Salt Lake*. NY. 1861. 1st ed. .... *$37.00–$45.00*

Page, Harry S. *Between the Flags: The Recollections of a Gentleman Rider*. NY. Derrydale Press. 1929. 1/850 cc, 8vo.. *$60.00–$90.00*

Page, Major Victor W. *Modern Aircraft*. NY. Henley. 1927. illus. green cloth. ....
.... *$15.00–$25.00*

Page, V. *Ford V-8 Cars & Trucks*. NY. 1940. .... *$30.00–$35.00*

Page, Victor W. *Model T Ford Car*. NY. 1917....................................... *$45.00–$65.00*

Pages from the Gutenberg Bible of 42 Lines. NY. 1940. ltd 2,000 cc, folio. ....
.... *$100.00–$125.00*

Paige, Satchel. *Maybe I'll Pitch Forever*. NY. 1962. 1st ed..................... *$35.00–$50.00*

Paine, A. B. *Mark Twain, A Biography*. NY. 1912. 3 vols. 1st ed. illus. . *$50.00–$95.00*

Paine, Albert Bigelow. *Mark Twain, a Biography*. NY. Harper. 1912. 3 vols. ....
.... *$35.00–$60.00*

Paine, Thomas. *Political and Miscellaneous Works*. Lon. Carlile. 1819. Vol. 1. boards..
.... *$60.00–$75.00*

Paine, Thomas. *Rights of Man*. Lon. 1791. 6th ed. .... *$200.00–$225.00*

Paley, Grace. *Enormous Changes at the Last Minute*. NY. Farrar, Straus & Giroux. 1974. 1st ed. author's first book, sgn, dj... *$75.00–$125.00*

Paley, Grace. *Just As I Thought*. NY. FSG. (1998). 1st ed. dj................. *$15.00–$45.00*

Paley, Grace. *Later the Same Day*. NY. 1985. 1st ed. dj. .... *$25.00–$30.00*

Paley, Grace. *Little Disturbances of Man*. Garden City. 1959. 1st ed. dj,......................
.... *$25.00–$125.00*

Palmborg, Rilla. *Private Life of Greta Garbo*. NY. 1931. .... *$40.00–$75.00*

Palmer, Abraham J. *History of theForty-Eighth Regiment of New York State Volunteers: 1861–1865*. NY. Veterans Assoc of the Regiment. 1885. illus..
.... *$80.00–$110.00*

Palmer, Brooks. *Book of American Clocks*. NY. 1950. 1st ed. dj............ *$40.00–$75.00*

Palmer, C. H. *Salmon Rivers of Newfoundland*. Bos. 1928. illus. fldg map. ....
.... *$75.00–$95.00*

Palmer, Frederick. *With Kuroki in Manchuria*. NY. Scribner's. 1904. illus. maps. ....
.... *$30.00–$85.00*

Palmer, Frederick. *With Kuroki in Manchuria*. NY. Scribner's Sons. 1904. 1st ed. illus. maps, red cloth. .... *$40.00–$85.00*

Palmer, Howard and J. Monroe. *Climber's Guide to the Rocky Mountains of Canada*. NY. Knickerbocker Press. 1921. 1st ed. illus. 16mo, 183 pp, maps. ...... *$65.00–$125.00*

Palmer, Peter S. *History of Lake Champlain*. NY. nd. 3rd ed. 250 pp, map. ....
.... *$50.00–$70.00*

Palmer, R. *Maine Birds*. Museum of Comparative Zoology. 1949. one of the scarcest state bird books.. *$90.00–$110.00*

Palmer, R. D. *Handbook of North American Birds*. Yale Univ Press. 1962. dj...............
.... *$40.00–$50.00*

Pankhurst E. Sylvia. *Suffragetter*. NY. 1911. 1st US ed. 517 pp, illus. *$65.00–$95.00*

Pankhurst, Christabel. *Great Scourge and How to End It*. Lon. 1913. 156 pp. ....
.... *$60.00–$75.00*

Pankhurst, E. Sylvia. *Suffragette Movement*. Lon. Longmans. 1931. 1st ed. 631 pp, dj, scarce. .... *$125.00–$150.00*

Pankhurst, E. Sylvia. *Suffragette Movement*. Lon. 1932. 2nd ptg, illus, dj...................
.... *$125.00–$150.00*

Panofsky, Erwin. *Albrecht Durer*. Princeton. Princeton Univ Press. 1948. 2 vols. 3rd ed.
.... *$60.00–$90.00*

Park, Mungo. *Travels in the Interior of Africa*. Lon. Newman. 1817. frontis, ¼ calf, red label. .... *$55.00–$75.00*

Parker, Dorothy. *After Such Pleasures*. NY. 1933. #189/250 cc, slipcase, sgn. ....
.... *$100.00–$125.00*

Parker, Dorothy. *Death and Taxes*. NY. Viking. 1931. 1st ed. dj. ...... *$100.00–$160.00*

Parker, Dorothy. *Sunset Gun*. NY. 1928. 1st ed..................... *$40.00–$60.00*

Parker, Robert B. *Judas Goat*. Bos. Houghton Mifflin. 1978. 1st ed. dj.....................
.... *$55.00–$125.00*

Parker, Robert B. *Pale Kings and Princes*. NY. Delacorte. (1987). 1st ed. dj. ....
.... *$22.00–$35.00*

Parker, Thomas V. *Cherokee Indians . . . Their Relations With the U.S. Govt*. NY. 1907. 1st ed. illus... *$65.00–$75.00*

Parker, William. *Life and Public Services of Justin Smith Morrill*. Bos/NY. Houghton Mifflin. 1924. 1st ed. illus. blue blind-stamped cloth.............. *$20.00–$30.00*

Parkinson, C. Northcote. *Devil to Pay*. Bos. Houghton Mifflin. (1973). 1st US ed. dj.. .... *$20.00–$40.00*

Parkman, Francis. *Book of Roses*. Bos. Tilton. 1866. 1st ed................. *$50.00–$75.00*

Parkman, Francis. *Francis Parkman's Works*. Bos. Little Brown. 1898. 11 vols. illus. frontis, teg.. *$100.00–$130.00*

Parkman, Francis. *History of the Conspiracy of Pontiac*. Bos. Little Brown. 1855. 4 maps.. *$70.00–$85.00*

Parkman, Francis. *History of the Conspiracy of Pontiac*. Bos. Little, Brown. 1855. 4 maps, original cloth. .... *$50.00–$75.00*

Parkman, Francis. *Old Regime in Canada*. Bos. 1874. 1st ed. map. ..... *$20.00–$35.00*

Parkman, Francis. *Oregon Trail*. Bos. Little Brown. 1892. 1st ed. illus. by Frederick Remington. .... *$125.00–$550.00*

Parkman, Francis. *Oregon Trail*. Bos. 1925. illus. by N C Wyeth and F Remington, ltd #907/975 cc. .... *$100.00–$145.00*

Parloa, Maria. *Camp Cookery*. Bos. Graves, Locke & Co. 1878. rbnd.......................... .... *$150.00–$200.00*

Parloa, Maria. *Miss Parloa's New Cook Book*. Bos. 1881. 1st ed. .... *$45.00–$55.00*

Parlour Magic. Phila. 1938. 1st US ed.. *$50.00–$60.00*

Parrish, Maxfield. *Poems of Childhood*. NY. Scribner's. 1904. 1st ed. illus. by Parrish. decorated cvr.. *$50.00–$130.00*

Parry, William Edward. *Journal of a Second Voyage for the Discovery of a North-west Passage from the Atlantic to the Pacific*. Lon. John Murray. 1824. 1st ed. illus. 26 plates, 5 charts, fldg maps. .... *$780.00–$925.00*

Parsons, C. G. *Inside View of Slavery*. Bos. 1855. 1st ed. 318 pp. .... *$75.00–$135.00*

Partington, Charles F. (ed.). *British Cyclopoedia of Natural History*. Lon. Orr & Smith. 1836. 3 vols. illus. plates, engr, marbled bds. .... *$60.00–$100.00*

Partisan Review. John Reed Club of NY. 1934. Vol I, No 1. incl "Studs Lonigan" by James T Farrell. .... *$25.00–$30.00*

Parton, James. *General Butler in New Orleans*. Mason Bros. 1864. illus. maps........... .... *$30.00–$45.00*

Parton, James. *Life of Andrew Jackson*. NY. 1861. 3 vols...................... *$45.00–$75.00*

Pasley. *Al Capone. The Biography of a Self-Made Man*. NY. 1930. 1st ed..................... .... *$15.00–$50.00*

Pasternak, Boris. *Doctor Zhivago*. Pantheon. 1959. 1st Amer ed........... *$45.00–$60.00*

Pasteur, M. Louis. *Inoculation Against Hydrophobia*. NY. 1886. wrps. *$30.00–$45.00*

Patch, Edith M. *Holiday Meadow*. NY. Macmillan Co. 1930. 1st ed. illus. yellow cloth. .... *$15.00–$20.00*

Patchen, Kenneth. *Before the Brave*. Random House. 1936. 1st ed. dj, author's first book. .... *$120.00–$225.00*

Patchen, Kenneth. *Hurrah for Anything*. 1957. 1st ed. wrps................. *$37.00–$45.00*

Paton, Alan. *Cry, The Beloved Country*. NY. 1948. sgn...................... *$125.00–$150.00*

Paton, Alan. *Oh, But Your Land Is Beautiful*. NY. 1982. sgn, dj............. *$30.00–$35.00*

Paton, Alan. *Too Late the Phalarope*. Capetown. 1953. 1st ed. dj. .... *$65.00–$100.00*

Patrick, Rembert Wallace. *Jefferson Davis and His Cabinet*. Baton Rouge. 1944. 1st ed. .... *$35.00–$50.00*

Patterson, A. *Notes on Pet Monkeys*. Lon. 1888. .... *$60.00–$85.00*

Patterson, J. H. *Man Eaters of Tsavo*. NY. St. Martin's Press. 1986. illus. rprnt. ....
.... *$15.00–$25.00*

Patterson, J. H. *In the Grip of the Nyika*. NY. Macmillan. 1909. 1st Amer ed. illus. photos.. *$70.00–$100.00*

Patterson, J. H. *Man-Eaters of Tzavo and Other African Adventures*. NY. Macmillan. 1927. revised. illus. photos. .... *$80.00–$110.00*

Patterson, Robert. *Narrative of the Campaign in the Valley of the Shenandoah*. Phila. 1865. map, sgn. .... *$112.00–$120.00*

Paul, Howard and George Gebbie (eds.). *Stage and Its Stars Past and Present*. Phil. Gebbie & Co. 1889. illus. vol 1 only, large folio. .... *$75.00–$100.00*

Paulding, James K. *Slavery in the United States*. NY. 1836. wrps. 312 pp. ....
.... *$100.00–$275.00*

Pauling, Linus. *No More War!* NY. 1958. sgn. .... *$40.00–$60.00*

Pauling, Linus and E. Bright Wilson. *Introduction to Quantum Mechanics*. NY/Lon. 1935. dj. .... *$30.00–$40.00*

Pauling, Linus and E. Bright Wilson. *Introduction to Quantum Mechanics with Applications to Chemistry*. NY. 1935. .... *$25.00–$35.00*

Paullin, Chas Oscar. *Commodore John Rodgers, Captain, Commodore and Senior Officer of American Navy*. Cleve. 1910. 1st ed. 434 pp. .... *$45.00–$75.00*

Pavlov, Ivan Petrovich. *Lectures on Conditioned Reflexes* . . . NY. 1928. illus. 1st ed in Eng. .... *$125.00–$150.00*

Payson, Howard. *Boy Scouts on the Range*. Burt. rprnt. dj. .... *$12.00–$15.00*

Peabody, F. *Education for Life. The Story of Hampton Institute*. 1918. 1st ed. ....
.... *$38.00–$70.00*

Pear, Fern Bissel. *Birds*. Akron. (1943). paintings of 12 birds. stiff linen. ....
.... *$18.00–$25.00*

Peary, Robert E. *North Pole*. NY. Stokes. 1910. 2nd ed. 373 pp, frontis, clr and b/w photos, fldg map. .... *$50.00–$70.00*

Peary, Robert E. *North Pole*. NY. Stokes. 1910. 1st ed. illus. fldg map. ....
.... *$90.00–$125.00*

Peary, Robert E. *Northward Over the Great Ice*. NY. 1898. 2 vols. 1st Amer ed. frontis, photo, charts and maps, ex-lib. .... *$35.00–$50.00*

Peck, J. M. *New Guide for Emigrants to the West*. Bos. 1836. 2nd ed. ....
.... *$150.00–$225.00*

Peckham, G. W. and E. G Peckham. *On the Instincts and Habits of the Solitary Wasps*. Madison, WI. 1898. .... *$30.00–$45.00*

Pedeschi, John B. *Books on the Horse and Horsemanship*. Lon. The Tate Gallery. 1981. illus. clr plates, dj. .... *$30.00–$60.00*

Peer, Frank. *Hunting Field.* NY. Mitchell Kennerly. 1910. 1st ed. cloth pictorial panel. .... *$50.00–$75.00*

Pendergast, A. *Cigar Store Figures.* Chi. 1953. 1st ed. illus. .... *$35.00–$40.00*

Pendray, G. Edward. *Coming Age of Rocket Power.* NY/Lon. Harper & Bros. 1945. 1st ed. illus. .... *$35.00–$60.00*

Pennell Joseph. *London Reverie.* Lon. 1928. illus. dj. .... *$30.00–$45.00*

Pennell, Elizabeth Robins. *French Cathedrals.* NY. 1909. illus. teg, plans and diagrams. .... *$25.00–$45.00*

Pennell, Joseph. *Pen Drawing and Pen Draughtsmen.* NY. Macmillan. 1920. illus. gilt, buckram. .... *$35.00–$80.00*

Pennsylvania Tours to the Golden State. Phila. 1890. wrps. illus. fldg map. .... *$75.00–$125.00*

Penzer, N. M. *Book of the Wine Label.* Lon. 1947. 1st ed. illus. .... *$38.00–$45.00*

Percival, A. S. *Optics, a Manual for Students.* Lon. 1899. 403 pp. .... *$20.00–$25.00*

Percy, Walker. *Lancelot.* NY. Farrar. 1977. 1st ed. dj. .... *$25.00–$50.00*

Percy, Walker. *Last Gentleman.* Farrar. 1966. 1st ed. dj. .... *$60.00–$125.00*

Percy, Walker. *Lost in the Cosmos.* Farrar, Straus & Giroux. 1983. 1st ed. dj. .... *$20.00–$35.00*

Percy, Walker. *Love in the Ruins.* 1971. dj. .... *$28.00–$35.00*

Percy, William Alexander. *Lanterns on the Levee.* NY. 1941. 1st ed. sgn, dj. .... *$50.00–$75.00*

Perelman, S. J. *Chicken Inspector.* Simon. 1966. 1st ed. dj. .... *$40.00–$50.00*

Perelman, S. J. *Chicken Inspector No. 23.* 1966. 1st ed. dj. .... *$15.00–$20.00*

Perelman, S. J. *Ill-Tempered Clavicord.* Simon. 1952. 1st ed. dj .... *$55.00–$70.00*

Perelman, S. J. *Listen to the Mockingbird.* Simon. 1949. 1st ed. dj. ...... *$65.00–$75.00*

Perkings, Charles E. *Pinto Horse.* CA. 1927. 1st ed. 76 pp, plates. ...... *$30.00–$45.00*

Perkins, D. A. W. *History of O'Brien County, Iowa.* Sioux Falls. 1897. illus. .... *$45.00–$65.00*

Perkins, G. *Report of the State Geologist on the Mineral Industries and Geology of Vermont.* Montpelier. Capital City Press. 1912. .... *$30.00–$40.00*

Perkins, James. *Annals of the West.* Cinc. 1846. 1st ed. maps. .... *$58.00–$70.00*

Perkins, Lucy Fitch. *Indian Twins.* Houghton. 1930. illus. .... *$18.00–$30.00*

Perkins, Lucy Fitch. *Italian Twins.* Houghton. 1920. illus. .... *$22.00–$40.00*

Perkins, Lucy Fitch. *Japanese Twins.* Houghton. 1912. illus. .... *$20.00–$40.00*

Perkins, P. D. and Ione Perkins. *Bibliography of Lafcadio Hearne.* NY. 1968. .... *$45.00–$60.00*

Perry Hand Book of Choice New Fruits, Ornamentals, Roses . . . Rochester. Perry Nursery. (1899). illus. .... *$80.00–$120.00*

Perry, J. H. *Romance of the Sea.* DC. National Geographic Books. 1981. illus. folio. ... . *$30.00–$40.00*

Perry, Louise. *Marine Shells of the Southwest Coast of Florida*. Ithaca. 1942. illus. 2nd ptg. .... *$28.00–$35.00*

Perry, Robert E. *Secrets of Polar Travel*. Century. 1917. 1st ed............ *$65.00–$85.00*

Perry, Thomas. *Big Fish*. NY. Scribner's. 1985. 1st ed. dj. .... *$35.00–$50.00*

Pesci, David. *Amistad*. NY. Marlowe & Co. (1997). 1st ed. dj sgn. .... *$50.00–$55.00*

Peterjohn, B. G. *Birds of Ohio*. Indiana Univ. 1989. dj. .... *$30.00–$45.00*

Peters, F. J. *Currier & Ives Railroad, Indian & Pioneer Prints*. NY. 1930. folio, dj....... .... *$35.00–$45.00*

Peters, Harry T. *America on Stone*. NY. Arno Press. (1976). rprnt of 1931 ed.............. .... *$70.00–$90.00*

Petersen, Wm. J. *Steamboating on the Upper Mississippi*. Iowa City. 1937. 1st ed. 575 pp. .... *$65.00–$85.00*

Petersham, Maud and Miska. *Story Book of Aircraft*. Phila. John C Winston Co. 1935. .... *$18.00–$35.00*

Peterson, R.T. *Field Guide to Western Birds*. Houghton Mifflin. 1941. 1st ed............... .... *$55.00–$75.00*

Peterson, Roger Tory. *Field Guide to Birds* . . . Bos. 1947. illus. 2nd ed. sgn. .... *$35.00–$45.00*

Peterson, S. *Living Tradition of Maria Martinez*. NY/SF. 1977. Special Southwest Museum ed. ltd 500 cc, sgn and nbr.................................... *$175.00–$275.00*

Peto, Florence. *Historic Quilts*. NY. 1939. 1st ed. illus. dj. .... *$55.00–$125.00*

Pettigrew, Thomas F. *Profile of the Negro American*. NY. D Van Nostrand Co. (1964). dj. .... *$10.00–$25.00*

Pfeiffer, Ida. *Last Travels of Ida Pfeiffer*. Harper & Bros. 1861. 1st US ed. .... *$65.00–$75.00*

Phair, Charles. *Atlantic Salmon Fishing*. Camden. John Culler & Sons. 1985. .... *$85.00–$125.00*

Pharmacopoeia of the United States. Phila. 1830. .... *$150.00–$225.00*

Phayer, Michael. *Protestant and Catholic Women in Nazi Germany*. Detroit. Wayne State Univ. 1990. 1st ed. cloth large....................................... *$20.00–$30.00*

Phelps, A. H. *Natural Philosophy for Schools, Families and Private Students*. NY. Huntington & Savage. 1846. lea. .... *$24.00–$30.00*

Philips, F. C. *Question of Color*. NY. Stokes. 1895. .... *$25.00–$35.00*

Phillippi, J. *Shakerism or the Romance of Religion*. Dayton. The Otterbein Press. 1912. 133 pp. .... *$50.00–$65.00*

Phillips, John. *China Trade Porcelain*. Harvard Univ Press. 1956. 1st ed. illus. clr and b/w. .... *$75.00–$185.00*

Phillips, Paul Chrisler. *Fur Trade*. OK. (1961). 2 vols. 1st ed. illus. slipcase. .... *$50.00–$100.00*

Phillips, W. J. *Maori Carvings*. New Plymouth. 1941. photos............... *$45.00–$70.00*

Phillips, W. S. *Indian Tales for Little Folks*. NY. Platt & Munk. 1928. illus. clr plates. ... . *$35.00–$50.00*

Phister, Harold Francis. *Facing the Light . . . Daguerreotypes.* Wash. Smithsonian. 1978. 1st ed. wrps... *$40.00–$55.00*

Phoenix, John. *Phoenixiana.* NY. Appleton. 1856. 1st ed. illus.......... *$100.00–$150.00*

Photographs by Cartier-Bresson. NY. Grossman. 1963. 1st ed. wrps. illus. ....
.... *$22.00–$30.00*

Physician's and Dentist's Directory of the State of Pennsylvania. Phila. Galen Gonsier. 1902. 1st ptg, illus, 458 pp. .... *$35.00–$48.00*

Piaget, H. E. *The Watch.* 1860. illus... *$100.00–$200.00*

Picard, Mary Ann. *Official Star Trek Cooking Manual.* NY. 1978. 1st ed. paperback, sgn.. *$12.50–$18.00*

Picasso, Pablo. *Desire. A Play.* NY. 1948. 1st ed. dj. .... *$25.00–$35.00*

Pictographic History of the Oglala Sioux. Lincoln. 1967. illus. by Amos Bad Heart Bull, boxed. .... *$37.00–$45.00*

Pictorial History of the 69th Infantry Division . . . 15 May, 1943 to 15 May, 1945. np. 1945. 93 pp.. *$70.00–$85.00*

Pictorial History of the Second World War. NY. 1944–65. 5 vols. illus. photos.............
.... *$45.00–$60.00*

Pictures of Old Chinatown. NY. Moffat Jard & Co. 1909. 2nd ptg, 57 pp, photos by Arnold Genthe. .... *$135.00–$150.00*

Pierce, Gerald S. *Texas Under Arms . . . Rep. of Texas, 1836-1846.* Austin. 1969. dj. ...
.... *$27.00–$35.00*

Pike, James. *Scout and Ranger. . .in the Indian Wars.* Cinc. 1865. 1st issue, plates,.......
.... *$450.00–$500.00*

Pike, Nicholas. *New & Complete System of Arithmetick.* Bos. 1808. 3rd ed. calf. ....
.... *$22.00–$45.00*

Pike, S. and S. Hayward. *Religious Cases of Conscience.* NH. Charles Peirce. 1808. lea.
.... *$45.00–$70.00*

Pike, Warburton. *Barren Ground of Northern Canada.* Lon. 1892. 1st ed. fldg maps...
.... *$85.00–$125.00*

Pike, Zebulon M. *Exploratory Travels Through the Western Territories.* Denver. 1889..
.... *$100.00–$125.00*

Pilling, James Constantine. *Bibliography of the Eskimo Language.* GPO. 1887. wrps..
.... *$55.00–$75.00*

Pincus, Gregory. *Eggs of Mammals.* NY. Macmillan Co. 1936.............. *$35.00–$40.00*

Pinkerton, Alan. *Gypsies and the Detectives.* NY. G W Carleton. 1880. 1st ed. pictorial cloth. .... *$25.00–$40.00*

Pinkerton, Allan. *Claude Melmotte, as a Detective & Other Stories.* Chi. 1875. 1st ed.
.... *$50.00–$65.00*

Pinkerton, Allan. *Claude Melnotte as a Detective.* Chi. W B Keen Cooke & Co. 1875. 1st ed. illus. wood engr plates. .... *$75.00–$100.00*

Pinkerton, Allan. *Strikers, Communists, Tramps and Detectives.* NY. Carlton. 1878. 1st ed. illus. wood engr. .... *$80.00–$100.00*

Pinkham, Lydia E. *Nature's Gift to Women.* Lynn, MA. Lydia Pinkham Medicine Co. (c 1917). illus. 32 pp. .... *$22.00–$35.00*

Pinkham, Lydia E. *Text Book upon Ailments Peculiar to Women.* Lynn, MA. Lydia Pinkham Medicine Co. (c 1875). printed wraps, frontis, 79 pp................ *$60.00–$85.00*

Pinter, Harold. *French Lieutenant's Woman.* Bos. Little, Brown. 1981. 1st ed. dj. .... *$35.00–$50.00*

Pinter, Harold. *French Lieutenant's Woman: A Screenplay with a Foreword by John Fowles.* Bos. Little Brown. 1981. 1st ed. dj. .... *$20.00–$25.00*

Pinto, Edward H. *Treen or Small Woodware Throughout the Ages.* Lon. (1949). 1st ed. illus. dj. .... *$32.00–$40.00*

Piper, Watty. *Cock, the Mouse, and the Little Red Hen.* NY. Platt & Munk Co. 1925. 1st ed. illus. pictorial boards. .... *$18.00–$30.00*

Pitchford R. and Combs, F. *Projectionist's Handbook.* 1933. 1st ed. illus. .... *$30.00–$40.00*

Pittenger, Peggy. *Morgan Horses.* So Brunswick. Barnes. 1977. 1st ed. *$50.00–$65.00*

Plath, Sylvia. *Ariel.* NY. Harper & Row. (1966). 1st ed. dj................... *$85.00–$100.00*

Plato. *Lysis, or Friendship* . . . NY. Limited Editions Club. 1968. illus. by Eugene Karlin 932/1,500 cc sgn. slipcase. .... *$20.00–$30.00*

Platt, J. C. *Remiscences of the Early History of Dark Hollow, Slocum Hollow, Harrison Lackawanna Iron Works.* Scranton, PA. 1889. brown cloth...................... *$40.00–$60.00*

Platt, Ward. *The Frontier.* NY. (1908). wrps. .... *$18.00–$22.00*

Plowden, E. *History of Ireland.* Lon. 1812. 2 vols. 2nd ed. ¼ leather..... *$50.00–$75.00*

Pocock, Roger. *Following the Frontier.* NY. 1903. .... *$85.00–$115.00*

Poe, Edgar Allan. *Fall of the House of Usher.* Cheshire House. 1931. illus. by Abner Epstein. ltd #136/1,200 cc, tan cloth. .... *$45.00–$60.00*

Poe, Edgar Allan. *Poetical Works of Edgar Poe.* Lon. 1858. 1st ed. thus, full lea, aeg, 247 pp, illus. .... *$150.00–$225.00*

Poe, Edgar Allan. *Tales of Mystery and Imagination.* NY. Brentano's. (1923). illus. by Harry Clarke. 1st US thus. pictorial label. .... *$80.00–$120.00*

Poe, Edgar Allan. *Works of* . . . Chi. Stone & Kimball. 1894. 10 vols. illus. 36 plates, teg, green cloth. .... *$275.00–$350.00*

Poe, Edgar Allan. *Works of Edgar A. Poe.* NY. 1902. 10 vols. library ed...................... .... *$75.00–$100.00*

Poe, Edgar Allen. *A Valentine.* Phila. 1849. 1st ptg in *Sartains* mag...... *$50.00–$60.00*

Poe, Edgar Allen. *Eureka.* San Francisco. Arion Press. 1991. illus. folio sgn. .... *$250.00–$300.00*

Poe, Edgar Allen. *Tales of Mystery and Imagination.* Tudor. 1935. illus. by Harry Clarke.. *$50.00–$100.00*

Pogany, Willy and Elaine. *Golden Cockerel.* NY. Thomas Nelson. 1938. 1st ed. illus. by Willy Pogany, red cloth. .... *$100.00–$175.00*

Pohl, Frederick. *Drunkard's Walk.* Gnome. 1961. 1st ed. dj.................. *$35.00–$55.00*

Point, Fr. Nicolas. *Wilderness Kingdom: . . . Indian Life in the Rocky Mtns, 1840–1847*. NY. 1967... *$25.00–$35.00*

Poisonous Snakes of the World. Wash. GPO. nd. illus. b/w and clr plates....................... ....*$40.00–$55.00*

Polk, James. *Treaty With Mexico . . .* 30th Congress, 1st Session. 1848. House Executive Document No 69. 74 pp. .... *$145.00–$175.00*

Polk, Willis. *Matter of Taste*. SF. Book Club of California. 1979. ltd 550 cc. illus. dj. ... .*$55.00–$80.00*

Polkinghorne, R. K. and M. I. R. Polkinghorne. *Toy-Making in School and Home*. Stokes. (1920). illus. green cloth... *$40.00–$60.00*

Pollard, Edward A. *First Year of the War*. Richmond. 1863. 1st ed. Confederate imprint. .... *$225.00–$300.00*

Pollard, Edward A. *Lost Cause Regained*. NY. 1868. .... *$36.00–$50.00*

Pollard, Edward A. *Lost Cause: A New Southern Hist. of War of the Confederates*. NY. 1866. .... *$75.00–$100.00*

Pollard, Edward A. *Southern History of the Great Civil War*. NY. 1865. 2 vols............. .... *$100.00–$125.00*

Poole, Ernest. *The Harbor*. NY. Macmillan. 1915. 1st ed.................... *$75.00–$100.00*

Poore, Ben Perley. *Life & Public Services of Ambrose E Burnside*. Prov. 1882. illus..... .... *$60.00–$85.00*

Poortenaar, Jan. *Art of the Book and Its Illustration*. Lon. Harrap. (1935). 1st ed. illus. ....*$80.00–$100.00*

Pop-up Book of Magic Tricks. NY. Viking. 1983. .... *$20.00–$30.00*

Pope, Dudley. *Black Ship*. Phil. Lippincott. (1964). 1st ed. dj. .... *$50.00–$75.00*

Pope, Dudley. *Ramage*. Phil. Lippincott. (1965). 1st US ed dj. .... *$55.00–$150.00*

Pope, Dudley. *Ramage and the Rebels*. Lon. Secker & Warburg. (1978). 1st UK ed. dj. .... *$35.00–$85.00*

Popular History of the Civil War in America. NY. 1884. 1st ed. illus. ... *$10.00–$15.00*

Porok, Byron Kuhn D. *Digging for Lost African Gods*. NY. Putnam. 1926. 1st ed. photos, fldg map, teg. .... *$60.00–$70.00*

Porter, Eliot. *Birds of North America*. E P Dutton. 1972. 1st ed. illus. dj. .... *$40.00–$60.00*

Porter, Gene. *Music of the Wild*. Garden City. 1910. 1st ed.................. *$95.00–$150.00*

Porter, Gene Stratton. *Birds of the Bible*. Cinc. 1909. 1st ed............. *$150.00–$200.00*

Porter, Gene Stratton. *Laddie. A True Blue Story*. Garden City. Doubleday. 1913. 1st ed. illus. blue cloth. .... *$40.00–$105.00*

Porter, Gene Stratton. *Magic Garden*. NY. 1927. 1st ed........................ *$35.00–$48.00*

Porter, Gene Stratton. *Michael O'Halloran*. Garden City. Doubleday. 1915. illus. 1st Amer ed. illus. cloth. .... *$55.00–$65.00*

Porter, Gene Stratton. *Moths of the Limberlost*. NY. Doubleday. 1912. 1st ed. .... *$75.00–$200.00*

Porter, Gene Stratton. *Song of the Cardinal*. Bobbs Merrill. 1903. illus. buckram........
.... *$80.00–$90.00*

Porter, Gene Stratton. *The Firebird*. Garden City. 1922. 1st ed. illus.... *$22.00–$35.00*

Porter, Gene Stratton. *What I Have Done With Birds*. Ind. 1907. 1st ed.......................
.... *$175.00–$225.00*

Porter, Gene Stratton. *White Flag*. NY. 1923. 1st ed. .... *$22.00–$65.00*

Porter, Katherine. *My Chinese Marriage*. NY. 1921. .... *$50.00–$65.00*

Porter, Katherine Ann. *A Christmas Story*. NY. 1958. 1st ed. .... *$30.00–$40.00*

Porter, Katherine Ann. *Ship of Fools*. Bos. 1962. 1st ed....................... *$20.00–$30.00*

Porter, Katherine Anne. *Leaning Tower*. NY. Harcourt Brace. (1944). 1st ed. dj. ....
.... *$50.00–$100.00*

Porter, Katherine Anne. *Ship of Fools*. Bos. Little, Brown. 1962. 1st ed. dj. ....
.... *$40.00–$60.00*

Porter, Kenneth W. *Jacksons and the Lees: . . . Massachusetts Merchants, 1765–1844*.
Camb. 1937. 2 vols. 1st ed. illus. dj..................................... *$65.00–$100.00*

Potter, Beatrix. *Peter Rabbit*. NY. (1920). wrps. illus. in clr.................. *$20.00–$30.00*

Potter, Beatrix. *Peter Rabbit Pop-up Book*. Columbia. 1983. .... *$35.00–$45.00*

Potter, Beatrix. *Pie and the Patty Man*. NY. 1905................................. *$45.00–$60.00*

Potter, Beatrix. *Story of Peter Rabbit and Other Stories*. Whitman. 1928......................
.... *$14.00–$18.00*

Potter, Beatrix. *Tale of Benjamin Bunny*. Lon. 1904. 1st ed. .... *$375.00–$495.00*

Potter, Beatrix. *Tale of Mr. Toad*. 1939. illus. dj. .... *$20.00–$35.00*

Potter, Beatrix. *Wag-by-Wall*. Bos. 1944. 1st ed. illus. by J J Lankes. dj. ....
.... *$125.00–$200.00*

Pound, Ezra. *70 Cantos*. Lon. 1950. 1st Eng ed. ltd 1,622 cc, dj. .... *$90.00–$120.00*

Pound, Ezra. *Classic Anthology Defined by Confucius*. Harvard Univ Press. 1954. 1st
ed. dj. .... *$50.00–$125.00*

Pound, Ezra. *Personae, The Collected Poems*. NY. 1926. 1st ed. .... *$75.00–$100.00*

Pound, Ezra. *Section: Rock Drill 85–95 de los cantares*. New Directions. (1956). 1st US
ed. 107 pp, dj,. .... *$75.00–$125.00*

Powall, Thomas. *Topographical Description of the Dominions of the United States of
America*. Pitts. Univ Pitt Press. 1949. 1st thus, illus............................ *$100.00–$150.00*

Powell, Agnes Baden. *Handbook for Girl Scouts*. 1917. 1st ed. .... *$30.00–$45.00*

Powell, Anthony. *At Lady Molly's*. Lon. Heinemann. (c1957). 1st ed. dj. ....
.... *$65.00–$75.00*

Powell, Anthony. *Venusberg & Agents and Patients: Two Novels*. NY. Periscope-
Holliday. (1952). 1st Amer ed. dj... *$50.00–$65.00*

Powell, J. W. *14th Annual Report of the Bureau of Ethnology*. Wash. GPO. 1896. illus.
maps... *$65.00–$95.00*

Powell, J. W. *Report on the Lands of the Arid Region of the United States*. DC. GPO.
1879. 2nd ed. fldg map in rear pocket. .... *$175.00–$225.00*

Powell, J. W, Mary C. Rabbitt, Edwin D. McKee, Charles B. Hunt, and Luna B. Leopold. *Colorado River Region and John Wesley Powell.* DC. GPO. 1969. 1st ed. illus. Geological Survery Professional Paper 669. .... *$45.00–$60.00*

Powell, John Wesley. *Fourth Annual Report of the Bureau of American Ethnology . . .* Wash. GPO. 1893. illus. clr lith. .... *$100.00–$138.00*

Powell, John Wesley. *Nineteenth Annual Report of the Bureau of Ethnology . . .* Wash. GPO. 1900. illus. photos. .... *$100.00–$150.00*

Power, John. *Handy-book About Books.* Lon. Wilson. 1870. 1st ed. illus. chromolithos. .... *$70.00–$100.00*

Powys, T. F. *Mr. Weston's Good Wine.* NY. Viking. 1928. 1st Amer ed. 317 pp. .... *$30.00–$40.00*

Poyas, Mrs. Elizabeth A. *Carolina in Olden Time.* Charleston. 1855. 1st ed............... .... *$50.00–$75.00*

Practical Aeronautics. 1917. 1st ed. illus.. *$40.00–$65.00*

Practical Guide to Homeopathy for Family and Private Use. Bos/Prov/Cinc. Otis Clapp/A F Worthington. 1892. 180 pp. .... *$60.00–$85.00*

Pratt, Joseph. *Year with Osler.* Balt. Johns Hopkins. 1949. fldg chart... *$65.00–$85.00*

Pratt, Parley P. *Voice of Warning and Instruction to All People.* Liverpool. 1881. full gilt lea.. *$65.00–$75.00*

Prebble, John. *Buffalo Soldiers.* NY. Harcourt, Brace and Co. (1959). 1st ed. dj. .... *$45.00–$65.00*

Prescott, W. H. *Conquest of Mexico.* NY. 1848. 3 vols. 1st ed. .... *$110.00–$125.00*

Prescott, William H. *History of the Conquest of Peru.* Phil. 1861. 3 vols...................... .... *$75.00–$100.00*

Prescott, William H. *History of the Reign of Ferdinand and Isabella.* Bos. Charles C Little & James Brown. 1839. 3 vols.................................... *$100.00–$200.00*

Price List. Manufacturers of and Dealer in Masonic Supplies. Cinc. John D Caldwell. 1883. wrps. illus, 40 pp. .... *$50.00–$75.00*

Price, Edity Ballinger. *Four Winds.* NY. Stokes. 1927. 1st ed. illus. sgn. .... *$70.00–$100.00*

Price, F. G. Hilton. *Old Base Metal Spoons.* Lon. Batsford. 1908. illus. decorated cloth. .... *$90.00–$125.00*

Price, George. *Modern Factory.* NY. Wiley. 1914. 1st ptg...................... *$50.00–$75.00*

Price, Reynolds. *Generous Man.* NY. Atheneum. 1966. 1st ed. dj.......... *$35.00–$50.00*

Price, Reynolds. *Permanent Errors.* NY. Atheneum. 1970. 1st ed. sgn, dj. .... *$50.00–$75.00*

Price, Vincent and Mary Price. *Treasury of Great Recipes.* NY. Ampersant Press. 1965. 1st ed. dj. .... *$50.00–$75.00*

Prideaux, Humphrey. *Old and New Testament . . . Hist.of Jews & Neighbouring Nations.* Balt. 1833. illus. fldg maps. calf.................................... *$50.00–$65.00*

Priest, Josiah. *American Antiquities and Discoveries in the West.* Albany. 1833. illus. fldg map, calf.. *$90.00–$135.00*

Priestley, J. *Discourses Relating to the Evidences of Revealed Religion*. Phila. 1796. 1st ed. lea... *$95.00–$120.00*

Priestley, J. B. *Angel Pavement*. Lon. 1930. ltd #842/1,025 cc, sgn. ...... *$40.00–$50.00*

Prieur, J. C. *Boyer's Royal Dictionary*. Dublin. 1796. full lea, 17th ed.. *$55.00–$85.00*

Prime, Samuel I. *Under the Trees*. NY. Harper. 1874. 1st ed. .... *$50.00–$90.00*

Prime, William C. *Boat Life in Egypt and Nubia*. Harper & Bros. 1857. 1st ed. red cloth. .... *$50.00–$85.00*

Prime, William C. *Tent Life in the Holy Land*. NY. (1857). sgn............. *$50.00–$75.00*

Prince, Nancy. *Narrative of the Life and Travels of Mrs. Nancy Prince*. Bos. 1853. original cloth. 89 pp. .... *$250.00–$300.00*

Pritchett, V. S. *Sailor, Sense of Humour, and Other Stories*. NY. Knopf. 1956. 1st ed. dj. .... *$30.00–$40.00*

Probable Termination of Mormon Troubles in the Utah Territory. GPO. 1858............. .... *$45.00–$55.00*

Proceedings of the Exec. of the U.S. Respecting . . . Insurgents. Phila. 1795. (Whiskey Rebellion). .... *$125.00–$175.00*

Proceedings of the Fifth Imperial Konvokation Held in Chicago, Illinois August 18 and 19, 1930. wrps. 16 pp.. *$40.00–$50.00*

Proctor, R. *Chance & Luck*. Lon. 1887.................................. *$50.00–$90.00*

Proctor, Richard. *Other Worlds Than Ours*. NY. Appleton. 1897. ½lea........................ .... *$25.00–$50.00*

Propert, W. A. *Russian Ballet*. NY. Greenberg. (1932). illus. .... *$150.00–$200.00*

Prosch, Charles. *Reminiscences of Washington Territory . . .* Seattle. 1904. sgn. .... *$95.00–$125.00*

Proulx, E. Annie. *Postcards*. NY. Scribner's. 1992. 1st ed. dj, sgn. .... *$300.00–$450.00*

Proulx, E. Annie. *Complete Dairy Foods Cookbook*. PA. Rodale Press. 1982. 1st ed. illus. bds, sgn.. *$50.00–$100.00*

Proulx, E. Annie. *Fine Art of Salad Gardening*. Emmaus, PA. Rodale. 1985. dj. .... *$75.00–$150.00*

Proulx, E. Annie. *Heart Songs*. NY. Scribner's. 1988. 1st ed. dj......... *$100.00–$350.00*

Proulx, E. Annie. *Heart Songs*. NY. Scribner's. 1988. 1st ed. wrps. dj, 1/1500 cc......... .... *$40.00–$100.00*

Prussian International Literature, Organ of the International Union of Revolutionary Writers. Moscow. 1934. bound vols 1, 2, 3. black cloth. .... *$50.00–$75.00*

Psalms of David by Isaac Watts. NH. Prentiss. 1803. lea...................... *$65.00–$85.00*

Publications of the Gratz College. Phil. Gratz Coll. 1897. Vol 1. a catalogue............... .... *$80.00–$100.00*

Punkin, Jonathan. *Downfall of Freemasonry*. published for the editor. 1838. 1st ed. illus. 159 pp, cloth... *$145.00–$200.00*

Purdy, James. *Children Is All*. NY. New Directions. (1961). 1st ed. dj.. *$30.00–$50.00*

Purdy, James. *Day After the Fair*. NY. 1977. 1st ed. dj. cloth bds. .... *$60.00–$75.00*

Purdy, James. *House of the Solitary Maggot*. Garden City. Doubleday. 1974. 1st ed. dj. .... *$25.00–$50.00*

Purdy, James. *I Am Elijah Thrush*. Garden City. Doubleday. 1972. 1st ed. dj. .... *$25.00–$45.00*

Purdy, James. *Narrow Rooms*. NY. Arbor House. (1978). 1st ed. dj. ..... *$30.00–$45.00*

Pursuit of Knowledge Under Difficulties . . . Lon. Charles Knight. 1830. 2 vols. .... *$20.00–$28.00*

Pusey, William Allen. *Wilderness Road to Kentucky*. NY. 1921. dj. .... *$58.00–$75.00*

Putnam, Carleton. *Race and Reason*. Wash. Public Affairs Press. 1961. cloth.............. .... *$60.00–$75.00*

Putnam, George Haven. *Books and Their Makers During the Middle Ages*. NY. Hillary House. (1962). rprnt. .... *$60.00–$90.00*

Putnam, George Haven. *Prisoner of War in Virginia*. Putnam. 1912. 1st ed. .... *$45.00–$60.00*

Putnam, George Palmer. *George Palmer Putnam*. NY. 1912. red cloth. *$35.00–$50.00*

Putnam, George R. *Lighthouses and Lightships of the United States*. 1933. illus. .... *$30.00–$45.00*

Pyle Howard. *Book of Pirates*. Harper & Row. (1949). illus. clr frontis dj. .... *$7.00–$14.00*

Pyle, Howard. *Howard Pyle's Book of Pirates*. NY/Lon. Harper & Bros. (1921). illus.. .... *$50.00–$100.00*

Pyle, Howard. *Men of Iron*. Harper. 1892. 1st ed. illus. .... *$55.00–$75.00*

Pyle, Howard. *Story of the Champions of the Round Table*. NY. Charles Scribner's. 1905. 1st ed. brown cloth. .... *$80.00–$120.00*

Pynchon, Thomas. *Crying of Lot 49*. Phila. Lippincott. 1966. 1st ed. dj......................... .... *$250.00–$500.00*

Pynchon, Thomas. *Gravity's Rainbow*. NY. Viking. (1973). 1st ed. spine faded, dj. .... *$650.00–$1,000.00*

Pyne, Henry R. *History of the First New Jersey Cavalry*. Trenton. 1871. 1st ed............ .... *$150.00–$200.00*

Quaife, Milo M. *Checagou: From Indian Wigwam to Modern City 1673–1835*. Chi. 1933. 1st ed. dj. .... *$20.00–$35.00*

Queen, Ellery. *Devil to Pay*. NY. Stokes. 1938. 1st ed. dj...................... *$30.00–$45.00*

Queen, Ellery. *Double, Double*. Bos. Little, Brown. 1950. 1st ed. dj..... *$25.00–$30.00*

Queen, Ellery. *Ellery Queen's Double Dozen*. NY. 1964. 1st ed. dj. ...... *$32.00–$40.00*

Queen, Ellery. *Murderer Is a Fox*. Bos. Little Brown. 1945. 1st ed. dj. . *$20.00–$30.00*

Queen, Ellery. *Origin of Evil*. Bos. Little Brown. 1951. 1st ed. dj. .... *$20.00–$40.00*

Queen, Ellery. *Queen's Bureau of Investigation*. Bos. Little, Brown. 1954. 1st ed. dj. ... . *$25.00–$35.00*

Queen, Ellery. *Ten Days Wonder*. Bos. Little Brown. 1948. 1st ed. dj. .. *$10.00–$18.00*

Queen, Ellery (ed). *To the Queen's Taste*. Bos. 1946. 1st ed. dj. .... *$25.00–$40.00*

Queeny, Edgar. *Prairie Wings*. NY. 1946. 1st ed. dj............................ *$150.00–$275.00*

Queeny, Edgar M. *Cheechako, The Story of an Alaskan Bear Hunt*. NY. Scribner's. 1941. photos. .... *$90.00–$125.00*

Question of Color. NY. 1895. .... *$33.00–$38.00*

Quick, Jim. *Trout Fishing and Trout Flies*. Castle Books. 1957. 1st ed. dj. .... *$20.00–$30.00*

Quiller-Couch, A. T. *Sleeping Beauty and Other Fairy Tales*. Lon. nd. illus. by Edmund Dulac.. *$125.00–$175.00*

Quiller-Couch, A. T. *Twelve Dancing Princesses*. NY. nd. illus. tip-in plates, dj............ .... *$90.00–$200.00*

Quiller-Couch, A. T. (ed.). *Oxford Book of English Verse, 1250–1900*. Ox. 1926. .... *$25.00–$85.00*

Quiller-Couch, Arthur T. *Old Fires & Profitable Ghosts*. NY. Scribner's. 1900. 1st Amer ed. 384 pp. .... *$100.00–$135.00*

Quincy, John. *Pharmacopoeia Officinalis & Extemporanea: or A Complete English Dispensary*. . . Lon. 1782. 15th ed. .... *$40.00–$60.00*

Quinn, Tom. *Working Retrievers*. NY. Dutton. 1983. illus. dj................. *$25.00–$35.00*

Quinn, Vernon. *Seeds, Their Place in Life and Legend*. Stokes. 1936. frontis. .... *$15.00–$22.00*

Quint, Alonzo. *Record of the Second Massachusetts Infantry 1861–65*. Bos. 1867. 528 pp. .... *$90.00–$150.00*

Quints, Dionne. *Growing Up*. 1935. .... *$35.00–$55.00*

Quiz Book upon the U.S.G.A. Rules of Golf. NY. Burr. (1914). 2nd ed. illus............... .... *$90.00–$316.00*

Radin, P. *Story of the American Indian*. NY. 1944. illus. enlarged ed. ... *$20.00–$30.00*

Radin, Paul. *Trickster: A Study in American Mythology*. NY. Philosophical Library. 1956. 1st ed. dj. .... *$22.00–$28.00*

Radio Amateur's Handbook. 1927. 2nd ed. softcvr................................ *$25.00–$35.00*

Radley, J. A. *Photography in Crime Detection*. Lon. 1948. illus. .... *$28.00–$40.00*

Raht, C. G. *Romance of Davis Mountains and Big Bend Country*. El Paso. 1919. 1st ed. illus. fldg map, plates. .... *$55.00–$100.00*

Raht, Carlysle Graham. *Romance of Davis Mountains and Big Bend Country*. El Paso. 1919. illus. drawings, photos, map. .... *$30.00–$45.00*

Raine, William M. *Guns of the Frontier*. NY. 1940. 1st ed. dj. .... *$35.00–$45.00*

Ralph, Julian. *On Canada's Frontier*. Harper & Bros. 1892. 1st ed. illus. by Remington. .... *$75.00–$95.00*

Ramsay, D. *History of the American Revolution*. Trenton. 1811. 2 vols. 2nd ed. lea. .... *$95.00–$125.00*

Ramsdell, Charles W. *Laws and Joint Resolution of Last Session of Confed. Congress*. Durham. 1941. .... *$45.00–$70.00*

Ramsey, Charles and Harold Sleeper. *Architectural Graphic Standards*. NY. John Wiley & Sons. (1947). illus. 3rd ed. .... *$35.00–$65.00*

Rand McNally. *Atlas of the World*. Chi/NY. Rand McNally & Co. 1908. illus. folio clr maps... *$60.00–$90.00*

Rand McNally & Co's New Dollar Atlas of the US and Canada. Chi. 1884. cloth, bds. .... *$40.00–$60.00*

Rand, Ayn. *Atlas Shrugged*. Random House. 1957. 1st ed. dj............. *$100.00–$250.00*

Rand, Ayn. *The Fountainhead*. Ind. Bobbs Merrill. 1943. 1st ed. dj............................... .... *$1,000.00–$1,200.00*

Rand, Ayn. *The Fountainhead*. Ind. Bobbs Merrill. 1943. rprnt.............. *$16.00–$20.00*

Rand, Ayn. *We the Living*. NY. Random House. 1936. 1st ed. dj.......... *$75.00–$100.00*

Randall, E. O. *History of the Zoar Society from Its Commencement to Its Conclusion*. Columbus. Press of Fred J Heer. 1899. 100 pp..................................... *$95.00–$135.00*

Randall, Henry. *Youatt On the Structure & Diseases of the Horse*. NY. Judd. 1865. .... *$24.00–$32.00*

Randolph Caldecott Graphic Pictures. Lon. 1883. illus. folio.............. *$85.00–$115.00*

Randolph, Cornelia J. *Parlor Gardener* . . . Bos. J E Tilton & Co. 1861. illus. 11plates. .... *$50.00–$75.00*

Randolph, Mrs. Mary. *Virginia Housewife*. Univ of SC Press. 1984. facsimile ed....... ....*$25.00–$35.00*

Ransom, John L. *Andersonville Diary*. NY. private ptg. 1881. 1st ed. .... *$95.00–$125.00*

Ransome, Stafford. *Japan in Transition*. Harper & Bros. 1899. illus. frontis, maps, red cloth. .... *$40.00–$50.00*

Ransome, Stafford. *Japan in Transition*. Harper & Bros. 1800. illus. maps, red decorated cloth, frontis. .... *$50.00–$65.00*

Raper, Charles. *North Carolina: A Study in English Colonial Government*. NY. 1904. 1st ed.. *$30.00–$35.00*

Rarey, John Solomon. *Modern Art of Taming Wild Horses*. Columbus. 1856. 1st ed. wrps. .... *$900.00–$1,500.00*

Rasmussen, Wayne D. (ed.). *Agriculture in the United States: A Documentary History*. NY. Random House. 4 vols. 1st ed.. *$185.00–$225.00*

Raum, Green B. *Existing Conflict Between Republican Gov. & South. Oligarchy*. Cleve. 1884. 1st ed.. *$48.00–$65.00*

Raum, Joan O. *History of the City of Trenton*. NJ. 1871. 1st ed. illus. fldg map............ .... *$35.00–$50.00*

Rawling, Charles J. *History of the First Regiment, Virginia Infantry*. Phila. 1887. 1st ed. .... *$275.00–$350.00*

Rawlings, Marjorie Kinnan. *Cross Creek Cookery*. NY. Scribner's. 1942. 1st ed. .... *$85.00–$125.00*

Rawlings, Marjorie Kinnan. *The Sojourner*. NY. 1953. 1st ed. dj......... *$30.00–$40.00*

Rawlings, Marjorie Kinnan. *The Yearling*. Scribner's. 1940. illus. by Wyeth, 12 clr plates... *$50.00–$75.00*

Rawlings, Marjorie Kinnan. *The Yearling*. Scribner's. 1938. 1st ed. dj........................
.... *$95.00–$125.00*

Rawls, Walton. *Great Book of Currier & Ives America*. NY. Abbeville. (1979). illus. clr
plates, folio, dj. .... *$85.00–$120.00*

Rawstorne, Lawrence. *Gamonia*. Phila. McKay. 1930. rprnt of 1837 ed. illus. with clr
plates. .... *$60.00–$100.00*

Ray, J. A. *Compleat Collection of English Proverbs*. Lon. Otridge. 1768. 4th ed. ....
.... *$70.00–$100.00*

Read, Rev. Hollis. *Negro Problem Solved*. Negro Universities Press. (1969). rprnt. ......
.... *$20.00–$30.00*

Reagan, R. *Speaking My Mind*. sgn. .... *$98.00–$125.00*

Rebold, E. *General History of Free-Masonry in Europe*. Cinc. 1868. .... *$35.00–$50.00*

Receipt Book of Melvina Poe. Augusta, GA. 1833. handwritten, leather, mar bds. ....
.... *$275.00–$315.00*

Redding, J. Saunders. *Stranger and Alone*. NY. Harcourt Brace and Co. 1950. 1st ed.
author's only novel, dj. .... *$100.00–$150.00*

Redmond, Pat H. *History of Quincy and Its Men of Mark*. Ill. 1869. 1st ed. Howes......
.... *$50.00–$100.00*

Redpath, James. *Public Life of Captain John Brown*. Bos. Thayer and Eldridge. 1860.
rebound. .... *$25.00–$85.00*

Redpath, James. *Public Life of Captain John Brown. . .With an Autobiography of His
Childhood and Youth*. Bos. 1860. 1st ed. .... *$90.00–$180.00*

Redpath, James. *Roving Editor*. NY. 1859. 1st ed. blue cloth, plates. *$100.00–$325.00*

Reed, Earl H. *Sketches in Duneland*. NY/Lon. John Lane Company. 1918. illus. sgn....
....*$50.00–$75.00*

Reed, Ishmael. *Flight to Canada*. NY. Random House. 1976. 1st ed. sgn, dj. ....
.... *$45.00–$60.00*

Reed, Ishmael. *Mumbo Jumbo*. Garden City. 1972. 1st ed. dj. .... *$35.00–$55.00*

Reed, John. *An Apology For the Rite of Infant Baptism . . . Modes of Baptism*. Prov.
1815. calf. .... *$25.00–$30.00*

Reed, John. *Daughter of the Revolution and Other Stories*. NY. Vanguard. 1927. 1st ed.
uncommon in dj. .... *$60.00–$85.00*

Reed, John. *War in Eastern Europe*. NY. Scribner's. 1919. illus. by boardman Robinson.
.... *$25.00–$35.00*

Reed, John A. *History of the 101st Regiment Pennsylvania Volunteer Infantry*. Chi. 1910.
.... *$40.00–$50.00*

Reed, William Howell. *Hospital Life in the Army of the Potomac*. Bos. William V
Spencer. 1866. 1st ed. .... *$95.00–$150.00*

Reeks, H. Caulton. *Diseases of the Horse's Foot*. Chi. 1918. .... *$37.00–$45.00*

Reeman, Douglas. *Winged Escort*. NY. Putnam. (1975). 1st US ed dj. .. *$25.00–$30.00*

Reese, A. M. *Alligator and Its Allies*. NY. 1915. illus. .... *$55.00–$75.00*

Reeves, J. E. *Hand-Book of Medical Microscopy.* Phila. 1894. 1st ed. illus. ....
.... *$37.00–$45.00*

Reeves, James J. *History of the 24th Regiment New Jersey Volunteers.* Camden, NJ. 1889. 1st ed. wrps. 45 pp. .... *$110.00–$135.00*

Regulations for the Care of Camels. Cairo. War Office Ptg Press. 1896. wrps. ....
.... *$55.00–$75.00*

Reichard, Gladys. *Spider Woman: A Story of Navajo Weavers and Chanters.* 1934. 1st ed. .... *$25.00–$48.00*

Reichenbach, W. *Six Guns & Bulls Eyes.* Sam Worth. 1936. 1st ed. dj. *$40.00–$50.00*

Reid, W. Max. *Lake George and Lake Champlain.* NY/Lon. Putnam. 1910. 1st ed. illus. blue cloth. small paste-down. gold lettering. teg. frontis maps. .... *$75.00–$100.00*

Reid, Carol McMillan. *Our Own Mother Goose.* WI. Whitman Pub Co. (1934). 1st ed. illus. tall pictorial wrps. .... *$10.00–$20.00*

Reid, Mayne. *White Chief: A Legend of North Mexico.* NY. 1875. .... *$22.00–$30.00*

Reid, Mrs . Hugo. *Woman, Her Education and Influence.* NY. 1847. wrps. ....
.... *$30.00–$45.00*

Reifenstahl, Leni. *People of Kau.* NY. Harper & Row. (1976). 1st Amer ed. illus. clr plates. .... *$50.00–$80.00*

Reilly, Catherine W. *English Poetry of the First World War: A Bibliography.* NY. St Martin's Press. (1978). 1st ed. .... *$50.00–$80.00*

Reinfeld, Fred and Harold M. Phillips. *Book of the Warsaw 1935 International Chess Team Tournament.* NY. Black Knight Press. 1936. 1st ed. .... *$40.00–$45.00*

Reinhardt, Col. G. C. and Lt. Col. W. R. Kintner. *Atomic Weapons in Land Combat.* Harrisburg. 1953. 1st ed. wrps. illus. .... *$20.00–$30.00*

Religious Folk Songs of the Negro. Hampton, VA. 1918. new ed. .... *$25.00–$40.00*

Remarks On a Scandalous Libel . . . Lon. 1713. wrps 2nd ed corrected with additions. 26 pp plus 16 pp of List of All the Members of the House of Commons. ....
.... *$75.00–$125.00*

Remarque, Erich Maria. *All Quiet on the Western Front.* Bos. Little Brown. 1929. 1st ed. dj. .... *$65.00–$125.00*

Remarque, Erich Maria. *Heaven Has No Favorites.* NY. 1961. 1st Amer ed. advance copy, dj. .... *$30.00–$35.00*

Remarque, Erich Maria. *Road Back.* Bos. Little Brown. 1931. 1st ed. second book, dj. .... *$60.00–$85.00*

Remey, Charles Mason. *Universal Consciousness of the Bahai Revelation.* Italy. (1925). tan bds. .... *$25.00–$35.00*

Remington, Frederic. *Crooked Trails.* NY. Harper & Bros. 1898. illus. by Remington. .... *$200.00–$275.00*

Remington, Frederic. *Done in the Open, Drawings by . . .* NY. 1904. folio. ....
.... *$80.00–$120.00*

Remington, Frederic. *Way of an Indian.* NY. 1906. 1st ed. illus. by Remington. ....
.... *$350.00–$475.00*

Remington, Frederic. *Pony Tracks*. NY. Harper. 1895. 1st ed. illus. by Remington. ......
.... *$300.00–$500.00*

Rennap, I. *Antisemitism and the Jewish Question*. Lon. Lawrence & Wishart. nd. 1st ed.
.... *$30.00–$45.00*

Rep. of Regents of NY on Longitudes of Dudley Observatory. NY. 1862. wrps. ....
.... *$30.00–$50.00*

*Report of the Cruise of the US Revenue Cutter Bear . . . November 27, 1897 to
September 13, 1898*. Wash. GPO. 1899. blue cloth, plates, map. .... *$85.00–$125.00*

Report of the Director of the Mint . . . During the Calendar Year 1888. Wash. GPO.
1889. .... *$20.00–$30.00*

Report of the Secretary of the Navy, Nov. 5, 1864. Richmond. 1864. 1st ed. wrps. 52 pp,
Confederate imprint. .... *$250.00–$350.00*

Report of the Special Commission Appointed to Investigate the Affairs . . . Wash. GPO.
1875. illus. cloth, spine lettered in gilt. .... *$100.00–$175.00*

*Report of the Watering Committee of the Select and Common Councils of
Philadelphia*. Phila. 1830. 1st ed. wrps. 18 pp. .... *$45.00–$60.00*

*Report on Indians Taxed and Not Taxed in the United States . . . Eleventh Census:
1890*. Wash. GPO. 1894. 683 pp, maps, plates. .... *$700.00–$1,200.00*

Report on Japanese Research on Radio Wave Propagation. US Army. 1946. 1st ed. ....
.... *$50.00–$65.00*

Report on the Census of Cuba, 1899. Wash. GPO. 1900. illus. photos. . *$48.00–$60.00*

Report on the Control of the Aborigines of Formosa. 1911. illus. maps. ....
.... *$75.00–$100.00*

Report on U. S. Geographical Surveys West of 100th Meridian . . . Wash. GPO. 1877.
illus. .... *$80.00–$120.00*

Reports . . . Joint Palestine Survey Commission, October 1, 1928. Bos. 1928. illus. ......
.... *$95.00–$125.00*

Reports of Explorations and Surveys to the Pacific Ocean. illus. plates. ....
.... *$150.00–$250.00*

Reports of Officers in Relation to Recent Battles at Pittsburg Landing. Wash. 1862. ....
.... *$75.00–$100.00*

Reuter, Edward Byron. *Mulatto in the United States*. NY. 1969. .... *$18.00–$25.00*

Revised Regulations for the Army of the United States. Phila. Lippincott. 1862. ....
.... *$75.00–$95.00*

Rey, H. A. *Zebrology*. Lon. Chatto & Windus. c 1937. illus. yellow paper. ....
.... *$75.00–$150.00*

Reynolds, E. W. *True Story of the Barons of the South . . .* Bos. 1862... *$40.00–$50.00*

Reynolds, George. *Book of Abraham*. Salt Lake. 1879. 1st ed. printed wraps. ....
.... *$40.00–$50.00*

Reynolds, Quentin. *Fiction Factory*. NY. Random House. 1955. 1st ed. dj. ....
.... *$35.00–$55.00*

Reznikoff, Charles. *By the Waters of Manhattan*. Charles Boni. 1930. 1st ed. paperback.
.... *$20.00–$65.00*

Reznikoff, Nathan and Charles Reznikoff. *Early History of a Sewing Machine Operator.* NY. Reznikoff. (1936). 1st ed. blue cloth, paper label......... *$165.00–$175.00*

Rheims, Maurice. *Flowering of Art Nouveau.* NY. nd. dj...................... *$85.00–$115.00*

Rhind, William. *History of the Vegetable Kingdom.* Lon. Blackie & Son. 1877. revised ed. .... *$120.00–$140.00*

Rhinegold & The Valkyrie. Lon/NY. 1914. illus. by Arthur Rackham, tip-in plates......... .... *$60.00–$75.00*

Rhoades, J. *Little Flowers of St. Francis of Assissi.* Lon. Oxford Univ Press. 1934. rprnt, 319 pp, full lea, gold-tooled, aeg... *$30.00–$40.00*

Rice, Anne. *Cry to Heaven.* NY. 1982. 1st ed. dj...................................... *$30.00–$45.00*

Rice, Anne. *Lasher.* Knopf. 1993. 1st ed. dj, sgn.................................. *$50.00–$60.00*

Rice, Anne. *Memnock the Devil.* NY. Knopf. 1995. 1st ed. sgn, dj......... *$45.00–$60.00*

Rice, Anne. *Mummy or Ramses the Damned.* NY. Ballantine. (1989). 1st ed. illus. Harlan Ellison's copy with his sgn bookplate. .... *$35.00–$65.00*

Rice, Anne. *Queen of the Damned.* Knopf. 1988. sgn, dj...................... *$45.00–$60.00*

Rice, Anne. *Tale of the Body Thief.* 1992. 1st ed. dj. .... *$30.00–$40.00*

Rice, Anne. *The Mummy.* Lon. 1989. 1st Brit ed. dj.......................... *$125.00–$175.00*

Rice, Anne. *Vampire Lestat.* NY. Knopf. 1985. 1st ed. dj, sgn. .... *$125.00–$285.00*

Rice, Anne. *Vampire Lestat.* NY. Knopf. 1985. 1st ed. dj................... *$150.00–$200.00*

Rice, Anne. *Witching Hour.* Knopf. 1990. 1st ed. dj sgn........................ *$30.00–$45.00*

Rich E. E. *Hudson's Bay Company, 1670–1870.* NY. Macmillan Company. (1961). 3 vols. 1st Amer ed. 6 plates, 2 fldg maps. .... *$100.00–$150.00*

Rich, Prof. George. *Artistic Horse Shoeing.* NY. 1890. .... *$35.00–$45.00*

Richards, Laura. *Captain January.* Bos. 1893. illus.............................. *$35.00–$45.00*

Richards, Laura E. *Golden Windows.* Little Brown. 1903. illus. .... *$30.00–$40.00*

Richards, Laura E. *Silver Crown.* Little Brown. 1906. illus. .... *$20.00–$40.00*

Richards, Laura E. *When I Was Your Age.* Bos. 1849. 1st ed................. *$20.00–$30.00*

Richards, Laura Elizabeth Howe. *Hurdy-Gurdy.* Bos. 1902. illus........ *$65.00–$85.00*

Richardson, A. E. *Old Inns of England.* Lon. 1942. .... *$25.00–$40.00*

Richardson, Albert D. *Secret Service, the Field, the Dungeon and the Escape.* Hartford. 1865. 1st ed. illus.. *$65.00–$145.00*

Richardson, Beulah. *Black Woman Speaks. . .of White Womanhood, of White Supremacy, of Peace.* NY. Amer Women for Peace. 1951. wrps. 12 pp. pictorial wrps. .... *$15.00–$45.00*

Richardson, Frank. *From Sunrise to Sunset: Reminiscence.* Bristol, TN. 1910. 1st ed. illus. .... *$90.00–$125.00*

Richardson, Frank. *Secret Kingdom.* Lon. (1911). 3rd ptg.................... *$50.00–$75.00*

Richardson, J. *Health & Longevity.* Phil. Home Health Society. 1912. illus. .... *$50.00–$75.00*

Richardson, James D. *Messages of the Presidents*. Bureau of National Literature. 22 vols.. *$75.00–$100.00*

Richardson, James (ed.). *Wonders of the Yellowstone*. NY. Scribner's, Armstrong. 1875. illus. fldg map... *$50.00–$80.00*

Richardson, Sir John. *Arctic Searching Expedition for Sir John Franklin*. NY. 1852.... .... *$60.00–$80.00*

Richmond Bicentennial Committee. *History of Richmont, Utah*. 1976. illus. photos. .. .. *$38.00–$50.00*

Richmond, Mary. *Day in the Life of a Spoiled Child*. New Haven. S Babcock. nd. wrps. 24 pp, 15 x 85 cm.. *$35.00–$50.00*

Rickard, T. A. *Copper Mines of Lake Superior*. NY. 1905. 1st ed. .... *$33.00–$45.00*

Rickett, H. *Wildflowers of the U.S.: The Southeastern States*. 1966. 2 vols. slipcase...... .... *$85.00–$120.00*

Riddle, Kenyon. *Records and Maps of the Old Santa Fe Trail*. FL. private pub. 1963. illus. fldg maps in rear pocket, rev. .... *$60.00–$75.00*

Rideing, William H. *Overland Express . . .* Ashland. Lewis Osborne. 1970. map 650 cc. .... *$30.00–$40.00*

Riefel, Carlos von. *Folio of Fruit*. Lon. The Ariel Press. 1957. illus. folio. dj............... .... *$50.00–$75.00*

Riggs and Carvie. *Modern Guns & Smokeless Powder*. Lon. 1892. .... *$48.00–$60.00*

Riggs, Lynn. *Big Lake. A Tragedy in Two Parts*. NY. 1927. 1st ed. dj. ... *$45.00–$60.00*

Riggs, Lynn. *Iron Dish*. Garden City. 1930. 1st ed. dj............................ *$22.00–$30.00*

Riggs, Lynn. *Russet Mantle and the Cherokee Night*. NY. 1936. 1st ed. dj. .... *$45.00–$125.00*

Riggs, Stephen R. *Dakota Grammar, Texts and Ethnography*. Wash. GPO. 1893........... .... *$60.00–$95.00*

Riggs, Stephen R. *Mary and I: 40 Years with the Sioux*. Bos. (1887). 2nd ed. 437 pp. .. .. *$35.00–$50.00*

Rights, Douglas LeTell. *American Indian in North Carolina*. NC. 1947. 1st ed............ .... *$50.00–$65.00*

Riis, Jacob. *Battle With the Slum*. NY. 1902. .... *$25.00–$45.00*

Riis, Jacob A. *How the Other Half Lives. . .the Tenements of New York*. NY. 1891. 1st ed. blue cloth, illus. .... *$125.00–$175.00*

Riker, James. *Revised History of Harlem*. NY. 1904. fldg map............. *$60.00–$95.00*

Riley, James Whitcomb. *Old Swimmin' Hole and 'leven More Poems . . .* Ind. 1891. 1st ed. 3rd state.. *$50.00–$75.00*

Rinehart, Mary Roberts. *Tenting Tonight*. Bos/NY. 1918. illus............. *$45.00–$60.00*

Rinehart, Mary Roberts. *Through Glacier Park*. Bos. 1916. 1st ed. illus. sgn. .... *$32.00–$40.00*

Rinehart, Mary Roberts. *When a Man Marries*. Tor. 1909. illus. 1st Canadian ed........ .... *$65.00–$75.00*

Rinhart, Floyd and Marion. *American Miniature Case Art*. South Brunswick. (1969). illus. plates, dj... *$40.00–$80.00*

Ripley, Eliza McHatton. *From Flag to Flag*. NY. Appleton. 1880. brown pictorial cloth. .... *$65.00–$80.00*

Ripley, Henry J. *Sacred Rhetoric*. Bos. Gould, Kendall & Lincoln. 1849. 1st ed........... .... *$25.00–$35.00*

Ripley, Mary. *Oriental Rug Book*. Stokes. (1904). clr illus. .... *$30.00–$45.00*

Ritchie, Leitch. *Ireland Picturesque and Romantic*. Lon. 1837. 1st ed. illus. engr, aeg.. .... *$85.00–$125.00*

Rivera, Diego. *Frescoes*. NY. (1929).................................... *$65.00–$135.00*

Rivers, George R. R. *Captain Shays, a Populist of 1786*. Bos. Little, Brown. 1897. 1st ed. .... *$65.00–$125.00*

Robbins, R. A. *91st Infantry Division in WWll*. Wash. 1947. 1st ed. illus. maps, photos. .... *$50.00–$60.00*

Roberts, Charles G. D. *History of Canada*. Bos. Lamson, Wolfe. 1897. 1st ed. illus. fldg map. .... *$15.00–$40.00*

Roberts, John. *Modern Medicine and Homeopathy*. Phila. Edwards & Docker. 1895. 1st ed. 69 pp. .... *$90.00–$125.00*

Roberts, Kenneth. *Arundel*. ME. Kennebunk. 1985. Centennial ed. ...... *$50.00–$75.00*

Roberts, Kenneth. *Black Magic*. Ind. Bobbs Merrill. (1924). 1st ed. author's fifth book, scarce. .... *$100.00–$135.00*

Roberts, Kenneth. *Concentrated New England*. Ind. Bobbs-Merrill. (1924). 1st ed. scarce. .... *$260.00–$300.00*

Roberts, Kenneth. *Europe's Morning After*. NY. Harper and Bros. (1921). 1st ed. author's first book. .... *$100.00–$300.00*

Roberts, Kenneth. *It Must Be Your Tonsils*. NY. 1936. sgn. .... *$55.00–$100.00*

Roberts, Kenneth. *Lively Lady*. Garden City. Doubleday, Doran. (1931). 1st ed. scarce, dj missing.. *$30.00–$45.00*

Roberts, Kenneth. *Lydia Bailey*. Garden City. 1947. 1st ed. dj. .... *$55.00–$85.00*

Roberts, Kenneth. *Moreau de St. Mery's American Journey*. NY. Doubleday. (1947). dj, blue cloth. .... *$15.00–$22.00*

Roberts, Kenneth. *Northwest Passage*. NY. 1937. 1st ed. wrps. inscrb dj..................... .... *$150.00–$250.00*

Roberts, Kenneth. *Rabble in Arms*. NY. Doubleday, Doran. 1956. dj.... *$10.00–$20.00*

Roberts, Kenneth. *Sun Hunting*. Ind. Bobbs-Merrill. (1922). first state, gilt cvr, scarce in dj... *$100.00–$400.00*

Roberts, Kenneth. *Trending into Maine*. Bos. 1938. 1st ed. illus. by N C Wyeth. dj. ... . *$75.00–$150.00*

Roberts, Kenneth L. *Why Europe Leaves Home*. NY. Bobbs Merrill. (1922). 1st ed. author's second book. no dj. .... *$250.00–$325.00*

Roberts, Morley. *Private Life of Henry Maitland: A Record Dictated by J. H.* Lon. Eveleigh Nash. 1912. 1st ed. .... *$80.00–$125.00*

Roberts, Thomas S. *Birds of Minnesota*. Minneapolis. 1932. 2 vols. 1st ed. clr plates. . ... *$100.00–$125.00*

Robeson, Eslanda Goode (Mrs. Paul Robeson). *African Journey*. NY. 1945. 1st ed. dj. .... *$45.00–$65.00*

Robeson, Kenneth. *Quest of the Spider: A Doc Savage Novel*. NY. 1935. .... *$95.00–$130.00*

Robeson, Paul. *Here I Stand*. Lon. Dennis Dobson. 1958. 2nd Brit ed. dj. .... *$35.00–$50.00*

Robie, Virginia. *Historic Styles in Furniture*. Chi. 1905. 1st ed. illus. ... *$35.00–$40.00*

Robinson, Bert. *Basket Weavers of Arizona*. Albuquerque. 1954. dj. ..... *$50.00–$75.00*

Robinson, Charles. *Kansas Conflict*. NY. 1892. 1st ed. .... *$95.00–$150.00*

Robinson, Edward Arlington. *Cavender's House*. 1929. 1st ed. dj. ...... *$30.00–$45.00*

Robinson, Edward Arlington. *Dionysus in Doubt: A Book of Poems*. NY. Macmillan. 1925. 1st ed. 1/350 cc, sgn, dj, slipcase. .... *$75.00–$175.00*

Robinson, G. *Travels in Palestine and Syria*. Paris. 1837. 2 vols. illus. half calf, maps, plates. .... *$150.00–$200.00*

Robinson, Jeffers. *Be Angry at the Sun*. NY. (1941). 1st ed. dj. .... *$35.00–$45.00*

Robinson, Leigh. *South Before and at the Battle of the Wilderness*. Richmond. 1878. wrps. .... *$75.00–$100.00*

Robinson, Rowland E. *Sam Lovel's Camps and Other Stories*. Rutland. Tuttle. (1934). Centennial Ed. .... *$30.00–$50.00*

Robinson, Rowland E. *Sam Lovel's Camps*. NY. 1893. .... *$20.00–$35.00*

Robinson, Rowland E. *Uncle Lisha's Outing*. Bos/NY. 1897. 1st ed. .... *$25.00–$35.00*

Robinson, S. *Kansas: Interior & Exterior Life*. Bos. 1856. .... *$35.00–$45.00*

Robinson, Samuel. *Course of Fifteen Lectures on Medical Botany*. Columbus. Pike, Platt & Co. 1832. .... *$125.00–$165.00*

Robinson, Selma. *City Child*. NY. Farrar & Rinehart. 1931. 1st trade ed. illus. by Rockwell Kent, bown cloth, dj. .... *$50.00–$100.00*

Robinson, Will. *Story of Arizona*. Phoenix. 1919. .... *$30.00–$65.00*

Robison, Capt. S. S. *Robison's Manual of Radio Telegraphy and Telephony 1919*. 1919. illus. 5th ed. .... *$30.00–$40.00*

Rockne, Knute. *Coaching*. NY. 1931. .... *$28.00–$35.00*

Rockwell, A. H. *Improved Practical System of Educating the Horse*. NY. 1971. illus. ... . *$25.00–$35.00*

Rockwell, Carey. *Danger in Deep Space*. Grosset & Dunlap. (1954). dj. *$6.00–$20.00*

Rockwell, Carey. *Robot Racket*. Grosset & Dunlap. (1956). dj. .... *$10.00–$14.00*

Rockwell, Carey. *Stand By for Mars*. Grosset & Dunlap. (1953). Tom Corbett, Space Cadet, dj. .... *$25.00–$30.00*

Rockwell, Carey. *Treachery in Outer Space*. Grosset & Dunlap. 1952. Tom Corbett #6, dj. .... *$15.00–$25.00*

Rockwell, George. *History of Ridgefield, Connecticut.* private printing. 1927. illus. blue cloth, gold lettering... *$40.00–$55.00*

Rockwell, Norman. *My Adventures as an Illustrator.* NY. 1960. 1st ed. slipcase, dj. .... *$40.00–$45.00*

Rockwood, Roy. *Through the Air to the North Pole . . .* NY. 1906. 1st ed. illus. .... *$32.00–$45.00*

Rocky Mountain Country Club. 1905...................................... *$45.00–$60.00*

Rodgers, Otis and Pat Mulkern (eds.). *Hobo From Texas.* np. 1950. 1st ed. thus, illus, pictorial wraps. .... *$50.00–$80.00*

Roe, F. G. *North American Buffalo.* Lon. David & Charles. 1972. 2nd ed, dj. .... *$35.00–$70.00*

Roehl, Louis M. *Harness Repairing.* Milw. Bruce. 1921. 1st ed. illus. . *$40.00–$65.00*

Roemer, Ferdinand. *Texas With Particular Reference to German Immigration.* San Antonio. 1935. 1st ed. wrps. .... *$100.00–$150.00*

Rogers, Alice Lang. *Poodles in Particular.* NY. 1951. illus.................... *$14.00–$18.00*

Rogers, Dale Evans. *Angel Unaware.* Revell. 1953. dj........................... *$15.00–$22.00*

Rogers, J A. *World's Great Men of Color.* NY. 1947. 2 vols................... *$50.00–$65.00*

Rogers, J. E. *Shell Book.* NY. 1908. illus... *$25.00–$50.00*

Rogers, Samuel. *Recollections of the Table-Talk of Samuel Rogers.* Lon. Moxon. 1856. calf and marbled bds. .... *$100.00–$150.00*

Rohmer, Sax. *Bat Flies Low.* NY. 1935. .... *$20.00–$35.00*

Rohmer, Sax. *Green Eyes of Bast.* NY. 1920. 1st ed. .... *$45.00–$75.00*

Rohmer, Sax. *Grey Face.* NY. Doubleday. 1924. 1st ed. .... *$15.00–$25.00*

Rohmer, Sax. *Hand of Fu Manchu.* McBride. 1917. 1st ed. .... *$40.00–$60.00*

Rohmer, Sax. *Island of Fu Manchu.* Garden City. 1941. 1st ed. Crime Club, dj............. .... *$100.00–$450.00*

Rohmer, Sax. *Moon of Madness.* Garden City. 1928............................. *$20.00–$40.00*

Rohmer, Sax. *Return of Dr. Fu Manchu.* NY. Grosset & Dunlap. dj. ..... *$55.00–$75.00*

Rohmer, Sax. *Tales of Chinatown.* NY. Doubleday. 1922. 1st ed. .... *$20.00–$30.00*

Rohmer, Sax. *White Velvet.* Garden City. 1937. dj. .... *$25.00–$35.00*

Rollicking Rhymes for Youngsters. Fleming Revell Co, Pub. 1902. 1st ed. illus............. .... *$27.00–$55.00*

Rollinson, John K. *Pony Trails in Wyoming . . .* Caldwell. Caxton Printers. 1941. inscrb by author. dj. scarce.. *$65.00–$95.00*

Rolvaag, O. E. *Giants in the Earth.* Harper. 1927. dj............................. *$65.00–$95.00*

Romance of the Oriental Rug. Tor. Babylon's Ltd. (1925). 1st ed. clr plates. .... *$35.00–$45.00*

Romantic Salt Lake City. Salt Lake. 1927. 1st ed. illus. printed wraps, photos. .... *$25.00–$35.00*

Ronalds, Alfred. *Fly-Fisher's Entomology.* Lon. 1883. illus. 9th ed. plates.................... .... *$125.00–$180.00*

Roop, Guy. *Villas & Palaces of Andrea Palladio, 1508–1580*. Milano. Arti Grafiche Francesco Ghezzi. 1968. illus. 1st ed in English, slipcase...................... *$70.00–$100.00*

Roop, Guy. *Villas and Palaces of Andrea Palladio*. Milano. Arti Grafiche Francesco Ghezzi. 1968. 1st Eng ed. illus. slipcase... *$70.00–$100.00*

Roosevelt, Eleanor. *This Troubled World*. NY. Kinsey. 1938. 1st ed. 47 pp, dj.............
.... *$65.00–$75.00*

Roosevelt, Eleanor (Anna). *It's Up to Women*. NY. Stokes. 1933.......... *$20.00–$30.00*

Roosevelt, Franklin D. *Happy Warrior, Alfred E. Smith*. Bos. 1928. 1st ed...................
.... *$35.00–$50.00*

Roosevelt, Theodore. *African Game Trails*. NY. 1910. 1st ed. illus. .... *$95.00–$150.00*

Roosevelt, Theodore. *Naval War of 1812*. NY. Haskell House. 1968. rprnt....................
.... *$30.00–$35.00*

Roosevelt, Theodore. *Outdoor Pastimes of American Hunter*. NY. 1905. 1st ed. illus. ..
.... *$60.00–$75.00*

Roosevelt, Theodore. *Ranch Life and the Hunting Trail*. NY. Century. 1896. illus. by Remington, 186 pp. .... *$120.00–$175.00*

Roosevelt, Theodore. *Through the Brazilian Wilderness*. NY. 1914. 1st ed. ....
.... *$67.00–$75.00*

Roosevelt, Theodore. *Wilderness Hunter*. NY. Putman's Sons. 1886. 1st ed. illus.........
.... *$95.00–$150.00*

Roosevelt, Theodore. *Wilderness Hunter*. NY. Putnam. 1893. illus. with b/w plates by Frost, Beard, Sandham, Eaton and Remington. .... *$50.00–$125.00*

Roosevelt, Theodore. *Winning of the West*. NY. 1900. 4 vols. illus. maps....................
.... *$25.00–$50.00*

Roosevelt, Theodore. *Winning of the West*. NY. 1900. 4 vols. .... *$70.00–$225.00*

Roosevelt, Theodore and Kermit. *East of the Sun and West of the Moon*. NY. Scribner's. 1927. 1st ed. photos, maps. .... *$60.00–$90.00*

Roosevelt, Theodore and Kermit. *Trailing the Giant Panda*. NY. Scribner's. 1929. 1st ed. photos, fldg map. .... *$50.00–$75.00*

Root, Edward W. and Phillip Hooker. *Contribution to the Study of the Renaissance in America*. NY. Scribner's. 1929. 1st ed. 242 pp, 1/750 cc.................... *$175.00–$225.00*

Root, S. *Primary Bible Questions for Young Children*. Atlanta. 1864. 3rd ed.................
.... *$125.00–$150.00*

Rosch, John. *Historic White Plains*. White Plains. Baletto-Sweetman. 1939. 1/1,000, fldg map... *$25.00–$40.00*

Roscoe, Theodore. *United States Submarine Operations in World War II*. Annapolis. Naval Institute Press. 1949. 1st ed. photos, fldg maps, tan cloth. .... *$45.00–$60.00*

Rose, Victor. *Texas Vendetta or the Sutton Taylor Feud*. Houston. 1956. rprnt..............
.... *$22.00–$35.00*

Roseman, Mill. *Strathmore Century: The 100th Anniversary Issues of the Strathmorean*. Westfield, MA. Strathmore Paper. 1992. illus. photos, facsimiles. .... *$60.00–$90.00*

Rosendahl, Commander C. E. *What About the Airship*. NY. 1938. 1st ed. dj...............
.... *$65.00–$80.00*

Rosengarten, A. *Romantic Revolutionary: Biography of John Reed*. NY. Knopf. 1975. 1st ed. illus. photos, dj.. *$35.00–$45.00*

Ross, Alexander. *Adventures of First Settlers on the Oregon or Columbia River*. Lakeside Press. 1928. .... *$40.00–$45.00*

Ross, Alexander. *Birds of Canada*. Tor. 1872. 2nd ed, brown cloth. ...... *$30.00–$60.00*

Ross, John. *Narrative of a Second Voyage in Search of a North West Passage*. Lon. A W Webster. 1835. 2 vols. 1st ed. illus. cloth views and charts. lithos. 9 hand clred............. .... *$450.00–$650.00*

Rosser, Mrs. Thomas. *Housekeepers' and Mothers' Manual*. VA. Everett Waddey Co. 1895. 1st ed. dark green gilt lettered cvr.................................... *$40.00–$60.00*

Rossetti, Christina. *A Pageant*. Lon. Macmillan. 1881. 1st ed. 198 pp......................... .... *$225.00–$300.00*

Rossi, Mario M. *Pilgrimage in the West*. Dublin. Cuala Press. 1932. 300 cc................. .... *$85.00–$175.00*

Roth, Cecil (ed.). *Haggadah*. Bos. Little Brown. 1965. illus. by Ben Shahn.................. .... *$90.00–$100.00*

Roth, Philip. *American Pastoral*. Bos/NY. Houghton Mifflin. 1997. 1st ed. dj.............. .... *$35.00–$40.00*

Roth, Philip. *Goodbye Columbus*. Bos. Random House. 1959. 1st ed. dj..................... .... *$300.00–$500.00*

Roth, Philip. *Great American Novel*. NY. 1973. 1st ed. dj..................... *$25.00–$40.00*

Roth, Philip. *Operation Shylock*. Simon & Schuster. 1993. 1st ed. dj. ... *$15.00–$25.00*

Roth, Philip. *Our Gang*. NY. Random House. 1971. 1st ed. dj.............. *$20.00–$35.00*

Roth, Philip. *Professor of Desire*. NY. 1977. 1st ed. dj......................... *$20.00–$35.00*

Roth, Philip. *When She Was Good*. Random House. 1967. 1st ed. dj..... *$35.00–$50.00*

Rothstein, T. *From Chartism to Labourism*. International Publishers. (1929). black cloth. .... *$25.00–$40.00*

Rowe, Samuel. *Perambulation of the Antient and Royal Forest of Dartmoor*. Lon/Exeter. 1896. 3rd ed. illus... *$50.00–$75.00*

Rowse, A. L. *Homosexuals in History*. Dorset. 1977. 1st Eng ed dj....... *$40.00–$55.00*

Roy, Arundhati. *God of Small Things*. NY. Random House. (1997). 1st Amer ed.......... .... *$35.00–$60.00*

Royce, Sarah. *Frontier Lady: Recollections of the Gold Rush and Early California*. New Haven. Yale Univ Press. 1932. 1st ed. dj................................... *$50.00–$70.00*

Royko, Mike. *I May Be Wrong, But I Doubt It*. Chi. 1968. 1st ed. .... *$24.00–$37.00*

Ruark, Robert. *Honey Badger*. NY. McGraw Hill. 1965. 1st ed. dj....... *$12.00–$25.00*

Ruark, Robert. *Old Man's Boy Grows Older*. NY. Holt, Rinehard & Winston. 1961. 1st ed. dj. .... *$50.00–$75.00*

Ruark, Robert. *Something of Value*. Garden City. 1955. 1st ed. dj. .... *$30.00–$45.00*

Ruark, Robert. *Use Enough Gun*. NY. New American Lib. (1966). 1st ed..................... .... *$45.00–$60.00*

Ruark, Robert. *Women*. NY. 1967. dj... *$50.00–$60.00*

Ruark, Robert C. *Horn of the Hunter*. NY. Doubleday. 1953. 1st ed. illus. dj. ....
.... *$70.00–$165.00*

Ruark, Robert C. *Horn of the Hunter*. NY. 1953. 1st ed. illus. .... *$70.00–$125.00*

Ruark, Robert C. *Old Man & The Boy*. NY. 1957. 1st ed. illus. .... *$45.00–$100.00*

Ruark, Robert C. *Uhuru*. Lon. 1962. 1st Brit ed. dj.............................. *$50.00–$65.00*

Ruark, Robert C. *Use Enough Gun*. NY. 1966. 1st ed. 1st ptg. illus. dj.....................
.... *$50.00–$65.00*

Ruark, Robert C. *Use Enough Gun*. NY. 1966. 1st ed. illus. dj. .... *$35.00–$75.00*

Rubaiyat of Omar Khayyam. NY. Doran. nd. illus. by Edmund Dulac... *$45.00–$65.00*

Rubin, Jerry. *We Are Everywhere*. 1971. 1st ed. dj................................ *$20.00–$25.00*

Ruess, Everett. *On the Desert Trails with Everett Ruess*. CA. Desert Magazine. 1940.
illus. .... *$200.00–$250.00*

Rugg, H. W. *History of Freemasonry in Rhode Island*. Prov. 1895. .... *$30.00–$45.00*

Rukeyser, Muriel. *Green Wave*. NY. Doubleday. 1948. 1st ed. dj. .... *$25.00–$60.00*

Rukeyser, Muriel. *Life of Poetry*. Current Books. 1949. 1st ed. dj. ...... *$75.00–$125.00*

Rukeyser, Muriel. *Selected Poems*. New Directions. 1951. 1st ed. dj. ... *$25.00–$40.00*

Rules and Regulations for the Field Exercise and Maneuvres of Infantry. NH. US War
Dept. 1817. lea bkd bds.. *$75.00–$100.00*

Rundell, Maria Eliza. *New System of Domestic Cookery . . .* Lon. 1849. illus. enlarged.
.... *$40.00–$50.00*

Rundell, Mrs. *New System of Domestic Cookery*. Lon. John Murray. 1818. By a Lady.
new ed. frontis. .... *$125.00–$150.00*

Rush, Benjamin. *An Account of the Bilious Remiting Yellow Fever . . .* Phila. Thomas
Dobson. 1794. 2nd ed. lea, rbckd... *$150.00–$275.00*

Rush, Benjamin. *Letters of the American Philosophical Society*. Princeton/Phil. 1951. 2
vols. 1st ed. djs. red cloth. .... *$45.00–$50.00*

Rush, Benjamin. *Medical Inquiries and Observations*. AL. 1979. rprnt. ....
.... *$50.00–$65.00*

Rushdie, Salman. *Jaguar Smile*. NY. Viking Press. (1987). 1st ed. dj.... *$15.00–$35.00*

Rushdie, Salman. *Midnights Children*. NY. Knopf. 1981. 1st US ed. pink dj................
.... *$300.00–$500.00*

Rushdie, Salman. *Moor's Last Sigh*. NY. Pantheon. 1996. 1st US ed. dj, sgn................
.... *$40.00–$65.00*

Rushdie, Salman. *Satanic Verses*. NY. 1989. 1st Amer ed. dj.............. *$45.00–$100.00*

Rushdie, Salman. *Shame*. NY. Knopf. 1983. 1st US ed. dj.................... *$25.00–$35.00*

Ruskin, John. *King of the Golden River*. Lon. (1932). 1st ed. wrps. illus. by Arthur
Rackham. dj.. *$150.00–$175.00*

Ruskin, John. *Letters and Advice to Young Girls and Young Ladies*. NY. 1879. ....
.... *$35.00–$45.00*

Russell, A. *Grizzly Country*. NY. Knopf. 1967. 2 vols. 1st ed. illus. dj... *$10.00–$20.00*

Russell, Bertrand. *A B C of Atoms*. NY. Dutton. 1923. .... *$25.00–$45.00*

Russell, Bertrand. *ABC of Relativity.* NY/Lon. 1925. 1st ed. .... *$75.00–$100.00*

Russell, Bertrand. *Analysis of Matter.* NY. Harcourt Brace. 1927. 1st Amer ed cloth. .. .. *$75.00–$125.00*

Russell, Bertrand. *Scientific Outlook.* NY. W W Norton & Co. 1931. 1st ed. .... *$35.00–$45.00*

Russell, Charles M. *Good Medicine.* Garden City. 1930. illus. .... *$50.00–$75.00*

Russell, George. *Tour Through Sicily in the Year 1815.* Lon. 1819. plates, clr fldg map. .... *$75.00–$100.00*

Russell, Keith. *Duck-Huntingest Gentlemen: Coll. of Waterfowling Stories.* 1977. ltd, slipcase, sgn. .... *$85.00–$125.00*

Russell, Prof. William. *Scientific Horse Shoeing.* 1901. illus. 6th ed. .... *$30.00–$45.00*

Russell, William Howard. *My Diary North and South.* NY. 1954. rprnt, dj. .... *$18.00–$25.00*

Russian. *International Literature Organ of the International Union of Revolutionary Writers.* Moscow, USSR. 1934. bound Vols 1, 2 and 3, black cloth. .... *$50.00–$75.00*

Rutherford, Livingston. *John Peter Zenger: His Press, His Trial . . . Bibliography of Imprints.* NY. 1904. 1st ed. illus. ltd 325 cc. .... *$150.00–$250.00*

Rutledge, Archibald. *An American Hunter.* NY. 1937. illus. by Lynne Bogue Hunt, 2nd ptg. .... *$18.00–$45.00*

Rutledge, Archibald. *Brimming Chalice.* NY. 1936. 1st ed. sgn, dj. .... *$95.00–$150.00*

Rutledge, Archibald. *Etiquette Among the Beasts.* np. 1981. .... *$18.00–$22.00*

Rutledge, Archibald. *Hunters Choice.* NY. Barnes. 1946. 1st ed. dj. ...... *$45.00–$65.00*

Rutledge, Archibald. *Plantation Game Trails.* 1921. 1st ed. dj. .... *$60.00–$85.00*

Rutledge, Archibald H. *Home by the River.* Ind. 1941. plates, sgn, dj... *$25.00–$35.00*

Ryder, Tom. *On the Box Seat.* Macclesfield. 1972. 2nd ed. dj. .... *$45.00–$60.00*

Rye, E. C. *British Beetles.* Lon. Lovell Reeve. 1866. 1st ed. illus. 1st separate ed. 113 pp. .... *$40.00–$55.00*

Rynhart, Susie Carson. *With the Tibetans in Tent and Temple.* Revell. 1901. illus. decorative cvrs. .... *$25.00–$45.00*

Sabatini, Rafael. *Strolling Saint. Tyrant.* Bos. Houghton Miflin Co. 1925..................... .... *$10.00–$25.00*

Sabin, Edwin L. *Building the Pacific Railway.* Lippincott. 1919............ *$25.00–$37.00*

Sabin, Joseph. *Dictionary of Books Relating to America.* NY. (1967). 2 vols. mini-print ed. .... *$270.00–$350.00*

Sabin, Joseph. *Dictionary of Books Relating to America . . .* Amsterdam. 1961. 15 vols. rprnt. .... *$950.00–$1,250.00*

Sachs, B. and L. Hausman. *Nervous & Mental Disorders from Birth Through Adolescence.* NY. 1926. 1st ed. illus. .... *$50.00–$85.00*

Sackville-West, Vita. *Daughter of France.* NY. Doubleday. 1959. 1st US ed. 336 pp, dj. .... *$45.00–$75.00*

Sackville-West, Vita. *Devil at Westease.* NY. 1947. 1st ed. dj. .... *$20.00–$25.00*

Sadler, William S. *Race Decadence*. Chi. 1922. 1st ed. dj .... *$27.00–$35.00*

Sagan, Carl. *Broca's Brain*. NY. (1979). 1st ed. dj .... *$25.00–$35.00*

Salaman, Malcolm C. *British Book Illustration*. Lon. The Studio. 1923. 1st ed. illus.... .... *$80.00–$110.00*

Sale, Edith Tunis (ed.). *Historic Gardens of Virginia*. Richmond. William Byrd Press. illus. ltd 1000 cc. .... *$75.00–$95.00*

Salinger, J. D. *Catcher in the Rye*. Bos. 1951. 1st ed. dj blue cloth. .... *$1,500.00–$2,000.00*

Salinger, J. D. *Complete Uncollected Short Stories*. Vols I and II. wrps. scarce............. .... *$250.00–$475.00*

Salinger, J. D. *Franny and Zooey*. Lon. Heinemann. 1962. 1st UK ed. .. *$45.00–$85.00*

Salinger, J. D. *Franny and Zooey*. Bos. 1961. 1st ed. dj .... *$45.00–$65.00*

Salinger, J. D. *Kitbook for Soldiers, Sailors & Marines*. 1943. 1st ed.. *$95.00–$150.00*

Salinger, J. D. *Nine Stories*. Bos. (1953). 1st ed. dj .... *$125.00–$500.00*

Salinger, J. D. *Raise High the Roof Beam, Carpenters*. Little Brown. 1963. 1st ed. 2nd state .... *$125.00–$175.00*

Salinger, J. D. *Raise High the Roof Beam, Carpenters*. 1963. 1st ed. 3rd issue, dj .... *$15.00–$40.00*

Salk and Salk. *World Population and Human Values*. NY. 1981. sgn, dj ....*$55.00–$70.00*

Salten, Felix. *Bambi's Children*. Ind. Bobbs Merill. (1939). 1st ed. scarce dj .... *$38.00–$50.00*

Salten, Felix. *Bambi, A Life in the Woods*. Simon & Schuster. 1928. ltd 1,000 cc........... .... *$50.00–$60.00*

Salten, Felix. *Bambi*. Simon & Schuster. 1928. 1st ed. .... *$40.00–$50.00*

Sampson, Ezra. *Youth's Companion*. Hudson. Nathan Elliott. 1816. 3rd ed. lea............ .... *$12.00–$25.00*

Samuels, Edward. *Ornithology and Oology of New England. . .with illustrations of many Species of Birds. . .* Bos. Nichols and Noyes. 1867. illus. plates, 583 pp.............. .... *$75.00–$95.00*

Sanborn, F. B. (ed.). *Life and Letters of John Brown, Liberator of Kansas . . .* Bos. 1891. 1st ed.. *$45.00–$55.00*

Sanborn, Helen. *Winter in Central America and Mexico*. Bos. 1887. 1st ed.................. .... *$32.00–$45.00*

Sanborn, Kate. *Old Time Wallpapers*. 1905. illus. ltd 975 cc, sgn and dated. .... *$100.00–$300.00*

Sanborn, Kate. *Truthful Woman in Southern California*. NY. 1893. 1st ed.................... .... *$15.00–$25.00*

Sandberg, Carl. *Breathing Tokens*. NY. Harcourt Brace and World. 1978. 1st ed. dj .... *$12.00–$20.00*

Sandburg, Carl. *Abraham Lincoln: The Prairie Years*. NY. Harcourt Brace. (1926). 2 vols. 1st trade ed. dj, slipcase. .... *$100.00–$350.00*

Sandburg, Carl. *Abraham Lincoln: The Prairie Years*. NY. Harcourt, Brace. 1926. 2 vols. 1st trade, sgn. .... *$75.00–$100.00*

Sandburg, Carl. *Abraham Lincoln: The War Years*. NY. Harcourt Brace. 1940. 4 vols. illus. slipcase.. *$60.00–$90.00*

Sandburg, Carl. *Always the Young Strangers*. NY. 1953. 1st ed. sgn, dj........................
.... *$30.00–$50.00*

Sandburg, Carl. *American Songbag*. NY. 1927. .... *$25.00–$75.00*

Sandburg, Carl. *Chicago Poems*. Holt. 1916. dj................................... *$20.00–$25.00*

Sandburg, Carl. *Early Moon*. NY. Harcourt Brace. (1930). 1st ed. no dj. ....
.... *$20.00–$40.00*

Sandburg, Carl. *Family of Man*. NY. MOMA. 1955. 1st ed. dj. .... *$20.00–$35.00*

Sandburg, Carl. *Good Morning America*. NY. Harcourt Brace. 1928. 1st trade ed. sgn, dj. .... *$85.00–$100.00*

Sandburg, Carl. *Good Morning America*. Harcourt. 1928. 1st ed. dj..... *$45.00–$55.00*

Sandburg, Carl. *Potato Face*. NY. Harcourt Brace. 1930. 1st ed. dj. ..... *$50.00–$80.00*

Sandburg, Carl. *Potato Face*. Harcourt. 1930. 1st ed. dj. .... *$50.00–$75.00*

Sandburg, Carl. *Remembrance Rock*. NY. 1948. 1st ed. dj. .... *$20.00–$30.00*

Sandburg, Carl. *Rootabaga Pigeons*. NY. 1923. 1st ed. illus............... *$75.00–$110.00*

Sandburg, Carl. *Steichen, the Photographer*. NY. (1929). 1st ed. 975 cc, sgn by Steichen and Sandburg, slipcase.. *$690.00–$1,700.00*

Sanders, Lawrence. *Anderson Tapes*. NY. Putnam. 1970. 1st ed. author's first book, dj. .... *$45.00–$60.00*

Sanderson, G. P. *Thirteen Years Amoung the Wild Beasts of India*. Lon. 1893..............
.... *$18.00–$25.00*

Sandoz, Mari. *Horse Catcher*. 1957. sgn, dj... *$25.00–$30.00*

Sandoz, Mari. *Old Jules*. 1935... *$5.00–$10.00*

Sandoz, Mari. *Son of the Gamblin' Man*. NY. Clarkson and Potter. (1960). 1st ed. sgn, dj. .... *$100.00–$150.00*

Sandoz, Mari. *The Cattlemen*. NY. 1958. dj... *$27.00–$35.00*

Sandoz, Maurice. *Fantastic Memories*. Garden City. Doubleday. 1944. 1st ed. illus. dj. .... *$85.00–$125.00*

Sandoz, Maurice. *The Maze*. NY. 1945. 1st ed. illus. by Salvador Dali. *$40.00–$75.00*

Sanger, Margaret. *An Autobiography*. NY. (1938). 1st ed. 504 pp, dj.... *$75.00–$85.00*

Sanger, Margaret. *My Fight For Birth Control*. NY. (1931). 1st ed. 360 pp. ....
.... *$65.00–$75.00*

Sanger, Margaret. *Woman and the New Race*. NY. Truth. 1920. 1st ed. dj, blue cloth...
.... *$22.00–$30.00*

Sanger, Margaret. *Woman and the New Race*. NY. Brentano. 1920....... *$12.00–$25.00*

Sanger, William W. *History of Prostitution*. NY. Eugenics Pub. 1939. .. *$15.00–$30.00*

Sanger, William W. *History of Prostitution*. NY. Medical Pub Co. 1921......................
.... *$18.00–$25.00*

Sangree, Allen. *Jinx: Stories of the Diamond.* NY. 1911. illus................ *$60.00–$90.00*

Sanial, Lucien. *General Bankruptcy or Socialism?* NY. Co-operative Press. 1913. wrps. .... *$35.00–$50.00*

Sansom, Joseph. *Travels in Lower Canada* . . . Lon. 1820. ¼ calf....... *$85.00–$125.00*

Santayana, George. *Sonnets and Other Verses.* Cambridge. 1894. 1st ed. ltd 450 cc..... .... *$150.00–$225.00*

Santee, Ross. *Bubbling Spring.* NY. Scribner's. (1949). 1st ed. dj......... *$20.00–$45.00*

Sanz, Carlos. *Bibliografia General de la Carta de Colon.* Madrid. Libreria General. 1958. 1st ed. wrps. 305 pp. .... *$125.00–$150.00*

Sarg, Tony. *Tony Sarg's Book of Animals.* Greenberg Pub. 1925. 1st ed. *$30.00–$40.00*

Sargent, Lyman Towers. *British and American Utopian Literature 1516–1975.* Bos. Hall. (1979). 1st ed. .... *$45.00–$80.00*

Saroyan, William. *Daring Young Man on the Flying Trapeze.* NY. Random House. 1934. 1st ed. dj. .... *$300.00–$400.00*

Saroyan, William. *Fiscal Hoboes.* NY. Valenti Angelo. 1949. 1st ed. wrps. ltd 250 cc. sgn... *$80.00–$100.00*

Saroyan, William. *Fragment by William Saroyan.* SF. Bender. 1943. 1st ed. wrps. ltd 150 cc. illus. woodcuts. .... *$50.00–$80.00*

Saroyan, William. *Get Away Old Man.* NY. Harcourt Brace. (1944). 1st ed. a play, dj.. .... *$75.00–$125.00*

Saroyan, William. *Hilltop Russians in San Francisco.* Stanford. Delkin. 1941. ltd 500 cc. illus. plates. .... *$40.00–$70.00*

Saroyan, William. *Human Comedy.* NY. Harcourt, Brace. (1943). 1st ed. illus. author's first novel. dj.. *$80.00–$120.00*

Saroyan, William. *Laughing Matter.* Doubleday. 1953. 1st ed. dj......... *$30.00–$55.00*

Saroyan, William. *My Heart's in the Highlands.* NY. (1939). dj......... *$75.00–$100.00*

Saroyan, William. *Native American.* SF. George Fields. 1938. 1st ed. illus. ltd 450 cc. sgn... *$80.00–$115.00*

Saroyan, William. *Rock Wagram.* NY. 1951. 1st ed. dj..................... *$20.00–$30.00*

Saroyan, William. *Saroyan's Fables.* NY. Harcourt, Brace. 1941. 1st ed. illus. ltd 1,000 cc. sgn, slipcase. .... *$40.00–$70.00*

Saroyan, William. *Three Times Three.* LA. Conference Press. 1936. 1st ed. ltd 1,000 cc. sgn... *$80.00–$125.00*

Saroyan, William. *Time of Your Life.* Harcourt Brace. 1939. 1st ed. dj. *$75.00–$100.00*

Sarton, George. *History of Science.* MA. Harvard Univ Press. 1952. .... *$25.00–$45.00*

Sarton, May. *A Reckoning.* NY. Norton. 1978. 1st ed. dj...................... *$15.00–$25.00*

Sarton, May. *Anger.* NY. 1982. sgn, dj.. *$30.00–$50.00*

Sarton, May. *Education of Harriet Hatfield.* NY. Norton. (1955). 1st ed. dj. .... *$20.00–$30.00*

Sarton, May. *Kinds of Love.* Jackson. Norton. 1970. 1st ed. dj............. *$20.00–$30.00*

Sarton, May. *Kinds of Love.* NY. Norton. 1970. 1st ed. dj..................... *$20.00–$30.00*

Sarton, May. *Miss Pickthorn and Mr. Hare*. NY. 1st ed. sgn, dj............. *$50.00–$65.00*

Sarton, May. *Plant Dreaming Deep*. NY. Norton. (1968). 1st ed. y....... *$12.00–$25.00*

Sarton, May. *Poet and the Donkey*. NY. Norton. (1969). 1st ed. dj........ *$15.00–$35.00*

Sarton, May. *Poet and the Donkey*. NY. 1969. 1st ed. dj....................... *$25.00–$30.00*

Sarton, May. *Recovering: A Journal*. NY/Lon. Norton. (1980)............. *$20.00–$30.00*

Sarton, May. *Shadow of a Man*. NY. Rinehart. (1950). 1st ed. no dj. .... *$40.00–$50.00*

Sarton, May. *Shower of Summer Days*. NY. Rinehart. (1952). 1st ed. 244 pp, dj, scarce.
.... *$50.00–$75.00*

Sartre, Jean-Paul. *Devil & the Good Lord*. Knopf. 1960. 1st US ed. dj. *$27.00–$35.00*

Sartre, Jean-Paul. *Existentialism*. Philosophical Library. 1947. 1st US ed. dj...............
.... *$45.00–$55.00*

Sartre, Jean-Paul. *Nausea*. CT. 1949. 1st US ed. dj. .... *$30.00–$55.00*

Sartre, Jean-Paul. *Situations*. 1965. 1st ed. dj. .... *$15.00–$25.00*

Sartre, Jean-Paul. *Theatre: Les Mouches, Huis-clos, Morts san sepulchre, La Putain Respectueuse*. (Paris). Gallimard. (c1947). 1st ed thus, 1/2,000 cc........ *$75.00–$100.00*

Sartre, Jean-Paul. *Wall and Other Stories*. New Directions. 1948. ltd ed. slipcase........
.... *$45.00–$75.00*

Sass, Herbert Ravenel. *Hear Me, My Chiefs*. NY. William Morrow. 1940. map frontis 2nd printing. .... *$8.00–$25.00*

Sassoon, Siegfried. *Memoirs of an Infantry Officer*. NY. 1931. illus. 1st US ed. dj. ....
.... *$25.00–$35.00*

Sassoon, Siegfried. *Nativity*. Lon. nd. 1st ed. dj. .... *$25.00–$35.00*

Satterlee, L. *American Gun Makers*. NY. 1940. 1st ed............................ *$35.00–$40.00*

Saundby, R. *Lectures on Bright's Disease*. Bristol/Lon. 1889. .... *$22.00–$25.00*

Saunders, Ann. *Narrative of the Shipwreck & Sufferings of. . .* Prov. 1827. 1st ed. wrps.
.... *$75.00–$85.00*

Saunders, Charles Francis. *Indians of the Terraced Houses*. NY. 1912. *$30.00–$45.00*

Saunders, Louise. *Knave of Hearts*. Racine, Wisconsin. 1925. illus. by Maxfield Parrish, folio, spiral bound.. *$500.00–$750.00*

Saunders, Ruth. *Book of Artists' Own Bookplates*. Claremont. Saunders Studio Press. 1933. 1st ed. ltd 360 cc, sgn and numbered... *$50.00–$75.00*

Savitt, Sam. *Around the World with Horses*. NY. Dial. 1962. 1st ed. oblong, dj. ....
.... *$30.00–$45.00*

Sawtelle, Mrs. M. P. *Heroine of '49*. San Francisco. 1891. .... *$35.00–$50.00*

Sawyer, Charles Winthrop. *Our Rifles*. The Cornhill Co. 1920. 1st ed. *$45.00–$65.00*

Sawyer, Ruth. *Tale of the Enchanted Bunnies*. NY. (1923). 1st ed. illus. dj, scarce........
.... *$105.00–$175.00*

Sayers, Dorothy L. *Omnibus of Crime*. NY. Payson & Clarke. 1929. 1st ed. dj. ....
.... *$40.00–$85.00*

Sayers, Dorothy L. *Strong Poison*. NY. Brewer & Warren. 1930. 1st Amer ed..............
.... *$40.00–$85.00*

Sayers, R. S. *LLoyds Bank in the History of English Banking.* Oxford. Clarendon Press. 1957. cloth. .... *$40.00–$60.00*

Sayler, Oliver M. *Russian Theatre.* NY. Brentano. 1922......................... *$50.00–$80.00*

Schaack, Michael. *Anarchy and Anarchists.* Chi. Schulte. 1889. 1st ed. fine................. .... *$150.00–$225.00*

Schaeffler, Casper. *Memoirs and Reminiscences Together with Sketches of the Early History of Sussex County, NJ.* . . Hackensack, NJ. Private printing. 1907. illus. ltd 250 cc, 187 pp. .... *$35.00–$50.00*

Schaldach, William J. *Coverts and Casts.* NY. 1943. 1st ed. illus. .... *$35.00–$45.00*

Schaldach, William J. *Fish by Schaldach.* Phila. 1937. ltd 1,500 cc.... *$80.00–$150.00*

Schaldach, William J. *Upland Gunning.* VT. 1946. illus. presentation copy, dj. .... *$100.00–$175.00*

Schell, William G. *Is the Negro a Beast?* Moundsville. 1901. 1st ed. .... *$40.00–$45.00*

Schenck, David. *North Carolina 1780–81.* Raleigh. 1889. 1st ed........ *$75.00–$100.00*

Schley, W. S. *Report of Greely Relief Exped. of 1884.* Wash. 1887. 1st ed. .... *$85.00–$110.00*

Schmookler, Paul. *Salmon Flies of Major John P. Traherne.* 1993. ltd and only ed. 300 cc, photos, lea, French hand-dipped clr paper over bds, slipcase, aeg. *$350.00–$600.00*

Schoenberger, J. *From Great Lakes to Pacific.* 1934. 1st ed................... *$50.00–$65.00*

Schoener, Allan (ed.). *Harlem On My Mind.* NY. Dell. 1979. 272 pp, illus. 2nd ed. wrps. .... *$40.00–$50.00*

Schoolcraft, Henry R. *American Indians; Their History, Condition and Prospects.* . . Rochester. 1851. illus. plates... *$150.00–$250.00*

Schoolcraft, Henry R. *Historical and Statistical Information Respecting the History, Condition and Prospects of the Indian Tribes of the United States.* NY. Historical American Indian Press. (1969). 6 vols. illus. maps, plates, facsimile. .... *$1,400.00–$3,000.00*

Schoolcraft, Henry R. *Journal of a Tour into the Interior of Missouri and Arkansaw* . . .*toward the Rocky Mountains.* . .*in the years 1818 and 1819.* Lon. Richard Phillips. 1821. fldg map... *$300.00–$650.00*

Schoolcraft, Henry R. *New York Historical Society.* NY. 1854. .... *$30.00–$55.00*

Schoolcraft, Henry R. *Report of Schoolcraft's Expedition Among the Northwestern Indians.* 1838. House Document #125, lea wrps, 16 pp. .... *$60.00–$100.00*

Schoolcraft, Henry R. *View of the Lead Mines of Missouri; Including . . . Observations on . . .Arkansaw and Other Sections of the Western Country.* NY. Charles Wiley & Co. 1819. 1st ed. copper engraved frontis and plates. .... *$350.00–$425.00*

Schooling, William. *Hudson's Bay Company, 1670–1920.* Lon. Hudson Bay Co. 1920. wrps. fldg map, 129 pp... *$65.00–$85.00*

Schoonmaker, W. J. *World of the Grizzly Bear.* Phila/NY. 1968. illus.... *$30.00–$40.00*

Schoonover, T. *Life of General J. Sutter.* 1895. 1st ed............................ *$60.00–$75.00*

Schreiner, Olive. *Story of an African Farm.* Westerham Press. 1961. illus. clr lith, drawings, 932/1,500 cc sgn. .... *$25.00–$35.00*

Schroter, Ludwig and Dr. C. Schroter. *Taschenflora des Alpen-Wanderers*. Zurich. Meyer & Zeller. 1890. illus. .... *$50.00–$80.00*

Schulberg, Budd. *Sanctuary V.* World. 1969. 1st ed. dj. .... *$20.00–$25.00*

Schulbert, Budd. *Harder They Fall*. Random House. 1947. 1st ptg, sgn, dj. .... *$65.00–$75.00*

Schulthess, Emil. *Antarctica*. NY. 1960. 1st Amer ed. plates................. *$60.00–$75.00*

Schultz, Charles M. *Good Grief, More Peanuts*. NY. 1956. wrps. .... *$30.00–$40.00*

Schultz, J. *Blackfeet Tales of Glacier National Park*. Bos. 1916............. *$45.00–$55.00*

Schulz, Charles M. *Snoopy and the Red Baron*. NY. 1966. 1st ed. dj. ... *$28.00–$38.00*

Schuyler, George W. *Colonial New York*. NY. 1885. 2 vols. .... *$150.00–$175.00*

Schuyler, Keith. *Lures*. Stackpole. (1955). dj. .... *$15.00–$22.00*

Schwatka, Frederick. *Summer in Alaska*. St Louis. 1893. illus............. *$45.00–$75.00*

Schweinfurth, Charles. *Orchids of Peru*. Chi. 1958. 2 vols. .... *$50.00–$60.00*

Schweizer, Charles H. *Billiard Hints*. LaCrosse, WI. 1906. .... *$20.00–$28.00*

Scott, Emmett. *Scott's Official History of the American Negro in the World War.* 1919. illus. .... *$20.00–$25.00*

Scott, Harold (ed.). *English Songbook*. NY. 1926. dj............................. *$25.00–$35.00*

Scott, Robert Falcon. *Scott's Last Expedition*. Lon. Smith, Elder. 1913. 2 vols. 3rd ed., teg. .... *$200.00–$260.00*

Scott, W. W. *History of Orange County, Virginia*. Richmond. 1907. 1st ed.................... .... *$85.00–$90.00*

Scott, Winfield. *General Scott and His Staff . . .* Phila. 1849. illus........ *$37.00–$45.00*

Scott, Winfield Townley. *Biography for Traman*. NY. 1937. 1st ed. scarce, dj. .... *$85.00–$125.00*

Scott, Winfield Townley. *To Marry Strangers*. NY. 1945. 1st ed. dj. ..... *$30.00–$75.00*

Scott, Winfield Townley. *Wind the Clock*. Prairie City, IL. 1941. sgn, dj....................... .... *$95.00–$125.00*

Scouting for Girls. NY. Girl Scouts. 1923. 5th ed. .... *$35.00–$50.00*

Scrivenor, Harry. *History of the Iron Trade*. Lon. 1854. 2nd ed. 321 pp...................... .... *$60.00–$75.00*

Scudder, S. H. *Tertiary Insects of North America*. Wash. 1890. 4to, 734 pp, map frontis, 28 plates (US Geological Survey, Vol 13)... *$125.00–$250.00*

Seale, Bobby. *Seize the Time*. NY. Random House. 1970. 1st ed. dj....... *$25.00–$40.00*

Seale, Bobby. *Seize the Time, the Story of the Black Panther Party*. NY. Random House. (1970). 1st ed. dj.. *$35.00–$50.00*

Seaman, Louis L. *From Tokio Through Manchuria with the Japanese*. NY. 1905. .... *$22.00–$35.00*

Seawell, Molly. *Ladies' Battle*. NY. 1911. 1st ed. 119 pp........................ *$30.00–$45.00*

Second Annual Report . . . Convict Labor. Wash. 1887........................... *$30.00–$40.00*

Secret Life of Salvador Dali. NY. Dial Press. 1942. 1st ed. illus. black cloth dj. ....
.... ***$95.00–$130.00***

Sedgwick, James. *Law of Storms*. Lon. Partridge and Oakey. 1852. illus........................
.... ***$45.00–$85.00***

Seeger, Alan. *Poems*. 1916. 1st ed. .... ***$30.00–$45.00***

Self, Margaret Cabell. *Morgan Horse in Pictures*. Phila. Macrae Smith. 1967. dj.........
.... ***$45.00–$65.00***

Selous, Frederick C. *African Nature Notes and Reminiscences*. Lon. Macmillan. 1908. 1st ed. illus. 13 plates. forward by President Roosevelt, cloth. .... ***$225.00–$285.00***

Sendak, Maurice. *In the Night Kitchen*. NY. Harper & Row. 1970. 1st ed. illus. Caldecott Honor book. .... ***$75.00–$120.00***

Sendak, Maurice. *Outside Over There*. NY. Harper & Row. (1981). 1st ed. illus. clr, dj.
.... ***$35.00–$45.00***

Sendak, Maurice. *Outside Over There*. NY. 1981. illus. by Sendak, dj.. ***$25.00–$40.00***

Sendak, Maurice. *Posters by*. Harmony, NY. 1986. 1st ed. dj. .... ***$28.00–$35.00***

Sendak, Maurice. *Works of Maurice Sendak 1947–1994*. Portsmouth. Peter Randall. 1995. 1st ed. dj. .... ***$85.00–$100.00***

Senefelder, Alois. *Invention of Lithography*. NY. Fuchs & Lang. 1911. trans by Muller.
.... ***$50.00–$70.00***

Senn, C. Herman. *Luncheons and Dinner Sweets. . .Ice Making*. Lon. 1st ed. illus. dj.
.... ***$15.00–$20.00***

Senn, Dr. Nicholas. *In the Heart of the Arctics*. Chi. Conkey. 1907. 1st ed. illus...........
.... ***$65.00–$125.00***

Sergeant, F. L. *Wright's Usonian House*. 1978. dj. .... ***$47.00–$60.00***

Serling, Rod. *Season to be Wary*. Bos/Tor. Little Brown & Co. (1967). 1st ed. dj. ....
.... ***$25.00–$60.00***

Serling, Rod. *Season to be Wary*. Bos. Little Brown. (1967). dj. .... ***$30.00–$45.00***

Service, Robert. *Ballads of a Cheechako*. NY. 1909. .... ***$6.00–$12.00***

Service, Robert. *Ballads of a Cheechako*. Tor. William Briggs. 1916. 1st ed. illus. green cloth. .... ***$40.00–$60.00***

Service, Robert. *Complete Poems of Robert Service*. NY. Dodd, Mead. 1945. 1st ed. inscr... ***$120.00–$350.00***

Service, Robert. *Rhymes of a Rolling Stone*. Tor. 1912. 1st ed. .... ***$60.00–$100.00***

Service, William. *Bar-Room Ballads*. Santa Fe. 1940. 1st UK ed dj. ...... ***$30.00–$40.00***

Seton, E. T. *Woodmyth & Fable*. Century. 1905. 1st ed....................... ***$115.00–$125.00***

Seton, Ernest Thompson. *Biography of a Grizzly*. NY. Century. 1900. 1st ed. ....
.... ***$45.00–$150.00***

Seton, Ernest Thompson. *Book of Woodcraft*. Garden City. 1921. illus. ***$30.00–$35.00***

Seton, Ernest Thompson. *Gospel of the Red Man*. NY. Doubleday Doran. 1936. 1st ed. dj. .... ***$50.00–$65.00***

Seton, Ernest Thompson. *Lives of the Hunted*. NY. Scribner's. 1901. 1st ed.................
.... ***$60.00–$80.00***

Seton, Ernest Thompson. *Monarch, The Big Bear of Tallac.* NY. 1904. 1st ed. illus. 1st imp. .... *$25.00–$50.00*

Seton, Ernest Thompson. *Rolf in the Woods.* Doubleday. 1911. illus. .... *$30.00–$45.00*

Seton, Ernest Thompson. *Two Little Savages.* NY. 1903. 1st ed. illus... *$40.00–$55.00*

Seton, Grace Thompson. *Yes, Lady Saheb.* NY/Lon. 1925. 1st ed. illus. photos. .... *$25.00–$45.00*

Seton, Grace Thompson. *Yes, Lady Shaheb.* NY. Harper. 1925. 1st ed. 1st ptg. illus..... .... *$35.00–$45.00*

Seton, Julia M. *Pulse of the Pueblo.* NM. 1939. presentation copy, sgn. *$25.00–$30.00*

Seuss, Dr. *500 Hats of Bartholomew Cubbins.* NY. Vanguard. (1938). 1st ed. dj. .... *$250.00–$450.00*

Seuss, Dr. *Horton Hatches the Egg.* NY. Random House. 1940. dj. .... *$25.00–$50.00*

Seuss, Dr. *More Boners.* NY. 1931.. *$40.00–$60.00*

Seuss, Dr. *Seven Lady Godivas.* NY. (1939). 1st ed. dj. .... *$144.00–$700.00*

Seuss, Dr. *Thidwick: The Big Hearted Moose.* NY. 1948. 1st ed. .... *$40.00–$80.00*

Seuss, Dr. *You're Only Old Once.* NY. (1986). 1st ed. ltd 500 cc, sgn. *$525.00–$600.00*

Seuss, Dr. *You're Only Old Once.* NY. Random House. 1986. 1st ed. dj. *$15.00–$30.00*

Seutonius, Caius. *History of the Twelve Caesars, Emperors of Rome.* Lon. Starkey. 1672. 12 copper plates.. *$80.00–$115.00*

Sewel, William. *History of the Rise, Increase and Progress of the Christian People Called Quakers.* Burlington, NJ. Isaac Collins. 1774. 812 pp............. *$100.00–$125.00*

Sewell, A. *Black Beauty.* Bos. 1890. illus. 1st Amer ed. .... *$200.00–$300.00*

Sewell, Anna. *Black Beauty: His Grooms and Companions.* Bos. 1890. 1st thus, American Humane Ed Soc. .... *$150.00–$295.00*

Sextus, Carl. *Hypnotism.* Chi. 1893. 1st ed. illus. .... *$30.00–$45.00*

Seymour, C. *Intimate Papers of Colonel House.* 2 vols. 1st ed. .... *$40.00–$60.00*

Seymour, Eaton. *Travelling Bears in New York.* Barse & Hopkins. 1915. illus. frontis. . ... *$90.00–$150.00*

Seymour, George Dudley, et al. *History of the Seymour Family . . .* New Haven. 1939. .... *$35.00–$50.00*

Seymour, Prof. W. P. *Seymour's Key to Electro-Therpeutics.* Newark. 1904. 2nd ed. ... . *$20.00–$30.00*

Sfinde, Julius. *Frau Wilhelmine.* Berlin. 1886. in German. .... *$25.00–$35.00*

Shackleton, Ernest H. *Heart of the Antarctic.* Phila. Lippincott. 1909. 2 vols. 1st Amer ed. illus, maps... *$400.00–$500.00*

Shackleton, Ernest H. *Heart of the Antarctic.* Phila. 1914. illus. fldg map, clr plates.... .... *$50.00–$75.00*

Shackleton, Ernest H. *South.* NY. Macmillan. 1920. 1st Amer ed. illus, map. .... *$140.00–$165.00*

Shackleton, Ernest H. (ed.). *Aurora Australis.* New Zealand. 1988. illus. rprnt, dj........ .... *$25.00–$30.00*

Shahn, Ben. *Haggadah for Passover*. Bos. Little, Brown. 1965. 1st ed. illus. trans by Roth. white cloth, gold lettered. .... *$100.00–$125.00*

Shakespeare's The Merry Wives of Windsor. NY. Stokes. 1910. 1st ed. illus. by Hugh Thomson. decorated cloth. .... *$85.00–$150.00*

Shakespeare, William. *As You Like It*. Lon/NY. Hodder & Stoughton. illus. paste in illus by Hugh Thomson. .... *$30.00–$100.00*

Shakespeare, William. *Comedies, Histories & Tragedies of Wm. Shakespeare*. 1939. 37 vols. illus. Ltd Ed Club, 8 slipcases. .... *$850.00–$950.00*

Shakespeare, William. *Dramatic Works*. Bos. Hilliard Gray. 1839. 8 vols. .... *$75.00–$100.00*

Shakespeare, William. *Midsummer Nights Dream*. Lon/NY. 1908. 1st ed. illus. by Arthur Rackham, clr plates.. *$100.00–$225.00*

Shakespeare, William. *New Shakespeare*. Cambridge. Univ. Press. 10 vols. 2nd ed. .... *$80.00–$120.00*

Shakespeare, William. *Romeo and Juliet*. NY. 1936. illus. dj. .... *$50.00–$75.00*

Shakespeare, William. *Shakespeare's Comedy As You Like It*. Lon/NY. nd. 1st ed. illus. 39 tip-in clr plates.. *$250.00–$350.00*

Shakespeare, William. *Shakespeare's Comedy of The Tempest*. Lon. 1915. illus. by Edmund Dulac. .... *$250.00–$300.00*

Shakespeare, William. *Tempest*. Lon. Heinneman. (1926). 1st ed thus. illus by Arthur Rackham. decorated black cloth.. *$120.00–$195.00*

Shakespeare, William. *Tragedy of King Lear*. Roycroft Shop. 1904. ½ suede. .... *$70.00–$100.00*

Shakespeare, William. *Works of*. Bos. Little Brown. (1861–65). 12 vols. .... *$75.00–$100.00*

Shakespeare, William. *Works of* . . . Lon/NY. The Nonesuch Press/Random House. 1929–33. 7 vols. .... *$1,200.00–$1,500.00*

Shakespeare, William. *Works of Shakespeare*. Lon. 1904. 10 vols. deluxe ed. ltd #197/500 cc. .... *$120.00–$135.00*

Shakespeare, William. *Works*. Lon/NY. 1892. 12 vols. boxed................ *$50.00–$75.00*

Shand, Alex Innes. *Gun Room*. Lon. The Bodley Head. 1905................ *$65.00–$75.00*

Shapiro, Karl. *White-Haired Lover*. NY. 1968. 1st ed. sgn, dj................ *$30.00–$45.00*

Sharp, H. *Modern Sporting Gunnery Manual* . . . Lon. 1906. small folio...................... .... *$30.00–$40.00*

Sharpe, Philips B. *Rifle in America*. NY. Funk & Wagnalls. 1947. illus. *$50.00–$60.00*

Shaw, Archer H. *Lincoln Encyclopedia*. NY. 1950. 1st ed. dj. .... *$30.00–$40.00*

Shaw, Edward. *Shaw's Civil Architecture*. Bos. 1852. .... *$40.00–$50.00*

Shaw, Edward Richard. *Pot of Gold. A Story of Fire Island Beach*. Chi/NY. 1888. .... *$85.00–$125.00*

Shaw, George Bernard. *Adventures of a Black Girl in Her Search of God*. Dodd Mead. 1933. illus. 1st Amer ed. dj. .... *$30.00–$45.00*

Shaw, George Bernard. *Intelligent Woman's Guide to Socialism & Capitalism*. NY. 1928. 1st Amer ed.. *$35.00–$90.00*

Shaw, George Bernard. *Intelligent Woman's Guide to Socialism and Capitalism*. NY. Brentano. 1928. 2nd US ptg, 495 pp, dj... *$25.00–$35.00*

Shaw, George Bernard. *Intelligent Woman's Guide to Socialism and Capitalism*. Lon. Constable. 1928. 1st ed. dj. .... *$45.00–$100.00*

Shaw, George Bernard. *Man and Superman*. NY. Heritage. (1962). slipcase................
.... *$20.00–$40.00*

Shaw, George Bernard. *Quintessence of Ibsenism*. Lon. Walter Scott. 1891. 1st ed. .....
.... *$100.00–$150.00*

Shaw, George Bernard. *Two Plays for Puritans*. NY. Limited Editions Club. 1966. illus. drawings by George Him, 932/1500 cc sgn slipcase. .... *$20.00–$30.00*

Shaw, George Bernard, (ed.). *Fabian Essays in Socialism*. Lon. 1899. pictorial and decorated cloth.. *$95.00–$120.00*

Shaw, Irwin. *Mixed Company*. Random House. 1950. 1st ed. dj. .... *$40.00–$50.00*

Shaw, Irwin. *Sailor Off the Bremen and Other Stories*. NY. Random House. (c1939). 1st ed. no dj. .... *$35.00–$45.00*

Shaw, Irwin. *Troubled Air*. NY. 1951. 1st ed. dj. .... *$35.00–$40.00*

Shaw, Irwin. *Young Lions*. NY. 1st ed. dj. .... *$35.00–$45.00*

Shaw, Robert. *Visits to High Tartary, Yarkand, and Kashgar*. Lon. John Murray. 1871. 1st ed. 2 fldg maps, 7 tinted plates.. *$300.00–$450.00*

Shaw, Thomas George. *Wine Trade and Its History*. Lon. nd................. *$37.00–$75.00*

Sheckley, Robert. *Is That What People Do?* NY. 1984. sgn, dj. .... *$15.00–$20.00*

Sheldon, Charles. *Wilderness of the Upper Yukon*. NY. 1913. illus. maps.....................
.... *$50.00–$75.00*

Shelley, Mary. *Frankenstein*. Univ Cal Press. 1984. 1st ed thus, dj........ *$50.00–$65.00*

Shelley, Mary W. *Letters of Mary W Shelley*. Bos. Bibliophile Society. 448 cc.............
.... *$50.00–$75.00*

Shelley, Mary Wollstonecraft. *Frankenstein*. Bos. Sever, Francis, & Co. 1869. 2nd Amer ed. 177 pp. .... *$350.00–$450.00*

Shepherd, Sam. *Operation Sidewinder*. NY. 1970. .... *$35.00–$40.00*

Sheridan, P. H. *Personal Memoirs*. NY. 1888. 2 vols. 1st ed. .... *$40.00–$85.00*

Sherman, Gen. *Memoirs of*. 1891. 2 vols. 4th ed. .... *$40.00–$70.00*

Sherman, John. *Recollections*. 1895. 2 vols. 1st ed. .... *$45.00–$65.00*

Sherman, S. M. *History of the 133rd Regiment, O.V.I.* Columbus. 1896. 1st ed. ....
.... *$95.00–$125.00*

Sherman, William Tecumseh. *Home Letters of General Sherman*. NY. 1909. 1st ed.....
.... *$40.00–$50.00*

Sherwen, Grayson. *Romance of St. Sacrement*. VT. Free Press Printing Co. 1912. 1st ed. illus. blue cloth. .... *$12.00–$20.00*

Sherwood, Mary Martha. *History of Little Henry and His Bearer*. Hartford. George Goodwin & Sons. 1822. 52 pp, 14 x 87 cm... *$70.00–$95.00*

Sherwood, Robert Emmet. *Queen's Husband*. NY. 1928. 1st ed. .... *$40.00–$45.00*

Shetrone, Henry Clyde. *Mound-Builders: A Reconstruction of the Life of a Prehistoric American Race*. NY. Appleton. 1930. 1st ed. illus. .... *$50.00–$80.00*

Shiel, M. P. *Children of the Wind*. NY. 1923. 1st US ed. .... *$30.00–$40.00*

Ship Figureheads and Other Wood Carving Art in the Nautical Collection of the SSTC of Boston. State Street Trust Co. wrps. illus. .... *$20.00–$30.00*

Shirley Temple Through the Day. Ohio/NY. The Saalfield Pub Co. 1936. 1st ed. illus. pictorial wrps. authorized ed. .... *$125.00–$150.00*

Shirts, Augustus F. *History of . . . Hamilton County, Indiana (1818 to Civil War)*. 1901. 1st ed. illus. .... *$65.00–$100.00*

Shoemaker, Henry. *Black Forest Souvenirs*. Reading, PA. Bright-Faust Printing Co. 1914. illus. plates, inscrb. .... *$60.00–$75.00*

Shriner, C. H. *Birds of New Jersey*. 1896. .... *$25.00–$45.00*

Shurtleff, Nathaniel. *Topographical and Historical Description of Boston*. Bos. 1871.. .... *$45.00–$75.00*

Shuster, George N. *Like a Mighty Army . . .* NY. Appleton Century. 1935. 1st ed. dj. .... *$30.00–$45.00*

Shute, Miss T. S. *American Housewife Cook Book*. Phila. 1878. .... *$30.00–$40.00*

Shute, Nevil. *On the Beach*. Lon. Heineman. 1957. 1st ed. dj. .... *$110.00–$150.00*

Shute, Nevil. *Ordeal*. NY. Morrow. 1939. 1st Amer ed. dj. .... *$25.00–$50.00*

Shute, Nevil. *Trustee from the Toolroom*. NY. William Morrow. (1960). 1st ed. dj. .... *$30.00–$40.00*

Sidney, M. *Five Little Peppers Grown Up*. Bos. 1892. 1st ed. .... *$20.00–$30.00*

Siebert, Wilbury H. *Vermont's Anti-Slavery and Underground Railroad Record . . .* Columbus, OH. 1937. 1st ed. illus. map, plates. .... *$50.00–$75.00*

Siegbahn, M. *Spectroscopy of X-Rays*. Lon. 1925. 1st Eng ed. .... *$40.00–$50.00*

Sikorsky, Igor I. *Story of the Winged-S with New Material on . . . Helicopter*. NY. 1942. illus. photos, inscrb, dj. .... *$40.00–$45.00*

Silko, Leslie Marmon. *Ceremony*. NY. Viking. (1977). 1st ed. dj. ..... *$100.00–$150.00*

Silverberg, Robert. *Lord Valentine's Castle*. Harper & Row. (1980). 1st ed. sgn, dj. .... *$20.00–$25.00*

Silverberg, Robert. *New Springtime*. Warner Books. (1990). 1st US ed. dj. .... *$14.00–$20.00*

Silverberg, Robert. *Shadrach in the Furnace*. Ind. Bobbs Merrill. (1976). 1st ed. dj. .... *$20.00–$35.00*

Silverberg, Robert. *Starborne*. Norwalk. Easton Press. (1996). 1st ed. ltd 1,500 cc, numbered and sgn, bound-in ribbon bookmark, laid-in Easton Press bookplate (not issued in dj). .... *$75.00–$85.00*

Silverstein, Shel. *Different Dances*. 1978. 1st ed. dj. .... *$100.00–$135.00*

Silverstein, Shel. *Giving Tree*. Harper & Row. 1964. .... *$20.00–$30.00*

Silverstein, Shel. *Light in the Attic*. Harper & Row. (1981). 1st ed. dj. .. *$15.00–$25.00*

Silverstein, Shel. *Take Ten.* Tokyo. Pacific Stars and Stripes. 1955. 1st ed...................... .... *$75.00–$135.00*

Simkins, Francis Butler and James Welch Patton. *Women of the Confederacy.* Rich/NY. 1936. 1st ed. dj. .... *$90.00–$125.00*

Simmon, Albert Dixon. *Wing Shots.* NY. Derrydale. (1936). 1st ed. illus...................... .... *$70.00–$100.00*

Simmons, Amelia. *American Cookery.* NY. 1958. ltd 800 cc, boxed....... *$35.00–$50.00*

Simms, Henry H. *Life of Robert M. T. Hunter.* Wm Byrd Press............. *$40.00–$50.00*

Simms, W Gilmore. *Lily & the Totem.* NY. 1850................................... *$35.00–$45.00*

Simpson, Charles. *Leicestershire & Its Hunts.* Lon. John Lane. (1926). illus. 28 clr. 55 b/w 75 cc sgn.. *$100.00–$150.00*

Sinclair, John L. *American Outpost.* NY. 1932. 1st ed. dj. .... *$70.00–$85.00*

Sinclair, John L. *I, Candidate . . .* Pasadena. (1935). 1st ed. .... *$15.00–$40.00*

Sinclair, Upton. *100%: The Story of a Patriot.* Pasadena. private ptg. (1920). 1st ed. .... *$100.00–$180.00*

Sinclair, Upton. *Mental Radio.* Lon. Werner Laurie. 1930. 1st ed. dj blue cloth............ .... *$45.00–$70.00*

Sinclair, Upton. *Millennium.* Viking. 1943. 1st ed. dj. .... *$20.00–$30.00*

Sinclair, Upton. *The Jungle.* NY. Doubleday. 1906. 1st ed. olive cloth. *$65.00–$150.00*

Singer, Isaac Bashevis. *Gimpel the Fool.* PA. Franklin Lib. 1980. 1st ed. dj.................. .... *$50.00–$70.00*

Singer, Isaac Bashevis. *Lost in America.* Garden City. Doubleday. 1981................... .... *$10.00–$15.00*

Singer, Isaac Bashevis. *Manor.* NY. Farrar Strauss & Giroux. 1967. 1st ed. dj. .... *$20.00–$40.00*

Singer, Isaac Bashevis. *Spinoza of Market Street.* Phil. Jewish Pub. (1961). 1st ed. dj... .... *$60.00–$150.00*

Singer, Isaac Bashevis. *Tale of Three Wishes.* NY. (1976). 1st ed. illus. by Irene Lieblich. dj.. *$20.00–$25.00*

Singer, Isaac Bashevis. *The Penitent.* Franklin Center. 1983. 1st ed. limited ed sgn....... .... *$70.00–$95.00*

Singer, Isaac Bashevis. *Young Man in Search of Love.* NY. Doubleday. 1978. 1st ed. dj. .... *$15.00–$25.00*

Singh, Kesri. *Tiger of Rajasthan.* Lon. Hale. 1959. 1st ed. illus. dj........ *$50.00–$65.00*

Singleton, Esther. *Shakespeare Garden.* NY. 1931. .... *$20.00–$25.00*

Singleton, Esther. *Social New York Under the Georges 1714–1776.* NY. 1902. 1st ed. .... *$30.00–$40.00*

Sinnett, A. P. *Occult World.* Bos. 1882. 1st ed. .... *$45.00–$85.00*

Siringo, Charles A. *History of Billy the Kid.* Austin. 1967. pictorial cloth.................... .... *$20.00–$30.00*

Siringo, Charles A. *Lone Star Cowboy.* Santa Fe. 1919. 1st ed. pictorial dark red cloth. .... *$100.00–$400.00*

Siringo, Charles A. *Riata & Spurs*. Bos. 1931. .... *$25.00–$35.00*

Siringo, Charles A. *Riata and Spurs*. Bos/NY. Houghton Mifflin. 1927. 1st ed. illus. pictorial cov. .... *$165.00–$275.00*

Siringo, Charles A. *Texas Cowboy*. NY. 1950. illus. by Tom Lea dj. ..... *$40.00–$75.00*

Siringo, Charles A. *Two Evil Isms*. Austin. 1967. illus. bds, facsimile. ....
.... *$40.00–$50.00*

Sisson, James E. II and Robert W. Martens. *Jack London First Editions*. Oakland. Star Rover House. 1979. 1st ed. illus. ltd 1,000 cc. .... *$60.00–$105.00*

Sitwell, Edith. *Shadow of Cain*. Lon. Lehmann. 1947. sgn, presentation copy from Margaret Mead. dj. .... *$55.00–$65.00*

Sitwell, Sacheverall. *Dance of the Quick and the Dead*. Lon. Faber & Faber. 1936. 1st ed. illus. dj. .... *$35.00–$47.00*

Sitwell, Sacheverell. *Gothick North*. Bos. Houghton Mifflin. 1929. plates.....................
.... *$30.00–$40.00*

Sketch of the 126th Regiment Pennsylvania Volunteers. PA. 1869. 1st ed. ....
.... *$95.00–$125.00*

Skinner, Otis. *Footlights and Spotlights*. Bobbs Merrill. 1924. ltd #27/500cc, sgn. ....
.... *$35.00–$45.00*

Skinner, Otis A. *Theory of William Miller, Concerning the End of the World in 1843*. Bos. Whittemore. 1840. 1st ed. .... *$150.00–$200.00*

Slang Dictionary. Lon. 1864. 2nd ed. .... *$40.00–$60.00*

Sloane, Eric. *Spirits of '76*. NY. Walker and Co. (1973). illus. white decorated cl over bds. pictorial dj. .... *$10.00–$24.00*

Sloane, T. O'Connor. *Electric Toy Making for Amateurs*. NY. Munn & Co. 1903. illus. .... *$35.00–$85.00*

Slocum, John and Herbert Cahoon. *Bibliography of James Joyce*. Westport, CT. (1977). illus. rprnt of 1953 ed. .... *$30.00–$60.00*

Slocum, Joshua. *Sailing Alone Around the World*. Lon. Samson, Low, Marston & Co. (c1900). 3rd ed. illus, pictorial cloth, aeg. .... *$38.00–$50.00*

Slocum, Joshua. *Sailing Alone Around the World*. NY. Century. 1900. 1st ed................
.... *$250.00–$400.00*

Slocum, Joshua. *Voyage of the Liberdade*. Bos. 1894. illus................ *$125.00–$255.00*

Slud, Paul. *Birds of Costa Rica*. AMNH. 1964. buckram....................... *$45.00–$60.00*

Small Homes. Ithaca, NY. Driscoll Bros & Co. c 1940s. pictorial wrps, for National Plan Service, 48 pp. .... *$35.00–$50.00*

Small, John. *Flora of the Florida Keys*. NY. pub by author. 1913........ *$75.00–$115.00*

Smiley, Jane. *Age of Grief*. NY. Knopf. 1987. 1st ed. dj. .... *$60.00–$150.00*

Smith, A. *Dental Microscopy*. Lon/Phila. 1895. plates. .... *$35.00–$45.00*

Smith, Adam. *An Inquiry Into the Nature and Causes of the Wealth of Nations*. Lon. 1930. 2 vols. djs... *$75.00–$130.00*

Smith, Adam. *An Inquiry Into the Nature and Causes of the Wealth of Nations*. Lon. 1811. 2nd Amer ed. .... *$200.00–$300.00*

Smith, Amanda. *An Autobiography* . . . Chi. 1893. 1st ed. .... *$45.00–$175.00*

Smith, Charles Hamilton. *Selections of the Ancient Costume of Great Britain and Ireland*. Lon. William Bulmer & Co. 1814. illus. folio 61 hand clred aquatint etchings. .... *$250.00–$350.00*

Smith, Charles W. *Beautiful Virginia*. Beautiful America Pub. illus. ...... *$50.00–$75.00*

Smith, Clark Ashton. *Other Dimensions*. Sauk City. Arkham House. 1970. 1st ed. dj. . ... *$30.00–$85.00*

Smith, Clark Ashton. *Tales of Science & Sorcery*. Sauk City. Arkham House. 1964. 1st ed. dj. .... *$50.00–$125.00*

Smith, Daniel. *Company K, First Alabama Regiment* . . . Prattville, AL. 1885. .... *$900.00–$1,000.00*

Smith, E. Boyd. *Song of Pocahantas and Captain John Smith*. Bos. 1906. 1st ed. illus. by Smith. clr plates.. *$125.00–$150.00*

Smith, Edward W. Jr. *Workaday Schooners*. Camden. Intl Marine. 1975. illus. photos, drawings, plans and descriptions, dj.. *$50.00–$65.00*

Smith, George W. *When Lincoln Came to Egypt*. Herrin, IL. Trovillion Private Press. 1940. 498 cc sgn by Smith. .... *$50.00–$75.00*

Smith, Gustavus Woodson. *Battle of Seven Pines*. NY. 1891. 1st ed. wrps. .... *$175.00–$200.00*

Smith, James Power. *General Lee at Gettysburg*. VA. nd. 1st ed........... *$50.00–$75.00*

Smith, Jerome V. C. *Natural History of the Fishes of Mass* . . . *Essay on Angling*. Bos. 1833. .... *$150.00–$175.00*

Smith, John Thomas. *Cries of London*. Lon. 1839. illus. 30 plates, cloth. .... *$275.00–$300.00*

Smith, Joseph. *Book of Mormon*. Liverpool. 1841. 1st Eng ed..... *$1,500.00–$2,500.00*

Smith, Joseph. *Pearl of Great Price*. Salt Lake. 1888. brown cloth. .. *$150.00–$200.00*

Smith, Martin Cruz. *Gorky Park*. NY. Random House. (1981). 1st ed. dj. .... *$20.00–$40.00*

Smith, Martin Cruz. *Gorky Park*. NY. 1981. 1st ed. dj. .... *$10.00–$20.00*

Smith, Martin Cruz. *Gypsy in Amber*. NY. (1971). 1st ed. dj............... *$60.00–$75.00*

Smith, Martin Cruz. *Indians Won*. NY. Belmont. (1970). 1st ed. wrps. .... *$100.00–$125.00*

Smith, Martin Cruz. *Rose*. NY. Random House. 1996. 1st ed. dj......... *$10.00–$20.00*

Smith, Mrs. *Female Economist . . . for the Use of Families*. Lon. 1810. ½ calf............. .... *$45.00–$65.00*

Smith, William Jay. *Spectra Hoax*. CT. Wesleyan Univ Press. (1961). 1st ed. illus. 4 plates.. *$20.00–$55.00*

Smith, Winston O. *Sharps Rifle*. William Morrow. 1943. 1st ed. .... *$60.00–$75.00*

Smucker, Samuel. *Life of Col. John Charles Fremont*. NY. Miller, Orton, & Mulligan. 1856. 1st ed.. *$35.00–$65.00*

Smyth, Henry Dewolf. *Atomic Energy for Military Purposes*. 1945. illus. 2nd ed. softcvr. .... *$35.00–$55.00*

Smyth, Henry Dewolf. *Atomic Energy for Military Purposes*. Princeton Univ Press. 1945. 1st ed. dj. .... *$90.00–$95.00*

Smythe, Frank S. *Kamet Conquered*. Lon. Victor Gollancz. 1933. 2nd imp, photos, maps... *$14.00–$20.00*

Smythe, Sarah M. *Ten Months in the Fiji Islands*. Oxford. John Henry & James Parker. 1864. maps, clr plates. .... *$325.00–$385.00*

Smythies, B. E. *Birds of Borneo*. The Sabah Society. 1981. pictorial bds. .... *$75.00–$100.00*

Snow White. 1978. printed in Czechoslovakia, 6 pop-ups. .... *$20.00–$25.00*

Snow, Alan. *How Dogs Really Work*. Bos. Little Brown & Co. 1993. 1st ed. illus. dj..... .... *$10.00–$25.00*

Snow, Jack. *Magical Mimics of Oz*. Chi. Reilly & Lee. (1946). illus. by Frank Kramer. .... *$75.00–$110.00*

Snow, Jack. *Shaggy Man of Oz*. Chi. Reilly & Lee. (1949). 1st ed. illus. by Frank Kramer. .... *$60.00–$110.00*

Snowden, James H. *Truth About Mormonism*. NY. 1926. 1st ed. illus. photos, scarce in dj. .... *$35.00–$50.00*

Snowden, R. *History of North and South America*. Phila. 1813. 2 vols in one, lea, maps. .... *$75.00–$100.00*

Snyder, Gary. *Earth House Hold*. 1969. 1st ed. sgn, dj. .... *$60.00–$85.00*

Snyder, Gary. *Old Ways*. City Lights. 1977. 1st ed. .... *$20.00–$25.00*

Snyder, Gary. *Regarding Wave*. Lon. 1970. 1st ed. dj............................ *$35.00–$45.00*

Solomon. *Why Smash Atoms?* Camb. 1940. 1st ed. .... *$30.00–$60.00*

Solzhenetsyn, Aleksandr. *Gulag Archipelago*. NY. Harper & Row. 1973. 3 vols. 1st ed. djs.. *$25.00–$75.00*

Solzhenitsyn, Aleksandr. *Oak and the Calf*. Harper. 1980. 1st US trade ed. dj. .... *$15.00–$25.00*

Solzhenitsyn, Alexander. *Cancer Ward*. Bodley Head. 1968. 1st Eng ed. dj. .... *$35.00–$40.00*

Solzhenitsyn, Alexander. *Lenin in Zurich*. Farrar. 1976. 1st US ed. dj.. *$20.00–$30.00*

Solzhenitsyn, Alexander. *One Day in the Life of Ivan Denisovich*. NY. Dutton. 1963. 1st ed. dj. .... *$15.00–$50.00*

Solzhenitsyn, Alexander. *Stories and Prose Poems*. Farrar. 1971. 1st US ed. dj. .... *$15.00–$30.00*

Some Accounts . . . Society of Friends Towards Indian Tribes (NJ & Pa). Lon. 1844. fldg map.. *$200.00–$350.00*

Somerville and Ross. *Sweet Cry of Hounds*. Bos/NY. Houghton Mifflin. 1937. 1st ed.. .... *$35.00–$45.00*

Somerville, H. B. *Ashes of Vengeance, a Romance of Old France*. McBride. 1923. illus. rust-clr cloth.. *$25.00–$35.00*

Somerville, Mary. *On the Connexion of the Physical Sciences*. Lon. John Murray. 1836. 3rd ed. .... *$30.00–$45.00*

Sommerville, Frankfort. *Spirit of Paris*. Lon. Adam and Charles Black. 1913. decorated cvr, teg, 169 pp, clr plates. .... *$60.00–$75.00*

Sonneck, Oscar G. T. *"The Star Spangled Banner . . . "*. GPO. 1st ed. illus. .... *$25.00–$45.00*

Sontag, Susan. *Trip to Hanoi*. NY. Farrar, Straus & Giroux. 1968. 1st ed. paperback. ... . *$45.00–$85.00*

Southern Songster . . . Liverpool. 1864. wrps. .... *$175.00–$225.00*

Southern, Terry. *Red Dirt Marijuana*. NAL. 1967. dj. .... *$35.00–$60.00*

Southwell, T. *Seals and Whales of the British Seas*. Lon. 1881. illus. *$175.00–$300.00*

Spalding's Official Base Ball Guide: Golden Jubilee, 1876–1925. NY. American Sports Publishing. 1925. wrps. illus. .... *$80.00–$120.00*

Spargo, John. *Karl Marx. His Life and Work*. NY. Huebsch. 1910. 1st ed. .... *$20.00–$65.00*

Spark, Muriel. *Driver's Seat*. Knopf. 1970. 1st US ed. dj. .... *$25.00–$30.00*

Spark, Muriel. *Hothouse by the East River*. Lon. Macmillan. (1973). 1st UK ed. .... *$35.00–$40.00*

Spark, Muriel. *My Best Mary*. Lon. 1953. 1st ed. dj. .... *$25.00–$60.00*

Spark, Muriel. *Prime of Miss Jean Brodie*. NY. Lippincott. 1961. 1st ed. dj.................. .... *$30.00–$40.00*

Spark, Muriel. *Prime of Miss Jean Brodie*. Lon. Macmillan. 1961. 1st UK ed. dj........ .... *$125.00–$150.00*

Sparks, Jared. *Life of George Washington*. Bos. 1839. 1st ed. illus. ...... *$65.00–$95.00*

Sparks, Jared. *Life of John Ledyard . . .* Cambridge. Hilliard & Brown. 1828. 2nd ed.. .... *$50.00–$100.00*

Sparrow, Walter Shaw. *Book of Sporting Painters*. Lon. The Bodley Head. 1931. illus. clr and b/w. dj. folio. .... *$150.00–$200.00*

Spears, John R. *Illustrated Sketches of Death Valley . . .* Chi. Rand McNally. 1892. 1st ed. illus. blue cloth map. .... *$300.00–$500.00*

Specimen Book of Monotype, Linotype & Foundry Type Faces, etc.Bos. 1941. 1st ed. .... *$28.00–$35.00*

Speck, Frank G. *Tutelo Spirit Adoption Ceremony*. Harrisburg. 1942. illus. photos....... .... *$25.00–$50.00*

Speer, Robert S. *Of One Blood*. Council of Women for Home Missions. (1924). wrps.. .... *$10.00–$25.00*

Speert, Harold. *Iconographia Gyniatrica*. Phil. F A Davis. (1973). 1st ed. illus. black cloth. .... *$60.00–$90.00*

Spence, Lewis. *Encyclopedia of the Occult*. Lon. Bracken Books. 1988. dj.................. .... *$18.00–$28.00*

Spencer, Ambrose. *Narrative of Andersonville*. NY. 1866. 1st ed. 272 pp. .... *$70.00–$85.00*

Spencer, Robert F. *North Alaskan Eskimo: A Study in Ecology and Society*. DC. GPO. 1959. 1st ed. 490 pp. Bulletin 171. .... *$85.00–$115.00*

Spender, Stephen. *Forward from Liberalism.* NY. Random House. (c1937). 1st Amer ed.
.... *$50.00–$65.00*

Spender, Stephen. *New Realism, a Discussion.* Lon. The Hogarth Press. 1939. 1st ed. printed wrps. .... *$40.00–$50.00*

Spender, Stephen. *Poems.* Lon. Faber & Faber. (1933). 1st ed. .... *$70.00–$80.00*

Spender, Stephen. *Poems of Dedication.* Lon. Faber & Faber. (1947). 1st ed. dj. ....
.... *$20.00–$40.00*

Spender, Stephen. *Trial of a Judge: A Tragedy in Five Acts.* Lon. Faber & Faber. (1938). 1st ed. inscrb,. .... *$55.00–$75.00*

Spenser, Edmund. *Prothalamion: Epithalamion.* Bos/NY. 1902. illus. ltd 400 cc, folio, dj. .... *$67.00–$85.00*

Sperry, Earle E. *Jerry Rescue.* NY. 1921. 16 pp. .... *$15.00–$25.00*

Spielmann, M. H. and Walter Jerrold. *Hugh Thomson . . .* Lon. A & C Black. 1931. illus. 13 clr plates. dj. .... *$85.00–$125.00*

Spillane, Mickey. *Kiss Me, Deadly.* NY. 1952. 1st ed. dj. .... *$45.00–$75.00*

Spillane, Mickey. *The Deep.* NY. Dutton. 1961. 1st ed. dj. .... *$40.00–$65.00*

Spiller, Burton L. *Firelight.* Derrydale. 1937. illus. by Lynn Bogue Hunt, ltd 950 cc. ....
.... *$180.00–$350.00*

Spiller, Burton L. *Grouse Feathers.* NY. 1947. illus. by Lynn Bogue Hunt. ....
.... *$50.00–$60.00*

Spivak, John L. *Georgia Nigger.* Lon. 1933. 1st ed. .... *$175.00–$250.00*

Splan, John. *Life With the Trotters.* 1889. presentation copy .... *$110.00–$125.00*

Splawn, A. J. *KA-MI-AKIN, the Last Hero of the Yakimas.* Portland. 1917. 1st ed. illus. photos, leather. .... *$90.00–$110.00*

Springs, Elliott White. *Rise and Fall of Carol Banks.* Garden City. Doubleday, Doran & Co. 1931. 99/200 cc. gray cloth paper label. .... *$75.00–$125.00*

Sprunt, A. *Florida Bird Life.* Coward McCann. 1954. dj. .... *$60.00–$75.00*

Sprunt, Alexander, Jr. *North American Birds of Prey.* Harper & Bros. 1955. 1st ed. dj.
.... *$25.00–$40.00*

Spryi, Johanna. *Heidi.* Phila. 1922. illus. by Jessie Willcox Smith. 1st ed. thus. ....
.... *$125.00–$175.00*

Spyri, Johanna. *Heidi.* Bos. Ginn. (1899). 1st ed. thus, 365 pp,. .... *$90.00–$125.00*

Spyri, Johanna. *Heidi.* John C Winston Co. 1927. clr plates. .... *$24.00–$30.00*

Squier, Ephraim G. *Lecture of the Condition and True Interests of the Working Man in America.* Albany. 1843. 16 pp, wrps. .... *$45.00–$55.00*

Squier, Ephraim G. *Nicaragua.* NY. Harper. 1860. rev ed. fldg map, 23 plates, original cloth, rbckd. .... *$95.00–$120.00*

Squier, Ephraim G. *States of Central America.* NY. 1858. illus. maps.. *$30.00–$50.00*

St. John Roosa, D. B. *Practical Treatise on the Diseases of the Ear.* NY. 1876. illus.....
.... *$42.00–$55.00*

Stafford, Jean. *Catherine Wheel.* NY. 1952. 1st ed. dj. .... *$20.00–$45.00*

Stafford, Jean. *Children Are Bored on Sunday*. NY. Harcourt & Brace Co. (1953). 1st ed. dj. .... *$30.00–$45.00*

Stafford, Jean. *Mountain Lion*. NY. Harcourt Brace & Co. (1947). 1st ed. dj. ....
.... *$70.00–$85.00*

Stalin, Joseph. *Leninism*. NY. International Publishers. 1928. 1st Amer ed. ....
.... *$60.00–$75.00*

Stanley, Dean. *Picturesque Palestine*. Lon. 1880–1884. 5 vols. plates. *$275.00–$350.00*

Stanley, Henry M. *Congo and the Founding of Its Free State*. NY. Harper & Bros. 1885. 2 vols. illus. 1st Amer ed. maps. .... *$150.00–$500.00*

Stanley, Henry M. *Congo and the Founding of Its Free State*. Lon. 1885. 2 vols. 1st ed. illus. maps, plates. pictorial cloth. .... *$600.00–$850.00*

Stanley, Henry M. *In Darkest Africa of the Quest, Rescue and Retreat of Emin, Governor or Equatoria*. NY. Scribner's. 1891. 2 vols. illus. fldg maps. *$80.00–$120.00*

Stanley, Henry M. *Livingstone Lost and Found*. Hartford. Mutual Publishing. 1873. 1st ed. illus. 782 pp. .... *$70.00–$85.00*

Stanley, Henry M. *Slavery and the Slave Trade in Africa*. NY. Harper & Bros. 1893. 1st Amer ed. illus by Frederick Remington. .... *$35.00–$50.00*

Stanley, Henry M. *Through the Dark Continent*. NY. Harper & Bros. 1878. 2 vols. illus. 1st Amer ed. illus. .... *$125.00–$180.00*

Stanley, Henry M. *Through the Dark Continent*. NY. 1879. illus. large 8vo, pictorial green cloth, 2 pocket maps. .... *$55.00–$70.00*

Stanley, Sir Henry Morton. *Autobiography. . .edited by His Wife*. Bos. Houghton Mifflin. 1909. 1st ed. photogravures, fldg map, teg. .... *$50.00–$70.00*

Stanley, W. H. *My Kalulu Prince, King & Slave*. NY. Scribner's. 1890. illus. ....
.... *$100.00–$150.00*

Stansbury, Howard. *Exploration and Survey of the Valley of the Great Salt Lake*. Phila. 1852. .... *$225.00–$425.00*

Star Trek. Random House. 1977. 4 fan-folded pop-ups. .... *$40.00–$55.00*

Star Trek Technical Manual. 1975. 1st ed. .... *$20.00–$25.00*

Stark, Francis R. *Abolition of Privateering and the Declaration of Paris*. NY. 1897.....
.... *$30.00–$50.00*

Starkie, Walter. *Scholars and Gypsies*. Berkeley. Univ Calif Press. (1963). 1st Amer ed. sgn, dj. .... *$25.00–$30.00*

Stathan, J. C. B. *Through Angola: A Coming Colony*. Edin. William Blackwood. 1922. 1st ed. illus. photos, plates, 2 fldg maps. .... *$50.00–$80.00*

Steamboats of Lake George 1817–1832. Albany. 1932. illus. 174 pp, maps, photos......
.... *$500.00–$700.00*

Stearns, Samuel. *American Herbal . . .* Walpole, MA. 1801. 1st Amer ed. lea. ....
.... *$1,000.00–$2,000.00*

Steele, Chester K. *Gold Course Mystery*. NY. George Sully. (1919). 1st ed. illus. ....
.... *$35.00–$45.00*

Steele, Matthew Forney. *American Campaigns*. Wash. 1909. 2 vols. 1st ed. ....
.... *$85.00–$125.00*

Stefansson, Vilhjalmu. *Farthest North*. NY/Lon. Harper. 1897. 2 vols. illus. 16 clr plates. 4 fldg maps in pocket. .... *$60.00–$90.00*

Stefansson, Vilhjalmur. *Adventure of Wrangle Island*. NY. 1925. 1st ed. illus. fldg clr map, sgn. .... *$75.00–$100.00*

Stefansson, Vilhjalmur. *Arctic Manual*. NY. 1944. 1st ed. .... *$28.00–$65.00*

Stefansson, Vilhjalmur. *Fat of the Land*. NY. 1956. 1st ed. sgn. .... *$35.00–$45.00*

Stefansson, Vilhjalmur. *Friendly Arctic*. NY. Macmillan. 1921. 1st ed. illus. cloth plates. 2 fldg pocket maps. sgn. .... *$100.00–$150.00*

Stefansson, Vilhjalmur. *My Life With the Eskimo*. NY. 1921. maps, inscrb, rprnt. .... *$40.00–$50.00*

Stefansson, Vilhjalmur. *Not By Bread Alone*. 1946. 1st ed. .... *$25.00–$30.00*

Steffansson, Vilhjalmur. *Friendly Arctic*. Macmillan. 1944. .... *$20.00–$25.00*

Stegner, Wallace. *All the Little Live Things*. NY. 1967. 1st ed. dj. .... *$35.00–$45.00*

Stegner, Wallace. *Beyond the Hundredth Meridian*. Bos. Houghton & Mifflin. 1954. dj. .... *$60.00–$85.00*

Stegner, Wallace. *Big Rock Candy Mountain*. NY. Duell, Sloan & Pearce. (1943). 1st ed. deep red cloth, dj. .... *$675.00–$1,000.00*

Stegner, Wallace. *Crossing to Safety*. Random House. (1987). 1st ed. dj. .... *$25.00–$35.00*

Stegner, Wallace. *Discovery! The Search for Arabian Oil*. Middle East Export Press. (1971). 1st ed. wrps. map endpapers, scarce 1st issue. .... *$60.00–$100.00*

Stegner, Wallace. *Gathering of Zion*. NY. McGraw-Hill. 1964. 1st ed. American Trials series, dj. .... *$50.00–$150.00*

Stegner, Wallace (ed.). *Beyond the Hundredth Meridian, John Wesley Powell*. Bos. Houghton Mifflin. 1954. illus. map endpapers, brown cloth, map, dj.. *$195.00–$225.00*

Stegner, Wallace (ed.). *This Is Dinosaur*. NY. Knopf. 1955. 1st ed. illus. photos, scarce, dj. .... *$100.00–$140.00*

Steichen, Edward. *Life in Photography*. Garden City. Doubleday. 1963. 1st ed. illus. photos. .... *$50.00–$80.00*

Steichen, Edward. *Life in Photography*. Garden City. 1963. 1st ed. illus. dj. .... *$50.00–$65.00*

Stein, Gertrude. *An Elucidation*. np. Transition. 1927. 1st separate ed. printed wrps..... .... *$200.00–$300.00*

Stein, Gertrude. *Autobiography of Alice B. Toklas*. NY. Harcourt Brace. 1933. 1st ed. dj. .... *$50.00–$350.00*

Stein, Gertrude. *Four in America*. New Haven. 1947. 1st ed. dj. .... *$45.00–$60.00*

Stein, Gertrude. *Lectures in America*. NY. Random House. (1935). 1st ed. dj. .... *$75.00–$200.00*

Stein, Gertrude. *Wars I Have Seen*. NY. Random House. (1945). 1st ed. dj. .... *$35.00–$45.00*

Stein, Gertrude. *What are Masterpieces?* LA. Conference Press. 1940. 1st ed. dj. .... *$125.00–$200.00*

Stein, Gertrude. *World Is Round.* Lon. 1939. dj. .... *$20.00–$30.00*

Steinbeck, John. *Bombs Away: The Story of a Bomber Team.* NY. Viking. 1942. 1st ed. illus. dj. .... *$80.00–$140.00*

Steinbeck, John. *Burning Bright.* NY. Viking. 1950. 1st ed. dj. .... *$80.00–$120.00*

Steinbeck, John. *Burning Bright.* NY. 1950. 1st ed. dj. .... *$45.00–$50.00*

Steinbeck, John. *Cannery Row.* NY. Viking. 1942. 1st ed. dj. .... *$35.00–$150.00*

Steinbeck, John. *Cup of Gold.* NY. Robert McBride. 1929. 1st ed. first issue of author's first book, yellow cloth, teg, dj, scarce.. *$3,500.00–$4,500.00*

Steinbeck, John. *Grapes of Wrath.* Viking Press. (1939). 1st ed. first issue, dj. ....
.... *$750.00–$2,000.00*

Steinbeck, John. *Letters to Elizabeth.* SF. Book Club of California. 1978. ltd 500 cc. dj.
.... *$70.00–$100.00*

Steinbeck, John. *Log From the Sea of Cortez.* NY. dj. .... *$100.00–$200.00*

Steinbeck, John. *Moon Is Down.* 1942. 1st ed. dj. .... *$35.00–$50.00*

Steinbeck, John. *Of Mice and Men.* Covici Friede. 1937. 1st issue, dj. ....
.... *$200.00–$550.00*

Steinbeck, John. *Red Pony.* NY. Covici Friede. 1937. 1st ed. ltd 699 cc. sgn, slipcase. .
.... *$700.00–$1,200.00*

Steinbeck, John. *Red Pony.* NY. (1945). illus. dj. .... *$50.00–$150.00*

Steinbeck, John. *Sweet Thursday.* NY. Viking. 1954. 1st ed. 1st issue. dj.....................
.... *$70.00–$100.00*

Steinbeck, John. *Sweet Thursday.* NY. Viking. 1954. 1st ed. dj. .... *$85.00–$125.00*

Steinbeck, John. *The Pearl.* NY. Viking. 1947. 1st ed. illus. dj. .... *$80.00–$140.00*

Steinbeck, John. *The Pearl.* NY. 1947. 1st ed. illus. dj. .... *$25.00–$50.00*

Steinbeck, John. *Travels With Charley in Search of America.* NY. Viking. (1962). 1st ed. dj. .... *$70.00–$125.00*

Steinbeck, John. *Travels With Charley.* Viking. 1962. 1st ed. dj............. *$25.00–$40.00*

Steinbeck, John. *Wayward Bus.* NY. Viking. 1947. 1st ed. dj................. *$40.00–$75.00*

Steinbeck, John. *Winter of Our Discontent.* NY. Viking. 1961. 1st trade ed. dj............
.... *$50.00–$90.00*

Steinbeck, John. *Winter of Our Discontent.* NY. (1961). 1st ed. dj. .... *$45.00–$70.00*

Steinbeck, John. *Winter of Our Discontent.* Heinemann. 1961. 1st Eng ed. dj. ....
.... *$25.00–$65.00*

Steinbeck, John and Edward F. Ricketts. *Sea of Cortez.* NY. Viking Press. 1941. 1st ed. dj. .... *$100.00–$150.00*

Steiner, Jesse Frederick and Roy M. Brown. *North Carolina Chain Gang . . .* Chapel Hill. 1927. 1st ed. .... *$100.00–$150.00*

Steiner, Stan. *Last Horse.* NY. Macmillan. 1961. 1st ed. illus. b/w and clr, dj...............
.... *$25.00–$30.00*

Steinmetz, Andrew. *Sunshine & Showers: Their Influence Throughout Creation: A Compendium of Popular Meteorology.* Lon. 1867. 432 pp. .... *$95.00–$150.00*

Stejneger, L. *Poisonous Snakes of North America.* Wash. 1895............. *$40.00–$60.00*

Stemons, James Samuel. *As Victim to Victims* . . . NY. Fortuny's. 1941. 1st ed. cloth....
.... *$40.00–$50.00*

Stephens, J. *Incidents of Travel in Yucatan.* NY. 1843. 2 vols. 1st ed. foldout plate, ex lib. .... *$60.00–$85.00*

Stephens, James. *Crock of Gold.* Lon. 1912. 1st ed. dj....................... *$125.00–$175.00*

Stephens, James. *Demi-Gods.* Lon. 1914. 1st ed. 1st issue. .... *$50.00–$75.00*

Stephenson, Neal. *Big U.* NY. Vintage. 1984. 1st ed. paperback scarce. ....
.... *$225.00–$400.00*

Sterling, Bruce. *Islands in the Net.* NY. Arbor House/William Morrow. (1988). 1st ed. dj. .... *$50.00–$100.00*

Sterling, George. *House of Orchids and Other Poems.* SF. Robertson. 1911. 1st ed. sgn, dj. .... *$85.00–$150.00*

Sterling, George. *Lilith.* SF. Robertson. 1919. 1st ed. ltd 300 cc. sgn. .... *$35.00–$60.00*

Sterling, Sara Hawks. *Lady of King Arthur's Court.* Phila. Jacobs. 1907. 1st ed. illus. .
.... *$45.00–$80.00*

Stern, Richard Martin. *Bright Road to Fear.* NY. (1958). 1st ed. dj... *$65.00–$100.00*

Stern, Richard Martin. *High Hazard.* NY. (1962). 1st ed. dj. .... *$20.00–$30.00*

Stern, Richard Martin. *Search for Tabatha Carr.* NY. Scribner's. (1960). 1st ed. dj. ....
.... *$40.00–$75.00*

Sterne, Laurence. *Life and Opinions of Tristram Shandy, Gentleman.* Basil. Legranc. 1803. 2 vols. mor. .... *$50.00–$100.00*

Stetson, George R. *Southern Negro As He Is.* Bos. 1877. 1st ed. .... *$75.00–$100.00*

Stevens, Abel. *History of the Methodist Episcopal Church.* NY. 1868. 4 vols. ....
.... *$30.00–$45.00*

Stevens, Hazard. *Life of Isaac Ingalls Stevens.* Bos. 1900. 2 vols. 1st ed. illus. ....
.... *$50.00–$85.00*

Stevens, John L. and W. B. Oleson. *Picturesque Hawaii.* np. Edgewood Pub. blue pictorial cloth.. *$80.00–$100.00*

Stevens, Thomas. *Around the World on a Bicycle, Vol.1.* NY. 1889. illus......................
.... *$35.00–$50.00*

Stevenson, Robert Louis. *Across the Plains.* NY. Scribner's. 1892. 1st Amer ed. cloth.
....*$75.00–$125.00*

Stevenson, Robert Louis. *Black Arrow.* NY. Scribner's. 1916. 1st ed. illus. by N C Wyeth. pictorial paste-down on cvr.. *$100.00–$150.00*

Stevenson, Robert Louis. *Catriona.* Lon. Cassell. 1893. 1st ed............. *$70.00–$90.00*

Stevenson, Robert Louis. *Child's Garden of Verses.* NY. (1929). illus. by Eulalie. scarce dj. .... *$35.00–$85.00*

Stevenson, Robert Louis. *David Balfour.* Scribner's. 1924. illus. by N C Wyeth...........
.... *$55.00–$60.00*

Stevenson, Robert Louis. *Fables.* NY. Scribner's. 1910. illus. 20 plates, tissue guards. .
.... *$30.00–$50.00*

Stevenson, Robert Louis. *Kidnapped.* Scribner's. 1946. illus. by N C Wyeth, rprnt....... .... *$40.00–$45.00*

Stevenson, Robert Louis. *Kidnapped.* NY. Scribner's Classic. 1913. illus. by N C Wyeth.. *$30.00–$200.00*

Stevenson, Robert Louis. *Strange Case of Dr. Jekyll & Mr. Hyde.* NY. 1930. illus. 1st thus.. *$50.00–$65.00*

Stevenson, Robert Louis. *Treasure Island.* Phila. 1930. illus. by Lyle Justis, No 1 of the Anderson Books. .... *$45.00–$55.00*

Stevenson, William G. *Thirteen Months in the Rebel Army . . . by an Impressed New Yorker.* Lon. 1862. 1st ed. 1st Eng ed. rbnd. .... *$50.00–$75.00*

Stewart, Elinore Pruitt. *Letters of a Woman Homesteader.* Bos. 1914. 1st ed. illus. by N C Wyeth. .... *$25.00–$37.00*

Stewart, Henry. *Shepherd's Manual.* NY. 1876. illus. .... *$27.00–$35.00*

Stewart, John J. *Mormonism and the Negro.* Utah. Community Press. 1963. 3rd ed cloth. .... *$25.00–$65.00*

Stickley, Gustav. *Craftsman Homes.* NY. 1909. 1st ed. .... *$125.00–$250.00*

Stieglitz, Alfred. *Georgia O'Keefe: a Portrait.* NY. MOMA. 1st ed. illus. dj, slipcase.... .... *$50.00–$80.00*

Stiles, Henry Reed, M.D. *Bundling, Its Origin, Progress and Decline in America.* Albany. 1869. 1st ed. 139 pp... *$85.00–$100.00*

Stiles, Robert. *Four Years under Marse Robert.* NY. Neale Pub. 1903. .... *$100.00–$300.00*

Still, A. T. *Autobiography of Andrew T Still.* Kirksville, MO. 1908. illus. 2nd ed. rev, 404 pp... *$85.00–$145.00*

Stillwell, Margaret Bingham. *Incunabula and Americana 1450–1800.* NY. Cooper Square. 1961. 1st ed. .... *$70.00–$100.00*

Stimson, F. J. *My Story.* NY. Scribner's. 1917. 1st ed. 3 plates.............. *$45.00–$60.00*

Stockham, Alice. *Tokology. A Book for Every Woman.* Chi. Sanitary Pub Co. 1883. 1st ed. 277 pp. .... *$75.00–$125.00*

Stockham, Alice B. *Tokology.* Chi. 1907. rprnt. .... *$30.00–$45.00*

Stocking, Amer Mills. *Saukie Indians and Their Great Chiefs Black Hawk and Keokuk.* Rock Island. Vaile. 1926. illus. red cloth, gold lettering.......................... *$50.00–$75.00*

Stockley, C. H. *African Camera Hunts.* Lon. Country Life, Ltd. (1948). 1st ed. illus. photos.. *$80.00–$100.00*

Stockman, David A. *Triumph of Politics, Why the Reagan Revolution Failed.* 422 pp, photos, dj. .... *$30.00–$45.00*

Stockton, Frank. *Pomonas Travels.* Scribner's. 1894. illus.................... *$50.00–$65.00*

Stockton, Frank R. *Girl at Cobhurst.* NY. 1898. 1st ed. .... *$45.00–$50.00*

Stoddard, Herbert. *Bobwhite Quail.* NY. Scribner's. 1932. illus............ *$50.00–$75.00*

Stoddard, John L. *Stoddard's Lectures.* Balch Bros. 1897. 10 vols. .. *$150.00–$200.00*

Stoddard, Lothrop. *Rising Tide of Color.* Blue Ribbon Books. (1920). brown cloth, dj. .... *$20.00–$50.00*

Stoddard, Solomon. *Guide to Christ . . .* NY. 1813. small lea............... *$30.00–$40.00*

Stoker, Bram. *Dracula.* NY. Grosset & Dunlap. (1931). illus. from the Universal picture, Photo-play ed. dj... *$60.00–$125.00*

Stoker, Bram. *Dracula's Guest and Other Weird Stories.* Lon. 1914. rprnt.................... .... *$35.00–$45.00*

Stoker, Bram. *Dracula.* Limited Ed Club. 1965. illus. sgn by Hoffman slipcase. .... *$175.00–$225.00*

Stoker, Bram. *Jewel of the Seven Stars.* NY. Harper. 1904. 1st Amer ed...................... .... *$70.00–$85.00*

Stoker, Bram. *Mystery of the Sea.* NY. Harper. 1904. 1st ed. .... *$75.00–$100.00*

Stoker, Bram. *Personal Reminiscences of Henry Irving.* NY. 1906. 2 vols. 1st Amer ed. illus. .... *$75.00–$125.00*

Stoker, Bram. *Under the Sunset.* Lon. Sampson, Low, Marston. 1882. 1st ed. author's first book... *$300.00–$1,000.00*

Stone, I. F. *Haunted 50s.* NY. 1963. 1st ed. dj... *$30.00–$40.00*

Stone, I. F. *Hidden History of the Korean War.* NY. Monthly Review Press. (1952). 1st ed. .... *$20.00–$35.00*

Stoney, S. G. *Plantations of the Carolina Low Country.* Charleston. 1938. 1st ed. dj, slipcase... *$85.00–$165.00*

Stoppard, Tom. *Arcadia.* Lon/Bos. Faber & Faber. (1993). 1st ed. .... *$60.00–$75.00*

Stories by American Authors. NY. Scribner's. 1896. 10 vols. red cloth. . *$45.00–$55.00*

Stories from the Old Testament. NY. Winston. 1938. illus. in clr by Maud and Miska Petersham... *$25.00–$30.00*

Story of Dark Plot or Tyranny on the Frontier. Warren Press. 1903. .... *$28.00–$35.00*

Story of King Arthur and His Knights. Scribner's. 1903. 1st ed. illus. by Howard Pyle. .... *$85.00–$115.00*

Story of the Fourth of July. NY. Kiggins & Kellogg. nd. wrps. illus. by Uncle Ned, 16 pp, 9 x 55 cm.. *$25.00–$40.00*

Story, A T. *Story of Wireless Telegraphy.* 1904. 1st ed. illus. .... *$45.00–$85.00*

Stout, Rex. *And Four to Go.* NY. Viking. 1958. 1st ed. dj..................... *$80.00–$125.00*

Stout, Rex. *Black Mountain.* Viking. 1954. 1st ed. dj............................ *$95.00–$125.00*

Stout, Rex. *Black Orchids.* NY. Collier. 1942. .... *$18.00–$30.00*

Stout, Rex. *Death of a Doxy.* Viking. 1966. 1st ed. dj. .... *$35.00–$100.00*

Stout, Rex. *Double for Death.* NY. Farrar & Rinehart. 1939. 1st ed. no dj..................... .... *$85.00–$175.00*

Stout, Rex. *Family Affair.* Lon. (1975). 1st UK ed. dj............................ *$35.00–$45.00*

Stout, Rex. *Golden Spiders.* NY. Viking Press. 1953. 1st ed. dj............ *$95.00–$120.00*

Stout, Rex. *Might As Well Be Dead.* Collins. 1957. 1st UK ed. dj. .... *$40.00–$55.00*

Stout, Rex. *Mother Hunt.* NY. Viking. 1963. 1st ed. dj. .... *$32.00–$40.00*

Stout, Rex. *Prisoner's Base.* NY. Viking. 1952. 1st ed. dj..................... *$65.00–$125.00*

Stout, Rex. *Red Box*. NY. Farrar & Rinehart. 1937. 1st ed. no dj. .... *$75.00–$100.00*

Stout, Rex. *Three at Wolfe's Door*. 1960. 1st ed. dj. .... *$100.00–$135.00*

Stout, Rex. *Too Many Women*. NY. Viking. 1947. 1st ed. dj .... *$70.00–$200.00*

Stout, Rex. *Triple Jeopardy*. 1952. 1st ed. dj. .... *$20.00–$30.00*

Stowe, Harriet Beecher. *Dred, a Tale of the Great Dismal Swamp*. Bos. 1856. 2 vols. 1st ed .... *$40.00–$55.00*

Stowe, Harriet Beecher. *Key to Uncle Tom's Cabin*. Bos. 1853. 1st ed. .... *$65.00–$150.00*

Stowe, Harriet Beecher. *Men of Our Times*. Hartford. Hartford Pub Co. 1868. 1st ed. illus. .... *$65.00–$150.00*

Stowe, Harriet Beecher. *Sunny Memories of Foreign Lands*. NY. 1854. 2 vols. illus..... .... *$200.00–$300.00*

Stowe, Harriet Beecher. *Uncle Tom's Cabin*. NY. Hurst. 1901. .... *$20.00–$30.00*

Stowe, Harriet Beecher. *Uncle Tom's Cabin; or Life Among the Lowly*. Bos. 1852. 2 vols. 1st ed. with no mention of "thousands" on the title pages. .... *$1,200.00–$2,500.00*

Strachen, Arthur W. *Mauled by a Tiger*. Edin. 1933. 1st ed. illus. .... *$35.00–$55.00*

Strachey, Lionel (trans). *Memoirs of an Arabian Princess*. NY. 1907. *$95.00–$115.00*

Strand, Paul. *Retrospective. 1915–1968*. large folio. .... *$90.00–$110.00*

Strange, Daniel. *Pioneer History of Eaton County, Michigan, 1833–1866 . . .* 1923. 1st ed. illus. .... *$60.00–$85.00*

Stratton, E. M. (ed.). *New York Coach-makers Magazine*. NY. Stratton. 1861. Vol. 3. illus. 46 clr plates. .... *$150.00–$175.00*

Street, Julian. *Abroad at Home*. NY. Century. 1916. illus. .... *$15.00–$30.00*

Striker, Fran. *Lone Ranger and the Silver Bullet*. 1948. 1st ed. dj .... *$20.00–$35.00*

Striker, Fran. *Lone Ranger and the Gold Robbery*. Grosset & Dunlap. 1939. Lone Ranger #3 .... *$40.00–$60.00*

Striker, Fran. *Lone Ranger and the Haunted Gulch*. Grosset & Dunlap. 1941. 1st ed. Lone Ranger #6, dj. .... *$35.00–$47.00*

Striker, Fran. *Lone Ranger and the Mystery Ranch*. 1938. 1st ed. dj ..... *$25.00–$35.00*

Striker, Fran. *Lone Ranger on Powderhorn Trail*. 1949. 1st ed. dj. .... *$20.00–$35.00*

Striker, Fran. *Lone Ranger Traps the Smugglers*. Grosset & Dunlap. 1941. Lone Ranger #7. .... *$35.00–$45.00*

Strode, Hudson. *Jefferson Davis, Confederate President*. Harcourt. 1959. wrps. dj. .... *$20.00–$30.00*

Strode, Hudson. *Story of Bermuda*. NY. Smith & Haas. 1932. 1st ed. illus. dj .... *$20.00–$30.00*

Strong, Anna Louise. *Children of Revolution . . .* Seattle. privately printed. 1926. wrps. 2nd print. sgn. scarce pamphlet .... *$50.00–$60.00*

Strong, Chas. J. and L. S. *Strong's Book of Designs*. Chi. Drake & Co. 1917. illus. oblong. .... *$100.00–$250.00*

Stuart, James. *Three Years in America*. NY. 1833. 2 vols. 1st Amer ed. *$50.00–$90.00*

Stuart, Jesse. *Kentucky Is My Land*. 1952. sgn, dj. .... *$50.00–$80.00*

Stuart, Jesse. *Man With a Bull-Tongue Plow*. NY. 1934. 1st ed. sgn, dj. ....
.... *$270.00–$300.00*

Stuart, Jesse. *Ride With Huey the Engineer*. NY. (1966). 1st ed. illus. by Robert Henneberger. dj... *$50.00–$100.00*

Stuart, Jesse. *Taps for Private Tussie*. NY. Dutton. 1943. 1st ed. dj. ...... *$50.00–$90.00*

Stuart, Moses. *Grammar of the Hebrew Language*. Andover, MA. Gould and Newman. 1838. 6th ed. calf-bkd bds. .... *$85.00–$125.00*

Sturgeon, Theodore. *More Than Human*. NY. 1953. 1st ed. dj. .... *$100.00–$150.00*

Sturgeon, Theodore. *Sturgeon in Orbit*. Lon. 1970. 1st Brit ed. dj. ... *$100.00–$150.00*

Sturgeon, Theodore. *Without Sorcery*. np (Phila). Prime Press. 1948. 355 pp, dj...........
.... *$30.00–$45.00*

Styron, William. *Confessions of Nat Turner*. NY. Random House. (1967). 1st ed. sgn, dj.
.... *$75.00–$150.00*

Styron, William. *Confessions of Nat Turner*. NY. Random House. (1967). 1st ed. dj.....
.... *$40.00–$75.00*

Styron, William. *Confessions of Nat Turner*. Franklin Center. Franklin Library. 1979. ltd, sgn. .... *$100.00–$125.00*

Styron, William. *Lie Down in Darkness*. Ind. Bobbs Merrill. 1951. 1st ed. author's first book, dj. .... *$120.00–$150.00*

Styron, William. *Set This House on Fire*. NY. Random House. (1960). 1st ed. dj. ....
.... *$40.00–$60.00*

Styron, William. *Set This House on Fire*. Lon. Hamish Hamilton. (1961). 1st UK dj. ...
.... *$40.00–$75.00*

Styron, William. *Set This House on Fire*. NY. 1960. 1st ed. sgn, dj. ...... *$55.00–$85.00*

Styron, William. *Sophie's Choice*. Random House. 1979. 1st ed. sgn, dj.......................
.... *$60.00–$75.00*

Styron, William. *This Quiet Dust*. np. Random House. (1967). wrps. dj.......................
.... *$20.00–$35.00*

Suckow, Ruth. *Bonney Family*. NY. 1928. 1st ed. ltd #66/95 cc, sgn, dj. *$35.00–$40.00*

Sue, Eugene. *Wandering Jew*. Lon. 1844–1845. 1st ed...................... *$275.00–$315.00*

Summer, Montague. *Vampire in Europe*. NY. Dutton. 1929. 1st US ed. *$35.00–$45.00*

Summers, Montague. *History of Witchcraft & Demonology*. Lon. 1973. rprnt of 1926 ed. dj. .... *$8.00–$12.00*

Sumner, Charles. *White Slavery in the Barbary States*. Bos. John P. Jewett. 1853. 1st ed. illus. wood engr. .... *$80.00–$120.00*

Sun Chief. *Autobiography of a Hopi Indian*. Yale. 1942. 1st ed. illus. 459 pp...............
.... *$28.00–$35.00*

Sunday School Almanac. NY. Carlton & Philips. (1854). wrps. illus. 32 pp, 112 x 73 cm.
.... *$20.00–$35.00*

Supplement. Wholesale and Retail Catalogue of Military Goods. NY. Francis Bannerman. 1905. pictorial wrps, 42 pp, illus. .... *$40.00–$50.00*

Surtees, R. S. *Hawbuck Grange.* Lon. nd. illus. .... *$50.00–$85.00*

Surtees, R. S. *Hunts with Jorrocks.* NY. 1908. illus. .... *$50.00–$85.00*

Susann, Jacqueline. *Every Night Josephine!* NY. 1963. 1st ed. dj, author's first book. .. .. *$150.00–$200.00*

Sutherland, C. H. V. *Gold: Its Beauty, Power, and Allure.* McGraw-Hill. 1969. 2nd ed. dj. .... *$25.00–$35.00*

Suthren, Victor. *In Perilous Seas.* NY. St Martin's Press. (1983). 1st US ed dj. .... *$35.00–$50.00*

Sutton, Margaret. *Mysterious Half Cat.* Grosset & Dunlap. 1936. Judy Bolton #9, dj. . ... *$10.00–$20.00*

Sutton, Margaret. *Seven Strange Clues.* Grosset & Dunlap. 1932. Judy Bolton #4, dj. . ... *$10.00–$20.00*

Sutton, Margaret. *Summer on the Farm.* NY. Grosset Dunlap. 1938. 1st ed. illus. pictorial dj. .... *$40.00–$65.00*

Sutton, Margaret. *Trail of the Green Doll.* Grosset & Dunlap. 1956. Judy Bolton #21, dj. .... *$14.00–$25.00*

Sutton, Margaret. *Vanishing Shadow.* Grosset & Dunlap. rprnt, Judy Bolton #1, dj...... .... *$10.00–$15.00*

Sutton, Richard and Emmy Lou Sutton. *An Arctic Safari. With Camera & Rifle.* . . . St Louis. C V Mosby. 1932. 1st ed. sgn and inscrb by author, 100 photos, dj. .... *$75.00–$90.00*

Swanton, John. *Indian Tribes of North America.* Wash. GPO. 1953. 726 pp, fldg maps. .... *$45.00–$65.00*

Swanton, John. *Indian Tribes of the Lower Mississippi Valley* . . . Wash. 1911. .... *$45.00–$60.00*

Sweeney, Robert L. *Frank Lloyd Wright: An Annotated Bibliography.* LA. 1978. dj. .... *$65.00–$90.00*

Sweet, Frederick A. *Miss Mary Cassatt.* Norman. (1966). 1st ed. illus. photos clr and b/w. sgn. dj. .... *$30.00–$45.00*

Swift, Jonathan. *Gulliver's Travels.* Lon. Ernest Lister. illus. clr plates by Jackson. .... *$75.00–$125.00*

Swinburne, Algernon. *Bothwell: A Tragedy.* Lon. Chatto & Windus. 1874. 1st ed. .... *$50.00–$85.00*

Swinburne, Algernon. *Chastelard: A Tragedy.* Lon. Edward Moxon. 1865. 1st ed. .... *$125.00–$165.00*

Swinburne, Algernon Charles. *Century of Roundels and Other Poems.* NY. 1883. 1st Amer ed. dj. .... *$40.00–$45.00*

Swinburne, Algernon Charles. *Erechtheus.* Lon. 1876. .... *$40.00–$55.00*

Swinburne, Algernon Charles. *Ode on the Proclamation of the French Republic, September 4th, 1879.* Lon. Ellis. 1870. 1st ed. wrps. .... *$80.00–$100.00*

Swinburne, Algernon Charles. *Springtide of Life.* Lon. Heinemann. (1918). 1st ed. illus. by Arthur Rackham. ltd 765 cc, sgn by Rackham. .... *$800.00–$900.00*

Swinton, George. *Sculpture of the Eskimo.* Tor. McClelland & Stewart. (1972). 1st ed. illus. .... *$50.00–$80.00*

Swope, John. *Camera Over Hollywood.* NY. 1939. illus. dj. .... *$95.00–$125.00*

Sylva, Carmen. *Pelefch-Marchen.* Bonn. 1886. author pseudonym for Elizabeth, Queen of Roumania, red cloth, gold lettering. .... *$25.00–$35.00*

Synge, John M. *Poems and Translations.* Churchtown, Dundrum. Cuala Press. 1909. 1st ed. 1/250 cc.. *$200.00–$250.00*

Szyk, Arthur. *Haggadah.* Jerusalem. 1956. 1st ed. mor, boxed......... *$100.00–$145.00*

Szyk, Arthur. *New Order.* NY. 1941. dj... *$125.00–$200.00*

Taber, Gladys. *Amber: A Very Personal Cat.* Lippincott. 1970. 1st ed. illus. dj.............. .... *$20.00–$45.00*

Taber, Gladys. *Daisy and Dobbin: Two Little Seahorses.* Phila. 1948. illus.................... .... *$18.00–$25.00*

Taber, Gladys. *Especially Spaniels.* Macrae-Smith. 1945. illus. 4th ptg, photos, dj........ .... *$10.00–$15.00*

Taber, Gladys. *First Book of Cats.* Franklin Watts. 1950. illus. .... *$18.00–$25.00*

Taber, Gladys. *First Book of Dogs.* NY. 1949. dj................................... *$25.00–$35.00*

Taber, Gladys. *Harvest of Yesterdays.* 1976. 1st ed. dj........................... *$10.00–$15.00*

Taber, Gladys. *Mrs. Daffodil.* Phila. Lippincott. 1957. 1st ed. dj. .... *$45.00–$60.00*

Taber, Gladys. *Reveries at Stillmeadow.* 1970. 1st ed. dj....................... *$22.00–$30.00*

Taber, Gladys. *Stillmeadow Cook Book.* Lippincott. 1965. 1st ed. dj..... *$25.00–$45.00*

Taber, Gladys. *What Cooks at Stillmeadow.* Phila. 1958. 1st ed. dj........ *$45.00–$60.00*

Taber, Grace. *Stillmeadow Kitchen.* MacRae Smith. 1951. illus. enlarged ed................ .... *$50.00–$100.00*

Tabor, Grace. *One Dozen and One.* Phila. Lippincott. 1966. 1st ed. dj.. *$15.00–$45.00*

Taft, J. A. *Practical Treatise on Operative Dentistry.* Phila. 1868. calf. . *$37.00–$45.00*

Tait, L. *Diseases of Women.* NY. 1879. .... *$40.00–$50.00*

Talbot, Eleanor W. *My Lady's Casket of Jewels and Flowers* . . . Bos. Lee & Shepard. 1885. 1st ed. illus. aeg. .... *$50.00–$100.00*

Talbot, Ethelbert. *My People of the Plains.* NY. 1906. illus. photos, teg. .... *$28.00–$40.00*

Talbot, Ethelbert. *My People of the Plains.* NY. 1906. 1st ed. .... *$52.00–$65.00*

Talbot, F. A. *Aeroplanes and Dirigibles of the War.* Phila. 1915. 1st Amer ed. illus. .... *$30.00–$40.00*

Tallent, Annie D. *Black Hills: or, the Last Hunting Ground of the Dakotas.* Sioux Falls. Brevet Press. 1974. 2nd ed. dj... *$25.00–$48.00*

Talmage, James E. *Vitality of Mormonism.* Bos. 1919. 1st ed. sgn by President George Albert Smith, rare. .... *$180.00–$200.00*

Tan, Amy. *Joy Luck Club.* NY. Putnam's. (1989). 1st ed. author's first book, dj............. .... *$100.00–$200.00*

Tan, Amy. *Kitchen God's Wife.* NY. Putnam. 1991. 1st ed. sgn, dj. .... *$50.00–$75.00*

Tan, Amy. *Kitchen God's Wife*. NY. Putnam. (1991). 1st ed. sgn, dj....... *$35.00–$50.00*

Tan, Amy. *The Hundred Secret Senses*. NY. Putnam. 1995. wrps. ed. dj, sgn. ....
....*$35.00–$45.00*

Tanner, Z. L. *Deep-Sea Exploration*. Wash. GPO. 1896. illus. drawings, fldg plates. ....
.... *$50.00–$85.00*

Tappan, David. *Lectures on Jewish Antiquities*. Bos. Hilliard and Lincoln. 1807. 1st ed.
.... *$95.00–$175.00*

Tarbel, Ida. *Business of Being a Woman*. NY. 1919. rprnt. .... *$25.00–$35.00*

Tarbell, Ida M. *In the Footsteps of the Lincolns*. NY. 1924. illus. .... *$30.00–$40.00*

Tarbell, Ida M. *Life of Abraham Lincoln*. NY. 1903. 5 vols. .... *$45.00–$50.00*

Tarbell, Ida M. *Life of Abraham Lincoln*. 1924. 4 vols. the Sangamon ed......................
.... *$60.00–$75.00*

Targ, W. *Bibliophile in the Nursery*. Cleve. 1957. 1st ed. dj. .... *$25.00–$35.00*

Tarkington, Booth. *Fascinating Stranger*. NY. Doubleday, Page. 1923. 1st trade ed. dj.
.... *$60.00–$80.00*

Tartt, Donna. *Secret History*. NY. Knopf. 1992. 1st ed. dj. .... *$50.00–$75.00*

Tasso, Torquato. *Jerusalem Delivered, an Heroic Poem*. Lon. Mawman. 1818. 2 vols.
trans. by J. H. Hunt... *$55.00–$80.00*

Tate, Allen. *The Fathers*. Putnam. (1938). 1st ed. dj........................... *$110.00–$140.00*

Tatham, Julie. *Clinic Nurse*. Grosset & Dunlap. 1952. Cherry Ames #13, dj. ....
.... *$14.00–$25.00*

Tatham, Julie. *Night Supervisor*. Grosset & Dunlap. 1950. Cherry Ames #11. ....
.... *$10.00–$14.00*

Taton, Rene. *General History of the Sciences*. Lon. Thames and Hudson. 1965–66.
3 vols.. *$150.00–$300.00*

Taverner, Eric. *Trout Fishing From All Angles*. Lon. Seeley, Service & Co. 1929. 1st ed.
illus. .... *$25.00–$60.00*

Taverner, P. A. *Birds of Canada*. 1938. rprnt.. *$30.00–$40.00*

Taverner, P. A. *Birds of Canada*. 1934. illus... *$35.00–$40.00*

Taverner, P. A. *Birds of Eastern Canada*. Canada Dept of Mines, Memois. 1922. ....
.... *$20.00–$25.00*

Taverner, P. A. *Birds of Western Canada*. Ottawa. 1926. 1st ed............. *$30.00–$40.00*

Tax, Sol (ed). *Evolution After Darwin*. Chi. Univ of Chi Press. 1960. 1st ed. dj............
.... *$45.00–$60.00*

Taylor, Bayard. *Eldorado*. NY. Putnam. 1850. 1st ed. 1st issue. 2 vols. 8 tinted plates,
original cloth.. *$400.00–$585.00*

Taylor, Griffith. *With Scott: The Silver Lining*. Lon. 1916. 1st ed. illus. maps...............
.... *$450.00–$700.00*

Taylor, Henry Dixon. *Church Welfare Plan*. np. 1984. illus. inscrb........ *$60.00–$75.00*

Taylor, J. *Lives of Virginia Baptist Ministers*. Richmond. 1838. 2nd ed. lea...................
.... *$35.00–$45.00*

Taylor, J. J. *Physician as a Business Man*. Phila. 1891. cloth................. *$25.00–$75.00*

Taylor, John L. *Memoir of His Honor Samuel Phillips, LL.D*. Bos. 1856. 1st ed. illus. . ... *$30.00–$75.00*

Taylor, Peter. *Happy Families are All Alike*. NY. McDowell and Obolensky. (1959). 1st ed. dj. .... *$80.00–$125.00*

Taylor, Peter. *Old Forest*. NY. 1985. 1st ed. dj. .... *$15.00–$22.00*

Taylor, Peter. *Oracle at Stoneleigh Court*. NY. 1933. 1st ed. dj. .... *$15.00–$22.00*

Taylor, Peter. *Summons to Memphis*. NY. Knopf. 1986. 1st ed. dj. .... *$22.00–$35.00*

Taylor, Peter. *Summons to Memphis*. NY. 1986. dj. .... *$15.00–$25.00*

Taylor, Rev. Wm. *Christian Adventures in South Africa*. NY. Nelson & Phillips. 1876. original cloth... *$35.00–$70.00*

Teerink, H. *Bibliography of the Writings of Jonathan Swift*. Phila. Univ of Penn Press. (1963). 2nd ed. dj. .... *$70.00–$175.00*

Telephone Appeals —1887. 1887. 1st ed. softcvr. .... *$125.00–$165.00*

Telephone Catalogue and Students' Manual for the Practical Instruction of Learners of Telegraphy . . .NY. J H Bunnell & Co. 1900. illus. printed wrps, 112 pp. .... *$40.00–$50.00*

Telescopes for Town and Country. Rochester, NY. Bausch & Lomb Optical Co. 1928. pictorial wrps, illus, 16 pp. .... *$40.00–$50.00*

Tell It All: The Story of a Life's Experience in Mormonism. Hartford. 1874................. .... *$25.00–$35.00*

Teller, Daniel W. *History of Ridgefield, Ct*. Danbury. 1878. illus. ¾ mor...................... .... *$50.00–$75.00*

Tennien, Mark. *Chungking Listening Post*. NY. Creative Age Press. 1945. 1st ed. illus. red cloth. map. endpapers. dj. .... *$12.00–$20.00*

Tennyson, Alfred. *Harold: A Drama*. Lon. Henry S King. 1877. 1st ed. *$25.00–$50.00*

Tennyson, Alfred. *Ode on the Death of Wellington*. Lon. Edward Moxon. 1853. printed wrps. .... *$35.00–$100.00*

Tennyson, Alfred. *Passing of Arthur*. Lon. Macmillan. 1884. 1st ed. printed wrps......... .... *$200.00–$300.00*

Tennyson, Alfred Lord. *Tiresias and Other Poems*. Lon. 1885. 1st ed. 12mo. .... *$60.00–$80.00*

Terkel, Studs. *Division Street: America*. Pantheon. 1967. 1st ed. dj....... *$28.00–$35.00*

Terkel, Studs. *Working*. Pantheon. 1974. 1st ed. dj. .... *$25.00–$30.00*

Terrell, John Upton. *War for the Colorado River*. CA. Arthur H. Clark Co. 1965. 2 vols. 1st ed. dj. .... *$110.00–$125.00*

Terrell, Mary Church. *A Colored Woman in a White World*. DC. National Association of Clred Women's Clubs. 1968. 1st ed. wrps. .... *$25.00–$35.00*

Terry, Adrian. *Travels in the Equatorial Regions of South America in 1832*. Hartford. 1832. 1st ed. 290 pp. .... *$100.00–$150.00*

Terry, Ellen. *Story of My Life*. NY. 1908. .... *$20.00–$35.00*

Terry, Ellen. *Story of My Life*. Lon. 1908. illus. ltd 1,000 cc, plates, teg, sgn. ....
.... *$125.00–$150.00*

Tesla, Nikola. *Experiments with Alternate Currents of High Potential and High Frequency*. NY. 1896. illus. .... *$95.00–$125.00*

Tesla, Nikola. *Lectures, Patents, Articles Published by Nikols Tesla Museum*. CA. 1973. rprnt, illus, wrps... *$60.00–$75.00*

Thacher, J. *American Revolution*. Hartford. 1861. illus. .... *$37.00–$55.00*

Thacher, James. *History of Plymouth Mass*. Bos. 1832. map.............. *$75.00–$200.00*

Thackeray, William Makepeace. *History of Pendinnis*. NY. Limited Editions Club. 1961. 2 vols. illus. clred plates by Charles Stewart, 932/1,500 cc sgn..... *$20.00–$30.00*

Thatcher, James, M. D. *History of the Town of Plymouth, From its First Settlement in 1620 to the Present Time. . . .* Bos. 1835. illus. map. .... *$135.00–$250.00*

Thayer, Tiffany. *Doctor Arnold*. (NY). Julian Messner. 1934. 1st ed..... *$30.00–$45.00*

Thayer, William. *Marvels of the New West*. Norwich. 1889. .... *$50.00–$75.00*

The Gift: A Christmas, New Year and Birthday Present. Phila. Carey & Hart. 1845. 1st ed. first issue, illus,.. *$200.00–$275.00*

Theory of the Universe. NY. 1868.. *$50.00–$65.00*

Theroux, Paul. *Black House*. Houghton. 1974. 1st ed. dj. .... *$30.00–$35.00*

Theroux, Paul. *London Embassy*. Bos. 1983. 1st Amer ed. dj. .... *$25.00–$32.00*

Theroux, Paul. *Mosquito Coast*. Houghton Mifflin. 1982. 1st ed. dj...... *$35.00–$50.00*

Theroux, Paul. *O Zone*. Lon. Hamish Hamilton. (1986). 1st ed. sgn, dj. ....
.... *$40.00–$50.00*

Theroux, Paul. *Saint Jack*. Bos. 1973. 1st ed. dj, sgn. .... *$95.00–$100.00*

Third Annual Report of the Geological Survey of Texas. Austin, TX. wrps..................
.... *$24.00–$50.00*

Third Marine Division. Wash. 1948. 1st ed. .... *$42.00–$50.00*

Thirkell, Angela. *High Rising and Wild Strawberries*. NY. 1951. 2 vols. 1st ed. djs. .....
.... *$25.00–$40.00*

Thirkell, Angela. *Love at All Ages*. NY. 1959. 1st US ed........................ *$18.00–$22.50*

This Is Japan. Asahl Shimbun. 1958. illus. slipcase, dj........................... *$40.00–$65.00*

Thomas, Dylan. *Beach of Falesa*. NY. Stein and Day. 1963. 1st ed. dj. .. *$15.00–$30.00*

Thomas, Dylan. *Child's Christmas in Wales*. CT. New Directions. 1954. 1st ed. dj........
.... *$60.00–$200.00*

Thomas, Dylan. *New Poems*. CT. New Directions. 1943. 1st ed. purple bds, dj. ....
.... *$60.00–$100.00*

Thomas, Dylan. *Portrait of the Artist as a Young Dog*. CT. New Directions. 1940. 1st Amer ed. no dj... *$15.00–$20.00*

Thomas, Dylan. *Prospect of the Sea*. Lon. Dent. (1955). 1st ed. dj........ *$45.00–$60.00*

Thomas, Dylan. *Quite Early One Morning*. CT. New Directions. 1954. 1st Amer ed. dj.
.... *$20.00–$45.00*

Thomas, Dylan. *Under Milk Wood*. New Directions. 1954. 1st ed. dj. ... *$30.00–$70.00*

Thomas, Dylan. *World I Breathe*. Norfolk. New Directions. (1939). 1st ed. ltd 700 cc.. .... *$95.00–$120.00*

Thomas, Fred D. *Darktown's Daily Dozen*. Exposition Press. (1948). illus. presentation copy from author. .... *$35.00–$50.00*

Thomas, Isaiah. *Holy Bible Containing the Old and New Testaments*. Worcester. 1800. .... *$120.00–$150.00*

Thomas, John J. *Farm Implements and Farm Machinery*. NY. Orange Judd. 1869. ed. illus. .... *$85.00–$125.00*

Thomas, Katherine. *Women in Nazi Germany*. Lon. 1943. 1st ed.......... *$25.00–$35.00*

Thomas, Lowell. *Old Gimlet Eye. The Adventures of Smedley D. Butler*. NY. 1933. 1st ed. sgn by author and Butler.. *$125.00–$175.00*

Thomas, Lowell, Jr. *Out of This World*. NY. Greystone Press. (1950). 1st ed. illus. dj map endpapers. .... *$17.00–$25.00*

Thomas, Will. *God Is For White Folks*. NY. Creative Age Press. 1947. 1st ed. dj.......... .... *$100.00–$135.00*

Thomas, Will. *God Is for White Folks*. NY. 1947. 1st ed. dj. .... *$15.00–$20.00*

Thomas, William Hamilton. *American Negro*. NY. Macmillan. 1901. 1st ed. cloth. .... *$175.00–$250.00*

Thompson Seton, Ernest. *Ernest Thompson Seton's America*. NY. 1954. 1st ed. 1st ptg, dj. .... *$20.00–$30.00*

Thompson, D. P. *History of the Town of Montpelier*. Montpelier. 1860. *$30.00–$50.00*

Thompson, George. *Narrative of . . . Attempting to Aid Some Slaves*. Hartford. 1854. cloth. .... *$60.00–$75.00*

Thompson, Henry T. *Ousting the Carpetbagger from South Carolina*. Columbia. Bryan Co. 1927. 2nd ed. illus. dj. .... *$60.00–$75.00*

Thompson, Hunter S. *Great Shark Hunt*. NY. Summit/Rolling Stone. (1979). 1st ed.... .... *$45.00–$75.00*

Thompson, James. *The Seasons*. NY. 1816. illus. woodcuts, lea............ *$40.00–$50.00*

Thompson, Jim. *Nothing More Than Murder*. NY. Harper & Bros. (1949). 1st ed........ .... *$25.00–$40.00*

Thompson, Kay. *Eloise in Paris*. NY. Simon and Schuster. 1957. 1st ed. illus. by Hilary Knight. .... *$250.00–$300.00*

Thompson, Lieut.-Col. R. R. *Fifty-Second (Lowland) Division*. Glasgow. Maclehose Jackson. 1923. illus. frontis. blue cloth. 11 maps in back of book....... *$150.00–$230.00*

Thompson, Margaret. *High Trails of Glacier National Park*. Caldwell. Caxton Printers. 1936. 1st ed. illus. photos, map, cloth, dj.. *$80.00–$100.00*

Thompson, Ruth Plumly. *Cowardly Lion of Oz*. Reilly & Lee. (1923). 1st ed. illus. by J R Neill, 12 plates, dj. .... *$300.00–$400.00*

Thompson, Ruth Plumly. *Gnome King of Oz*. Reilly & Lee. (1927). 1st ed. illus. by J R Neill, 12 plates.. *$200.00–$350.00*

Thompson, Ruth Plumly. *Hungry Tiger of Oz*. Reilly & Lee. 1926. illus. by J R Neill pictorial green cvr. .... *$200.00–$400.00*

Thompson, Ruth Plumly. *Lost King of Oz.* Chi. (1925). illus. by John R Neill. 12 clr plates. .... *$140.00–$250.00*

Thompson, Ruth Plumly. *Purple Prince of Oz.* Reilly & Lee. (1932). 1st ed. illus. by J R Neill, 12 plates. .... *$600.00–$700.00*

Thompson, Ruth Plumly. *Wishing Horse of Oz.* Reilly & Lee. (1935). 1st ed. illus. by J R Neill, 12 plates. .... *$225.00–$400.00*

Thompson, Ruth Plumly. *Yellow Knight of Oz.* Reilly & Lee. 1930. illus. b/w. brown cloth. .... *$100.00–$150.00*

Thompson, Susan Otis. *American Book Design and William Morris.* NY. 1977. illus. dj. .... *$50.00–$70.00*

Thompson, W. G. *Training-Schools for Nursing.* NY. Putnam. 1883. 1st ed. .... *$90.00–$150.00*

Thompson, Zadock. *Geography and Geology of Vermont . . . State & County Outline Maps.* VT. 1848. illus. maps. .... *$50.00–$85.00*

Thompson, Zadock. *History of Vermont.* Burlington. 1842. illus. engr. . *$30.00–$75.00*

Thomson, J. J. *Corpuscular Theory of Matter.* Lon. 1907. 1st ed. .... *$55.00–$100.00*

Thoreau, Henry David. *Cape Cod.* NY. Bromhall. 1951. cloth. .... *$12.00–$20.00*

Thoreau, Henry David. *Cape Cod.* Bos. Ticknor & Fields. 1865. 1st ed. .... *$500.00–$700.00*

Thoreau, Henry David. *Maine Woods.* Bos. 1864. 1st ed. orig green cloth. .... *$400.00–$450.00*

Thoreau, Henry David. *Men of Concord.* Bos. Houghton Mifflin. 1936. illus. by N C Wyeth, dj. .... *$45.00–$60.00*

Thoreau, Henry David. *Walden or Life in the Woods.* Bos. The Bibliophile Society. 1909. 2 vols. illus. ltd, slipcases. .... *$600.00–$900.00*

Thoreau, Henry David. *Walden, or Life in the Woods.* Peter Pauper Press. illus. slipcase. .... *$20.00–$45.00*

Thoreau, Henry David. *Walden.* Bos. 1854. 1st ed. .... *$1,600.00–$3,000.00*

Thorne, Diana and Albert Payson Terhune. *Dog Book.* Akron. Saalfield. (1932). 1st ed. illus. clr plates. .... *$60.00–$90.00*

Thorpe, T. E. *Dictionary of Applied Chemistry.* Lon. Longmans Green & Co. 1898. 4th impression. .... *$15.00–$22.00*

Thrasher, Halsey. *Hunter & Trapper.* 1863. .... *$65.00–$100.00*

Three Bears. Wis. Whitman Pub Co. (1927). 1st ed. illus. linen-like finish. .... *$15.00–$30.00*

Thrum, I. *Hawaiian Folk Tales.* Chi. 1912. illus. .... *$45.00–$100.00*

Thurber, James. *Fables For Our Time.* NY. 1940. 2nd issue. .... *$25.00–$40.00*

Thurber, James. *Is Sex Necessary.* NY. 1929. author's first book. ...... *$350.00–$500.00*

Thurber, James. *Wonderful O.* NY. Simon & Schuster. (1957). 1st ed. illus. clr, dj. .... *$25.00–$50.00*

Thurman, Arnold. *Folklore of Capitalism.* New Haven. 1937. 1st ed. . *$85.00–$115.00*

Thurston, Robert. *History of the Growth of the Steam-Engine.* NY. 1878.....................
.... *$45.00–$60.00*

Thwaites, Reuben and Louise Kellogg (ed.). *Documentary History of Dunmore's War 1774.* Madison, WI. Wisconsin Historical Society. 1905. 1st ed. illus. 1/1,000 cc, 472 pp, maps.. *$100.00–$225.00*

Tillotson, John. *Palestine, Egypt and Syria with the History of the Jews.* Phila. clr maps, illus. .... *$70.00–$85.00*

Tilman, H. W. *Ascent of Nanda Devi.* NY. Macmillan. 1937. 1st ed. photos, maps, dj. .
.... *$55.00–$75.00*

Tilton, Theodore. *Sexton's Tale.* NY. Sheldon. 1867. 1st ed. author's first book. ....
.... *$35.00–$60.00*

Tjader, Richard. *Big Game of Africa.* NY. Appleton. 1910. 1 vol. 1st ed. map, plates...
.... *$225.00–$250.00*

Tocqueville, Alexis de. *Democracy in America.* NY. 1840. 2nd Amer ed. cloth.............
.... *$100.00–$250.00*

Tocqueville, Alexis de. *Democratie en Amerique.* 1849. 2 vols. .... *$50.00–$100.00*

Todd, W. E. C. *Birds of the Labrador Penninsula and Adjacent Areas.* Tor. 1963. illus.
.... *$50.00–$75.00*

Todd, W. E. C. *Birds of Western Pennsylvania.* Univ of Pittsburgh. 1940. ....
.... *$70.00–$85.00*

Toffler, Alvin. *Future Shock.* NY. 1970. dj... *$15.00–$20.00*

Toklas, Alice B. *Alice B. Toklas Cook Book.* NY. Harper & Bros. 1954. 1st ed. illus......
.... *$35.00–$50.00*

Toler, Ernst. *Man and the Masses.* Garden City. 1924. 1st ed. 109 pp, photos. ....
.... *$60.00–$75.00*

Tolkien, J. R. R. *Father Christmas Letters.* Bos. Houghton Mifflin. 1976. 1st ed. ....
.... *$55.00–$80.00*

Tolkien, J. R. R. *Lord of the Rings.* Bos. Houghton, Mifflin. 1963. 3 vols. boxed. djs...
.... *$50.00–$75.00*

Tolkien, J. R. R. *Pictures.* Bos. Houghton Mifflin. 1979. 1st Amer ed. slipcase.............
.... *$65.00–$80.00*

Tolkien, J. R. R. *Smith of Wooton Major.* Bos. Houghton, Mifflin. 1967. illus. by Pauline Baynes, 1st Amer ed. dj.. *$50.00–$75.00*

Tolkien, J. R. R. *The Hobbit.* Bos. Houghton Mifflin. (1968). green decorated cvr........
.... *$70.00–$85.00*

Tolkien, J. R. R. *The Hobbitt.* Bos. 1966. illus. no dj. .... *$25.00–$50.00*

Tolkien, J. R. R. *The Silmarillion.* 1977. 1st ed. dj. .... *$45.00–$100.00*

Tolkien, J. R. R. *Tree and Leaf.* Bos. Houghton Mifflin. 1965. 1st Amer ed. 112 pp, dj.
.... *$50.00–$65.00*

Tolley, Cyril. *Modern Golfer.* NY. 1924. illus....................................... *$30.00–$50.00*

Tolstoi, Alexis. *Vampires: Stories of the Supernatural.* NY. 1969. 1st Eng language ed. dj. .... *$40.00–$50.00*

Tomes, Robert. *Battles of America by Sea and Land.* NY. 1878. 3 vols. illus.................
.... *$145.00–$175.00*

Tooker, William W. *Indian Place-Names on Long Island* . . . NY. 1911.......................
.... *$35.00–$40.00*

Tooley, R. V. *English Books with Coloured Plates.* Lon. Batsford. (1954). 1st ed. illus.
.... *$80.00–$120.00*

Tooley, R. V. *Maps and Map-makers.* Lon. BT Batsford. (1949). 1st ed. illus. dj...........
.... *$25.00–$35.00*

Towne, H. R. *Treatise on Cranes.* Conn. 1883. .... *$40.00–$50.00*

Townsend, William John. *Madagascar: Its Missionaries and Martyrs.* Lon. S. W. Partridge. illus. wood engr, brown cloth, gilt lettering. .... *$50.00–$80.00*

Train, Arthur. *Mortmain.* NY. Appleton. 1907. 1st ed............................ *$30.00–$45.00*

Train, Arthur. *Page Mr. Tutt.* NY. Scribner's. 1926. 1st ed. dj. .... *$30.00–$35.00*

Train, Arthur. *World of Thomas Kelly.* NY. Scribner's. 1917. 1st ed. inscrb, dj..............
.... *$25.00–$35.00*

Train, Arthur. *Yankee Lawyer—The Autobiography of Ephraim Tutt.* NY. 1943. 1st ed. illus. dj.. *$35.00–$50.00*

Travels in South Eastern Asia. NY. Sunday School Union. 1838. illus.. *$10.00–$20.00*

Traven, B. *March to Caobaland.* Lon. Robert Hale. 1961. 1st ed in Eng, dj................
.... *$50.00–$115.00*

Traver, Robert. *Anatomy of a Fisherman.* McGraw Hill. 1964. 1st ed. dj.....................
.... *$125.00–$250.00*

Travers, P. C. *Maria Poppina* . . . NY. Harcourt Brace. 1968. 1st ed. illus. by Mary Shepard. dj.. *$30.00–$50.00*

Treece, Henry. *Haunted Garden.* Lon. 1947. 1st ed. dj. .... *$30.00–$45.00*

Tremaine, Marie. *Bibliography of Canadian Imprints, 1751–1800.* Tor. 1952. ....
.... *$90.00–$150.00*

Trevelyan, Francis Miller. *World in the Air.* NY & Lon. Putnam. 1930. 2 vols. 1st ed. cloth. dj.. *$75.00–$100.00*

Trevers, Frederick. *Uganda for a Holiday.* Lon. Smith Elder. 1910. 1st ed. 2nd impr. illus. photos, plates.. *$60.00–$90.00*

Treves, Sir Frederick. *Land That Is Desolate.* NY. Dutton. 1912. illus. 1st Amer ed.....
.... *$30.00–$50.00*

Trevor, William. *Family Sins.* Viking. (1990). 1st Amer ed. dj. .... *$25.00–$35.00*

Trevor, William. *Old Boys.* NY. 1964. 1st ed. dj................................. *$85.00–$100.00*

Trial of Andrew Johnson, President of the US. Wash. GPO. 1868. 3 vols.....................
.... *$50.00–$100.00*

Trilling, Lionel. *Liberal Imagination.* NY. Viking. 1950. 1st ed. dj........ *$25.00–$35.00*

Trilling, Lionel. *Middle of the Journey.* NY. 1947. 1st ed. sgn. .... *$45.00–$65.00*

Trimble, Harvey M. *History of the 93rd Regiment Illinois Volunteer Infantry.* Chi. 1898. illus. fldg map.. *$125.00–$150.00*

Trip Around the World in an Automobile. McLoughlin Bros. 1907. wrps. illus. lithos. .
.... *$50.00–$80.00*

Triscott, C. Pette. *Golf in Six Lessons*. Phila. nd. 1st ed. illus............... *$30.00–$40.00*

Trollope, A. *West Indies and the Spanish Main*. NY. 1860. 1st Amer ed. *$70.00–$90.00*

Trollope, Anthony. *Bertrams*. The Folio Society. 1993.......................... *$40.00–$55.00*

Trollope, Anthony. *Can You Forgive Her*. Lon. 1864. 2 vols. 1st ed. illus. ....
.... *$135.00–$250.00*

Trollope, Anthony. *Chronicles of Barsetshire*. Bos. Lauriat. 1926. 6 vols. illus. ....
.... *$150.00–$175.00*

Trollope, Anthony. *Last Chronicle of Barset*. Lon. 1867. 2 vols in one. ....
.... *$110.00–$125.00*

Trollope, Anthony. *North America*. Phil. Lippincott. 1862. 2 vols in one. 1st Amer ed. .
.... *$100.00–$200.00*

Trollope, Anthony. *Small House at Allington*. NY. Harper & Bros. 1864. 1st Amer ed.
cloth. .... *$100.00–$150.00*

Trollope, Anthony. *Vicar of Bullhampton*. NY. Harper. 1870. 1st Amer ed. ....
.... *$175.00–$225.00*

Trollope, Frances. *Life and Adventures of Jonathan Jefferson Whitlaw*. Lon. 1836. 3
vols. 15 engr... *$250.00–$350.00*

Trotsky, Leon. *Stalin*. NY. Harper & Bros. 1941. 1st Amer ed.............. *$30.00–$50.00*

Trotter, William. *On the Rearing and Management of Poultry*. Lon. 1852. wrps. illus. .
.... *$28.00–$35.00*

Trowbridge, Bertha Chadwick. *Old Houses of Connecticut*. New Haven. Yale Univ.
1923. 1,000 cc. sgn. teg... *$100.00–$150.00*

Trowbridge, J. T. *South: A Tour of Its Battlefields and Ruined Cities* . . . CT. 1866. 1st
ed. illus. .... *$45.00–$55.00*

Trowbridge, J. T. *Vagabonds*. NY. Hurd & Houghton. 1869. 1st ed. illus. ....
.... *$60.00–$90.00*

Truman, Harry. *Memoirs by Harry S. Truman*. Garden City. 1955, 1956. 2 vols. 1st ed.
sgn, dj. .... *$350.00–$380.00*

Truman, Margaret. *Harry S. Truman*. NY. 1973. photos. .... *$35.00–$45.00*

Truman, Margaret. *Murder in Georgetown*. NY. Arbor House. 1986. 1st ed. dj...........
.... *$10.00–$27.00*

Truman, Margaret. *Murder in the CIA*. 1987. 1st ed. dj......................... *$6.00–$10.00*

Truman, Margaret. *Murder in the CIA*. NY. Random House. 1987. 1st ed. dj..............
.... *$20.00–$25.00*

Truman, Margaret. *Murder in the Smithsonian*. 1983. 1st ed. dj........... *$10.00–$20.00*

Truman, Margaret. *Murder in the White House*. 1980. dj...................... *$18.00–$25.00*

Truman, Margaret. *Murder on Embassy Row*. 1984. 1st ed. dj. .... *$12.00–$18.00*

Trumbull, Benjamine. *Compendium of the Indian Wars of New England*. Hartford.
Edwin Valentine Mitchell. 1926. 1st ed. wrps. ltd 400 cc. .... *$75.00–$100.00*

Trumbull, James Hammond. *Natick Dictionary*. DC. GPO. 1903. 1st ed. 347 pp. Bulletin 25. .... *$50.00–$125.00*

Tschopik, Harry. *Navaho Pottery Making*. Cambridge, MA. 1941. illus. printed wrps, plates. .... *$60.00–$75.00*

Tuckerman, A. *Index to the Literature of Thermodynamics*. Wash. 1890. inscrb. .... *$50.00–$75.00*

Tuckerman, A. *Short History of Architecture*. NY. 1887. illus. calf .... *$75.00–$95.00*

Tudor, Tasha. *Corgiville Fair*. NY. Crowell. 1971. illus. dj. .... *$38.00–$50.00*

Tudor, Tasha. *Fairy Tales by Hans Christian Anderson*. NY. Oxford Univ Press. (1945). 1st ed. illus. dj. .... *$85.00–$125.00*

Tudor, Tasha. *First Delights*. NY. (1966). 1st ed. inscrb. .... *$130.00–$150.00*

Tudor, Tasha. *Give Us This Day—The Lord's Prayer*. NY. (1987). 1st ed. inscrb, dj...... .... *$35.00–$65.00*

Tudor, Tasha. *Night Before Christmas*. Chi. Rand McNally. 1975. illus. by Tudor. tall 4to. .... *$65.00–$85.00*

Tudor, Tasha. *Night Before Christmas*. Chi. Rand McNally. 1984. 9th ptg. .... *$35.00–$40.00*

Tullidge, Edward W. *Life of Brigham Young*. NY. 1876. 1st ed. .... *$60.00–$80.00*

Tunis, Edwin. *Wheels, a Pictorial History*. Cleve. World. 1954. 1st ed. illus. dj. .... *$35.00–$65.00*

Turbott, E. G. (ed.). *Bullers Birds of New Zealand*. East West Center Press. 1967. dj. .. .. *$60.00–$80.00*

Turner, L. M. *Contributions to the Natural History of Alaska*. DC. GPO. 1886. 1st ed. illus. 26 litho plates. .... *$40.00–$80.00*

Turner, William. *Transfer Printing on Enamels, Porcelain & Pottery*. Lon. 1907. illus. .... *$115.00–$150.00*

Tuttle, Charles. *An Illustrated History of the State of Wisconsin*. 1875.. *$55.00–$75.00*

Tuttle, Florence Guertin. *Awakening of Woman*. NY. Abingdon Press. (1915). 1st ed. dj. .... *$60.00–$75.00*

Twain, Mark. *Adventures of Huckleberry Finn*. NY. The Heritage Press. (1940). illus. by Norman Rockwell slipcase. .... *$20.00–$40.00*

Twain, Mark. *Adventures of Tom Sawyer*. 1876. 1st Amer ed. 2nd ptg. .... *$450.00–$1,250.00*

Twain, Mark. *Curious Republic of Gondour*. NY. Boni & Liveright. 1919. 1st ed. 140 pp, dj. .... *$350.00–$800.00*

Twain, Mark. *Dog's Tale*. Lon. Anti-National Vivisection Society. 1903. wrps. First separate ed, original stiff wrps. .... *$200.00–$350.00*

Twain, Mark. *Europe and Elsewhere*. NY. Harper. (1923). 1st ed. 406 pp, intro by A B Paine, dj. .... *$700.00–$900.00*

Twain, Mark. *Extract from Captain Stormfield's Visit to Heaven*. NY. Harper & Bros. 1909. 1st ed. .... *$100.00–$125.00*

Twain, Mark. *Following the Equator*. Hartford. Amer Pub Co. 1897. 1st ed. first state 8vo, 712 pp, blue cloth. .... *$125.00–$250.00*

Twain, Mark. *Innocents Abroad* . . . NY. Limited Editions Club. 1962. illus. by Fritz Kredel, 932/1,500 cc, sgn. slipcase. .... *$40.00–$65.00*

Twain, Mark. *Letters From the Earth*. NY. Harper & Row. 1962. blue cloth, dj. .... *$45.00–$75.00*

Twain, Mark. *Life on the Mississippi*. NY. Heritage Press. (1944). illus. by Thomas Hart Benton. .... *$10.00–$15.00*

Twain, Mark. *Life on the Mississippi*. Bos. 1883. 1st ed. 2nd state.... *$125.00–$150.00*

Twain, Mark. *Life on the Mississippi*. 1883. 1st Amer ed. 1st issue... *$250.00–$550.00*

Twain, Mark. *Mark Twain's Autobiography*. NY. Harper. 1924. 2 vols. illus. teg. .... *$40.00–$60.00*

Twain, Mark. *Mark Twain's Sketches, New and Old*. Hartford. 1875. 1st ed. 2nd state. illus. blue cloth. .... *$20.00–$40.00*

Twain, Mark. *Prince and the Pauper*. NY. Grosset & Dunlap. 1921. dj. rprnt. .... *$8.00–$15.00*

Twain, Mark. *Pudd'nhead Wilson* . . . Hartford. 1894. 1st US ed....... *$100.00–$185.00*

Twain, Mark. *Roughing It*. NY. Time Life Books. imitation brown leather. .... *$15.00–$20.00*

Twain, Mark. *Tom Sawyer Abroad*. NY. Grosset & Dunlap. 1924. illus. dj. .... *$12.00–$20.00*

Twain, Mark. *Tramp Abroad*. NY. Limited Editions Club. (1966). illus. by David Knight, 932/1,500 cc sgn slipcase. .... *$25.00–$35.00*

Twain, Mark (Clemens, Samuel L). *Innocents Abroad*. Leipzig. Bernhard Tauchnitz. 1879. 2 vols in 1. Authorized ed. 1st ptg, 16mo, half lea, inscrb. ..... *$800.00–$1,000.00*

Twenty Sixth Annual Catalogue of Fancy Goods and Toys . . .Bos. Cutter, Hyde & Co. 1870s. illus. .... *$65.00–$75.00*

Twiss, Travers. *Oregon Territory, Its History and Discovery*. . . NY. Appleton. 1846. 1st Amer ed. 264 pp. .... *$180.00–$225.00*

Tyler, Anne. *Accidental Tourist*. Knopf. 1985. dj. .... *$20.00–$35.00*

Tyler, Anne. *Accidental Tourist*. NY. Knopf. 1985. 1st ed. dj. .... *$50.00–$175.00*

Tyler, Anne. *Dinner at the Homesick Restaurant*. NY. Knopf. 1982. 1st ed. dj. .... *$45.00–$60.00*

Tyler, Anne. *Saint Maybe*. NY. Knopf. 1991. 1st ed. dj. .... *$50.00–$85.00*

Tyler, Anne. *Searching for Caleb*. NY. Knopf. 1975. 1st ed. dj. .... *$175.00–$200.00*

Tytler, Patrick F. *Historical View of the Progress of Discovery on the More Northern Coasts of America*. Edin. 1832. cloth fldg map. .... *$90.00–$120.00*

U.S. Camera. NY. 1945. .... *$30.00–$50.00*

U.S. Camera. 1953. .... *$12.00–$20.00*

U.S. Camera. 1936. .... *$25.00–$50.00*

U.S. Camera. 1943. .... *$15.00–$25.00*

U.S. Cartridge Company's Collection of Firearms. US Cartridge Co. nd. cat. .... *$35.00–$50.00*

Ude, Louis Eustache. *French Cook.* Phila. 1828. rbkd with leather. .. *$295.00–$375.00*

Ulrich, Arthur. *Colt: A Century of Achievement.* Hartford. 1936. illus. pictorial cvr...... .... *$30.00–$40.00*

Underhill, Ruth. *Here Come the Navaho.* KA. Bureau of Indian Affairs. 1953. illus. pictorial wrps. .... *$12.00–$45.00*

Underhill, Ruth. *Workaday Life of the Pueblos.* AZ. Bureau of Indian Affairs. 1954. illus. pictorial wrps. .... *$15.00–$20.00*

Undertakers' Specialties. Catalogue No XVII. Albany or Rochester, NY. National Casket Co. August, 1903. illus. paper-cvred cloth wrps, 120 pp............... *$50.00–$75.00*

Underwood, L. H. *With Tommy Tompkins In Korea.* Revell. (1905)...... *$25.00–$35.00*

Underwood, Rev. J. L. *Women of the Confederacy.* Neale. 1906. 1st ed....................... .... *$145.00–$175.00*

United States Bureau of American Ethnology. *Twenty eighth Annual Report. Smithsonian Institution.* Wash. 1912. illus. 102 plates. .... *$125.00–$175.00*

Universal Indian Sign Language. Boy Scouts. 1929. .... *$32.00–$45.00*

Updike, Daniel Berkeley. *Printing Types.* Cam. 1927. 2 vols. 1st ptg of 2nd ed., dj...... .... *$75.00–$100.00*

Updike, Daniel Berkeley. *Some Aspects of Printing, Old and New.* New Haven. Rudge. 1941. 1st ed.. *$30.00–$45.00*

Updike, John. *Bech Is Back.* NY. Knopf. 1982. dj. .... *$14.00–$35.00*

Updike, John. *Hoping for a Hoopoe.* Lon. Victor Gollancz. 1959. 1st Eng ed. author's first book, dj.. *$65.00–$125.00*

Updike, John. *Hugging the Shore.* Knopf. 1983. 1st ed. dj.................. *$22.00–$27.00*

Updike, John. *Month of Sundays.* NY. Knopf. 1975. 1st ed. dj. .... *$20.00–$35.00*

Updike, John. *Odd Jobs.* NY. Knopf. 1991. 1st ed. dj. .... *$40.00–$50.00*

Updike, John. *Of the Farm.* Knopf. 1965. 1st ed. dj. .... *$100.00–$125.00*

Updike, John. *Pigeon Feathers.* NY. 1962. 1st ed. dj........................... *$50.00–$135.00*

Updike, John. *Poorhouse Fair.* NY. Borzoi. 1959. 1st ed. dj............... *$85.00–$100.00*

Updike, John. *Problems and Other Stories.* NY. Knopf. 1979. 1st ed. dj...................... .... *$15.00–$65.00*

Updike, John. *Rabbit at Rest.* NY. Knopf. 1990. 1st ed. dj..................... *$20.00–$40.00*

Updike, John. *Rabbit Is Rich.* NY. Knopf. 1981. 1st ed. sgn, dj........... *$85.00–$100.00*

Updike, John. *Rabbit Redux.* NY. Knopf. 1971. 1st ed. .... *$15.00–$30.00*

Updike, John. *Rabbit Redux.* NY. Knopf. 1971. 1st ed. dj..................... *$25.00–$30.00*

Updike, John. *Rabbit Run.* NY. Knopf. 1960. 1st ed. dj. .... *$50.00–$100.00*

Updike, John. *Same Door.* NY. Knopf. (1959). 1st ed. cloth-bkd bds. dj...................... .... *$85.00–$100.00*

Updike, John. *The Centaur.* NY. Knopf. 1963. 1st ed. dj. .... *$35.00–$50.00*

Updike, John. *Trust Me*. NY. 1987. 1st ed. dj. .... *$18.00–$25.00*

Updike, John. *Twelve Terrors of Christmas*. NY. Gotham. (1993). 1st ed. wrps. illus. by Edward Gorey. sgn by author and illustrator....................................... *$100.00–$160.00*

Updike, John. *Witches of Eastwick*. NY. Knopf. 1984. dj. .... *$12.00–$30.00*

Updike, Wilkins. *History of the Narragansett Church*. Bos. 1907. 3 vols...................... .... *$75.00–$125.00*

Upham, Charles. *Salem Witchcraft* . . . Bos. Wiggin & Lunt. 1867. 2 vols. wrps. green cloth. .... *$175.00–$250.00*

Upham, Elizabeth. *Little Brown Bear*. Platt & Munk. (1942). illus. by Marjorie Hartwell. .... *$65.00–$125.00*

Urban, John W. *In Defense of the Union*. Wash. 1887. 1st ed. illus. ..... *$35.00–$45.00*

Uris, Leon. *Exodus*. NY. Doubleday & Co. 1st ed. dj. .... *$30.00–$85.00*

Uses of Elleman's Embrocation. Slough. 1902. 3rd ed. illus, 188 pp..... *$35.00–$45.00*

Utah. Hastings House. 1941. black cloth.. *$35.00–$45.00*

Vaillant, George C. *Aztecs of Mexico*. NY. Garden City. 1950. illus. dj. tan decorated cvr and endpapers. .... *$25.00–$40.00*

Valk, M. H. A. van der. *De Profeet Der Mormonene Joseph Smith Jr*. Kampen. 1921. illus. photos.. *$80.00–$95.00*

Van de Water, Frederic F. *Glory Hunter: a Life of General Custer*. Ind. Bobbs Merrill. (1934). 1st ed. illus. plates, maps.. *$85.00–$135.00*

Van Dine, S. S. *Green Murder Case*. NY. Scribner's. 1928. 1st ed. no dj...................... ....*$10.00–$20.00*

Van Dine, S. S. *Canary Murder Case*. NY. Scribner's. 1929. Photoplay ed. dj. .... *$100.00–$150.00*

Van Dine, S. S. *Gracie Allen Murder Case*. NY. Scribner's. 1938. 1st ed. dj. .... *$100.00–$250.00*

Van Dine, S. S. *Bishop Murder Case*. NY. Scribner's. 1929. 1st ed. dj... *$35.00–$50.00*

Van Dine, S. S. *Dragon Murder Case*. NY. Scribner's. 1933. 1st ed. dj........................... .... *$120.00–$200.00*

Van Dine, S. S. *Dragon Murder Case*. Grosset & Dunlap. 1933. dj. ...... *$20.00–$30.00*

Van Dine, S. S. *Scarab Murder Case*. NY. 1930. 1st ed. dj................. *$100.00–$225.00*

Van Dyke, Henry. *Travel Diary of an Angler*. Derrydale Press. 1929. illus. ltd 750 cc. .... *$225.00–$250.00*

Van Dyke, Theodore S. *Southern California*. NY. 1886. 1st ed. sgn.. *$100.00–$125.00*

Van Gieson, Judith. *Raptor*. NY. (1990). 1st ed. dj. .... *$30.00–$125.00*

Van Gulik, Robert. *Chinese Bell Murders*. Lon. Michael Joseph. 1958. 1st ed. dj......... .... *$200.00–$300.00*

Van Gulik, Robert. *Chinese Bell Murders*. NY. Harper & Bros. 1959. 1st Amer ed. dj. .... *$55.00–$75.00*

Van Gulik, Robert. *Chinese Lake Murders*. NY. 1960. illus. 1st US ed...................... .... *$75.00–$100.00*

Van Gulik, Robert. *Chinese Nail Murders*. NY. Harper. 1961. 1st Amer ed. dj.............. .... *$65.00–$175.00*

Van Gulik, Robert. *Haunted Monastery*. NY. Scribner's. (1969). 1st ed. dj. .... *$40.00–$65.00*

Van Gulik, Robert. *Judge Dee at Work*. NY. 1973. dj. .... *$25.00–$35.00*

Van Gulik, Robert. *Monkey and the Tiger*. NY. Scribner's. 1965. 1st US ed. dj............ .... *$40.00–$75.00*

Van Gulik, Robert. *Murder in Canton*. NY/Lon. 1966. 1st Amer ed. dj. *$30.00–$75.00*

Van Gulik, Robert. *Necklace and Calabash*. Scribner's. 1967. 1st ed. dj. .... *$40.00–$60.00*

Van Gulik, Robert. *Red Pavilion*. Kuala Lampur. Art Printing Works. 1961. 1st ed. no dj as issued... *$300.00–$350.00*

Van Gulik, Robert. *Willow Pattern*. NY. Scribner's. 1965. 1st ed. dj..... *$50.00–$85.00*

Van Loan's Catskill Mountain Guide and Bird's-eye View . . . NY. 1879. illus. maps... .... *$175.00–$225.00*

Van Ness William P. *An Examination of the Various Charges Exhibited Against Aaron Burr*. NY. Ward and Gould. 1803. 1st ed. complete with errata.......... *$120.00–$130.00*

Van Rensselaer, Stephen. *American Firearms*. NY. Century House. (1947). red cloth. . ... *$25.00–$55.00*

Van Ronk, Dave and Richard Ellington. *Bosses' Songbook . . . Modern Political Songs of Satire*. NY. 1959. 2nd ed. wrps. .... *$65.00–$75.00*

Van Urk, J Blan. *Horse, the Valley and the Chagrin Valley Hunt*. NY. Richard Ellis. 1947. 700 cc teg.. *$75.00–$100.00*

Van Urk, J. Blan. *Story of American Foxhunting*. NY. Derrydale. 1940 and 1941. 2 vols. ltd 950 cc. sgn, djs.. *$450.00–$595.00*

Vanderveer, Helen. *Little Slam Bang*. Volland. 1928. .... *$15.00–$30.00*

Vargas, Alberto. *Vargas: The Esquire Years*. NY. Alfred Van der Marck eds. 1987. 1st ed. dj. .... *$40.00–$60.00*

Variety Inc. *Radio Directory 1937–1938*. 1937. 1st ed. .... *$45.00–$60.00*

Varney, Almon. *Our Homes and Their Adornments; or How to Build, Furnish, and Adorn a Home*. Detroit. J C Chilton. 1885. illus. 486 pp. .... *$50.00–$85.00*

Vassall, Henry. *Football: The Rugby Game*. NY. 1890. 1st ed................ *$65.00–$95.00*

Vaughan, B. F. *Life and Writings of Rev. Henry R. Rush, D.D* . . . Dayton, Oh. 1911. 1st ed. .... *$55.00–$75.00*

Veblin, Thorstein. *An Inquiry into the Nature of Peace and the Terms of Perpetuation*. NY/Lon. Macmillan Co. 1917. 1st ed...................................... *$50.00–$75.00*

Veblin, Thorstein. *Theory of the Leisure Class* . . . NY/Lon. Macmillan Co. 1917. 1st Amer ed. green cloth. .... *$100.00–$150.00*

Verdelle, A. J. *Good Negress*. Chapel Hill. Algonquin. 1995. 1st ed. dj. *$48.00–$60.00*

Verne, Jules. *In Search of the Castaways*. Phila. Lippincott. 1874. illus. 1st Amer ed.... .... *$125.00–$200.00*

Verne, Jules. *Journey to the Centre of the Earth.* NY. Scribner's. 1906. cloth.................
.... *$25.00–$40.00*

Verne, Jules. *Michael Strogoff.* NY. Grosset & Dunlap. 1965. illus. dj... *$15.00–$25.00*

Verne, Jules. *Mysterious Island.* Scribner's. (1920). illus. pictorial cvr, endpapers, 14 clr plates by Wyeth. .... *$25.00–$40.00*

Verne, Jules. *North Against South, a Tale of the American Civil War.* Lon. 1888. illus. by L Benett. .... *$90.00–$125.00*

Verne, Jules. *Their Island Home.* NY. 1924. 1st US ed............................ *$40.00–$50.00*

Verne, Jules. *Tour of the World in Eighty Days.* Bos. Osgood. 1873. 1st Amer trade ed. red cloth... *$150.00–$300.00*

Verne, Jules. *Twenty Thousand Leagues Under the Sea.* NY. Heritage Press. (1956). slipcase.. *$20.00–$30.00*

Verne, Jules. *Voyages et Adventures du Capitaine Hatteras.* Paris. Hetzel. 1867. illus. wood engr, aeg.. *$60.00–$90.00*

Verne, Jules. *Winter in the Ice.* Bos. 1876. .... *$25.00–$35.00*

Verne, Jules. *Wreck of the Chancellor.* Bos. 1875. 1st US ed. .... *$20.00–$30.00*

Verplanck, William E. and Moses W. Collyer, *Sloops of the Hudson.* Port Washington. (1968). rprnt.. *$20.00–$40.00*

Verplanck, William E. and Moses W. Collyer, *Sloops of the Hudson.* NY/Lon. Putnam. 1908. 1st ed. .... *$50.00–$100.00*

Vibert, Henri. *All About Dogs.* Q-W Laboratories. 1921. wrps. illus. .... *$18.00–$25.00*

Victor, O. *History of the Southern Rebellion.* NY. 4 vols. illus. .... *$165.00–$225.00*

Vidal, Gore. *Dark Green Bright Red.* NY. Dutton. 1950. 1st ed. dj...... *$75.00–$130.00*

Vidal, Gore. *Myra Breckinridge.* Little Brown. 1968. 1st ed. dj. .... *$28.00–$35.00*

Vidal, Gore. *Season of Comfort.* NY. 1949. 1st ed. dj............................ *$25.00–$40.00*

Vidal, Gore,. *Lincoln.* NY. Random House. (1984). uncorrected proof. . *$40.00–$50.00*

View Book of the Alaska Highway. Tor. nd. wrps. 16 images................. *$35.00–$50.00*

Visscher, William Lightfoot. *Thrilling and Truthful History of the Pony Express.* Chi. Rand McNally. 1908. 1st ed. illus... *$50.00–$60.00*

Vladislav, Jan. *Italian Fairy Tales.* Lon. Hamlyn Pub Co. 1971. illus. dj.....................
.... *$25.00–$35.00*

Von Chamisso, Adelbert. *Peter Schlemihl.* Lon. Hardwicke. 1861. 3rd ed. illus. by George Crhikshank. .... *$50.00–$80.00*

Vonnegu, Kurt. *Player Piano.* NY. Scribner's. 1952. 1st ed. of author's first book, dj. ..
.... *$300.00–$450.00*

Vonnegut, Kurt. *Canary in a Cat House.* NY. 1962. sgn, dj.............. *$100.00–$125.00*

Vonnegut, Kurt. *Galapagos.* NY. Delecorte. 1985. 1st ed. dj................. *$25.00–$35.00*

Vonnegut, Kurt. *God Bless You, Mr. Rosewater.* Holt Rinehart Winston. 1965. 1st ed. dj.
.... *$95.00–$125.00*

Vonnegut, Kurt. *Jailbird.* np. 1979. 1st ed. dj...................................... *$25.00–$30.00*

Vonnegut, Kurt. *Palm Sunday.* Delacorte. 1981. 1st ed. dj. .... *$15.00–$30.00*

Vonnegut, Kurt. *Precautionary Letter to the Next Generation*. np. 1988......................
.... *$18.00–$30.00*

Vonnegut, Kurt. *Slapstick*. NY. Delacort Press. 1973. 1st ed. dj. .... *$12.00–$35.00*

Vonnegut, Kurt. *Slaughterhouse Five*. NY. 1969. sgn, dj. .... *$175.00–$300.00*

Voth, H. R. *Oraibi Natal Customs and Ceremonies*. Field Columbian Museum. 1905.
illus. Vol VI, No 2.. *$35.00–$50.00*

Voth, H. R. *Oraibi Oaqol Ceremony*. Field Columbian Museum. 1903. illus. Vol VI,
No 1. .... *$85.00–$130.00*

Voth, H. R. *Oraibi Summer Snake Ceremony*. Field Columbian Museum. 1903. illus.
Vol III.. *$95.00–$145.00*

Voyage Through the Islands of the Pacific Ocean. NY. Lane & Scott. 1851. rev cloth.
.... *$90.00–$120.00*

Vrooman, J. J. *Forts and Firesides of the Mohawk Valley*. Phila. 1943. 1st ed. ltd 106 cc.
.... *$65.00–$90.00*

Wa-Sha-Quon-Asin (Grey Owl). *Tales of an Empty Cabin*. Lon. Lovat Dickson. 1936.
illus. 2nd printing. brown cloth. .... *$35.00–$50.00*

Wack, Henry Wellington. *Story of the Congo Free State*. NY. 1905. 1st ed. illus. ....
.... *$125.00–$175.00*

Wain, Louis. *Fun For Everyone*. Lon. Nister. nd. illus. b/w, clr. .... *$50.00–$70.00*

Wainwright, John Howard. *Rhymings*. NY. D Appleton & Co. 1860. purple cloth sgn.
....*$30.00–$40.00*

Wakefield, H. R. *Clock Strikes Twelve*. WI. Arkham House. 1946. 1st US ed, dj. ....
.... *$40.00–$65.00*

Wakefield, H. R. *They Return at Evening*. NY. Appleton. 1928. 1st Amer ed. 266 pp, no
dj. .... *$65.00–$75.00*

Wakefield, J. *History of Waupaca County, Wisc*. Waupaca, WI. 1890. 1st ed.................
.... *$60.00–$85.00*

Walcott, Mary Vaus. *Illustrations of North American Pitcherplants*. DC. Smithsonian
Inst. 1935. 1st ed. illus. folio, 34 pp, portfolio with ties, 1/500 cc....... *$175.00–$225.00*

Walden, Arthur T. *Dog Puncher on the Yukon*. Bos. Houghton Mifflin. 1928. ....
.... *$25.00–$35.00*

Waley, Arthur. *More Translations from the Chinese*. NY. Knopf. 1919. 1st Amer ed. ...
.... *$40.00–$50.00*

Walker, Aldace F. *Vermont Brigade in the Shenandoah Valley*. VT. 1869. illus. maps. ..
.... *$35.00–$100.00*

Walker, Alice. *Color Purple*. NY. Harcourt, Brace, Jovanovich. 1982. 1st ed. dj, sgn. ...
.... *$950.00–$1,000.00*

Walker, Alice. *Color Purple*. NY. 1982. sgn, dj.................................. *$325.00–$450.00*

Walker, Alice. *Temple of My Familiar*. Harcourt. 1989. ltd 500 cc, sgn, dj, slipcase.......
.... *$85.00–$100.00*

Wall, E. G. *Handbook of the State of Mississippi*. Jackson. 1882. 1st ed. illus. ....
.... *$85.00–$125.00*

Wallace, Alfred R. *Australia.* Lon. Edward Stanford. 1879. 1st ed. illus. 2 clr maps, pictorial cloth... *$195.00–$250.00*

Wallace, Alfred Russel. *Darwinism* . . . Lon. Macmillan & Co. 1889. 1st ed. bds. ....
.... *$140.00–$160.00*

Wallace, Alfred Russel. *Malay Archipelago* . . . NY. Harper & Bros. 1869. 1st Amer ed.
.... *$75.00–$100.00*

Wallace, Anthony F. C. *King of the Delawares: Teedyuscung 1700–1763.* Phila. 1949. 1st ed. dj. .... *$40.00–$60.00*

Wallace, Dillon. *Long Labrador Trail.* Chi. 1923. illus. sgn. .... *$22.00–$30.00*

Wallace, Dillon. *Lure of the Labrador Wild.* NY. Fleming H Revell Co. (1913). 11th ed. illus, map. .... *$25.00–$35.00*

Wallace, Dillon. *Lure of the Labrador Wild.* NY. Revell. 1905. 16 plates.......................
.... *$35.00–$45.00*

Wallace, Edgar. *Clever One.* Doubleday Crime Club. 1928. 1st ed. dj.. *$35.00–$50.00*

Wallace, Edgar. *Day of Uniting.* Mystery League. 1930. 1st ed. dj. ...... *$50.00–$60.00*

Wallace, Frederick William. *Wooden Ships & Iron Men.* NY. .... *$30.00–$45.00*

Wallace, Isabel. *Life and Letters of General W. H. L. Wallace.* Chi. 1909. 1st ed. illus.. .... *$95.00–$125.00*

Wallace, Lew. *Ben-Hur, Souvenir Album Scenes of the Play.* Klaw & Erlanger. 1900. illus. pictorial cvr, flashlight photos by Byron...................................... *$50.00–$100.00*

Wallace, Lewis. *Ben-Hur.* NY. Harper & Bros. 1908. .... *$35.00–$80.00*

Wallace, Susan E. *Land of the Pueblos.* NY. 1888. 1st ed. illus. photos. *$75.00–$95.00*

Waller, Robert James. *Bridges of Madison County.* NY. Times Warner. 1992. 1st ed. author's first book, dj... *$70.00–$100.00*

Walsh, J. H. *Every Horse Owner's Cyclopedia.* Phila. Porter & Coates. 1871. 1st ed. illus. .... *$30.00–$45.00*

Walt Disney's Pinocchio's Picture Book. Whitman. 1940. wrps. illus. *$125.00–$150.00*

Walter Camp's Book of College Sports. NY. 1893. 1st ed. .... *$50.00–$75.00*

Walton, Evangeline. *Cross and the Sword.* NY. Bourcgy & Curl. (1956). 1st ed. dj. ......
.... *$55.00–$65.00*

Walton, Evangeline. *Virgin and the Swine.* Chi. 1936. 1st ed. dj. ...... *$100.00–$175.00*

Walton, Evangeline. *Witch House.* Sauk City. Arkham House. 1945. 1st ed. dj. ....
.... *$50.00–$100.00*

Walton, Evangeline. *Witch House.* Arkham House. 1961. dj................. *$45.00–$50.00*

Walton, Isaac. *Compleat Angler.* 1931. illus. by Arthur Rackham, #49/775 sgn by Rackham. .... *$550.00–$650.00*

Walton, Isaac and Charles Cotton. *Compleat Angler.* Lon. Richard & Henry Causton. 1772. illus. 10 engraved plates. 8th ed. .... *$100.00–$150.00*

Walton, Isaac and Charles Cotton. *Complete Angler, or Contemplative Man's Recreation.* Lon. 1784. illus. 4th ed. slipcase. .... *$350.00–$450.00*

Walton, Isaac and Charles Cotton. *Complete Angler.* NY. 1848. ¾ lea, bds. ....
.... *$50.00–$60.00*

Walton, Isaak. *Compleat Angler*. Phila. McKay. (1931). 1st Amer ed. illus by Arthur Rackham. .... *$275.00–$300.00*

Walton, Izaak. *Compleat Angler*. NY. Caxton Press. 1937. blue cloth... *$30.00–$45.00*

Walton, Izaak. *Compleat Angler*. NY. Heritage Press. 1948. slipcase.... *$20.00–$45.00*

Walton, Izaak. *Compleat Angler*. Lon. J M Dent. 1896. illus. .... *$45.00–$55.00*

Walton, Izaak. *Universal Angler*. Lon. Marriott & Brome. 1676. ...... *$700.00–$850.00*

Walton, Izaak and Charles Cotton. *Compleat Angler*. NY. Heritage Press. 1948. illus. green cloth, slipcase. .... *$10.00–$20.00*

Warbey, William. *Vietnam: The Truth*. Lon. 1965. 1st ed. .... *$25.00–$30.00*

Ward, Artemas. *Grocer's Hand-Book and Directory for 1883*. Phila. Grocer Pub. 1883. 1st ed. illus. .... *$80.00–$120.00*

Ward, Austin. *Male Life Among the Mormons or The Husband in Utah*. Phila. 1863. ... . *$45.00–$60.00*

Ward, Henshaw. *Charles Darwin* . . . Ind. Bobbs Merrill. 1927. .... *$20.00–$30.00*

Ward, Maria. *Female Life Among the Mormons: A Narrative of Many Years' Personal Experience, by the Wife of a Mormon Elder*. NY. 1857. .... *$75.00–$250.00*

Warhol, Andy. *"A."* NY. 1968. 1st ed. dj. .... *$35.00–$45.00*

Waring, John Burnley (ed.). *Examples of Weaving and Embroidery*. Lon. Day & Son. illus. 14 chromolitho plates. folio. .... *$100.00–$150.00*

Warner, Charles Dudley. *My Winter on the Nile, Among the Mummies and Moslems*. Hartford. American Publishing. 1876. 1st ed. .... *$80.00–$120.00*

Warren Report. GPO. 1964. 26 vols. .... *$900.00–$1,500.00*

Warren, Henry Mather. *To and Fro*. Phil. Wm F Fell Co. 1908. illus. pictorial gold-stamped cloth. scarce. .... *$50.00–$75.00*

Warren, John. *The Conchologist*. Bos. 1834. 1st ed. illus. presentation copy, lea, bds. . ... *$115.00–$130.00*

Warren, Lillie E. *Defective Speech and Deafness*. NY. Edgar S Werner. 1895. 116 pp.. .... *$50.00–$75.00*

Warren, Robert Penn. *Meet Me in the Green Glen*. NY. 1971. 1st ed. presentation copy, sgn. .... *$100.00–$225.00*

Warren, Robert Penn. *Wilderness*. Random House. 1961. 1st ed. dj. ..... *$50.00–$30.00*

Warshburn, Robert Collier. *Life and Times of Lydia E. Pinkham*. NY. 1931. 1st ed. 221 pp, illus. .... *$25.00–$35.00*

Washington's Farewell Address to the People of the United States.Troy. The Washington Benevolent Society. 1810. frontis. .... *$25.00–$45.00*

Washington, Booker T. *Story of My Life and Work*. Tor. Nichols. 1901. illus. .... *$25.00–$55.00*

Washington, Booker T. *Up From Slavery*. NY. Doubleday, Page. 1901. 1st ed. photos. .... *$40.00–$70.00*

Washington, Booker T. *Working With the Hands*. Doubleday. 1904. 1st ed. .... *$55.00–$75.00*

Washington, Booker T. (ed.). *Negro in Business.* Bos. Hertel, Jenkins. 1907. 1st ed. illus. photos.. *$145.00–$170.00*

Watanna, Onoto. *Heart of Hyacinth.* NY. 1904. clr plates, boxed. .... *$20.00–$50.00*

Watanna, Onoto. *Heart of Hyacinth.* Harper. 1903. 1st ed. illus. teg..... *$25.00–$75.00*

Watanna, Onoto. *Japanese Blossom.* NY. Harper. 1906. 1st ed. clr plates.....................
.... *$30.00–$50.00*

Watanna, Onoto. *Japanese Nightingale.* Harper. 1901. 1st ed. illus. ..... *$17.00–$30.00*

Waterman, Jonathan. *High Alaska: A Historical Guide to Denali.* NY. American Alpine Club. 1988. 1st ed. photos, route photos, maps, dj. .... *$40.00–$50.00*

Waters, Ethel. *His Eye Is on the Sparrow.* NY. 1951............................ *$25.00–$35.00*

Waters, Ethel. *His Eye Is on the Sparrow.* Garden City. 1951. 1st ed. cloth, dj.............
.... *$15.00–$20.00*

Watkins, Sylvestre. *Anthology of American Negro Literature.* NY. The Modern Library. (1944). light green cloth. .... *$8.00–$45.00*

Watson, Elizabeth C. *Metropolitan Mother Goose.* NY. nd. wrps. illus. by Emma Clark.
.... *$15.00–$25.00*

Watson, Francis Sedgwick. *Operative Treatment of the Hypertrophied Prostate.* Cupples & Hurd. 1888. 167 pp. photogravures. .... *$100.00–$140.00*

Watson, John F. *Historic Tales of Olden Times.* Phila. 1833. 1st ed. illus. lea, 316 pp. .
.... *$50.00–$85.00*

Watson, Wilbur J. *Bridge Architecture.* NY. 1927. illus......................... *$50.00–$75.00*

Watson, William. *Adventures of a Blockade Runner.* Lon. 1892. .... *$100.00–$155.00*

Watts. *Watts' Divine Songs For the Use of Children.* New Haven. 1824. illustrated wrps.
.... *$60.00–$75.00*

Watts, Rev. Isaac. *An Arrangement of the Psalms, Hymns and Spiritual Songs of . . .* Bos. James Loring. 1818. .... *$70.00–$100.00*

Wauchope, R. *Handbook of Middle American Indians, Vol 1.* Austin. 1964. illus. dj. ....
.... *$25.00–$35.00*

Waugh, Evelyn. *Brideshead Revisited.* Bos. Little Brown. 1946. 1st Amer trade cd. dj.
.... *$30.00–$125.00*

Waugh, Evelyn. *Edmund Campion.* Sheed & Ward. (1935). 1st ed. dj. *$30.00–$125.00*

Waugh, Evelyn. *Helena.* Bos. Little Brown. 1950. 1st ed. dj,................. *$35.00–$50.00*

Waugh, Evelyn. *Love Among the Ruins.* Lon. 1953. 1st ed. dj. .... *$35.00–$45.00*

Waugh, Evelyn. *Mr. Loveday's Little Outing and Other Sad Stories.* Lon. Chapman & Hall. (1936). 1st ed. .... *$50.00–$125.00*

Waugh, Evelyn. *Tourist in Africa.* Lon. Chapman & Hill. 1960. 1st ed. illus. b/w photos, dj. .... *$30.00–$65.00*

Waugh, Evelyn. *When the Going Was Good.* Bos. Little Brown. 1947. dj. ....
.... *$40.00–$55.00*

Waugh, F. A. *American Apple Orchard.* NY. Judd. illus.......................... *$28.00–$40.00*

Waugh, F. A. *Landscape Gardening.* NY. 1899. 1st ed. .... *$32.00–$45.00*

Waugh, Frank A. *Textbook of Landscape Gardening*. NY. Wiley. 1922. 1st ed. illus.....
.... *$35.00–$45.00*

Weaver, Clarence E. *Sketches of Richmond Virginia* . . . Central Pub. illus. b/w photos.
.... *$50.00–$65.00*

Weaver, Lawrence. *Small Country Houses*. Lon. Country Life. 1914. 1st ed. illus. ....
.... *$50.00–$100.00*

Weaver, Warren A. *Lithographs of N. Currier and Currier & Ives*. NY. Holport. (1925).
1st ed. illus.. *$50.00–$80.00*

Webb, Walter Prescott. *Texas Rangers*. Houghton Mifflin. 1935. 1st ed. illus...............
.... *$52.00–$60.00*

Webb, William Seward. *Calif. and Alaska, and Over the Canadian Pacific Railway*. NY.
1890. illus. ltd to 500 cc.. *$120.00–$155.00*

Weber, Carl J. *Fore-Edge Painting*. Irvington-on-Hudson. 1966. illus. dj......................
.... *$165.00–$200.00*

Weber, Rev. Francis J. *Bibliography of California Bibliographies*. Ward Ritchie Press.
illus. slipcase, 1/500 cc.. *$65.00–$85.00*

Webster, Daniel. *Private Correspondence of Daniel Webster*. Bos. Little Brown. 1857.
1st ed. illus.. *$50.00–$100.00*

Webster, Noah. *American Spelling Book*. NY. 1804. illus. woodcuts. ..... *$50.00–$65.00*

Webster, Noah. *An American Dictionary of the English Language*. Merriam. 1849.......
.... *$75.00–$175.00*

Webster, Thomas. *An Encyclopedia of Domestic Economy*. NY. 1845. 1st ed. ....
.... *$65.00–$125.00*

Wee Gee. *Naked City*. NY. Essential Books. 1945. dj......................... *$150.00–$200.00*

Weeden Toy Steam Engines. New Bedford, MA. Weeden Manufacturing Corp. 1939.
pictorial wrps, illus, 19 pp.. *$65.00–$75.00*

Weeden, Howard. *Songs of the Old South*. NY. 1900. 1st ed. illus. clr plates.................
.... *$85.00–$125.00*

Weegee. *Weegee's Creative Camera*. Garden City. Hanover House. 1959. 1st ed. illus.
.... *$80.00–$120.00*

Weeks, John. *History of Salisbury, VT*. Middlebury. 1860. .... *$90.00–$100.00*

Wehr, Julian. *Popeye and the Pirates*. NY. Duenewald Pub. (1945). illus. by Sagendorf,
with four animations by Wehr. .... *$125.00–$200.00*

Weld, Isaac. *Travels Through the States of North America and the Provinces of Upper
and Lower Canada During the Years 1795, 1796, and 1797*. Lon. 1799. 1st ed. 464 pp,
plates, maps laid in, small folio.. *$320.00–$400.00*

Well, H. G. *Ann Veronica*. NY. 1909. 1st ed. dj. .... *$75.00–$100.00*

Well, Samuel R. *New Physiognomy of Signs of Character*. Fowler & Wells. 1883. illus.
brown decorated cloth. .... *$40.00–$55.00*

Wellman, Manly Wade. *After Dark*. Garden City. Doubleday. 1980. 1st ed. dj.............
.... *$35.00–$65.00*

Wellman, Manly Wade. *Lost and the Lurking*. Garden City. Doubleday. 1981. 1st ed. dj.
.... *$25.00–$65.00*

Wellman, Manly Wade. *Old Gods Awaken*. Garden City. Doubleday. 1979. 1st ed. ......
.... *$30.00–$65.00*

Wells, Carolyn. *Folly for the Wise*. Bobbs Merrill. 1904. 170 pp, illus. . *$45.00–$65.00*

Wells, Carolyn. *Marjorie in Command*. NY. Grosset & Dunlap. 1910... *$10.00–$18.00*

Wells, Carolyn. *Merry-Go-Round*. Russell. 1901. 152 pp, illus by Peter Newell............
.... *$120.00–$150.00*

Wells, Emma M. *History of Roane County, Tennessee, 1801–1870*. Chattanooga. 1927.
1st ed. illus... *$55.00–$75.00*

Wells, Frederic P. *History of Newbury, Vermont*. St Johnsbury, VT. 1902. illus. fldg
plans, ¾ mor. .... *$40.00–$55.00*

Wells, H G. *Tono-Bungay*. Lon. Macmillan. 1909. 1st ed. .... *$50.00–$75.00*

Wells, H. G. *Adventures of Tommy*. NY. Stokes. (1929). 1st ed. illus. red cloth. ....
.... *$35.00–$75.00*

Wells, H. G. *First and Last Things*. NY. 1908. 1st US ed........................ *$40.00–$50.00*

Wells, H. G. *Invisible Man*. NY. Edward Arnold. 1897. 1st Amer ed. 279 pp, orange
cloth. .... *$600.00–$1,150.00*

Wells, H. G. *Invisible Man*. Lon. 1897. 1st ed. .... *$1,000.00–$2,000.00*

Wells, H. G. *Men Like Gods*. NY. Macmillan. 1923. 1st ed. .... *$25.00–$45.00*

Wells, H. G. *New Worlds for Old*. Lon. Constable. 1908. 1st ed. red cloth.....................
.... *$85.00–$100.00*

Wells, H. G. *Tales of Space and Time*. NY. Doubleday & McClure. 1899. 1st Amer ed.
.... *$45.00–$65.00*

Wells, H. G. *Time Machine*. Random House. 1931. illus. by W A Dwiggins. clr plates..
.... *$30.00–$50.00*

Wells, H. G. *Time Machine*. Lon. 1927. dj.. *$125.00–$165.00*

Wells, H. G. *When the Sleeper Wakes*. Lon/NY. Harper & Bros. 1899. 1st ed. illus........
.... *$85.00–$120.00*

Wells, Helen. *Island Nurse*. Grosset & Dunlap. 1960. Cherry Ames #21, dj..................
.... *$14.00–$17.00*

Wells, Helen. *Jungle Nurse*. Grosset & Dunlap. 1965. Cherry Ames #25.....................
.... *$30.00–$40.00*

Wells, Helen. *Student Nurse*. Grosset & Dunlap. 1943. Cherry Ames #1, dj.................
.... *$12.00–$20.00*

Wells, Helen. *Veterans' Nurse*. Grosset & Dunlap. 1946. Cherry Ames, #6, dj. ....
.... *$8.00–$12.00*

Wells, Henry P. *City Boys in the Woods*. NY. Harper. (1889). 1st ed. illus. ....
.... *$30.00–$80.00*

Wells, Tom. *Confederate Navy*. AL. Univ of Alabama. 1971. dj............. *$35.00–$45.00*

Welo, Samuel. *Practical Lettering*. Chi. Drake. (1930). 1st ed. illus. ..... *$30.00–$50.00*

Welty, Eudora. *A Curtain Green: A Book of Stories*. Garden City. Doubleday Doran.
1941. 1st ed. author's first book, dj. .... *$850.00–$1,000.00*

Welty, Eudora. *Bride of the Innisfallen and Other Stories*. NY. Harcourt Brace. (c1955). 1st ed. 2nd issue, dj. .... *$150.00–$190.00*

Welty, Eudora. *Delta Wedding*. NY. (1946). 1st ed. dj........................ *$100.00–$200.00*

Welty, Eudora. *Golden Apples*. NY. Harcourt Brace. (1949). 1st ed. no dj. ....
.... *$45.00–$60.00*

Welty, Eudora. *Golden Apples*. NY. Harcourt Brace. (1949). 1st ed. dj. ....
.... *$125.00–$150.00*

Welty, Eudora. *In Black and White*. Northridge. Lord John Press. 1985. sgn. ....
.... *$165.00–$250.00*

Welty, Eudora. *One Writer's Beginnings*. Camb. 1984. dj. .... *$30.00–$40.00*

Welty, Eudora. *Ponder Heart*. Harcourt. (1954). 1st ed. sgn, dj. .... *$75.00–$125.00*

Welty, Eudora. *Robber Bridegroom*. Garden City. Doubleday Doran. 1942. 1st ed. dj. . .
.... *$100.00–$500.00*

Welty, Eudora. *Robber Bridegroom*. Garden City. Doubleday, Doran. 1942. 1st ed. blue cloth sgn and inscrb. .... *$750.00–$1,000.00*

Welty, Eudora. *Short Stories*. NY. Harcourt Brace. (c1949). 1st ed. 1/1,500 cc, no glassine dj present. .... *$55.00–$100.00*

Welty, Eudora. *Wide Net and Other Stories*. NY. 1943. 1st ed. dj...... *$350.00–$500.00*

Wentz, Robert W. Jr. *Portsmouth A Pictorial History*. Donning. illus. b/w photos. sgn dj. .... *$30.00–$45.00*

Weslager, C. A. *Delaware Indians: A History*. New Brunswick. Rutgers Univ Press. 1972. 2nd ed. dj.. *$30.00–$40.00*

West, Benjamin. *New England Almanack For 1776*. Prov. 1775. .... *$125.00–$150.00*

West, James E. *Lone Scout of the Sky*. NY. Boy Scouts of America. 1927. 1st ed. illus. green cloth. .... *$20.00–$50.00*

West, James E. *Lone Scout of the Sky*. NY. 1927. Boy Scout Book. ...... *$15.00–$18.00*

West, Jerry. *Happy Hollisters and the Indian Treasure*. Doubleday. 1953.....................
.... *$10.00–$20.00*

Westerners Brand Book. Chi. 1st ed. vol XV11. .... *$40.00–$75.00*

Westminster Shorter Catechism Ratified . . . Presbyterian Church in Augusta, Georgia.Virginia. (Confederate Imprint). 1861. wrps. .... *$95.00–$125.00*

Westwood, T and T. Satchell. *Biblioteca Piscatoria: A Catalogue of Books on Angling . . .* Lon. 1883–1901. ¼ blue mor and blue cloth, teg, complete with 1901 supplement, orig supplement wrps preserved.. *$150.00–$250.00*

Wetmore, Mrs. Helen C. *Last of the Great Scouts: The Life Story of Buffalo Bill*. Duluth. 1899. 1st ed. illus. plates.. *$75.00–$175.00*

Whall, W. B. *Sea Songs & Shanties*. Glasgow. 1920. illus. 4th ed......... *$50.00–$75.00*

Wharton, Edith. *Crucial Instances*. NY. Scribner's. 1901. 1st ed. .... *$85.00–$200.00*

Wharton, Edith. *Custom of the Country*. NY. Scribner's. 1913. 1st ed. . *$50.00–$90.00*

Wharton, Edith. *Ethan Frome*. NY. Scribner's. 1911. 1st ed. .... *$250.00–$450.00*

Wharton, Edith. *Fruit of the Tree*. NY. Scribner's. 1907. 1st ed. 633 pp. ....
.... *$25.00–$50.00*

Wharton, Edith. *Gods Arrive*. NY. Appleton. 1932. 1st ed. dj. .... *$125.00–$150.00*

Wharton, Edith. *House of Mirth*. NY. Scribner's Sons. 1905. 1st ed. 1st issue. teg........
.... *$75.00–$150.00*

Wharton, Edith. *Italian Villas and Their Gardens*. NY. 1904. 1st ed. illus. by Maxfield Parrish. decorated cloth. .... *$700.00–$750.00*

Wharton, Edith. *Old New York, New Year's Day*. NY. Appleton. 1924. 1st ed. illus. by E C Caswell, dj. .... *$60.00–$125.00*

Wharton, Edith. *Sanctuary*. NY. Scribner's. 1903. 1st ed. illus. by Walter Appleton Clark, 184 pp, scarce. .... *$150.00–$250.00*

Wharton, Edith. *Son at the Front*. NY. Scribner's. 1923. 1st ed. red cloth. ....
....*$25.00–$100.00*

Wharton, Edith. *Summer*. NY. 1917. 1st ed. dj. .... *$65.00–$95.00*

Wharton, Edith. *Tale of Men and Ghosts*. Lon. Macmillan. 1910. 1st Eng ed. 438 pp.
.... *$45.00–$55.00*

Wharton, Edith. *The Children*. NY. 1928. 1st ed. dj. .... *$75.00–$125.00*

Wharton, Edith. *Xingu and Other Stories*. NY. 1916. 1st ed. .... *$60.00–$75.00*

Wharton, Edith (ed.). *Book of the Homeless*. Scribner's Sons. 1916. illus. gray bds.
.... *$50.00–$80.00*

Wheeler, F. G. *Billy Whiskers at the Fair*. Akron. 1909. 1st ed. illus. plates..................
.... *$30.00–$35.00*

Wheeler, Opal. *Stephen Foster and His Little Dog Tray*. NY. E P Dutton & Co. (1941). 1st ed. illus. dj. .... *$22.00–$30.00*

Where to Hunt American Game. MA. 1898. 1st ed. illus...................... *$50.00–$75.00*

Whilt, James W. *Mountain Memories*. Chi. W B Conkey. 1925. illus. sgn by author.....
.... *$20.00–$30.00*

Whipple, Maurine. *Giant Joshua*. Bos. 1941. 1st ed. dj........................ *$45.00–$60.00*

White, Alma. *Ku Klux Klan in Prophecy*. NJ. 1925. 1st ed................. *$150.00–$275.00*

White, E. B. *Charlotte's Web*. NY. (1952). 1st ed. illus. by Garth Williams, dj. ....
.... *$200.00–$450.00*

White, E. B. *Charlotte's Web*. NY. 1952. dj...................................... *$22.00–$35.00*

White, E. B. *Fox of Peapack and Other Poems*. Harper. 1938. 2nd ed. sgn and dated. ...
.... *$60.00–$75.00*

White, E. B. *Here Is New York*. NY. Harper and Bros. 1949. 1st ed. dj. . *$25.00–$50.00*

White, E. B. *Stuart Little*. NY. 1945. dj. .... *$50.00–$175.00*

White, James. *Early Life and Later Experiences . . . of Elder Joseph Bates*. Battle Creek. 1877. illus. 320 pp... *$115.00–$150.00*

White, Mrs. Alma. *Titantic Tragedy . . .* Bound Brook. Pentecostal Union. 1913. ....
.... *$25.00–$50.00*

White, Rev. Gilbert. *Natural History and Antiquities of Selborne*. Lon/NY. Routlege & Sons. illus. wood engr, mor and mar bds.. *$70.00–$100.00*

White, W. Edward. *Covered Bridges of New Hampshire*. Plymouth, NH. (1942). illus. pictorial wrps. .... *$25.00–$40.00*

Whitehead, Alfred North. *Science in the Modern World*. NY. 1925. 1st ed. .... *$40.00–$50.00*

Whitehead, Don. *FBI Story*. NY. 1956. sgn by Hoover dj. .... *$45.00–$50.00*

Whitehead, Russell F. *Architecture of the American Colonies and the Early Republic*. NY. Helburn. (1927). 2 vols. illus. photos... *$60.00–$80.00*

Whitehouse, Eula. *Texas Flowers In Natural Colors*. Austin. 1936. 1st ed. illus in clr, illus by author, inscrb by author. .... *$35.00–$65.00*

Whitman, Roger B. *Motor-Car Principles*. NY. Appleton. 1909. rev. ed. illus............. .... *$60.00–$80.00*

Whitman, Walt. *Good-Bye My Fancy: 2nd Annex to Leaves of Grass*. Phila. David McKay. 1891. 1st ed. teg... *$50.00–$100.00*

Whitman, Walt. *Leaves of Grass*. Mount Vernon. Peter Pauper Press. 1943. illus. 1/1,100, folio. .... *$95.00–$125.00*

Whitman, Walt. *November Boughs*. Phila. 1888. 1st ed. .... *$90.00–$325.00*

Whitney, Ada. *Mother Goose for Grown Folks*. NY. 1859. 1st ed. sgn........................... .... *$125.00–$250.00*

Whitney, Harry. *Hunting with the Eskimos*. NY. Century. 1910. 1st ed. illus. fldg map. .... *$50.00–$75.00*

Whitney, Orson F. *Poetical Writings of . . .* Salt Lake. 1889. 1st ed. orig lea, aeg. .... *$75.00–$100.00*

Whitted, J. A. *History of the Negro Baptists of North Carolina*. Raleigh. Edwards & Broughton. 1908. 1st ed. illus. .... *$195.00–$225.00*

Whymper, C. *Egyptian Birds for the Most Part Seen in the Nile Valley*. Lon. 1909. illus. .... *$70.00–$85.00*

Whymper, Frederick. *Travel and Adventure in the Territory of Alaska*. Harper & Bros. 1871. illus. .... *$65.00–$85.00*

Wickersham, Hon James. *Old Yukon*. Wash. Washington Law Book Co. 1938. 1st ed. illus. .... *$28.00–$75.00*

Wickersham, James. *Bibliography of Alaskan Literature 1724–1924 . . .* Cordova. 1927. .... *$225.00–$275.00*

Wiggin, Kate Douglas. *Birds' Christmas Carol*. 1912. illus. .... *$18.00–$27.00*

Wiggin, Kate Douglas. *Diary of a Goose Girl*. Bos. 1902. 1st ed.......... *$20.00–$30.00*

Wiggin, Kate Douglas. *Old Peabody Pew*. Bos/NY. 1907. 1st ed........... *$35.00–$50.00*

Wiggin, Kate Douglas. *Penelope's Irish Experience*. Bos. 1902. illus. aeg.................... .... *$50.00–$60.00*

Wiggin, Kate Douglas. *Rebecca of Sunnybrook Farm*. Bos. Houghton Mifflin. 1903. 1st ed. .... *$100.00–$135.00*

Wiggin, Kate Douglas. *Rebecca of Sunnybrook Farm*. Bos. Houghton, Mifflin. 1903. 1st ed. 3rd ptg. pictorial cloth. .... *$35.00–$50.00*

Wiggin, Kate Douglas. *Rebecca of Sunnybrook Farm*. NY. Houghton Mifflin. 1903. 1st ed. 1st state binding... *$150.00–$225.00*

Wight, J. B. *Tobacco: Its Use and Abuse*. Columbia, SC. 1889.............. *$20.00–$35.00*

Wightman, Orrin. *Diary of an American Physician in the Russian Revolution. 1917.* Brooklyn. Daily Eagle. 1928. 1st ed. photographs,, 230 pp, sgn presentation copy. .... *$95.00–$125.00*

Wilcox, Walter Dwight. *Rockies of Canada.* NY/Lon. 1900. .... *$75.00–$100.00*

Wilde, Oscar. *Canterville Ghost.* Bos. J W Luce. 1906. 1st separate ed. illus, tri-clr slate cloth, teg. .... *$100.00–$125.00*

Wilde, Oscar. *Critic in Pall Mall.* Lon. Methuen and Co. (1919). 1st ed. fine. .... *$75.00–$150.00*

Wilde, Oscar. *Epigrams and Aphorisms.* Bos. Luce. 1905. 1st ed. .... *$45.00–$100.00*

Wilde, Oscar. *Fisherman and His Soul.* SF. Ransohoff's. 1939. .... *$125.00–$180.00*

Wilde, Oscar. *Happy Prince.* NY. Stokes. (1913). illus. pictorial cloth. . *$25.00–$55.00*

Wilde, Oscar. *Impressions of America.* Sunderland. Keystone Press. 1906. 1st ed. ltd 50 cc. .... *$60.00–$100.00*

Wilde, Oscar. *Irish Poets and Poetry of the Nineteenth Century.* SF. Book Club of California. 1972. .... *$30.00–$50.00*

Wilde, Oscar. *Poems of Oscar Wilde.* NY. 1927. illus. .... *$30.00–$65.00*

Wilder, Thornton. *Angel That Troubled the Waters and Other Plays.* NY. Coward-McCann. 1928. 1st ed. ltd 775 cc. sgn. .... *$70.00–$100.00*

Wilder, Thornton. *Bride of San Luis Rey.* NY. 1962. 1,500 cc, slipcase. .... *$100.00–$150.00*

Wilder, Thornton. *Cabala.* NY. 1926. 1st ed. .... *$100.00–$360.00*

Wilder, Thornton. *Theophilus North.* NY. (1973). 1st ed. presentation copy, sgn, dj. .... *$80.00–$100.00*

Wildflowers of Palestine. 1895. .... *$50.00–$60.00*

Wildridge, T. Tindall. *Dance of Death in Painting and in Print.* Lon. Redway. 1887. 1st ed. illus. wood-cut plates, hand-clred frontis. .... *$120.00–$185.00*

Willard, Frances E. *How to Win.* NY. 1887. 4th ed. .... *$50.00–$65.00*

Willard, Frances E. *Woman in the Pulpit.* Chi. Woman's Temperance Pub Co. 1889. 1st ed. .... *$85.00–$125.00*

Willard, Signey. *Hebrew Grammar.* Cambridge, MA. 1817. 1st ed. calf-bkd bds. .... *$225.00–$285.00*

Willett, Mortimer and Peter. *Great Racehorses of the World.* NY. St. Martins. 1970. 1st US ed. .... *$35.00–$45.00*

Williams, Garner F. *Diamond Mines of South Africa.* NY. Macmillan. 1902. 1st ed. fldg map, plates. .... *$125.00–$200.00*

Williams, Joseph J. *Hewbrewisms of West Africa. From Nile to Niger with the Jews.* NY. Dial Press. 1930. 1st ed. maps. .... *$50.00–$80.00*

Williams, Morris. *Stair Builder's Guide.* NY. David Williams Co. (1914). illus. 256 pp. .... *$55.00–$75.00*

Williams, Mrs. *Neutral French . . .* pub by author. 1841. .... *$50.00–$75.00*

Williams, S. Wells. *Middle Kingdom.* NY. 1883. 2 vols. wrps. rev ed. 2 fldg frontis, pocket map. .... *$150.00–$225.00*

Williams, Tennesee. *Roman Spring of Mrs. Stone*. NY. 1950. 1st ed. dj. *$50.00–$75.00*

Williams, Tennessee. *Cat on a Hot Tin Roof*. NY. 1955. 1st ed. dj....... *$75.00–$100.00*

Williams, Tennessee. *Cat on a Hot Tin Roof*. Secker. 1956. 1st Eng ed. dj...................
.... *$75.00–$90.00*

Williams, Tennessee. *Glass Menagerie*. NY. Random House. 1945. 1st ed. dj. ....
.... *$65.00–$80.00*

Williams, Tennessee. *One Arm and Other Stories*. NY. New Directions. (1948). 1st ed. ltd 1,500 cc. slipcase. .... *$80.00–$120.00*

Williams, Tennessee. *Rose Tattoo*. New Directions. 1951. 1st ed. dj.... *$60.00–$125.00*

Williams, Tennessee. *Streetcar Named Desire*. NY. New Directions. (1947). 1st ed. 171 pp, bds, dj. .... *$250.00–$350.00*

Williams, W. *Appleton's Northern and Eastern Traveller's Guide*. NY. 1855. illus. maps.
.... *$85.00–$130.00*

Williams, William Carlos. *Complete Collected Poems, 1906–1938*. Norfolk, CT. New Directions. (c1938). 1st ed. dj. .... *$150.00–$225.00*

Williams, William Carlos. *Kora in Hell*. SF. City Lights. (1957). wrps. 2nd ed,. ....
.... *$60.00–$75.00*

Williams, William Carlos. *Life Along the Passaic River*. Norfolk, CT. New Directions. 1938. 1st ed. dj. .... *$75.00–$250.00*

Williams, William Carlos. *White Mule*. Norfolk, CT. New Directions. 1937. 1st ed. dj.
.... *$200.00–$450.00*

Williamson, Henry. *Salar the Salmon*. Bos. Little Brown. 1936. 1st ed. dj. ....
.... *$40.00–$50.00*

Williamson, James J. *Mosby's Rangers*. NY. Sturgis & Walton. 1909. rev. and enlarged.
.... *$75.00–$125.00*

Wilson, Angus. *Hemlock and After*. Viking. 1952. 1st Amer ed, dj. .... *$15.00–$20.00*

Wilson, Capt. James. *Missionary Voyage to the South Pacific Ocean, in 1796, 1797 & 1798: In the Ship Duff*. Lon. Chapman. 1799. plates, fold-out charts, 395 pp, very scarce treasure.. *$225.00–$550.00*

Wilson, Colin. *Philospher's Stone*. NY. Crown. (1971). 1st Amer ed. dj. *$35.00–$40.00*

Wilson, Dixie. *Pinky Pup*. Chi. Volland. (1922). illus. by Erick Berry.. *$70.00–$125.00*

Wilson, Edmund. *Boys in the Back Room: Notes on California Novelists*. SF. Colt Press. 1941. 1st ed. 1/500 cc, dj. .... *$95.00–$200.00*

Wilson, Edmund. *Poets, Farewell*. NY. Scribner's Sons. 1929. 1st ed. dj......................
.... *$475.00–$600.00*

Wilson, Edmund. *Travels in Two Democracies*. NY. Harcourt, Brace. (c1936). 1st ed. dj.
.... *$125.00–$250.00*

Wilson, Elija N. *Among the Shoshones*. SLC. 1910. 1st ed. .... *$200.00–$250.00*

Wilson, F. P. *The Keep*. NY. Morrow. 1981. 1st ed. dj. .... *$30.00–$45.00*

Wilson, Joseph Thomas. *Black Phalanx; A History of Negro Soldiers of the U.S.* CT. 1888. 1st ed. illus.. *$175.00–$250.00*

Wilson, Mitchell. *American Science and Invention*. NY. Bonanza Books. 1960. ....
.... *$25.00–$35.00*

Wilson, R. L. (ed.). *Antique Arms Annual*. Stevens. 1971. 1st ed. illus. ....
.... *$70.00–$100.00*

Wilson, Rev. Edward F. *Missionary Work Among the Ojebway Indians*. Lon. 1886. 1st ed. illus. .... *$75.00–$150.00*

Wilson, T. *Biography of the Principal American Military & Naval Heroes*. NY. 1821. 2 vols. .... *$55.00–$65.00*

Wilstock, Frank J. *Wild Bill Hickock*. Garden City. 1926. .... *$15.00–$22.00*

Wimsatt, Genevieve. *Chinese Shadow Shows*. Camb. Harvard Univ Press. 1936. 1st ed. illus. dj. .... *$50.00–$80.00*

Winchester and Hotchkiss Repeating Fire Arms, Rifled Muskets, Carbines ... of All Kinds. New Haven, CT. Winchester Repeating Arms Co. 1884. illus. printed wrps, 68 pp.
.... *$175.00–$225.00*

Winkfield, Unca. *The Female American*. Vergennes, VT. 1814. 2nd ed. 12mo, 270 pp, calf, scarce. .... *$150.00–$250.00*

Winslow, John. *Famous Planes and Famous Flights*. NY. The Platt & Munk Co. (1940). 1st ed. illus. pictorial cvr. .... *$20.00–$50.00*

Winter, William. *Life of David Belasco*. NY. 1918. 2 vols. 1st ed. illus. *$40.00–$50.00*

Winthrop, Theo. *Canoe and the Saddle*. Bos. Ticknor & Fields. 1863.. *$30.00–$55.00*

Winthrop, Theodore. *Canoe and the Saddle*. Bos. Ticknor & Fields. 1863...................
.... *$75.00–$100.00*

Wirt, Mildred A. *Ghost Beyond the Gate*. Cupples & Leon. 1943. Penny Parker # 10, dj.
.... *$13.00–$40.00*

Wise, Isaac M. *Judaism: Its Doctrines and Duties*. Cinc. Office of the Israelite. (1872). 1st ed. .... *$150.00–$375.00*

Wise, Jennings C. *Long Arm of Lee*. VA. J B Bell. 1915. 2 vols. .... *$95.00–$200.00*

Wise, John. *Vindication of the Government of New-England Churches*. Bos. 1772. 2nd ed. .... *$100.00–$150.00*

Wistar, Isaac Jones. *Autobiography of . . .* Wistar Institute. illus. b/w photos. fldg map in rear. .... *$65.00–$85.00*

Wodehouse, P. G. *Bachelor's Anonymous*. Simon & Schuster. 1974. dj. *$20.00–$30.00*

Wodehouse, P. G. *Bill the Conqueror*. NY. 1924. 1st Amer ed. .... *$50.00–$75.00*

Wodehouse, P. G. *Carry On, Jeeves!* NY. 1927. 1st US ed.................... *$45.00–$65.00*

Wodehouse, P. G. *Code of the Woosters*. Lon. 1938. 1st ed. .... *$35.00–$50.00*

Wodehouse, P. G. *Golf Without Tears*. NY. 1924. 1st ed. .... *$60.00–$85.00*

Wodehouse, P. G. *Inimitable Jeeves*. Lon. 1923. 1st ed. .... *$40.00–$50.00*

Wodehouse, P. G. *Love Among Chickens*. Lon. 1936............................. *$35.00–$40.00*

Wodehouse, P. G. *Piccadilly Jim*. Lon. 1924................................... *$30.00–$40.00*

Wodehouse, P. G. *Prince and Betty*. 1912. 1st ed.................................. *$50.00–$65.00*

Wodehouse, P. G. *Thank You, Jeeves*. Lon. 1934. 1st ed. .... *$75.00–$85.00*

Wodehouse, P. G. *Uncle Fred in the Springtime*. NY. 1939. 1st ed. dj. ... *$40.00–$55.00*

Wodehouse, P. G. *Uneasy Money*. Lon. 1934. .... *$30.00–$35.00*

Wodehouse, P. G. *Very Good, Jeeves*. NY. Doubleday. 1930. 1st US ed. 340 pp. ....
.... *$50.00–$65.00*

Wolf, Simon. *American Jew As Patriot, Soldier and Citizen*. Phila. 1895. 1st ed. ....
.... *$65.00–$75.00*

Wolfe, Humbert. *Troy*. Lon. Faber & Gwyer. 1928. 1st ed. illus. ltd 500 cc. sgn. ....
.... *$90.00–$150.00*

Wolfe, Thomas. *From Death to Morning*. NY. 1935. 1st ed. dj. .... *$100.00–$225.00*

Wolfe, Thomas. *Of Time and the River*. NY. Scribner's. 1935. 1st ed. black cloth, green and gilt-stamped front board and spine, dj .... *$100.00–$275.00*

Wolfe, Thomas. *Web and the Rock*. NY. Harper. 1939. 1st ed. dj. ...... *$125.00–$150.00*

Wolfe, Thomas. *Web and the Rock*. NY. Harper. 1939. 1st ed. 695 pp, dj. ....
.... *$70.00–$125.00*

Wolfe, Thomas. *You Can't Go Home Again*. NY. Scribner's. (1940). 1st ed. 743 pp, dj.
.... *$125.00–$150.00*

Wolfe, Tom. *Bonfire of the Vanities*. 1987. 1st ed. dj. .... *$40.00–$60.00*

Wolfe, Tom. *In Our Time*. NY. 1980. 1st ed. dj .... *$60.00–$75.00*

Wolfe, Tom. *Mauve Gloves & Madmen, Clutter & Vine*. Farrar. 1976. 1st ed. dj. ....
.... *$40.00–$50.00*

Wolfe, Tom. *Painted Word*. 1975. dj .... *$20.00–$40.00*

Wolfe, Tom. *Purple Decades*. NY. Farrar, Strauss & Giroux. 1982. 1st ed. dj ....
.... *$15.00–$35.00*

Wolfe, Tom. *Radical Chic and Mau-mauing the Flak Catchers*. NY. Farrar, Straus & Giroux. 1970. 1st ed. 1st ptg. dj .... *$35.00–$50.00*

Wolfe, Tom. *Right Stuff*. NY. Farrar, Straus & Giroux. (1979). 1st ed. inscrb, dj. ....
.... *$60.00–$100.00*

Woman's Kingdom. NY. 1869. illus. 1st Amer ed .... *$22.00–$30.00*

Wood, Alphonso. *American Botanist and Florist*. NY. A S Barnes. 1875. ....
.... *$18.00–$25.00*

Wood, Edward J. *Curiosities of Clocks and Watches From the Earliest Times*. Lon. 1866. 1st ed .... *$150.00–$220.00*

Wood, Edward J. *Giants and Dwarfs*. Lon. 1868. 1st ed. .... *$58.00–$75.00*

Wood, Nancy. *Clearcut. The Deforestation of America*. SF. (1971). 1st ed. wrps. illus. photos .... *$30.00–$50.00*

Wood, Nancy. *Hollering Sun*. NY. (1972). 1st ed. illus. photos .... *$55.00–$70.00*

Wood, Robert Williams. *How to Tell the Birds from the Flowers*. NY. Dodd, Mead. (1917). illus. 20th ed. .... *$10.00–$20.00*

Wood, Wales W. *History of the Ninety-fifth Regiment Illinois Infantry Vols*. Chi. 1865. 1st ed .... *$145.00–$175.00*

Wood, Walter. *Harvesting Machines*. NY. 1882. wrps .... *$30.00–$40.00*

Wood, William. *General Conchology: A Description of Shells*. Lon. 1835. illus. 60 hand-clr plates, 1.2 green mor, marbled bds, ex lib. .... *$300.00–$400.00*

Woodbridge, Hensley C., John London and George Tweney, comps. *Jack London, A Bibliography*. Georgetown, CA. Talisman Press. 1966. 1st ed. illus. ..... *$60.00–$120.00*

Woods, Stuart. *Deep Lie*. NY. (1986). 1st ed. dj. .... *$25.00–$50.00*

Woods, Stuart. *Grass Roots*. NY. (1989). 1st ed. dj. .... *$45.00–$65.00*

Woods, Stuart. *Run Before the Wind*. NY. (1983). 1st ed. dj. .... *$75.00–$125.00*

Woodworth, Jim. *Kodiak Bear*. Harrisburg. Stackpole. 1958. illus. with b/w photos. dj. .... *$75.00–$100.00*

Woolf, Virginia. *Flush*. Lon. 1933. 1st ed. illus. by Vanessa Bell, dj ...... *$50.00–$75.00*

Woolf, Virginia. *Reviewing*. Lon. Hogarth Press. 1939. 1st ed. illus..... *$75.00–$100.00*

Woolf, Virginia. *The Waves*. Lon. 1931. 1st ed. dj................................ *$75.00–$225.00*

Woolf, Virginia. *The Years*. NY. Harcourt, Brace. 1937. 1st Amer ed. dj....................... .... *$75.00–$100.00*

Woolf, Virginia. *The Years*. Lon. Hogarth. 1937. 1st ed. dj................ *$200.00–$400.00*

Woolf, Virginia. *Three Guineas*. Lon. Hogarth. 1938. 1st UK ed. .... *$45.00–$60.00*

Woolf, Virginia. *Writer's Diary: Being Extracts from the Diary of Virginia Woolf*. Lon. Hogarth Press. 1953. 1st ed. dj... *$70.00–$85.00*

Woolfe, Virginia. *Contemporary Writers*. NY. 1965. 1st US ed. dj......... *$40.00–$50.00*

Woolner, Frank. *Grouse and Grouse Hunting*. NY. Crown Pub. (1970). illus. yellow cloth. pictorial dj.. *$25.00–$45.00*

Worcester, J. E. *Geographical Dictionary*. Bos. Cummings & Hilliard. 1823. 2 vols. calf. .... *$45.00–$65.00*

Wordsworth, William. *Sonnets of . . .* NY. Peter Pauper Press. slipcase. *$15.00–$25.00*

Wordsworth, William. *The Prelude*. NY. Appleton. 1850. 1st US ed. *$250.00–$300.00*

Work, John W. *American Negro Songs and Spirituals*. NY. Bonanza Books. 1940. illus. dj. .... *$55.00–$75.00*

World Encompassed: An Exhibition of the History of Maps. Balt. Walters Art Gallery. 1952. 1st ed. illus. 60 plates, pictorial wrps....................................... *$100.00–$150.00*

Wormley, A. E. *Israel Yesterday and Today*. Bos. Beauchamp. 1918. 1st ed. .... *$60.00–$80.00*

Worthington, T. *Brief History of the 46th Ohio Volunteers*. Wash. 1877–1880. wrps. ... . *$75.00–$100.00*

Wouk, Hermann. *Caine Mutiny*. Garden City. Doubleday. 1951. 1st ed. dj................... .... *$125.00–$200.00*

Wouk, Hermann. *Caine Mutiny*. Franklin Center. Franklin Library. 1977. ltd, sgn........ .... *$100.00–$125.00*

WPA. *Alaska*. 1943. .... *$25.00–$35.00*

WPA. *Anthology of Writers in Fed. Writer's Project*. .... *$50.00–$75.00*

WPA. *Boston Looks Seaward the Story of the Port*. Bos. 1941. illus. ..... *$25.00–$40.00*

WPA. *California*. NY. Hastings House. 1945. 1st ed. .... *$30.00–$45.00*

WPA. *Cape Cod*. 2nd ptg. .... *$30.00–$35.00*

WPA. *Cavalcade of the American Negro*. Chi. 1940. .... *$50.00–$75.00*

WPA. *Florida: A Guide to the Southernmost State*. NY. Oxford. (1944). 3rd ptg, 600 pp, photos, maps in rear packet. .... *$15.00–$22.00*

WPA. *Iowa*. NY. 1938. 1st ed. pocket map, dj. .... *$30.00–$40.00*

WPA. *Key West*. NY. 1949. 2nd ed. dj. .... *$14.00–$20.00*

WPA. *Maine, A Guide Down East*. 1937. illus. pocket map, dj. .... *$20.00–$35.00*

WPA. *Maritime History of New York*. NY. 1941. illus. dj. .... *$20.00–$35.00*

WPA. *Maryland*. NY. 1941. 5th ptg. .... *$15.00–$25.00*

WPA. *Michigan*. Ox. 1941. 1st ed. pocket map, dj. .... *$30.00–$40.00*

WPA. *Minnesota*. NY. Viking Press. 1938. 1st ed. map, dj. .... *$45.00–$50.00*

WPA. *Montana*. 1st ed. map, dj. .... *$35.00–$100.00*

WPA. *Negroes of Nebraska*. Lincoln, Nebraska. 1940. 1st ed. .... *$45.00–$60.00*

WPA. *New Orleans City Guide*. 1938. map. .... *$22.00–$30.00*

WPA. *New York City Guide*. Random House. 1940. map, dj. .... *$28.00–$35.00*

WPA. *New York City Guide*. 1939. pocket map. .... *$30.00–$40.00*

WPA. *North Dakota*. Fargo. 1938. 1st ed. .... *$37.00–$50.00*

WPA. *South Dakota*. NY. 1952. 2nd ed. maps, dj. .... *$40.00–$50.00*

WPA. *Texas, A Guide to the Lone Star State*. NY. 1940. 1st ed. illus. dj. *$24.00–$35.00*

WPA. *Wyoming*. 1st ed. map, dj. .... *$60.00–$95.00*

Wrensch, Frank A. *Harness Horse Racing in the United States and Canada*. Van Nostrand. (1951). 2nd ed. illus. .... *$20.00–$30.00*

Wright & Ditson's Lawn Tennis Guide for 1895. wrps. .... *$25.00–$45.00*

Wright Olgivanna. *Our House*. NY. 1959. 1st ed. dj. .... *$30.00–$35.00*

Wright, Frank Lloyd. *An American Architecture*. NY. Horizon. 1955. 1st ed. ....
.... *$55.00–$65.00*

Wright, Frank Lloyd. *An Organic Architecture*. Camb. MIT Press. 1970. 3rd ed. rprnt.
.... *$50.00–$75.00*

Wright, Frank Lloyd. *Drawings for a Living Architecture*. NY. Horizon Press. 1959. 1st ed. illus. 255 pp. .... *$600.00–$950.00*

Wright, Frank Lloyd. *Future of Architecture*. NY. Horizon Press. 1953. 1st ed. dj. ......
.... *$95.00–$115.00*

Wright, Frank LLoyd. *Genius and the Mobocracy*. Lon. 1949. 1st ed. dj. ....
.... *$200.00–$300.00*

Wright, Frank Lloyd. *Japanese Print and Interpretation*. NY. 1967. 1st ed. boxed. ......
.... *$90.00–$250.00*

Wright, Frank Lloyd. *Living City*. 1958. 1st ed. dj. .... *$55.00–$67.00*

Wright, Frank Lloyd. *Natural House.* NY. Horizon. 1954. 1st ed. illus........................
.... *$80.00–$120.00*

Wright, Frank Lloyd. *Natural House.* Horizon Press. 1954. 1st ed. dj. ....
.... *$100.00–$150.00*

Wright, Frank Lloyd. *On Architecture.* NY. 1941. 1st ed. .... *$95.00–$125.00*

Wright, Frank Lloyd. *When Democracy Builds.* Univ of CA. 1945.... *$75.00–$125.00*

Wright, Frank Lloyd. *Works of . . .* NY. Bramhall House. 1965. illus. The Wendingen Edition, 163 pp, dj. .... *$100.00–$155.00*

Wright, G Frederick. *Ice Age in North America.* NY. 1890. illus. maps, 622 pp. ....
.... *$50.00–$75.00*

Wright, G Frederick. *Ice Age in North America.* Appleton. 1889. 1st ed. ....
.... *$70.00–$100.00*

Wright, Gordon and the US Equestrian Team. *Horsemanship.* Tryon, NC. Gordon Wright. 1958. 1st ed. slipcase. .... *$45.00–$58.00*

Wright, H. B. *Long Ago Told Legends of the Papago Indians.* 1st ed. illus. facs dj. ....
.... *$450.00–$675.00*

Wright, H. B. *Shepherd of the Hills.* A L Burt. 1907. 1st ed. .... *$45.00–$70.00*

Wright, Harold B. *Uncrowned King.* The Book Supply Co. 1910. .... *$30.00–$40.00*

Wright, Harold Bell. *Devil's Highway.* NY. 1932. dj. .... *$150.00–$275.00*

Wright, Harold Bell. *Mine With the Iron Door.* NY. 1923. 1st ed. dj..... *$25.00–$65.00*

Wright, Harold Bell. *Re-Creation of Brian Kent.* Chi. Book Supply Co. (1919). 1st ed. dj. .... *$100.00–$130.00*

Wright, Henry. *History of the Sixth Iowa Infantry.* Iowa City. 1923...... *$55.00–$65.00*

Wright, Olgivanna. *Our House.* NY. 1959. 1st ed. dj..................... *$50.00–$65.00*

Wright, Richard. *Black Boy.* NY. (1945). 1st ed. dj. .... *$65.00–$90.00*

Wright, Richard. *Black Power.* NY. Harpers. (1954). 1st ed. dj............. *$30.00–$60.00*

Wright, Richard. *Native Son.* NY. 1940. 1st ed. dj............................ *$200.00–$300.00*

Wright, Richard. *The Outsider.* NY. Harper. 1953. 1st ed. .... *$20.00–$30.00*

Wright, Thomas. *History of Domestic Manners and Sentiments in England During the Middle Ages.* Lon. Chapman & Hall. 1862. 1st ed. illus. aeg, bound by Zaehnsdorf. ......
.... *$100.00–$150.00*

Wright, William. *Grizzly Bear.* NY. Scribner's. 1909. 1st ed. illus. photos by author.....
.... *$75.00–$195.00*

Wright, William. *Grizzly Bear.* NY. 1913. illus.................... *$40.00–$75.00*

Wulff, Lee. *Atlantic Salmon.* NY. A S Barnes. 1958. illus. b/w. 1/200 cc. sgn. slipcase.
.... *$275.00–$325.00*

Wyatt, Colin. *Call of the Mountains.* NY. Beechhurst Press. (1953). 1st ed. illus. no dj. large blue cloth. .... *$15.00–$30.00*

Wyatt, Thomas. *Manual of Conchology.* NY. 1838. 1st ed. illus. 36 litho plates...........
.... *$65.00–$140.00*

Wyeth, Betsey James. *Wyeth at Kuerners.* Bos. 1976. 1st ed. dj. .... *$60.00–$90.00*

Wyeth, Betsy James. *Christina's World*. Bos. 1982. 1st ed. illus. oblong folio, dj.......... .... *$50.00–$75.00*

Wyeth, Betsy James (ed.). *Letters of N. C. Wyeth 1901–1945*. Bos. 1971. 1st ed. dj. .... *$50.00–$75.00*

Wyeth, Betsy James (ed.). *Wyeths: The Letters of N.C. Wyeth*. Bos. Gambit. 1971. 1st ed. dj sgn by author. .... *$75.00–$125.00*

Wylie, Eleanor. *Orphan Angel*. NY. Knopf. 1926. 1st ed........................ *$20.00–$75.00*

Wylie, Elinor. *Collected Poems*. NY. Knopf. 1932. 1st ed. dj................ *$25.00–$50.00*

Wylie, Elinor. *Mr. Hodge & Mr. Hazard*. NY. Knopf. 1928. 1st ed........ *$30.00–$60.00*

Wylie, Elinor. *Nets to Catch the Wind*. Lon. Knopf. 1928. 1st British ed. dj................. .... *$35.00–$50.00*

Wylie, Elinor. *Nets to Catch the Wind*. NY. Harcourt, Brace. 1921. 1st ed. dj. author's first book.. *$100.00–$175.00*

Wylie, Philip. *Murderer Invisible*. NY. 1931. 1st ed. .... *$35.00–$50.00*

Wyss, Johann. *Swiss Family Robinson*. NY. Limited Editions Club. 1963. illus. by David Gentleman, 932/1,500 cc sgn, slipcase. .... *$20.00–$30.00*

X, Malcolm. *Autobiography of Malcolm X*. NY. Grove. 1965. 1st ed. illus. photos, dj. .. .. *$650.00–$800.00*

Yardley, Herbert. *Chinese Black Chamber*. Bos. Houghton & Mifflin. 1893. 1st ed. dj. .... *$25.00–$45.00*

Yates, Richard. *Special Providence*. NY. Knopf. 1969. 1st ed. dj. .... *$25.00–$50.00*

Year Book Boston 1913. Boston Architectural Club. blue cloth, gray bds, pictorial paste-down, illus. .... *$18.00–$25.00*

Yeats, William Butler. *Hour-Glass*. NY. Macmillan. 1904. 1st Amer ed. .... *$75.00–$150.00*

Yeats, William Butler. *In the Seven Woods*. NY. 1903. dj..................... *$95.00–$125.00*

Yeats, William Butler. *Per Amica Silentia Lunae*. NY. 1918. 1st Amer ed. .... *$35.00–$45.00*

Yeats, William Butler. *Plays for an Irish Theatre*. Bullen. 1911. 1st ed. *$25.00–$35.00*

Yeats, William Butler. *Synge and the Ireland of His Time*. Churchtown, Dundrum. Cuala Press. 1911. 1st ed. .... *$200.00–$275.00*

Yeats, William Butler. *Words upon the Window Pane: A Play in One Act*. Dublin. Cuala Press. 1934. 1st ed. 1/350 cc. .... *$200.00–$250.00*

Yolen, Jane. *Dragon's Blood*. Delacorte Press. (1980). 1st ed. dj. .... *$20.00–$25.00*

Yolen, Jane. *Neptune Rising, Songs and Tales of the Undersea Folk*. NY. (1982). 1st ed. sgn, dj. .... *$25.00–$35.00*

Yolen, Jane. *Sister Light, Sister Dark*. NY. 1988. 1st ed. sgn, dj. .... *$25.00–$35.00*

York, Alvin C. *Sergeant York*. Garden City. Doubleday Doran & Co. 1928. 1st ed. decorated cloth sgn by York. .... *$200.00–$300.00*

Youatt, William. *Sheep*. NY. 1865. illus. .... *$60.00–$85.00*

Youatt, William. *The Horse*. NY. Leavitt & Allen. nd. illus. 448pp. .... *$55.00–$67.00*

Youmans, Eliza. *Descriptive Botany* . . . NY. Appleton & Co. 1985. ...... *$20.00–$25.00*

Young Lady's Friend. By a Lady. Bos. 1837. .... *$35.00–$40.00*

Young, Alexander A. *Manual of Phrenology*. Phila. Perkins. 1837. 1st ed. wrps............
.... *$140.00–$175.00*

Young, Ann Elizabeth. *Wife #19*. Hartford. 1876. 1st ed. illus. 605 pp.. *$70.00–$85.00*

Young, Brigham. *The Resurrection*. Salt Lake. 1884. 2nd ed, printed wrps..................
.... *$40.00–$65.00*

Young, Clarence. *Jack Ranger's School Victories*. Cupples & Leon. 1908. #3, dj. ....
.... *$15.00–$35.00*

Young, Clarence. *Motor Boys on the Atlantic*. Cupples & Leon. 1908. #6, dj...............
.... *$40.00–$60.00*

Younghusband, Ethel. *Glimpses of East Africa and Zanzibar*. Lon. John Long. 1910. 1st
ed. illus. photos, fldg map, teg. .... *$60.00–$100.00*

Yount, George C. *George C. Yount and His Chronicles of the West*. Rosenstock. 1966.
1st ed. illus. fldg map. .... *$40.00–$50.00*

Zaharias, Babe Didrikson. *Championship Golf*. NY. Barnes. 1948. 1st ed. illus. photos.
.... *$25.00–$40.00*

Zaharias, Babe Didrikson. *This Life I've Led*. NY. Barnes. 1955. 1st ed. illus. photos dj.
.... *$25.00–$95.00*

Zahm, J. A. *Quest of El Dorado*. NY. Appleton. 1917. 1st ed. cloth. ..... *$40.00–$75.00*

Zahm, The Reverend J. A. *Through South America's Southland*. Appleton. 1916. illus.
frontis, teg, blindstamped. .... *$20.00–$35.00*

Zangwill, Israel. *Children of the Ghetto*. Lon. 1892. 3 vols. 1st ed.... *$125.00–$150.00*

Zeisberger's Indian Dictionary. Cambridge. John Wilson & Son. 1887.......................
.... *$140.00–$160.00*

Zeitlin, Ida. *Gessar Khan*. NY. 1927. 1st ed. illus.................................. *$50.00–$60.00*

Zelazny, Roger. *Doorways in the Sand*. Harper & Row. (1976). 1st ed. dj. ....
.... *$25.00–$35.00*

Zelazny, Roger. *Eye of Cat*. NY. Timescope Books. (1982). 1st ed. dj sgn....................
.... *$15.00–$25.00*

Zelazny, Roger. *Sign of Chaos*. NY. Arbor House. (1987). 1st ed. dj..... *$12.00–$25.00*

Zelazny, Roger. *Sign of the Unicorn*. Garden City. 1975. 1st ed. dj....... *$30.00–$45.00*

Zelazny, Roger. *Trumps of Doom*. NY. (1985). 1st ed. dj .... *$25.00–$35.00*

Zeller, Mrs. H. *Wild Flowers of Holy Land*. Lon. 1876. illus. 2nd ed. 54 plates............
.... *$95.00–$120.00*

Ziegler, Rev. Winfred. *Wyoming Indians*. Laramie. 1947. wrps. illus. ... *$20.00–$30.00*

Ziemann and Gillette. *White House Cook Book*. Chi. 1903. illus. plates.....................
.... *$35.00–$45.00*

Zinsser, Hans. *Rats, Lice and History*. Bos. 1945. rprnt. .... *$35.00–$45.00*

Zogbaum, Rufus Fairchild. *Horse, Foot, and Dragoons*. . . NY. Harper & Bros. 1888.
1st ed. illus. by the author, 176 pp, pictorial cloth, teg......................... *$180.00–$200.00*

Zollinger, Norman. *Meridian*. NY. Forge. (1997). 1st ed. dj. .... *$15.00–$25.00*

Zolotow, Charlotte. *I Have a Horse of My Own*. Crowell. 1964. 1st ed. dj sgn..............
....*$18.00–$45.00*

Zolotow, Charlotte. *New Friend*. NY. Abelard & Schuman. 1968. 1st ed. dj.................
....*$14.00–$22.00*

Zolotow, Charlotte. *River Winding*. NY. Crowell. (1970). dj inscrb........ *$25.00–$35.00*

Zolotow, Charlotte. *Sky Was Blue*. Harper & Row. 1963. 1st ed. illus. dj sgn. ....
....*$35.00–$40.00*

Zolotow, Charlotte. *White Marble*. NY. Abelard-Schuman. 1963. 1st ed. dj. ....
....*$20.00–$25.00*

Zorn, Anders. *Etching of Anders Zorn*. NY. Empire State. 1923. 1st ed. illus. ....
....*$50.00–$80.00*

Zucker, A. E. *Chinese Theatre*. Bos. 1925. illus. ltd #329/750 cc, slipcase. ....
.... *$195.00–$250.00*

Zuckerman, Solly. *Monkeys Men and Missiles* . . . NY. W W Norton. 1989. ....
.... *$20.00–$25.00*

Zweig, Arnold. *Case of Sergeant Grischa*. NY. Viking. 1928. 1st ed. dj. *$20.00–$40.00*

Zweig, Stefan. *Amok*. NY. Viking. 1931. dj. .... *$30.00–$50.00*

Zweig, Stephen. *Marie Antoinette*. NY. 1933. dj................................. *$20.00–$35.00*

Zwemmer, Samuel. *Arabia: The Cradle of Islam*. NY/Chi/Tor. Fleming Revell. (1900). 1st ed. illus. red pictorial cloth. maps. photos... *$35.00–$75.00*

Zwemmer, Samuel. *Childhood in the Moslem World*. NY/Chi/Tor. Fleming Revell. (1915). 1st ed. illus. reddish cloth. .... *$75.00–$125.00*

Zwemmer, Samuel. *Heirs of the Prophets*. Chi. Moody Bible Institute. 1946. illus. dj. .
.... *$200.00–$400.00*

BIBLES LISTING

✳

The Book that in many's eyes doth share the glory
That in golden clasps locks in the golden story.

—WILLIAM SHAKESPEARE
ROMEO AND JULIET

Leif Laudamus, seller of fine and rare books in Leyden, Massachusetts, and one of a rare few dealers in Bibles, offered some general guidelines to help sort out some of the mystery and misconceptions that confuse most people about Bibles.

Although the Bible has been on the best-seller list since Gutenberg made it readily available, Bibles in general are not collectible. "Nevertheless," Leif says, "current collector interest is high," but hastens to list some caveats for the novice and uninitiated. "For every edition of interest," Leif continues, "there are literally hundreds of scant or no interest."

When a Bible gets into the 19th century, it is less likely to have any real value. In general, Leif says, American Bibles must be published before 1800 to be of value. On the other hand, to be of value, European Bibles should be published before 1700. And again, after 1800, ask for counsel from a credible bookseller on whether or not you have a prize. Some later editions are interesting, he added, so don't rush to discard your book imprudently.

What else makes a Bible valuable besides its age? Well, you might one day run across the first Bible printed in a particular place, country, state, or city. Or the first Bible printed in any language, such as the Eliot or Natick Bible printed for the Natick colony of "praying Indians," west of Boston, completed in 1663. The first Bible printed, translated, or edited by a woman would be a prime example of a significant exception.

Also, Bibles owned by famous people, miniature Bibles called "thumb" Bibles, hieroglyphic Bibles, other unusual Bibles in fine bindings, or those printed for children.might also be valuable.

Most people think of the family Bible—old, leather-worn, and bearing the ancient script of a long-deceased ancestor as surely a valuable treasure. This is true, indeed, not in dollars, but in the pleasure and fortune of having a precious family heirloom tucked away safely or prominently spotlighted in your home.

Listed below are some Bibles of value:

American Bible. "The Eliot" or "Natick Bible." Cambridge, MA. 1663. Indian language translation. scarce. .... *$175,000.00-$250,000.00*

American Bible. Phila. 1790. 2 vols. 1st Amer ed of the Douai or Roman Catholic Bible. .... *$6,500.00-$10,000.00*

American Bible. Trenton. 1791............................ *$1,000.00-$1,300.00*

American Bible. Phila. 1794. pocket size..................... *$75.00-$100.00*

American Bible. Windsor, VT. 1812. .... *$800.00-$1,000.00*

Bible. Edin. 1817. red mor. aeg....................................... *$25.00-$35.00*

Bible. NY. American Bible Society. 1831. lea. ....*$24.00-$35.00*

Bible. Lon. Edward Whitechurch. 1541. 6th ed. folio. sheep binding. .....
.... *$1,900.00-$2,500.00*

Bible Atlas. . . . Phila. American Sunday School Union. 1827. colored maps, 9 leaves, 135 x 11 cm..................................... *$95.00-$115.00*

Bible in English. Oxford. Baskett. 1717. 2 vols. large folio. many errors. called the "Vinegar Bible" for a proofreading error in Luke XX, word "vinegar" substituted for "vineyard." .... *$600.00 - $900.00*

Bible in English. The Oxford Lectern Bible. Ox. 1935. designed by Bruce Rogers. large folio.....................................*$6,000.00-$8,000.00*

Biblia Sacra Polyglotta. Lon. 2 vols. folio. .... *$250.00-$270.00*

Gospel of Matthew in the Mpongwe Language. Gaboon. West Africa. 1850. .... *$145.00-$250.00*

Holy Bible. Phila. Bible Society of Phila. 1812. lea. stereotype ed.........
....***$125.00-$225.00***

Holy Bible. Lon. 1963. 3 vols. .... ***$75.00-$95.00***

Holy Bible, Containing the Old and New Testaments. Cooperstown, NY. 1839. lea. .... ***$30.00-$45.00***

Holy Bible, Containing the Old and New Testaments. Phila. 1796. illus. large folio. 376 un-numbered leaves. 16 engr plates. 2 maps. full calf. gilt. .... ***$1,500.00-$2,000.00***

Holy Bible. Oxford. 1817. Clarendon Press. 3 vols. lea. *New Testament Translated into the Cree Language*. Lon. 1876. lea. ....
.... ***$150.00-$200.00***

Holy Bible Containing Old & New with Apocrypha. Isaiah Thomas. 1791. engr. calf. .... ***$1,100.00-$1,400.00***

Holy The Great Book, Old Testament, and New Testament. Lon. 1861. Cree language. calf. .... ***$500.00-$850.00***

Jerusalem Bible. Garden City.1970. illus. by Salvatore Dali. 32 colored plates. .... ***$300.00-$500.00***

Magil, Joseph. *Magil's Linear School Bible. The 5 Books of Moses.* NY. 1905. .... ***$15.00-$24.00***

New Testament. Lon. 1616. 136 pp. mor. .... ***$75.00-$100.00***

New Testament. Lon. 1816. folio. silver hinges and clasps. ....
.... ***$1,200.00-$1,400.00***

Old & New Testament & Apocrypha. Boston. Hinkley. ltd. 488 cc. 14 vols.. ***$175.00-$250.00***

Psalms, Hymns, and Spiritual Songs of The Rev. Isaac Watts. Bos. 1852. .... ***$10.00-$15.00***

The Birth of Christ from the Gospel According to St. Luke. Golden Cockerell Press. 1925. ½ lea. over bds. 370 cc. .... ***$95.00-$150.00***

The Holy Bible. Hartford. 1842. lea.. ***$350.00***

The Holy Bible. Harford. 1845. steel engr, 2 maps...... *$60.00-$75.00*

The Holy Bible. Hartford. 1845. 2 maps. .... *$50.00-$75.00*

The Holy Bible Contained in the Old and New Testaments and the Apocrypha. Bos. (1904). 14 vols. full lea. .... *$250.00-$300.00*

Yates, Elizabeth. Joseph, *The King James Version of a Well-Loved Tale.* Knopf. 1947. 1st ed. dj. .... *$15.00 - $22.00*

DEALERS

✳

We wish to thank the dealers listed below who responded to our request for information. Most of them, except where a specialty is noted, are general booksellers covering a broad field of subjects.

Abracadabra Booksearch
International
3606 Chalkstone Cove
Austin, TX 78730
512-502-9042

Alan & Mary Culpin, Booksellers
32 S. Broadway
Denver, CO 80209
1-800-545-2665

American Booksellers
102 West 11th St.
Aberdeen, WA 98520

An Uncommon Vision
1425 Greywall Lane
Wynnewood, PA 19096-3811
610-658-0953

Antiquarian and Collectible
Books
Rodger & Joan Bassett
P.O. Box 536
Fullerton, NE 68638
308-536-2377

Artis Books
201 N. Second Ave.
Alpena, MI 49707
517-354-3401

Barbara B. Harris Books
8 Morgan Way
Gilford, NH 03246
603-524-5405

Barry R. Levin
Science Fiction & Fantasy
720 Santa Monica Blvd.
Santa Monica, CA 90401
310-458-6111

Benchmark Books
3269 S. Main St., Suite 250
Salt Lake City, UT 84115
801-486-3111

Bev Chaney Jr. Books
73 Croton Ave.
Ossining, NY 10562

Bibliomania
129 Jay St.
Schenectaday, NY 12305
518-393-8069

Bolerium Books
2141 Mission, Suite 300
San Francisco, CA 94110
1-800-326-6353

Bookcell Books
Box 506
Haverford, PA 19041
610-649-4933

Brick House Bookshop
RFD 3, Box 3020
Morrisville, VT 05661
802-888-4300

Callahan & Co. Booksellers
P.O. Box 505
Peterborough, NY 03458
603-924-3726

Cattermole
20th Century Children's Books
9880 Fairmont Rd.
Newberry, OH 44065
216-338-3253

Center for Western Studies
Box 727, Augustana College
Sioux Falls, SD 57197
605-336-4999 or 1-800-727-2844

Dan Wyman, Books
47 Dartmouth St.
Springfield, MA 01109
413-733-9065

Daniel Gallagher Bookseller
P.O. Box 381
Charlotte, VT 05445
e-mail: gallagherbooks@usa.net

David M. Lesser
One Bradley Rd. #302
Woodbridge, CT 06525
203-389-8111

DeWolfe & Wood
P.O. Box 425
Alfred, ME 04002
207-490-5572

Edwin Glaser
P.O. Box 1765
Sausalito, CA 94966
415-332-1194

Emmett Harrington
P.O. Box 27236
San Francisco, CA 94127
415-587-4604

Ethnographic Arts Publication
1040 Erica Rd.
Mill Valley, CA 94941
415-383-2998, 332-1646

Foundations Antiques
Stephen Smith
148 N. Main St.
Fair Haven, VT 05743
802-265-4544

Frances L. Robinson
US Rt 2, 81 South St.
South Hero, VT 05486
802-372-6622

Freeman Fine Arts of
Philadelphia, Inc.
1808 Chestnut St.
Philadelphia, PA 19103
215-563-8236

George Kolbe
Fine Numismatic Books
P.O. Drawer 3100
Crestline, CA 92325-3100
909-338-6527

Heinoldt Books
1325 W. Central Ave.
South Egg Harbor, NJ 08215
609-965-2284

High Meadows Natural History
Books
1198 Clear Creek
Boise, ID 82709
208-323-0328

Hurley Books
1752 Rt. 12
Westmoreland, NH 03467
603-399-4342

J & J House
731 Unionville Rd.
Rt. 82, Box 919
Unionville, PA 19375
215-444-0490

James Cummins, Bookseller
699 Madison Ave.
New York, NY 10021
212-688-6441

James W. Beattie Rare Books
105 N. Wayne Ave.
Wayne, PA 19087
215-687-3347

Julian J. Nadolny
121 Hickory Hill Rd.
Kensington, CT 06037
203-225-5353

Just Good Books
P.O. Box 232
Belgrade MT 59714-0232

Ken Andersen
P.O. Box 621
Auburn, MA 01501
508-832-3527

Ken Lopez
51 Huntington Rd.
Hadley, MA 01035

Knollwood Books
P.O. Box 197
Oregon, WI 53575-0197
608-835-8861

L & T Resspess Books
P.O. Box 1604
Charlottesville, VA 22902
804-293-3553

L. W. Currey, Inc.
Water St., Box 187
Elizabethtown, NY 12932
518-873-6477

Leif Laudamus
752 Greenfield Rd.
Leyden, MA 01301-9418
413-774-5722

Lyders Fine Books
P.O. Box 250
Peacham, VT 05862
802-592-3086

Michael Canick Booksellers
80 East 11th St., Room 430
New York, NY 10003
e-mail: canick@panix.com

Monroe Street Books
Dick & Flanzy Chodkowski
7 Monroe St.
Middlebury, VT 05753
802-388-1622

Mordita Books
P.O. Box 79322
Houston, TX 77279
713-467-4280

Nouveau Rare Books
P.O. Box 12471
5005 Meadows Oak Park Dr.
Jackson, MS 39211

October Farm
2609 Branch Rd.
Raleigh, NC 27610
919-772-0482

Orpheus Books
11522 NE 20th St.
Bellevue, WA 98004-3005
360-776-4912

Peninsula Books
451 N. Madison
Traverse City, MI 49684-2112
1-800-530-6737

Poor Richard's Books, Ltd.
968 Balmoral Rd.
Victoria B.C. Canada V8T 1AB
604-384-4411

Richard Adelson Antiquarian
Booksellers
Jane & Richard Adelson
HC 69, Box 23
North Pomfret, VT 05053
802-457-2608

Roy C. Kulp
Handwritten Americana
Box 264
Hatfield, PA 19440
215-362-0732

Rudolph Wm. Sabbat
6821 Babcock Ave.
N. Hollywood, CA 91605
818-982-4911

Ruth Woods
Oriental Books & Art
266 Arch Rd.
Englewood, NJ 07631
201-567-0149

Second Life Books, Inc.
P.O. Box 242, 55 Quarry Rd.
Lanesborough, MA 01237
413-447-8010

Stan Clark Military Books
915 Fairview Ave.
Gettysburg, PA 17325
717-337-1728

Steve Finer
Box 758
Greenfield, MA 01302
413-773-5811

The Eloquent Page
Donna & Marilyn Howard
21 Catherine St.
St. Albans, VT 05478
802-527-7243

The Inquisitive Sportsman Books
Box 1811
Granite Falls, WA 98252
360-691-7540

The Printer's Shop
4546 El Camino Real B10 #207
Los Altos, CA 94022
415-941-0433

The Unique Antique
Jonathan Flaccus
P.O. Box 485 Main St.
Putney, VT 05346
802-387-4488

Thomas Cullen
Rockland Bookman
Box 134
Cattaraugus, NY 14719
716-257-9116

T. N. Luther, Books
P.O. Box 429
Taos, NM 87571
505-776-8117

Tom Munnerlyn Books
P.O. Drawer 15247
Austin, TX 78761-5247
e-mail: thomas@texas.net

Trotting Hill Park Books
P.O. Box 1324
Springfield, MA 01101
413-567-6466

Waverly Auctions
4931 Cordell Ave.
Bethesda, MD 20814
e-mail:
www.waverlyauctions.com

William L. Parkinson, Books
P.O. Box 40
Hinesburg, VT 05461
802-482-3113

RECOMMENDED PERIODICALS AND RESEARCH RESOURCES

✳

AB Bookman's Weekly. PO Box AB. Clifton, NJ 07015. This weekly magazine is arguably the most valuable single source of information currently available for the serious bookman. It includes articles and commentary on specialty markets, personalities in the business, as well as an extensive advertising section of want lists and books for sale. May be the most widely disseminated magazine in the trade, seen all over the world by more dealers and collectors than any other current publication in the field.

AB Bookman Yearbook. PO Box AB. Clifton, NJ 0701. This treasure is included in the package when subscribing to the weekly magazine, or it can be bought separately. Its features include:
—Bookseller Associations Directory
—Geographical listings of dealers
—Categorical listings of dealers
—Dealers' permanent want lists
—Directories of specialty publishers
—Remainder houses
—Bookselling services
—Directories of auction houses
—Information about foreign dealers
—Advertisements

A Collector's Guide to Hard Cover Boy's Series Books 1872-1993. E. Christian Mattson and Thomas B. Davis. Mad Book Co. 273 Pollydrummond Rd. Newark, DE 19711. (302) 738-0532.

American Book Prices Current. Box 1236. Washington, CT 06793. The annual compilation of realized prices of books sold at auction. It lists sales of $50 or more. While an excellent investment, the volumes are expensive and your best bet is to find a good library that carries the books in the reference department.

The Antiquarian Booksellers Association of America (ABAA). Membership Directory. 50 Rockefeller Plaza. New York, NY 10020. A comprehensive listing of dealers in the association. This may overlap the directories in the *AB Yearbook* somewhat, but it is more complete and well worth the price.

Book Collecting. By Allen Ahearn, a guide to values for the first book by an author.

Book Collecting as a Hobby. By P. H. Muir. Out of print, but worth finding.

Book Prices Used and Rare. E. Zempel and L. A. Verkler (eds.). Spoon River Press. 2319-C West Rohmann. Peoria, IL. 61604-5072. A price guide.

Bookman's Price Index. Gale Research, Inc. Detroit, MI. 48226-4094. A pricing resource.

Civil War Books. Tom Broadfoot. 1907 Buena Vista Circle. Wilmington, NC 28405.

Civil War Books, Confederate and Union. Ronald R. Seagrave. Sgt. Kirkland's Museum and Historical Society, Inc. 912 Lafayette Blvd. Fredericksburg, VA 22401-5617.

Collected Books. The Guide to Value. By Allen and Patricia Ahearn. This guide offeres information identifying first editions of books in hand

Identification of First Editions–A Pocket Guide. By Bill McBride. Hartford, CT. 06105. Pointers for identifying first editions from various publishers over the years.

Price Guide for Children's & Illustrated Books for the Years 1850-1960. By E. Lee Baumgarten.

Seminar-Workshops on the Out-of-Print and Antiquarian Book Market. Contact Book Seminars, Inc. PO Box 660. Lodi, NJ 07644-0660 for information and application forms.

Synsine Press. Box 6422. Rheem Valley, CA 94570. Children's series book.

The Insider's Guide to Old Books, Magazines, Newspapers and Trade Catalogs. By Ron Barlow and Ray Reynolds. Windmill Publishing Co. El Cajon, CA 92020.

The Used Book Price Guide. Compiled by Mildred Mandeville. P.O. Box 82525. Kenmore, WA 98028. "Mandeville" has been a standard for dealers for decades, offering extensive lists of books and current prices, but subject to the usual cautions as to errors or fluctuations in the markets that pertain to any regularly produced price guides.

US-Iana. By Wright Howes. R. R. Bowker, Co. New York. A bibliography of books on the United States.

ABOUT THE AUTHORS

PAT GOUDEY started out thirty-two years ago to become an English teacher and writer, then switched her college major to psychology. As fate would have it, she became a writer after all. Her first experience in the publishing trade came with a job as an editorial assistant in the college text department of Prentice-Hall, Inc., in Englewood Cliffs, New Jersey, where she learned about editing and publishing up close.

While her children were growing, she worked as a newspaper reporter for the community weekly, *The Sharon Advocate,* in Sharon, Massachusetts. She moved up to managing editor before leaving to establish an editorial service, write magazine features, and put together the first and second editions of *The Official Price Guide to Old Books* with her partner (and mother), Marie Tedford.

In 1996, after a two-year detour as Assistant to the General Manager of a performing arts center in Foxboro, Massachusetts, where she worked on a broad spectrum of projects including public relations, graphic arts, advertising, audience services, and contract issues, she returned to writing full time.

She is married and the mother of two grown sons.

Ever since MARIE TEDFORD was old enough to get lost in her local library, she has had a passion for books. She started out as a book scout for John Westerberger, the Yankee Peddler, in Rochester, New York, twenty-some years ago. One cold day in January, the worst month of the winter, Marie and a small band of intrepid Vermont booksellers negotiated snow-packed roads to the town of Ludlow and began the Vermont Antiquarian Booksellers Association. Learning the book trade is a never-ending journey, Marie says, no plateaus, only heights to soar. When she isn't beating the bush for books, she writes non-fiction and has written three children's books for an educational publisher. She lives in Underhill, Vermont, with her husband, Ted, and their daughter, Laurie. Marie is a general bookseller and her bookroom is open by appointment or chance.